THE
SCIENCE OF SOCIETY

PUBLISHED UNDER THE AUSPICES OF THE SUMNER CLUB
ON THE FOUNDATION ESTABLISHED
IN MEMORY OF
PHILIP HAMILTON McMILLAN OF THE CLASS OF 1894
YALE COLLEGE

THE
SCIENCE OF SOCIETY

BY

WILLIAM GRAHAM SUMNER

*Late Professor of Political and Social Science
in Yale University*

AND

ALBERT GALLOWAY KELLER

*Professor of the Science of Society
in Yale University*

VOLUME I

NEW HAVEN
YALE UNIVERSITY PRESS
LONDON : HUMPHREY MILFORD : OXFORD UNIVERSITY PRESS

TO

THE MEN WE HAVE TAUGHT

Χαίρετε, φίλτατοι, ἦ ῥα διαμπερές, εἰς ὅ κε γῆρας
ἔλθῃ καὶ θάνατος, τά|τ᾽ ἐπ᾽ ἀνθρώποισι πέλονται.

CONTENTS

VOLUME I

Preface.

PART I

INTRODUCTORY

Chapter I. Starting-Points.

* An asterisk after a section-number indicates that there is in the *Case-Book* a section corresponding to that number.

PART II

SELF-MAINTENANCE: INDUSTRIAL ORGANIZATION

EXPLANATORY NOTE

Inasmuch as the authors aim always at a display of the inter-connection of society's institutions—to that end employing a re-iteration of cross-reference—it seems proper to equip each volume not alone with its own table of contents but also with those of pre-ceding and succeeding volumes. For this reason the following Tables of Contents of Volumes II, III, and IV are here inserted.

CONTENTS

VOLUME II

PART IV

SELF-MAINTENANCE: RELIGION

VOLUME III

PART V

SELF-PERPETUATION

Chapter LIV. Posterity.

Chapter LV. Family-Organization.

Chapter LVI. Transition to the Patriarchate.

Chapter LVII. Relationships and Family-Life.

Chapter LVIII. Retrospective.

Part VI

Self-Gratification

Chapter LIX. Pleasure.

PREFACE

The genesis of this book is recorded in the preface to *Folkways* as falling within the year 1899. It has been in the writing, therefore, for some twenty-seven years. Much has happened in the interval to delay its completion. From 1899 to about 1905 or 1906, Professor Sumner wrote along as steadily as his college duties and his condition of health and strength allowed. Never seeming to feel that he had enough material, he still continued to read a great deal; and his progress was retarded, also, by an increasing fatigue in composition. The work of six or seven years was represented by a lengthy draft of parts of this book, consisting of a great number of cases thrown into rough order and connected by a varying amount of comment and generalization. Fragments of this manuscript were nearly ready for the printer; other parts were no more than sketched; certain blocks of materials had not been attacked at all. At about this time he arrived at the topic of the "Mores," which he had located pretty far on in his plan, under a section called by him "The Mental Outfit" (at a point well along in Part IV of this book). He had been telling me that he was about two-thirds through his first draft.

For some time thereafter he spoke of being occupied with "the section on the mores," and finally told me one day that this topic had run away with him. "I have a chapter," said he, "of two hundred thousand words. That's too long for a chapter; I think I'll make a book of it." This is what he did, for he set aside his original project and devoted all his efforts to the volume called *Folkways*, which was published in June, 1907. "My next task," he wrote, in the preface to that book, "is to finish the sociology." But he was now much wearied by the writing of *Folkways* and did not have the energy to return at once to his original undertaking. Then, early in 1908, he suffered an irreparable misfortune in losing for some months all use of his right hand. He was never able to write with any comfort or speed thereafter, though, true to his indomitable purpose, he trained his left hand to substitute after a fashion until his right regained enough strength in some measure to resume duty.

Not alone did he suffer from this handicap, but his general physical vigor was on the decline. He told me that he could do little at best, that the labor of composition was almost unendurable to him, and that *Folkways* would be his last book. He said that all he had written on the general treatise must now be done all over again in the light of *Folkways* and that he never could rise to the task. I offered to assist to the extent of my time and powers, but he refused, asserting that "it wouldn't be fair," and added: "It will be your book now; I'll give you all I've got and you go ahead." I could not accept such terms, and we finally compromised upon the dual-author title-page. During that fall I was able to cover a part of the ground laid out under Self-Maintenance, an early section which he had neglected because, as he said: "I was afraid I might be tempted to write a treatise on political economy, and I have sworn never to do that." I secured his criticism and approval upon something over a hundred pages of written matter (expanded now into Chapters IV-VI, below). This was the extent of our personal coöperation.

Upon December 26, 1909, Professor Sumner suffered a final breakdown in health and was wholly disabled between that date and his death, on April 12, 1910. The enterprise of a seasoned scholar[1] thus devolved upon a man in his thirties, and he has had to grow up to it as he could.

Professor Sumner enjoined upon me, when we were talking over the work I had set out to do upon his collections and manuscripts, that he wanted me to be bound in no degree whatsoever by what he had written; that I was to change it, both as to detail and to structure, as my best judgment dictated; that "the dead hand" was not to figure in any way at all. I have therefore been perfectly free to omit, to add, and to alter as I saw fit; and I have done so in the spirit which he indicated. I am thus responsible for the book as it stands. He cared for nothing whatever except the truth, and I hope I have worn his mantle in that respect, if in no other.

It is next to impossible, in view of all the writings and re-writings, through sixteen years—work that has been done largely in intervals often short and widely inconsecutive—to apportion the parts contributed by the two authors of this book; and I much

[1] See Starr, *Life of William Graham Sumner*.

doubt whether it would be worth while if it were practicable. But I
can indicate on broad lines the main elements which each of us has
put into the common stock. Professor Sumner collected by far the
larger number of cases; he classified and re-classified them over a
number of years; in so doing he gradually developed the salient
features of the system here set forth; he got the outline of it down
on paper, in his manuscripts; and he provided, in *Folkways*, an
analysis of the basic societal phenomena, the mores. I have gathered some thousands of additional cases; have worked over, re-
classified, added and rejected, translated where necessary, and
written up the body of evidence anew; have considerably altered
the system, though always within the main outlines of it; have
extracted from the manuscripts left by Sumner to me everything
which I thought important and relevant; and have made explicit
and emphatic the conception of evolution in the mores—an idea
implicitly recognized in Sumner's writings but explicitly denied by
him.[2] It is my opinion that he had confused evolution and progress, and would certainly have come to subscribe to the view here
taken as to the paramount and vital matter of adjustment of
mores and institutions to societal life-conditions. I cannot go into
detail concerning the shares of the two authors in the actual text
further than to say that there are comparatively few passages of
any length or consecutiveness which stand exactly as Professor
Sumner left them, and no whole chapters, except that Chapter
LVIII remains almost as he left it; §§458, 459, 460, 461, and 463
are likewise mainly in his words. Sentences and short passages of
his are embedded throughout the text, many of them will be recognizable to one familiar with his style. The idea of the *Case-Book*[3]
as a device to relieve the text, while at the same time indicating the
inductive nature of the method employed and permitting scrutiny
and criticism of the bulk of the evidence, is an expedient which
occurred to my mind a few years ago.

There is nothing to say, in preliminary, of the system here set
forth. If it is vocal at all, it will speak for itself; if it cannot, no
amount of heralding can or ought to lend it an equivocal significance. Throughout, the aim has been simplicity and clearness; the

[2] See Keller, *Societal Evolution,* 247-248, and note at end of that volume.
[3] This *Case-Book* is volume IV of this edition.

audience we both have visualized has been the college student and the general reader. We have felt that the qualities at which we aim ought not utterly to alienate the specialist.

This book does not set out to criticize anyone or to exhibit the only true way of eliciting the truth. It intends, however, to speak bluntly. We object to the "considerate" handling by scientists of what seem to them false or futile positions; that appears to us treachery to the truth. We present a body of unruly facts and the conclusions which we have been able to wring from them by the employment of what we conceive to be scientific methods. Occasionally we find ourselves constrained to offer criticism of other writers; but that is far from being our main objective.

Among a number of points upon which one becomes sadder and wiser by reason of much experience, is this: that there is an inevitable antagonism between induction and exposition. The latter cannot be accomplished by introducing the whole work-shop. It must have some guiding principles. Yet, however honestly such generalizations have been arrived at by the scrutiny of many cases, if they are set first, either in a treatise as a whole or in its constituent sections or paragraphs, the presentation bears a resemblance to deduction which the reader reared, as most readers are, on deduction, or the displeased critic, is not slow to seize upon. It is probably impossible to avoid such appearances except in a very technical and minute investigation. That this situation is capable of worrying even a profound master of science is proved by the reiterated assurances throughout the *Origin of Species* that the author of that fortuitously shortened work has in hand quantities of extra evidence, which he promises to publish later on, for the conclusions he reaches. All that can be done here is to state the conclusions arrived at and then cite representative cases both in support and in contravention of them, in text and *Case-Book*, so as to dispel the impression of deduction from minds from which it can be dispelled.

If a book of this sort, which deals with masses of evidence, is not to become an encyclopædia, it must be terse where it can and turn over much to its cases. It has been necessary throughout to refrain from developing all the implications of the instances cited.

They have been placed in their setting, as we have seen it, and should be studied as part of the demonstration. Much has been left for discussion. It is hoped that this plan will lend to the whole something of the advantage of the legal case-book.

This seems to be the place to introduce several matters of detail concerning the cases. First of all, it is likely that a larger accumulation would have modified our conclusions to some extent. The temptation has been to go on gathering materials. However, there is no end to that process, for vistas of uncertainties are ever opening with more knowledge, and there comes a time when harvesting must be begun if it is to be done at all. Next, except where otherwise indicated, the evidence has been taken direct from the sources cited. We have carefully reproduced the words of our authorities, and have not sought to better either their grammar or even their punctuation. Translations have been made with the utmost fidelity to the original, consistent with rendering the passages into English of an idiomatic order. There is one partial exception here, however. Among the thousands of excerpts taken by the senior author there have been a number concerning which it was uncertain whether they were direct quotations or paraphrases. Many of the citations about which there was uncertainty have been compared with the originals, and with varying result. There has not been time to verify each and all of them, were that necessary. In none of the checked-up cases, however, has any author quoted, whether literally or by paraphrase, been misrepresented. The paraphrases have expressed the essential sense of the passages. In view of this situation, it is quite probable that excerpts occur in quotation-marks which are not exact reproductions of the original and others without quotation-marks which are. And, finally, the persons acting as copyists for the senior author have been occasionally detected in error, for instance, in the matter of exactitude in the reproduction of correct volume-numbers. Much effort has been expended in rectifying such mistakes, but it is not to be hoped that every one of them has been caught. It has not been thought worth while to spend the time and money necessary to the detection of a relatively few insufficiencies of an insignificant order. Errors are more likely to remain undiscovered in connection with quotations from the Russian and Polish, inasmuch as the junior author does not command those languages.

It has been our policy to reduce our lists of cases where we can refer to standard collections of data, such as Frazer's *Golden Bough,* Westermarck's *History of Human Marriage,* Seligmann's *Der Böse Blick,* or Letourneau's several works; we shall refer out of hand to such authorities, with the proviso, however, that the reference is to their materials and does not imply, unless so stated, an adherence to their conclusions. In respect to Sumner's *Folkways* the case is a little different, for its collections have lain, in good part reclassified, before the writer; I have used the materials from which it was constructed over again with entire freedom. Again, we have no idea of rejecting Spencer, Morgan, and others because they are "old." The case is not dissimilar to that in which Darwin figures; men call him old and out-of-date, but they go back to his collections of data constantly, not having been able, apparently, to assemble anything comparable in all these years. Facts do not become "old," nor, indeed, the conclusions drawn from them by men of power. Lippert's *Kulturgeschichte* is over forty years old, but its essential value of

1886-1887 is still with it; in any case, that work has so deeply influenced both authors that the spirit of it pervades large parts of this book, whether or not the foot-notes give notice to that effect. We pay to this master and to Herbert Spencer our respectful homage.

Further, we have avoided protracted citation of evidence where, in our judgment, the reader is likely to be able to supply cases out of his own unconsciously made collections—where, as is the common saying, the point is "self-evident." This is a loose use of that word. There will be a good many points commonly accepted by readers as self-evident, which we think we have proved untrue. The sort of "self-evident" which we mean is "evident from the experience of life," or "familiar from general reading," and not "evident" because of falling in with prejudice or bias or accepted doctrine about "eternal verities" or "the order of the universe." If we state it properly, we need cite no evidence whatever that property is monopoly; but we subscribe to no "self-evident" proposition about property being robbery. One is true; the other is but a deceptive jingle.

It has been our method to cleave rather closely to primitive phenomena. This has been done with a purpose, as the sections on evidence, toward the end of this book, explain; nevertheless we have not refrained from employing materials derived from even highly civilized society when they have served our purpose. For that purpose is to show genetic series. Further, we do not hesitate to suggest the applicability of our conclusions, from what is in any case by far the longest stretch of societal evolution, to phenomena of the present day. Indeed, as we have found by experience, the implications from the study of primitive society as to the mores and institutions of civilization are so compelling that our students have spontaneously recognized the fact and have over and again made applications for themselves. It was a wise remark of Wilken[4] that we "have to go to school to the nature-peoples" in order to comprehend the complex phenomena of modern culture.

It remains, among these more or less miscellaneous remarks concerning our procedure, to say a word concerning our use of terms. In general we strive to employ words in their ordinary signification. There is no point in trying to wrench a word that is in common use over to mean something highly recondite or technical or widely removed from ordinary understanding. If a term has a good many shades of meaning, like "society," for example, it is necessary to specify which one of these we are going to talk about. It is only when the connotation of a word is highly vague, as is the case with "custom" or "social," or perverted from its scientific signification, as "sociology" has been, that there is any real justification for new terminology. It is always preferable, in our opinion, to use the current term in the current sense, wherever this does not sacrifice accuracy. We believe, for example, that the conception of "magic" has remained virtually constant. What is today in people's minds, when they use the term, corresponds well enough with what has been in the minds of men on earlier stages of civilization. What we mean by magic is about what anyone means by it; but it is possible to make explicit much that is implicit, and therefore ignored, in the term as popularly employed. One more illustrative case, from a slightly different angle. Under the subject of spirit-possession, we have treated of various types and degrees and illustrated them as fully as we could from the materials we had. Whether, in so doing, we have seemed to strain

---

[4] In *Verspreïde Geschriften*, II, 329.

the conception of possession must be left to the reader's judgment, when he has reflected upon the cases. But he may realize that we are always viewing societal phenomena with an eye to their earlier phases rather than to their often highly rationalized contemporary forms. It will probably be agreed that a number of the phenomena cited are "somewhat like possession," though objection may be raised to their classification under that topic. The question is then in order: What are they more like? If we are accused of making "a kind of metaphysical extension of the term," the accusation is an admission that we are classing likes together, which is what, and all, that we are trying to do.

It hardly needs be said that when we use "primitive" we do not always mean "savage." There are plenty of primitives among civilized peoples. Even scientists may be primitive in everything else except their narrow specialties.

If some such caveats as the above be kept in mind, we are confident that our terminology will not constitute a stumbling-block to anyone, whether he is a layman or a specialist. Unless there is some specification to the contrary, our terms mean what they say to the intelligent layman; for it is to him, above all, that we address ourselves.

It is evident at a glance that this book seeks perspectives. In laying out so comprehensive a plan it has been necessary to assign weight and space, or no space at all, as the case seemed to us to demand. We have doubtless distributed emphasis in a manner that will seem to some erratic or unjustifiable; but we believe that we have attained a perspective, however faulty. Along with that purpose we have sought throughout to display interrelations. This has been done by the use of several devices: sections that aim to tie up strands horizontally, so to speak, by cutting across the direction of the main topics; copious cross-references; and a certain distribution of cases. The last of these devices involves a degree of blurring of classification; for, although we have located most of the instances of a particular practice in one place, yet there will be found in other connections what seem to be cases gone astray—sometimes deliberately so misplaced with the purpose of exhibiting or recalling the close connection of topics which the exigencies of exposition have separated. Some instances under the topic of taboo, for example, belong, strictly speaking, to avoidance in the ghost-cult; they are put where they are in order to bring out more vividly the genetic connections involved.

There is, further, a sort of stage-direction that must be set down before going forward to the text. For the understanding of whole sections of this book, the reader must be aware of prospects as well as retrospects; there must be presupposed a certain acquaintance with other sections which have to come later.

The whole thing cannot arrive at once, as it does in actual life; in any analysis something must precede and something else must follow. No matter what the choice of order, it is inevitable that what is not yet developed shall be, to some degree, anticipated. This may be a hard saying, but a little reflection will reveal its reasonableness. We shall try to move from point to point in such manner as to render the necessity of forecasting as little troublesome as may be; our frequent cross-references are designed to further this purpose.

It is our intention, likewise, to leave as few issues as possible hanging in uncertainty. Says George Eliot, in her *Essays*, reviewing Lecky on Rationalism: "The writer impresses us as being in a state of hesitation concerning his own standing-point, which may form a desirable stage in private meditation but not in published exposition." Desiring not to deserve thrusts of this sort, we shall not feel it necessary to go much into issues which are plainly under judgment, but confine ourselves, rather, to those which seem capable of settlement at some period short of eternity. In general, we seek the sense of societal customs and institutions. That means to us their expediency as adjustments in living, whether or not we can come to any conclusion as to their origin. Nor do we regard it as enough merely to exhibit them as adjustments, so proved because of their survival; we hope to show also how and to what adjustment has been made.

Adjustment, as our first chapter states, is the key-word to this book. It is our opinion that no one should undertake to study the evolution and life of human society without having first acquired for himself at least a layman's knowledge of Darwinian evolution. For many years no treatise competent to instruct the layman concerning this theory has been available; but that lack has been supplied. Henshaw Ward's *Evolution for John Doe* is wholly adequate for the purpose. It makes clear that cardinal fact about evolution, which has so often escaped attention, that it is simply and essentially a theory of adjustment. Our book assumes but little antecedent preparation; but it does assume a layman's knowledge of evolution.

When it comes to making acknowledgments for encouragement

and assistance in a protracted enterprise, the junior author knows that he speaks for his associate as well as for himself when he mentions first of all the body of students who have passed through our classes and to whom this book is dedicated. There are numerous passages in the following chapters which were suggested during the give-and-take between instructor and student; and several which are set down in the language of some undergraduate because the point in question was returned by him, upon some test-paper, much better expressed than originally in the lecturer's words. To the several thousands who have sat beneath our instruction, the authors here return thanks for the invaluable life-experiences accorded the teacher of such men. The senior author, in an autobiographical sketch, has spoken for us both. "My relations with students and graduates have always been of the pleasantest, and I think that there can be but few relations in life which can give greater satisfaction than these."

Some years ago, several graduates banded together to form an informal Sumner Club, one of the objects of which was to assist in the dissemination of the ideas associated with Sumner—what was long ago denominated "Sumnerology"—and, in particular, to help the junior author to go forward more speedily with the book now published. Their encouragement, which for some years took the material form of a contribution toward secretarial expenses, manifested itself, at length, in a subsidy of size ample for the completion of the work. To the original nucleus of the Club a number of admirers of Sumner were added, bringing the list somewhat above thirty. These men have made the completion of this book possible within a much shorter time than it would otherwise have demanded; but the encouragement which they have extended to me is but in small part referable to their material contributions. Through their organizer and secretary, Julius C. Peter, from whom needed reassurance has been forthcoming at every period of dejection, I thank them in the name of us both. As for Mr. Peter himself, any conventional acknowledgment of his interest and friendship would be wholly insufficient.

We owe much to Professor Maurice R. Davie, who is not only a heavy contributor to this enterprise by reason of the work he has done on the *Case-Book*, but has also lent invaluable aid and highly useful criticism at all points. I have been blessed with several searching critics of the whole manuscript in the persons of Mr. Henshaw Ward, Professor James E. Cutler, Dr. Harris E. Starr, and Professor Edwin D. Harvey; and have profited by the loyal aid and keen criticism of Professor Esther L. Brown, who was my secretary for several years. Her part in this book has been no inconsiderable one. I have confined myself to naming those only who have had to do with the whole of the manuscript; if I were to list the colleagues, students, and friends who have assisted me more casually, this preface would be much extended. I hereby thank them all—they are aware of their identity—in the name of both authors, but assure them, at the same time, that I have gone my own way, after listening to their criticisms and admonitions, and that no one of them, or of those whom I have named, is responsible for any of the defects of the published book. I am keenly alive to many shortcomings which they have pointed out but which I have been unsuccessful, I fear, in amending, as well as to many others revealed only to my own private misgivings.

A. G. KELLER.

New Haven, January 18, 1926.

PART I

INTRODUCTORY

CHAPTER I

STARTING-POINTS

§1. Adjustment. The adjustment of men to their surroundings is the controlling thought of this book. The surface of the earth is the arena on which they work out their destiny. To this floor of a deep ocean of air men, like animals and plants, are held down, there to be exposed to the play of changeless natural forces. The only interest that "Nature" manifests in them is that they shall live and reproduce. This they have succeeded in doing solely by compliant adjustment to their life-conditions; the cleverness which they have come to show in detecting the nature of these conditions and then in suiting conduct to them— a feat sometimes interpreted as lordship over nature—has lessened in no degree their submissiveness to the inalterable. Concerning the process by which adjustment is attained there exists a growing certitude. The process is evolution; for the essence of evolution is the adjustment of life to life-conditions. It has become the dominant mode in thought; so pervasively commanding is it that even those who reject what they take to be evolution are yet always thinking on evolutionary lines and speaking in evolutionary terminology. Evolution has been received, wittingly or unwittingly, into the mental outfit of the race.

This book concerns itself only indirectly with the evolution of physical man and with the physical differences between race-types. Such matters have been reviewed by the science of anthropology. Holding with the anthropological conclusion that all men are essentially alike, we start here with MAN. The one other element at the basis of our treatment is the set of life-conditions, or environment, to which man must secure adjustment if the race is to go on. Environment is multiform, but its most salient feature, so far as effectiveness in determining the forms of human society is concerned, is earth-surface, or LAND. Upon this arena, we repeat, has the destiny of mankind been accomplished. There is nothing surer than that men are earth-born and earth-nourished. That fact long ago impressed itself upon mankind and was recognized in the ascription of motherhood to the Earth. Land is that upon which, and out of which, men live. It signifies primarily standing-room, or emplacement, which is theoretically the first of needs; in practice, however, it means the source of subsistence. Life comes from it and returns to it.

The ultimate elements offered for a scientific study of the evolution and life of human society are, then, MAN and LAND; given these, there arises at once the necessity of adjustment between them.

§2. The Man-Land Ratio. How much land there is to how many men is the fundamental consideration in the life of any society. The ratio between these two factors means the ratio of numbers to sustenance, or of mouths to food; for the fact that all food comes in last analysis from the earth should not be let slip because it is obvious. This relation of numbers to sustenance affords a firm, unspeculative, unselected footing for a science of society. It is a matter of observation and of recorded experience. It is also determinative for organic life in general. Where Mother Earth has more children than she can nourish, they die or exist in misery; where beasts or men are fewer, they get more nourishment and may live on in comfort. This simple and objective relation furnishes, we say, a firm footing for a science of society; we start with an incontrovertible and, indeed, implacable fact of life, and not with any speculative considerations.

Adjustment between men and land involves a struggle between men. Numbers are always surging up against the limit of subsistence, and the mouths do not close upon the food without a preliminary contest which decides who is to have it. This is the familiar struggle for existence, or competition of life, with the powerful urge of self-preservation behind it, and its type is a reflection of the man-land ratio. If there are few men to much land, the struggle is lighter; if the reverse, it is searching and destructive. For the moment we are ignoring what men can do to alter the terms of the ratio—that will appear with advancing analysis—but the ratio is always there, at the base of things.

The type of the struggle, determined by the ratio, next claims attention. Human beings, and many animal species as well, pursue the contest in association. To fight in a body, instead of single-handed, has become a human custom. This is because it constitutes an expedient adjustment. In so doing, men develop concurrent ways or customary methods of meeting life-conditions. Societies are characterized by these ways, as when we speak of hunting, pastoral, or agricultural tribes. The maintenance-ways, by which an actual living is acquired, are tested constantly and convincingly on the realities of life; if life-conditions change and they do not respond, the result is speedily apparent, even to a limited intelligence. There are also other ways, which represent adjustment to less tangible realities such as sex-difference or the luck element. These are not checked up so promptly or directly or conclusively. If they fall out of adjustment, misery ensues, as it does upon any form of maladjustment, but its cause is not so apparent as in the case of the maintenance-ways. Customs of this order, farther removed from objective test, are those out of which develop marriage-systems, family-organization, religion, and government. In general, the adjustment of these is to the maintenance-organization rather than directly to physical realities. Since, however, they are bound to retain consistency with the maintenance-organization, they must needs adjust, even though indirectly, to the physical realities to which that basic organization responds—which means that the relation of numbers to sustenance underlies and is finally determinative of all human usages, not of the maintenance-ways alone.

Out of the blocks of customs thus evolved and controlled issue all human institutions. Hence the type of society's institutions derives ultimately from the ratio of men to land. This is equivalent to saying that the type of society and of societal life goes back to that ratio; for the life of any society lies in the evolution of its institutions, since they are its adjustments to its life-conditions. Any science that sets out to study society's life must examine it in society's institutions; there is no other way to study it. To understand the institutions it is necessary to review their development; and if that is followed back to a simple and objective root-relation in the numbers-sustenance ratio, which holds for other forms of organic life as well, there is a reassuring sense of firm ground under foot so that one can go forward with more confidence.

The man-land ratio may be viewed as a special case of the law of supply and demand, for that law is not one of prices only but of the whole societal order. A group stands upon its land with its task before it. The career-interest of its members is at stake in its policy. The needs of the men are the demand; the apt materials of the earth, after they are extracted and fitted to serve human needs, are the supply. The two must be equal, for the needs and desires, which know no limit, must be curtailed to the fact of what is; nevertheless, the law of supply and demand also works towards a limit at which the distribution would conceivably give to each member of the group his maximum satisfaction from the kind and quantity of useful things on hand. Such a distribution is not practically attainable. It is a task of policy to approach as near to it as possible.

Unoccupied land cannot be said to be a demand for men. Underpopulation is the demand for men.[1] Underpopulation is a number of men insufficient to exploit the land of the group to its maximum on a given stage of the arts. Parts of the globe are, at the present time, underpopulated. Hence there is a demand for men; hence life is highly valued and the loss of a number of lives is regarded with horror; hence the terms of the career-interest are favorable to unskilled laborers and non-capitalists; hence wages rise and interest falls; hence the expense of high education for all children born in a community can be thrown on the capital of the community; hence democracy is the political fashion; hence social schemes of world-beatification are rife and are not altogether absurd; hence the poor and ignorant are popular. The conjuncture is favorable to the men and against the land because land is plentiful and laborers are wanted, and there is plenty of capital (food and tools) for their outfit.

§3. Society. A sufficient definition of the science of society is now in our minds: it is the science which investigates the evolution and life of human society. One must not fail, though, to disengage this term "society" from its tangle of meanings and confine it to a single sense; otherwise he cannot hold steady that which he is to examine. If an observer could peer down through the air-ocean and view the human creatures living and moving about upon its floor, he would notice that they do not live each unto himself, but together. From his position of distance and detachment, in fact, he would lose the individual man in the masses of men, and could make out only clusters of various size. These would present themselves as discharging the usual function of organic groups: the maintenance and the reproduction of life. A group of human beings liv-

---

[1] Sumner, *Coll. Ess.*, III, 109 ff.

ing in a coöperative effort to win subsistence and to perpetuate the species: such is the conception here offered of a human society.

This definition has, like the man-land ratio, the advantage of resting squarely upon the well-known facts of all organic life. Indeed, our starting-points are located so close to the organic range that we have but to omit the word "human" from this definition in order to have a definition of any non-human society: for instance, a swarm of bees. It needs no comment to demonstrate the objective quality of a conception of society which locks immediately with facts observable in nature. At the same time our definition obviously excludes not a few forms of human association from the title of society: a club, for example, or a lodge, or a political party, or a trade-union, or a monastery, or a college. High "society" may not be a society. It is indispensable for our definition that there shall exist coöperative activities in self-maintenance and self-perpetuation.

Given a human group in an environment, and given also—though we have not yet come to them—differences, chiefly of sex and age, existing between its members, then the science of society sets out to trace all the ensuing types of adjustment which produce societal organization, functions, and structure, that is, evolution and life. The conditions of the definition set no limitation on the size of the group that is taken to constitute a society: the family satisfies the conditions, as does the nation, or even the whole race of mankind. The proportions of the group and the space occupied by it depend upon the distribution of the food supply, upon the means of transportation and communication, and, beneath these and other factors, upon the conditions of the struggle for existence. The whole human race constitutes, at least potentially, a society; for the life of mankind on earth is subject to conditions and forces which are as wide of scope as the earth or the race, and the tendency of events toward the progressive unification of the world's peoples into a societal unit is a matter of observation.

Wherever there is free and actual communication and coöperation in the struggle for existence, where the stage of civilization, the code of manners and morals, the doctrines of rights, duties, and powers, the apparatus of scientific and literary information, and the stock of knowledge are substantially the same, there is a culture-area. The ties of societal organization run through the whole, in spite of state lines and positive political barriers, or differences of race, creed, language, or form of government. A culture-area is, then, a good deal like a society, and may turn into one. World-commerce tends to make the culture-area of civilization a single society by combining the whole in one struggle for self-maintenance. State-legislation works against this by fostering differences, enacting tariffs, and otherwise. It is characteristic of our time that the economic and intellectual forces tend to identify culture-area and society while the political forces seek to identify the state with the society.

§4. Organization. Organization—specialization plus coöperation—is not sufficient alone to form a society; it must be organization for the discharge of the two characteristic societal functions. It is not admissible to regard large combinations, such as churches or conventions, as societies; for the term has then no real definition and the science employing it is doomed to barren wanderings over a vague domain. Unorganized groups of people, again, may perform societal functions without being societies. A chance concourse of persons—the audience at a theater, the worshippers in a church (even if habitually the same persons),[2] the passengers on a train or on a steamer—is not a society. Occasions arise when such a group wishes to perform societal functions; then organization becomes necessary. Any one of these groups could be sharply defined, but the cases serve to show that mere strictness of demarkation is no element in a definition of society.

There are two thousand persons on a ship, consisting of crew and passengers. The group has absolutely fixed boundaries and is segregated from all other human beings. The crew is under stringent disciplinary organization, while the passengers are not organized at all. If the ship should be wrecked upon an uninhabited island, the officers would no doubt superintend the landing of the whole party, with such stores as could be saved. The disciplinary organization would then, perhaps, break down, the authority of the officers being no longer recognized; but if time went on and rescue was despaired of, the whole party would have to go to work to produce food and otherwise take up the struggle for existence. It would fall into an organization primarily dictated by the customs of the society from which it came, but modified as experience

2 The little congregations or church-groups in the old Puritan days in New England were usually societies.

revealed that these customs were maladapted to the conditions. The party might thus turn into a society. Several novels have been written about this imagined situation. Reflection upon it will clarify further the conception of what a society is and is not.

The conception of organization requires some sharpening, for there are in it other elements beside the basic ones of differentiation and coöperation. Up to the highest developments of modern civilization differentiation of function, invention of appropriate new structure, adaptation, perfection, coöperation, and rhythmic effort under command and discipline have been the steps of advancing organization. Advancing organization has been the key to new power, and it has been the conserving element also, for by its reactions on population it has prevented the dissipation of the gains in the maintenance of a great number of worthless creatures. The individual and the minor group have their own narrower interests, purposes, and views of policy which they try to impose on the whole of which they are parts; this is the element of differentiation and liberty. The organization restrains and constrains the individuals to a common purpose and, while hostile to liberty, gives aid and protection and is the sustaining structure within which individual life goes on in security. The two elements alternate in their preponderance where the life of the group is prosperous.

We have to live in the societal organization. It dominates us, and to it we are constrained to make concessions of our liberty of unrestricted action. Its might is greater with higher civilization, even though the latter, through its institutions, endows each member of society with a sphere of individual activity so widened that his experience of individuality, liberty, and independence far surpasses anything which men on lower civilization can know. It is to be noted that organization is built upon inequality; it produces new inequality from one step to another because some adapt their individual effort to the organization more intelligently than others; it requires a hierarchy of managers which has more and more ranks as the organization becomes wider and more complex; it is aristocratic because it automatically selects the more fit for its positions of greater power; it requires sterner discipline as it becomes larger because it then becomes more impersonal; it gives an imperial position to those who, selected from all, stand out at last as fit to be commanders-in-chief. To resist these tendencies, which are inherent in organization, is to resist culture, which is an issue out of organization.

§5. **Preponderance of the "Masses" in Society.** Any person of sense would agree, in the abstract, that no society is correctly viewed except as a whole. This whole is composed mostly of "common people." It is hard for an outsider to realize the brute bulk of the "masses,"[3] and still harder to enter into their ways of thinking and acting—so strong is the human tendency to assume the prevalence throughout society of the qualities and habits of action

[3] Sumner, *Folkways*, §§47 ff.

and thought encountered in one's own circle of life. Often the observer knows of no other environment and code of behavior than his own, and his mental construction of the life-conditions and mode of existence of other classes is as unchecked by fact as was the once accredited phantasm of the "noble savage." Particularly is this the case with beginners or casual students of the social sciences. A college student, by the very fact that he is in the institution, is privileged over the thousands who get no such chances; but it is hard for him to see that he must not judge all mankind by himself and those about him. He can easily fall into the habit of guessing and theorizing, which goes with half-culture, without feeling the need of studying facts before forming conceptions.

It is imperative for a student of society to realize at the outset that, by very virtue of the fact that he has time and opportunity to study, he belongs to a relatively small and favored class, and always to check up his thinking by the reflection that it is the masses who constitute the body of society and who ultimately determine its evolution and life. It is the masses who carry the ways and customs,[4] and society moves only as their relatively inert bulk lurches this way or that. This fact appears unmistakably in history, but has been recognized, in institutions for the freer expression of public opinion, only within comparatively recent times.[5] The sole winning course for the student of society to adopt is to become so alive to this situation as to rid himself of his provinciality—of race, nation, class, or other local grouping—and see society as a whole. He may thus secure an approach to that scientific dispassionateness which has enabled natural scientists to attain their enviable reputation and results.

§6. Association. Weismann[6] remarks that from the thirteenth to the eighteenth century the study of natural science was confined to repeating and extending the work of Aristotle. There was nothing new, depending upon personal observation, and no test of his statements, even about familiar objects. No one noticed the error of assigning eight legs to the fly instead of six—even though the

---

4 Sumner, *Folkways*, §52.
5 Keller, *War to Peace*, ch. VIII.
6 *Evol. Theory*, I, 12.

fly, one might add, was always standing on four and polishing up the others on the very desk of the mediæval scribe. This same Aristotle[7] once said that man was a "politikon zoön," that is, a being of urban characteristics. In this generalization he was, of course, thinking of Greeks; he did not take in the antipodes because he did not know about them. But his term has been translated, without the citation of clear parallels—for there was no such generality of conception, in those days—as "social being"; and then the fly-episode has been repeated.

It is characteristic of man as we ordinarily encounter him that he is found in the society of his fellows. This fact has been lightly accounted for by the dictum that he is a "social animal," is "gregarious," or has a "herd-instinct." Such explanations do not explain. They amount to a re-statement of that which is to be elucidated: "man is social because he is social." They have often furnished a useful major premise from which to deduce acceptable conclusions as to man's exceptional or, at any rate, not sub-bestial nature and endowment; for you can always get out into your conclusion everything you have once packed into your major premise. We do not believe that man was outfitted with any innate quality of sociability implanted in his germ-plasm, but that the tendency to associate is acquired rather than inherited, and that man's association with his kind is a product of societal rather than of organic evolution. Association is another of those long-standing usages which, like "natural rights,"[8] are referred to "nature" because their origin is not known.

Association, it is true, is found in nature as a product of organic evolution. Bees and ants have societies that meet the terms of our definition of society except for the adjective "human." Some there are who wish to assume this and that about the earliest human relations because it would be so unpleasant otherwise. What can be known, in contradistinction to sentimental guesses and thin speculation, is that a number of human beings about the earth live in a condition of marked atomism, and that association decreases as we go back toward the "nature-man."[9] There is no doubt about

[7] *Politika*, I, §2, 10, 15; III, §6, 3. The term translated "by nature" means "natural" in a sense broad enough to include the mores.

[8] §§456, 171, below.

[9] §9, below.

the survival-value of association; the saying that in union there is strength witnesses to a deep-seated popular appreciation of its benefits. Man is found to have hit unwittingly and early upon this expedient for living; but that does not prove him "instinctively gregarious." The misleading element in such pronouncements is the impression conveyed that man hurried eagerly into association in somewhat the manner of a pointer-pup on his first hunt, trembling with excitement and longing, bursting in the prospect of expressing a preëxisting instinct. The implication is that man always loved his fellows, rejoiced in their companionship and sought it, happily practised mutual aid, and thereby exhibited some heaven-sent quality that distinguished him from the beasts that perish; that association was a "natural" process as "natural rights" are averred to be natural, and that disassociative forces were not present or were negligible.

§7. **Drawbacks to Association.** Brief reflection, if it is candid, will convince any man that association with his fellows has its drawbacks. Any association, including a human society as here understood, exacts payment for whatever benefits it confers. It is clarifying to ask one's self whether society is a great club, enjoying privileges and advantages by nature, with free membership for everybody; or whether it is a gild of workers, with high admission fees and strict rules of general welfare, which imposes heavy penalties on dissenters, and confers no privileges except a costly insurance against certain massive ills.[10] The thinking man is aware that the latter of these alternatives corresponds with the facts; he knows that each is born into society, whether or no, and receives its discipline through childhood, and that at maturity at the latest he must begin to pay dues of labor and sacrifice, that he may be permitted to carry on his struggle inside it and through it. He is content because he can realize that the benefits of association are worth the cost; while the masses of men, who do not reflect upon this matter at all, live along on lines now become habitual and in ways so inveterate as to exclude the very conception of other ways. Misguided people may even set out to destroy the safeguards under whose protection alone society, including the bomb-

10 §197, below.

throwers, can live. What the cases drawn from the life of primitive societies show is that the capacity to live in society is not there at the outset, but has to be won. It is not hereditary in the race but traditional in custom. Incontinently to assert its presence at the outset, or to assume that it is the result of rational choice and resolution, is to ignore the facts in favor of a chosen premise or selected thesis—which may have been excusable in the uninformed past but is so no longer. Association has at length, and with difficulty, become a characteristic habit of mankind because of its high survival-value in the evolution of civilization.

No form of association exists into which men can enter without sacrificing, in particular, personal liberty. Crusoe could do what he liked upon his island—howl, go naked, cast aside all manners and propriety—because there was no one else present upon whose sphere of self-realization he might infringe. When Friday joined him, Crusoe had to subject himself to limitations which amounted to the curtailment of perfect freedom. When he returned to London, that freedom was sure to suffer further inroads; there were conventions about street-behavior, for example, of which he had been hitherto quite independent. If he joined a club or a church, he had to conform to house-rules or ritual. Examples are numerous and obvious of the inevitable surrender of personal freedom in the society of one's fellow-men. Such renunciation does not thrust itself upon consciousness any more than does the unheeded pressure of the atmosphere, except upon occasion. Life is lived out amidst limitations and under a discipline of which, knowing nothing different, men are for the most part unconscious. But the acceptation and toleration of such discipline is not "natural," as can be seen in the case of children. It takes discipline and then more discipline to rear an acceptable member of society; and the main reason why we have too few of such is because early discipline has been lax.

If, without training, a child took naturally to being controlled and limited, as one must be in society, the assertions about social animals, social instincts, and the rest would be more plausible. As it is, all those qualities which are indispensable to membership in society have to be learned, like language, by each generation anew; no one is "to the manner born"; no one spontaneously limits his own freedom. Much less does the savage instinctively gravitate toward such limitations on his liberty. If there is anything he prizes in life, it is this same personal freedom;[11] and if he presently comes to sacrifice part of it, that is only because he is compelled by circumstances to do so. Societal bonds were forced upon lawless men by the necessities of the struggle for existence; association was a species of insurance which one could not afford to be without. It was not, however, conferred upon the beneficiary without cost; the premiums of the policy were the sacrifices made. It is not that primitive man reflected upon the situation and acted purposefully in the light of his conclusions; it is that if he advanced in the direction of the winning expedient, he lived on into the next period, while the less adaptable or less fortunate dropped out and left the prize of existence to him and his like.

Men have to be driven to think in terms of society and very few come to do so. What they can sense without trouble is the individual interest, and some can come to recognize that of the limited group. But the interest of the larger group speedily vanishes if confronted with that of the smaller. World-interests rapidly dissolve before the real or supposed interest of the state, as do the national interests in the face of the local. The forces leading to integration and to the inviolability of the extended peace-group can never avail against the more definite sense of the interest of the smaller society. No amount of outcry about the interests of the larger group can get attention when those of the smaller are believed to be in jeopardy.

§8. Advantages of Association. Despite its drawbacks, association has prevailed, for evolution lays hold upon and fosters the expedient which has utility. The utilities of association, which mean the advantages of life in society, are manifold and decisive. Association both augments and economizes power. Fifty men working in coöperation can do things that the same fifty men acting separately cannot; they can pull, one at a time, at a rope attached to a heavy weight, and the latter does not move; they pull no harder, but at the same time, with someone to mark rhythm for them, and the shift is made. Herein lies the paradox that a society

11 Lippert, Kgchte., I, 41; cases under §9, below.

is greater than the sum of its parts. The extra power is due to organization; it is the superiority of a dozen policemen to a mob of hoodlums. Then there are the manifold economies attending on specialization, as in division of labor, by which men save time, effort, and materials, and yet get a better product. These can be realized only in association. The offensive against nature can be managed better under organization, and so can the defensive, against both nature and fellow-men. Without trying to list all the advantages of association, it is clear enough that men possessing no more than the ones that have been indicated are bound to prevail in the competition over those who have them not, or who have them in lesser degree. The stress of competition enforces an ever closer association. The formation of society was thus a winning expedient in the art of living.

It is a subtle and mysterious fact that a collective body of human beings manifests a life of its own which is something else than the sum of the lives of its members. Artificial social creations, such as corporations, have the same character.[12] A society shows this phenomenon more strongly than any other collective body.

In general, the extent and complexity of the bonds of association vary directly with the height of civilization. They are now incredibly far-reaching and complicated. The world is becoming one mighty association for the winning of subsistence. The product of the Javanese native appears on the breakfast-table of the Maine fisherman, and what is occurring in Timbuctoo is no longer a matter of ignorance or indifference to London. But the present and recent extension of human association should not lead us to infer that it has always been characteristic of men. It is not by chance that the Latins designated stranger and enemy by the same term, *hostis*. As we retrace the course of civilization toward its beginnings, we note a progressive shrinkage in both the extent and the complexity of association and, along with this, an increasing hostility of group to group and man to man; and we arrive at length at the stage of civilization revealed by the most backward peoples—which is a state of things generally not visualized by those who talk confidently about the social instinct—and there

12 Pollock and Maitland, *Hist. Eng. Law,* I, 472.

discover facts that jar heavily upon suave theories concerning man's social nature and proclivities.[13]

§9*. Primitive Atomism. If, as we go back over the course of evolution, we encounter less and less perfect types of association, the inference is that beyond the range of our information, in the unknown past, the measure of association approaches zero. Indeed, there are observed cases where the close-knit world-society of civilized mankind finds its prototype in the scarcely more than temporary and scattering kin-groups of the Australian natives or of the African Bushmen and Pygmies. Not only are these societies small, unstable, and disconnected, but their members harbor sentiments toward outsiders and even toward each other that cannot, by any stretch of the imagination, be interpreted as brotherly. Where men are existing with slight resources on the edge of catastrophe—and, except in certain favored spots, we take this to have been the original state[14]—they are full of hostility, suspicion, and other anti-social feelings and habits. We have cases in which the struggle for existence is intense, and in which the competition of life has taken on its harshest form, because the men have not been able to rise to a coöperative effort in higher organization, so as to overcome their difficulties. The fact that they may have retrograded from some happier estate to these depths has no bearing upon the matter; for whether they have gone up or down, according to our notions, their life represents an adjustment to their hard conditions, and falls into the evolutionary series back toward its beginnings.[15]

Of the Teda, or Tubu, a tribe of the Sahara, it is reported:[16] "The competition of all for the possession of the wretched and meager resources of life makes each one ruthless, suspicious, and crafty. Each strives to hurt the other, if the other stands in his way; and all stand in one another's way in this land of need. Each one is eager to get an advantage over the other, not in a comparatively legitimate way, but by shutting him out of all chance of competing for the prize or by robbing him of it. To this end the Teda steals, lies, and murders if need be. Hence we find that he flees the society of men and builds his lonely hut in a hidden cleft of the rocks. We see that if he encounters the

[13] Chs. XIV, XV, below, *passim.*
[14] §§32, 93, 146, below.
[15] §§454, 455, below.
[16] Nachtigal, *Sahara,* 246, 247, 274, 425, 438 ff. (quoted), 454, 455.

footprint of a tribe-comrade on the path through the desert, he is filled with anxiety and fear, and that he chooses the night by preference as the time for his enterprises. Thus each lives for himself, and every thought of his fellow-tribesmen, every feeling of sympathy with them in a tribal life, every effort for a common tribal welfare, is foreign to him. Common danger from without or common plundering expeditions alone unite the tribe, never combined labor or common participation in harmless public entertainment. Public tribal life does not exist. In their public assemblies they practise only sophistical argumentation and crafty distortions of law and right. These meetings often end in bloodshed." Custom forbids them to go about in their own dwelling-places armed, but they nevertheless carry the superseded weapons of their childhood, even there, and both men and women quarrel and inflict injuries upon one another. Everyone on a journey seeks to elude a fellow-countryman and at home lives as far as possible from his neighbor. If two meet, they assume attitudes of defense and so remain during the conversation. Negotiations with a stranger are carried on weapon in hand—one in each hand—and the parties do not look at each other, except for an occasional glance, but fix their eyes on the horizon or on the ground. "Here we have the notion of right of men who are always hungry, always in misery, and who have naturally a greedy disposition." Where the environment is less desolate this situation is correspondingly relieved of its savagery.

A shorter companion-piece is furnished by a people of Madagascar who are said to live in such constant suspicion and dread of an enemy that they never wash in their houses, but only in the open air; and even then they wash only one side of the face at a time, leaving one eye open and one hand grasping gun or spear.[17]

A prime characteristic of atomistic peoples and, in general, of tribes of low civilization, is their impatience of anything which infringes upon their liberty.[18] The following cases, while still illustrative of atomism, view it as a revolt against limitation incident to association.

Dundas[19] describes how the people of a certain African district took an oath binding one and all to confess in case the British government discovered a breach of local law which they were planning. Two men were arrested, and then not only was the oath disclosed contrary to agreement but all denied complicity. "Thus the fact that a number of Akamba could combine even to the extent of binding themselves by oath did not show a very unanimous spirit among them after all. And this is a very common experience with the Akamba, no matter how sacred an act may be to them, despite all supernatural terrors which one would suppose sufficient to bind them to a common interest, the discordant spirit is yet stronger, and nothing lacks more in their composition than a unanimous feeling. . . . They never could submit to a common chief, or join to oppose a common enemy. Above all the Mkamba prizes his independence, to be subject to anyone or bound by anything beyond mere family

[17] Sibree, *Great Afr. Isl.*, 286.
[18] §7, above.
[19] In JAI, XLIII, 487-488.

ties is hateful to him. Often small settlements are found in isolated places where water is scarce, where their fields are constantly destroyed by wild beasts, just where we should expect to find the villages close together, but it is just in such places that we find them farthest apart and entirely strange to each other. . . . If a Mkamba meets another on the road he has nothing to say to him, and will probably look away, for he is a stranger and does not concern him. This attitude has often been put down to surliness, but I hold that this is not correct—it is much more due to his desire for independence closely connected with another characteristic. The Mkamba is much too mistrustful and suspicious to make it possible for him ever to work to any extent in combination with others. His mind runs along dark and complicated lines, with a distinct inclination for things mysterious and distorted."

Of the Nigerian head-hunters it is reported that "they have such a strong love of freedom and conservatism, that I do not think they would relinquish their liberty nor take to any European customs without compulsion, and as that would be contrary to our principles, we let them alone so long as they keep the roads open and remain peaceful. The tax imposed is merely to remind them that they are no longer able to indulge in their little hobby of collecting the skulls of their neighbours without serious consequences."[20] The Jibaro Indians of Ecuador "are by nature impulsive and choleric, qualities that among them frequently give rise to disputes and quarrels which may degenerate into sanguinary feuds. Their unbounded sense of liberty and their desire to be independent, not only of the whites but also of each other, is one of the reasons why they do not live in villages but each family separately, for in this way conflicts are more easily avoided. . . . The family's sense of justice as well as the duty to the deceased now require that revenge shall be taken, and the supposed wizard is assassinated. This murder naturally awakes the desire for blood revenge on the part of the family thus outraged, and so a blood feud is begun which, as is easily understood, has a tendency to make itself permanent."[21]

It is necessary, though not easy, to shake off impressions about early society derived from legendary accounts of original felicity or from the appealing imaginings of eloquent eighteenth-century philosophers about the "state of nature." Despite the revelations of science, these are still much with us. Men who are in a desperate situation as regards self-maintenance show the disposition of the tribes just cited; they are atomistic and anti-social. Individual self-interest prompts action with them; and that interest is incapable of seeing its satisfaction under limitations imposed by the general interest. There was no Arcadian peace and simplicity in the elder ages. Men always quarreled, and if they did not fight it was because they were too broken, cowed down, or cowardly. It

[20] Tremearne, in JAI, XLII, 148.
[21] Karsten, "Jibaro," in BAE, Bull. LXXIX, 8-9.

was only as time went on that peace was found to be a more expedient policy. Peace was a benefit to be striven for; it did not come as a natural boon. The more backward the savage is, the less he knows about methods other than the nearest ones for the attainment of self-preservation; and there is no recourse closer than force, and no suspicion of others more vivid than the misgiving that they are preparing to use force. Familiarity with violence is common to all animal life. Under civilization the individual gets away from it; but it cannot be said that societies have yet done so. Hostility and war are what we are moving away from, and also what we fall back upon whenever the supporting structure of civilization breaks down. It is the primordial thing, like poverty. Generalization as to the warlike or unwarlike disposition of the savage must take account of many varying types; but it is fair to infer that mutual suspicion and fear were the rule among the scattered groups of early man, competing as they were for a precarious sustenance.[22]

§10. The Evolution of Association. The fact is that the stress toward adjustment, even among those tribes that have plenty of spirit for a fight, makes insensibly for peaceful association; there is an ever-present tendency toward the formation and extension of the "peace-group."[23] But this is a very different matter from the exhibition of an innate instinct; as well say that man has an instinct for trade because in the course of time he develops a commercial organization. We cannot credit the savage with the natural ability to perceive societal expediency, particularly if it runs counter to what he sees as his personal interest; and so we must conclude that he was driven into societal life by factors acting automatically upon self-interest. Association started, like all other social habitudes, with action in response to need; it proved, under test, to possess utility for living, and so became habitual. It was, then, a matter of adjustment to life-conditions, and in particular a response to driving forces, productive of discomfort, that were and are coercive to activity and also to the discrimination of expedient from inexpedient action. Such an expla-

22 Sumner, *Coll. Ess.*, I, 7; §139, below.
23 Ch. XV, below; Keller, *War to Peace*, chs. IX, X.

nation of association involves no assumptions but only simple inferences from attested fact.

The organization of society has been and is natural, in the sense of being spontaneous, unconscious, and automatic. It is not, in its origin, artificial or designedly disciplinary, like that of an army or an orchestra. Historically it has been produced by the process of trial and failure; the organization which grew up was the one that gave most satisfaction with least pain. From time to time the elements of the situation changed, and then the organization had to adapt itself anew. It did so without rationally conceived and visualized purpose, without reflection or analysis.

In general, life in society is a species of insurance. Insurance is something which man has had to develop against the chances of life, although he could not realize its nature and function until long ages had passed. Its function is the reduction of the risk-element in life to a constant; the substitution of a small, recurring, calculable loss for a possible ruinous and incalculable one.[24] Living within a peace-group, a man enjoyed a security which he paid for by the limitation of his freedom, by services rendered, and by payments in goods; outside of his group, he was a prey to the mischances of life just as any one is exposed to fire-hazards if his property is uninsured. It is clear that early man was bared, in the absence of an apparatus of protection, to ruinous calamities: starvation, cold, violence. He needed protection; association afforded it; and he was forced into association whether he willed or not. Under primitive conditions no one was so forlorn as the unattached man; banishment was a punishment equivalent to death. All that could save a man was the evidence, certified to by the tribal mark, that he had some one to avenge him. Cain had to have a special protective mark or the first person who met him would have put an end to him.[25] Hence tentatives arising as variations in custom developed, if they tested out on experience, to provide a form of insurance against life's mishaps. The face of the policy was security; the premiums were payments of various description. We still make them in the same old form.

24 §197, below.
25 Gen., IV, 15.

§11. **The Socializing Forces.** Plainly association is a decisive advantage in the struggle for existence, and those who developed it were of the fit. By their survival it was bound to prevail. But were there not identifiable forces that were stressing men toward it? There are two of these whose identity is revealed in our definition of society; they are the natural impulses that stimulate to self-maintenance and self-perpetuation: hunger and sex-love. Human beings share them both with the rest of animal life. Besides these, there are two others, which are specifically human, and which demand the existence of a society as an arena for their exhibition, namely, vanity and ghost-fear. "Vanity" appears here as a ranking representative of a set of impulses—including also those calling for sense-gratification or mere pleasure—that stress toward self-gratification, that is, toward the attainment of satisfactions over and above those of the very basic needs of existence.

Hunger, love, vanity, and fear have operated with great power on all peoples. We call them the socializing forces because, being the stimuli that drove men into society and held them there, they may be said to have socialized mankind. But for the action of these forces there could have been no society at all. However, this is not to say that they have made solely for peace and association; they are also the war-forces, and as such, at any rate in immediate result, they have been dissocializing in their effect. They are what forced men to action of some kind—action that has often been, and at the outset usually was, predatory: war for plunder, over women, for glory, for some religious end. It is not unheard of that the same forces should produce results apparently diametrically opposed; the fall of the stone and the ascent of the balloon are alike due to gravitation. And the final adjustment, superseding violence, even though attained through violence, has been peaceful association.[26] Hunger, love, and even vanity, in part, are instinctive, but the stress toward association which they combine to create, is not. We believe that this quartet of forces, understood as we shall endeavor to present them, is exhaustive for general purposes.

This socializing process got under way with extreme slowness and its course has been marked by frequent lapses or retrogressions. War may unite the

26 §§144, 145, and ch. XV, below.

aggressors or the assaulted; it makes the body of victors coherent; but it dis-integrates the vanquished. In Africa the destructive and desolating effects of violent raids by plunderers and slave-stealers are described by most of the explorers. Says Sir H. B. Frere:[27] "We find polygamy and slavery continually at work dissolving the cohesion of old political institutions in the old civilized races of Asia and Africa. In an uncivilized society like that of Zululand they prevent such cohesion ever taking place. They help to keep the Kaffir tribes in perpetual unrest and barbarism, by destroying the germs of civilization and preventing its growth." Slavery is perhaps the most peculiar curse under which the human race has ever fallen. It accumulates force and produces organization without which culture could not have been won, and then it turns into a sort of societal disease which is fatal to strength and organization. Polygyny is primarily in the industrial organization—in fact, marriage in general was originally almost a form of slavery which worked out into a different institution—but with the development of wealth and luxury it en-courages excess and vice and these corrupt a society to its core. Blood-revenge is the most primitive sanction of justice, peace, and order—without the law of retaliation to start with, it is hard to see how our modern systems could have developed; but it turns into a custom of private war which makes any societal order impossible. It then affords a striking example of an institution which has far outgrown its original function and has become an independent force. Feud and vendetta are irrational hate and hostility raised to a duty which preponderates over every other interest. These illustrations should carry the point that there are dissocializing forces and that they are often the same which we have seen to have been, under other circumstances, socializing.

§12. Hunger and Sex-Love. The term "hunger" is here ex-tended, beyond its special meaning, to cover sensations of lack, due to insufficient preservation or repair of bodily energies, and accom-panied with other related or derived discomforts. The prime mate-rial needs of the body are food to promote its growth and repair its waste, and protection in the form of clothing and other shelter. Hunger is here taken to be the sense of physical discomfort that impels to their satisfaction; it works out into the stimulus to the pursuit of material well-being. Perhaps "want," though more vague, would be a better term; but "hunger" recalls more vividly the underlying and ultimate facts. The characteristic of food-hunger is its rhythmic manifestation over short intervals. Wast-age of the body never ceases, and restoration must be frequent. Hunger rises slowly and steadily, like a long wave, pushing an organic being toward a state where satisfaction is sought at almost any cost. It is, imperative as no other of the forces is, for the penalty of non-satisfaction is enfeeblement and death. It is, in

[27] In JAI, XII, 266.

short, the basic impulse of life. The less vital forms of material want are less peremptory, and easily shade off into the desire for something over and above the necessities for mere existence, that is, into a strain after a standard of living. Where the eye is upon superfluities, either of quantity or quality, rather than bare necessities, there self-maintenance passes over toward self-gratification, and vanity-wants and pleasure-wants supersede hunger-wants. In general, hunger-wants are readily recognizable, and the corresponding satisfactions, being material, are soon verified and identified. If a man—even a savage—is hungry or cold, he knows what is the matter with him and what to do about it. There is not much place for theorizing or illusion. Self-maintenance is very near to realities. This is why the adjustment of the maintenance-ways is quicker and surer than that of the more derived ways, such as those belonging to self-gratification, marriage, or religion.

Our use of the word "love" refers to sex-passion and its immediate derivatives. The stimulus in this case is primarily the discomfort of an undischarged function; but the term is taken to include the sequels of mating and, in particular, the mother-love common to female animals. It also includes conjugal and paternal affection, when these appear, and even romantic love, when that form, at length, late in time, arrives. If one is constrained to believe paternal love, or any other form of family affection, to be a societal development, he need never feel that way about mother-love.

Primary sex-love is, as compared with hunger, unsteady, transitory, and violent. It is a variable over against a constant. It possesses no such massive rhythm or impassive persistence. It is a gusty thing, to be reckoned with occasionally—among animals, seasonally—and not perennially. There are no demonstrated penalties of a physical nature attendant on its postponement and restraint, though there are terrible sanctions upon irregularities in its satisfaction. Love, marriage, and the family have been justly glorified in poetry and fiction as affording the highest human felicity; but it is to be noted that sex-love alone, however compulsive, and even though it may be, for a period, enthralling to the exclusion of all other considerations, even that of existence,

is essentially a passing thing. No enduring human relations have
ever been formed upon it alone.[28]

Hunger and love are sufficient by themselves to form a society,
as the cases of animal societies show. They are primordial appetites, universal at least among the higher animals; they can be
described in terms of physiology, as the other socializing forces
cannot. They impel to the two essential activities of preserving
the present generation and of providing its successor. They force
self-preservation and race-preservation. They represent, viewed
in the large, the pain of maladjustment; all pain, indeed, is a
warning, rude though it may be kind, that life and life-conditions
are not in harmony. The ensuing discomfort leads to acts primarily aimed at relief and resulting in readjustment. Without
the activities to which hunger urges, the human stage would be
cleared very shortly; without those to which love impels, the cur-
tain would fall upon the tragedy, comedy, or farce after a span
of life allotted to one generation.

The impulsion of these vital interests is not only primordial in
human life but also permanent. Observers who penetrate below the
surface always find them. A character of Locke's[29] remarks on
"the countless ways in which different nations and different folks
look at the same thing . . . the same old principles of human life
—food, sleep, love, marriage, self-protection, law, order, the primitive essentials. Every section of society I've come across wants to
be happy, just to enjoy these elementary sanctions. And yet every
section seems to get at them in the most roundabout ways. And it
would be a very wise man who could say that one is right and
another is wrong."

Corresponding to the former of these two forces is a great set
of ways that pass into institutions, which may be termed with
brevity the maintenance-organization of society, including as its
chief arm the industrial organization; and corresponding to the
latter are the fundamental organizations of marriage and the
family. The two motives and their outworkings cross back and
forth and intertwine; that they severally and jointly impel to
association is self-evident. Anyone can see that human beings must

28 §§334, 335, below.
29 *The Coming of Amos*, 253.

coöperate in self-maintenance and self-perpetuation. We do not
intend, of course, to leave it at that; the elaboration of the obvious sometimes discloses relations not visible on the surface. In
one sense, the rest of this book is no more than a demonstration
of the effectiveness of the forces now under preliminary review.

§13. Impulses to Self-gratification. There are human activities over and above those securing mere maintenance, which are,
at the same time, not motived by the sex-love just considered or
the ghost-fear presently to be instanced. What these activities
have in common is that they minister to self-gratification; and it
is this fact that leads us to consider them together. The impulses
behind them are vanity and the various forms of the desire for
pleasure. They have resulted in no massive institutions, such as
property, government, or religion. They are diversified and show
no such integration. Nevertheless they are significant and important. They are typified by vanity, though they are not by any
means all referable to it, or even closely allied to it. To vanity can
be referred war for glory, ornamentation of various types, much
of ceremonial—in short, such activities as aim at the display of
superiorities in individual or group. It is evident enough that
vanity calls for an audience and supports rather than originates
association; and the same is true, in good measure, of the other
impulses toward self-gratification. Further developments belonging to this category are art in its various forms, gaming and
gambling, the use of intoxicants and narcotics—various forms of
catering to the senses, neutralizing boredom, and otherwise making
life more interesting. Although none of these is indispensable to
society's maintenance or perpetuation, the impulses behind them
are strong. Vanity, for instance, may on occasion thrust aside all
other considerations, to the result even of sacrificing individual
or group-existence. It evokes especial exhibitions of human energy.
Also men have always been willing to overlook necessities in the
desire to possess luxuries. And if vanity be extended or rarified to
cover pride, personal dignity, honor, ambition, and other less
crude impulses to the expression of individuality of person, class,
or wider group, it will be seen that such a sentiment deserves all
the importance assigned it in its selection as the chief representa-

tive of motives to self-gratification. In general, the development of practices in self-gratification implies an antecedent development of the maintenance-organization, by which energy is freed for activities not productive in themselves. Existence has to be assured before people can play about or practise ostentation very much.

§14. Ghost-fear. There is a fear which is felt in the face of physical suffering, economic loss, humiliation of pride; it is a form of shrinking from natural and earthly mishap; it is a fore-warning of the pain that announces maladjustment. The fear which is now in question is not such. It is uneasiness in the presence of the weird and unearthly, as typified to the primitive mind by the ghosts of the dead—a fear of the supernatural, an appalling, grisly, hair-raising, helpless terror, and an abiding one. It is of the night and darkness, when churchyards yawn and graves give up their dead. Such a sentiment is typically human, and is the product of human association. Fear, like vanity, is not so primordial as hunger and love; it is derived rather than primary, and cannot be explained in terms of physiology. Like vanity, however, it is primary for our purposes, since the most primitive of men exhibit it. Whether it was present from the beginning is immaterial; we have to work with it all through the stages of societal evolution of which we know. It becomes a socializing force, for men have always held to each other in the face of it, and have developed, in the cult, joint methods of confronting the supernatural menace. Fear, therefore, is socializing in the sense of holding society together rather than in that of producing the original association. It is a force of tremendous power, and around it develop massive institutional forms. The cult is a social bond of the first order. It seems to one, while he is concentrating for the time upon this force and its doings, that it is the strongest of all that affect the life of society; but the same conviction arises from the study of each, in turn, of the forces that have been named.

§15. Elemental Needs. The foregoing impulsions are original in human nature, in the sense that there are no peoples known who have failed to take account of them. It is possible that a few isolated tribes have exhibited an absence of ghost-fear, but the limited evidence for its lack seems inconclusive.[30] A realization of these impulsions brings home the fact that elemental needs exist. Such needs are always present and obvious to unobstructed vision; but it is not the fashion to say much about them; they are too coarse and crude to pleasure the yearning soul. Attention is fixed upon what are regarded as "higher things"—upon desires and aspirations—and the underlying vital needs are lost to sight. It is essential for one who wishes to understand the evolution of society to penetrate beneath the play of mere desires to the fundamental natural needs, as these are to be viewed in their rude and naked form among peoples not yet in possession of the societal power necessary to relegate them to the background; for that cannot be done until society is strong enough, especially in its maintenance-organization, to attend to their satisfaction and yet leave men free to experiment with higher desires.

Desire and elemental need are two different things. The former is a product of experience and is capable of indefinite intensification; from one satisfaction it reaches out to the attainment of a second. It contains also an element of idealization—a straining after something not yet, and perhaps never, realizable—and an attendant enthusiasm. It is apt to embody illusion, and sometimes only repeated disillusionment can crush it out; for enthusiasm blinds men to the facts which determine what they can attain. In civilized society, with its literature and representative arts, there is such stimulation to desire, for the most part unaccompanied by any critical sense, that people act largely from desire, not from the promptings of elemental needs; and this is, again, the reason why the consequences of what they do, individually or collectively, often differ so widely from what they expect on the basis of their motives and purposes. Civilized life often looks like a chaos of inconsistent desires and strivings. Among the unsophisticated fore-runners of civilization, who could not get far away from elemental need, the socializing forces focussed the energy of societies upon coöperative and parallel efforts, so that when men acted in association, producing the collective phenomena of societal life, they emerged into a comparatively clean-cut societal organization.

[30] §322, below.

The success of our predecessors' adjustment has built for us, as it were, a smooth platform above the elemental crudities, upon which we may, with limitations, flit about after uncertainties with some impunity; and it is a good thing we can, for such experimentation is of the very essence of civilization. Still it is salutary to realize that the primordial things are down there, right below the platform, and are as ready to swallow us up, if we pursue some will-o'-the-wisp over the edge, as they were to set their grip upon the first cave-men.[31]

§16. **Antagonistic Coöperation.** Brought into association and held there by compulsion, men strive on in proximity, and with the sacrifice of personal freedom, to realize hunger-interests, love-interests, and the rest. The fellow-members of a society collide on occasion, but they push on as a body in the same direction. Doing things together secures accumulated impact against obstacles; it involves rhythm, and rhythmic applications of force have their characteristic efficacy. A body of soldiers may cross a shaky bridge safely by breaking step, while their movement in rhythm will sway the structure to its fall. Coöperation, however, for all its expediency, is brought to pass not because the individuals want to coöperate, but because they have to; the only way to get on is to sink differences, endure sacrifices and limitations, and work together because custom, which promotes the expedient, demands it. Coöperation is worth the price, though, it must be understood, such assessment of a customary usage is never worked out rationally by early man; he lives on into it unconsciously. It is clear that most coöperation has in it, in primitive days at any rate, suppressed antagonisms that are overborne by practical advantages; it is quite as wrong to assume mutual good-will as the basis of human coöperation as it would be to suppose its existence between the bee and the clover or the rhinoceros and the tick-bird. There is no love lost between the ponderous, nearsighted pachyderm and its alert, sharp-eyed parasite, though the former, as the host of thousands of ticks, forms a feeding-ground for the latter, and the latter, by nervous twitterings, warns the former of im-

31 Keller, *Soc. Evol.*, 177-179.

pending danger.[32] That the native, when he wishes to express his dependence upon another, calls him "my rhinoceros," is quite irrelevant to the real relation of beast and bird.

In view of the various facts now before us concerning association, it is evident that the term "antagonistic coöperation"[33] may be justly applied to many of the forms of joint activity of men. There are few major cases of coöperation into which the antagonistic element does not enter. The term will be needed and illustrated, over and over again, in the course of this book.

§17. Custom. Since there is no absolute solution for the problems of life, the interests of men are not satisfied in all cases by the same adjustments. What is found in societal life is a variety of forms of coöperation, that is, of corporate ways of realizing interests. Institutions differ as between different parts of the world at any one time, and also as between different times in any one part of the world. Still, because both men and their life-conditions are pretty much alike, there is a general similarity between the expedients adopted for the realization of interests in all places and times. They have a family likeness. They all reflect the inveterate conditions of life on earth. Divergences are seen, often obviously and always upon reflection, to be due to local circumstances. These considerations suggest the presence of some general process, with laws behind it, which works on imperturbably beneath the complexities of society's life and institutional forms, down in the region of the elemental needs. Society adjusts itself to its life-conditions by this process, which we term societal evolution. But before we enter upon a sketch of that process, it is necessary to go back to those "ways" out of which institutions develop, and acquire a somewhat more definite conception of them.

If one reflects upon the life of some society which he can view with detachment because it is remote from his interests, particularly a primitive society, he is presently impressed by the power of local custom. Here are those "ways" to which allusion has been made. People do this and refrain from doing that solely because of their traditional codes of conduct. If a native is asked why he

---

32 Livingstone, *Mission. Travels*, II, 584-585.
33 §462, below.

will not eat fish, or marry his cousin, or leave off servility before the chief, he will reply that it is because his ancestors abstained from eating such food, contracting such alliances, or showing anything but obsequiousness to constituted power. The answer will assert that ill is sure to result from non-conformity to the local standards of behavior. One's conclusion is that primitive peoples are ruled by custom. "There are pounded into every Indian . . . from the moment he first breathes, the ideas and the outlook of his particular group, which is a very limited one; and so his point of view and his genius are hedged in. Rousseau and Voltaire were wrong. The 'savage' has less personal liberty than any of us. Even his mind is cramped, and he conforms religiously to the *mores* of his time and place; for that inheres in being a savage."[34]

Since primitive times much development has taken place; yet who would care to deny that the masses of mankind, even that part of them that dwells in a civilized country, are still creatures of custom? Let the observer try to keep his eye in the same focus of detachment while looking about him, and he will see the masses still adhering almost wholly to custom, and even the enlightened freed only to a degree from its domination. From the time and manner of eating to the time and mode of worship; from the mode of dressing infants to the fashion of enshrouding the dead—all is prescribed in the local code, and departure from it is rare. The unconventional is, in fact, penalized; so that it is not only easier to adhere to custom, but uncomfortable or dangerous to break away from it. These facts are obvious when once correctly visualized, and have been enlarged upon by men of vision in all ages.

In truth, the power of custom over life is one of those matters of fact to which men constantly appeal without reflection or analysis. Custom is by its nature a floating and undefined conception, and is accepted as a sort of pervasive and irreducible feature of life. In its varieties it is highly interesting and can be profusely and edifyingly illustrated, but to deal with it scientifically is difficult. It lends itself to irresponsible speculation just because it is so diffuse, evasive, and resistant to scientific devices for analyzing phenomena, reducing them to orderliness, and handling them in the search for truth. And yet a science of society, if it is to be pene-

34 Walton and Waterman, in AA, XXVII, 26.

trating and revealing, must overcome that resistance; for all of society's forms and institutions are found, when reduced to lowest evolutionary terms, in custom. It is the germ of them all. Nothing in the societal realm is more original, underived, and elemental. The study of custom is, for a science of society, what the study of the cell is for biology.

§18*. Folkways and Mores. The senior author of this book, during the composition of his original survey, became so impressed by the fundamental character of custom or convention that he turned aside to an analysis of it, as to an unforeseen but inevitable preliminary to a science of society. The result was a volume called *Folkways*, subtitled "a study of the sociological importance of usages, manners, customs, mores, and morals."[35] In that study the author undertakes to relieve the conception of custom of that indefiniteness and intangibility to which allusion has been made. It was found necessary to adopt the terms "folkways" and "mores" to cover social usages and traditions, in order to evade the set of vague connotations that cling about the more familiar terms.

The present book is constructed, as its original projector felt that it must be, and as his collaborator heartily agrees, upon the conception of the mores. It is impossible to convey that conception fully by summary, for the transfer of an idea which may, after acceptance, seem simple and obvious, can be definitively accomplished only by presenting a weight of concrete evidence. No amount of reasoning offers a substitute for plain facts, such as *Folkways* sets forth in profusion. Nevertheless the conception of the mores developed in that work must find place at this point, even though it must be expressed in dogmatic form and with the severest brevity.

§19. Development of the Folkways. The first task of life is to live, and every moment brings necessities that must be satisfied at once. These are requirements of adaptation, and the sign of their presence is pain. In the beginning is need; and in response to need ensues action, not reflective thought. Upon the experience of pain there follows an attempt somehow to allay the discomfort by satis-

[35] See iii of the Introduction to *Folkways*.

fying the need. There is no experience of the relation of means to ends, to serve as a guide, and "the method is that of trial and failure, which produces repeated pain, loss, and disappointments." New needs are always appearing, which have to be met in the same clumsy and floundering way. Such tentatives form a case of variation, with the several variants of unequal value in the struggle to live. Some of them relieve the situation, however, and the fact is noticed. "Pleasure and pain, on the one side and the other, were the rude constraints which defined the line on which efforts must proceed. The ability to distinguish between pleasure and pain is the one psychical power which is to be assumed. Thus ways of doing things were selected, which were expedient. They answered the purpose better than other ways, or with less toil and pain. Along the course on which efforts were compelled to go, habit, routine, and skill were developed."

Here are no real assumptions, any more than in the development of the man-land ratio, but rather simple facts of experience.

Thus far it is the individual that has occupied the foreground. But the individual never developed folkways, which are mass-phenomena; and mass-phenomena are the only sort of phenomena upon the study of which a science of society can be built. From now on, in the development of the folkways, the individual drops out; for the next step is "a concurrence towards that which proved to be most expedient. All at last adopted the same way for the same purpose; hence the ways turned into customs and became mass-phenomena. . . . The operation by which folkways are produced consists in the frequent repetition of petty acts, often by great numbers acting in concert or, at least, acting in the same way when face to face with the same need. The immediate motive is interest. It produces habit in the individual and custom in the group. It is, therefore, in the highest degree original and primitive. By habit and custom it exerts a strain on every individual within its range; therefore it rises to a societal force to which great classes of societal phenomena are due."

Clearly the development of the folkways is wholly unpremeditated. "It is of the first importance to notice that, from the first acts by which men try to satisfy needs, each act stands by itself, and looks no further than the immediate satisfaction. From recurrent needs arise habits for the individual and customs for the group, but these results are consequences which were never conscious, and never foreseen or intended. They are not noticed until they have long existed, and it is still longer before they are appreciated. Another long time must pass, and a higher stage of mental development must be reached, before they can be used as a basis from which to deduce rules for meeting, in the future, problems whose pressure can be foreseen. . . . The origin of primitive customs is always lost in mystery, because when the action begins the men are never conscious of historical action, or of the historical importance of what they are doing. When they become conscious of the historical importance of their acts, the origin is already far behind."

§20. The Mores. After practising certain folkways for an extended time, people acquire the conviction that they are indispensable to the welfare of society. They come to believe that their own ways are the only right ones, and that departure from them will involve calamity. It is with the addition of this welfare-element that folkways become mores. To illustrate: the removal of the hat when a civilian meets a woman on the street is in our folkways, while the practice of monogamy belongs to our mores. We do not regard neglect of the former usage as dangerous to society, though it is discreditable to the individual; but we are so convinced as to the expediency of the latter that we will promptly and severely repress the polygamist, and that in the interests of society. There is a real distinction in analysis between a folkway and a mos, but it is a discrimination for the laboratory rather than for actual practice. Settled folkways surrounding a vital interest are always taking on the welfare-element and receiving religious sanction, thus becoming mores. It is out of the mores rather than the folkways that institutions develop, and in a study of institutions, such as we present, the former term is naturally more in evidence. Anyone who uses the two terms very much finds it in any case unprofitable if not impracticable to insist upon consistency in discriminating between them; as evolutionary categories, they shade imperceptibly into one another.

The welfare-element in the mores is powerfully reinforced by a conviction which is in the minds of all primitive peoples and appears in survivalistic form upon high stages of civilization. The dead are supposed to harbor an intense prejudice in favor of the mores which they found good while in life, and to guarantee them with the supernatural power which is now theirs. Religion comes to be the redoubtable sanction of the mores, and with its entrance upon the scene they become uniform, universal in a society, imperative, and, over long periods, invariable.

Putting the foregoing considerations together, we arrive at a definition of the mores: they are the popular habits and traditions, when they include a judgment that they are conducive to societal welfare, and when they exert a coercion on the individual to conform to them, although they are not coördinated by any authority. Human life, "in all ages and stages of culture, is primarily controlled by a vast mass of folkways handed down from the earliest existence of the race, having the nature of the ways of other animals, only the topmost layers of which are subject to control, and have been somewhat modified by human philosophy, ethics, and religion, or by other acts of intelligent reflection."

We are told that "it is difficult to exhaust the customs and small ceremonial usages of a savage people. Custom regulates the whole of a man's actions,— his bathing, washing, cutting his hair, eating, drinking, and fasting. From his cradle to his grave he is the slave of ancient usage. In his life there is nothing free, nothing original, nothing spontaneous, no progress towards a higher and better life, and no attempt to improve his condition, mentally, morally, or spiritually."[36]

All men act in this way with only a little wider margin of voluntary variation. "The mores are social ritual in which we all participate unconsciously. The current habits as to hours of labor, meal hours, family life, the social intercourse of the sexes, propriety, amusements, travel, holidays, education, the use of periodicals and libraries, and innumerable other details of life fall under this ritual. Each does as everybody does. For the great mass of mankind as to all things, and for all of us for a great many things, the rule to do as all do suffices. We are led by suggestion and association to believe that there must be wisdom and utility in what all do. The great mass of the folkways gives us discipline and the support of routine and habit. If we had to form judgments as to

[36] Macdonald, in JAI, XX, 140.

all these cases before we could act in them, and were forced always to act rationally, the burden would be unendurable. Beneficent use and wont save us this trouble."[37]

§21. The Mores in Evolution. The folkways and mores are, as we have several times stated, institutions in their lowest terms. In their developed form institutions are very complex and their essentials difficult to disengage and identify; but their simple and informal beginnings, which are direct, habitual, unconscious, unpremeditated adjustments to life-conditions, are less confusing and baffling. They are nearer to nature and may be studied with fewer intrusions of the subjective element and of bias. Thus examined, they reveal at once their evolutionary quality in the very fact that they constitute adjustments to life-conditions. This book will substantiate that fact in almost every paragraph. For a systematic treatment of evolution in the mores we must again refer to a separate publication by one of the present writers,[38] and again limit ourselves to a brief and dogmatic statement of contentions there advanced.

Adjustment of the mores to society's existing life-conditions is the fact of observation to be explained. It is accounted for by the combined action of variation in the mores, selection among the mores, and transmission of the mores. The first of these is technically demonstrable only by the citation of thousands of well-known instances; it is here assumed to be self-evident. That selection occurs is shown by the fact, among others, that the path of society's advance from primitive conditions to high civilization is strewn with the débris of discarded customs and institutions. All through history, codes and institutions have risen as variations on what went before, have persisted long enough, at least, to get into the records, and then have lasted on for a long time—always under considerable alteration of detail—or have passed away. Such is the result of the action of selection. Variations that have weathered

37 Sumner, *Folkways*, §68.
38 Keller, *Societal Evolution*, a Study of the Evolutionary Basis of the Science of Society. See pages 328-330 for the relation of the two authors of this book to the conception. Briefer and simpler statements are to be found in Keller, *Through War to Peace*, chs. VI, VII, XIV, XVIII, and in Keller, "Societal Evolution," being ch. V of Lull and others, *Evolution of Man*.

the selective process have become candidates for transmission over longer periods through imitation and tradition, so that they have come, in some instances, to be widespread over space or time, or both. An institution like slavery shows a distinct life-cycle, from small tentatives, through an almost if not quite universal prevalence, into a state of decay befitting that which has become a maladjustment.

Here are the processes of variation, selection, and transmission. The first originates in the individual, who throws out tentatives in response to need felt personally; the third takes place through the eye and ear, and passes the mores over from generation to generation and also between contemporaries. The process of selection demands a little more attention, even in a summary. It is mainly automatic and unplanful, especially on the primitive stage; but so, for that matter, are variation and transmission. If purposeful reasoning, followed by action in the light of it, comes in anywhere, it is in variation, when that factor takes the form of experimentation. Selection, automatic or not, calls for conflict and competition, which are furnished primarily by the struggle for existence and then by the struggle for a better quality of existence. Competition never ends; and it is well that it does not if the attainment of better adjustment, which must be through the agency of selection, is desirable. The crudest form of selection is by way of violence, or war; it is also the final resort at any period, the last argument, the *ultima ratio*. Codes and institutions go down to destruction along with the men who practise them. Selection takes place also through peaceful competition, industrial, political, and other. Chiefly in these lighter forms does it reveal a certain relation between sets of mores that should be borne in mind throughout any study of societal evolution. This relation is as follows.

The mores that have to do with self-maintenance, being closest to natural conditions, are checked up more speedily and obviously on the life-conditions than are the rest of the mores. Poor methods in hunting are revealed to be such much more readily than are inexpedient religious practices. Causes of discomfort and failure are here more easily identifiable, impressing even the untrained mind. Hence the maintenance-mores tend to follow changing life-conditions pretty closely; that is, they are least insulated against selection, least subject to benumbing tradition, more sensitive. They are adjustable as the rest of the mores are not. The rest of the mores, however, take their tone from the maintenance-mores, as from a sort of basic theme; the former experience a strain toward consistency with the latter. The superstructure—those mores which are farther removed from the ground of natural conditions—must conform to the foundation-lines of the maintenance-mores. This is a relation which will be illustrated frequently, as we go on. It follows that selection operates indirectly upon the forms of property, marriage, religion, and government, as compared with its action upon forms of industry. If the industrial type changes from, say, a pastoral economy to an agricultural, gradually there appears a characteristic alteration in those customs which are more remote from pragmatic test. There is a pastoral type of general societal organization, as well as of industry. An appreciation of this relation amounts to the possession of a key to not a few doors that one wants to open as he explores the structure of society.

The tendency is prevalent to read into the primitive mind the sophisticated, sentimental, and other ways of viewing life which freedom from the raw struggle for existence has allowed civilized man to develop; indeed, it is regarded as somewhat sordid and "materialistic" to regard the lofty superstructure of societal life as resting upon an indispensable basis in the maintenance-organization. Sentimentalists revolt at the idea much as they do at the derivation of man from animal ancestry. Nevertheless there can be no scientific investigation of society any more than of physical man apart from a willingness to follow the facts wherever and however far they lead.

As an illustration of a picturesque but false interpretation confronted by one which, though materialistic, is true, take the following. "It has often been a subject of remark by visitors to the Nilgiri Hills that the Todas have chosen the most beautiful spots for their dwellings, and interest has been taken in the love of beauty in nature which this choice shows. I think there can be little doubt that the choice of suitable dwelling-places has been chiefly determined by the necessity of a good water-supply, and if possible of a double water-supply, and the Todas have chosen the beautiful spots, not because they are beautiful, but because they are well watered. Their choice has been dictated, not by a love of beautiful scenery, but by the practical necessities of their daily life."[39] This instance remotely recalls the pleased surprise of the lady who believed that this was the best possible of worlds, when she came to perceive that rivers ran so conveniently near to cities.

Numerous instances could be assembled to illustrate adjustments of the mores to sudden changes in the environment produced by the contact of a higher civilization with a lower.[40] Here, as elsewhere, the maintenance-mores are, so to speak, the file-leaders for the rest. The superiority of the white man's tools has forced the Australian stone tomahawk and wooden digging-stick out of the field; the iron crowbar easily attained supremacy.[41]

Fletcher and La Flesche[42] remarked how "the various environments in which the Omaha people lingered as they moved westward left their impress on the ceremonials of the tribe. Some of these . . . were lost and the relation of others to the welfare of the people suffered change." These authors cite a number of examples in point and go on to a general survey of adjustments which is worth reproduction in full.

"With the coming of the trader and the introduction of iron implements and other articles for daily use new conditions confronted the Indians; they were no longer obliged to make all the articles required for use and the time formerly occupied by the long and wearisome process of chipping and rubbing stone was now left free. Furthermore, the stimulus for acquiring skill in the old-time industries was withdrawn. The new iron implements which had brought about this change in conditions had been acquired by bartering pelts. Barter was not new to the people. It had long been practised between various tribes; minerals, seeds, shells, and other articles had found their way by this means into regions remote from their natural environment, but it is safe to say that up to the time of the coming of the white trader no Omaha had slain animals for merely commercial purposes. The barter in pelts established by the trader was therefore different in character from any barter that had been practised between tribes and was destined to give rise to a new industry among the Indians—that of hunting for gain. Heretofore hunting had been carried on in order to secure food and other necessities—clothing, shelter, and bone with which to make implements; moreover it had been conducted with more or less religious ceremony, which had directed the Omaha thought toward . . . [their Great Spirit], as the giver of the means by which to sustain life, as shown in the rites connected with the annual buffalo hunt and planting the maize. The quest of game for profit introduced new motives for hunting and also of cultivating the soil, motives not consonant with the old religious ideas and customs; consequently under their influence such customs slowly but inevitably fell into disuse. The effect on the Omaha mind of their obliteration was to weaken the power of ancient beliefs and to introduce new standards, commercial in charac-

39 Rivers, *Todas*, 26.
40 Keller, *Soc. Evol.*, chs. V, VIII; Muntz, *Contact*.
41 Horne and Aiston, *Cent. Aust.*, 11.
42 In BAE, XXVII, 261, 614-615.

ter; as a result the Omaha became less strong to resist the inroads of new and adverse influences which came with his closer contact with the white race.

"The new character given to hunting produced permanent effects not only on the thought of the people but on their ancient mode of life. The stimulation of hunting as an avocation weakened the influence of the old village life, created different standards of wealth, enhanced the importance of the hunter, and greatly increased the labors of the women in preparing pelts and skins for the market. There is good reason to ascribe to the last-named condition an impetus to the practice of polygamy among the Omaha. There was no special working class in the tribe nor could labor be hired. In the old time one woman could scarcely give proper attention to all the skins secured by a good hunter; still less could she do the additional work occasioned by the pressure of trade."

Evidently group-adjustment through the mores is a never-ending indispensable. Its success is adjudged by what happens to numbers. When we say that such and such tribes are not succeeding in the struggle for existence, we mean that as the biologist does: they are not increasing in numbers. That is, as in nature, because their adjustments to life-conditions are not apt enough; but for their isolation doubtless many of them would never have survived to become objects of study.

§22. Evolutionary Series. Having scanned the process by which societal adjustment is attained, we are in a position to realize that the actual societal forms which result from it must constitute an evolutionary series; that is, a succession of forms developing out of preceding forms, in a connected order, with survival of the fittest expedients. This book deals with such series rather than with the process itself. The series of marriage-forms, for example, runs from the slightest of regulation through to the exclusive form called pair-marriage. The forms of government which correspond to various sets of life-conditions, over space and through time, fall likewise into a series, which begins with an informal council of elders or a vague chieftainship and winds up, thus far, with a highly organized "democracy." Monogamy and the single-toed equine foot are equally forms of adjustment to life-conditions, secured by the action of regular evolutionary factors. It is with the tracing of such series that this book has chiefly to do. Only we need an understanding of how the process is working in order to get at the sense of the phases, and of the change of phases, of societal forms and institutions. The survey of the results of a process shed additional light upon the process itself. Studies in the camel-series certainly illuminate the process of organic evolution, and similarly a review of the property-series or the family-series should clarify the general process of societal evolution. In that sense, we shall be studying the process, in its results, throughout this book; for presently we shall embark upon a protracted review of the essential nature and successive phases of society's instruments of adjustment—its mores and institutions.

§23. Society and the Individual. If society is to be studied in the evolutionary series of its institutions, the length of the perspective involved means that the individual is pretty much lost to sight. The subject-matter of a science of society can be nothing else than a society. It is a pity that everything cannot be studied at once, but the human mind is not constituted so as to do that. A society lives and evolves in accordance with laws of its own; the individual can be left to the sciences which make a business of investigating his body and mind. We believe societal phenomena to be due to the operation of impersonal, automatically acting forces which transcend altogether the range of individual powers and control and produce effects characteristic of themselves alone. Such a conception provides, to our view, the sole reason for existence of a science of society and assures to it a distinctive range of its own. The individual cannot be left utterly out of account any more than can the molecular composition of an ivory ball used in a physics experiment; but if the object of study is the ball, or the society, it is just and proper to deal with it as an entity, not as a sum of its constituent elements.

The individual has a function of surpassing importance as a source of variation in the mores; he is the indispensable leader-off in the evolutionary process, for without variation no process can take place. He may even set afloat a mutation. For present purposes, however, it is immaterial how or through what agency a variant derives its origin. When it comes into the range of our investigation, concurrence has taken place some time since; it is already a mass-phenomenon, to be dealt with as such. We are convinced that this way of looking at things frees our treatment from a current tendency, which we regard as confusing and unproduc-

tive, to refer societal results to conscious, reasoned, and purposeful action on the part of the individual. There is a view of society
—as of woods from among the trees—which may be got by preoccupation with the individual, his psychology, and his "choices";
then there is another—as of the woods from a detached position—
which promises superior clarity and perspective in that it envis-
ages society as a whole. The latter we regard as a more commanding vantage-point for the observation and assessment, not only of
historic societal phenomena, but also of those formations and dis-
solutions that are taking place as our own day passes.

If we extend our perspective, look over and beyond the individual, and think
in terms of societies, we can see, for example in the late world-conflict,[43] the
alignment and confrontation of societies in pursuit of their group-interests
under their codes—vast forms going about their prodigious affairs, uncon-
cerned, above the fighting, dying, unregarded mortals. The movements of the
contending societies are seen to be impersonal and automatic, after the manner of bodies acted upon by gravitation or capillary attraction, and the individual is lost to identification as he blends into the composite mass. The world-
conflict, thus seen—and, as we believe, correctly seen—appears as a powerful
selective agency in the evolution, not alone of the several societies, but of
human society itself. Here was a vast laboratory of selection—the greatest
laboratory the student of society has ever seen or heard of—for what was
going on before his face was no less than the most gigantic exhibition of selection between codes of mores that the world has ever witnessed. Such a crisis-
time affords glimpses of the cosmic process—glimpses that one can never
catch, of truth that will remain veiled to him, so long as he does not ascend
in thought to a plane where individuals and their doings cease to distract him.
And what is true of a crisis-time is true, in its measure, of any other time also.

In adhering to this point of view, we present a way of looking at
the succession of societal phenomena, including those that are contemporary, which must be judged by what is rendered visible. No
amount of preliminary defense of the method adopted counts for
anything. The contention is that the life of society is so long and
wide that a far-reaching perspective of mass-phenomena is required in order to make out the course and sense of its evolution.

§24. Land, Men, and Mores. Environment, or land, may be
considered as a stage, and men as the actors. The latter must adjust to the former. As a society, they do this through the expedients of folkways and mores. These are evolutionary products,
brought into adjustment through the combined action of varia-

[43] Keller, *War to Peace,* ix, chs. II-IV.

tion, selection, and transmission. The maintenance-mores respond most speedily and convincingly to changes in the type of the struggle for existence; then the rest of the mores follow after those of maintenance. If we reflect upon the determinative influence upon the type of the struggle for existence exerted by the population-land ratio, and then upon the formative action of that struggle upon the mores, it becomes ever clearer that our study of the science of society starts out with a set of objective and even obvious considerations.

It should be understandable that a master-strand like this one of the man-land ratio will not regularly show through the fabric that is woven upon it. It would be monotonous in the extreme to insist upon dissecting down to fundamentals in the case of every detailed and ramifying usage encountered; every twig cannot be faithfully carried back to the trunk. It is enough in most cases to trace it to the branch that supports it; if the connection of that branch to the main stem is accepted, the ultimate provenance of the twig is not a matter of doubt.

From what precedes it might be inferred that we regard the man-land ratio as a universal explanation of societal phenomena. A disclaimer on that point is entered forthwith. Only the tyro in the study of human society dares to risk much on the single cause. That we have distinguished love, vanity, and ghost-fear as three of the quartet of socializing forces indicates that we are not proposing to settle down to any doctrinaire demonstration of economic determinism. What we shall have to say concerning the intertwining of various factors will reveal many instances of multiple causation. The classification which we have adopted makes allowance for the entrance of a number of factors aside from the purely economic ones.

Our contention is briefly this: that if society is to endure, no considerations whatever can take precedence over success in self-maintenance, that is, in the food-quest and in the provision of protection of all kinds to life. "The first task of life is to live." Success in self-maintenance depends upon racial qualities of several types; nevertheless those qualities may be present in the highest degree and yet, unless the earth provides sufficient sustenance, men may fail. They fail in any case if there are too many of them; they will succeed with a minimum of effort if they are few in comparison with resources; the sort of struggle they will be forced to make will vary according to the proportion of numbers to resources.

What they can do in ranges outside of material self-maintenance cannot but vary, and will be seen to vary, with the type of struggle they have to maintain in order to supply basic necessities. Ways outside of self-maintenance proper must take their general tone from self-maintenance-ways. In many cases their details of tone will be seen, on thorough inspection, to be set by their dependence upon prior success in maintenance. When this relation is evident and direct, we shall not omit the calling of attention to it; where it is not, where a usage is merely a characteristic growth on a branch which itself has been shown to be vitally connected with maintenance, we shall not parrot the man-land ratio to no profit.

Thus far we have not sought to distinguish men from men, or land from land, in our basic ratio. In the long perspective it does not matter what men are on what land; the ratio holds just the same. In fact, we might quite as readily work out an animal-land or a plant-land relation. But it is possible now to sharpen our terms somewhat, and to consider how the original ratio has been modified by the application of the human mind. For not only do men, when they begin to adjust mentally rather than physically, strike out on a different plane of evolution from that of the rest of the organisms, but they accomplish, among other things, no less than an alteration in both terms of the deep-rooted numbers-land ratio.

CHAPTER II

MODIFICATION OF THE MAN-LAND RATIO

§25. The Law of Population. The man-land ratio is a rough formula or synthesis, blocked out in comprehensive terms and indicating in broadest outline the fundamentals of the subject before us. Both terms of the ratio might be subjected to an analysis which would reveal them to be highly composite. As for man, some ethnologists do not doubt that the several races of mankind are differently endowed by nature; and any race will split up into thousands of sub-divisions capable of being set off, on various "natural" criteria, from one another. Similarly with land: considered as the ultimate source of life-necessities, it reveals a variety of types of "biological intensity"[1]—meaning the amount of flora and fauna available, the plant and animal substances usable without progressively destroying them. Neither term of the ratio is, then, fixed once and for all, but both fluctuate.

Such fluctuations, so far as they refer to natural diversities in land or men, can be noted and then ignored; for in whatever combination races of alleged innate high, low, or medium grade may meet high, low, or medium grade land, the ratio still obtains. What cannot be ignored is the capacity of men, through the development of folkways, to alter the terms of the ratio.

The ratio between numbers and land is something that plants and animals cannot alter. If their increase is such as to press heavily upon their food-supply, the only possible immediate outcome, apart from migration, is such elimination of numbers as will leave the survivors provided for. Over a long period, structural adjustments might take place which would enable more individuals to live upon the same area; but even so the immediate mortality would be little if at all decreased. Animal and plant life tends to increase up to the limit of the supporting power of the environment; it cannot advance beyond that dead-line. The case of man is different; he is an animal with superior capacities for speedy adjustment which enable him to operate upon the numbers-land

[1] Ratzel, *Anthropogeog.*, II, 205 ff.

ratio. By the invention of various methods of getting more food out of the land, he virtually increases that term of the ratio, a feat which allows of a rise in human numbers. We call these adjustments of his the arts of life, or, briefly, the arts. When they deal directly with the extraction from nature of the prime necessities of life, chiefly food, they include the instruments and processes of hunting, herding, and tillage, all of which are, directly or indirectly, ways of exploiting land. And men can also operate upon the other term of the ratio, for they can practise limitation of their own numbers. This is generally put into operation, not so much to avoid the worst as to maintain a standard of living that is traditional, or to attain to a higher one. Thus the arts are seen to be operating upon the land-side of the basic ratio, and the standard of living upon the man-side.

The foregoing considerations may be gathered up, prior to analysis, into a law of population. Numbers vary directly with the arts and inversely with the standard of living. To align this law of human population with the one which covers the case of plants and animals, all that is necessary is the proviso that the modifying arts and standard of living shall remain constant—thus: Population tends to increase up to the limit of the supporting power of the environment (land), on a given stage of the arts, and for a given standard of living. This is, it will be noted, simply a more explicit rendering of the bare man-land ratio. The rest of this chapter will be devoted to the disclosure in finer detail of the ways by which men have altered the terms of that ratio through the development of the arts of life and of the standard of living. It should never be lost to sight that those alterations have taken place through the evolution of folkways and mores, for both the arts and the standard of living belong among these basic adjustments.

§26. Numbers and Civilization. The question of numbers is paramount in the organic world. Successful adjustments are those permitting of numbers, while dwindling species are approaching extinction. The same is true in the societal range. The sum of men's adjustments to their life-conditions is their culture, or civilization. These adjustments, it has been seen, are attained only through the combined action of variation, selection, and transmission. There must be numerous and frequently recurring variations for selection to operate upon, if the process is to work out into a high degree of civilization; and this cannot be, unless there are many individuals present who are striking out on various tentatives in the realization of interests. Variation calls for numbers. Nor can selection appear in full vigor unless the competition is keen. Selection, too, demands numbers. And the products of selection cannot attain to any extended transmission, so as to spread both lineally to subsequent generations and laterally to contemporaries, unless there is some density of population. Civilization is therefore a function of numbers in contact. On the other hand, numbers cannot increase greatly unless the adjustments to life-conditions are successful, especially those that have to do with the food-quest. "Whilst food is to be had, there is no fear of wanting people."[2] "Where there is bread there will be men, but we cannot say that where there are men there will be bread."[3]

Barriers to free contact are typically anti-cultural; anything that hinders exchanges acts as an isolating factor preventive of the wide socialization of achievement. One of the most effective of insulators is difference of language. This is taken up, along with other similar factors, in a later connection.[4] A single example may lend enforcement at this point. Speaking of Kordofan, Seligmann[5] remarks on "the multiplicity of languages spoken within its bounds. The inhabitants of neighbouring hills only a few miles apart may speak languages mutually unintelligible and even on the same *massif* [land-elevation]— when this is of moderate size—there may be two or three communities speaking different languages and coming little into contact one with another, though their habits, customs and beliefs are fundamentally the same."

There is, indeed, a school of anthropological thought which minimizes the parallel origination of culture-phenomena as compared with the contagion or acculturation resulting from race-contact. Rivers,[6] who is less fanatical than some others in his adherence to this point of view, states it as follows; the passage is quoted because, apart from any dispute about theory, it brings out sharply the services of contact in promoting culture. "The assumption which underlies the whole construction of this book is the importance of the contact of peoples in the history of human culture. It has been the main task of this volume to show how all the chief social institutions of Melanesia, its dual organization, its secret societies, its totemism, its cult of the dead, and many

2 Townsend, *Poor Laws,* in *Overstone Tracts,* III, 443.
3 Zacharias, *Bevölkrgsfrage,* 43.
4 §§79, 137, 167.
5 In JAI, XL, 507.
6 *Melan. Soc.,* II, 595.

of its less essential customs, such as its use of money, its decorative art, its practice of incision and its square houses, have been the direct outcome of the interaction between different and sometimes conflicting cultures. . . . The Oceanic evidence points unmistakably to degradation and even to disappearance as the result of isolation, and suggests that the mixture of peoples will have to be taken much more into account by the historians of human culture than it has been in the past. Indeed, the study of this part of the world suggests that the contact and interaction of peoples have furnished the starting-points of all the great movements in human history which we are accustomed to regard as Progress."

Population among tribes of low civilization is sparse; such people are not succeeding in the struggle for existence because they have not developed culture, and their lack of numbers halts that development. Their degree of societal adaptation is not high enough to allow of a reduction of the death-rate by an augmentation of the food-supply and of protection from the elements and from violence. Here is a case of the supporting and interlocking action of societal factors: population fails to increase because culture is backward, while at the same time the arts do not improve with any promptness by reason of lack of numbers. Even upon a low stage of the arts, however, civilization has been capable of development where the natural supporting power of the environment has allowed of considerable numbers despite the backwardness of culture. The first foci of civilization were precisely where environmental conditions combined to favor numbers and the contact of numbers: in the river-bottoms of the warmer temperate sections of the Old World—in China, India, Assyria, and Egypt.[7] Numbers made possible the development of the arts; then the arts improved to support a still larger population; then the added numbers, in turn, stressed the arts to further advance. Thus the process rolled up on itself. An advanced civilization and a relative density of population are destined to occur conjointly.

§27. Action of the Arts of Life. The effect of the arts is to multiply land in the matter of its supporting power. Hence they attack the problem of living at its root; for in the relative abundance of air, water, and some other necessities, the supreme (because limited) requisites are food, clothing, and shelter, all of which are ultimately land-derived. The sense of the development of

[7] Gregory, Keller, and Bishop, *Phys. and Comm. Geog.*, ch. X.

the arts is that it bears upon the antagonism between the natality and mortality of men. It enlarges the conditions of survival around a group of human beings. The arts change the plane upon which natality and mortality are operating, and the limit at which they become equal is moved. Among savages, population might thus become stationary, with natality and mortality equal, when each soul had a hundred square miles, while the same conditions might not appear among civilized men until there were a thousand souls to each square mile.

If natality is conceived of as positive or aggressive, mortality is negative, and may be figured as the obstacle, barrier, or restraint against which natality beats. Here we have before us the struggle for existence in the simplest conception of it. Death is not the problem, but life. That anything should be, means that it triumphs over nothingness, and that its continued existence must be maintained by constant victories, procured by apt adjustment to nature's laws, to wrest from her all that it needs to maintain its vital energy. Life is active and implies growth, self-aggrandizement, maturity, and decline. It reaches a climax and is spent. It contains in itself decline, decay, and death; that is to say, when its initial energy is spent and its power of assimilation is exhausted, it storms the opposing barrier in vain. It follows that if anything moves the barrier farther away, natality will increase and will spring up to press against it as hard as ever. It is the arts which set the barriers of mortality farther off by winning more subsistence with the same labor, or by increasing human defenses against cold, heat, and the elements, or by giving men more advantage in the competition of life with other organisms. The arts are always operating on the land-side of the man-land ratio—weighing down the scale-pan on that side, let us say, so that a greater and greater weight of living beings can find place in the other pan, and equilibrium still be preserved.

The arts of life, as the term is here used, should not be confounded with other arts which more directly counteract mortality; such are the prophylactic and healing arts. These operate on numbers, not by way of land, but immediately; they attend to the preservation of life irrespective of the presence of resources for its support. They lay heavier burdens upon the population-side of the ratio which the land-side must weigh up to equilibrium. Likewise does the establishment of peace, law, and order result in the preservation of numbers, and so add to the strain upon the land-element. Such developments of culture are always forcing the arts of life.

The effect of advance in these arts, however stimulated, upon numbers and civilization, may be illustrated by reference to a set of simple types. There are four orders of effort by which societies are found to be maintaining themselves directly off the land. These have been called the primary maintenance-activities and are extractive; they are collection (the mere gathering of food and other natural products), hunting, animal-raising, and plant-culture. There are no other methods in the field for getting a living so directly out of land. Of course the living does not consist of dirt, even for earth-eaters, but of plant and animal substance; so that, strictly speaking, the land is not directly exploited. In comparison, however, with these four methods, such processes as those of mining, manufacture, and commerce are indirect; they will not maintain a population by their own immediate winnings. To these four direct types of maintenance there correspond four types of societal economy: the collection stage, the hunting stage, the pastoral stage, and the agricultural stage. It is true that such "stages" are abstractions, in the sense that there are few peoples, and perhaps none at all, who belong exclusively in any one of them. All such categories, like the "stone age," "bronze age," and the other "ages," are devices for exposition rather than observable realities. If we are forewarned not to fall into the category-fallacy,[8] we may profitably employ these stages as a background before which to portray the effect of advance in the arts of life upon population.

The term "stages" implies that we have here a sequence of types, proceeding from simpler to more complex. Evidently hunting could not come before collection, nor animal-raising before hunting, nor agriculture on any intensive scale before the possession of domestic animals. The Australians, having no domesticable animals, never got beyond the hunting stage, and the same is true of many tribes of American Indians; what agriculture the latter had

8 §456, below.

was accomplished with the hoe. Cattle-raisers who have lost their herds have dropped back into a hunting economy for which they had become unfitted; and, on the other hand, hunting peoples may acquire a domestic animal, as the Alaskan Eskimo did at the hands of the United States government,[9] and become successful herders. The settlers in this country sometimes dropped from agriculture to hunting or even collection, as the result of losses and calamity; while the history of the American West exhibits a steady progression represented by the successive waves of trappers, cowboys, and farmers.

Grinnell[10] says that the Cheyenne Indians used to live in villages and cultivate the soil; then, having moved west beyond the Missouri River and got the horse, they became a typical tribe of bison-hunters, "possessing energy and courage, and taking rank as one of the most hardy and forceful tribes of the great central plains." They entered the plains first on mere hunting journeys, returning with meat to their villages; later on they stayed longer, and gradually gave up the agriculture they practised while still living their old village life. "Knowing the conservatism of Indian women, we may feel certain that they would not easily have laid aside the agricultural practices"; wherever there was a chance of returning during the summer, they would have planted.

§28*. The Collection Stage. The stage upon which men acquired food and other prime necessities by simply collecting what their bare hands could seize upon is inferential; but the inference to it is not remote or strained. It must have occurred; for its chief and determining characteristic is the absence of all tools and weapons, and there must have been a time when these had not yet been contrived. Several peoples on the low hunting stage approximate to this status, and accident has reduced members of even highly civilized nations to it. It is the original condition to which men revert when they lose all the acquisitions of culture. The conditions of life on this stage have been reconstructed, in story form, by several authors.[11]

If the arts of life are undeveloped and man is dependent upon what he can gain as a naked animal, the amount and quality of his sustenance are limited. For physically he is, as the savages well realize, inferior in power, speed, and other qualities to most of his

[9] N. Y. *Times,* March 22, 1914; May 24, 1915; March 11, 1921. Statements from the Bureau of Education are quoted.

[10] *Cheyenne,* I, 1, 12, 253.

[11] London, *Before Adam;* Waterloo, *Story of Ab.*

fellow-animals. It is with his mental and societal adaptations that he attains his parities and superiorities. And so, when forced to exist by the collection of available plant and animal food, his successes cannot be conspicuous. In order to get enough to support life, he must have recourse to an extended range of land. The supporting power of any given area is necessarily small, since it can be worked out only in the most superficial and extensive manner. Hence an art-less population, at the limit of this available supporting power of land, must remain sparse. Population, thus quantitatively limited, was also kept down in quality. For the food-supply, besides being meager, was both irregular and of low quality. In a very true sense, men are what they eat and how they eat it. Some of the races that most closely approach the collection stage show in their physical type the effects of alternate repletion with food of poor quality and starvation over extended periods.[12] Inevitably, the whole matter of living is highly hazardous and subject to the element of chance or luck.[13]

Since any area is speedily worked out, population on this stage must also be constantly on the move. This is a necessity that has significant results of several kinds. Even if it does not directly affect numbers to any considerable degree, it hampers the development of settled and improved adjustments: instruments, processes, capital, and other agencies that ease the struggle for existence. As the rolling stone gathers no moss, so are the wandering peoples prevented from gathering civilization; in general the amount of culture developed by a tribe varies inversely with its degree of nomadism. Thus this initial stage seems to contain within itself strong elements preventive of emergence from itself.

There seems to be no place here for the development of foresight. Life has to be lived from day to day. Even the African Bushman, who has his tools and weapons, is called by Fritsch[14] "the unfortunate child of the moment." But foresight is one of the most elementary and elemental qualities productive of civilization.[15] The inferential condition represented by the collection stage

12 Spencer, on "Primitive Man Physical," in *Prin. Soc.*, I, ch. V.
13 §§194 ff., below.
14 *Eingeb. S.-Afrikas*, 418.
15 Lippert, *Kgchte.*, I, 3 ff. *et passim*.

is therefore one of apparently stagnant and dismal destitution. It is one of the reasons for regarding the evolutionary point of view as a hopeful one that human society, by its own unaided and mainly unconscious efforts, in response to forces and incitements that have always been and always will be in the field, has managed to lift itself, here and there, to the plane of civilization.

This inferential stage has been introduced, as are the references to very low civilizations, by way of securing a point of departure for a subsequent and fuller treatment of stages that have come more fully under observation. There is an inveterately persistent delusion in men's minds, embodied in legends of some golden age far back in time, that the race began in felicity and fell by reason of accident or ritual sin. Nothing can be farther from the truth as revealed by the patient and unindoctrinated researches of science. The truth, to science, is quite the reverse; for it sees that human society began in the depths, and that, where it has attained the heights, this has been accomplished by a normal development under the stress of forces which can any day be seen at work.

§29. The Hunting Stage. The hunting stage is characterized by the possession of weapons, which are at the same time tools. These may be regarded as extensions or projections of the body's physical endowment.[16] The hammer, for example, is the lengthened arm with a harder and heavier fist at the end; the mill represents more powerful "molars." Such implements stand for an advance in the arts of life. A given range is worked more intensively through their use than it can be by mere collection. Hence more people can live on and from a unit area. Not only is there more food, together with more adequate clothing and shelter, but it is of better quality and diet is more diversified. This makes for an increase of quality, as well as of quantity, in population. And the weapons enable their owners also to defend and to hold what they have against the onslaughts of competitors in the struggle for existence.

The determinative factor in respect to status of numbers is the relation between the birth-rate and the death-rate—natality and mortality; and the fundamental consideration as to the latter is the fate of the young. If we wish to exterminate the mosquito we

16 Lippert, *Kgchte.*, I, 66-67, 284-285.

attack the young—even the unborn—not the mature. It is by lowering the death-rate of the young rather than that of the adults that human population increases. The better food obtainable by the use of implements, and its more suitable preparation for children's needs, secured chiefly through the agency of fire, operate both to increase the birth-rate and also to lower the death-rate during the critical period of child-life. Better and more digestible food renders possible earlier weaning, and so the earlier restoration of women to child-bearing. Weaning is often delayed among savages until even the fourth or fifth year. One author[17] speaks of seeing a boy who had learned to smoke before he was weaned: "I myself have seen a small rascal run up to his father, take the cigarette from his mouth, puff away, and shortly afterwards resume his meal at his mother's breast." Of course the woman who nurses her young for only a year will normally bear more children than one who nurses them, and is likely to remain sterile, for two or three times as long.[18] The better the substitutes for mother's milk, the larger the birth-rate. The case with respect to the infant death-rate, though more significant still, needs little elaboration. Among the Australians, who are on a low hunting stage, the nature of the food has much to do with the question of population. The children cannot eat roots and berries until they have nearly all their teeth. Infanticide is practised on a large scale.[19] An infant is plainly better off, as the hunting stage evolves, in respect to the fundamental wants of food and protection. Thus there is a considerable increase of population on the hunting stage, as compared with that of the collection stage.

The superior quality of sustenance leads inevitably to a better physical type of population; and there is an enhancement of quality in lines other than the physical. Since sustenance is surer, there appears an emancipation from the element of chance, which engenders a mood of confidence. Nothing succeeds like success. The weapons and tools are capital and represent insurance against the chances of life. The savage hunter is not seldom a good deal of a man, in his way; he has his qualities of bravery, coolness in

17 Hagen, *Papua's*, 233.
18 For practices connected with nursing, etc., see §409, below.
19 Ratzel, *Vkde.*, II, 54.

facing danger, ingenuity, and he has also his opportunities; for his implements—weapons, tools, traps, fire—tend to free his energies from mere animal routine. Not so much time and effort have to be put in on meeting mere existence-needs; there is more that can be utilized for further advances in the arts.

Much of the time and strength spent, on a less developed economy, in wandering about while extensively and superficially exploiting the land, is saved for something else. If a unit area is going to be more intensively worked over, it is not necessary to cover so wide a range. There can at least be semi-permanent headquarters around which the ranging is done; and, as will be recalled, the less there is of wandering the more there is of civilization. Foresight develops to reach beyond the immediate need; the very fact, indeed, that tools and weapons are made at all indicates the presence of that quality in some strength. In short, from the hypothetical stage where there were no arts of life, there has been an advance all along the line. Numbers increase with the arts; civilization increases with the numbers; that means more and better arts; then numbers again increase toward their limit under the new conditions; and so the process goes on.

There have been some estimates of the supporting power of unit areas upon this stage. Whereas under difficult environmental conditions, as among the Eskimo or the Australians, the native needs a good many square miles for his support, more favorable circumstances allow of a population of as high as one, or even several, per square mile.[20]

Of the Australians we learn that "in their original condition of life the natives never stayed long in one place. They shifted from one camping ground to another perpetually. It does not seem that the whole local group always lived and moved about as one body. A single family, that is a man and his wife or wives and their children, often travelled and hunted by themselves. . . . When some particular article of food became very plentiful in the country of one group they invited their neighbours to come and stay with them. Thus the inland natives visited those on the coast when fish was plentiful. . . . This state of things shows very clearly that the unit of social life . . . was the family. . . . Such a unit might move about by itself without reference to the movements of the other families of the local group."[21]

The foregoing citation portrays the type of wandering characteristic of tribes on the low hunting stage; it is in sharp contrast with the mass-migra-

20 §32, below.
21 Brown, in JAI, XLIII, 146-147.

tions of certain pastoral peoples. The quotation which follows illustrates the general break-up of the whole system of living which results when the traditional maintenance-organization is thrown out of adjustment by changes in life-conditions. The people in question are the Omaha Indians who had recently been forced to give up hunting owing to the sudden extinction of the bison-herds. "Contact with the white race was increasing daily and beginning to press on the people. The environment was changing rapidly, and the changes brought confusion of mind to the old people as well as to many in mature life. The beliefs of the fathers no longer applied to the conditions which confronted the people. All that they formerly had relied on as stable had been swept away. The buffalo, which they had been taught was given them as an inexhaustible food supply, had been destroyed by agencies new and strange. Even the wild grasses that had covered the prairies were changing. By the force of a power he could not understand, the Omaha found himself restricted in all his native pursuits."[22]

§30*. The Pastoral Stage. The Animal-Raising or Pastoral Stage has all the arts of the hunting stage, out of which it develops, plus one of exceeding importance: the domestication of animals. It is often not far removed from the preceding stage, and the cattle-raising is scarcely more than the stocking of a preserve with game. The animals are branded or otherwise rendered identifiable, are turned loose to run wild, and have to be caught much as wild animals are, with lasso or other device. They are scarcely in captivity, strictly speaking, so loosely are they attached to man; but they are not altogether wild either. This is a transition between the hunting and the developed pastoral stages.[23] For our purposes domestication means breeding in captivity; it is therefore considerably more than taming, and normally includes that. The domestication of animals, as a case of appropriation of energy out of nature, will be given special attention later on;[24] in this place we shall pass it over the more briefly, and consider only its bearing upon the law of population.

This notable improvement in the arts very materially extends the supporting power of the land and so allows of a great increase of numbers over the figure for the hunting stage. Sustenance is more copious, better in quality, more regular. The land is utilized more intensively—in fact, it may be cleared of vegetation altogether by the grazing and close cropping of cattle and sheep.

22 Fletcher and La Flesche, in BAE, XXVII, 29.
23 §117, below.
24 §§94 ff., below.

Thus population can become more dense and remain in closer contact. The effect upon the birth-rate and death-rate of infants, through the utilization of animal milk, is very powerful. Much less is left to chance. The herds are capital and form insurance against the ills of life; the herders live upon the interest of their capital, so to speak, keeping the body of it intact. Even when very hungry, the Teda will not kill one of their numerous goats.[25] It takes a much severer calamity, such as cattle-plague, to reduce herders to destitution, or to throw them back upon the hunting stage, than it does to overwhelm the hunting tribe. Hence a heightening of confidence and of other qualities leading to continued success; hence also a further freeing of energies from the animal-routine of food-getting and assimilation. Holub[26] says of one of the pastoral tribes of South Africa that their herds make them lazy but evoke whatever nobler emotions they have. There is a further development of foresight, of the arts, and of civilization in general, and a higher potency is lent to the mutual action and reaction between numbers and civilization.

The pastoral stage has been called also the nomadic stage. It would thus appear to be the extreme antithesis of sedentary life—farther away from it than hunting is. Yet, though wandering and civilization do not go together, cattle-raising is generally to be ranked as a more civilized occupation than hunting. The apparent paradox is due to the fact that the ancient agricultural peoples attached this name to the pastoral tribes about them, who afforded the most evident contrast, within their experience, to themselves and their own mores. The wanderings of genuinely and typically pastoral peoples are indeed spectacular. They practise a seasonal mass-migration, reappearing however in the same regions at regular intervals. This migration is imposed upon them by the distribution of the water-supply and the exhaustion of pasture-areas. It is no wonder that they came by the distinctive title of nomads; yet their movements were of a different type from that of the hunters, being migratory and less desultory. They moved about as a body, as a society, not as individuals or segregated small family-groups. They populated a shifting emplacement rather

25 Nachtigal, *Sahara*, I, 268.
26 Capstadt, 203.

copiously.[27] They did not have to travel so light that they could
not take with them all the implements and gear that represented
the material part of their adjustments to life-conditions. Hence
they did not sacrifice, by their migratory habits, so much of the
culture that they were in the way of developing. They had their
greater numbers, and these remained in proximity and contact.
Their nomadism, though striking in its manifestations, did not
have as a consequence the negation of organization that the less
evolved types of wanderings and of land-exploitation involved.

§31*. The Agricultural Stage. The Agricultural Stage is initiated by the domestication of plants and, provided that tillage is
to advance beyond a mere hoe-culture, presupposes the domestication of animals. Agriculture represents a momentous advance in
the arts of life, with a corresponding effect upon numbers, for it
immensely extends the supporting power of land. The food-supply
is more copious, of better quality, and more variegated. Utilization of land advances in intensiveness to actual penetration beneath the surface, an entrance upon basic resources which has not
appeared in the superficial skimmings of preceding stages. It
takes four acres of pasture, we are told, to equal, so far as food
is concerned, one acre of plowed land.[28] Further, when methods of
brand-tillage and the use of manure have been discovered, the land
is not merely exploited but its productivity is restored and maintained. Population may increase to limits hitherto unimagined,
and may remain in closer contact than ever before. The birth-rate
and the death-rate of infants maintain a favorable ratio. Capital,
which is insurance against mischance, by its accumulation renders
existence less hazardous. In all these and other respects the agricultural stage represents a distinct advance over anything that
went before; the details of comparison need not be recited. Slavery
and private property in land are two important adjustments that
accompany agriculture;[29] and there are other scarcely less imposing ones. In general, as Lippert[30] points out, the plant is a
better teacher of foresight than the animal, so that an education

27 §32, below.
28 Dudgeon, *Land Question* (China), 9.
29 §§100, 103, 118, 123, 124, below.
30 *Kgchte.*, I, 245-246.

is enforced upon the agriculturist that fits him for civilized life more thoroughly than is possible upon less developed stages.

Further than this, the temper of agricultural peoples is something new as compared with that of hunters and herders. The virtues of the hunter are, in a word, militant; and they remain those of the herder, for animal-taming and domestication are direct sequels to hunting. The nature of these occupations calls for much the same qualities as does war; in fact, hunting and fighting differ little, in their origin, except in the matter of the identity of the prey. Hunters and pastoral nomads have been typically warlike throughout their course. The agriculturist has no such characteristics fostered in him by contact with plant-life. He becomes, in a word, industrial. His qualities are those of patience and perseverance in labor rather than of aggressiveness and violence against animal and human competitors. He thus falls into sharp contrast with the herder, whose ways are not his and whom he inspires with contempt and dislike. "Shame," says the Tuareg, "enters the family with the plow."[31] The antagonism between herder and tiller is traditional, and is based largely upon the fact that their interests inevitably fall into conflict; it not seldom results in the domination of the former over the latter.[32]

"The Todas are a purely pastoral people, limiting their activities almost entirely to the care of their buffaloes and to the complicated ritual which has grown up in association with these animals. The Badagas are chiefly agriculturists; the Kotas are artisans and mechanics; and both supply the Todas with part of their produce. There is here a well-marked instance of division of labour, in which the labour of the Todas is reduced to a minimum. Their privileged position is usually held to be due to the tradition that they are the 'lords of the soil,' and the produce which the Todas receive from the other tribes is supposed to be of the nature of tribute."[33]

The collision of the two types of self-maintenance is graphically illustrated in the mutual hostility of the "Fence-Men" and "No-fence Men"—the latter determined to range at large and to have no barriers, the former intent upon reserving special claims to special areas of improved land. In the Chin Hills "the fields are not fenced and no one hesitates to shoot strange cattle which stray into his fields."[34] In the western states of this country much strife arose between tillers and herders about fences. Should the tillers be compelled to fence the cattle out, or the herders be compelled to fence their cattle in? It is understandable that the resentful cowboy should add to his kit a pair of tin-

31 Gautier, in *Geog. Jr.*, Jan., 1921, 10.
32 §102, below.
33 Rivers, *Todas*, 6.
34 Carey and Tuck, *Chin Hills*, I, 211.

ner's shears and despoil all the wire fence he encountered; and that the farmer should be enraged to the point of manslaughter by his losses from the trampling of his crops.

This antagonism is broadly a result of collision between the nomadism of the herder and the sedentary habits of the tiller. For agriculture, as it advances in efficiency, demands a progressive renunciation of movement from place to place. The tiller stays by one piece of improved land, investing in it more and more of his labor and capital and seeing it gain steadily in value. From short-season crops he advances at length to the planting of vines and trees whose bearing-period will outlast his own life-time. He wants title in perpetuity and has no idea at all of abandoning his holdings and moving on. He thus automatically develops a degree of foresight clear beyond that of any previous stage; for while the hunter may look ahead a few days or weeks, and the herder a few months or years, the tiller's outlook can hardly cover less than years, and generally extends over decades. This is part of his industrial character, set deep in his mores. The highly sedentary quality of agriculture has its dominant effect in the rapid accumulation and retention, partly through the art of writing, of culture or civilization. Here is a contrast with preceding stages, upon which nomadism and civilization have not gone together. The highest of developing civilizations have all been typically agricultural; and except on the basis of agriculture no high culture has ever developed. By staying in one place and holding, without loss or diffusion, the gains of successive generations, a real civilization can be built up and retained. This point needs no elaboration, for a little reflection upon self-evident conditions and upon historical facts will carry it. Here let there be noted, yet again, the mutual interplay of numbers and civilization: no civilization without numbers; civilization, through the arts of life, allowing of increasing numbers; the increased numbers offering opportunity for an increase of the arts and of civilization; and so on in alternation.

§32*. Degrees of Density in Population. Before the development of an agricultural economy the density of population cannot be very great;[35] and on that stage the number per unit of land

---

[35] Lippert, *Kgchte.*, I, 88, 89.

varies widely in proportion to the degree of intensiveness attained by the local type of tillage. Where that degree is high, as it has been in parts of Belgium, for example, a country's population may run to over six hundred to the square mile.[36]

Lugard[37] reports that in British and French tropical Africa, an area of seven million square miles, the population does not average over 8.5 per square mile. It is unevenly distributed, owing both to the nature of the several regions and to tribal warfare, slave-raiding, and unchecked epidemics. The desert part of the Sudan supports only one per two square miles. He divides British tropical Africa into a western and an eastern section: the former includes Nigeria with a figure of 52.2 per square mile; Cameruns, 20.8; Gold Coast, 19.8; Togoland, 27.5; Sierra Leone, 60.2; Gambia, 58—average, 44.6. The eastern group is: Sudan, 3.9; Somaliland, 4.9; Kenya, 10.5; Uganda, 26.4; Zanzibar, 192.8; Tanganyika, 10.9; Nyasaland, 30.4; N. Rhodesia, 2.8—average, 7.5. The grand total average is 14.4.

It should be realized that advances in agricultural technique, while they may not be reflected in a dense population over the actual farming lands, yet, combined with parallel improvements in the arts of transportation, support a density otherwise impossible in manufacturing, commercial, and other centers which are themselves barren, so far as the production of basic life-necessities is concerned. Other and more derived adjustments to life-conditions, trade, for example, are secondary to the types of self-maintenance now before us and are dependent on them. With every advance of the arts of life, the limit set to the increase of numbers is loosened up and moved on. Several millions of people now live on the island of Manhattan and its environs (the area of New York City is now not far above three hundred square miles) where once no more than a few hundreds of Indians could exist; it is estimated that if the growth of this population were to keep up at its present pace there would be, in about a century, a city of over a hundred millions.[38]

An essential fallacy lurks in the assertion that beasts of draft and burden, or machines which utilize wind, falling water, steam, or electricity, displace men. The beasts, if this were true, would be doubly harmful to men, since they require land for their sustenance and thus compete with men for the food-

[36] Boulger, in *Encyc. Brit.* (11th ed.), III, 669.
[37] *Brit. Trop. Afr.*, 45.
[38] Ogburn, quoted in N. Y. *Times,* May 13, 1923. This prognostication has been criticized. See also an address by L. I. Dublin, referred to editorially in N. Y. *Times,* May 15, 1925.

supply. If an island could support a mean population of a million human beings, without any natural power available, the introduction of a thousand oxen, which would do the work of five thousand men, would not reduce the population (reckoning five souls to each laborer) to 975,000; it would raise it at least to 1,025,000, and probably still higher. The million could either increase or live better. In truth, five thousand men would be displaced only in the sense of being set free to do what no one could do before. Of course if a million oxen and a million horses were introduced into a country like Japan in a single year, the effect upon the men who were living by muscular labor would be disastrous on account of the suddenness and greatness of the disturbance in organization. Evidently it would be impossible to get and introduce animals to the number suggested in any one year. Machines cannot be introduced into all industries for which they are suitable as soon as they are invented; there is an element of friction, which is beneficial since it gives time for readjustment. The displacement of labor, in this sense, though it may be accompanied with the pain incidental to all readjustment, has been the very thing men have striven for and profited by. If a farmer and his sons had to draw their own plow, they would strain every nerve to save enough to buy a yoke of oxen, which would displace their labor. Their wives and daughters have ceased to spin and weave since steam began to do it, and they do not complain that their labor is displaced; they buy the cloth and shoes and hats that were formerly manufactured locally out of the gains from the displacement of their men's labor in favor of a better adjustment in the arts. Meanwhile, along with greater ease in living, the population has steadily increased.

The three states that may occur, owing to degree of density in population, are underpopulation, mean population, and overpopulation, of which the first and third, and especially the first, display a long range of gradation. In the first, the man-land ratio favors man; in the second, there is a state of equilibrium which, however, is always unstable; in the third, all the penalties of societal maladjustment are in evidence.

"In general, then, when the men are too numerous for the means of subsistence, the struggle for existence is fierce. The finer sentiments decline; selfishness comes out again from the repression under which culture binds it; the social tie is loosened; all the dark sufferings of which humanity is capable become familiar phenomena. Men are habituated to see distorted bodies, harsh and frightful diseases, famine and pestilence; they find out what depths of debasement humanity is capable of. Hideous crimes are perpetrated; monstrous superstitions are embraced even by the most cultivated members of society; vices otherwise inconceivable become common, and fester in the mass of society; culture is lost; education dies out; the arts and sciences decline. All this follows for the most simple and obvious of all reasons: because a man whose whole soul is absorbed in a struggle to get enough to eat, will give up his manners, his morals, his education, or that of his children, and will thus, step by step, withdraw from and surrender everything else in order simply to maintain existence. Indeed, it is a fact of familiar knowledge that, under the stress of misery, all the finer acquisitions and sentiments slowly but steadily perish.

"The converse of this statement, however, is true. . . . If the subsistence of men is in excess of the number of men, all the opposite results are produced, for in that case the demand is in excess of the supply."[39]

§33. **Underpopulation.** A population may be so sparse that there is no adequate organization of industry on the stage of the arts. This state appeared in the Anglo-American colonies; it is characteristic of frontier-societies. Such new settlements of civilized men attempt to form new societies upon the scale of organization, including subsistence-capital, tools, machines, and stock, all combined, which they knew in the old society that they left. These elements need to be coördinated in some due relation to one another and to the numbers. It is not possible that this should be brought about all at once; even if it were, equilibrium would be upset by the influx of immigrants, the introduction of more machines, or any other change in any element. The industrial history of Anglo-America shows innumerable illustrations of the cases which may occur under the fluctuations of these elements and of the effect which they produce on the notions of men about economic policy; our currency and tariff notions have taken their origin in experiences of this kind.[40]

In a new colony there never can be strong and highly developed institutions of learning, religion, literature, fine art, or other forms of culture. A frontier-society is the chance for the non-possessor and unskilled laborer to win a new status for himself and his children. It cannot at the same time be a place for artists, littérateurs, scientific men, and the highest professional and skilled laborers to prosecute their specialties. As a society works out of this frontier-condition, the differentiations that appear along with

[39] Sumner, *Coll. Ess.*, III, 120-121.
[40] Sumner, *Coll. Ess.*, III, 289 ff.

advancing population produce reactions, adjustments, and higher combinations to the advantage of all.

All the phases of the relation of the human group to the land can be found in the Middle Ages. In the later period, examples of overpopulation, on the extent of land which could be united in one economic unit and under the arts then existing, are frequent; it was a relief to carve out new tilled land upon the waste when there was more waste than was needed under the manorial system. This meant the increase of the land-side of the numbers-land ratio by plain addition. The great pestilence of 1348 acted through all Europe as a reducer of population, and through the following century the effect is visible on the whole society in every one of its institutions and customs. The Hundred Years' War had the same effect in France; there was a relative and temporary underpopulation. Great areas returned to wilderness and then were reoccupied as free land. These movements did not affect solely the economic status of the people;[41] men who made new holdings on the waste or who went into military colonies on the frontier were freed from traditional tenures; they entered into a new contract-relation which was rational and advantageous.[42]

The discovery of America had the same effect on a grand scale. The land of America did not become freely available until the end of the eighteenth century, but then the effect on Europe was incalculable, and it continued through the nineteenth century. The effect of steam-transportation on the ocean could be immediately expressed in terms of so much land added to the territory of western Europe. Not only those who migrate, but those who stay at home, find the competition of life greatly alleviated. Migration means the addition of land to our basic ratio, and it is an effective remedy far beyond the actual number who migrate, for all who go leave also more room for those who remain. The country of destination is almost sure to be underpopulated; it gains economically by immigration, while offering a new standard of living to the immigrants and a change of status after a few generations. It would be possible now for nearly the whole globe to be united in one economic unit but for obstructive policies. The ensuing status would be one of underpopulation— in other words the world as a whole is still underpopulated, though it is thought by some that world-population is reaching the saturation-point.[43]

Culture is developed when the social pressure due to density of population reaches a degree at which life brings a stress on men. There is need of a stimulus in necessity, together with a surplus energy beyond what is needed to keep up the struggle for existence under the circumstances—conditions which are not fulfilled where life is too hard or too easy.[44] The surplus energy is avail-

[41] D'Avenel, *Hist. Écon.*, has done a great service by pursuing in detail the economic movements of the thirteenth, fourteenth, and fifteenth centuries and showing how they were controlled by the relation of the population to the land under the changes in numbers and arts.

[42] Lippert, *Kgchte.*, II, 584.

[43] Pearl, in N. Y. *Times*, Oct. 8, 1922.

[44] Gregory, Keller, and Bishop, *Phys. and Comm. Geog.*, §§146-148.

able for discovery, invention, and the production of tools and
machines, that is, for the development of cultural adjustments at
a more rapid tempo.

§34. **Concentration.** Underpopulation upon the higher stages
is more advantageous for culture than upon the lower. Urban life is
more favorable to it than is rural life. Interchange between the two
from time to time is more favorable still. What is needed is nearness, interchange, mutual help and stimulus, mutual give and take.
It is only in a dense population that the products of human handiwork and culture can be so assembled that they act through the
senses upon members of the society. In the presence of products
of the past lies a constant suggestion of what may be produced in
the future. Travel multiplies these suggestions and increases the
influence of them by the stimulus to attention which comes from
newness and variety. A greater density of population overcomes
the laxity and shiftlessness which come from easy circumstances
and indifference. It imposes order and discipline which are highly
advantageous to culture. This discipline is irksome, especially
when it comes as something new and strange. It is a diminution of
liberty. It is to be noticed that in Anglo-American society there
has been a steady trend away from liberty toward organization,
order, and discipline. There have been constant complaints of this
course of things on the part of those who found it irksome. As men
come nearer together they always lose liberty. If each family lived
on a quarter-section, what each did would make little difference to
any other; fire-risk, sanitary danger, noise, quarreling would not
reach from one to another. In a city street there must be rules of
movement, and in a tenement-house general safety requires universal restraint.[45]

The greater social pressure which comes from greater density
of population and severer competition has put the spur to energy
and enterprise. Recent generations of Americans have shown a
marvellous response to this stimulus, which was wanting in the
eighteenth century. It would perhaps be wanting now in the new
states if it were not for their close relation with the older ones;
for in these it is felt, and they offer a type of culture which is

[45] Keller, *Soc. Evol.*, ch. X.

adopted and pursued. The fact that the population of the earth is
scattered over it in different degrees of density produces relations
between the groups which are causal in respect to the development
of culture. This may be seen, not only in the relation of the older
to the younger states of the American Union, but also in that of
all newer countries to western Europe.

In part, the modern rush of population to cities is due to a
desire to get into the movement of culture. In its grosser forms
this goes back to impatience of dullness, love of excitement, vanity,
and frivolity, which, however, are only the attendant evils of a
great movement. The cities show the effects of density through all
its stages of high activity, intense competition, grand achievement,
disease, failure, sacrificed men and women, ruin, pauperism, prostitution, and crime. They exhibit a high combination, an intense
power, a great sustained activity, which cannot be achieved without great social pressure. With them comes a heavy risk. There
are great victories and great catastrophes: some are caught up to
giddy heights of prosperity; others are swept away into gulfs of
ruin and shame. It is true that when human beings are brought
into a certain degree of nearness there is a maximum of healthful
and reproductive reaction; yet as they come still nearer and
nearer, in masses, they become more and more dangerous to each
other. Air, soil, and water may be fouled; infectious diseases
spread with great rapidity; and, along with the sanitary risks, the
vices, crimes, and follies, the passions and appetites, the currents
of emotion and whim in a crowd, grow up to larger proportions
and at a progressive ratio as the concourse grows denser. Although
pauperism, prostitution, vagabondage, mendicancy, and crime are
not due solely to overpopulation, still all social reactions are intensified by closeness of contact. There is produced a set of strong
influences which have the educational character of mores.

§35. Effect of Degrees of Density. In sum, therefore, the different stages of concentration present different opportunities of
human welfare which are always environed by the necessity of
moderation and wisdom in the use of them. With increasing density comes enhanced opportunity, and with it more highly developed power; but there arrives also greater and greater risk,

rising to crises in which emerge on one side transcendent achievement, on the other immeasurable catastrophe.

It follows that the progressive increase of population is that change in the elements of the societal situation which is the immediate and usual stimulus to readjustments productive of effects on all details of the societal structure, functions, and relations. These changes constitute phases of civilization, under which customs, mores, philosophies, and institutions undergo changes. It is evident that on all stages of culture, and at all densities of population, the relations of the society to its life-conditions will present parallels in respect to the relations of interests, the pessimistic or optimistic trend of the accepted philosophy, the predominance of militarism or the contrary. Social pressure, if low, produces freedom and equality (democracy); if high, it results in classes, wide social distinctions, and discipline. Castes are developed more or less completely in different ages but in like cases. Feudalism has been evoked many times in different periods and places; for it is a societal phase which is normal when society must form again out of anarchy. Ghost-fear is an almost universal faith and, in the form of daimonism, is a world-philosophy which is not by any means extinct, even in Christendom. The medicine-man is a functionary of the widest dispersion and of constant recurrence; he is a product of the case and of the world-philosophy. Endogamy and exogamy, bride-price and dowry, polygyny and monogamy, mother-family and father-family, rise in response to similar societal states on very different stages of culture, and persist or decline as their expediency endures or wanes.

§36. The Arts-Policy. Through ages men have accepted the fact, consciously sometimes, but for the most part unreflectingly, that the arts of production must be brought to sustain whatever weight of numbers is to be put upon them; and have consequently bent available powers to their improvement rather than to their relief. This was the natural, self-evident, and concrete means of meeting the pressure of population on land, and men have come to feel that it cannot fail. They have gone on manipulating the man-land ratio upon the land-side, and have encountered a high measure of success in so doing. They have, on the other hand, paid but

slight attention to the numbers-side of the ratio, lightly and unreflectingly confident that somehow the arts of production could be
brought forward to make the land sustain the weight of whatever
numbers might be attained.

Men have not underestimated the importance of production; in
fact, to most of us "industry" means production; rather have we
driven the willing horse with little attention to the enormous increase of his load. We have not lacked cases in the past when numbers have pressed so heavily upon the supporting power of the
land that calamity and high mortality have resulted; such experiences, however, have led us to develop the arts of production only
the more energetically rather than to consider some limiting policy
on population. This attitude has been encouraged by the opening
up of new land; for in each case where that has occurred, the arts
of production already developed by us have been applied under
most favorable conditions. The new lands have relieved the pressure of population in other lands, either by drawing it off or by
contributing to its sustentation. Now, however, it is being realized
ever more clearly that the once new lands are growing old, and
that there are no more undeveloped areas like those opened up by
the Discoveries. Consequently, while the effort to develop the arts
of life has in no wise abated, there is appearing a set of factors
that tend automatically to limit numbers, and even a conscious
program of control. It has come to be seen that, baldly stated,
hunger and sex-love cannot be satisfied to the full at the same
time.[46]

Although the term "arts-policy" has been used to head this
topic, it is not to be understood that the development of hunting,
tillage, or any other type of maintenance was a real "policy"—
that it took place because men visualized the interests of society
and consciously strove for their realization. Even on the highest
stages of civilization, those who can perceive societal interest as
distinguished from, and often in opposition to, individual interest,
and then consciously strive to realize it, are very few in number.
What men are vividly aware of is individual pain and pleasure,
individual goals and ambitions. When they are striving for their

[46] See Janke, *Übervölkerung*, 222, for a crude but graphic version of this
fact.

own interests, they are working for something objective and concerning the nature of which also they themselves are, on the whole, the best judges. They put forth variations, which are then exposed to selection. Only with the development of a scientific understanding of the nature of society and of the laws of its life, can its massive interests be adequately appreciated and rationally furthered. When it is said that men have given the bulk of their attention to the development of the arts that multiply land, instead of to the restriction of numbers, that means that society, through the action of its constituent members, has found its joint and corporate interest served by the former type of adjustment rather than the latter. The race has had no actual "policy"; that term is used in a metaphorical sense. Societal law is personified in "society" as natural law is in "nature"; the way things went was such that "society" might be figured, for convenience of expression, as having pursued an arts-policy instead of a limitation-policy.

§37*. Limitation of Numbers. Limitation of population occurs upon the most primitive stages. It is due either to an approach to the saturation-point, where numbers, because they actually are not supported, fall off through starvation, reduction in vitality, or lack of protection against fellow-competitors, animal or human; or it is referable to beliefs and practices irrelevant to the matter of physical sustentation, as, for example, the killing of twins or widows, due to daimonistic beliefs, or the separation of man and wife during the protracted nursing of the child.[47] Savages can have no real "population-policy"; if their practices are dignified by that term, it is because of what is read into them.[48] A real population-policy implies a deliberate and purposeful group-direction of group-destiny, as in a modern exclusion-law against immigration; it is not present where an individual family limits its numbers with an eye solely to its own interests. It is doubtful whether any society can boast of more than a fragmentary population-policy; among primitive folk, certainly, there is no societal control over numbers except that which is traditional in the mores.

[47] §409, below.
[48] Keller, *Soc. Evol.*, 93-94.

If a tribe is militaristic, and loses numbers as a result, that cannot be regarded as a population-policy; it is merely a sort of prolongation of the struggle for existence. Abortion, infanticide, military or religious celibacy—though such usages may amount to a loss of numbers, they do not constitute a policy with respect to numbers. They sometimes look, in retrospect, like deliberate measures; but even if, in a few cases, nature-peoples assert that they kill infants or the old because "there are too many" or "there is not food enough," such practices are traditional rather than rational. The general reply given to questions, here as elsewhere, is that these things are done because the ancestors did them. The religious and other ceremonial surrounding such acts, revealing as it does the motives of the actors, is unmistakable evidence that whatever the effects on population may be, they are automatic and unplanned.

There are examples, in the islands of Melanesia, Polynesia, and the East Indies where population had reached a state of approximate equilibrium with its environment. During thousands of generations, experience in the struggle for existence had produced an unconscious population-practice consisting of rules, customs, and taboos, by which the numbers were held within the limit set by the food-supply and the arts available. Of course such a state of things could not continue after the societies in question had been brought into contact with the rest of the world. Commerce came to them as a destroyer.

If we drop the idea of a population-policy as of something deliberately contrived in the interests of society, and regard the term "numbers-policy" as being metaphorical, just as in the foregoing case of the "arts-policy"; if we realize that all the usages that go under both terms are simply phenomena of the mores; and if we recognize that an aggregate of individual purposes does not constitute a societal purpose, for no one visualizes the needs of the society; then we are in a position to ask how the usages under review came about in the course of evolution of the mores. And this brings us around to the consideration of a factor already casually referred to, but deserving of much attention and reflection, the standard of living. Roughly outlined, this standard represents a customary or anticipated level of existence below which people do not wish to fall. Nothing can bring it down more quickly than the pressure of numbers upon resources. Its development means that those shall not live, or shall not be born, whose presence will enforce a lower quality of existence on the ones already here. Parents of several children refrain from having others because, if they do, they must renounce a standard of living which they have set up for themselves and their limited domestic circle. Whereas, therefore, the arts of life provide for increased numbers by the improvement of maintenance, the standard of living operates to limit numbers by reducing the rate of reproduction. It must be taken account of in any study of human population. It is evident already, then, that the proviso, "for a given standard of living," belongs in the law of population; but its full bearing cannot be appreciated until that standard is examined from several points of view.

§38. The Standard of Living. In the present connection it is desirable to keep before us, as an unifying thought, the relation of the standard of living to natality and mortality. Nature will see to it that, through famine, pestilence, and war, population will be prevented from exceeding the limit of the supporting power of the land. When it is at that limit, natality cannot exceed mortality. But this does not mean that the limit is a dead-line, on one side of which is well-being and on the other side utter destruction. It is no artificial boundary like a state line, a single step over which carries from one state into another; it is a zone, rather, of increasing ill-being, as a society traverses it from underpopulation toward overpopulation. And whether society is or is not succeeding in pushing the whole zone of transition farther off, through development of the arts, it is always setting its own limits, in the mores,[49] somewhat this side of the natural limit, and thus creating a margin that serves as a defense against disaster. Society holds natality down as against mortality at some point short of the place where "nature" assumes control; and it does this by the development of some standardized conception of satisfactory living, beyond which, in the direction of the natural limit, people are restrained by the mores from venturing. This means, primarily, that they will not propagate beyond the capacity of the environment, on their stage of the arts, to support them according to their customary notion of what satisfactory living is. Population

[49] Sumner, *Folkways*, §§168–169; ch. LIV, below.

increases to the end of resources, but the point at which the end
of the resources is conceived to be reached is determined by the
standard of living. Here is the baldest exhibition of that standard.

People who live under a high standard have a wide reserve by means of
which to encounter disaster. When the Irish peasants had multiplied up to the
number which could exist on a potato diet, and no one of them had furniture,
clothing, jewelry, or other capital beyond the most petty supply of the cheap-
est kind, then, when the potatoes were blighted in a single night, they died of
starvation before help could be brought. Without the adjustment in the arts
of life represented by transportation and communication the mortality would
have been much greater. People who live regularly on meat and wheat can fall
back upon three or four cheaper grains and vegetables before they need starve
to death. If they have clothes, books, tools, jewelry, pictures, and other resources, all these can be sacrificed to tide over a disaster. Disasters are generally temporary, and the vital question always is in regard to the ability to
hold out until they pass. A high standard of living acts as an accumulator of
the natality-power. In its concrete form it appears as capital, a store which
can be used against an access of mortality. Here is another aspect of the
margin between the societal and the natural limit of numbers.
It is very remarkable that the people of the United States should have been
characterized by such a high standard of living when they were in such easy
circumstances in respect to the struggle for existence, for a high standard is
generally the result of tense effort of sharpened faculties put forth in a severe
though winning struggle. The French peasantry are also remarkable for a high
standard; but with them it takes the form of frugality, utilitarian marriages,
restriction of births, and some severity towards the old. It is practised by
them under a severe competition of life, and is in part a product of arbitrary
legislation about the division of land; for by their system of inheritance holdings would be subdivided down to small fragments if there were many children
in each generation.

As it develops, the standard of living is not describable in simple
and unqualified terms. Presently comes an idealization of the
actual and customary notion of well-living, an enhancement
toward which men reach out. There is a sort of inkling of what
might be, and this is gradually attached to the standard, or thrust
under it, so that it lifts somewhat. It easily springs up to the
limit of what is possible, and is prone to range beyond. At each
stage of societal existence new wants arise and the visualized satisfaction of them enters into the standard. What is seen is a set of
prospective adjustments to life-conditions, called for by needs
that have sprung out of present adjustment and whose entrance
has made of the latter, in so far, a maladjustment. What is
wanted is something a little farther ahead on the present road.
The standard becomes thus a moving, non-static conception; yet

at recurrent intervals of comfortable living, and sometimes for long ones, it appears as what is rather than as what may be. It tends also, like the mores in general, to become fixed in tradition, sanctioned by religion, and thus bereft of variability and resistant to readjustment. And it may retrograde so as to narrow the margin between the line fixed by society and that established by nature for an equilibrium between natality and mortality. It is really a sort of indicator as to the character and destiny of a society. If the standard of living remains steady and traditional, sensitiveness to life-conditions and consequent adaptability are shown to be weak, whereas an ever more ambitious standard, implying discontent with what is in comparison with what may be, indicates responsiveness to environment together with some qualities of imagination and foresight. Variability and adaptability can then be counted upon. The analogy with the individual is enlightening: with the self satisfied, the present is the standard and stagnation is the result, while the contrasting type does not call upon the passing moment to remain but storms forward to what is beyond.

What the standard of living works out is quality of population rather than quantity. Indeed, there is always an antagonism between numbers and quality; "we must have few men, if we want strong men."[50] If more and better are demanded by each unit, the number of units must halt or decline. The standard of living means a better share to fewer people. By advance in the standard of living, increase of numbers is deterred, neutralized, or even transformed into a decrease. By preventing births, it has the same effect on quality as is produced by thinning out a garden and assuring to the comparatively few survivors what all would otherwise have had to struggle for.

The clearest case of the effect of the standard of living on numbers is that of birth-control. A man and his wife, for example, cherish a standard of living that includes higher education for their children, that is, a development of quality. It is clear to them that there is no reasonable prospect of realizing their aims if the family is large—as large, say, as their grandparents' families. Then one thing or the other—quality or numbers—must be renounced; and if they cling to the standard of their ambitions, the number of births is controlled and the size of the family limited. The only other alternative is an

[50] Sumner, *Soc. Classes*, ch. V.

extraordinary and successful effort to increase income, that is, so far as this family-group is concerned, to advance the production of its arts of life. The normal course in these days is to limit numbers, the degree of limitation being determined by some combination of considerations. No such deliberate and purposeful action is shown by society at large. We shall return to this direct type of influence of the standard of living on numbers a little later on.

§39. **Characteristics of the Standard.** It is doubtful whether the standard of living can be convincingly portrayed without pursuing it into its more modern phases. In them, at any rate, it is to be seen in familiar form, with but little distortion due to nearness. The standard of living seems to be individualistic. It resembles honor. It is a sense of what a man owes to himself, his wife, and his children. He must find the spring of it within himself. But the mores of the surrounding society and of the class to which he belongs are what awaken and sustain it; they surround a man with models, stimuli, help, and open to him chances and possibilities; then the individual may execute variations about the societal norm. He did not create that norm; rather was he born into it, for it is in the mores; and his function in regard to it is his regular function as respects the mores. The standard of living is by no means to be confused with the sentiment of the man who thinks that he is a fine fellow to whom the world owes three meals a day and many other comforts. To give anybody things that he wants, without exacting any return from him, raises his appetite and his sense of right to demand, not his standard of living. Education is a case in point; for while people have come to demand it as a right, yet far more is offered than is taken. Benevolence has often lowered and pauperized its beneficiary by degrading his self-respect, which is the flower of his standard. For that is a demand which a man addresses to himself, and it is to be answered only by toil and self-denial. If he sets his standard high, he will have to make a long preparation to be able to reach it. It is a most mischievous error to suppose that the standard of living is an engine which is at the disposal of the social philosopher and projector. It is rather the fine bloom of character and morality, and is a by-product to be indirectly cultivated rather than a resource which may be assumed to be at hand. It is like honor in this respect also; for honor, while inestimable as a regulator of life, is most effective and real when least is said about it, and when least outright use is sought to be made of it.

Within the broad bounds of a national standard of living there are class-standards; in fact, the former is a sort of generalization of the latter, resuming their common elements. The lowest classes have the least effective standard; that is partly the cause, as it is certainly the barometer, of their position. The standard begins to tell upon those who care for decency and order. In the middle classes it is sometimes sordid and unlovely and takes the form of a social ambition for which there is little to be said. It is strongest among the educated classes; indeed, education might be regarded as a process for raising its degree. It is a familiar fact that the natality of social classes varies inversely with the height of their standards of living. The motives formative of the standard and of capital are similar. In general, the former helps to create the latter or to prevent consumption of it. Capital is, however, the great fortification of human welfare; it is that which most powerfully operates to push farther away the natural limit of numbers. Thus the standard of living is effective to differentiate men; and, being a class-phenomenon, it reacts to intensify and integrate classes and to render them hereditary through the education of children. This tells far more in an old country. Better food and clothing, athletic exercise and sport, travel, fine art, and literature are privileges of the possessing classes, which are recruited all the time from those with a high standard of living. At the same time these latter are nourishing vital resistance by virtue of which they can endure the assaults to which all classes are subject. The peril of the high-standard class comes, in generations, from luxury, which is the opposite of the virtue by which that class was created.

Most of the difficulty in moving from class to class is connected with the adoption of a new set of mores, including chiefly new standards of living. Enriched poor people do not, we are told, enjoy big houses; they live in the kitchen. They dread servants as spies and wasters, and suspect them of perceiving and ridiculing the maladjustments of which they themselves are uncomfortably conscious. Others do not want gardens, pianos, libraries, pictures, yachts; for these things bring unaccustomed care and problems. Educated barbarians return to barbarism to get peace, freedom from care, and leisure. For all it is early education that sets habitual and traditional standards, and it is hard for the old dog to learn new tricks. For one who has never eaten, bathed, or dressed according to a higher standard, to do so, despite his discomfort, raises tone. The sense of pride which comes from living in a separate house, on a better street, from having carpets on the floor, keeping children neat and well-clothed, having books about, sending a son to college, travelling, entertaining, having a summer home, is a social safeguard.

The standard of living is almost wholly a product of the mores within a class or small social group. It is apparent why it has been called a psychological or ethical product, though that is a misleading designation. It is the measure of decency and suitability in diet, dress, residence—in material provision for comfort in living—which is traditional in a group. It is a class idea. The standard is upheld by the fear of derogating from class "respectability" and incurring the disapproval or contempt of one's nearest fellow-men. It varies from one industrial group to another; what is thought coarse and gross in one class is not regarded as out of the way, that is, unconventional, in another. The mores of the class determine the whole.

Thus the society's standard of living is a composite in the mores, made up of the standards of classes or other sub-groups in their different degrees. There arises a strong disinclination to run down or lose caste. This disinclination imposes action which restrains natality and thus enters into the law of population.

§40. **Drawbacks of the Standard.** The standard of living does not set aside the pains and perils of the law of population. By virtue of it a large fraction of any old and dense population is condemned to celibacy; for monogamy itself, which rules out many persons, chiefly women, from parenthood, goes with a higher standard of living and is, indeed, one of the expedients for attaining it.[51] Also, since the standard tells most upon the people with high education and strong moral feelings but not possessed of ample incomes, it prevents that class from becoming, in proportion to its numbers, the parents of the next generation. On the other hand, since the poorest and least responsible have the lowest standard of living, it is they who procreate the next generation. Nor are the rich and great, who are emancipated from care in this matter, and may marry young and have large families, the best of parents. It is asserted that, as a consequence, society is being recruited predominantly from the top and the bottom—chiefly from the latter, where the numbers are—while its strength, vigor, and hope are in the middle. This is the most weighty criticism which could be made on existing society. Much has been said in this connection of "race-suicide," meaning in the first instance

51 §§400, 401, 432, 433, below.

class-suicide, and of counter-selection.[52] It is feared by some that the emancipation of woman, with the consequent stimulation for her of a "career-interest," may operate in the same direction.

Whatever else such phenomena may signify, they strongly support the correlation between the standard of living and natality. It is also contended that diversity in the standard of living, by intensifying class-differences, must result in the continuance and intensification of class-strife.

The minority of children who now enjoy advantages of culture and training, and profit by them, will actually if not openly rule their generation, and the others will serve them in the ranks of the army, or of industry, or of politics. Popular education for the masses goes just far enough to make social war certain, although popular education is absolutely indispensable in order to find out and develop the powers which exist in the society. At the same time that it differentiates the leaders, popular education plants the seeds of undiscipline in their subordinates. The high standard of living by enforcing celibacy helps to produce vice: illicit relations, illegitimacy, prostitution. It encourages mercenary marriages and acts harmfully, therefore, on the status of women who inherit nothing. They are driven into crowded and ill-paid occupations unless they have opportunity, courage, and ability to make their way into others. In fact, the high standard of living, with the removal of prejudices and restrictions of birth or class, is a process of selection which is good for the best but bad for the worse. The "respectable classes" and the "disreputable classes" are thrown into more glaring contrast and the moral effect on all who feel that they have passed from the former into the latter is a new force to depress them still farther. The high standard of living, by acting to defer marriage until a later time in life, lessens the chance that the parents can live to bring up their children, and to care personally for their education. Late marriages increase the number of orphans.[53] This must be regarded as an important offset to its advantages.

Thus the high standard of living substitutes voluntary pain for natural pain; anxious forethought and care, together with all the sacrifices, strains, and stresses connected with its elevation, for the ruder and more "natural" sufferings incurred by letting nature take care of the matter.

Where people have the tradition that children shall begin to earn at the age of ten or twelve, the notion of educating them up to the eighteenth or twentieth year is a new demand on life and an irksome strain, for, instead of getting help from their children, parents have a heavier burden to be borne over a longer time. Every extension of life's burdens means more care and anxiety; and men's recoil before them, especially on the primitive stage, is represented, among other things, by the recourse taken to intoxicants and

[52] Keller, *Soc. Evol.*, ch. VI.
[53] Farr, *Vital Statistics*, 45.

narcotics. The upper classes and the more civilized peoples assume that the lower and uncivilized want what they themselves do, and will make sacrifices to get it. Often they do not feel such wants at all; and if they do, the magnitude of the sacrifice required of them to attain satisfaction is not appreciated. It is often so great that, if the struggle is made, the satisfaction does not seem proportionate to it. In some cases the self-abnegation shown in renouncing the satisfactions, which really releases from exertion, may come to be regarded as praiseworthy. That is a counsel of despair or ineptitude. There is often a dilemma here which can be expressed in the homely terms: "Live like a hog and you will behave like one; behave like a hog and you will live like one." How can both terms of the correlation be raised at once, when one conditions the other?

Though the standard of living is a societal policy which unquestionably works for better societal adjustment, it has very important drawbacks, and every gain is won at a sacrifice. All that men can do is to find a policy by which, within the conditions of their existence, they can offset good and ill so as to gain as much as possible, even though it be but a little.

§41. **Predatory Standard-Seeking.** Most of the foregoing discussion of the standard of living has been carried on with civilized conditions in view. But there are groups or classes in any, even partially developed society that enjoy a position of superior power and well-being over the rest; and they, sensing the fact, cherish and have the force to try to realize a more developed standard. In so far as they attain it, they exclude other classes from multiplication. A noble or rich man will practise polygyny to the detriment of a number of poor men who are limited to one wife, a shared wife, or no wife at all. This may have, theoretically, but small effect upon general numbers; the rich man, however, has also the right to the products of the arts for his offspring—to the detriment, perhaps to the death or loss of vitality, of the poor man's progeny. The former may be able to divert the arts to the production of articles of luxury or ostentation, where that means a lessening of the food-supply of the group as a whole. The standard of living casts upon the arts an extra burden of production; amply to maintain numbers they now have to support not only the whole population on a living scale but some of them on a heightened and more costly scale. Every advance in the standard of living lays this extra burden upon the arts if they are not to be relieved, in compensation, of some of the weight of numbers to be supported on the old scale. This is as near a mathematical certainty as anything in the societal range can be. No one planned that men should profit thus unequally, and in so far exhibit a predatory quality in their standard-seeking; it came about in the course of evolution and shows in retrospect the logic and rationality of the inevitable.

More directly predatory is the action of the powerful in robbing the weaker of products of the arts, that their own standard of living may rise. In their own interest, groups of men, whether classes in a society or tribes and nations, have always been trying to attain a chosen standard of living by appropriating the results of others' application of the arts to land instead of themselves applying the arts; and when they have succeeded in so doing, the other claimants have had to go without and have suffered for it in the matter of numbers. Very recent is the development of a measure for realizing a standard of living where the aspirants pay the price for themselves, namely, prudential restraint. This is practised where the standard cannot be realized at others' expense or where the conviction exists in the mores that it ought not to be so attained.

Predatory standard-seeking has been a favorite occupation of nations. Although within the peace-group there were some limits set on exploitation of fellow-members, the outsider has always been legitimate prey. History is full of examples. The most cynical advancement of the contention that the great and powerful nations, in order to live more fully, have a right to exploit the smaller and weaker has been disposed of by a world-conflict in recent times. One nation wanted a "place in the sun," where it could realize a grandiose vision of exalted living; and the ensuing contest issued in a decrease of population not contemplated even by the aggressor—not for himself, at any rate.[54] This decrease, apart from actual war-casualties, has been due to the imposition of a weight upon the arts of maintenance so great that they could not support the numbers, even after the virtual collapse of the standard of living.

§42. Prudential Control.[55] It is only of late that men have

[54] Keller, *War to Peace,* ch. III, 60 ff. *et passim.*
[55] See Keller, "Birth Control," in *Yale Rev.,* VII, 129 ff., for a fuller treatment.

come to pay much attention to the man-side of the man-land ratio. This is one reason for presenting the standard of living chiefly through modern cases. It is not that men have at length come to the point where they can think in terms of a society; except for a very few, on a limited number of issues, that is not yet. Of late people have learned, nevertheless, to some degree, to follow their own interests by the negative method of limitation, along with the positive one of straining for further development of the arts. They have gained some knowledge of the reproductive process and how to adjust to it, as they earlier learned the facts of natural law and adjusted to them by the development of the arts of life. This is due in good part to the pressure resulting from the rapid filling up of the earth's available land. Formerly it was possible to ease the pressure by draining the overflow into new countries; now there are no more increments of land to be opened and so utilized, as there were in the centuries succeeding the Discoveries. It is also only of late that interests have been so rapidly multiplied, by the development of communications and otherwise, that even peasants now have aspirations of which formerly only the noble and rich could conceive. Many satisfactions, in fact, have been brought within the range of even the thrifty poor that the wealthiest of two centuries ago could not have got, because they did not exist. Hence a constantly increasing standard of living and an ever stronger impulse to limit here in order to realize there.

This impulse has been rendered effective by an increase of knowledge as to methods of control. There is no way, we suppose, of estimating the amount of control actually exercised; but anyone who denies its presence is self-deceived. There has been no biological change recorded whereby contemporary married pairs are less fecund than their great-grandparents; nor can it be believed that what is sometimes called "oldfashioned continence" has become the practice. Nature put into operation within this range what is probably the most powerful passion known in the organic field; but she did not see fit to endow mankind at the same time with the power to resist it or neutralize it altogether. It has been limited and set within the legalized boundaries of marriage by some of the strongest inhibitions ever developed by society; but the very power which holds it so marvellously to these limits has prescribed its

satisfaction within them. Every attempt to secure further renunciation has been in vain. These are facts, not views, and must be
taken into account, together with a number of implications and
corollaries not developed here. Of a consequence the birth-rate
could decline, as the result of a general societal movement for
direct birth-control, only with the knowledge of means preventive
of conception. So long as people did not know much about the
process they could not do much to arrest it. Thus, while it has
been long practised by certain elements in the population, birth-
control as a societal phenomenon could not be other than modern.
As a rational program for whose realization, in the interest of
society, knowledge is deliberately to be disseminated, it is of the
present day. It has yet to make its way against an imposing barrier of mores before it gets much beyond the program-stage.

§43. The Limitation Policy. Taken in the metaphorical sense,
the word "policy" may be applied to the method of limitation as
it was to that of the arts. The relation between the standard of
living and numbers, as it appears in the modern family, exhibits
circumscribed limitation as a deliberately planned recourse. But
the case from family life, and from a very recent phase of it as
well, should not be permitted to mislead. We are studying society
in the large, and in that perspective view the varied motives of
individuals or of families, in the pursuit of their interests, merge
into a composite and impersonal whole. What we find is that
societies with the highest standards of living show a lowered
natality, while those whose standard is crude produce the "swarm-
ing, spawning multitudes," whose presence, in turn, keeps the
standard depressed. Although within recent years all the most
highly civilized nations, beginning with France, have made much
ado over their declining birth-rate, no such wail has come from
India. Quite the reverse: a cry of despair has been heard from
those who have been working for her uplift, and it has been wrung
from them because they see all the benefits conferred in the matter
of improving the arts quickly neutralized by an overwhelming
wave of numbers. Then famines have occurred and those who
practised no restraint have been carried through, if at all, by

those who did. The parable of the wise and foolish virgins has been often enough applicable to the doings of societies.

It is the more civilized nations which have practised limitation; it is also the most cultured classes in any nation that follow this practice; and it is the most farsighted and thrifty families in any class who aim at quality rather than numbers of progeny. The slums continue to show an undiminished fecundity. The fact stands out that it is the possessors of the most numerous and varied interests and the highest standard of living who are most sensitive to environmental influences that affect all interests, and who have the knowledge necessary to expedient adaptation. A multiplication of interests, or wants, is the most characteristic mark of culture, in individual, family, class, or nation. Hence the higher classes act as a sort of indicator for the society at large. They show a lowered birth-rate before the rest, and might even be said to practise limitation vicariously for the others. The latter then straggle along, by self-adjustment or through imitation, in their degree and capacity; and when the nation as a whole attains a higher level of sensitiveness, that is, when it is, as a society, more highly civilized, it comes to stand among other nations in a position analogous to that of the indicator-class among other classes.

It can never be expedient to bring children into the world to die in infancy. The physical expenditure of the mothers and the capital expenditure on the children while they live, to say nothing of the nerve-strain of care, anxiety, and grief upon the parents, are pure loss. It would be a far better bargain to get the increase by immigration, so far as mere quantity goes; on that criterion, to restrict immigration by law would be as foolish as to restrict marriages and births by law. It can never be an object to an industrial society, not cynically preoccupied with the production of "cannon-fodder," to increase numbers after the population is sufficient to allow of an expedient organization of industry according to the existing stage of the arts. Those who are not born never suffer and cause no problems; those who are born have so much the more room. Economy is just as expedient in reproduction as in economic production. That group will be strongest, other things being equal, which reproduces in the strictest conformity with its life-conditions and preserves all it procreates.

"The statistician will doubtless long continue his fashion of confidently estimating the importance, and predicting the survival, of populations, from their quantity and rate of reproduction alone; but at all this, as naturalists, we can only scoff. . . . It is the most individuated type that prevails in spite, nay, in another sense, positively because of its slower increase. In a word, the survival of a species or family depends not primarily on quantity but on quality. The future is not to the most numerous populations, but to the most individuated."[56] The only qualification here needed is that in war brute numbers count as they do not elsewhere.

The conclusion is irresistible that as the world advances from a condition of underpopulation toward greater and greater density, limitation is sure to increase. On the frontier, where there is much land and few men, numbers are desirable; there is no restriction, even upon immigration, except, perhaps, that of criminals. On the other hand, a relative scarcity of land, as in a settled country, means that numbers are at a discount instead of a premium; then the adjustment becomes, not increased fecundity, but a diminished reproduction.[57] Only in case the arts can multiply land by rapidly increasing its productivity can the natality of frontierdays remain a proper adjustment to life-conditions; only in that case can the periodic natural reductions by famine, disease, or violence be avoided. It is the arts that must carry any increasing burden of numbers. Some theorists believe that they will always rise to the occasion, to meet any and all demands of population;[58] but as peoples have become more sophisticated they act as if they did not share that view. They do not think the situation out in terms of society's interests; they act from a variety of motives in striving to satisfy personal and local interests. It is the logic of their acts that indicates the presence of distrust in the all-sufficiency of the arts and the logic of acts, whatever their motives, can never be lightly passed over by the student of society. Interests of all kinds are affected by the changing life-conditions of any period, and in reacting upon them, as presented in multifarious cases and varied form, the masses of individuals unite to pro-

[56] Geddes and Thomson, *Evol. Sex*, 295; Ratzenhofer, *Soc. Erkennt.*, 111-112.

[57] Sumner, *Coll. Ess.*, III, 109 ff.; Keller, *Soc. Evol.*, ch. IX.

[58] Dublin, "The fallacious propaganda for birth-control," in *Atl. Mo.*, CXXXVII, 186 ff. See also editorial comment on an address by Dublin, in N. Y. *Times*, May 15, 1925, and a typically impassioned letter in N. Y. *Times*, April 5, 1925.

duce a common adjustment in the mores—in this case, a limitation
of numbers. Then, as is the inveterate way with a natural process,
the adjustment is seen in retrospect to be logical and is taken to
be a case of rational procedure.

This is the case with limitation. So far as the interests of society
go, it has always been automatic. Individuals, families, and perhaps other small and local groups have seen their petty interests
subserved by limitation and have been rational in adopting that
policy for themselves. If an occasional individual has proved to
himself and a few others that it would be a good thing for society,
that does not say that any of them put it into practice for society's sake. When it has come about as a more general usage, this
is not because of any one's thinking or advocacy, but because
people with more wisdom and forethought have put it into practice for their own interests and have been imitated in so doing by
others whose horizon was likewise limited to local considerations.
Thus would it get into the mores in the regular, unconscious, unplanned, unspoken, unheeded, unrecorded way. The conclusion
which we reach concerning prudential restraint is that unless the
arts can bring land to support rapidly, progressively, and indefinitely increasing numbers, with a progressively advancing standard of living, limitation of fecundity is the only recourse to evade
the Malthusian checks; and we ourselves do not expect the arts,
despite their marvellous performances of the past and present, to
meet such a requirement.

§44. Inevitability of the Law of Population. No subject is
more obscured by prejudice and established notions than this one
of population. A dispassionate study of it shows that we turn and
twist within the play of natality and mortality so that we change
the point at which they act upon us and so for a time think that
we have defeated them. We do, in fact, win space inside of them.
We do that by getting more knowledge of them, and in general of
the world in which we live; then we learn how to deal with them.
But we never defeat or escape the forces in the field. Overpopulation means just the same thing for the people of Belgium as for
those of Bengal or of an island in Melanesia. The phenomena of
it, physical, mental, social, and political, are always the same,

allowance being made for the plane of civilization. The sanctions
of right knowledge and wise conduct under the law are the most
awful which men experience. The notion that we defeat and escape
them is always due to a misapprehension of facts. The people of
the United States have been living in a state of underpopulation.
Few of them have known anything about it. It is the explanation
of their power, wealth, prosperity, liberty, democracy, and all the
other happy circumstances which they generally attribute to their
institutions, and often solely to their political system or even to
some party in power. The institutions are a consequence, not a
cause.

During a period when a large extent of unoccupied land is available and the
arts are advancing at a very high rate, as has been the case in America, the
connection between land, men, the arts, and the standard of living is not close
and severe. The play of forces is veiled. The situation, instead of being recognized as a phase of the combinations, is interpreted as a refutation of the
theorem. Political, social, economic, and moral doctrines are accepted as true
which affirm the possible universal beatification of mankind and assume that
the societal organization, the relation of classes, the policy of state freedom,
justice, and the rest are all open to human caprice and arbitrary determination. The elasticity and free play which are allowed between economic conditions and natality, under the circumstances of the time, give opportunities for
happiness such as no other men have enjoyed. Doctrines are relatively true
which would not be true at any other time—at any rate, they are not immediately disproved on the cold facts of experience, because they do not come
to the test. There is no harsh friction between the components of the societal
process.

It has been said[59] that "there is no solution of the social question which is satisfactory if it neglects the law of population."
That is profoundly true, in the same sense in which it is true that
there is no solution of perpetual motion which is satisfactory if
it neglects the law of gravitation.

We find that any possible policy has only a very narrow field of
operation and that of its effects, even though some will be such as
are desired, others at the same time will be quite the reverse. If
we lessen one evil, we create at best another only a little smaller,
and we find ourselves squirming in the grasp of forces which,
through all changes, remain undiminished. If mischief is not to be
done there must be a correct knowledge of the forces.

It is by virtue of the law of population, which expands upon the

[59] Kautzky, quoted by Zacharias, *Bevölkrgsfrage,* 65.

man-land relation, that there is a science of society. So long as the outside boundary and final limits are natural and fixed forces —natality over against mortality; vital vigor over against disease and death—which are determining the growth or decline of society, an investigation has all the elements of a true science. Whether it has in view the whole race or a single or composite society, it has a defined field capable of observation and controlled by law. It is dealing with natural necessity, and it may go on until it has duly studied the elements by which all the phenomena of society are produced. Since the human race is bound in with all other organisms under laws of life which are part of the universe, human society is itself a phenomenon of the universal order. It is a product of forces in which there is no caprice or accident. The forces are acting within conditions that are a part of the whole. This whole has been, is, and will be, through some span of time. It is as immaterial what went before or will come after as it is whether, as a matter of fact, there is a fourth dimension of space. We live within that span of time in which this universe may be accepted as constant, just as we live within Euclidean space. Such are the bounds of all the sciences.

CHAPTER III

DIVISIONS OF THE SCIENCE OF SOCIETY

§45. Society a Living Whole. It is impossible to get a comprehension of any complex societal structure without taking it to pieces, somewhat as one takes down an automobile. The mind cannot understand either the whole or the interrelation of the parts without the employment of that expedient. Yet it is not always realized that when analysis is done the results are dead, unreal, and misleading unless the investigator or student frees himself from his categories and, enlightened but not hampered or bound by what analysis has taught him, re-assembles the parts and rises to a view of the intricately interlocking action of all the factors. Neat piles of springs, bolts, wheels, and other parts, lying about on the floor, are not an automobile. They must be put together before there is anything fit to be called by that name or that acts like a motor vehicle. Similarly with a society: it is not composed of sets of institutions that have been analyzed out and separately examined; it is the whole of them acting together. If we take society and societal life down into its components, we must put them together again and try to see them in their involved interaction; thus only shall we form a real conception of them. Throughout this book the authors seek every occasion to suggest the presence of such interaction. That is all we can do—to suggest. There is no way to portray at once the whole intricacy of society and societal life. But if the mind remains alert to the shortcomings of all analysis and classification, and alive to the need of forming composite impressions, the conception of society as a living whole ought to break over it as the various sets of its institutions are passed in review.

Says Rivers[1] of his study of Melanesian society: "This book shows how hopeless it is to expect to understand human culture if we limit our attention to any one of its component elements. In the more complicated examples of human culture, specialism may be inevitable, though even here it needs to be assisted by the work of those who may lack the completeness and exactness of the specialist, but yet understand the principles of more than one science.

[1] *Melan. Soc.*, II, 594.

In the study of the ruder varieties of human culture, such specialism is far less needed and is far more prohibitive of progress. The constituent elements of such cultures as those of the Melanesian, Australian or African are so closely interwoven with one another, it is so difficult or impossible to disentangle these elements, that the work of the specialist in social organisation, religion, language or technology must be unfruitful and soulless."

§46. Institution-Building. With this caution or reservation we turn to the classification of society's institutions; and we begin with their lowest terms, the mores. The mores cover all details of action in society, but they are not unclassifiable. They tend to form accretions about nuclei; and the nuclei are interests. Certain of these interests are weak and transitory; others strong and constant. About the latter type the accretion is more copious and forms a body of related practices. A perennial interest is never more than approximately satisfied, and there is always about it a sort of shifting envelope composed of obsolescent, mature, and nascent mores—of mores in all degrees of adjustment, running from actual maladjustment to untried variation. For example, it is a salient fact of societal life that it is lived by two sexes. It is to the interest of both sexes, to offspring, and to the society at large that there shall be some regularity in sex-relations. Mores develop which secure such regularity in some degree. Then the basic life-conditions change, or the sex-interest for other cause ceases to be satisfied, or so well satisfied, and the mores are altered through selection among constantly rising variations.[2] When the set of practices which has gathered about this dominant interest becomes recognizable as constituting a related group, we call it marriage or the family, and refer to it as an institution.

One might say that every major interest of man gathers about itself a conglomerate of practices to secure its satisfaction. Then under the selective test some of these mores show a survival-value inferior to that of others and are selected out. This generally occurs through the medium of the taboo: Thou shalt not. What is left after the action of the taboo, which is, on the primitive stages, virtually decisive,[3] is likely to last on for some time and so to become traditional. Indeed, certain of the surviving practices may seem to have some permanent or "absolute" character, which,

[2] Keller, *Soc. Evol.*, chs. II, III.
[3] §§268, 269, below.

when once the knowledge of origins is lost, lends to them the spurious quality of "natural." Such is the "natural right" to life, that results from the taboo: Thou shalt not kill.[4] The action of the taboo in institution-building may be likened to that of the sculptor upon the raw block of stone; as someone quaintly put it, he knocks off the superfluous corners and protuberances, chisels away the slighter irregularities, and reveals the statue that was seated there in the mass of stone all the time.

§47. The Major Institutions.

Mores gather, then, about interests, and develop, where the interests are salient, into institutions. Aligned with the social forces, and of course resulting from their action, are what we might call the hunger-interest, the love-interest, the gratification-interest, and the fear-interest: the interests involving the self-maintenance, self-perpetuation, and self-gratification of society, and its relations with the supernatural. About these basic, permanent, and engrossing interests the mores have formed in their characteristic way and upon them the taboo has exercised its distinctive function.

The result has been the development of massive institutions or blocks of institutions, corresponding to three of the four interests, and of a numerous but far less integrated galaxy of minor institutions in the case of one of them—the gratification-interest. These are:

I. the institutions of societal self-maintenance, including the industrial organization, property, war for plunder, and the regulative organization—all corresponding to the hunger- or preservation-interest;

II. those of societal self-perpetuation, including marriage and the family—corresponding to the love-interest;

III. those of societal self-gratification, including more or less unrelated societal forms, such as practices of ostentation in dress, ornament, social etiquette, war for glory, and other particulars, and forms of pleasure-seeking, such as games, gambling, the use of stimulants and narcotics, dancing, play-acting, and the fine arts—corresponding to the gratification-interest; and

IV. those of religion in the broadest sense, including animism,

---

[4] Keller, in *Unpopular Review*, VII, 286 ff.; §172, below.

daimonism, and their derivatives—corresponding to the fear-interest.

All of these institutions interpenetrate, as do the interests that summoned them into being. Property, for instance, goes back in no small degree to vanity; marriage is not by any means to be connected solely with sex and love; gambling does not find its sole motive in pleasure-seeking; dancing is often religious in nature; and religious practices are not unresponsive altogether to the hunger-interest or to that of sex. Each of these interests produces consequences on the domain of the others which are often, indeed, foreign to its own satisfaction. These cross-relations will reveal themselves as we go on. We intend, however, to adhere to our four-fold division, regarding its categories as typical. In no case of evolution is there a possibility of drawing hard and fast distinctions. Categories run into one another across zones of transition, and no such zones are clean-cut but all are blurred. When it comes to the order of treatment, however, we are led to adopt a sequence based in part upon considerations not introduced hitherto. It remains to explain these and to state the sequence.

§48. Order of Treatment. Of the two basic activities of any society, self-maintenance is naturally cast for first entrance. Since types of maintenance correspond to types of environment, the former are here distinguished upon the basis of the latter. The environment encountered by men may be regarded as consisting of three main types. There is first the natural or physical environment of inorganic nature, flora, and fauna; and maintenance within it results primarily in the industrial organization. There is, second, the social environment of fellow-men; and adjustment to it summons into being an organization of offense, defense, and regulation, including chiefly the military organization and government. In these two types of environment men must compete with their plant, animal, and human fellows; indeed it may be said, somewhat metaphorically, that they compete with inanimate nature. In an age of steam and electricity, a man who has only muscular power to offer in the industrial organization competes with coal. He is equal to so many pounds of it. In addition to these two types of environment, men feel themselves in confrontation with a third also, the world of ghosts and spirits; and the corresponding form of societal self-maintenance is religion.

This specifically human construction, in the way of a third environment, deserves brief comment here at the outset; it has been called the "imaginary environment," because the earliest ideas about it rest upon evidence which enlightenment considers illusory. To the primitive mind, however, it is as actual as the surroundings perceptible to the senses, and the outstanding prosperity-policy on that stage is one of adjustment to it. Maladjustment to it as a life-condition is taken to be as serious—at least as serious—as in any other range. As one author has put it, religion is the struggle for existence prolonged beyond the grave.[5] The fear-factor is, at least on occasion, even more actual, peremptory, constant, and compelling than any other of the socializing forces; and so we wish to give it a place in the forefront of our treatment. It is to be noted that Spencer[6] begins almost at once with the primitive ideas about the imaginary environment; they are so powerful and pervasive in their effects that they should be taken into account early in any scientific study of human society. Anyone who reviews the evolution of religion with a mind free of prepossession presently senses the fact that it too is a prime expedient in maintenance. This inclusion of religion under a broadened conception of societal self-maintenance is not at all in the interest of fussy classification, but carries with it essential ideas of the interrelation of societal forms.

The foregoing provides for the maintenance-institutions. Self-perpetuation and self-gratification remain. These, however, do not call for analysis and classification according to the types of environment to which they constitute societal adjustments. They follow naturally after the forms of maintenance, self-gratification, as productive of no great institutions, bringing up the rear. In that position, also, since it is intimately connected with all that goes before— one might almost say that it has no important institutions of its own because it exists as a sort of growth upon the maintenance- and perpetuation-institutions—whatever treatment is allotted to it will serve as a sort of retrospect of ground that

[5] Lippert, *Kgchte.*, I, 29.
[6] *Prin. Soc.*, I, chs. VIII ff.

has been covered. The position and space accorded to self-gratification are by no means evidence of its insignificance.

Our arrangement returns, therefore, essentially to our definition of society: I. Self-Maintenance, including (a) the Industrial Organization, (b) Property, (c) the Regulative Organization, and (d) Religion; II. Self-Perpetuation, including Marriage and the Family; III. Self-Gratification, comprising a variety of societal forms not comparable in degree of organization with the foregoing.

General considerations involving certain more abstract matters connected with the science, in so far as they are touched upon at all, will be relegated to the concluding Part of this book. In such postponement we are reversing the usual order; but we believe that the college student and the general reader (a pair to whom, before all others, we are offering this book) will come to the more abstract generalities respecting nature of evidence, limitation of the field, relation of theory to practice, and the rest, with more interest and a better understanding, if they have first followed the course of a systematic demonstration accompanied with concrete cases in evidence. Such generalities, wherever they appear in a treatise, and provided they are scientifically arrived at, have to be written last; and they might as well take their natural place. Hence also our introductory chapters have been held down to what we consider an irreducible minimum.

PART II

SOCIETAL SELF-MAINTENANCE

CHAPTER IV

INDUSTRIAL ORGANIZATION: FACTORS

§49*. Original Destitution. In a highly civilized and organized society there is no struggle for existence. One may try to maintain himself, and fail, or not try at all; but he will not be allowed to die of hunger or cold or by violence, if his predicament is known. It is regarded as a sort of disgrace to a modern community if people perish within it of starvation or exposure. Societal organization has achieved the power to set up against nature barriers that protect all who come under the range of that organization.[1] But this is a power acquired in relatively recent time. Disguise it as he may, and refuse to look the facts in the face as he will, man's cleverest and most desperately wrought out adjustments have, on many antecedent stages of societal evolution, failed to secure him existence. The earlier adaptations came hard; famines occurred and a large death-rate ensued while men were groping about to better the arts of maintenance, or, worse still, were yet in the stage of suffering and futile grumbling which preceded the putting forth of effort in adjustment. Formerly the Maori of New Zealand were much pinched for food in the winter—the "grumbling months"; "they had no other name for them, being a blank in their calendar, as they could do nothing but sit in their smoky huts, with eyes always filled with tears."[2]

It is a mistake to think that man's earlier mental adaptations could have been voluntary and pleasurable; they were painful and were forced upon him against his will. When, however, he had broken through his inertia, under pressure, enough times, there was added to his make-up an impulse toward self-realization—a "career-interest"[3] which caused him, with progressively less frequent lapses, to strain toward a standard of living. This struggle for a standard or quality of living, rather than for mere existence, is a specifically human development. It is a phase into which, for

---

[1] Keller, *Soc. Evol.*, 67 ff.
[2] Taylor, *Te Ika*, 341; Holm, *Ethnol. Skizze*, 120.
[3] Ratzenhofer, *Soc. Erkennt.*, 56 ff.

men alone, the struggle for existence issues. It has come to replace the primitive type of struggle.

Our minds should be free, in this connection and from the outset, of the error involved in carrying back along the course of evolution, as a basis of interpretation, ideas and conceptions which belong to our own stage and era. It has already been observed that the science of society begins at the bottom, allowing for man conditions of existence in no respect milder than those encountered by other creatures, and finding in him the same elemental impulses and general stamp that characterize organic life through its successive stages. No myth was ever farther from scientific truth than that which represents mankind as starting in a state of nature in which there were peace, love, truth, justice, gratuitous abundance, liberty, and equality. Investigation of primitive conditions shows men in destitution—worse off, in fact, than many of the animals.

Even in the islands of Oceania, often reputed as an earthly paradise, there was an unremitting struggle to live. Of the D'Entrecasteaux islanders it is reported that "their hospitality would not stand the strain of frequent demands, and they object to being imposed upon much as we do. They have to work hard enough to gain a livelihood under ordinary conditions, and cannot afford to be burdened with outsiders. There is no idle sitting under a tree and allowing the bread-fruit to drop into their mouths, as a writer once ludicrously stated of the South Sea Islanders. The gardens must receive unremitting care and attention during the greater part of the year, if the yam harvest is not to be a failure and the natives faced with starvation. It is not so much that the work is heavy, though some portions of it are, but it has to be continuous."[4] Of this same region Finsch[5] writes that there is no paradisaical innocence, but the struggle for existence everywhere.

"When man came to take his seat at the banquet of life, he found the places all occupied, and to get a seat he was forced to expropriate a crowd of table-companions who were no less ravenous than he."[6] All the knowledge that men possess, all the arts, capital, and societal organization, are due to toil and sacrifice. What is to be explained is wealth, not poverty. It is an ultimate fact that man has nothing with which to support life. Poverty is not "caused"; it is there; it is the zero-line from which all else is reckoned. You do not need to be told how to become poor any more

[4] Jenness and Ballentyne, *D'Entrecasteaux*, 205-206.
[5] *Samoafahrten*, 107.
[6] Bourdeau, *Monde Animal*, 130; Sumner, *Coll. Ess.*, II, 217 ff., 233 ff., on the Banquet of Life and the Boon of Nature.

than how to fall down an elevator-shaft. All you have to do is to let yourself go. It is movement in the other direction that demands toil and thought. Wealth is not spontaneous and natural, but is societal and produced. All wealth-production is an effort to abolish poverty by putting something in the place of nothing. The work of civilization is to soften the conditions of the struggle. The modes of civilization are labor, knowledge, and organization. Vice, strife, error, and ignorance annul wealth-production, and thus lead back toward the starting-point. That which has brought us where we are is not the kindly current of a gentle stream, but the desperate strain of toughened sinews against a boisterous current; and the ultimate incitement to any activity has been the discomfort of the endangered or unsatisfied physical organism.

§50. **Coercion to Organization.** Since no human being could long exist without experiencing hunger—for bodily waste never ceases, while restoration is periodic—activities of self-maintenance must begin at once. Whether they are the right or best for the end in view is unknown. Experience proves, corrects, and warns. The immediate purpose, until a high stage is reached, is not to do right, but to live and to realize pressing interests. The first of these maintenance-activities must be the appropriation of certain chemicals (food) out of the environment. There is no other place to start than with food. Very many advances of mankind owe their origin to the food-interest and stand regularly in its service; clothing comes largely from plants that were originally selected for attention on account of their edible seeds. The struggle for existence rests on the fact that nature gives us only raw materials; we must work to get at them and adapt them. The competition of life is due to the fact that the natural supply of means of sustenance is limited.

The prime necessity is to get. This is accomplished in association; but, however small the society, there must develop at once ways of getting which become habitual, in brief, maintenance-mores. Such practices are directed primarily at what we now call production, and when an inclusive institution has formed out of them, it becomes the Industrial Organization. Furthermore there are competitors in the field, and it is hardly less vital to hold the gettings than to acquire them in the first instance. Hence a defensive organization. It is also possible to live by robbing others of what they have got, and here is the basis of an offensive or predatory organization. The defensive and offensive organizations are one, and form the Military Organization. It is directed mainly by the "we-group"[7] against the "others-group." But even within the "we-group" there are conflicts of interest in both getting and holding; there must be authority capable of keeping order. Hence the Regulative Organization. These organizations overlap in the discharge of their functions; all three are typical developments, mainly out of the maintenance-mores.

Organization, let it be recalled, proceeds through specialization followed by integration. First comes distribution of functions, then variation in structure to correspond to it. When functions are extended, as where infantry and artillery branch off from a single parent form, and are perfected, there follows a more marked adaptation of structure. Coöperation, or integration, brings specialization "to bear"; and along with it arrives the possibility of developing rhythm, or reiteration at intervals of time, and discipline under some form of leadership.

§51. The Industrial Organization. This is a set of adjustments including combinations, that has now become highly complex and refined. It has been necessary at every step to develop structure and apparatus. We are rapidly coming to see that history, in its most important sense, is a record centered about the evolution of this organization. By what stages have men struggled along through untold generations in the effort to get subsistence out of the earth for a larger number, or in larger measure for a given number? This is the question of human history. Other things which have been done or have come to pass are consequential, inferential, incidental, or range themselves around this central and absorbing interest. The chief concern and importance attaching to these latter—education, science, art, institutions, mores, morals, statecraft, literature, fashion, war, glory, religion—is in the question as to how they have reacted again upon the central interests.

[7] Keller, *Soc. Evol.*, 58 ff.

"Peary once turned to one of his Eskimo hunters who sat pensively outside the skin tupik (tent) on a brilliant Arctic summer day and said: 'Of what are you thinking, Tauchingwaq?' The brown native shrugged and smiled. 'I do not have to think, Pearyaksuak (Great Peary). I have plenty of meat.' "[8]

"The one great impulse prevailing everywhere in the history of civilization is self-maintenance. In it both that which is human and that which is brutal are united and distinguished. In it are presented, according to its extent, animal instinct and the seal and sign of humanity."[9] "The possession of the materials of civilization underlies the possession of intellectual culture. Intellectual creations come as a luxury after the satisfaction of the bodily needs. Therefore every question about the origin of civilization resolves itself into this question: What will favor the development of the material prerequisites of civilization? . . . Those gifts of nature are the most valuable for man, therefore, which open to permanent activity the fountains of force which dwell within him."[10] The processes of the industrial organization, once started, are cumulative. "A tool makes another tool without disappearing in the process [as seed does in the corn], like fire which kindles another fire. The second tool makes a third. Often a tool, once obtained, gives a possibility at the next step, by the same labor, of producing a better product. This is the point of departure for the enormous multiplication of the possessions of men, which, with its tendency to geometrical increase, is always going forward, which has become the creator of all material, and therefore of all intellectual, culture, but which gives to the former its more obvious tendency to an accelerated course."[11]

The pressing need of adjustment to changing conditions is the sharpest spur to human activity. It is very difficult for peoples who have a settled economy in an isolated station to be other than passive. Changing life-conditions force the conquest of inertia, one advance stresses to another, and activity succeeds passivity. Energy "is the child of education under the pressure of a widely outreaching form of maintenance; the consequence of life among forms and in regions of a strange type." Tribes that encounter changing conditions and become alert to adjust and learn are like travelled people.[12]

Although the modern type of the industrial organization is so complex and refined, and the primitive so simple and rude, there are two basic factors common to both, and to all intervening members of the series. These are Labor and Capital, representing respectively, as will presently appear, pain and self-denial. That from the beginning men perform labor and practise self-denial is in itself sufficient evidence that they are under compulsion, for they do not want to do either of these things. "We may affirm in general that on the lowest grade of civilization people always do what they want to do, and, as a rule, undertake what is useful only

[8] Green, F., "Eskimos," in N. Y. *Times,* Oct. 10, 1926.
[9] Lippert, *Kgchte.,* I, 3; Keller, *Soc. Evol.,* 141 ff.
[10] Ratzel, *Vkde.,* I, 17.
[11] Müller, *Ursprung,* 45.
[12] Lippert, *Kgchte.,* I, 42-48; 172 (quoted).

when compelled."[13] The fact that, for certain types of men, work becomes a satisfaction in and for itself or as a sort of drug against various mishaps and miseries, does not mean that it was anything but an unpleasant necessity for the primitive or is anything else for the masses of mankind to-day. And even if one is inclined to hold reservations as to labor, certainly economizing and saving are, in themselves, wholly repellent to undisciplined minds and tolerable to the enlightened only as means to an end.

It is by labor that men lift the burdens of life's ills and carry on culture; and it is when their labor is consolidated in capital, which raises the energy to a higher power, that it becomes strongly effective. After the lowest stage is passed, human society lives on subsistence-capital and multiplies the power of its labor by production-capital, in the form of implements, and by the natural forces which are brought into play through apparatus and machines. Population and capital are therefore the concrete forms in which we meet with the functions of societal self-maintenance—and self-perpetuation as well, for nutrition and reproduction go together[14]—when we turn to the practical processes of society as they are presented to observation and experience.

§52. **Foresight.** Certainly behind both the putting forth of labor and the accumulation of capital lies the development of power, in some degree, of representing the future; of foreseeing the chances of ill that it may hold and of providing such insurance against them as may be possible. It is foresight that incites to labor and to the accumulation of capital—foresight enforced by the repetition of bitter experience. Where this quality is rudimentary, labor is fitful and capital scarcely represented; where it is strongly marked, labor becomes steady and highly organized and capital is accumulated in profusion. Life on the lowest stages has scarcely any outlook over space or time. In space, with the exception of the mother-instinct, it does not go beyond the person; in time, the primitive type of mankind is, as we have already heard, "the unfortunate child of the moment," living from day to day, if not literally from moment to moment, without thought of what is

13 Ratzel, *Vkde.*, I, 57.
14 §340, below.

ahead.[15] In anticipating future needs he is less efficient than instinct-directed animals. It is the development of non-instinctive foresight that distinguishes the man; he comes gradually, in his mores, to subordinate the present to the future with some regularity instead of uniformly and childishly sacrificing the future interest, which he visualizes vaguely if at all, for the present interest whose crude bulk crowds his slight perspective. The index of this alteration is the willingness to labor and save; and the results of toil and economy then furnish the basis for a still wider and deeper extension and penetration of foresight.

We need to begin here with the warning that apparent cases of laziness and thriftlessness on the part of native peoples, especially the men,[16] are not always what they seem to be. They are often explicable if the local circumstances and mores are known. Certain beliefs, like that in magic, amount to the discount of the value of work; so do several others, as the following quotation from a veteran missionary will show. It may be said that natives hold views and engage in practices, merely because they like them, which countenance or even promote thriftlessness and sloth. That is another story and raises an issue that can be answered only by an extended demonstration of the automatic nature of societal evolution.

Of the Upper Congo native, Weeks[17] writes: "Visitors will sometimes find him lounging about the town, and thoughtlessly condemn him as lazy, whereas four times out of five, if they inquired, they would find that he is resting after a long bout of arduous work. He may have just returned from a trading journey lasting three to four months, during which time he has had rough sleeping places, insufficient food, and difficult roads to traverse; or he may have returned only yesterday from a fishing expedition, sleeping in rough shelters for three months, isolated from his fellows, and fishing during the night as well as the day so as to take advantage of the season; or it may be he has just returned from his twelve months' engagement for the white man, and his pay has been taken from him on one pretext or another, and the only way he can now get any compensation for his year's work is to live for a few weeks on those who have robbed him of his money. They have 'eaten his pay,' he will now eat their food. Or, he may have been away for months making a large canoe which he has finished, and it is now floating on the river, and he is resting before he commences another, and in the meantime he is trying to find a buyer. Then again he may be well to do, and have no need of work. His father or uncle may have been a keen trader, and has left his heir sufficient to live upon. If he were an Englishman he might be showing the soles of his boots in a Pall Mall club window, and be called a 'gentleman,' but being a native of Africa he smokes under his own shade tree, and is called by the ignorant a 'lazy nigger.' Give him 'piece-work,' and above all a guarantee that he will

[15] Fritsch, *Eingeb. S.-Afr.*, 418; Lippert, *Kgchte.*, I, 22.
[16] §64, below.
[17] In JAI, XXXIX, 135-136.

enjoy the fruits of his labour, and you will see him work as I have seen him—
equal to any white man doing *piece-work.*"

It is very difficult to rise from improvidence to a higher level. "Remarkable
is the often noted fact that . . . natives, when they have been for some time
in the service of Europeans, lose their happy disposition and take on a sullen,
gloomy character. This is to be explained only by the fact that such servants
gradually get from their masters the habit of worrying over the future and
that their temperament does not endure engrossment with such care."[18] Furthermore, there is an element of conservatism and inertia in the mores themselves, as the following will illustrate. "It is a curious fact that one tribe never
imitates another in its principal mode of fishing. I have seen an Upper river
native make and use a cast net such as he had seen our Accra carpenters use,
but I have never seen a man of one tribe imitate a man of a neighbouring tribe
in his peculiar mode of fishing. They have traps common to all, but each tribe
has its own principal mode peculiar to itself. I have twitted a native of Mon-
sembe about not following or even trying the successful mode of fishing pursued by the Libinza people, and he has replied, 'We could not catch fish like
them if we tried; that is their way, and we have ours.' " This author[19] goes on
to mention another and even more striking reason for the stoppage of advance
upon lower levels. "During my more than twenty-five years' teaching of the
Congo natives, both on the Lower and the Upper River, I have noticed that up
to the age of fourteen and fifteen, the boys and girls—especially boys—are
very receptive, and easily taught; but after that age comparatively few make
real advance in learning. After the age of fourteen or fifteen they have to
make a continuous effort to retain any book knowledge they may have received.
This may be due in some measure to their thoughts being centred on other
matters, as trade journeys, fishing, and hunting on their own account, and
later on building their houses and looking about for a wife, and procuring
the necessary articles for paying the marriage money and meeting the expenses of the feast, etc. I have also thought that the following is a great factor
in causing their mental growth to practically stop at the above age. For generations boys on arriving at the age of fifteen had learned all their fathers had
to teach them respecting fishing, hunting, wood-craft, paddling, and women.
If they showed a special aptitude for fishing, hunting, etc., they followed their
'bent' in that particular, and simply became proficient by practice, and their
successes were generally put to the credit of their charms." Here should be
noted the fact that where magic is accredited with results attainable only
through industry, there can be no great impulse to solid achievement. "They
never initiated new ways of building (until after the arrival of the white man),
or new ways of hunting, or fishing, etc., but only carried on those modes they
had gained from their fathers, and which were mastered by the time they were
fifteen years old."

While we are on this topic, we may take a glance at the question as to
whether emergence from his native state really benefited the savage after all.
Frequently it threw him totally out of adjustment to the environment in which
he had to live. There is much misapprehension on this score, for it is generally
assumed that the "lower" races gain in happiness as the result of learning

[18] Fritsch, *Eingeb. S.-Afr.,* 56; Lippert, *Kgchte.,* I, 39.
[19] Weeks, in JAI, XXXIX, 128, 131.

what the "higher" peoples have to teach them. Lugard,[20] a veteran colonial administrator, speaks as follows: "We are perhaps somewhat too apt to take it for granted that the introduction of civilization must add to the happiness of the natives of Africa. The ascent of man to a higher plane of intelligence, self-control, and responsibility is a process not unattended with pain. We in England would not hesitate to prefer our present culture to the barbarism of our woad-painted ancestors, but who shall say that we are either happier or physically fitter than they?" Under conditions of primitive life, the author goes on to say, there are many crudities and much suffering. "It is the weak who suffer. Women, after the first flush of youth, lead a life of perpetual toil and slavery. The aged and the sick succumb to the law of the survival of the fittest. On the other hand, the enhancement of the value of life to the individual brings with it apprehension. From the ability to realise cause and effect spring many sources of fear unknown to primitive man. A more highly-developed brain and nervous system increase the sensibility to physical pain. . . . It is impossible to strike a balance of the immediate profit and loss to the native populations by the advent of civilization." Again and again are encountered comments such as the following: "It may truthfully be said that the native, with his little, gets more real enjoyment out of life than do many of our wealthy white people with riches at their command. He has fewer wants and cares, and, above all, is not greedy for riches. Hence we find more contentment and true enjoyment of life in the homes of these humble people than in many homes of our own race."[21]

In view of evidence of this sort, it might well be questioned whether the inertia and conservatism of the savage man do not constitute a protective element that sets the brakes against a "progress" which, for him, is nothing else than a rush into maladjustment. The pace of early culture is necessarily and also expediently slow; because the day was one of small things it should not be held in contempt any more than is childhood.

§53⁴. Labor. Men are not so well aware as they might profitably be that they can "make" nothing. The operations of men consist in moving things into or out of the way of natural forces, and in combining, deflecting, or dissipating forces, by taking advantage of what knowledge has been gained concerning their ways and adjusting interferences accordingly.[22] Nothing is "created"—indeed, much energy is "lost"—in that transformation of one form of natural force into another upon which man prides himself. The heat stored up in coal is set free by putting the coal into the way

20 *Brit. Trop. Afr.*, 90, 91.
21 Jones, *Thlingets*, 211.
22 Keller, *Starting-Points*, chs. IV, V; Keller, *War to Peace*, ch. XVIII.

of a flame; it is metamorphosed in turn into the expansive power
of vapor, into linear motion, into circular motion, into reversed
circular motion, into a series of blows or more intricate movements
—a loss of the original energy of the fuel taking place at every
step. The power in the coal is deflected and divided, its place of
incidence is changed, but nothing is "created."

The operations of men can be exerted only upon materials furnished, permanent qualities and all, by nature; the activities of
the mind respecting them are reflections on experiences in the past
and conclusions as to the meaning of them, with inference as to
what is best to do in the present and future whereby these materials may be endowed with utilities for men. Metals, shell, bone,
fibers, hair, are made into weapons, implements, dress. This operation is labor, and it is a characteristically human activity. Tool-
making, wherein the human organs are strengthened and extended,
and both those organs and also things in nature are imitated in the
form of artifacts, is specifically human.[23] Spiders work at web-
spinning and bees construct honey-combs; yet these operations
are largely the externalization of some bodily secretion. Even if
birds and animals, for instance, beavers, collect materials entirely
outside themselves and build them into independent structures
resembling those of man, yet these activities are directed by instinct, never improving under conscious experimentation. With
some little qualification, therefore, it may be held that labor distinguishes man from other animals.

In labor it is seen that man's bane is his blessing. Labor is not
by any means a curse, as the ancient writers will have it. When
nature offers man a food-supply which requires little labor to
adapt it to immediate use, the effect is to make him lazy and good
for nothing; he develops no considerable civilization.[24] Yet labor
is irksome, and leisure, besides being agreeable, is an indispensable
condition for the production of auxiliary capital, or of ornaments,
and for the reflection by which knowledge grows. At some point
every individual must determine the line between labor and leisure,
and societies fix such a line in their mores. The standard of living

---

[23] Lippert, *Kgchte.*, I, 281, 284-285, 300.
[24] Gregory, Keller, and Bishop, *Phys. and Comm. Geog.*, §§146 ff.

is the limit at which the last increment of effort equals the last increment of satisfaction.

The savage knows as well as the civilized man that more work will bring more product; but increments of labor become more and more irksome and increments of the same products give less and less present satisfaction. There is a diminishing return in satisfaction and an increasing return in the pain of effort. Everyone has to determine for himself the point at which the last increment of labor and the last increment of gain are equal. The savage man hates labor so much and has an eye so single to immediate satisfactions that he locates this point only a little way along the line of exertion. Leisure and labor meet one another, for him, at a point where the pains of insistent hunger are not strongly felt. Laziness is often so pronounced "that anyone who, so to speak, has an atom of food in the house, will not go to work before he is driven to it by hunger—which, so long as affairs go poorly, he tries to forget by sleeping."[25] Leisure is often, though not always, devoted by primitive men to pure sloth. It includes play, that is, self-gratification, and is not altogether lost time with respect to cultural advance, for play wins skill and mental training for the savage just as it does for children, who, while hating work, will work hard at play.

Quite foreign to the nature-man is the modern conception of the time-element in labor. Natives are never in a hurry and do not work up to a set point of time at which a task must be done.[26] The juncture at which the use of the time-measure begins is important in the history of civilization; we ourselves live by time-pieces during the whole course of waking life, for time has become to us a sort of fetish to which we surrender the control of most of our actions.[27]

§54. Incentives to Labor. All coercions and incentives which induce men to work harder or more regularly are, in so far, favorable to culture. Newly evoked wants have this effect. On the lowest stages few incentives carry appeal except such as gratify the

25 Von Rosenberg, *Geelvinkbaai*, 88.
26 Von Götzen, *Afr.*, 121.
27 Day, "The Man who knew Gods," in *The Crow's Nest*.

appetites without delay. Intoxicating drinks and tobacco have had this effect; they have availed to get work out of aborigines where other inducements have failed. Planters have preferred bibulous laborers who would quickly squander their earnings and return to work after brief intervals instead of retiring in princely affluence upon their accumulated few hundreds of pesetas or dollars. Hence the rôle played by ardent spirits in the contact of civilized and uncivilized. So weak is the representative power that a man of undeveloped intelligence—even an immigrant or peon—will look at a reward that is dangled before his eyes and agree to work a long time for it. A tropical laborer is offered fifty dollars for five years' labor, and accepts; he sees only the fifty dollars. Beads, wire, cloth, and other like goods have appealed to vanity, and have exerted a strong incentive to labor when once they have won their way and have been sanctioned by fashion. Knives, guns, and other superior weapons offered in trade have become, after the savage has become acquainted with the advantages of them, strong incentives to the collection of furs and ivory. Useful tools and utensils win their way far more slowly and much later. They represent surrender and resignation to steady and apparently endless exertion.

The economic results of the contact between civilized and uncivilized are likely to be destructive to the latter. The incentives to which they are exposed may be excessive. The evil effect of strong alcoholic drinks is more readily understood than are some other aspects of the case, and is a matter of wide knowledge and regret; but it is not so much worse than the effects of other factors inherent in contact to destroy whatever culture the natives had and to exterminate them. Incentives of strange and alien origin, like fire-arms, always throw a simpler organization out of adjustment to normal occasions and conditions in the case as it stands. There are reactions to correspond and crises ensue; game is rapidly destroyed, for example, and then famines come. Incentives may therefore result in demoralization unless there is a reserve of steadying training to offset the effect. We have cases of this presented to us in school-life, when prizes are offered. Civilized men are strongly influenced by excess incentives all the time—now more than ever before. The sight of wealth won in a few years acts in civilized society as an impulse to strenuous and prolonged effort far beyond the equilibrium-point between present strain and present gain. The result is overwork, excitability, and nerve-damage, with demoralization from either success or failure of effort; for the moral training that enables men to fail or to succeed with equanimity is rarely adequate to meet the strain of either eventuality. The savages show us a crude phase of a process to which all mankind are subject.

When, further, we compare primitive conditions with those of a high civilization, we must remember that only where the industrial organization is large and powerful does it present a great variety of products to strive for, allowing of change from one to another. When it is primitive and weak, the range of satisfactions is narrow and the gain from more product speedily falls below the pain of more labor; and along with this goes the fact that the stimulus of a future good depends upon the ability of the mind to represent to itself a satisfaction which is as yet imaginary. The history of civilization presents a long scale over which these elements have varied and combined to produce societal forms ranging all the way from those of the savage, who will work no more when hunger is stilled, to those of the civilized man whose possible and future satisfactions are so great that by all the labor of which he is capable he never reaches the point where the final increment of pain is equal to the next increment of satisfaction.

§55. **Capital.** The significance of this term, as we use it, is energy stored up against the struggle for self-maintenance; and we shall distinguish subsistence-capital, which explains itself, and auxiliary or production-capital, like tools, which is usable in further production. This distinction need not be sharpened at this point.[28] If a man or society has capital, he or it does not need to struggle for the means of living either so hard or so long as does the non-possessor; the capitalist, in fact, may intermit effort for a time, or for good and all, if he has a sufficient store. We think of the energy-storing agency as a human one, for capital "is labor accumulated, multiplied into itself—raised to a higher power, as

[28] §84, below.

the mathematicians say."[29] That nature is more complaisant in one
place than in another, and that the element of chance[30] is always
present—whereby, for instance, a lucky imbecile has become the
possessor of much capital—are facts which, though they bear
upon the accumulation and distribution of capital, are incidental
to our conception. Capital is essentially a result of human foresight, however unconsciously manifested, and is rendered possible
by consistent renunciation of the present in favor of the future.
It is the outcome of self-denial and is a product of societal evolution.

Foresight is shown not only in the storing up of resources in
modern fashion, but in even the most artless cases of appropriation out of nature, such as the taking up and retention of a conveniently shaped stick or stone. Such an action is really capital-
creating and renders the future less insecure; it exhibits that
departure from the status of the animals which works out into the
greater security enjoyed by man in the presence of a hostile environment. But the staff and stone, the prototypes of most later
and derived weapons and tools, were at most of slight and accidental superiority over any club or missile that could be caught
up from the ground, until man had put into them something of
himself by working them into more useful form, by materializing
in them certain of his ideas.[31] Such procedure, however, could not
have been enforced, in many if any cases, by immediate necessity;
to have the better weapon in time of need, energy must have been
invested in its fabrication in anticipation of such time. Action on
the spur of the moment could scarcely have created capital; some
forecasting of the future, however unpremeditated, must have
taken place before possible future pain, likely to be caused by the
absence of the worked-up article, could have been balanced against
taking present "pains" in the storage of energy, and could have
outweighed the latter.

The development of capital in the form of tools, weapons, and
the more complicated types of cultural apparatus lends to men,
in the course of time and experience, such a feeling of security in

29 Sumner, *Soc. Classes,* 62.
30 §§194 ff., below.
31 Keller, *Soc. Evol.,* 19.

self-maintenance that they are led to ignore the conditions set over human life in the forces of nature, and to get their attention so riveted upon their own achievements as to regard these—in the absence of some great cataclysm or of candid reflection—as the determining factors of life. Nevertheless there is enough of truth behind such exaggeration to warrant the statement that the development of capital and that of civilization go together.[32] Brief reflection will evoke evidence enough for this correlation. Hence the folly of some thoughtless people who have inveighed against capital as such; it is as great as that exhibited by one who would decry labor. Capital and labor are the two legs upon which civilization stands and moves. The possession of capital is important enough to show an elemental survival-value throughout societal evolution. Whether the concomitants that go along with capital, or with labor, are right and moral is neither here nor there, for we are now encountering yet another aspect of the inevitable.[33]

§56. The Simpler Terms of Maintenance. Capital and labor in their more developed stages, as well as the industrial organization in general, have received much attention from many able men. It is far from our purpose to enter the field of modern economics, which we regard as a branch of the science of society that has, by reason of long and intensive cultivation, become independent.[34] In offering, however, an analysis of the industrial organization in its simpler terms, we do not renounce the hope of lengthening the perspective of the modern specialist and of exhibiting the operation in lower terms of forces and factors sometimes lightly regarded as recently evolved or created. Even upon the primitive stage both labor and capital are massive and complex factors requiring analysis for their understanding. Spencer and others have acquainted us with the conception of organization as a matter of integration succeeding differentiation. In the case of the industrial organization this means specialization of economic function accompanied by that coöperation without which any and all specialization must remain sterile; a coöperation expressly provided for

---

[32] Sumner, "The Power and Beneficence of Capital," in *Coll. Ess.*, II, 337 ff.
[33] §169, below.
[34] §459, below.

in our definition of society, as a condition indispensable to society's existence.

Allusion has been made to another method, not industrial or economic, by which societal self-maintenance is attained, namely, by military organization. It calls for mention in this connection; for it allows, first, of defense of what has been gained through industry and, second, of the appropriation of the winnings of others. A defensive force is a species of insurance, costly but necessary so long as predatory activities on the part of others are possible. An offensive force has been, in some cases, the prime and almost the sole agency for self-maintenance upon the spoils of others. War for plunder has certainly been a maintenance-activity, and the war-organization cannot be denied its distinct economic function. In addition, the arts of war are always contributing to or being adapted to the needs of industry and peace. Its relation to the organization for self-maintenance is, however, but one aspect of war. There is war for glory, which is self-gratification; war to satisfy political as distinguished from economic earth-hunger;[35] and war to propagate the faith. The most significant function of war is in the evolution of the regulative system, or government; and we prefer to postpone any general treatment of military organization until it can be brought into its most appropriate setting.[36]

[35] Sumner, "Earth Hunger," in *Coll. Ess.*, II, 31 ff.
[36] Chs. XIV ff., below.

CHAPTER V

LABOR: SEX-SPECIALIZATION

§57. Specialization by Sex. Specialization, the factor which leads off in organization, takes place between unlikes; and the greatest opportunity for specialization lies between extremes of unlikeness. The organization for self-maintenance began, as organization is wont to begin, where there was the greatest differentiation between the factors present in the field, that is, between man and woman. For there exists among human beings no other dissimilarity, whether of age, temperament, social position, or anything else, that approaches in scope, constancy, and universality that of sex. The fact that *Homo* is a bi-sexual organism remains, and will ever remain, one of the steadfast and inexorable ultimates of human life, to which, through mores and institutions that take shape about the attending interest, adjustment will be made. Primary and secondary sex-differences constitute, as between man and woman, a series of essential contrasts, thorough-going, all-pervasive, inevitable, and immutable, such as do not exist as between man and man and woman and woman. It follows, of course, that if sex-specialization was the first specialization, then sex-coöperation was the first coöperation. Some peoples are so weak in general coöperation that they resemble boys picking up chestnuts from the ground, with no one to go up the tree and shake for all; but even such peoples have sex-coöperation in some form of sex-union.

Since these differences of sex represent a life-condition of an elemental order, adjustments to which are to be noted in all the divisions of our subject, we shall take up the general case here and now, that it may be before us almost from the outset. In the following general characterization of the sexes, and chiefly of woman, much of the evidence is derived from observations on non-primitive subjects; but we believe the underlying differences to be characteristic of sex and that their general type is of all stages and times.

§58. Sex-differences. No amount of reasoning, complaining, or protesting can alter the fact that woman bears children and man does not, and that the former is rendered periodically weaker than the latter, not only by reason of the accompaniments and sequels of child-birth but also because of more frequently recurrent incapacities incidental to female sex-life. Maternity is a disability in the struggle for existence, and a special peril.[1] Even if woman and man were equal in physical strength and alertness at ordinary times, as seems to be the case among some primitive tribes,[2] women would be periodically the weaker. Such inequality is due to what might be called primary sex-differences; and with these might be classed also the instinct of mother-love, which handicaps the female individual in the interest of the species.[3] Furthermore, among the higher animals, the male is regularly more powerful than the female, and is often endowed with fighting weapons—a superior outfit, to account for which Darwin developed the theory of sexual selection.[4] It is obvious that, within the human race, the male is regularly larger and stronger than the female. "In general, the stature of the women of any race may be taken as about one-sixteenth less than that of the men. Thus in England a man of five feet eight inches and a woman of five feet four inches look an ordinary well-matched couple."[5] That "the preponderance of the adult man over the adult woman in total stature and bulk is fairly obvious and well established," is a conclusion drawn after the examination of much evidence.[6] It requires no demonstration, except, perhaps, a reference to the records of athletic history, to justify the statement that woman cannot vie with man, even when she is not under her special sexual handicap, in strength, speed, and other qualities which must once have been all-important for living. Ellis[7] reports that woman's rate, rapidity, and precision of movement are inferior to man's; that, while she tires less easily at her own level of routine action, she gives way speedily at man's level, which is that of intense concentration for a time, or of intermittent spurts of energy. She lives at a more continuous, lesser

1 Hegar, *Geschlechtstrieb*, 20.   2 §336, below.
3 §335, below.
4 In *Descent of Man* and *Selection in Relation to Sex.*
5 Tylor, *Anth.*, 57.   6 Ellis, *Man and Woman*, 41.
7 *Man and Woman*, ch. VII.

tension, is passive rather than aggressive, industrial rather than militant.

The female nervous system is less stable than the male, being more affectable and susceptible to neurasthenia, hallucinations, hypnotic influences, and hysteria. The last of these terms is derived from the Greek *hystera*, meaning "womb." Woman dreams more and is more likely to become abnormal under anæsthesia. Female mediums are commoner than male, and witches figure more prominently in the history of manias and persecutions than do their male counterparts. "Nervous as a witch" is one of those folk-summaries whose import, in proverbs, apothegms, and the like, we do not hold as lightly as we once did.[8] In her mental processes, woman is characterized by intuition and feeling rather than by logic. "She can seldom carry an idea to its logical conclusion, passing from term to term; somewhere there is a solution of continuity."[9] She is quick to perceive and alert to act; of nimble wit as compared with the more massive and deliberate processes of man. She does not think things out as steadily but proceeds by indirection rather than by dogged frontal attack. Deduction comes to her more readily than induction; and she has shown much less mental power in activities demanding the latter. She is imitative rather than original, doing the appointed rather than the self-appointed task; she is therefore, as any teacher knows, more docile, patient, and amenable to discipline. "Men," says Goethe,[10] "strain after freedom; women after usage."

Geddes and Thompson[11] think that males live at a loss, are more katabolic, disruptive changes tending to preponderate in the sense of alterations in their living matter or protoplasm, while females live at a profit, are anabolic, constructive changes predominating in their life, whence child-bearing. This is the great difference of sex. Man, says Reclus,[12] "was by instinct a ferocious beast, woman was by function a mother." Ellis[13] remarks that "the method of attaining results by ruses is so habitual among women that . . . deception is 'almost physiological.' The same fact is more ungraciously stated in the proverbs of many nations, and in some countries it has led to the legal testimony of women being placed on a lower footing than that of men." "Coyness and caprice have become a heritage of the sex," writes Galton,[14] "together with a

8 §310, below.
9 George, in *Atl. Mo.*, CXVI, 726. Illustrations are cited.
10 *Tasso*, Act II, Sc. I, 1013-1022.   11 *Evol. of Sex*, 26.
12 *Prim. Folk*, 58.   13 *Man and Woman*, 174.
14 *Human Faculty*, 57.

cohort of allied weaknesses and petty deceits, that men have come to think venial and even amiable in women, but which they would not tolerate among themselves." Lecky[15] has a very good comparison of the moral traits of men and women. Locke,[16] a shrewd observer, writes: "There are mental states in which a woman has no point of view at all. She wanders over an ill-defined circular area of vision. That is why, in such conditions, you can never pin a woman down with a shaft of logic and compel her surrender, as you can compel that of a mere man." Ostwald[17] questions women's capacity to be "cultural pioneers"; he thinks no woman has been found in the ranks of such hitherto and that the occurrence "probably will not take place at any period that can be foreseen." The case of Madam Curie, he thinks, is still incomplete. This is not because women have been oppressed; his cases of great men show that the chief food of geniuses has been books which women could have utilized without special training, just as many men have done, had not their interests lain in another field. Women who have done something in science have attached themselves to male teachers and have gone along with docility in the path on which they were started. Further, genius usually shows itself early in life, and women have been able to attend higher institutions of learning long enough now for some results to appear if that were possible. This whole situation is biologically quite comprehensible. The author holds the orthodox German opinion about women, but what he says can be adjudged apart from the knowledge of that somewhat disconcerting fact.

§59. Sex-Mores.[18] "Women are said to be mentally more adaptable. This is shown in their tact, which is regarded as a product of their desire to adapt themselves to the stronger sex, with whose muscular strength they cannot cope. If a woman should resist her husband she would provoke him, and her life would be endangered. Passive and resigned women would survive. 'Here at any rate we have *one* of the reasons why women are more passive and resigned than men.' Their tact is attributed to their quicker perception and to their lack of egoism. 'The man, being more self-absorbed than the woman, is often less alive than she to what is going on around.' "[19] The foregoing would point to natural selection as the agency productive of sex-qualities; but this is not by any means the whole story. Girls are in very early childhood accustomed to inhibitions strengthened by affection and imitation; so are boys, but girls are subjected, from the outset, to a greater number. There are many more things that boys may do, and girls not do, than *vice versa*. And the girls are more influenced by sentiment

---

15 *Europ. Morals*, 357.   16 *Red Planet*, 18.
17 *Grosse Männer*, 417-420.   18 Sumner, *Folkways*, ch. IX.
19 Sumner, *Folkways*, §359 (based chiefly upon Campbell, *Nervous Org.*, especially 53 ff., 56, 223).

and are in more constant intimacy with the mothers who keep up the inhibitions, to say nothing of the precepts, without interruption. Hence the girls are trained to docility, whether or not they are born to it. The notion of doing what is "right," that is, what parents, teachers, pastors, and other authorities, especially if beloved, have always presented as right, becomes part of their being, and the habit of conforming conduct to it comes to be a norm of life. It promotes conservatism. Especially does all this apply to woman's own status, her relations to men, in and out of marriage, and to all that concerns sex-relations. Women acquiesce and submit without reflection or struggle in whatever pain and loss this system of notions, rules, standards, and dogmas brings to them individually, and they do it so unconsciously that they are not aware of pain from it—certainly not of any suffering comparable with the pangs incident to breaking through the bonds of mores and law.

The conservatism of women, to which allusion has been made, has been observed by many commentators on human nature. It is unquestionably a matter of the mores; just how far, however, it is to be referred to a more recondite source in biological differences, is not clear.

Dundas[20] says that, "like all Africans the Mkamba is strictly conservative, he can brook no change or alteration. . . . Particularly opposed to improvements and new-fangled ideas are the women, who are, on the whole, far more intractable and stubborn than the man. Her wishes do not go far, but what a woman wants she will have, and I have known not a few cases where women have committed suicide when forcibly restrained from getting their own way."

Rivers,[21] who was an experimental psychologist, believes that, despite the evident influence of the mores, the Toda women were mentally inferior to the men. "In all my work with the men, it seemed to me that they were extremely intelligent. They grasped readily the points of any inquiry upon which I entered, and often showed a marked appreciation of complicated questions. They were interested in the customs of other parts of the world, and appeared to grasp readily the essential differences between their own ways and those of other peoples. It is very difficult to estimate general intelligence, and to compare definitely the intelligence of different individuals, still more of people of different races. I can only record my impression, after several months' close intercourse with the Todas, that they were just as intelligent as one would have found any average body of educated Europeans. There were marked individual differences, just as there are among the more civilised, and it is probable that I saw chiefly the more intelligent members of the community.

[20] In JAI, XLIII, 488.   [21] *Todas,* 20-23.

. . . Some of the younger women, when examined by various tests, showed as ready a grasp of the methods as any of the men, but most of the elder women gave me the impression of being extremely stupid. It was often obvious that they were not attending and were thinking far more of their personal appearance and of the effect it was having on the men of the party than of the task they were being set, but even when a liberal discount was made for this, it seemed to me that they were distinctly less intelligent than the men."

There develops, as a fact of observation, a code for each sex, covering behavior all the way from the details of boy and girl life to the "double standard of morality." What is to be especially noted is that the divergence goes back always to the fact of sex, and basically to the physical sex-differences represented at last analysis by the condition that the female carries the ovum and the male the spermatozoön. "As structural complexity increases, the female generative system becomes more and more complex. All this involves a great expenditure of energy, and we can clearly see how an ovum-producing organism would benefit by being spared the additional effort required for seeking out and impregnating another organism, and how, on the other hand, organisms whose main reproductive feature is simply the production of the spermatozoön would be better fitted for the work of search and impregnation if unhampered by a cumbersome female generative system. Hence the advantage of the sexes being separate."[22] The female bears the passive, relatively heavy, inert, impregnatable ovum; the male the active, light, impregnating spermatozoön. The female is the sought, the male the aggressive seeker. Other sex-differences of a physical, mental, and social character follow upon this basic diversity. There is no "equality" of the sexes, thus differently endowed from the outset. There is no equality between an etching and a sonata, for there is no measure common to them; and the case is similar as between man and woman. The sexes are complementary one to the other, as we shall see, but "equality is an incongruous predicate" in the case. The sums of the characteristics accordant with sex, when set over against each other, form a sharp contrast representing a cleavage through the whole societal structure. It is futile to try to argue or denounce away such vital differences. The only way to make the sexes equal would be to get back along the course of evolution and interfere at the point where bi-sexual-

22 Campbell, *Nervous Org.*, 29.

ity first appeared. As well attempt to argue away or decry gravitation or capillary attraction.[23]

§60. Sex-Codes. The mores are acquired characteristics and are not inherited but transmitted from generation to generation by imitation and inculcation.[24] Even in babyhood the sex-codes begin to form, and in early and almost sexless childhood their divergence is clearly marked. In the code of boyhood it is contemptible to play with dolls, however much the small urchin shame-facedly longs to do so; while the girl enacts the mother from the beginning. Then comes puberty, with all its subtle awakenings, and the codes draw farther apart. The young man must be manly, though it does not do, despite recent exhibitions of "emancipation," for the young woman to be altogether mannish; while the latter must be feminine, the former may not be effeminate. Objects of imitation and courses of education are diverse for the sexes; they are more nearly alike now than ever before, but the irreducible fact of sex is always implicit. Why must girls be escorted, chaperoned, and otherwise protected? Why is a parent more terrified at the thought of a young daughter rather than a young son wandering into some low part of a big city? The latter may be robbed or assaulted with intent to kill. That is bad enough. But the boy cannot be so abused that the consequence is lifelong shame and impairment of career and destiny. Why is there a "double standard"? Because only one of the sexes has borne across the ages the unconcealable physical consequences of transgression of chastity, and so has been exposed to the punishment for it which the mores have demanded. This is not "fair"; but then it is not fair either that women alone should suffer the childbirth pangs. Nature cares nothing about our ideas of fairness and equality; it is our business to realize them as we can. A genuine standard of sex-morality is lived up to by some men now, where once it was not within the mental horizon of anybody; the code of the enlightened and chivalrous gentleman, his sense of personal honor and of that

[23] See a vigorous and plain-spoken article by Sedgwick, "Feminist Revolutionary Principle is Biological Bosh," in N. Y. Times, Jan. 18, 1914. We know of nothing else from high authority which treats the sex-differences so thoroughly in such brief compass. Explosion of comment in N. Y. Times, Feb. 15, 1914.

[24] Keller, Soc. Evol., ch. VII.

due his future wife and the mother of his children, demands it of
him. He will not use his superiority in physical strength to beat
a woman, nor yet his exemption from consequences in order to
impose upon her in much more coarse and cowardly ways.

Notions of conduct befitting sex, though of inexhaustible number and variety, all go back with different degree of directness to
the primal sex-distinctions.

Primitive peoples insist upon sex-distinction in very concrete ways. Until recently the older Cheyenne men wore a breech-clout as a sign of sex; up to
about 1900 the Northern Cheyennes all wore it under the trousers, and also
"the string about the waist, next to the skin." If they took it off they thought
that they would lose their manhood. The string upon which the clout hangs is
as important as the clout itself; little boys wear the string, with no clout.[25]

Drinking, swearing, expectorating, slouchiness of person and
dress, and other such habits seem worse in a woman than in a man.
The dowdy woman is seldom condoned, even if she is exhibiting
simply the eccentricities of genius. Women are coming to smoke,
but they confine themselves, as yet, to dainty cigarettes. The
feelings revolt at the idea of a female butcher or pugilist. Many
occupations of this order are regarded as distinctly unfeminine;
and while the traditional prejudice against woman in the professions is declining, there is still a feeling that she is more in place
as a nurse than as a doctor. To some extent she must drop femi-
ninity when she enters the lists with men; she must not, says one
lawyer, use any of the traditionally feminine arts to soften the
judge or jury. Coming into direct competition with men, she must,
in a sense, surrender much of the chivalrous consideration long
accorded her in the mores; for every privilege attained carries
with it the renunciation of immunities incident to exclusion from
it. Despite the change of ideas, however, as to what women may
do—and it must be remembered that they have penetrated, long
ere this, into activities, such as play-acting, that had been strenuously and traditionally denied them—for the great bulk of mankind there will always be, while sex exists, standards of conduct
based upon sex, just as there are standards based upon the lesser
diversities of age, occupation, social position, and the rest.

§61. Sex-Destiny. It is necessary to outline the general case as

[25] Grinnell, *Cheyenne*, I, 221.

respects sex-contrasts to form a background before which, presently, to set forth the special case, namely, sex-division of labor. In view of the foregoing it is clear that women are the destined mothers and home-makers. Love and marriage are said to be incidental to man's career, while they are to woman, the very career itself: "Man's love is of man's life a thing apart, 'Tis woman's whole existence."[26] If one is inclined, in the light of recent events, to differ with this view, he must yet recall that it correctly represents the sentiment of long ages of recorded and unrecorded time, as well as the axiom revealed in usage by the masses of present-day mankind.[27] Why have women never occupied the eminent positions in societal life: in the state and church, in science and art, in the professions, in the industrial organization, and elsewhere? Partly, doubtless, because of lack of the physical and mental powers called for; partly, too, because of the absence of a measure of opportunity open to men; but also, in largest degree, because they have been otherwise interested and occupied. Many a modern woman has gladly sacrificed a public career for a domestic destiny, and that in an age when the mores have not proscribed the former and prescribed the latter. How much the more insistent must the call to domestic life have been in former times, when instinct and convention united in their impulsion; for it requires no profundity of ethnographical or historical knowledge to demonstrate that the sphere assigned to woman was that of marriage and the family.[28] A quaint piece of evidence as to the relatively secluded life of woman is given by Haddon[29] in an article on the study of tattooing: "The tattoo patterns of the women should alone be studied, because the men are often tattooed with foreign patterns when on their travels."

We take it to be self-evident that women have seldom or never vied with men in most branches of what might be called the reputation-producing activities of life. Where are the female counterparts of the eminent inventors, merchants, captains of industry, explorers, scientists, historians, poets, musical composers, statesmen—to mention at random a list of careers in each of which men have gained world-wide renown? The names of women fit to rank

26 Byron, *Don Juan*, I, CXCIV.   27 §5, above.
28 Chs. L, LI, below.   29 In JAI, XXXV, 113.

even with the second-rate and third-rate men are almost as conspicuous by their rarity as would be those of women who might
enter the singles of a championship tennis tournament in serious
competition with men.[30] The female counterpart of Napoleon or
Columbus is not forthcoming, for very obvious reasons, it may be
said: women have not been fitted for war or the hardships of discovery; as a sex they have been unsuited. Furthermore it cannot
be believed that women have been so systematically deprived of
opportunity through the ages as not to have developed cases of
eminence in other lines, had they not been inhibited, not by man,
but by their sex and its concomitants. Under conditions of great
oppression, men of talent have emerged. All who have attained
eminence have not had freedom, education, and privileges. And in
some lines, certainly, women have had all the opportunity that men
have enjoyed—in music, for instance. Yet where is the woman who
ranks, not with Beethoven, but with much lesser masters? It is
incredible to us that, with all the actual and alleged subjection of
women, they would not have shown more instances of eminence if
they had had it in them, or had they not been under a constant
stress in another direction that distracted their minds as from a
minor interest to a major. And we take this major interest to have
been the attraction of marriage and the family, something which
goes straight back to sex.[31] In this field the most decisive successes
remain unrecorded; but we dare affirm that if superiority in
woman's particular sphere conferred such public renown as is
gained by eminence in the outer activities, man would be outranked

[30] On one occasion, the two leading tennis players of the world, of opposite
sex, went on the court for a practice set. "Our national champion then conclusively proved what the world's champion man tennis player could do to the
best woman player by taking the set at love without the slightest exertion. For
the first three games of the set Mlle. Lenglen played hard, then, evidently convinced that she had no chance, slackened her efforts and several times asked
Tilden to give her thirty each game. But he jokingly insisted she was too
good a player to receive any such handicap and played out the set." Tilden
has said that whenever he played a woman he had to cut down the speed of
his shots fifty per cent in order to allow her to reach them in time to make
any sort of return. A prominent player has estimated that Mlle. Lenglen was
about number fifty on a world-list, the forty-nine players ahead of her all
being men.—N. Y. *Times*, Aug. 29, 1926.

[31] Baruch, "Why Women Lack Great Originality," in N. Y. *Times*, Aug. 4,
1915; Traquair, "Women and Civilization," in *Atl. Mo.*, CXXXII, 289 ff.

in the domestic range as much as woman appears to be in the world of recorded eminence. "The hand that rocks the cradle rules the world." The fact is that each sex is superior in its own domain.

§62. Woman and Marriage. A famous artist who refused, at length, to take any more young women as students, gave as his reason that his promising female pupils were too likely to marry and renounce a career. The relatively low wages of women, the economists tell us,[32] have been due to the fact that most girls in business or industry regard such employment as temporary; they often engage in it, in fact, solely for the sake of the pin-money or the social life to be derived from employment. It is not serious business leading to promotion and a career; it is a sort of stage between school and marriage. In the past this state of mind has been unfavorable to union organization.

An official of the New England Telephone and Telegraph Company has stated that a majority of their operators quit work to be married, after an average duration of service of between four and five years. It is well known that telephone companies are obliged to train and keep available a considerable body of substitutes to replace such defections. Of the two hundred girls in the employ of another company, thirty were, in June, 1915, about to be married; the news item reads rather dolefully: "No sooner has a girl become competent than she promptly announces her engagement, and another new girl must be taught."[33] Cases need not be multiplied; one more will be enough. A large knitting-mill was led to discontinue group life-insurance on female help and, in reply to a request for reasons, stated that the form of insurance in question, so far as women were concerned, was an absolute failure. The communication goes on: "Women are simply not as much interested as men in the future. They are not accustomed to the thought of providing for someone after their death. Considerable evolution in our economic conditions will have to take place before women will be interested in the insurance line on an equal basis with men. At present their thoughts and environment are molded on entirely different lines, and something for the present appeals to them much more strongly than any promise for the future. In our case, we have substituted for this a proviso that we give all our female employees, instead of group insurance, one per cent of the total salary they have received from us during the period of employment. This one per cent is given them at the time they leave for marriage. We have asked them to practically vote on this proposition; they have unanimously voted in favor of the aforementioned bonus, and against a continuation of group insurance."[34]

[32] Hobson, *Evol. of Capitalism,* ch. XII.
[33] Assoc. Press dispatch for Dec. 30, 1915; New Haven *Journal-Courier,* June 12, 1915.
[34] Personally communicated by a correspondent.

§63. The Sexes are Complementary. The fact is that sex, instead of being a comparatively unimportant and superficial difference between man and woman, is a deep-seated structural diversity, "affecting probably every organ, every tissue, and every cell of the entire body."[35] "The division of the human race into two sexes is the most important of all anthropological facts."[36] It becomes at least one of the most important of all facts for a science of society, forming as it does a major life-condition to which society must adjust as it adjusts to other equally basic conditions.[37] The outlines of the general case of sex-differentiation being now before us, we turn to the necessary reflection of this differentiation within society's maintenance organization. If man is, by nature, active, aggressive, and not limited, while woman is passive (so much so, we are told, that even in case of suicide, she adopts passive methods),[38] patient, and limited in her sphere of action, there is here a case of diversely endowed beings capable of advantageous coöperation. One sex acts under high pressure, the other under low pressure; one revolts at monotony, the other takes naturally to routine; one shows a restless pursuit of the new and untried, the other an "organic conservatism." It is unnecessary to summarize the physical, mental, and social differences involved in sex; but it is clear enough that the sexes are complementary. That being the case, the peculiar utility of their coöperation may be inferred on general principles. It would appear that, ignoring reproduction, the man-woman combination is stronger for success in living than that of man with man or woman with woman. Many soldiers of this generation have observed the reluctance of their fellows who were assigned to "kitchen police"; it is for men really a punitive task. Many will recall the bickerings and paltry sophistry over whose turn it might be to attend to the kitchen-functions of a man's camping-party. Those duties, however, are precisely the ones that women in general would by nature prefer as against drilling, bayonet-practice, fighting, or even wading all day in trout-streams. "Woman's work" was not thrust upon her wholly by superior force.

[35] Sedgwick, "Feminist Revolutionary Principle," in N. Y. *Times*, Jan. 18, 1914.

[36] Sumner, *Folkways*, §360.   [37] §331, below.

[38] Ellis, *Man and Woman*, 334 ff.

Since it is more difficult to see man's advantage than woman's in sex-coöperation, let us reconstruct a situation with his standpoint chiefly in mind. Suppose the background to be the early hunting stage, and the use but not the generation of fire[39] to be understood. Two men are pursuing the struggle for existence together, and they have no women. At best they must take turns doing what they do not want to do or have no special capacity for doing; there will hardly be any specialization, in the absence of enslavement (for which our stage is too primitive), whereby one constitutes himself the ranger and the other the headquarters. Yet the extra weapons and utensils, and especially the fire, must be tended and carried safely, and the person who is doing that cannot be hunting freely. There is no natural and inevitable specialization of function in such masculine association because the associates are too nearly alike. The details of inconvenience, cross-purposes, clashing of will, and so on, can be supplied without difficulty. Suppose now that of the two associates one is a woman, and, to make the case the more conclusive, suppose her encumbered with her young. The differentiation of function carries itself out spontaneously. The woman, even if she is able, does not wish to range far and wide; she is well content to tend the fire and to move slowly, laden with the joint possessions, to the next resting-place, leaving the man relieved of whatever may hinder the full prosecution of activities along his line. She gets in return some protection for herself and her young and the remnants or superfluity of his quarry. He comes back to an abiding-place and to the protecting and comforting blaze; there is no uninteresting transportation or routine drudgery for him to do; he may sleep or loll and smoke; and yet the headquarters have been shifted conveniently to his movements.

Situations on this order, obviously schematic, but entirely justified by what we know of primitive life, can be reconstructed to satisfy our desire for rational explanation of what developed without forethought or analysis, in the mores. Even among pastoral nomads, "when the men go out in the mornings to hunt, they give the women directions as to whither they shall move; and after they tire of hunting they meet at the appointed spot in the evening,

[39] §§88, 90, below.

find the camp in order and the meat already cooking over the fire."[40] Though, to simplify the situation, we have taken only two individuals, sex-coöperation is readily visualized as a mass-phenomenon.

§64. Coercion of Woman. Reports on primitive peoples sometimes inform us that the men force the women to do the drudgery. Undeniable as such evidence may be, it is incorrect to assume that it includes the whole story or that primitive women feel themselves tyrannously oppressed and wronged by their men. Travellers see the women hoeing incessantly in the field, while the men loaf about the camp; but they have not seen the men on the night-hunt while the women slept in the lodges. It is regarded as good economy that the savage, after the strenuous exertion of hunting, lies about while his wife drudges.[41]

"Fatigues of hunting wear out the body and constitution far more than manual labor," and the Indians' "manner of rambling through the woods to kill deer is a very laborious exercise, as they frequently walk twenty-five or thirty miles through rough and smooth grounds, and fasting before they return to camp loaded." The Indian "affects not to feel the weight of dragging a deer 100 to 150 pounds weight through a considerable tract of forest."[42] Grinnell[43] says that the Cheyenne division of labor was fair. The men had to be unencumbered so as to be ready to fight. Hunting, regarded by us as mere sport, was to them strenuous toil. Before they got horses and fought so much, both sexes used to carry heavy loads. Lugard[44] protests against the popular impression of the native man's universal laziness; he "cannot think why Europeans persist in assuming that a native lives in degrading idleness unless working for a European. . . . It has long been the fashion to speak of the African as naturally lazy, leaving work to his women, and contented to lie in the sun and eat and drink. . . . The fertility of the soil, his few wants, the physical capacity of his women for manual work, are all prompting causes for idleness, yet except when relegated to reserves, or when his status as a slave deprives him of all incentive, he is usually industrious. . . . The free pagan tribes in West Africa often cultivate more than it seems possible to consume. There is no question of merely 'scratching the surface,' and the deep trenches in the Yoruba yam-fields show how thoroughly his work is done."

Thus the labor required of the savage man within the limits of his wants was often very intense in degree; on the hunting expedi-

40 Olsen, *Primitivt Folk*, 77.
41 Geddes and Thomson, *Evolution of Sex*, 269; Dellenbaugh, *No. Amer.*, 333; §53, above.
42 Carr, in *Smithson. Rep.*, 1891, 510, note.
43 *Cheyenne*, I, 127, 128, 257.   44 *Brit. Trop. Afr.*, 400-401.

tion some of its forms involved the highest strain of muscle and nerve for a period; and the same may be said of war. It was, for men of the type under consideration, physiologically necessary that these labors should alternate with periods of complete relaxation. "The tasks demanding powerful muscular development, and the resulting capacity for intermittent spurts of energy, involving corresponding periods of rest, fall to the man; the care of children and the domestic industries, calling for energy more continuous, but at a lower tension, fall to woman."[45] Woman received, in the sex-division of labor, the functions that were of a routine nature; the drudgery, the work that had no stimulus of adventure, involved no nervous strain, and was endless and disagreeable to man. If our preceding analysis of sex-differences is even an approximation to the truth, this distribution of function lay along lines of natural propensity.

It is possible to get a thoroughgoing insight into sex-specialization only by according proper weight to these considerations. Yet it would be foolish to suppose that man, in those stages where chivalry was not, failed to use his sex-superiorities for what they were worth. He was superior in brute force; and that was not all. As our cases presently to come will show, man specialized in hunting and war. This meant that he developed the apparatus corresponding and became the wielder of weapons of offense and defense. Boys were early trained in the use of these, while girls, besides being unfitted physically for the use of a number of the weapons, especially those that were thrown, received little or no practice in such exercises; they were trained to the domestic tasks. Even if man had been physically the weaker, his weapons would have secured him dominance over woman, as they did over the beasts that were so much more powerful than he. And even this is not all. There is no other such school for discipline and organization as that afforded by hunting and war. Men, specializing in these lines, learned to subordinate themselves to a leader and to combine their strength. "In co-operation," we are told,[46] "women have always been weak"; and another authority,[47] while he does not feel sure that "habits of war produced a sense of the advantages of

<hr>

[45] Ellis, *Man and Woman*, 1.   [46] Mason, *Woman's Share*, 160.
[47] Ellis, *Man and Woman*, 11.

specialized and subordinated work," yet concludes: "In any case the fact itself is undoubted, and it has had immense results on civilization." Hence, even if the women had been the physical equals of men, and had possessed fighting-apparatus, but without military discipline, they would still have been subject to coercion by men. In view of these facts, and of the combination of contempt and fear which often represented man's attitude toward woman,[48] it is to be expected that he would have coerced and oppressed her; and the facts prove that he did. It is a mistake to believe that she was at any time utterly defenseless;[49] the savage man is frequently sadly henpecked; but in general, whether or not she would have chosen the sort of tasks with which she is found to be busied, she had to perform them anyhow or else suffer for her omissions or reluctance. In fact, she fell in contentedly with the current mores, than which she knew nothing different, and did not resent the loss of "rights" of which she had not dreamed.

§65. Man's Encroachment. Dominant as he was, man did not hesitate to encroach upon occupations which woman had originally developed, or had come to practice, if his interest led him that way. There is here some difference of opinion about woman's share in the origination and early practice of the arts. It is asserted by some that she originated them all, or, at any rate, a large proportion of them.[50] This seems to us a ridiculous generalization. For, to take only one opening for criticism, it is clear enough that many of the arts of peace are contributions from the arts of war.[51] Yet if anything is demonstrated it is that war and the apparatus of war were man's all-but-exclusive monopoly. The tools that were once weapons, or are modified from weapons, plainly predominate upon the early stages.[52] War is a sort of forcing process for the development of expedients of all sorts which are then carried over into the uses of peace. This consideration alone is enough to dispose of sweeping assertions accrediting to woman the origination of the arts; and our cases will reveal a distribution of industries between the sexes hard to account for on any such theory. Some of the arts were doubtless originated by women, some by men, and

48 §§388, 389, below.   49 Ch. L, below.
50 Mason, *Woman's Share*.   51 §143, below.
52 Tylor, *Anth.*, 184 ff.

some of them by both sexes working together. The question of origins, here and elsewhere, is to us largely a matter of indifference,[53] except as some curious theory about them is seized upon for a selected purpose, such as, in the present case, the exaltation of the services of one sex over those of the other, with consequent indictment of man as a brutal represser and despoiler. All such moral judgments are out of place in science. Man acted in pursuit of his interests as he saw them, and without restraints now in vogue in the mores. If he became interested in some characteristic pursuit of woman, whoever originated it, he did not hesitate to encroach on her sphere. She could not reciprocate, for he had the power and she had not. Unfair, perhaps, in our eyes, but not in hers, or his.

Whether or not the weaker sex was "fairly" treated, the encroachments of man had their cultural results. Irrespective of his motives in taking over from woman that which interested him, leaving to her the occupations and drudgery that remained to him unattractive, it is undeniable that he introduced into what he laid hold of an element that made for success. Having taken up the occupations of woman, he "specialized them and developed them in an extraordinary degree."[54] Cooking and dressmaking are to us of the present age traditional woman's work; yet men have been the most eminent chefs, and even the most outstanding designers and "creators" of fashions—including women's. Man, when he had taken over a typical woman's art, introduced into its prosecution a superior strength, an added element of inventiveness, and, above all, the power of organization that he had learned in hunting and war. Take the case of tillage, which is as probably an art originated by woman as any other. It is supposed that the woman, being tied to the fire and the child, had to make use of the vegetable food, such as roots and seeds, available within a limited range; that she came to know the identity and quality of such supplies; and, at length, advanced to the art of planting.[55] In any case, the rude beginnings of tillage, among tribes not yet practising anything deserving the name of agriculture, are found in the hands of the women. Then, in the course of societal life, either

---

[53] §451, below.   [54] Ellis, *Man and Woman*, 11.
[55] Lippert, *Kgchte.*, I, 251, 447, 452, 617.

because hunting and herding fall off, or because tillage becomes important enough to emerge from its lowly stage as woman's work, man turns his attention to the despised occupation. Woman has, let us say, brought it within his range of vision and interest, and he begins to apply to its prosecution whatever special strength and means he possesses. Among the latter is the superior power of the domesticated animal or the enslaved man, won as a product of hunting or war. There is no real agriculture until some such power is applied, for only then, as a rule, is the soil more than scratched. With the plow appears real agriculture; and the process of applying power and contrivances goes on up to the present. Few, if any, of these applications and inventions are connected with the name of a woman, a condition duplicated all along through the mechanic arts, where the Howes, Arkwrights, or Edisons are all men. To tillage man applied also the expedient of organization, and the result was to raise this form of self-maintenance to a position of commanding importance.[56]

The following summary, while it has its inaccuracies, states the case with substantial correctness. "Primitive women have in their hands all the industries, and, in consequence, the rudiments of most of the arts. But when we get beyond the rudiments the position begins to change, and when we reach fully differentiated arts, even among savages, we find that they are almost exclusively in the hands of men. Miklucho-Maclay, speaking of Papuan art in Northeast Guinea, remarks: 'I have been struck by the absolute absence of ornament on the pottery, the clay easily lending itself to all sorts of ornamentation; this lack of ornament is due to the fact that the manufacture of pottery is exclusively confided to women, who are not usually very artistic by nature. I have found confirmation of this ancient and just observation even among Papuan women. I am able to state that I have never seen the slightest ornament invented or executed by a woman.' If we turn to the pure artistic impulse, as manifested in the higher stages of culture, we find that the supremacy of men in painting is unquestionable. In the evolution of music women have played a very small part. . . . It is remarkable that although women are so strongly drawn to religion, they have done almost nothing to give classic expression to that mysticism which is the kernel of religion everywhere. . . . In poetry women have done much more than in either mysticism or metaphysics. . . . In fiction women are acknowledged to rank incomparably higher than in any other form of literary art. . . . There is at least one art in which women may be said not merely to nearly rival but actually to excel men: this is the art of acting. . . . Even in the matter of cooking we may see how emphatic is the tendency for an art to fall into the hands of men. All over the world cooking, as an industry, is women's business, yet wherever cooking

[56] §§64, above and 67, below; Keller, *Soc. Evol.*, 141 ff.

rises from an industry to become something of an art it is nearly always in the hands of a man."[57]

One authoress[58] contends that women have had no chance, that they have always risen to the opportunity when they got it. She thinks they have an "inferiority complex" due to suggestion. Men geniuses have had to have a favorable environment—approval of what they did, as in art—in order to rise; though women have the same need, they have never had the same opportunity. There is no question here of women being mentally inferior; Spencer[59] has met that argument. They are different. The traditional attitude is expressed by Antigone:[60] "We needs must bear in mind that we are women, not fitted to contend with men; and so that we are ruled by the stronger."

§66. Reactions of Sex-Specialization.

Lippert,[61] starting with the idea that man and woman tended naturally to have to do with the supply, respectively, of animal and vegetable food, assigns sex-qualities of disposition, at least in some degree, to preoccupation with these special forms of food-production.

"On the side of meat food there is an excess of effort and of satisfaction, in constant alternation with torpor and need. All attention is concentrated upon food-winning, which is, with all its dangers, the honorable field of manly activity, while to the preservation of what has been got, to the foresight that leads to thrift, there is assigned an opposite valuation. There is early developed on the side of vegetable food, on the other hand, a reverse relationship: here is required, in general, less of courage, daring, and virile tension of strength than of reliance, endurance, and foresight in collecting and storing . . . virtues that we see appearing at a very early period as specifically feminine." It may be interpolated that, among certain Indians, the women stored up the grain in the ground away from the men, who would eat even the seed.[62] "As is so often the case, causes and results here form a closed circle. The sex-characters, thus differently developed, are not the original ones, for it is only out of an exclusive preoccupation with a special group of food-materials that they have been derived; yet it is the original and natural necessity that has led the sexes out upon such one-sided careers—careers in whose course, then, their whole characters cannot but derive distinctive qualities."

Such progressive differentiation, growing gradually within the mores, could not but confirm the specialization of function which lay deep in nature.

Sex-specialization in labor, with all its features that are repellent to cultured taste, plainly constituted an expedient adjustment in the organization for society's self-maintenance. It has always

[57] Ellis, *Man and Woman*, 316.

[58] Parsons, in *Yale Review*, XIV, 739 ff.

[59] *Social Statics*, 73 ff.   [60] Sophocles, *Antigone*, 61 ff.

[61] *Kgchte.*, I, 245.   [62] Wood, in *New Eng. Prospect*, 106.

revealed a strong survival-value. That such specialization and coöperation formed one of the reasons for existence of marriage and the family must have struck the reader already, and will be presented to him again.[63] In some cases, as in the so-called matriarchal system,[64] woman became able to impose the terms of coöperation on man; as a rule, however, her relative weakness and her burdens and disabilities incident to her sex worked out into her subordination and even virtual enslavement. She continued to coöperate because she had to, or because she had come to know nothing different. Where hunting was good, or herding successful, so that man attained to a high-class food-supply which was also a steady one, he felt less vital need of woman's contribution. He had learned in the meantime, however, the advantages to be gained from the coöperation of a sex so differently endowed from his own, and was able to enforce a joint action originally compulsory in natural conditions. Women might then become less coöperators than slaves. "A man should drink, fight, and hunt, and the portion for women and slaves is work."[65]

Sex-specialization, followed by coöperation, constitutes the first form of organization in self-maintenance; but it is important to note that it works out naturally into another, namely, slavery. Men assumed almost exclusively the external group-relations, which were chiefly militant, while to the women fell a large share of the industrial activities and, in case of war, the maintenance of the fighters. This militant specialization on the part of the men then resulted, with the conquest and subordination of another group, in a further differentiation and organization within the society—an organization based upon further coercion, but running no longer along the primordial lines of sex, and a differentiation resting no longer upon biological characters, but upon social distinctions.[66] Thus did specialization between man and woman help to render possible that between man and master.[67]

[63] §§335, 337, below.
[64] §§416 ff., below. Perhaps the mother-family was an eventually unsuccessful variation whereby coöperation was confined largely within the bounds of one sex.
[65] An adage of the Siyins, in Carey and Tuck, *Chin Hills*, I, 186.
[66] Keller, *Soc. Evol.*, 73 ff.   [67] §71, below.

§67*. Specialization in the Food-Quest. When the attempt is
made to classify even the more primitive sex-occupations, the student realizes anew, as he scans his cases, the extreme complication
of whatever has to do with societal life. Some occupations, to be
sure, are tabooed to women, and there are others which are virtually forbidden to man because they are "woman's work" and he
is ashamed to pursue them. Indeed, one does not need to go much
out of his way to collect examples of this detail of the mores, for
it is still to be observed in our own society and age. It is to be
noted, however, as indicating the preferred position of man, that
there are few, if any, cases where man's work is considered by
woman to be beneath her; she may be unable to do it, or not permitted, but she would feel no shame in being seen at it. When men
are scarce, as in a case mentioned by Nansen,[68] where a village had
only five men in a population of twenty-one, women sometimes
adopt the life of men completely. A man, on the other hand, has
to be lost to shame before he will submit to the degradation of
becoming a woman; in one of the Hill Tribes of India, if a man is
unable or too lazy to do his work, he puts on woman's dress and
consorts with the women.[69] The taboo is more peremptory for
woman than for man; she is kept in her place much more strictly
than he in his. The relative positions of the sexes approach those
of master and servant; the latter may not engage in activities
that characterize the master, while the master may do anything
which his dignity will allow.

If we exclude, for the time being, the arts of manufacture, and
confine ourselves to the direct winning of the food-supply and to
offense and defense, we find almost no cases where hunting and
fighting are not the exclusive affairs of the men; and it further
appears that when an advance has been made from the hunting
to the domestication of animals and the cattle-raising stage is in
evidence, it is the men who attend to the herds. On the other hand,
where agriculture is not developed, the search for vegetable food
is prevailingly the duty of the women; where it is pursued otherwise than as the major occupation of the society, men seldom have
much to do with it; and where it is all-important, among less

68 *Esk. Life*, 124.
69 Lewin, *S. E. India*, 255; §310, below.

advanced peoples, women seldom escape from a considerable share
in its labors. Woman thus seems to be peculiarly identified with
tillage. Wherever the man hunts and fishes for a living, the division of labor impels the woman to open up other and supplementary means of support; she, and he too, on occasion, may be forced
to live on the plant-products which she can either collect or cultivate. In her sphere she is forced to win her own knowledge.[70] Hence
she is, though in a far less exclusive sense, for man presently penetrates her preserve while she does not enter his, identified with the
tilling of the soil as man is with the chase and with war. Man takes
hold of and directs tillage only after a time during which woman
has been gradually raising it to a position of significance.

When the men are on the low hunting stage, the women are still
practically collectors.

In Australia, "it is the man's business to obtain animal food, but the women
have to dig for eatable roots in the scrub and to search for mushrooms and
palm nuts, fruit, grass seeds, honey, sweet resin, and the manna of the gum
trees."[71] "A man," said a native, "hunts, spears fish, fights, and sits about;"[72]
what the women do can be inferred without difficulty. The fixedness of this
sex-specialization is marked: "when a tribe of blacks on the coast range of
Queensland move camp, the men, women and children spread out in a long
line or semi-circle, driving all before them. No woman, unless perhaps an old
gin, dares to throw her waddy [club] at a startled wallaby or kangaroo-rat,
but she will attract the attention of the nearest man or boy to its presence;
and if a man pass an edible root, he will tell the woman next him to dig it."[73]
These cases come, of course, from records of human life on one of the lowest
stages known to us; but they are matched in other parts of the world. Among
the Coroados of Brazil, "while the man is solely occupied with the chase, war,
and making his arms, all domestic cares fall on the women. They plant and
collect the harvest, if this species of cultivation has been introduced among
them; look in the woods for Spanish potatoes and fruit."[74]

On a higher stage of the hunting economy, women fall pretty
much out of account as food-producers. The case of the Plains
Indians is representative.

Herding, like its parent-activity, hunting, is a typical man's
occupation; and if it is combined with tillage, it is almost sure to
be the man who represents the former and the woman the latter.
Specialized as she was in an occupation regarded as inferior, and

70 Von den Steinen, *Zent. Bras.*, 214.
71 Semon, *Aust. Bush*, 207.   72 Howitt, *S. E. Aust.*, 738.
73 Roth, in JAI, XVI, 120.
74 Spix and Martius, *Travels*, II, 246.

one certainly inconsonant with a nomadic life, woman was likely
to become relatively less useful as a partner and coöperator.[75] Her
position under the pastoral régime was analogous to her status
where hunting was so productive, on the American prairies, for
example, as to render man almost independent of her contribution
to joint maintenance.

Of the Tungus it is said: "Along with this life of wandering there goes a
strict division of labor in the family. The men employ themselves only in
hunting, fishing, and the care of the herds, while the women have to attend
to the whole house-keeping without man lifting his finger in aid. They have
to pitch the *yurts*, secure fuel, cook, and keep utensils and clothes in order.
Every free moment, besides, is utilized for the domestic economy; for instance,
in tanning skins, sewing clothes, or preparing ornaments for the husbands, for
themselves, or for the children. Before the man goes out to hunt in the morning, he advises his wife whither she shall move and where he will meet her in
the evening."[76] The function of the woman in constituting "headquarters"[77] is
still in evidence, although the Tungus are largely herders. The South African
natives, as typical herdsmen, show a characteristic sex-specialization. Of the
Hottentots we read: "The tending of the cattle, butchering, and the preparation of hides were essentially man's work; while the erection of houses, after
the supports had been raised with man's aid, the preparation of food, and all
the domestic cares were woman's. Thus woman had the lion's share of the
work." Similarly, to take another example from the same region, in the case
of the Kaffirs: "Aside from activities connected with hunting, it is chiefly
cattle-tending that appeals to the male Kaffir as his most appropriate labor;
and he attends to it, even down to the milking, alone, without calling on the
women. . . . The hide, when removed, awaits further working-over at the
hand of man, so that no one of all the activities connected with cattle falls
to the woman. . . . The erection of the cattle-kraal is regarded as much too
important a thing to be entrusted to the women."[78] Here is to be observed the
development in the mores of a sex-taboo respecting cattle. In Uganda, likewise, no woman may touch a cow's udder; the men do all the milking.[79] Among
the Bechuana this taboo had curious consequences in determining a subsequent
specialization: the suppression of their supply of arms and ammunition compelled them to take to agriculture; but among such of them as had the plow,
since women were never allowed to touch the cattle, the men were obliged to
do the work.[80]

If the herders are less nomadic, women take up the cultivation of the soil.
Thus among the Alur and other East Africans the man gets food and watches
the cattle while the woman keeps house and cultivates the fields.[81]

[75] §386, below.   [76] Hiekisch, *Tungusen*, 79.
[77] §63, above.
[78] Fritsch, *Eingeb. S.-Afr.*, 325, 85, 86, 87.
[79] Ratzel, *Vkde.*, I, 458.
[80] Holub, in JAI, X, 11; *Sieben Jahre*, I, 422-423; *Capstadt*, II, 214.
[81] Stuhlmann, *Mit Emin*, 502.

Many instances parallel to these are to be found in widely separated parts of the earth. Woman seems to have an affinity, and man an antipathy, to the soil. Religion may support the connection of the woman with the domesticated plants. They are female like her; and "like is best known by like."[82] While, however, among tribes whose agriculture is rudimentary this type of division of labor by sex has been characteristic, it must be realized that woman's contribution was oftentimes, and might become at any time, an indispensable one.

Among certain tribes of Brazil, although the men were capable hunters, the supply of vegetable food won by the women was of the greatest importance on account of its reliability. Hunting was more subject to chance. The women sought roots with a sharp stick, climbed the palm trees for the fruit, and collected nuts.[83] With the Shans of Farther India, "the wife does all the homework and a large share of the outdoor work as well. So important a member of the household is she considered, that, in most of the States, a widower is exempt from all taxation."[84] "The appellation *pasigadong*—the means of getting *gadong,* or food—is jocosely applied by the Batak to his wife; for the field labor, above all things, is done, among the gallant Bataks, by the women."[85] Such a status for woman is fraught, however, with danger of decline, as man's power increases, into one of enslavement. The little agriculture that has been carried on by the Bechuanas has been at the hand of woman, the men being accustomed to buy two or three women to plant their grain while they were employed in killing game, selling the ivory or ostrich feathers thus obtained, and lying otherwise idle.[86] Sometimes, however, the fact that woman, even though all but enslaved, is the bread-winner redounds to her advantage. "If a man hits his wife on the head and stuns her, and renders her incapable of work for a few days, then it follows that until she can get out to her gardens again, the noble hitter has to go short of food. The man finds that he cannot dispense these lordly taps on his wife's head without hitting himself at the same time in a very tender spot; so he regulates his conduct accordingly."[87]

As agriculture gains in importance, man is found taking first a small, then a gradually increasing share in the once unattractive industry. His beginnings along this line had to do with the heavier or grander tasks, and only in the case of need. In a number of cases, the men clear the ground, leaving to the woman the less interesting, more monotonous duties, like weeding; she has full control of the lowly yams, while he attends to the bananas.[88] Then,

[82] Karsten, "Jibaro," in BAE, Bull. LXXIX, 60; §214, below.
[83] Von den Steinen, *Zent. Bras.,* 490.   [84] Woodthorpe, in JAI, XXVI, 26.
[85] Wilken, *Vkde.,* 5.   [86] Holub, in JAI, X, 11.
[87] Abel, *New Guinea,* 57-58.   [88] Bromilow, in AAAS, 1909, 474.

as the cultivation of the soil comes to be a dominant interest, the sexes share for a time more nearly equally in it, until eventually man takes it over as his.

"Looking after cattle throughout the world is usually the work of men, while, in agriculture, the usual rule is that the bulk of the work is done by women, the men only intervening to carry out the more difficult or arduous tasks, such as cutting down trees and clearing the ground, which bulk largely in the agriculture of those peoples who only use a plot of ground for a limited time and then allow it to relapse into wildness."[89] Sometimes the men go at their part of the field-work in such an intensive manner as to make one doubtful whether primitive agriculture was always a mere scratching of the earth. "The ground must first be cleared of scrub and grass, then ploughed with pointed sticks, the ends of which have been hardened in the fire. Several men stand in a row and drive their sticks into the ground, then with a united heave turn over one long sod of earth, leaving a continuous furrow. Occasionally women help in this, but the work is rather heavy, and generally the heavier work is left for the men to do."[90] Again, however, "men rarely," if ever, cultivate, one woman can raise sufficient food to keep two or three men."[91] Certain Bushmen use the digging-stick "to unearth roots and tubers. This is usually the work of the women and girls. I have never heard of the men digging, or, indeed, doing anything except attend to their weapons and the chase." As these people are hardly out of the collection stage, it would appear that the first rudiments of soil-manipulation belonged to females; there is a legend of this people which seems to support such a view: "In the beginning of things, a long, long time ago, when the men and women of the early race lived upon the earth, so my father told me, the men lived by hunting and the women by gathering grass seeds."[92]

Not always, however, do the men seem physically more able to perform the harder labors; how much of their inability is referable to the mores and how much to weakness of physique is difficult to say. "Very little use has been made of the Akamba for labour, partly owing to their inability to stick to any work, but more so owing to their inborn indolence. Work is to the Mkamba nothing short of a misfortune; when he does take to it a very little discomfort, such as he would otherwise not notice, will completely incapacitate him, while he has then the appearance of undergoing the deepest misery. . . . Even when food is short there are hundreds of young men capable of becoming useful workers who would sooner starve than take to employment. . . . But if the men are unfit for hard work, the women are exceedingly tough and hardy, and whereas a man can rarely carry more than a 45-lb. load, most women will easily shoulder 60 lbs. I have seen women carrying as much as 140 lbs. At an early age also the men become useless for work, while the women will continue to labour up to a great age."[93]

[89] Rivers, *Soc. Org.*, 147-148.
[90] Jenness and Ballentyne, *D'Entrecasteaux*, 123.
[91] Roscoe, in JAI, XXXII, 38.
[92] Dornan, in JAI, XLVII, 49, 78.
[93] Dundas, C., in JAI, XLIII, 490-491.

§68*. Specialization in Handicrafts. The instances presented, parallels and approximations to which abound, serve to indicate the persistence, chiefly in the food-getting activities, of the division of labor by sex, and of notions and provisions associated with it. Coming now to the handicrafts—to occupations that are not directly productive of a food-supply—one encounters a series of cases considerably more tangled and complex than those just reviewed. There lie before us, as we write, about two hundred excerpts from seventy or more books or articles dealing with the ethnography of toward a hundred particular tribes. There are also several generalizations covering several or many tribes taken together, as "the American Indians," or "the East Africans." All the tribes are on the primitive stage, that is, their ways are representative of those existing among "nature peoples" throughout the world. Of the sex-occupations reported, about twenty have been pretty consistently mentioned, and of these an account has been taken. From our lists we derive five categories of sex-occupations:

(1) almost or quite exclusively of males: weapon-making, canoe-building;

(2) almost or quite exclusively of females: grain-grinding, carrying, "gathering," drink-making;

(3) prevalently of males (in the hands of men more than twice as often as in those of women, and in order of prevalence): sewing, weaving;

(4) prevalently of females (in the same general proportions as the preceding and in order of prevalence): water-carrying, pottery-making, house-work, trading, hide-preparation, spinning, care of children, cooking, fire-tending, wood-getting;

(5) mutually pursued (running from male prevalence to female): house-building, clothes-making, basketry.

This list represents no more than a rough guide to generalization respecting sex-division of labor in the handicrafts; it is realized that a larger collection of cases would somewhat alter these categories; but since we have generalized cautiously and propose to continue to do so, the above classification will serve as a convenient charting of the course. Further instances, scattered under different topics throughout this book, will be found to corroborate the essentials of this classification.

Though most of the evidence for the foregoing statements has been relegated to the *Case-Book*, there are several cases to be cited here. In East Africa, "the daily tasks of the native village in its original form were apportioned as follows: The men took upon themselves: (1) the general conduct of family affairs, both internal and in relation to the whole community; (2) the herding of stock; (3) the rougher work, such as felling of trees, and the breaking up of the soil preparatory to cultivation; (4) the manufacture of household implements and utensils, and also the making of clothes and ornaments, including most of those worn by women, and of arms (excepting those made by smiths); (5) hunting and honey collecting and, above all, warfare. To the women fell: (1) the tilling of the soil after it was broken up, sowing, weeding, and reaping; (2) the fetching and carrying of firewood and water; (3) the preparation of food and the milking of cattle. . . . Other labours are shared by both sexes; thus, in the building of a hut the frame is made by men whilst the thatching is done by women; the guarding of crops shortly before harvesting is done by old and young of both sexes. Now if we compare these various duties we shall see that there was very great difference in the labours. The work of the men might be described as skilled labour, that of the women being unskilled. When ordered government was established, the two most important duties of the men were eliminated, namely, warfare and the conduct of government, but the women's duties were in no way affected." The author quoted[94] says elsewhere that "to the native it is as inconceivable that a man should, for instance, fetch and carry water as that a woman should bear arms; similarly a woman would no more contemplate fashioning a bee-hive than would a man cook the family food. I think that if we could enter into the native's thoughts we should picture to ourselves that it is for the man to perform the hardest and most skilful work, to provide for the family wealth and welfare, and at the same time to give protection to the family, while the woman's sphere is the provision of all home comforts."

It is common enough for the men to make man's utensils and weapons and the ceremonial implements, while woman fabricates household articles and clothing;[95] still, there are many cases where specialization runs quite contrary to expectation. In Samoa the cooking devolved on the men and "all, even chiefs of the highest rank, considered it no disgrace to assist in the cooking-house occasionally."[96] In British Central Africa, sewing was man's work, upon which no woman ever thought of encroaching; hence the resentment against the missionaries who felt it their duty to set matters right by instructing the women in an art which "ought" to be feminine.[97]

There should be at least one illustration of the principle that where a certain specialty is important because of its religious connections, it falls to the man. It is part of his function as a public person, whereas the woman has little part in the life of society at large. "Certain specializations of industry

[94] Dundas, C., in JAI, XLV, 301-302.
[95] Grinnell, *Cheyenne*, I, 172; section on woman's work, 209 ff.
[96] Turner, *Samoa*, 112. [97] Werner, *Brit. Cent. Afr.*, 271.

according to sex are widely found throughout the world. Thus, canoe building is almost always, if not invariably, confined to men, while the art of making pottery by hand is almost universally practised by women, men only following this occupation when the potter's wheel is used." This, of course, makes it more interesting. "A rule of wide application is that occupations involving religious ritual, i.e. involving knowledge of manual or verbal rites implying appeal to higher powers, are practised by men, while occupations devoid of this sacred aspect are open to women. . . . The process of making canoes and gongs is far more than a merely practical art, and is accompanied throughout by ritual of a religious kind, apparently designed to appease spirits and ancestral ghosts, including the spirit of the tree, or some ancestral ghost believed to be resident in the tree, from which the canoe is made. It therefore constitutes an instance of the differentiation of occupation according to sex."[98]

§69. General Conclusion as to the Arts. The most general conclusion to be drawn from our collections of evidence as to sex-specialization is that, within any limited group, the occupations of men and women are seldom the same, or interchangeable. The sexes have few duties in common; "even as beasts of burden they seldom work in pairs." Beyond this generality, if an attempt is made to be more specific as to the handicrafts, it could not be far from the truth to conclude that man, pursuing in his hunting and warfare a closely specialized activity, must have himself developed the arts of making the weapons and other devices for which he alone had need. This is what the above classification yields. Such a conclusion, we are reminded, has an immediate bearing upon the generalization concerning the origination and early practice of the arts by women.[99] It might be thought that the "arts of peace" were more likely to be developed by woman than by man, preoccupied as he was in warfare and the chase; but it is indiscreet to wish to universalize any such generalization, however logical it appears upon its face. It must be realized, once again, that the germs of very many, at least, of the handicrafts lay precisely within the primordial arts of strife as practised against beast and fellow-man; and that the ages have witnessed constant contributions from the arts of violence to those of peace—all the way from the primitive hatchet to poison gas. It matters very little, however, that women were the originators of this and that detail of the industrial organization if real effectiveness came only with the encroachment of man. It would correspond with the facts to conclude that proficiency in the application and organization of force enabled man to coerce woman to whatever activities repelled him most; while there was no reason at all why he himself should keep out of that occupation which revolted him least or which he might even fancy.

This general conclusion from the cases is in harmony with that derived from the review of physical and other sex-differences. The items under 2 and 4 in the preceding paragraph[100] (occupations exclusively and prevalently of women), are mainly drudgery; and where men engage in the more toilsome labors of 4 and 5 (the latter covering occupations mutually pursued), it is sometimes stated, or at any rate implied, that men's share is what women cannot measure up to physically, or what is more interesting. Men, for instance, raise the frames of houses or break up the soil; they get wood or tend fire, but only "at need";[101] they attend to the children, in order that the women may get back to their labors in the field;[102] they decorate, but do not make, the pottery,[103] just as they cultivate the luxury-product. The care of shrines is woman's; the knowledge of its contents, ceremonies and rituals is man's.[104] Nothing stands out more clearly than that the man did what he wanted to much more consistently than did the woman; so that sex-specialization was not due to sex-propensities alone, except as man's superiorities evoked a tendency to dominate and domineer. Even so, however, the women came to accept their tasks, to us uninteresting and monotonous, as the appropriate ones and to see nothing unfair in them, just as they regarded their repasts upon the leavings of the men's meals as in the natural order of things.

It is a significant aspect of the relations of the sexes, and worth reiteration, that shame connected with doing the work of the other sex is exhibited almost exclusively by man; it is reported, for instance, that though division of labor is a natural thing among African negroes, the sexes helping each other in case of need, yet in the presence of a stranger a man is ashamed to do a woman's

[100] §68, above.
[101] Dorsey, in BAE, III, 266; Ratzel, *Vkde.*, I, 155.
[102] Von den Steinen, *Zent. Bras.*, 335; Ella, in AAAS, 1892, 622.
[103] Ellis, *Man and Woman*, 6, 316.
[104] Fletcher, in AA, IV, 734.

work. Men will not carry children, except on a journey.[105] Among
the natives of the New Hebrides it is thought undignified for a
male to carry a burden like a woman; but women may carry a pig
between them on a pole, like the men.[106]

In short, all of these items and notions get into the mores, show
or do not show survival-value under selection, and are transmitted
or not transmitted from generation to generation as the traditional code. Had it not been for the fact of sex and the complementary abilities and disabilities connected with it, no such mores
and codes could have appeared. The domination of man was inevitable; under it the coöperation of the sexes developed as we find it,
and the human race moved on toward what it has become. If there
is any fault to be found with the process, in the matter of its
unfairness or its oppressiveness, the complaint must be carried
back and lodged against whatever power produced bi-sexuality in
Homo; for, given that condition, the consequences are inevitable.
It is a great error to charge woman's present position to man's
base behavior in the past. That behavior, however detestable from
the standpoint of our later code, could not have been otherwise.
It was not deliberately planned out, but lived into automatically.
And it is a still greater error to wish to ignore the basic and
derived sex-differences, in the mutual adjustment to which were
laid down the fundamentals of a sex-code that has been tested by
the ages.

105 Ratzel, *Vkde.,* I, 155.   106 Gray, in JAI, XXVIII, 129.

CHAPTER VI

LABOR: FURTHER SPECIALIZATION: COÖPERATION

§70. Specialization other than by Sex. Bi-sexuality is one of the few elemental life-conditions; and no science of society can get far on its way without taking account of it. The search is vain for another distinction between human beings which is so sharp, persistent, and primordial as sex. But sex-differences are not the only dissimilarities between members of society. Some are old, others young; some are sound of body, others sickly or crippled by accident; some are endowed over others in mental powers, coördination of hand and eye, cleverness and perseverance in this or that direction. Aiston[1] says that "in the old days, before the advent of the whites in this country, practically all the stone tools and weapons were made by the old men. The young men and the women looked after the finding of food for the camp. The old men sat down at some convenient water-hole where there was a supply of stone for tools and wood for weapons, and put in their time in keeping the young men supplied." All is variation and inequality; and adjustability is thus rendered possible. Livingstone[2] reports the tradition of a man, evidently of superior mind, who left his Barotse countrymen, came down the river, took advantage of the falls, and led out a portion of the water there for irrigation. He was a sort of culture-hero. Even though ordinarily the difference between man and man is much slighter than that existing between this negro and his fellows, nevertheless the smaller diversities may afford a basis for specialization and coöperation. Inequality is the very precondition of organization and progressive adjustment. This has been encountered in typical or even extreme form in sex-specialization, where marriage normally supplies the arena of coöperation. If specialization and coöperation otherwise than by sex, however small their degree, are competent to secure positive additions to power and also economies of effort, then, as forms of the mores, these modes were bound to become valuable for survival

<hr>

[1] Horne and Aiston, *Cent. Aust.*, 105.   [2] *Mission. Travels*, I, 233.

to groups practising them. Thus they have come, in more and more perfected form, to characterize societies that have been successful in self-maintenance. No society is so low that it displays no such forms of organization; and as the several ascending stages of civilization are attained, there is developed a correlative complexity and interplay of these same forms.

§71. Coercion to Activity. It must not be thought, however, that human beings adopted this organization rationally or entered upon it with satisfaction. They came beneath it by necessity, being under compulsion to fit into the industrial organization, even at the price of individual liberty. Society, we recall, never existed as a great and free club save in the minds of the ill-informed, the misinformed, the visionary, or those whose views have been the reflections of preconceived ideas. In many primitive societies the waking hours of all the members are devoted to unremitting toil; there are really no non-laborers. In general, the amount of labor performed varies about some group-average set in the mores— that this average seems to us low has nothing to do with the forming of a judgment as to how it is lived up to. And if, in certain cases, it appears that non-laborers exist, it is yet true, first, that they are always conceived to be contributing to the general welfare something particularly necessary and arduously wrought out, as an offset to their exemption from ordinary tasks (as, for instance, in the case of the medicine-men);[3] and, second, that the very fact of their exemption reveals a prior non-exemption—prior, that is, to the development of the mores which secure their eventual immunities. It is likewise a common misconception to ascribe to such privileged offices as that of king or priest a status of ease and freedom from effort and care. These officials were subjected to strains of a different and more searching order than the constant and monotonous low-pressure of the common herd.

In one Brazilian tribe, unmarried or widowed men and women are supported by the community and not held to labor. The alleged motive here is family integrity, marriage and the family being held very pure.[4] This is a rare case; but everyone is familiar with the exemption of the sacerdotal classes from labor, and with that of parasitic classes in a more modern time. It is safe to

[3] §320, below.
[4] Ehrenreich, in *Königl. Mus. Vkde.*, II, 28.

say that there never were non-laborers or drones, as such, in the difficult primitive times; everyone was supposed to render some equivalent for his preservation. Even the professional beggar in Spain acted as a fulcrum for the lever of charity which was to elevate his benefactors' souls to heaven.[5]

It is only in later and more humanitarian times, when capital has been laid up and the struggle for existence is not universal, near, and menacing, that a member of society is excused for not "pulling his own weight," and invited to eat though he has not worked. Primitive theory, however mistaken its premises, was too chronically in the presence of stubborn fact to allow of such vagary; there was no "bounty of nature" to draw upon, and the homely proverb about "rooting or dying" would have met instant applause.

Despite the pressure brought upon members of a group to find their places and get to work, no grand-scale specialization beyond that of sex emerges until, somewhat late in the evolutionary course, a special sort of coercion comes into action. Sex-specialization goes back to biological differences; the type about to be considered finds the unlikeness upon which it must be based in differences that are social. These social differences come to exist between conqueror and conquered, when the latter is allowed to live, that is, between master and slave. It is quite reasonable to conclude that sex-specialization provided the ground for specialization based upon conquest; for it allowed the man to concentrate on the development of a military organization. Then came the conquest and enslavement of other men. It is our intention to treat of slavery, in other connections, later on;[6] so that it is to be mentioned here rather than developed. In the present connection it is clear that its introduction led speedily to a specialization in labor, for the victors were enabled to choose between the more desirable and the less desirable functions, and the vanquished, if allowed to live, existed under tolerance and beneath the menace of an impending or postponed visitation of force. They were obliged to do the hardest and most unpleasant things, thus not alone relieving the master but also flattering his vanity. As he watched them slaving, his heart might swell as erstwhile on the battle-field: "Unfortu-

[5] Oliveira Martins, *Civ. Iber.*, 271-273; 283-286.
[6] Ch. X, below.

nate are the parents whose sons oppose my might !"[7] The introduction of slaves had a considerable effect also upon the occupations, and so upon the social status, of their conquerors' women.[8] This form of specialization, as well as that by sex, had a high survival-value, chiefly because it resulted in the performance of an amount of labor which would never have been done except under the powerful compulsion represented by the ownership, with attendant powers, of the master over the man.[9]

§72*. Rudimentary Specialization. It remains to illustrate some of the earlier and simpler forms of intra-group specialization other than by sex or by enslavement. In all primitive cases the group must be small, for organization, civilization, and numbers are all intricately interconnected.[10] A 'society within which specialization other than by sex or by enslavement is literally not to be found is inferential rather than observable. Despite the often alleged uniformity of savages, which the best observers do not find, there must always be present, in some degree, certain inherited or acquired abilities and disabilities, such as physical or mental endowment or accumulated experience, upon which differentiation may or must be based. These elements of strength and weakness, experience and inexperience, are sure to result in some small specialization, even in the absence of personal coercion. The Eskimo resort to violence as little as any native peoples of whom we know; yet rudimentary specialization in hunting, housebuilding, and other occupations occurs. These rudimentary cases are not to be overlooked; they form the germ of what comes later on. There is an indeterminate point at which specialization comes to be recognized as such; and it is of importance to realize that this point is not reached at a leap but by transitions. Specialization is not clearly recognizable until certain individuals devote all or most of their time to a single activity.

It is said of the Ostiaks that "they have no craftsmen among them; everyone makes everything for himself."[11] The same might be said, judging by the same criterion, of a number of backward societies, Bushmen, Fuegians, most

---

[7] Homer, *Iliad*, VI, 127.　　　[8] §§385, 386, 387, below.
[9] §104, below.　　　[10] §26, above.
[11] Kondratowitsch, in *Globus*, LXXIV, 289.

Australians,[12] and some others. Homer's[13] Cyclopes, as an epitome of what was at that time regarded as plain savagery, exhibit the same picture.

If it is realized that rudimentary specialization preceded any definite forms, it is possible to view the crafts emerging from a sort of conglomerate into identifiable shapes.

As a typical instance of this stage of evolution take the case portrayed by Homer;[14] because of its completeness and its unconsciousness, the Homeric evidence surpasses any record of a society by an outsider. In ancient Greece, specialization of craft or trade is found only on the broadest lines; a man could turn his hand to almost any task. The first specialization approaching distinctness was that of the smith, who did almost all the work in metals. He derives his name and the names of his tools from the metal copper, but his operations were not confined to it. He worked in gold, silver, tin, and iron; and his function did not stop even there, for he sewed the leathern parts of shields and otherwise supplemented his main work. There is in Homer no clearly marked case of division of labor in the manufacture of any single product.

These facts, together with others recorded in the *Case-Book,* afford a perspective of specialization within a simple society, so far as the construction of two long tales, in which the incidents and facts of common life play an uncommonly prominent part, has had occasion to refer to its several phases. It is plain from the foregoing that with little differentiation goes little definiteness of specialization, and with slight advance in technique,[15] little consistency in the same. Temporary attention to certain employments, determined mainly by local interest or chance, seems to be the stock form, from which there is little departure, except that the ordinary man seems less easily convertible into the smith than into any other craftsman. This Greek case is typical of many.

From such evidence can be derived an idea of how simple peoples drift unpremeditatedly into specialization. It is always to be noted that a precondition for a developed system lies in the opportunity for exchange—a market for the specialty. The presence of such opportunity explains the superiority of certain groups over others in the development of distinct crafts, affording yet another instance of how numbers and proximity promote civilization. Thus the Central Australians had specialists in hut-building, who were in great demand and were borrowed from camp to camp.[16] It is of interest, at this point, to note what handicrafts first gain identity;

[12] See Ratzel, *Vkde.,* under these names.
[13] *Odyssey,* IX, 106 ff.; Keller, *Hom. Soc.,* 3-4.
[14] Keller, *Hom. Soc.,* 80-84, where full references to the text are given. On the nature of Homeric evidence, see Keller, in *Am. Jr. Soc.,* IX, 37 ff.
[15] Consider the tools of the smith. Keller, *Hom. Soc.,* 55.
[16] Horne and Aiston, *Cent. Aust.,* 19, 20.

they are, in general, those which demand for their prosecution some uncommon knowledge or special training.

It is thought by some that stone-workers were the first real specialists, because stone was probably the first substance worked which called for special skill.[17] Certainly stone-working became specialized to a remarkable degree where metal did not supplant the stone; consider the perfection of prehistoric flints. Of the Australians it is said that "not all were good weapon-makers. Some specialised in the making of the stone tools and usually confined themselves to these alone. Very often a man specialised in only one tool, and made nothing but that."[18] Catlin[19] states of the Indians that the operators "seemed to have reduced the art of flaking to almost an absolute science with division of labor, one set of men being expert in quarrying and selecting the stone, others in preparing the blocks for the flaker." Among the Shasta Indians, the making of arrow-points is a craft which many attempt, but in which only a few attain pronounced superiority.[20]

While stone-working is doubtless long antecedent to the use of metals, the expert in smithery, where he exists, is likely to stand out as the ideal craftsman of primitive times. In ancient Greece there was a smith-god; in Scandinavia the smith was in close connection with the spirit-world. With striking unanimity primitive peoples have regarded the smiths as sorcerers, according them, as a consequence, a position of enviable or unenviable distinction in society.[21] They often formed an endogamous and racially distinct group in a society. The smith and smelter being usually the same person, this craftsman was likely to become fixed in abode in the neighborhood of the ore-deposits. When itinerant he has sometimes been of the gypsy type. His dwelling or shop was a sort of community meeting-place, like the country store, and is thought to have been a forerunner of the public lodging-house.[22] Among the Sea Dyaks of Borneo, "the blacksmith, with the exception of the *manang*, or doctor, is the only person in the village whose time is solely occupied by a profession or trade."[23] Synge explains the Irish phrase, "the words of women and smiths" as follows: "This

---

[17] Lippert, *Kgchte.*, I, 282; Wilson, *Arrowpoints*, in USNM, 1897, pt. I, 857.
[18] Horne and Aiston, *Cent. Aust.*, 106.
[19] Sellers, in *Smithson. Rep.*, 1885, pt. I, 875.
[20] Ratzel, *Vkde.*, II, 593.
[21] §§310, 320, 352, below; Lippert, *Kgchte.*, II, 215 ff.; Wilken, in VG, III, 39; Gröndal, in *Annaler*, 1863, 104; Nachtigal, *Sahara*, I, 443-444.
[22] Lippert, *Kgchte.*, I, 604, 630; II, 220-222; Homer, *Odyssey*, XVIII, 328; Keller, *Hom. Soc.*, 81.
[23] Roth, *Sarawak*, II, 236.

phrase is almost a quotation from an old hymn of Saint Patrick. In Irish folklore smiths were thought to be magicians, and more or less in league with the powers of darkness."[24] The reason why the smiths got such distinction was because they acquired a species of dexterity that was not the obvious extension in degree of what everyone else was doing. Metal-working, often including mining— for there was not, in the early stages, enough differentiation within the craft to separate the two—was a very different thing from, say, wood-working; in the minds of the easily impressed primitives, it came to possess a certain magic quality which aligned it with the work of the magician. Baldwin's *The Sampo* is a set of stories based upon the Finnish Kalevala. The hero is a smith and the tales are full of his wizardry.[25] Even in relatively modern times there have been all sorts of, to us, superstitious notions about the nature of metals.[26]

Smithery is a pronounced type of early specialization; and the case of other crafts, as they came along, is not dissimilar. Rivers[27] makes a good deal of the fact that when division of social function first appears it is often in connection with religion. He cites canoe-makers as a special group of craftsmen practising a ceremonial process of manufacture, with formulæ to be uttered at various stages. First a general range of specialization is vaguely marked off; then comes an intensification of cultivation of the specialty, an accumulation of experience, differentiation within the original range, and at length a sort of schooling of novices and, it may be, a gild-like organization.

§73. The Organizing Function of Might. The earliest and most elemental forms of organization for societal self-maintenance go back, whatever strand be followed up, to force. All members of early society discharged functions that they did not like to discharge under the compulsion of life-conditions as metamorphosed into the authority of the mores, of law, or of some person or group possessed of superior power. In connection with our preceding

---

[24] Meyerfeld, "Letters of Synge," in *Yale Rev.*, XIII, 695.
[25] Especially pp. 11, 25, 35, and ch. VI.
[26] §307, below; Thorndike, *Magic*, index *sub* "metals," "metallurgy," "alchemy."
[27] *Soc. Org.*, 147, 148, 150; §161, below.

generalities, it is of importance to note the following three conclusions.

First, that the organization, created by force, or by the stress of conditions in which there were inequality and "injustice," is the historical germ out of which civilization has come. Whether this organization was moral or not, or whether some other organization would have been more conducive to societal welfare, is a quite idle and irrelevant question. It is a popular saying that might does not make right, and it is true; but might makes what is, and has been, in all history. Might can make right only if what is is right. That which is, however, may be a passing maladjustment, as well as a nascent or mature adaptation.[28] What is right is a matter of opinion. There are many who do not think that our various wars have been right; but these wars are irrevocable facts, and their consequences run on. Might made them; the right of them is now only a matter of academical discussion. The weal or woe of today and tomorrow are with the might of them. What is done or happens, and the play of our reflective judgment about that which is done or happens, are two very different things. The former is an object of study that we may know facts with which we must deal; the latter is an object of study that we may judge what it will be wise to do in some future case. This way of force is the direction that things took; and mankind did not perish but lived on to run its course through later stages. This fact alone is important to us.

Second, the institutions of marriage and of industry began together. They are seen to be interlocked at the beginning, and will be found to have run parallel to one another and to have been correlative ever since.[29]

Third, the societal functions of war and industry, and the classes of producers and fighters, are primordial. In any stable order these two classes must be provided to perform these two functions, and their adjustment to one another must be suitable and adequate.[30] It is by this advantage to society, indeed, that the societal sanction to marriage as an enforced servitude of women is largely accounted for.

28 §169, below.   29 §341, below.
30 §§144, 167 ff., below.

§74. Specialization as Adaptation. The topic of primitive division of labor, on lines other than those of sex, is one which verges upon the range of the economist. Most general economic treatises, in the course of forays into the earlier conditions, explain in all essentials the virtues of specialization and coöperation. The aspect of the matter to which we wish to give attention is that which opens back toward the beginning of things rather than forward toward the modern conditions which form the natural station of observation of the economist. We wish to present specialization of economic function as one of the characteristic responses or adjustments of man in the struggle for existence; one which, in addition, since the specializing person cannot supply his own general needs, entails the further response involved in the development of exchange and its increasingly complex mechanism. These general considerations regarding adaptation apply also to what immediately follows, on inter-group specialization, and should be recalled in that connection; but they are needed at this point by way of tying up the strands of specialization and coöperation already spread before us.

Plants, animals, and human societies succeed in the competition of life by reason of exhibiting variations leading to better adjustment to life-conditions. The plant or animal develops, under pressure, its new detail of structure; the society, likewise under pressure, as the preceding paragraphs have shown, evolves its new tool or method—its advance of power. Evidently an enforced economy in the struggle for existence, such as results from division of labor, is often quite equivalent to an enforced positive acquisition; put in a different way, the knowledge of how to avoid a difficulty is equally valuable, so far as the immediate preservation of life is concerned, with the acquisition of power to surmount it. This division of labor, enlisting, as it does, propensity and habit, is an economy, for it is an elemental way of pursuing the line of less resistance. Specialization of function is shown in lowly organisms, and with advance in the scale of life it becomes ever more marked. In fact, what we call advance in that scale is largely so termed because of the progressive differentiation of function exhibited. In view of the utility of the expedient of specialization plus coöperation, that is, organization, in the struggle for societal self-maintenance, it would be strange indeed if the groups showing favorable variation toward such organization did not survive and grow strong where unorganized groups perished or fell away. No matter how little superior in expediency the specialization in one group may be as compared with another, it has selective value; for in these evolutionary matters it is never a question of a superlative, but always of a comparative.

§75*. Conditions of Group-Specialization. The preceding cases of specialization or division of labor are all intra-group affairs. There is another type of specialization, that existing between groups, which deserves particular attention; for the form of coöperation that goes along with the inter-group type is exchange or trade; and trade is the forerunner of civilization. It is easily understandable, granted the possibility of inter-tribal exchange, that there should be a common specialization on the part of all or most of the members of a tribe. The control of some natural monopoly such as a flint-deposit or a salt-bed, a special dexterity somehow acquired, or even mere chance, have lent to some societies an advantage in the struggle for existence, indisputable, but attainable only through identical specialization on the part of many. Even among the backward tribes of Australia, small groups fashion different things for which they have the raw material or to make which they have special opportunity, and then exchange with one another.[31] Such a superiority in the maintenance-mores could not but possess survival-value in any society's evolution, and would come more and more definitely to distinguish the favored group. Examples of this group-specialization abound.

A case of tribal specialization resting upon a natural monopoly is that of the Chibcha Indians of Colombia, who exported the rock salt which abounded in their territories, receiving in return cereals which they could not raise on their barren soil.[32] A similar case is reported from the Albert Nyanza region.[33] In Mashonaland whole villages make iron exclusively, and trade for what they need; other villages specialize in pottery-making.[34] Villages of potters occur in Uganda,[35] while the Caribs in Guiana, and the Nu-Arawaks, among the

---

[31] Ratzel, *Vkde.*, II, 57.   [32] Nadaillac, *Preh. Amer.*, 463.
[33] Stuhlmann, *Mit Emin*, 267.   [34] Bent, *Ethiopians*, 45.
[35] Ratzel, *Vkde.*, I, 455.

Shingu tribes, are the potters.[36] Ratzel[37] finds, indeed, a prevailing group-specialization among the Indians as a whole. There is no point in multiplying examples; the following description may serve to illustrate the detail of inter-group specialization and coöperation through trade; it is typical enough to stand for the generality of cases.

Im Thurn[38] says that there exists among the Guiana Indians a rough system of division of labor between the tribes, and that this serves not only the purpose of supplying all of them with better made articles, but also brings the different tribes together and spreads among them ideas and news of general interest. Each tribe has some manufacture peculiar to itself, and its members constantly visit other tribes, often hostile ones, for the purpose of exchanging the products of their own labor for such as are produced by the other tribes. These trading Indians are allowed to pass unmolested through an enemy's country.

Of all the tribes on the coast the Warraus make by far the best canoes, and supply them to neighboring tribes. In the same way, far in the interior, the Wapianas build boats for all the tribes of that district. The Macusis make *ourali* for poisoning arrows, the darts of blow-pipes, and an abundance of cotton hammocks. The Arecunas grow, spin, and distribute most of the cotton which is used by the Macusis and others for hammocks. They also supply all blow-pipes, for these are made of the stem of a palm, which, growing only in and beyond the Venezuelan boundary of their territory, are procured by the Arecunas, doubtless in exchange, from the Indians of the native districts of that palm. The Tarumas and Woyowais have a complete monopoly of the manufacture of the graters on which Indians of all tribes grate their cassava. They are also breeders and trainers of hunting-dogs. These distribute their graters and dogs through the Wapianas, who act as middlemen. The true Caribs make the best pottery, the Arawaks make fiber hammocks of a kind peculiar to them.

To interchange their commodities, the Indians make long journeys. The Wapianas visit the Tarumas and Woyowais, carrying canoes, cotton hammocks, knives, beads, and European goods. Leaving the canoes they walk back, carrying a supply of cassava-graters and leading hunting-dogs. The Macusis visit the Wapianas to obtain graters and dogs, for which they give *ourali*-poison and cotton hammocks; and these in turn carry such graters and dogs as they do not require, together with their own *ourali* and cotton hammocks, to the Arecunas, who give in return cotton and blow-pipes, or to the true Caribs, who pay in pottery. In this way travellers with news and goods pass from district to district.

This quotation exhibits the fact that group-specialization must be accompanied by inter-group exchange. Division of labor between the sexes or classes within a group calls for coöperation; and exchange or trade is the form which coöperation takes when specialization is group-wise. Between man and woman, specializing

---

[36] Von den Steinen, *Zent. Bras.*, p. 215.

[37] *Vkde.*, II, 593.

[38] *Ind. of Guiana*, 270, and ch. XIV. Summary in Mason, *Invention*, 364-365.

sexwise, there could not exist anything recognizable under the name of trade; we call their form of coöperation, in most cases, marriage. Again there is the type of coöperation corresponding to the master-man specialization, which we know as slavery. The term trade is reserved in usage for wider coöperations. While exchange inside a group was doubtless the germ of all trade, yet it was of so informal, incidental, and inconsecutive a nature as scarcely to repay detailed investigation. It is when groups have begun to specialize, and each to make a quantity of objects of a certain sort greater than it can possibly use, relying meanwhile upon other groups to supply what it is thus forced to neglect, that trade worthy of the name must already be present. Specialization of labor is sterile without coöperation. In all that has been said of the former the presence of the latter has, of necessity, been implied. It may take on, within the group, the form of matrimony or enslavement or barter or any other relationship that involves a mutualization or exchange, equitable or otherwise, of the product of effort. The relationship may be thoroughly distasteful and the coöperation in a high degree antagonistic. In any case the dual process is not, either in its primitive stages or in many of its more evolved ones, the outcome of rational reflection, but is set in motion automatically and unconsciously. It is in the "natural order." It passes into the mores and so into the range of societal selection.

To be noted in passing is the fact that an exchange cannot be called trade so long as what one group transfers to another does not represent a diminution of the former's resources; the transfer of fire, for example, or of ideas, cannot be considered as trade, for when these have been given the original stock yet remains intact. The sharing of fire and of ideas is a special case.[39]

Thus we find trade evolving along with group-specialization in the process of self-maintenance; or, more broadly, it is identified as one of the sub-adjustments of the industrial organization, which is itself the major adaptation of society in the struggle for existence. Primitive peoples have seized upon this expedient of trade to a greater extent and with more energy than they are sometimes thought to have done. That stone has been carried afar is shown

[39] Lippert, *Kgchte.*, I, 282; §91, below.

by the distances from the quarries at which artifacts of peculiar stone have been found.[40] After the conquests of the Aztecs their subjects were oppressed by expert traders until revolt was the regular order.[41] A number of backward peoples are enthusiastic traders in their way; in any case there is no such feeling of contempt for the merchant as was sometimes exhibited in antiquity.

In East Central Africa, trade in food and pottery is carried on by the women. Labor is not derogatory and skill in handicraft is esteemed; "even chiefs are not ashamed to be smiths or basket-makers, though their natural preference is for trade. Markets are sometimes established on the neutral ground between several villages, where an important chief has buried his . . . fetish."[42]

§76*. Trade and War. At this point we must work in another strand by inquiring as to what group-relations preceded exchange, and by observing how the latter evolved out of the former. There is some evidence as to the unwarlike character of primitive tribes, but it does not invalidate the fact that they came into collisions of interest in the competition of life and knew no better way of adjustment than by fighting it out.[43] The cases where there is some substitute for a general battle are significant of a former stage where there was no mitigation of conflict. As survivals in the ceremonies attendant on marriage point back to "marriage by capture,"[44] so do those in the early forms of trade witness to antecedent robberies and to an earlier inter-group relationship marked by suspicion and fear. There are, indeed, actual cases of the absence of trade, where it would be advantageous to both parties, owing purely to the prevalence of almost unintermittent hostilities. Again, where some feeble exchange may actually exist, its development is precluded by strongly anti social sentiments.[45] The examples which we have to cite exhibit several stages of enmity and distrust that have formed, in a number of places, the preliminaries to the development of trade. The reader will note in these cases that it is plainly the unreflective consensus of the parties concerned that the advantage of recurrent opportunities to trade completely outweighs a single chance to loot. The savage,

[40] Lippert, Kgchte., I, 282, 291, 296, 297.
[41] Nadaillac, Preh. Amer., 287.
[42] Torday and Joyce, in JAI, XXXV, 408.
[43] §139, below.   [44] §§358, 360, below.
[45] §9, above.

in restraining his natural impulse, could not analyze the matter; what he did lay in the body of accepted and unquestioned procedure—in his code of mores.

So experienced an ethnologist as Peschel[46] says: "We may assume that commerce has existed in all ages, and among all inhabitants of the world." To this universal the exception may be taken that even in modern times some tribes have revealed a very vague idea of barter, or none at all, as, for example, the Andamanese, Australians, Patagonians, and Fuegians, when first encountered by the whites.[47]

What we are especially concerned to show here is how a period of some sort of peaceful exchange grew out of one of violence and by reason of being a more expedient adaptation in the struggle for existence, supplanted it. Consider the rudimentary quality of exchange where two members of two neighboring tribes approach one another, each with spear poised and eyes fixed upon the other. They move in crouching posture into sufficient proximity to drop each the article offered and snatch up the one proffered; and then, retiring watchfully backward in the same style, finally rise and take to their heels. A false move or a stumble during the progress of this sort of commerce turns peace into violence and trade into slaughter. This is, perhaps, an extreme and even ridiculous case, but there are not a few of the peoples of the earth who show mutual suspicion in a degree scarcely inferior. The whites had to trade in force, and well-armed, with the Herero; they had to meet force with force, or be robbed. If the natives outnumbered them, they simply kept the arms they came to examine for purchase and could not be stopped. Firmness resulted in the parties remaining friendly and avoiding future trouble.[48] Again, "when the Brazilian savages want to trade with one another, they mutually lay their weapons aside, and side by side; and then, the trade being closed—as indicated by the repetition of certain words several times by both parties—both sides seize their weapons at the same instant." The recounter regards this procedure as survivalistic.[49] Again, "when living among the Macusi, I was often amused," says Im Thurn,[50] "by a number of those Indians rushing into my house, . . . who with bated breath, half in joy, half in terror, used to point through the window to some party of their enemies, the Arecunas, coming with cotton balls and blow-pipes for exchange. It is these traders who carry with them the latest news."

Professional intermediaries exist in trade, as they do in war; often they are women, sometimes boys dedicated and trained to the function from earliest years.[51] In both cases they are recognized noncombatants, which allows the short inference that trade was so near to war that only the recognizedly unwarlike were free of suspicion. Although such a system is not always admittedly based upon mutual distrust and fear, that idea is not far away. "In earlier days, previous to the advent of the whites," says Niblack[52] of the

[46] *Races,* 210.
[47] Letourneau, *Commerce,* chs. I-IX, *passim.*
[48] Büttner, *Walfischbai,* 94, 95.   [49] Von Martius, *Beiträge,* I, 94.
[50] *Ind. of Guiana,* 271.
[51] Letourneau, *Commerce,* 76; §384, below.
[52] In USNM, 1888, 337.

Indians of the northwest coast, "the trading was carried on less systematically and with more formality on account of the feuds between the different tribes."

Among unsophisticated peoples, like the Herero, who have no words for "buy" and "sell," but merely for "barter," a merchant in the European sense "is always a deceiver" because he seeks to win something by exchange. They see no labor in the merchants' operations that calls for payment.[53] The early Greeks applied vituperative epithets to all Phœnicians.[54] Indeed, the orthodox mediæval view of the merchant was far from flattering. It is characteristic of the trader that he depends upon "trade-friends" to protect and support him during his sojourn among strange tribesmen; no one man of one tribe can trade forthwith with all the members of another, but cleaves to those with whom he has eaten dog or pig.[55]

§77*. Transitional Forms. One of the most curious forms of early exchange is that known as "silent barter," "dumb barter," or "deposit barter." The classic case is one reported by Herodotus;[56] the Carthaginians, he says, relate the following.

"There is a country in Libya and a nation beyond the Pillars of Heracles, which they are wont to visit, where they no sooner arrive than forthwith they unlade their wares, and having disposed them after an orderly fashion along the beach, leave them and returning aboard their ships, raise a great smoke. The natives, when they see the smoke, come down to the shore, and laying out to view so much gold as they think the worth of the wares, withdraw to a distance. The Carthaginians upon this come ashore and look; if they think the gold enough, they take it and go their way, but if it does not seem to them sufficient, they go aboard once more and wait patiently. Then the others approach and add to their gold, till the Carthaginians are content. Neither party deals unfairly with the other, for they themselves never touch the gold until it comes up to the worth of the goods, nor do the natives ever carry off the goods till the gold is taken away."

This ancient report is corroborated by more recent ones referring likewise to the West African coast. Miss Kingsley,[57] first recalling the same sort of story from a Venetian writer of the fifteenth century, continues: "To this day there is a form of silent trade still going on in Guinea. The writer has often seen on market roads in many districts, but always well away from Europeanized settlements, a little space cleared by the wayside, and neatly laid with plantain leaves, whereon were very tidily arranged various little articles for sale—a few kola nuts, leaves of tobacco, cakes of salt, a few heads of maize, or a pile of yams or sweet potatoes. Against each class of articles so many cowrie shells or beans are placed, and, always hanging from a branch above, or sedately sitting in the middle of the shop, a little fetish. The number of

[53] Büttner, *Walfischbai*, 27. There is a relation between the words *tauschen* and *täuschen*, *Handel* and *Händel*, that is more than a play on words.

[54] Keller, *Hom. Soc.*, 25, 272.

[55] Hagen, *Papua's*, 216-221; §150, below.

[56] *Hist.*, IV, 196. The translation is from Ridgeway, *Standards*, 83.

[57] *W. Afr. Studies*, 243-244, 248-249 (quoted).

cowrie shells or beans indicates the price of the individual articles in the various heaps, and the little fetish is there to see that anyone who does not place in the stead of the articles removed their proper price, or who meddles with the till, shall swell up and burst." Miss Kingsley thinks this device is practised mostly for convenience, one person being thereby enabled to have several shops open at but little working expense; but she has seen it employed as a method of trading between tribes that are at war with one another. She sees in it a sense of personal insecurity and a tendency to leave dangerous traffic in the hands of the gods. The relation between dumb barter and a status of mutual hostility is, however, unmistakable.

Other cases of silent barter are to be found here and there over the earth.[58] They all reveal suspicion and fear. The parties dare not trade over a counter unless that counter, so to speak, is too wide for either party to reach across it with a weapon. It is plain enough that the device of silent barter is calculated to obviate something that is normal and usual when strangers meet, namely, violence. Generalization upon the cases reveals that the expedient before us is put into operation only in dealings with, or between tribes of a markedly primitive type; that it is a substitute for either non-intercourse or hostilities. Hence it must be a very primitive form of exchange, developed, as a better expedient in living, out of the relations of antagonism that preceded—such relations as, for instance, those sometimes called group-slavery,[59] where a nomadic tribe periodically robs a sedentary population of agriculturists.

Another transitional form between war and trade is called "peaceful access." The distribution of desirable materials is not uniform over the earth; the only way to have them is to go and, some way or other, get them. It appears that natural deposits of flint, salt, and other desirables were fought over in early times and changed hands again and again; sometimes, however, it is found that a tribe within whose range deposits occur is accustomed to admit aliens to participation in such wealth, generally in return for some payment. The transition from the former to the latter state of affairs may be made out from the following series of cases.

A branch of the Zuñi Indians once held the region of the Lake of Salt, in south central New Mexico; this deposit "they guarded so jealously that their wars with the Keresan and other tribes to the south-south-eastward were

---

[58] Grierson, *Silent Trade;* Letourneau, *Commerce,* 10, 12, 16, 78, 149, 168, 173, 314, 409, 529; Schrader, *Aryans,* 352.
[59] §102, below.

caused—as many of their later wars with the Navajo have been—by slight encroachments on the products of the lake to which the Zuñis laid claim."[60] That the natives of southeast Australia "had often to fight their way to the mines of red ochre and freestone slabs is not surprising, when one remembers that these places were the property of the tribes in whose country they were situated. These expeditions were a trespass on them, and interfered with the barter which the owners of the mines no doubt carried on with other tribes.[61] "Tribal possession is a well-defined entity." A certain tribe owned the Beltana deposit of ochre. "To these a message-stick was sent when red ochre was required, and presents, in return for permission to mine it, followed."[62] Again, in Australia, "the Dieri annually send an expedition of able-bodied men to the *pitcheri* country on the Herbert River, Queensland, about 250 miles away. The party has to pass through land of several hostile tribes and must fight its way."[63] Once, in ancient Germany, two peoples fought for the salt-wells; and long afterwards a similar conflict took place between the Burgundians and the Alemanni.[64]

Gradually, however, these deposits or other natural resources were opened up to outsiders, and within the region peace was enforced. In some cases the Australian expeditions were allowed transit through tribes at war.[65] "It is wellknown that the celebrated 'red pipe-stone quarries' were held as sacred and neutral ground by all the [Indian] tribes which were accustomed to gather there for the purpose of procuring this rare, and, to them, valuable stone. No matter what feuds may have existed between tribes, or what deadly enmities may have been held by individuals, when workers met in these quarries it was always in a state of peace, even if their differences would not allow friendly intercourse."[66] Again, "in some places in Victoria there are seen the quarries where in former times the natives broke out the trappean rocks for their hatchets. Large areas are covered with the débris resulting from their labors; and it is stated, on good evidence, that natives from far distant parts were deputed to visit these quarries, and carry away stone for implements. When one or two natives were selected by a distant tribe to make a journey for the purpose of procuring diorite or basalt from such quarries, they carried with them credentials, showing exactly their object. If they faithfully pursued their object, and tarried no longer in any place than was necessary, they appear to have been allowed to proceed without molestation, and to have been treated as guests—not always as welcome guests, but with such protection as the host gives to those that, perhaps unwillingly, he entertains. If, however, they interfered in the quarrels of any tribe, violated any custom, or seemed not really anxious to hasten the journey, they were treated as enemies, and sometimes pursued and killed."[67] There were formerly definite trading-routes between water-holes. If traders kept to those paths they were not molested.[68]

[60] Cushing, in BAE, XIII, 352-355. [61] Howitt, *S. E. Aust.*, 713.
[62] Horne and Aiston, *Cent. Aust.*, 34.
[63] Howitt, in JAI, XX, 76. The *pitcheri* is a bush whose twigs are used, dried, as a narcotic.
[64] Möller, *Salz*, 6; Lippert, *Kgchte.*, I, 619-620.
[65] Tylor, *Anth.*, 281.
[66] Smith, in *Smithson. Rep.*, 1884, pt. I, 871.
[67] Smyth, *Vict.*, I, 359.
[68] Horne and Aiston, *Cent. Aust.*, 20.

It is to be noted that in most cases there was something, even though of trivial value, given in return for the peaceful access; that is, there was here a beginning of trade. "The simplest form of commerce on the western contiment," says Mason,[69] "does not seem to have been in the hands of peddlers; but certain necessary articles like salt and other minerals existed in mines or quarries situated inside the boundaries of certain tribes. The owner did not dig the material and carry it about to sell or exchange it, but the people who wanted the article had to go after it and pay some kind of tribute for the privilege." Certain tribes held veins of turquoise or kalaite; others were settled near salt marshes; one fortunate group had in front of its village large veins of mineral paint for adorning pottery.

Piracy is yet another transitional form between war and trade. When a stranger presented himself at the door of a Homeric house, he was asked in a matter-of-fact manner whether he was on business or roving like a pirate;[70] in the one function as in the other, he was evidently welcome if he came in peace, and the question conveyed no implications. The functions of trader and pirate were easily interchangeable according to circumstances. The Phœnicians, for example, were quite willing to get something for nothing by looting prospective customers who appeared in numbers inferior to their own, and by consistent kidnapping.[71] Frontier-trade has often exhibited a similar tendency to revert to violence; and the persistence of piracy has been a serious interference with commerce from very early times down almost to the present.[72] It is not necessary to rehearse details; the point at issue is that piracy is another witness to the once close connection between war and trade.

§78*. Exchange in the Industrial Organization. We shall not follow exchange any farther, for in so doing we shall verge upon the field of economics. It is common knowledge that exchange has developed its own mechanism, moving from simple barter by gradual adjustments up to its complicated modern form; advancing from a standard of value and circulating medium, combined in the form of a characteristic commodity or dominant ware, to the standards and media that have survived many selections and are

[69] In USNM, 1894, 586.
[70] Homer, *Odyssey*, III, 71-74; IX, 252-255.
[71] Keller, *Hom. Soc.*, 90 ff.
[72] Ratzel, *Vkde.*, II, 428; Montero y Vidal, *Piratería, passim;* Worcester, *Philippine Isl.*, 150 ff.; Lala, in *Leslie's Pop. Mo.*, May, 1900.

in use today in high civilization. Letourneau[73] compares salt to our gold coin; the cowrie-shells, so often in use as a medium of exchange, to our subsidiary coinage. The evolution of money is highly typical of the automatic adjustment-process; any adequate sketch[74] of it reviews the earlier members of an evolutionary series whose later forms have become incredibly complicated.

It can be seen from the evidence now before us that trade, as a special development in the organization for societal self-maintenance, takes its origin in group-specialization, and represents certainly one of the factors that brought mankind into peaceful inter-group relations. In this respect *commercium* and *connubium* support each other, justifying the Romans in their yoking together of the terms; and there is a widespread custom whereby markets are put under both civil and religious sanction, as places of peace.[75] It can be seen that the advance of specialization between groups, plus the extension of group-coöperation through exchange, tends to expand and strengthen the maintenance-organization until its field of operation covers the whole world; and until the advances in organization originated by the most effective races have come to be, in the degree which circumstances will allow, the patrimony of all mankind. Moreover, with the transmission of the basic maintenance-mores there goes a general advance in culture along all lines.[76] In theory we are obliged to conclude that those forces which oppose or hinder group-specialization according to resources and propensity, or block inter-group exchange, are retrogressive elements; they tend to weaken, render ineffective, and stunt the development of that organization which has been built up, through a long series of automatic and inevitable adjustments, for the maintenance of society.

§79. Exchanges in General.[77] In the development of civilization the exchange of materials and of ideas has been of an importance second only to their origination. For by exchange all the new departures that have turned out well for their originators have been

---

[73] *Prop.*, 468-469.   [74] Sumner, *Folkways*, ch. III.

[75] §§356, 142, 146, 150, 151, below.

[76] Keller, *Soc. Evol.*, 141 ff.; 232 ff.; Gregory, Keller, and Bishop, *Phys. and Comm. Geog.*, ch. XIII.

[77] Adapted from Keller, *Starting-Points*, ch. VII.

transmitted to other peoples, back and forth; and each of several communicating groups has been able to profit by a set of adjustments which include the best that any and all of them have succeeded in hitting upon. Intercommunication is a prime essential. Men must not only know what is going on in the minds of other men, so as to compare and mutually adopt ideas, but, still more important, especially among backward tribes which can most readily deal with ideas when embodied in things, they must be able to see and handle those things—in this case, other peoples' products. They can communicate by speech or writing; but they must also bring products to each other; and to do that they must learn to overcome distance. This calls for transportation of men and things. And when men get into proximity, they must have some method of peaceably exchanging their products; hence the mechanism of trade, including money, measures and weights, credit, and other commercial devices. They must, further, make their products desirable to one another; hence the methods of appeal, chiefly by suggestion, practised by the trader.

All these are adjustments in the art of living, and are, as such, comparable with the invention of tools and weapons. The exchange of products precedes that of ideas or processes, at least on the primitive stage. It should not be understood, however, that hard and fast lines of distinction can be drawn between these two forms of exchange; the transfer of products is hardly possible without a simultaneous transmission of ideas, for the products are themselves ideas expressed in material form.

The first and prime instrumentality for the exchange of anything between human beings is language.[78] It might be called a tool without stretching that term out of all recognition; it is, at any rate, no organic product, but a societal one. That a series of customary sounds, selected and arranged by nobody, should form a language which has a regular, logical, and complicated structure of its own, is a fact that never ceases to amaze. Not all languages have the same structure, but, whatever the type, it is as fully subject to law as are the movements of the planets. Language did not leap to an elaborate and logical structure, with all the parts of speech distinct, at once; it developed gradually, through varia-

[78] Sumner, *Folkways,* §§135 ff.

tion, selection, and transmission, in adjustment to needs. It furnishes one of the best cases of evolution in the societal field. Nobody made it; everybody made it. The various languages have grown by gradual and almost imperceptible changes; they are evidently the handiwork of whole peoples—as are the rest of human institutions as well, though we are sometimes deceived into thinking otherwise.

Allied with language is writing, as a means for the preservation and transmission of ideas and culture across time and space. Literature discharges an important function in acquainting peoples with one another's characteristics; the novel has been highly effective in that way. Exogamy and slavery, as well as trade, have assisted in the transmission of culture. By all these means exchanges are effected between human societies and there is brought to pass what has been called a "cross-fertilization of culture." Though the results attained transcend the compass of self-maintenance, yet all the processes of exchange start within that range. The subject of exchanges, viewed broadly, reinforces strongly the contention that civilization is a function of numbers in contact.

CHAPTER VII

CAPITAL

§80*. **Primitive Improvidence and Thrift.** Without entering any farther into the details of either specialization or coöperation in labor—for our concern is less with the apparatus of self-maintenance than with its organization—we pass on to the other great factor, capital, which stands shoulder to shoulder with labor at the beginning of things, so far as success in societal self-maintenance is concerned. No tribe which has implements or fire or domestic animals could be said to be without energy stored up against the struggle for existence;[1] for such possessions assure their holders the possibility of living longer and better. No tribes are without capital; they could not have held their own and remained in existence without it. Complete lack of capital could exist only in that inferential past which must of necessity have preceded stages of which we have information, in which man was still performing structural adaptation along with other animals. There are real cases, however, of tribes with little capital, and many examples of groups with no more than rudimentary foresight—a quality prerequisite to the accumulation of capital.

The Bushmen, Australians, Veddahs of Ceylon, and Fuegians hardly ever hoard for the future.[2] The Central Australians want all their food at once, so as to have a good gorge; then they are resigned to "go one big fella hungry." Growth of plants from the seed is quite beyond their ken. In one of their ceremonies seed is thrown broadcast, but it is first crushed and is incapable of sprouting. When they move they leave their stone utensils lying about. If they need more they make them. No one will ever take the abandoned articles, so they will still be there at return.[3] Of the tribes on Geelvink Bay, New Guinea, it is said that their characteristic trait is sloth, which is so marked "that any one who has, so to speak, an atom of food available will not go to work until he is driven to it by hunger," a sensation which "he tries to forget as long as possible by sleeping."[4] A single tool is enough, until it wears out, for a Papuan; he has no idea of providing a successor beforehand.[5] It is reported of the Haida Indians that they often, through feasting or improvidence, eat up all the dried berries before spring and were it not for a few

<hr>

[1] §55, above.   [2] Letourneau, *Prop.*, 38-39.
[3] Horne and Aiston, *Cent. Aust.*, 7, 8, 18.
[4] Van Rosenberg, *Geelvinkbaai*, 88.   [5] Hagen, *Papua's*, 219.

bulbs which they dig while awaiting the halibut-season, numbers of them would starve to death.[6]

Again, sixteen rations, enough for two days, were eaten at one meal by eleven Mohaves, who then threatened to desert the expedition unless the quantity of food was increased. This may have been a case of over-reaching, but another typical instance where such a motive could not be present was "that of an Apache woman at one of the military posts in Arizona, who, on receiving her rations for the week, consumed all the food at a sitting," trusting to her ability to pick up enough sustenance to tide her over till the next issue-day.[7]

It might be thought that there existed some reason for this prompt assimilation, for food once eaten could not be taken away; and it is certain enough that insecurity prevented hoarding all through the primitive time. Periods of repletion and of semi-starvation regularly succeeded one another. Lack of foresight is displayed even more plainly in the wanton destructiveness of some primitive peoples. Certain of the Australian blacks invariably kill immature animals and birds whenever opportunity offers.[8] The aborigines of Tasmania "are an extremely improvident race, for although dependent almost entirely upon their hunting for subsistence, yet they will slaughter indiscriminately, long after they have supplied themselves with sufficient for their present use."[9] The rifle was a curse to the Eskimo, for it enabled them to decimate the seals for the mere pleasure of killing. The Nootka-Columbian Indians do not hoard; they often destroy extra canoes and blankets.[10]

The improvident destruction of natural resources is not a thing confined to savages; but the distinction between primitive and so-called civilized vandalism is clear enough: the savage cannot know any better, while the civilized barbarian ought to know better if he does not.

On the other hand, even among very backward peoples the beginnings of foresight are to be found, and often a high development of it along certain lines; and where it is not evenly distributed over a group, the thrifty are found resolutely protecting themselves, so far as possible, against the improvident.

We have seen that the Indian women in New England had to hide the seed from the men, lest they devour it all.[11] Again, of the Indians, "the corn is stowed in caches, and they keep the situation of these caches secret as if found out they would have to supply every needy neighbor." This, it is added, "may occasion a famine, for some are so lazy that they will not plant at all, knowing that the more industrious can not refuse to divide their store with them."[12]

[6] Niblack, in USNM, 1888, 277.
[7] Hoffmann, in BAE, XIV, pt. I, 287.
[8] Curr, *Aust. Race*, I, 82.   [9] Roth, *Tasmania*, 48.
[10] Bancroft, *Nat. Races*, I, 191.   [11] Wood, *New Eng. Prospect*, 106.
[12] Loskiel, *Mission*, 68.

It is a form of improvidence to squander resources on luxury, and savages are found exhibiting it often in an even more crass degree than civilized man. Further, there are in the savage mind certain lacunæ by reason of which he apparently cannot rise to foresight or, even if he can forecast somewhat, is not able to summon the energy to live up to the lights he possesses. A pair of illustrations will bring out these points.

Certain Nigerian tribes are good agriculturists. "They raise a great deal of guinea-corn and millet every year, but unfortunately make most of it into beer, so that from June to October they are usually in a state of semi-starvation, and have nothing but some bitter roots and what they can buy or steal."[13] The other difficulty is typified by the savage's "different conception of the value of time. To the native one day is the same as another. Tell him to come tomorrow and he will probably turn up the day after, fully believing that he has kept the exact letter of his word. It is very annoying to the white man, no doubt, but the native can hardly be blamed. Perhaps it is partly this indifference to temporal considerations which makes the native somewhat improvident. The Olegana people allowed their domesticated pigs to root up the sweet potatoes, though they knew that food was scarce. The Bwaidoga natives, again, planted sweet potatoes when the yam crop failed, but omitted to erect any fences round them; later they complained that the wild pigs ravaged their gardens."[14]

Perhaps a transitional form between improvidence and its opposite is offered by communities the majority of whose members are industrious, but which tolerate with various degrees of patience the worthlessness of the ne'er-do-wells. There are peoples who will share, even grudgingly, yet invariably, with their worthless members because they are unfortunate enough to include in their mores an element of communalism;[15] consider the Indians mentioned just above.

Among the Eskimo, generally so industrious and thrifty, there is a quota of black sheep. A young man, starting out in life with gun and ammunition, will soon, with energy, be able to make a kayak from the spoils of the hunt; and then he can procure the skins of marine animals to construct an oomiak and tent. Thus he may work up through the stages of local importance until he becomes the head of a gens or family, including his brothers and sisters with their wives, husbands, and children. But some men are too improvident to prepare the skins when they have the chance, and are then unable to own a kayak, which prevents them from providing themselves with an oomiak and tent. These persons live with others or by themselves, and pass a wretched

13 Tremearne, in JAI, XLII, 143.
14 Jenness and Ballentyne, *D'Entrecasteaux*, 208.
15 Ch. XV, §271, below.

existence, scarcely noticed by their fellows even during a season of abundance.[16] There are good-for-nothings here, even under conditions of great stress, but improvidence is evidently at a discount.

Gradually groups are driven, as a whole, to thrift, and it comes to characterize their mores. The natives of Victoria are not so improvident as is generally supposed: they take great care of birds' nests, sink wells, and protect the natural water-holes against the encroachments of animals. They cover the springs with stones and branches, and show, by burning off the grass, and in many other ways, that they foresee future needs.[17] Certain Melanesians, while they would let the rest of their houses rot, were careful to preserve the big boards. These "are often 4 metres long by one broad and 25 to 50 mm. thick, and in the old days of stone tools, took a long time to make and were really valuable on account of the labour expended on them."[18] The rest of the house was flimsy and easily replaceable. The foresight originally shown in hewing the boards bred the thrift exhibited in saving them. And so on up to cases of really remarkable thrift: taboos on game (game-laws), storage, and accumulation. "A side-light on the frugality and farsightedness of the Hopi is shown by their storage of a reserve supply of corn for two years."[19] One of the most striking exhibitions of thrift appears in the customs that tend to neutralize funeral waste and the losses incurred by sacrifice to the gods.[20] Typical of these usages is the sacrifice of images of things rather than of the things themselves.

Thrift and self-denial mean the accumulation of capital: and that allows of the storage of reserve strength and energy. The essential power of capital emerges more clearly when we see it in the form of a surplus of articles each of which is directly or indirectly of use in the struggle for existence. The man, for instance, who has a hundred cattle is a capitalist in almost a modern sense, for he may live off his interest, the increase of the herd, and yet maintain his principal, the herd, intact. There is a similar storage of articles useless in themselves but conveying title to goods of direct utility; surplusage is laid up in the form of some characteristic commodity or preëminent ware, such as salt, pelts, ivory, cattle, or some more evolved form of money. This means insurance against or emancipation from the vicissitudes of the struggle for existence. When capital comes to be a surplus, it begins to exert more effectively its characteristic influence on a society; for it becomes subject to unequal division and rapid accumulation. It is power not only over nature but also over fellow-competitors.[21] In

[16] Turner, in BAE, XI, 240.   [17] Smyth, *Vict.*, I, 143.
[18] Seligmann, *Melanesians,* 90.   [19] Hough, in AA, X, 35.
[20] §234, below.
[21] Sumner, "Power and Beneficence of Capital," in *Coll. Ess.,* II, 337 ff.

the armory of any group, it is a potent weapon with which to fight the battle of life. Its possession constitutes, therefore, a distinct superiority for the thrifty society. It is a societal adjustment of the first order.

Says Ratzel,[22] rather expansively: "The lowest stage of civilization is exactly the one where the accumulation of riches is an affair of the greatest importance, because without riches there is no leisure, and without leisure there is no ennoblement of the mode of life and no intellectual progress."

§81*. Motives to Accumulation. Thrift is in the mores of a society and is primarily the product of automatic selection[23] rather than of reasoned choice. Though this is true, we are not thereby prevented from identifying the forces under which men act, however unpremeditatedly, in developing their codes of conduct. At the outset it is to be understood that, the wants of the moment once satisfied, the alternatives that confronted primitive man were capital-formation or idleness. Every group, we know, must settle to an equilibrium between its labor and the conditions of its environment; and this amount of labor becomes customary and traditional. Less labor would result in the loss to the group of vigor or numbers; more would afford it a surplus. For the attainment of a status where present leisure would not be preferred to a foreseen surplus, some special stimuli are needed; and here the socializing forces of hunger, love, vanity, and fear are found competent to develop capital, as they have been seen to be effective in producing association itself.

It is obvious that the remembered agonies of famine or thirst, or the fear lest fire be lost, would force men toward foresight in food-storage, water-storage, and fire-preservation. To take a less primordial case, men early learned prevision from acquaintance with the palm-tree, on account of its slow growth and the penalties of negligence. The Wanika of East Africa align the destruction of the coco-palm with matricide, because it gives them food as a mother does. The palm was early protected by a sort of intertribal law.[24] It would be easy to multiply such instances: the change of the seasons, the peculiarities of flora and fauna, and many another life-condition forced men, at peril of destruction, to learn fore-

[22] *Vkde.*, I, 86.   [23] Keller, *Soc. Evol.*, ch. III.
[24] Lippert, *Kgchte.*, I, 251, 329, 247, 249; Rohlfs, *Reise*, 70.

sight and gather capital. Hunger, in its generalized sense,[25] furnished the motive for such adjustments in self-preservation.

To get a wife, again, took capital; someone, if not the groom, must make an expenditure. The close interrelation of marriage and property is an ever-recurring phenomenon.[26] Vanity and the other impulses leading to self-gratification have always been powerful incentives to capital-building. In this connection it must be realized that the wants of the primitive man are not at all to be inferred from those which are felt by his cultured descendants; the uncivilized set small value upon many classes of satisfactions that appeal to the civilized, just as the less cultivated in our own society are indifferent to many of the things for which the cultivated strive and without which they are unhappy. The savage will labor for the sake of rum, or gewgaws, when nothing else will move him; that which ministers, not to self-maintenance, but to self-gratification, is often the key to the situation. The uncivilized, somehow in possession of a surplus, not seldom spend it luxuriously and do not use it as capital at all.

Further, there were strong incentives to accumulation that lay in the desire for social recognition.[27] Vanity lurked behind most of these. Without gifts to the chief there was no chance of social position any more than there was for the wifeless man. The ability to pay fines for real or fictitious infringements of both regular and specially contrived regulations was all that kept a man, not only in good standing, but in any standing at all. In many places membership in the secret societies was that which distinguished the man of account from the man of no account, or from the women; and such social position had to be paid for. Plutocracy and venality are not at all phenomena of a modern high civilization. The chief himself must be wealthy, give gifts and entertain profusely, and practise ostentation in general, if he is worthily to clothe his office in the eyes of his subjects. Such conditions of life and ideas of men were capable of evoking the sustained exertion and the forethought that must needs precede the acquisition of capital.

25 §12, above.   26 §341, below.   27 §166, below.

Weeks[28] is so impressed by the Upper Congo natives' desire for a grand funeral that he thinks it may account for certain offensive traits. The case is chiefly one of ostentation, but makes transition to the next topic, the influence of religion upon capital-formation. The negro's "apparent generosity is innate selfishness, for he only gives that he may receive more in return, and be the giver black or white he will complain bitterly if the return present is not so large as his greed imagined it should be. Perhaps this trait in his character may be accounted for by his desire to have a grand funeral—the talk of the village or the country side. For this he will save and scheme, lie and steal, rob his neighbours, his wives, and his children to hoard up cloth, etc., for his own burial."

If a man required capital to maintain his position in relation to nature and to fellow-man, he needed it no less imperatively for self-maintenance in the face of the environment of ghosts and spirits. He needed it to acquire for himself a future life of any consequence, or, indeed, a future life at all; for among primitives it is not the poor but the rich who may look beyond the grave with confidence. There is nothing about the needle's eye or Abraham's bosom in primitive religion. The savage had to have capital in view of the world to come. He required it, in a word, that he might straightway sacrifice it. This was in reality the utilization of wealth to produce more wealth, for the gods were the reservoir of all well-being. Part of what he had gathered was utterly destroyed in the effort to pass it over as a propitiatory gift to supernatural beings; and part of it went out of his own possession and use into the hands of human representatives of the superhuman powers. Gifts to the shaman were no less imperative for welfare and social recognition than gifts to the chief. Further, where accumulations were not destroyed and did not go wholly to the priesthood, they were often distributed in small amounts among many beneficiaries. This custom of sharing, it is to be noted, amounts to a dissipation of capital and is preventive of a wholesome inequality.[29]

§82. Religion and Capital. At first sight it appears that ghost-fear operated wholly against the accumulation of capital. It led to considerable actual destruction of goods; and then, again, it created a surplusage of things relatively or quite useless for self-maintenance. Stone graves, with their alignments and mono-

<hr>

[28] In JAI, XXXIX, 135.   [29] §129, below.

liths and, in more developed form, pyramids and obelisks—these
are striking examples of the kind of surplusage called for by crude
religious ideas. Viewing the matter from a slightly different angle,
we find the accumulation of even a rudimentary surplus checked
by religious considerations. In cases where provision for the
future is wellnigh absent, the explanation is, for example, that
nothing must be saved lest it tempt evil spirits to come. There is
a popular superstition, even in parts of Europe, that fine weather
will ensue if no fragments of meals remain. Further, the practices
based upon the conception of the other world in terms of this one
check the accumulation of capital from one generation to another,
in that they negative inheritance; the dead man's belongings must
go with him to the other world, and each generation must begin
where its predecessor did.[30] That compounding of possessions,
upon which increase of power and security in self-maintenance so
largely depends, is at most rudimentary.

In such manner religion, on the face of it, has run counter to
the formation of capital. Still it must not be concluded that the
inmixture of religion in the organization for self-maintenance, or
of vainglorious or luxurious squandering, or of sharing, was an
unrelieved evil. It was doubtless better that a surplus should be
produced only to be dissipated than that one should not be produced at all; better that a new generation should be forced to
overcome its inertia in beginning over again than that it should
repose in sloth upon efforts that went before. Even now there are
cases where the absence of a patrimony would have been beneficial
to the beneficiary. The wide prevalence of cult-waste shows that
the practice must have had some strong utility upon a certain
stage of society's evolution.

Religion did, in fact, hinder the wide accumulation of capital
in the hands of individuals; but it also concentrated it in those of
the priesthood. Perhaps an accumulation was lodged with the
latter which would never have been assembled but for the spur of
ghost-fear.

Even the individual got from his sacrifices something that was
worth its cost, namely, a sense of security and a peace of mind. It
is not, however, in any case, the ephemeral individual, nor a few

[30] §206, below; Lippert, *Kgchte.*, I, 39, 244.

generations of him, but the long-lived society, that here engages interest. The fact is that the priesthood turned back, unpremeditatedly, a part of the capital dedicated to the dead, as a provision for them in the life beyond—and so, in theory at least, forever lost—into the development of that which became, at length, art and science. Such capital was transmuted, not annihilated. This matter deserves attentive consideration when the case shall be before us in all its aspects.[31] Ghost-fear afforded, at the very least, discipline in forethought and saving, even though the individual were not himself to profit directly by his efforts, a training behind which lay a compulsion strong enough to overcome the inertia and shiftlessness of primitive man. Wherever religious ideas intrude, as Lippert[32] remarks, there are factors at work other than the purely natural ones. Human notions enter as components into the parallelogram of forces, and there is a confusion and intricacy in the combination such that they cannot be analyzed out as the operation of natural forces can be. Though the idea of the savage that the ghosts of the dead need food may seem laughable, nevertheless the grandest creations of civilization, reaching down with power into our own time, stand in evolutionary connection with the later phases and derivatives of that now obsolete notion.

If a surplus is indispensable for insurance against hunger, to get a wife, to minister to vanity, and to discharge religious obligations, what stronger compulsions against inertia could be imagined?

§83. Capital and Class-Distinction. Though systematic sharing of capital, not to mention its destruction, under the impulse of vanity or ghost-fear, was inevitable in its day, the system that had immediate possibilities in it was the one which favored accumulations and preserved them intact. If capital ever was actually communal, it could not remain so; for it is inevitably subject to unequal division and very early appears as an instrument of power of man over man. Fashion supported this differentiation; when one individual is distinguished by possessions, others want them, and so the mode arises. Thus the successful gather to themselves an accumulation which they expend on court, luxuries, re-

---

[31] §§329, 330, below.   [32] *Kgchte.*, I, 33; II, 605.

tainers, gifts to maintain power, and so on. These possessions produce a profit and an increase, and capital rolls up on itself. Thus the power of it increases and the breach widens between rich and poor, strong and weak; abundant stores of useful things have always given a sense of freedom and independence, as against the humility and dependence of non-possessors.[33] The possession of capital goes with political and social power as cause and effect, or as effect and cause. Of the kingship Telemachus exclaims: "Sayest thou that this is the most evil thing among men? Not at all ill is it to be king; for speedily one's house becomes affluent and himself more renowned."[34]

It is generally the chiefs who do the lending, as in New Britain, where one man often holds deposits of shell-money for a number of others; he is generally one who is feared and who has a good reputation for valor. His house is then the rallying-point in times of trouble for all who have deposits with him. He thus becomes a person of influence and power, because, no matter how bad he may be, the hearts of the depositors are with their treasure, and they rally round his house to defend their deposits and hence to defend him.[35] This illustration exhibits the tendency of even a minor obligation to create a relation of dependency and retainership. The rich chief is a banker, and is on the way to become trader for household or tribe.[36]

Position in the social scale is, among many peoples, so closely connected with wealth that a true plutocracy exists. As is normal, the possessors are the defenders of the *status quo*—it suits them well enough; they have succeeded under it—and the non-possessors are for various reasons in a position of such abject helplessness that they fall in readily with the traditional code. It is always to the advantage of the holders of capital that law and order shall prevail; the anarchy that ensues upon the break-up of settled rule is fatal to accumulations. Capital makes, therefore, for conservatism of viewpoint; it is "the have-nots" who are discontented with conditions under which success eludes them.

The possession of capital works over characteristically into the general societal structure by way of the debt-relation. Those who have no capital must borrow from those who have, either to live at all, or in hope of better things, or to attain some essential

[33] Schurz, in *Deut. Geog. Blätter,* XX, I, 58.
[34] Homer, *Odyssey,* I, 391-393.
[35] Von Pfeil, *Südsee,* 68; Danks, in JAI, XVII, 309.
[36] Niblack, in USNM, 1888, 251.

of respectability such as a wife or membership in the secret society, or otherwise to preserve or elevate their standard of living. To induce the loan some present must be given, which is the germ of interest.

In the Upper Congo region "to ask for and expect interest on a loan was very strongly condemned by all; but if a person in difficulty promised 150 [metal] rods in return for a loan of 100, nothing was said, as it was not regarded as interest but as a gift for help in difficulty. Of course no one had rods to spare until such a promise was given."[37] Sometimes a loan may be forced upon a stranger or even a comrade, which he must accept unless he wishes to offend the lender[38]—a case alignable with mutual gift-giving.

If, now, mischance attends the borrower, or if he is sluggish and careless, he speedily falls into a subordinate position to the lender, which may vary all the way from a shadowy clientage or retainership to plain slavery.[39] It needs but a slight acquaintance with primitive interest-rates to see that there was but small chance of repayment. In the case of the Batak, "anyone who borrows a hundred florins has two hundred to pay at the end of a year, four hundred at the end of two years, and so on."[40] Even among peoples of a higher grade of civilization, rates were very high.[41] Hence the prevalence and hopelessness of debt-slavery. It turns speedily into a status from which the debtor has no expectation of emerging. So eager was a man to get back his capital that, undeterred by considerations that prevailed under kin-group solidarity, he seized the debtor's person or the offspring of his body. Thus the entrance of capital into the societal organization produces a change of status in its members which is to all intents and purposes as permanent as if it had been brought about by war and conquest. Though the subject of slavery is to be taken up more generally elsewhere,[42] a few instances of the debt-relation are in place here.

In New Britain, if the borrower is a young man, and has borrowed to buy a wife, or if someone has bought a wife for him, he is somewhat at the bidding of the lender until the obligation is paid.[43] Among the Igorrotes of Luzon

37 Weeks, in JAI, XXXIX, 422.
38 Ratzel, *Vkde.*, II, 267 (Banks Isl.).
39 Consider the case of the *ambil-anak* marriage, in §363, below.
40 Wilken, *Vkde.*, 423.   41 Letourneau, *Prop.*, 355-358.
42 Ch. XIII, §105, below.   43 Danks, in JAI, XVII, 309.

there are debtor-slaves, who pay by labor.[44] Two-thirds of the Yakuts are in debt, and one-third so hopelessly that every year's income is swallowed up in the interest due the rich.[45] In the time of Jeremiah, there were many Israelitish slaves who had got into this sad situation by reason of their debts.[46] Among certain Nilotic tribes defaulting debtors are enlisted in the standing army.[47]

Further, it is not the borrower alone who runs a risk of enslavement: his fellows may be enslaved for his debts; there is here a group-solidarity in responsibility.[48]

Among the Guinea Coast tribes the creditor has the right to demand payment in full, at any time, and without notice. If the debtor cannot pay, the creditor may seize him, or his family, or slaves, and sell them.[49] In Togo, "it is customary in general, and is in a certain sense the law, that the creditor may hold the relatives of the debtor until the obligation is settled, as surety—that is, as slaves."[50]

Thus a good deal is made of the debt-relation, a fact which witnesses to a lively interest in capital and property. The debtor was sometimes a malefactor, to be punished, on occasion by death.[51]

"The Aryan debtor also, like the malefactor, was fastened to the post till he redeemed himself by payment of the debt, either personally or by his friends. Thus it was ordained, the thief and other debtors being put on a par with him. It was a cruel means of pressure, and cruelty was its primary object. There he stood, unable to move, exposed day and night to all weathers—burning heat by day, cold by night, and rain—and no doubt the creditor, or, if more than one, each one of them, had full license to slake their vengeance by flogging him, without taking into account the amount of the debt; and if his friends did not compassionately supply him with food and drink he must assuredly have starved. This explains the 'thousand deaths' of the man at the stake; the most terrible view we get of the Aryans."[52]

There may be interpolated at this point a singular case of intertribal indebtedness resulting from a peculiar style of payment for mutual tribal services. The relation operates not unlike *commercium* and *connubium* to form a reciprocal obligation leading to contacts and transfer of culture.

"The completion of certain masks used by chiefs in dancing, the building of a canoe, the erection of a totem, and of a house, calls for a feast, the primary

[44] Blumentritt, *Igorroten*, 93.
[45] Sieroshevski-Sumner, in JAI, XXXI, 426.
[46] Jer., ch. XXXIV; Buhl, *Israeliten*, 102.
[47] Ratzel, *Vkde.*, I, 462.   [48] §§176 ff., 274, below.
[49] Ellis, *Tshi*, 300.   [50] Klose, *Togo*, 210.
[51] Ratzel, *Vkde.*, I, 83.
[52] Ihering, *Evol. of the Aryan*, 54-55.

purpose being to pay those who did the work. These items are tribal property, and all tribal property must be made, built or erected by those of another tribe than the one owning them. This is the process of Thlinget settlement. They are perfectly satisfied with this method, though they must wait months or even years before a feast can be given and a settlement effected. While they do not keep books, yet every one remembers accurately what is due him until he has been paid, no matter how long the settlement is put off. The women, especially, keep tab on every one under any obligations to their families."[53]

The topic of intra-group class-distinction as based on capital works out, in later times, into ranges where the phenomena are far less simple, clean-cut, and concrete; the modern issues, nevertheless, follow the lines of the primitive ones, and exhibit the function of capital as persisting upon its original path. Among other revelations derivable from a review of the industrial organization as it operates to produce social distinctions, is the conviction that it promises no satisfaction at all to sullen envy or rancorous discontent. None has been vouchsafed. It has been provided only that those who yield to such passions in destroying others shall destroy themselves. There is no promise of satisfaction to the most honorable ambition for a better social status save through the formation of capital, which will always be an individual rather than a class-achievement. Those who are fond of talking about "social problems" make their initial error in consenting to discuss capital-accumulation, with its accompanying rise of status, as a class-problem. Classes as classes do not rise. Variation is in the hands of the individual. Individuals rise; and if we say that a class has risen we mean only that many individuals of it have come up in the world. The wage-receiver has his advantage over the slave or the serf in being able to employ his labor as he judges best for his own interest, and to accumulate capital for himself. If an individual of that class wants to escape from its disadvantages and uncertainties, he can do so only by the same processes which we have seen operative in the whole industrial history of mankind—by migration or the acquisition of capital. If he is to acquire capital, he can do that only by the same methods which have been always used: by restraining his consumption below the capital distributed to him in wages, saving the difference, and winning its assistance for continued labor. He possesses, in the modern indus-

[53] Jones, *Thlingets*, 137-138.

trial system, one high advantage, namely, that he is not utterly bound up with the fate of his class, so far as that is affected by an increase of population within it.

Sentimentalists speak of the "laboring classes" as if there were really some such category, strictly and permanently marked off from all others. They lay little stress upon the indispensability of capital to any improvement in the position of any man. They regard the laborers as a class which must exist, consist of the same elements, and move as a whole. They represent it as having no responsibilities of its own or for itself, but as possessing claims and constituting a burden for somebody else. It is not strange, if such views are disseminated, that there should be an increase in the number of those who marry without forethought or provision, consume their earnings in common luxuries, declaim about their rights, and wait to be taken care of by the state (which can mean only by those who have been industrious and prudent), while they repeat the philosophy that nothing is true which is disagreeable, and that a man has a natural right to everything he wants. If someone comes forward and complains that any law or institution of society bears unjustly on him, and that he has a grievance, he is entitled to prompt attention and redress. But if he sets up a general arraignment of nature because she has made life too hard, so that he is not competent to cope with it, he cannot call upon his fellow-men for redress as for a right. The most that can be demanded is that the laws of life be fairly and patiently explained to him, and the means of self-help, so far as the efforts of men have availed to discover them, be set before his intelligence. More than this lies in the province of the poet and romancer; it is not within the range of the scientist.

It is here that we have to observe the connection of one generation with the next, which the popular notions in fashion for the last century have obscured. If a man has been prudent, temperate, and virtuous, his highest reward is to see his children grow up in health and vigor of body and mind, and to be able to secure them against the harshest hardships of life through the capital which he has saved. If he has been vicious, idle, and extravagant, his heaviest penalty is to see the fruits of his vices in the diseases, weakness, or misery of his children, and to realize that they will be left upon the lowest level of opportunity to live out their years or to make a career. The love of children acts as one of the strongest motives to industry and economy, and for the right-minded it must also act as a restraint on vice and a stimulus to virtue. It is the chief interest under which the race keeps up a continuous aggression, in its successive generations, against the natural obstacles to development. As an industrial force it ranks among the highest and strongest, and the state sees itself obliged, in its own interest, to guarantee bequests and inheritance.

§84. Production-Capital. Labor, because it presents itself in objective form, as a natural necessity, is more readily understandable than is capital. The latter is more remote, derived, and secondary and so more open to misconception. Yet the two are always closely interlocked, whether that embrace be the clinch of mortal antagonism, the formal salute of dissimulated suspicion, or the rare clasp of friendly coöperation. Some perspective of this agelong interrelation will appear as certain later phases of the evolution of capital are reviewed.

Whether or not man began his course in regions where nature provided abundant resources, multiplication must sooner or later have driven him into areas where such abundance was not to be enjoyed. If then he were to get time to fashion a tool or weapon, he must either work longer hours for a time to collect food enough for his support while engaged on that task, or go hungry while so employed—in either case, for the sake of a foreseen advantage. The lowest races show most distinctly the aim of man, according to his knowledge and ability, to lower the amount of effort expended upon the satisfaction of the needs by which he finds himself beset in life. Violence and accident apart, this aim could be accomplished only by labor and self-denial in the face of present good for the sake of future good. This process has made headway by the smallest stages, unconsciously and under necessity. If a store of goods has been reserved from present consumption, its employment performs a special function: when consumed it is transmuted, as it were, into a weapon or tool which, although it cannot itself be eaten, worn, or otherwise directly applied to the satisfaction of animal need, yet raises its possessor to a higher grade of security in living. Such an important function in a stock of goods so used, and in the product of that use, differentiates it from the goods daily consumed to satisfy needs directly and finally.

The time has now come to differentiate to some degree the two forms of capital to which allusion has earlier been made.[54] These

[54] §55, above.

are subsistence-capital and production-capital. The latter is a
development out of the former that accompanies advancing organization and progressive success in the struggle for societal
self-maintenance. It might be said to appear in marked form only
after the struggle for existence has passed into the struggle for a
standard of living. Capital comes eventually to differ from what
it has been on the lowest stages in the way in which it is employed.
This new form of utilization consists in sustaining the laborer
during continued labor, not during idleness. Such labor is expended in a manner involving a certain delay or an extended
period of industry to secure the product in view; though the
capital-goods are consumed just as other goods are, the result is
not simply to sustain life during the period but to perpetuate, in
another form, the surplus once accumulated. There must be a
stock of capital, and its accumulation involves industry without
present reward, that is, again, self-denial. The final outcome is a
great gain in the struggle for self-maintenance, which must be regarded as a reward, in the natural order of things, for the self-
denial that has been practised. The possessor of such production-
capital enjoys an immense advantage in the competition of life
over any who have not similar resources.

When capital comes to be a product of labor, reserved from
mere enjoyment, and used to assist production, we are already
somewhat removed from the primitive stage. This is the form of
capital which most deeply interests the economist, and we have no
intention of trenching upon his analysis of it. What we wish to
show here is that, although this form is characteristic of a more
developed organization, nevertheless its germs are to be made out
upon earlier stages of societal evolution. It is not characteristic
of them; in a sense, the distinction between the two types of capital is not in itself, upon the primitive stages, of enough importance to call for much attention; but because production-capital
is of such significance in more highly developed societies it is desirable to exhibit its beginnings. It is possible to observe its presence and gradual growth through the now familiar "stages of
societal self-maintenance."

§85. Capital among Hunters, Herders, and Tillers.[55] So soon as the men of a community were generally supplied with weapons, the hunting economy appeared. Under it, capital, albeit undergoing a great extension and diversification, remained obtainable only by the same processes as before, with the single addition that capital already won could be used as a means for its own further development. Division of labor and organization were at the same time advanced. Population, so long as it was below the limit of the hunting economy, increased rapidly and was vigorous and prosperous. Its approach to that limit was marked by decrease in game and by a less well sustained existence for the tribe. Wars, disease, and migrations continually opened gaps which were, however, steadily filled. Tribes found themselves jostled against one another and engaged in struggles in which the weaker perished or were driven off the hunting-grounds. Then came the domestication of animals as a transition to a new economy.

Beasts kept in herds furnished steady supplies of food without the fitful exertion, the alternate surplus and want, of the hunting stage. Capital was extended to include the herds, and there was a corresponding development of weapons, utensils, and the rest. It is on this stage that the element of care and self-denial in the formation of capital is especially striking: for the animals demanded attention by day and night, had to be moved from one water-supply to another and from pasture to pasture, and must be particularly attended to at the time of breeding. Population once more underwent rapid and vigorous increase, and gradually the elements of care and self-denial advanced to high and stringent degrees. The decisive point was reached when the grazing-grounds were so occupied that it was difficult to change often enough to get pasturage sufficient to keep the herds up to full vigor and fecundity. Human care must then economize to the utmost what there was, and must prevent waste and loss with anxious concern. Once again, at length, a situation is reached where migrations, involving war, are necessary, or else another advance in culture must be won.

This last step is found in the settlement of the population in fixed abodes, with food taken directly, by tillage, from the earth.

[55] §§29 ff., above.

Here is the agricultural stage, with possibilities that have not yet been exhausted. On this stage, the most significant development of capital is in seed for successive crops and in food to sustain labor during cultivation. The period of production is now long and the delay in restoring capital corresponds. Capital, in the two forms mentioned, is absolutely essential to life, on this stage; the whole stock produced on earlier stages, in food-supply, tools, utensils, and gear, is strained to support the advance. Permanent dwellings are now substituted for tents, and towns are built. The first rude tillage of the soil by implements such as existed on the previous stages is so painful that new tools, constituting a new development of capital, are invented for new needs. Beasts of burden had been used before, but now that an increased force is needed in tilling, it is attained by the fuller utilization and training of animals. As different stretches of land produce with advantage different crops, roads become necessary for transportation, and commerce extends. Vehicles are invented and improved.

However great and complicated the developments of capital, up to the latest refinements, it presents the same phenomena as already described. It is found in the same way, applied in the same way, costs the same abstinence and self-denial, and confers advantages of the same sort. These last make the product greater where capital is used than where it is not used. An increase of product furnishes profits on capital. If land could produce at best a crop no greater than the seed, or if a man could raise as large a crop by cultivating land with his fingers as by employing a hoe or plow, there would be no profits. It is because the natural facts are otherwise that a part of the product falls to capital. As we go from herding to tillage an acre of land bears more rent. When tillage is possible it is the advance in rent that forces advance in cultivation. Land often requires artificial irrigation or the destruction of growing trees or the drainage of swamps; and the artificial appliances for such purposes, whose invention is gradually forced because the necessary amount of land to support a growing population cannot otherwise be obtained, are another development of capital. They involve sustained taboo and self-denial and cannot be repaid in one season's crop.

Capital makes also for property-rights.[56] The advantage in the competition of life accruing from its possession cannot be enjoyed unless there is an exclusive ownership of the capital. Acquisition arouses the envy and covetousness of those who have not and who dread the process of acquiring. Here arises the conception of property-rights, which we find developed as to chattels among the most primitive tribes of which we have knowledge. The authority and force of the community follows the developments of the natural facts and forces and gives sanction to them. Communities, coerced into solidarity by the struggle with other groups, plundered and robbed each other, but short experience proved that the necessity of internal unity, if there were to be external strength, must forbid the attempt of one man within the group to take things from another.

After a certain period of common property in land, the need of applying capital in increased amounts to assist cultivation, in order to supply increasing numbers, and the impossibility of persuading anyone to save and apply capital unless he could be assured the use of the land for a long period, led to private property in land. It was impossible otherwise to obtain from the land a sufficient supply of food. There was also an effect upon social status; for as population increased the descendants of the first appropriator could not live upon the land which had supported him and his. However much men might improve the means of cultivation, sooner or later this point must be reached. If land was divided and subdivided from generation to generation, the share of the inheritor, at last insufficient to support his existence, would have to be sold, and so new aggregates would be formed. This produced a landless class and constituted what has been discovered in recent times to be "the social problem," although it is only the old crisis which we have seen on all the earlier stages, in a new form. The remedy is not altered; it consists in migration or in a higher organization of society.

§86. **Services of Capital.** Those who have labor and self-denial behind them are not situated in life as those are who have labor and self-denial before them, any more than those who are strong

[56] §§123, 124, below.

and well are situated as those are who are diseased and ill. The difference is based on natural facts which are as positive and clear as any physical facts, and it is interwoven with the whole industrial, social, and moral fabric of society. The notion that birth into one or another set of social circumstances is an accident is one of the strangest that ever won wide assent. If a certain man begets a son, the circumstances of nationality, social environment, industrial surroundings, family-relationships, physical perfections and imperfections, traits of character, special appetites, traditions and faiths, philosophy of life, and all the rest into which a child is born, are all determined by the position in which the father has placed himself and by the relations which he has formed. They are different for the son of that father from what they would be for the son of this one. For a father, then, to overlook all this, is to put himself singularly out of the correct point of view for appreciating the responsibilities of life.

Capital has raised organization to ever higher degrees of complexity and efficiency. It has set men free in the only sense in which they are free—as a man standing by an engine which is doing his work for him is free—and it has emancipated women, in so far as they have been emancipated, from the drudgery that was their lot. Whatever diminishes capital works against societal welfare, for capital is the fund that pays the cost of existence. It staves off poverty, pauperism, neglect of children, ignorance, and, to some extent, vice. The question as to what we can do is answered by the question as to how much capital we have.

As the capital is constantly consumed and reproduced, it can be redistributed in successive periods of production. The marriage-rate rises or falls with the amount of subsistence-capital, so that capital of that type is a demand for men[57] and causes an increase in population. When there is a change in the distribution of capital so that subsistence-capital is transmuted into machines, it is withdrawn from the demand for men. Wages fall, the marriage-rate is lowered, and population declines. Later the machines increase subsistence-capital in an enormous ratio and produce a counter-movement. In our own time these efforts have overlapped and been confused. The constant introduction of machines has

[57] Sumner, *Coll. Ess.*, III, 109 ff.

given to this period the character of a constant increase of sus-
sistence-capital, advance in wages, demand for men, and growth
of population. Especially has the demand for men followed the
line set by the increase of machinery.

We have now noted the two main factors of the organization for
societal self-maintenance, namely, labor and capital; and have
observed how deeply and diversely they penetrate into one another
and into the general life of society. Especially in regard to capital
does it appear that its first accumulation by the race must have
been through processes so long and painful as to surpass and baffle
imagination. No true conception of society's maintenance organization can be gained without constantly reckoning with this pair
of factors, both in themselves and in their bearings and outreachings. When account has been taken of them, the broadest outlines
of the industrial organization are identified; to fill in this framework with detail would take many volumes.

CHAPTER VIII

THE APPROPRIATION OF ENERGIES: FIRE

§87. The Technique of Self-Maintenance. This book has to do with matters of societal organization rather than with mechanism or apparatus; still the outlines of the maintenance-organization must be filled in with enough detail to suggest its substance. The functions in organization of labor and capital have been surveyed; the question now arises as to what is actually done in effecting adjustment between societies and their life-conditions. This leads to the consideration of the mechanism or apparatus of self-maintenance; to inventions or findings, in the broadest sense, including implements, methods, processes, economies, and so on. The only way to present these with any fullness would be to embark upon the making of a sort of encyclopædia of technology, touching upon everything from architecture to yam-culture. This is impossible; to cover the subject of pottery-making alone would take several volumes. What we are going to do is, first of all, to stick to the undeveloped forms of maintenance-apparatus; then, into or across these we propose to sink three shafts, as geologists penetrate strata to get samples, or make three cross-cuts, hoping thus to display in its essentials the type of invention and craftsmanship developed by less sophisticated men in dealing with their material life-conditions. The three achievements chosen as typical of maintenance-adjustments will be the utilization of fire, the domestication of animals, and the enslavement of men.

In the last analysis the activity of mankind in relation to nature consists in the discovery, appropriation, and transformation of that which exists in nature.[1] The forms of natural or "raw" energy upon which man has drawn, to transform them into that which is useful for the preservation of his life and the furthering of his projects, have been classified by an eminent chemist[2] into the following five categories: mechanical energies, heat, light, electric and magnetic energies, and chemical energies. For those whose

[1] §52, above; Keller, *Starting-Points,* chs. IV, V.
[2] Ostwald, *Energet. Grundlagen,* 13-14.

interest is concerned mainly with the early phases of the industrial organization, the last of these types is the most significant. Chemical energy, as Ostwald[3] remarks, is of greater manifoldness than the other forms and is associated with ponderable bodies; it is more easily stored and transported and—a fact of great import to our study—is the form of energy upon which all organisms, including man, are entirely dependent for all their activities. Ostwald, whose theory is that the relation of society to the energies in nature is its fundamental relation, goes on to show that human systems and economies of one kind and another are directed toward the maximum use, or to the minimum waste and neutralization, of these several nature-given resources. The essence of this contention may be expressed in a form more appropriate to our subject, namely, that all other and more derived mores and institutions of society are determined by the type of the industrial organization;[4] for the latter is the basic organization in the pursuit of the struggle for existence.

The appropriation of chemical energies is to be illustrated by the three examples announced above, in which the derivation is, respectively, from the inorganic, the organic, and the human world. From fire, beasts, and fellow-men are appropriated forms of energy which "lie outside the epidermis" of those who use them, and are available, to use the terminology of physics, for all sorts of "work."[5] It is primarily in connection with the discovery, appropriation, and transformation of such nature-forces that men perform, in association, those characteristic mental adaptations to environment by which societal self-maintenance is assured.

It is necessary here to digress briefly on a matter of presentation as adopted in this book. In this chapter and the two following will be sketched the appropriation of three forms of energy out of nature, together with some account of how they have been utilized. The occasion is offered thereby to extend our treatment of institutions "laterally" as well as forward and back. What is meant by this is as follows. For the purpose of comprehending and presenting a complex whole, it has been necessary to divide societal institutions into several categories, the chief of which are the industrial, regulative, religious, and marital.[6] In the main, an analysis must take these up one by one, and

[3] *Energet. Grundlagen*, 19-20; 111 ff.
[4] §21, above.
[5] Ostwald, *Energet. Grundlagen*, 82; Mason, in USNM, 1894, 239.
[6] Ch. III, above.

separately, starting each time with the earlier members of each evolutionary series and advancing, as it were longitudinally, along the line of development toward the later members. We cannot do otherwise than cover one set of institutions at a time and carry it through its series, without much attention to other series that really run laterally or side by side with it, as, for instance, marriage runs parallel with property. Such sections of the societal structure may be set apart from one another for purposes of study and exposition, but, as has been indicated before, the apprehension of the mutual interlacing and interdependence of them all is to the investigator one of his most enlightening results, as well as, perhaps, his most formidable revelation as to the difficult nature of his enterprise. Wherever opportunity presents itself, perhaps both in and out of season, we shall seek to bring these separated lines of institutional development into connection by a sort of lateral tying-up process, so that the student may not fail to realize that the strands which have been held apart and viewed one by one really intertwine and even blend with one another to form a single living whole. There must be cross-strands, or woof, along with those of the warp, if the fabric and its pattern are to be made out truly, as a whole.

Therefore, while the topics chosen to illustrate the concrete aspects of the maintenance-organization will be treated in their economic bearings, they will also be followed directly into their religious, political, or other phases. For while the bulk of any topic taken up in this book falls within one or another of our main divisions, there is no subject whatever that is wholly economic, or familial, or political, that is, without its relations to all the other sets of mores and institutions. Says Lippert,[7] on the occasion of an anticipatory reference to the function of fire in religion: "In the history of civilization threads of all kinds interlace. No one can be followed up without touching a number of others, and we cannot sever any single portion of the web without sacrificing insight into the course of the separate strands. That nearly every strand which we can directly follow leads us into a mesh of social relations is a fact that will be less surprising to the reader than that we can so seldom advance for a space without falling into the purlieus of cult or religious ideas." Minor "lateral" allusions will appear regularly in this book, in foot-note cross-references chiefly; and now and then there will be a topic, like the one before us, which can be utilized to afford a deliberate and wider cross-sectional view.

§88*. The "Taming of Fire." Among examples of this process of energy-appropriation, another can scarcely be found which is so far-reaching in its consequences as is, to use Lippert's[8] expression, the "taming of fire." It is selected as an example of appropriation from the inorganic world. The use of fire is very ancient and, so far as direct evidence goes, universal; no tribes have been found which have preserved any clear remembrance of its introduction, and even legendary materials afford but vague indications on this score.

[7] *Kgchte.*, I, 278.　　　　[8] *Kgchte.*, I, 250.

The Yakuts told Sieroshevski of peoples on islands in the Arctic Sea who did not have fire;[9] and the natives of Tasmania were at one time supposed by colonists to be unacquainted with it.[10] This type of "evidence" is about all that can be found in ethnographic works. Concerning certain Papuan tribes it is reported:

"They told me that they well remembered the time when they baked without pots. . . . In my questioning I at length succeeded in bringing out the fact that the present inhabitants of the Maclay coast still know through tradition of the time when they had as yet no fire. It is very peculiar and very interesting that the same thing was told me in different localities."[11]

Isolated reports of this nature may be of a certain significance, but when it comes to actual observation, it is certain that over the whole earth no fireless tribe of men has been found.[12] The diluvial man had it, and even knew how to generate it,[13] and the lowest of historic or contemporary tribes possess it, even though they do not own any fire-making apparatus. Man is scarcely man till he is in possession of fire; or, to put it in another way, when man got control of fire, a chasm was opened between him and all other creatures which was never closed again.[14]

There are many climates in which man could not possibly have come to dwell without this element; in its absence his habitat could include only tropical regions, and not all of these. Hence the wideness of man's dispersal, unparalleled in the geographical distribution of organisms, must be regarded as one of the results of the discovery and appropriation of fire. Further, since it is in the cooler regions only that the necessary conditions for the development and accumulation of civilization have been found to exist, it is fair to say that the use of fire has been a precondition to the rise of culture. That is, the feat of adaptation represented by this basic "invention" has drawn in its train a sequence of feats whose possibility lay in the initial conquest.

Some wish to go still farther back on the evolutionary trail and to refer the physical development of *Homo,* and in particular the differentiation of function between hand and foot, the importance of which has been so often emphasized,[15] in good part to the use of fire. Certainly one of the prime needs

9 Sieroshevski-Sumner, in JAI, XXXI, 654.

10 Roth, *Tasmania,* 96.

11 Miklucho-Maclay, in *Berl. Ztsft. für Ethnol.,* XV, 574, quoted in Hagen, *Papua's,* 204.

12 Kl. Nachr., in *Globus,* XCIII, 162.   13 Ranke, *Mensch,* II, 433.

14 Lippert, *Kgchte.,* I, 250; Starcke, *Prim. Family,* 257.

15 Tylor, *Anth.,* 42 ff.

of man, living amidst a hostile and physically better endowed animal environ-ment, was protection in the inevitable struggle for existence. It seems that such protection was to be attained in good part, as it is still attained by most primates, through an arboreal life. Tree-dwellings, indeed, are not unheard of in the reports of modern ethnographers. It is likewise true that the erect posture of man, that followed upon the specialization of hand and foot, could scarcely have developed apart from sojourn upon the flat ground-surface. What allowed him to descend to the earth made him what he then became. But there was only one element in nature, mastery over which enabled men to spend the night as well as the day upon the earth-surface, and that was fire; for it is universally feared by animals and dazes them. Hence with the posses-sion of fire there came to man, or to his precursor, that possibility of a terres-trial existence which drew after it significant structural changes, extending by way of the hand and its power of manipulation even to the brain, which are now recognized as specifically human.[16]

§89. Utilities of Fire.

In considering utilities of a more re-stricted order—those, at any rate, which are found capable of being prized by nature-peoples—it is astonishing, at first sight, to note that the effectiveness of fire in the arts, or for cooking, or even for protection from the wild beasts, is not that which appeals most strongly to the primitive man. What seems to him of sur-passing importance is the service of fire in its relation to the imaginary environment; for, though his universe is peopled with perils that belong to the natural world, these are slight in com-parison with those inhering in the supernatural.[17] The light and, to some extent, the heat of fire are regarded as most efficacious agencies in dealing with the ghosts and spirits;[18] the flame is thought to be effective where the most perfect of weapons are of no avail. Within the circle of fire-light there is a semblance of day, while without are night and its shapes and "voices."

Examples abound. The Samoans are afraid of the spirits at night unless the fires are burning;[19] the Eskimo keep their train-oil lamps burning all night on account of superstitious fears.[20] The Hyperboreans use fire for light, mak-ing scarcely any attempt to secure heat from it.[21] Chinese servants refuse to sleep unless a lamp burns in the room all night. An employer states that he "has not equipped his servants' quarters with electricity because a small kero-sene lamp is vastly cheaper than electric lighting."[22] In Chaldæa, man was

[16] Lippert, *Kgchte.*, I, 69.   [17] §§201, 236, 243, below.

[18] §§227, 317, below; examples in Harvey, *Chinese Animism;* De Groot, *Relig. Syst.*, VI, *passim.*

[19] Ella, in AAAS, 1892, 644.   [20] Nansen, *Esk. Life*, 81.

[21] Reclus, *Prim. Folk*, 30.

[22] Personal communication from Professor Harvey.

supposed to need, in his war against the evil spirits, every help he could get. Fire was his most efficacious ally, the greatest enemy of the evil spirits; for it put them to flight and dissipated their power. The Chaldæan never moved a step except in fear of them, especially at night, and even in his own house.[23]

This quality of fire will appear, over and over again, in different connections. No adequate idea of the place of fire in primitive life can be gained without a realization of its significance in that which has to do with the supernatural.

Concerning the other utilities of fire, there is found among primitive peoples, as should be expected from the above and on general principles, no perspective of their relative importance. The use of artificial heat for warming the body, which is, in many localities, even decisive for existence, receives the attention usually accorded to the matter-of-course. If the Sudanese negroes are accustomed to carry, on cold mornings or after a rain, a burning piece of wood with which they warm the body now in this place and now in that,[24] this is merely a very crude form of an everyday usage. Utilities of fire in the arts, later developed as they are, and more novel, appeal to the savage mind with greater force. If the developing utilities of fire in the industrial organization are examined in the light of science, they are seen to have been of the highest significance, both in their immediate results and in the series of societal consequences which they set in motion. Take the function of fire in connection with food.

Of surpassing significance was the employment of fire in cooking. The possession of the art is regarded by the savages themselves as a mark of distinction, and the term "raw-flesh-eaters" is a term of contempt. Thucydides refers to the backwood tribes of interior Greece as "Omophagoi" (Raw-Eaters).[25] The earliest cooking, of course, scarcely deserves the name; the African Bushmen simply throw their meat into the fire, leaving it there only long enough to get the taste of burning.[26] It is thought that the significance of a crude cooking process, like the habitual consumption of raw flesh, betokens a fireless ancestry at no remote age.[27] Cooking, however, even in its cruder stages, meant the liberation of human energy, through the lessening of the demands upon its

23 Maspero, *Hist. Anc.*, I, 635.   24 Junker, *Afrika*, I, 330.
25 Tylor, *Anth.*, 265; Thucydides, *Hist.*, III, 94; Keller, *Soc. Evol.*, 59-60.
26 Ratzel, *Vkde.*, I, 64.   27 McGee, in BAE, XVII, pt. I, 189.

store, for purposes less immediate than the mere preservation of existence. Cooking amounts to a sort of predigestion. It breaks up and softens foods to a greater degree than milling or even chewing. Although cooked food may be less digestible than raw, under the conditions of the modern cuisine, in earlier times the raising of the temperature of the food, as well as the division of it into more minute particles, amounted to a shortening of all processes preceding intestinal assimilation.

It is plain that this meant the freeing of vital energy for other things than digestion; and such a result was naturally most salutary, as well as revolutionary, in the primitive days of rough and indiscriminate diet. The Australians, for example, have exhibited revolting performances in the line of gorging raw blubber to such repletion that they lay helpless and in agony, or comatose, while digestion was arduously going on.[28] In such case there was not much energy left over for higher activities. With the better preparation of food and the shortening of the assimilative process, there must have come more frequently recurring opportunity for those mental adjustments through inventions of various sorts which are the bases of civilization. This is one of the most significant services of fire to man. The custom of cooking food, in its very universality, shows an unmistakable survival-value.

In connection with the cooking appear also the well-known processes of preservation through smoking and drying. It is an evidence of progress in thrift, as well as a stimulus to further advance, when stores against the future can be thus deliberately and successfully laid aside. The service of heat in food-preservation has been known from very primitive times; the discoveries of a Pasteur along this line are direct descendants of the primitive ones.

Cooking undoubtedly led to the lessening of infant mortality and probably to an increase in the birth-rate; for it provided food better adapted to young children, especially at the age of weaning, and probably also shortened the nursing-period, so that the strain on the mothers was lightened. This meant not alone the enlargement of the original group but, as the result of increased man-power, its extension by incorporation of other groups; and it is

[28] Letourneau, *Soc.*, chs. II, III; Mason, *Invention*, 103.

out of numbers and the contact of numbers that higher civilization, that is, a more apt set of adjustments, arises. Hence on both
counts, by the liberation of energy and the increase of numbers,
the utilization of fire has proved itself of great significance. It
has permitted of the growth of population also through its connection with the arts. In hunting, the grass was set on fire to assist
the chase; in agriculture, brand-tillage was common[29] and fire
was widely used in the separation of chaff and grain; in the
mechanical arts, it was indispensable. In the working of wood,
horn, and bone it was the agency used to harden and bend. It
supplemented the axe in felling trees and hollowing out their
trunks to make dug-outs; it "opened the door of the primitive
races to the use of metals"; it lengthened the working-hours by its
light; it had its uses in war—it was, in short, practically universal and all-pervasive in its contribution to self-maintenance. A
moment's reflection will reveal its indispensability to modern civilization. The "taming of fire" was perhaps the most momentous
single "invention" of man.

Turner[30] cites a pair of examples of tree-felling by fire which may illustrate a widespread but not generally familiar process. On Bowditch Island,
"they sometimes burned the trunk of a tree to make it fall, but as the fire
occasionally ran up the heart of a tree and destroyed it all, they usually cut
away at the trunk with their shell hatchets, day after day, until it fell. It
took ten, fifteen, and thirty days to fell a tree. Another plan was to dig down
and cut the roots." In contrast with these islanders, the New Caledonians,
using a slow fire close to the ground, felled their trees in four days. They
"burned off the branches also, and, if for a canoe or house-post, the length
of log required. If for a canoe, they cut a hole in the surface of the log,
kindled a small fire, and burned down and along, carefully drop, drop, drop-
ping water all around, to confine the fire to a given spot; and in this way they
hollowed out their logs for the largest canoes." The Bowditch islanders used
the same method in hollowing buckets out of solid blocks of wood.

§90. "Keeping" Fire. When all these and many more detailed
utilities of fire have been listed, the conception of its importance
to society is not yet complete. It entered as a major factor of
existence, allowing no disfavor of climate to limit the distribution
of mankind but permitting the higher development of vigorous
races in the less hospitable regions; and since its use was universal,
its effects could not have been less than universal. Even aside from

29 Tylor, *Anth.*, 218.   30 *Samoa*, 270, 343.

the momentous rôle it played in religion, its influence is to be traced throughout the whole societal structure. To understand some of its earlier societal effects it is necessary to realize that it was utilized long before it could be artificially generated. There must be no confusion between three distinct things: the knowledge of fire, the use of fire, and the production of fire. Evidence goes to show that, even after generative processes were known, the flame was guarded carefully from going out; any survival, such as "perpetual fire," points back to a time when preservation of the vital spark was a powerful incentive to watchfulness and forethought.[31]

Thus the Andamanese, not knowing any way of producing fire, show much care and skill in avoiding its loss; "if more than a few hours' absence is anticipated on a hunting or fishing expedition, in addition to the supply of provisions, some one takes a smouldering log, which he is expected to keep burning, and to kindle into a blaze whenever it is required."[32] Certain of the Papuans have no means of generating fire. "In the huts, therefore, there were always preserved the live coals of a very slow-burning wood, so that in a Papuan village the fire next to never goes out. However, should that happen, the coast-dwellers of this region fetch fire from the mountain villages, whose inhabitants understand the art of fire-making." Brands were always carried along on the march.[33] Similarly in East Africa, "one meets constantly with scattered pieces of extinguished charcoal which show that the path is much frequented by the natives; for they, not having matches, are obliged to keep the fire always lighted in order to give it to one another, blowing on it constantly and carrying it thus from place to place."[34] And it is rather startling to find Homer,[35] who nowhere mentions a method of fire-generation, when he is casting about for a simile calculated to convey the exceeding care with which Odysseus hid himself in fallen leaves, hitting upon the scrupulous covering of the "seed of fire." "As when one hides a brand in black ashes—one who dwells on a far-away field with no neighbors—saving the seed of fire, so that he may not have to kindle from some other source, thus did Odysseus cover himself with leaves."

It must not be thought that the anxious preservation of fire always goes with absence of the art of generation. The latter is often a very tedious process, especially in damp weather.[36] In any

[31] This aspect of fire is developed by Lippert, *Kgchte.*, I, 259-279.

[32] Man, in JAI, XII, 150, 357.

[33] Finsch, *Samoafahrten*, 47; Finsch, *Ethnol. Erfahr.*, II, 62; Hagen, *Papua's*, 204.

[34] Vanutelli e Citerni, *L'Omo*, 315-316.

[35] *Odyssey*, V, 488-491; XX, 123.

[36] Hough, in USNM, 1888 and 1890, presents a full survey of this topic.

case, the advantage of preserving the flame, however got, could not fail to impress even a rudimentary intelligence.

Though the African Pygmies understand the generation of fire, yet with their primitive appliances they have great difficulty in getting it, and therefore keep one going all the time. They set fire to some large trunk, which they keep smoldering for months.[37] On the west coast of Australia, the best way the native has of preserving fire is in the so-called fire-sticks, the dark brown, velvety-looking center of Banksia stalks, which is very retentive of fire and burns slowly. These sticks are about eight inches long, and a bag of them will last all day.[38] Among the Herero, the friction-process was always onerous, and the flame was carefully guarded, its custodian being the daughter of the household. If the fire went out, it was regarded as an omen of ill fortune."[39] The Aino require from two to two and one-half hours to make fire with their apparatus; for the Botocudos fire-making is long and laborious; while even among the Pawnees, "sometimes it would take four men to make a fire, one relieving another as they grew tired."[40] The Tupi of Argentina could make fire by friction or percussion, "but they seldom need to, for in their huts the fire never goes out, and they always carry a fire-brand with them in their wanderings."[41] On Easter Island "the method of obtaining fire requires considerable preparation of material and patience on the part of the operator. . . . The difficulty of preserving suitable material in a perfectly dry state led to the custom of keeping up a perpetual fire in each community. . . . The flames were as carefully watched and attended as the celestial fire."[42] Even in Norway, in the sixteenth century, people avoided the trouble of using flint and steel, and went around begging a light.[43]

This matter has been gone into rather fully by way of illustrating the care and responsibility that inhere in the possession of fire, especially during the less familiar period when artificial generation is unknown or when its methods are rude and uncertain. Fire was a recognized advantage "great enough to bow the rebellious factor of human inertia beneath its schooling." It was lucky that a period of fire-keeping preceded the discovery of processes of generation; for the difficulty in getting and preserving fire was a compelling educational factor.[44] Care and education went together; and in the cooler climates anxiety lest the vital possession be lost must have been dominant, impelling to an extra degree of

[37] Burrows, *Pigmies,* 199; Burrows, in JAI, XXVIII, pt. I, 40; Stuhlmann, *Mit Emin,* 452.

[38] Taylor, *Te Ika,* 357.   [39] Fritsch, *Eingeb. S.-Afr.,* 232.

[40] Hough, USNM, 1890, 398; Wied, *Brasilien,* II, 18; Grinnell, *Folk Tales,* 257.

[41] Ambrosetti, in *Globus,* LXXIV, 245.

[42] Thomson, in USNM, 1889, 471, 472.

[43] Lund, *Norges Hist.,* 186.   [44] Lippert, *Kgchte.,* I, 279.

foresight, and coöperating toward the cultural superiority of these latitudes. Whatever imposed emphatically upon the improvident primitive, as fire-preservation did, a care for the future, could not but have exerted a powerful influence upon all his doings, not alone upon his activities in self-maintenance.

The whole fabric of societal life is woven together very closely; the destiny of no single part is independent of that of the rest; but the master-strands go back, as any evolutionist would expect, to the nature of the organization for self-maintenance. In this struggle the possession of fire was of the high importance indicated in preceding passages. Hence it could not but play a significant and far-reaching rôle in all phases of society's life. Fire appears in the field of marriage and the family, of government, and of religion. By reviewing in their most general lines the wider societal consequences of the possession, and especially of the keeping of fire, there may be attained that cross-sectional view of the interlacings of institutions to which allusion was made at the beginning of this chapter.

§91. Fire and Socialization. The necessity of keeping the fire had a direct bearing upon the organization of the primitive family. Traditionally woman has always been the attendant or presiding spirit or priestess of the hearth; and the facts bear out the tradition. Given the natural conditions which rendered woman relatively passive as compared with man, the tending of the fire, in the differentiation of function based upon sex-unlikeness, naturally fell to her. The fire constituted the headquarters of the primitive family, and the hearth has remained the center of the domestic economy through the ages. Fire was of great efficacy, then, in defining the most primitive form of specialization and coöperation, that is, of organization. It follows from the above that the fire and hearth, coming to be the center of the family, were almost synonymous with family-organization.

When an Australian family takes up a new abode, a fire is started before a shelter is built; fire is more important than the hut, and is the real center of family life.[45] Among the Yakuts, "fire is often presented as a protector and as a symbol of the family and the *sib* [kin-group]. A youth who comes to find a wife dare not pass beyond the strip of light, which falls from the household

45 Ratzel, *Vkde.*, II, 49.

fire, to go over on the women's side of the house. This would be improper. The same is true for any other person who does not belong to the family. A betrothed man, until he has paid the whole of the bride-price, has no right even to light his pipe at the fire of his affianced; but a wife brought home to the house of her husband, and taking her place in his family, ought first of all to go around behind the fire and cast into it a little butter or fat, to put three splinters into it, and to blow them to a blaze. In general women ought not, as far as they can avoid it, to pass over the strip of light in front of the fireplace; their domain is behind it."[46] In India, the newly wedded pair formerly "brought to their own home a portion of the sacred fire which witnessed their union and which, when once kindled on their own family hearth, had to be maintained ever afterwards for use in all domestic ceremonies and sacrifices, including the last sacrifice of all, the final burning of their own bodies at death."[47] "The Buryat fears to be without children, and a childless man says sadly, 'The fire of my hearth will go out.' The strongest Buryat oath is 'May my fire be extinguished!' "[48] In ancient Rome, "Vesta was the flame, the life of the home, the fire which burned on the domestic altar; it was the center of the family, the symbol of its perpetuity."[49]

If we look about for the real central point of the primitive family, says Lippert,[50] we find it in the common fire. This forms forthwith, and in a manner still more real than does community of blood, the characterizing mark of those who belong together. The members of the Hindu family are "designated in downright manner as 'those who cook together.' " The blood-bond remains, of course, the real one; but a wandering life precludes the persistence of the memory of a blood-bond. "The common fire, on the other hand, characterizes the contemporary and actual status of new families, and from that stage on it can be said that a family is constituted of those persons who have a common fire, who use fire from the same source."[51] This survival-symbol[52] whereby the community of fire in a sense supplants that of blood comes out in the fact that portions of the family, when they split off, take their fire from the ancestral hearth, that is, keep the same fire. The Herero father gives the son who is founding a family of his own a brand from the paternal hearth with which to start the new

[46] Sieroshevski-Sumner, in JAI, XXXI, 106.
[47] Monier-Williams, *Brāhmanism*, 354.
[48] Czaplicka, *Aborig. Siberia*, 139.
[49] De Marchi, *Culto Privato*, quoted in *Année Soc.*, 1897, 192.
[50] *Kgchte.*, I, 265.
[51] Jolly, in *Grund. d. Indo-Ar. Philol.*, II, 76.
[52] §456, below.

household fire.[53] Further, the use of fire in the wedding ceremony signifies the joining of a family bond.

When the Unyamwesi bride has kindled the first fire with a quirl-stick, she is already the guardian of the hearth;[54] elsewhere in Africa the bride's mother must light the first fire in the house of the young couple. In ancient India the use of sacred fire in the wedding ceremonies is general: "the solemn act and the irrevocable union took place before the enkindled Agni" [Ignis], and here the bride was given over to the groom, who led her about the fire three times, keeping it to the right. After the ceremonies, "the new husband must now see to the house-fire, which he keeps ever burning, the sign of his being a householder." The fire had a room as its sanctuary and was shown great reverence: it was never blown upon with the mouth; nothing impure was ever thrown into it; and it was never used for warming the feet.[55] Similar ritual is performed in modern India.[56] In Transcaucasia the bride is led three times around the hearth and then sits facing it.[57] Among the Kirghiz there are ceremonies at the door and at the fire-place; the Bulgarian bride is seated by the fire, and the White Russian upon the tile stove.[58] The ancient Germans had the ceremony of marching three times around the fire.[59] When the Roman bride entered the house of the groom, she was received with fire and water—*aqua et igni accipi;* "the ceremony of water and fire symbolized the inclusion of the bride into the hearth and house fellowship of her husband." The bridal veil was in origin flame-colored, and was called *flammeum.*[60]

Not the family-bond alone, but the wider, political and religious bond is symbolized by a common fire; and there is as much care taken in keeping it as the savage was capable of. The "eternal" character of such central fires recalls, as a survival, the earlier stages of fire-keeping.

When the Herero son takes fire from the paternal hearth he thus links himself with the paternal household; and as the off-shoot groups grow larger and more numerous their common fire comes to be a tribal symbol. Among these same Herero, the most important fire-place is that before the hut of the chief; "it forms the central point of the whole settlement and at the same time the chief place of sacrifice. The extinguishment of this fire would be looked upon as an omen of ill fortune, and the daughter of the chief , , , is therefore specially entrusted with its custody. If they change their dwelling-place, she has

[53] Fritsch, *Eingeb. S.-Afr.,* 232.
[54] Stuhlmann, *Mit Emin,* 80, 538, 390.
[55] Zimmer, *Altind. Leben,* 311; Monier-Williams, *Brāhmanism,* 363-364; Gubernatis, *Usi Nuz.,* 168-169; Hopkins, *Relig. India,* 270-271.
[56] Thurston, *S. India,* 1-3; "Royal Marriage at Kolhapore," in JASB, II, 311 ff.
[57] Von Haxthausen, *Transkaukasia,* II, 22.
[58] *Russian Ethnog.* (Russ.), II, 188, 482, 106.
[59] Weinhold, *Deut. Frauen,* I, 407-408.
[60] Rossbach, *Röm. Ehe,* 361, 364; Gubernatis, *Usi Nuz.,* 162.

to bring the fire along."[61] Many tribes of North America maintained an eternal fire before the Europeans came.[62] "The general council of the Five Nations was held at Onondaga, where there has, from the beginning, been kept a fire continually burning, made of two great logs, whose flames were never extinguished."[63] The council-fire was a symbol of political unity; and was employed by the Indians when they called the Thirteen Colonies the "Thirteen Fires." Again, the essential features of the Greek *prytaneion*, which was consecrated to Hestia, the hearth-goddess, were its perpetual fire and its hearth, the latter differing from other hearths in that it was the hearth of the city, the common hearth.[64] In the earlier Homeric time, the epithets applied to the lover of intra-group strife include his exclusion from the hearth: he is said to be "brotherless, lawless, hearthless."[65] Whenever the Greeks sent out a colony, fire was taken along from the central hearth, or *prytaneion*, of the metropolis.[66]

If the inferences to be drawn from these instances are put together, it becomes clear enough that the fire-factor entered very early and penetrated very deep into family and tribal life, taking on at length a distinctly political tinge. As a typical and marked survival, it became a symbol of the greatest significance, corresponding to a vital actuality in the struggle for existence of the far past.

There is a respect in which fire differs from all other human possessions—at least from all other possessions of primitive man —with the exception of ideas. It can be given to another without depletion of the giver's store; it can be conferred and kept, at one and the same time. Precisely this exceptional quality of fire renders it of an especial educative value, upon the primitive stage, in the direction of socialization. Amidst the life-conditions of some Australians, for example, there is little or nothing to be gained by intertribal coöperation, since there is small chance for specialization in complementary activities. In fact, two of these natives, if collecting food together, would impede each other and strife would probably result. Yet if one of them had lost his fire, he must either sink back to a lower stage of living or seek those relations with another which interest in self-preservation had led him, up to that time, to avoid. Something could be given which, though costing nothing, might assure a return in kind in case of need.[67] In other terms, here was a species of insurance[68] cheaply

[61] Fritsch, *Eingeb. S.-Afr.*, 232.　　[62] Ratzel, *Vkde.*, II, 684.
[63] Carr, in *Smithson. Rep.*, 1891, 537, note.
[64] Mason, *Woman's Share*, 262.　　[65] Homer, *Iliad*, IX, 63-64.
[66] Keller, *Colon.*, 42.　　[67] Lippert, *Kgchte.*, I, 266.
[68] §197, below.

taken and yet capable of breaking down the barriers to a wider socialization.

Given the ideas seen in above paragraphs to be connected with the use of fire derived from a common blaze, the thin edge of the wedge is forced the deeper. "Just as in Rome, according to the evidence of the poets, there was no pretext closer at hand for improperly slinking into any strange house—none that attained its end with less danger—than to assert that one wanted to get fire, in the same way, we must think, there was also created forthwith a safe-conduct which led securely from tribe to tribe and could open the way to any other kind of intercourse."[69] If there are put together the two facts, first, that fire was practically the most indispensable element to primitive man and, second, that it was, at the same time, precisely that one thing among his few possessions which could be freely given and exchanged, a further and important increment is added to the conception of the rôle which fire, while yet kept and passed about, was competent to play.

§92*. **Fire and Religion.** Fire thus plays its part in the industrial organization and in that of the family and community. But this is not yet all; for it comes to be far more than an instrument or a symbol. An element of such extraordinary importance, entirely apart from its peculiar qualities, could not fail to take on a significance not of this world. It is not surprising, when we recall what was, in the eyes of primitive men, the chief value of fire, to find it no less than a fetish of the first magnitude. This aspect of the subject cannot be treated in full in the present place, for it belongs under the topic of fetishism;[70] but it is important to gain some present realization of the added power with which this form of appropriated energy could now, being metamorphosed into a spirit, operate within and upon the life of society. The fetishistic quality of fire has entered largely into some of its functions as outlined above; it is probably the main reason for fire having become the symbol it has been seen to be. One should recall the quotation from Lippert,[71] who remarks how all social strands make connection with the cult and religion.

[69] Lippert, *Kgchte.*, I, 266-267. [70] §§247 ff., below.
[71] §87, above.

How widely fire has been identified with religion appears from the essential agreement of a great variety of notions about the nature and service of fire; for these ideas all seem to accord in the matter of the connection of fire with spirits. It is itself a spirit; or it is the habitation of a spirit; or it exercises a controlling power over spirits. This unity of conviction in a variety of conceptions calls for illustration at this point, although the full significance of fire in the family and community organization and, above all, in religion, can be grasped only after the evolution of each of these organizations and especially religion, with its characteristic premises and perspectives, has been traced.

The Mongols of northern Siberia regard fire as a divinity, or at least as a spirit. It purifies and grants wealth and happiness; hence it is the protector of households, the hearth is a sanctuary, and fire lighted in the *yurt* (tent) purifies and consecrates it. It is a sin to put into the fire anything that will give out a bad smell, or to spit into it, or pour on it anything unclean—or even clear water. It is a sin to put it out; it must be allowed to go out of itself. It is forbidden to step over it, to vituperate it, to strike it with any instrument, or to chop anything beside it. Offerings to it are what will brighten the flame, such as wine, butter, and fat; and to this day the Tatars of the Yenesei, Yakuts, and Tungus will drink no wine or tea without first pouring out a few drops on the fire. Fire is the sole purifier: after a death the yurt was purified by fire; and all articles carried between two fires were believed to be purified within and without. Fire was even conceived to neutralize poison. Some diseases, as well as conflagrations, were supposed to be due to the wrath of the offended flame. To put the fire out vexed the spirit; it was better to let him have his own way and satisfy himself.[72]

To the Yakuts "the spirit of fire is a grey-haired, garrulous, restless, eternally fussy old man. What he is whispering and shuffling about so perpetually few understand. The *shaman* [sorcerer] understands it, and also the little child whose ear has not yet learned to distinguish human speech. The fire understands well what they are saying and doing round about it; therefore it is dangerous to hurt the feelings of the fire. . . . It will not do to cast into the fire rubbish which adheres to the shoes, for that would cause headache. It is sinful to poke the fire with an iron instrument, and the wooden poker with which they do stir it up must be burned every week, or there will be bad luck in the house. A good house-mistress always takes care that the fire may be satisfied with her, and she casts into it a bit of everything which is prepared by its aid. No one ever knows what kind of a fire is burning on the hearth of his house; therefore it is well to conciliate it from time to time, by little gifts. The fire loves, above all, fat, butter, and cream. They sprinkle these often upon it."[73]

In the Old Testament it is forbidden to make sons and daughters pass

[72] Shchukin, *Shamanism* (Russ.), 30-31.
[73] Sieroshevski-Sumner, in JAI, XXXI, 106.

through the fire.[74] Even among modern peoples expressions such as "tried by
fire," and conceptions such as that of purgatory, carry on ideas of the above
order into the realm of survivals. The "need-fire," and the "Johannis-feuer,"[75]
through which unmarried young people leaped in order to secure the growth
of the flax and continued health, are such survivals. In White Russia when a
wedded pair is led from the church, they go into the house through a fire
built before the gate; and elsewhere in Russia the horses are driven through
a ditch, in which a fire has been built, to render them healthy—this fire being
kindled by friction of two sticks and called the living fire.[76] Anyone who had
been present beside a corpse or at a burial must formally smoke out the death-
poison, or air it out; the Tzar especially was always kept from such pollution.
Stern,[77] who reports this, says that in his boyhood he saw peasants jump
about the Johannis-feuer, not any longer naked, as once, but merely with bare
feet. No one took offense at it on that particular day. Another observer found
this jumping through the fire regarded as of doubtful propriety; it had come
under the disapproval of the clergy.[78] At a christening-feast in the Highlands,
the father placed a basket of food across the fire and handed the infant three
times over the food and flame. Mothers were afraid of a fairy who changed
newborn infants. To test the child, a great fire was made and the child hung
in front of it, or in a basket over it, as near as possible without harm. If it
was a changeling, it would disappear up the chimney. It was an old custom
in England and Scotland to carry fire around the houses and fields, on the
last night of the year, in order to secure fertility and prosperity.[79]

The fetishistic character of fire is further established by the
fact that certain peoples hesitate to give it away because of its
peculiar nature, especially at certain holy periods. Again, there
has been a widespread belief that fire could become old and con-
taminated, with the result of causing calamity, unless it was renewed or cleansed. Of this idea that fire grows old, or becomes
defiled and impure, thus necessitating periodical generation of new
fire, many instances occur; and it is to be noted that the new and
pure flame must be obtained by ancient methods, such as the friction-process, or in some peculiar and ritual way indicative of the
solemn and spiritual nature of the process and the product.

The Iroquois believed that the appearance of disease among them was due
to the fire having become "old." To dispel the calamity they put out all fires
and set about making "new fire," which was done by the friction-method. New
fire was probably made at their winter feast.[80] "Fire-making formed an im-

[74] Lev., XVIII, 21; Deut., XVIII, 10; XII, 31.
[75] Tylor, *Anth.*, 261 ff.; Weinhold, *Deut. Frauen*, I, 287.
[76] *Russian Ethnog.* (Russ.), I, 104, 266.
[77] *Russland*, 72-73, 355.
[78] Danielevski, *Fugitives from New Russia* (Russ.), 55.
[79] Gomme, *Village Life*, 111, 113, 147.
[80] Hough, in USNM, 1888, 546.

portant feature of a number of ceremonies. New fire was made in the Green-corn ceremony of the Creeks, . . . the White-dog feast of the Iroquois, the New-fire and Yaya ceremonies of the Hopi, and among many other tribes in widely separated localities. There are also many legends and myths grouped about the primitive method of obtaining fire at will. The Cherokee and other southern tribes believed that a perpetual fire burned beneath some of the mounds in their country, and the Natchez built their mounds with a view, it is said, of maintaining a perpetual fire."[81] The Aztecs generated their new fire annually, with special ceremonies, every four years and every fifty-two years; all the old fires were allowed to die out and the new was obtained with a fire-drill. The Hopi produce new fire each November.[82] In old Serbia a boy and a girl between eleven and fourteen years of age are chosen to make the new fire. They go into a hut without a window, undress completely, and do not speak while the boy makes fire by saw-friction.[83] On the twelfth of January of every year, at Burghead, on the coast of Scotland, a tar-barrel was burned; and as it fell to pieces the fisherwives endeavored to get a lighted bit of it to kindle fire on the cottage hearths. It was considered lucky to keep this flame all the rest of the year.[84] Such a case is plainly allied to that of the African tribesmen who put out all fires in the village when some hut was struck by lightning and immediately kindled new fires therefrom.[85]

The foregoing cases demonstrate the magical or fetishistic quality of fire. That it became, farther along the path of evolution, an object of actual worship, forming the characteristic spirit of certain developed religions, is well known.[86] Thus this natural element, this form of energy appropriated out of nature, came to enter into the life of society in an intimate and all-pervasive way possible only to a factor with a strong strain of the supernatural about it. Fire-worship is connected, in the minds of most readers, with the Persians.

In Persia fire "remains more distant from man; being an earthly form of the eternal, infinite, godly light, no death, no uncleanness can be allowed to enter it, as it is here below the purest offspring of the good spirit, the purest part of his pure creation. Its only function is to repel the fiends with its bright blazing. In every place where Parsis are settled, an everlasting fire is kept, the Bahram fire, which, 'preserved by a more than Vestal care,' and ever fed with perfumes and dry well-blazing wood, whichever side its flames are brought by the wind, it goes and kills thousands and thousands of fiends, as Bahram does in heaven. If the necessities of life oblige us to employ fire for profane uses, it must be only for a time an exile on our hearth, or in the oven of the potter, and it must go thence to the Right-Place of the fire . . . the

[81] Hough, in HAI, I, 460.
[82] Dellenbaugh, N. Amer., 252, 368, 370; Fewkes, in AA, III.
[83] Titelbach, "Das Heilige Feuer bei den Balkenslaven," in Int. Archiv. f. Ethnog., XIII, 1.
[84] Gomme, Village Life, 98.   [85] Mason, Invention, 87.
[86] Lippert, Kgchte., II, 442-444.

altar of the Bahram fire, there to be restored to the dignity and rights of its nature."[87]

To the Avesta-people fire was "the symbol of moral purity and a powerful means for repelling demons. In night and darkness the evil fiends do their work, but the fire generates light and brightness and scares off the hellish spirits. The hearth-fire as the center of the house is at the same time the symbol of steady domicile, and the latter quality, again, is the characteristic which distinguishes the pious and the believers from the godless."[88] The extinction of the fire signifies "the abandonment of the dwelling and the occupation of its place by the evil spirits of barrenness and unfruitfulness. Fire is to the peoples tribally related to the Iranians a highly revered god; but it forms in the nature-religion of the Iranians the very central point of religious reverence, and has maintained this preferred position in the Zoroastrian system also. The latter now has conferred upon the ideas of light and darkness a spiritual form: the former becomes the original source of all moral good, the latter the bearer of all that furthers the powers of evil."

These Iranian ideas do not stand alone; "the Iranian religion," Justi[89] goes on, "in its fire-cult accords . . . with many others: Semitic, Egyptian, Indian, Greek, Roman, even Aztec; and the extraordinary reverence for this element is certainly to be ascribed in no small degree to the circumstance that, even in the pre-Zoroastrian period, the fire-cult was already quite in the foreground."

It should be recognized, finally, that in systematic fire-worship there is formed yet another societal bond; and the fire-myths could not but unite, to some degree, fellow-believers.[90]

§93. Summary. We have examined, in the foregoing, and at some length, the place in the life of human society taken by one of the chemical energies appropriated out of nature. We have touched upon its importance as a factor in the organization for societal self-maintenance, without, however, attempting to develop in any detail the technological aspects of the subject, either in primitive or in modern times. To gain an adequate idea of the importance of fire to the races of the present day and to our own civilization, one needs only imagine its absence, with the consequent cessation of most forms of industry and the lowering of efficiency in the struggle for existence to such a degree that, at least in the cooler climates, mankind must disappear. This aspect of the matter does not call for scientific demonstration. That which is not at all apparent, apart from investigation into the

[87] Müller, *Sacred Books of East,* IV: Zend-Avesta, pt. I, lxxxix ff.
[88] Geiger, *Ostiran. Kultur,* 253.   [89] *Persien,* 71-72, 74.
[90] Spencer, *Prin. Soc.,* §§622 ff.

long course of societal evolution, is the all-pervasive societal influence of the use of fire; and one of the reasons why it is not evident is that this influence was exerted prior to the acquisition of means easily and readily to generate the element. There was a painful slowness in the development of such means, interrupted as it must often have been by periods of retrogression; here, however, is encountered no more than a type of the process of invention in general, which only in recent times has somewhat broken away from the arduous accretion of small increments.

It has been our intention, in the present connection, to emphasize the less obvious societal relations into which the fire-factor has entered. Pursuing this course, we have found fire of great significance in the family and tribe, thus becoming eventually of an almost political importance. And when to its other qualities that of a fetish had been added, fire was equipped for entrance into many relationships within the societal structure. Thus we see how an element in nature, the product of natural chemical processes, becomes, when appropriated by man for his purposes, a factor endowed with a versatile effectiveness in the life and evolution of society.

CHAPTER IX

APPROPRIATION OF ENERGIES: ANIMALS

§94. Man and Other Animals. The case of fire is perhaps the most thoroughgoing of any as illustrating the appropriation of energies out of the inorganic world; yet one might dwell at length upon the utilization of mechanical forces and, in modern times, of electricity. These have had effects of great moment, both in their direct applications, and also indirectly, upon the societal structure. Books could be written upon the development of tools and weapons, the use of metals, of steam-power, gunpowder, and so on.[1] Our program, however, calls for a survey of three typical examples of energy-appropriation, and the next in order are organic energies. It is possible to choose between plant and animal energies, and the latter have been selected. Having covered the general case in our first example, we shall be able to treat the other two—the appropriation of animal energies and of human energies—more summarily and, to some degree, from a different angle.

Turning to the relations of man and animal, we find that primordially they must have been those of unmitigated hostility in the competition of life. In this struggle, as Darwin[2] long ago pointed out, there exist the most complex relations; and certain of these are relations of helper and helped. In the most highly organized insect societies, one species of insect comes to be dominated by another and to constitute a subordinate group of helpers; certain warrior-ants are, indeed, so highly specialized in consequence of the division of function in practice between them and their helpers, that they are unable, alone, to maintain themselves and their young. But in the case of man there seem to have been at the outset no relations such as these; the animals were hostile and dangerous or they were timorous and avoided his neighborhood. They were all man's enemies; the whole of nature was

---

[1] See the chapters on some of these topics in Lippert, *Kgchte.;* and, for an example of thoroughness, Beck, *Gchte. des Eisens.*

[2] *Orig. of Species,* chs. III and VIII.

against him and he had to prevail, if at all, through setting his brains at work to offset his relative physical inferiority. In his days of unequal contest with formidable competitors he had to respect their superiorities, and he learned from them. Many of the forms of animal life are still unalterably hostile to man, and can in no way yet conceived be rendered of any utility or comfort to him. Poison-bearing insects and other menaces exist in the environment as irreconcilably hostile elements, imperilling by their presence the life of man and of society. Several forms of disease are due to microscopic fauna.[3]

Into the competition with fellow-creatures, however, man turned his powers of mental adjustment;[4] and the dominance which he has attained is a measure of the effectiveness of intellectual adaptation over physical. The weak and small animals first become his prey, while the strong ones remain dreaded competitors. The line between the two classes rises with the development of the arts of life, until most of the beasts that had been in the latter class fall into the former. Man's weapons and other materialized ideas enable him to take advantage of the animals at every turn; and the result is like that attained by any species that has evolved a superior type of adaptation: that species prevails in the struggle for existence. It is necessary only to allude to the annihilation of animal foes wherever civilization has become well rooted; or to the development of whole systems of offense against them, as, for instance, a large part of the system of medicine and sanitation. Nevertheless when men had reduced the animals to a position where they were his prey rather than he theirs, he had barely begun the history of his relations with them. He had appropriated their dead bodies, it is true, but that represented only the rude and obvious beginnings of the taking of what they had to give. There is potential energy in dead meat, but there is more, and in a greater variety of forms, in the living organism. It is with the taming and domestication of the animals that the present topic really begins.[5]

[3] Gregory, Keller, and Bishop, *Phys. and Comm. Geog.*, §150, and, in general, chap. VIII, where man's relations with flora and fauna are worked out in an elementary way.

[4] Keller, *Soc. Evol.*, 18 ff.

[5] Mason, in AA, I, 50, calls this "zoötechny."

§95. Domestication. First, as to the possibility of appropriation of animal forces out of nature, it is to be noted that not all
of the continents are equally rich in domesticable fauna. Australia, offering as its ranking form of animal life the marsupial,
afforded little chance of selection for domestication; and much the
same might be said of South America, the Pacific Islands, and
some other regions. In fact, no one of the continents really contained a variety of domesticable animals comparable to that shown
by parts of Europe and Asia.[6] Great as has been the alteration
of the wild types under domestication, it has not been sufficient to
have rendered of much value to man such animals as the giraffe,
the kangaroo, or the larger of the carnivora. Hence, though other
factors must be assigned their proper weight in the matter of
domestication, the presence or absence of fauna apt for the process must often have been determinative. There is evidence that
practically every animal likely to be at all available for man's
purposes has been recurrently held by man under conditions favorable to the proof of such availability.

Galton[7] cites a number of instances selected from many showing how the
most diverse of animals have been kept as pets or otherwise attached to human
groups. "I infer," he concludes, "that every animal, of any pretensions, has
been tamed over and over again, and has had numerous opportunities of becoming domesticated. But the cases are rare in which these opportunities have
led to any result. No animal is fitted for domestication unless it fulfils certain
stringent conditions. . . . My conclusion is, that all domesticable animals of
any note have long ago fallen under the yoke of man. In short, that the animal
creation has been pretty thoroughly, though half unconsciously, explored, by
the every-day habits of rude races and simple civilizations."

Thus the character and disposition of the animal enters as an
important factor into domestication; the appropriation of animal
energies is not equally easy in all parts of the earth.

If the character of the animals forms an important condition,
certainly that of the men can do no less; it must have been entirely decisive as between sections about equally endowed with
domesticable fauna. From Darwin[8] we learn that while most of our
domestic animals must have received their first domestication at
the hand of the savage or rude barbarian, the appropriation of

6 Gregory, Keller, and Bishop, *Phys. and Comm. Geog.*, §§157 ff.
7 *Human Faculty*, 243 ff. (244-245 quoted).
8 *Orig. of Species*, ch. I.

their qualities and forces could have been but crude and inadequate before the development of at least the rudiments of civilization. From this may be concluded, incidentally, that the appropriation of animal forces, in more than rudimentary fashion, must have taken place long after that of fire; there is no such elemental need for the former as for the latter.

It is easy to see the reasonableness of Darwin's position. Australia affords a combination of low civilization and no domestic animals of importance; the Americas show few and inferior ones, even in the region of the Inca civilization; and ethnological Africa, that is, Africa south of the Sahara, completes the picture. Almost all the valuable domestic animals we have—and the same is true, for the same reasons, of the plants—go back to the regions of early civilization, the temperate river-regions of Eurasia. Darwin's explanation of this fact is that savages cannot secure isolation of strains; they seldom possess more than one breed of a species. The conclusion is that any incipient breed, unconsciously developed by the savage through preservation of animals with qualities that pleased him, tends to run down, in the absence of artificial isolation through various forms of enclosures, to the level of pre-domestication. Thus it would appear that no appropriation from the animal world, in the absence of exceptional conditions such as self-isolation, becomes consistent and its products stable until civilization has attained to some degree of advancement; that is, domestication cannot profitably be considered apart from artificial selection in breeding.

As yet no distinction has been drawn between taming and domestication. Such a distinction is of importance. An animal is tamed when it is no longer "wild"; when it endures or seeks the proximity of man and lives in a sort of fellowship with him. There are varying degrees of tameness. An animal is not truly domesticated, on the other hand, until it can be bred, that is, until it will reproduce in captivity. Thus the elephant is tamed, but not fully domesticated, for the cases are very few where it will breed when out of its native habitat, even though removed but a relatively short distance therefrom.[9] This breeding in captivity leads to unconscious, and finally to conscious, artificial selection, that is,

9 Darwin, *Orig. of Species,* ch. I.

to breeding in the special, transitive sense. Since, in general, the animal forces appropriated out of nature are those of domesticated animals, what there is to say on this topic assumes domestication as an antecedent process.

§96*. **Artificial Selection.** Darwin[10] enumerates several conditions favorable to artificial selection, which may be condensed as follows: (1) large numbers; (2) propagation in great numbers and at a quick rate; (3) ease in preventing crosses; (4) high value set on the animal or plant. Of these conditions, the first and second, taken together, secure copious chances for selection and allow of a rapid sequence of choices, as the generations pass in quick succession before the selector; the third secures isolation; the fourth, attention. This list, nearly complete for our purposes, may receive one additional item, which Galton[11] suggests, namely, adaptability. To be successfully domesticated, animals must be present in large numbers, must breed copiously and rapidly, must be relatively easy to isolate from indiscriminate crossing, must have a high value set upon them, and must be adaptable to conditions imposed.

One who approaches the question of the utility of domesticated fauna is confronted by a multiplicity of varied examples; their prime utility was, however, their service as a food-supply. The evidence, especially that of the cult,[12] all points that way. Animals and plants which no one thinks of nowadays as food-possibilities, for instance, the dog and the fiber-plants, were once employed almost wholly as food and, indeed, are still so employed by backward peoples. The only competing motive to hunger, as an incentive to domestication, was vanity; for some of the animals that were early domesticated had the general character of trophies,[13] or were purely ornamental or amusing, as, for example, the parrot. Other and less elemental utilities revealed themselves later on in the evolutionary course.

To the race the utility of animal energies cannot have vied with that of fire; for, while the domestication of certain animals has meant the persistence of certain relatively local groups, no animal

---

10 *Orig. of Species*, ch. I.   11 *Human Faculty*, 271.

12 §324, below.   13 Spencer, *Prin. Soc.*, II, §§349 ff.

or group of animals has been absolutely indispensable, as was fire, to the dispersal and survival of large sections of the race, and least of all to the development of specifically human traits.[14] Although the dog in polar America, the reindeer in northern Asia and Europe, the camel in the desert, have been determining influences of a high order upon the destinies of arctic and desert populations, it is entirely conceivable that the race should have been able to increase and to occupy most of the inhabited portions of the world if domestication had never taken place at all. Hence the utility of the forces derived from the animal world has never approached that of forces which go back to an inorganic source.

Nor would the energies appropriated from the animal world have attained a fraction of their import apart from the molding activity of man. Whereas fire remains the same element after its "taming" as before, the utility of animals depends very largely upon changes wrought in them by art. They are "artificialized," sometimes out of all but a semblance to what they were. In other words, the animals, to be of high utility to man, must have been bred and selected; that is why mere taming is insufficient. As soon as animals began to breed in captivity, there developed an unpremeditated and unmethodical artificial selection; man naturally favored those animals which he had found most useful to his interests, and sacrificed them, when necessity came upon him, last of all. Even this selection, unsystematic as it was, meant that the type of animal was sure to be altered in the direction of human needs; and out of this humble beginning there developed a methodical breeding whose results, now that it has been in operation and subject to deliberate improvement these many centuries, are truly astonishing. It would seem that the marvel in the energies appropriated out of the inorganic world lay in their own constant nature and in the discovery of their applications; while in the case of the organic energies it resided in the activities of man, transformative as they have been of what he originally appropriated.

By means of artificial selection the potential utilities of the animals have been realized in ever greater measure; to a certain degree they have been made what man has come to wish them to be. The dog has a keener scent, or greater tenacity, or enhanced

14 §88, above.

attachment to man—a very "instinct of service"; the sheep furnishes better meat or a thicker coat of finer wool; the horse is stronger, or faster, or smaller, or larger. In the case of animals, and of plants as well, man has captured, as it were, some of the forces in nature originally arrayed against him, and has made them his allies; he has then drilled them and molded them, accumulating the variations or preserving the mutations which they presented, when favorable to his interests. Thus he has acted directly upon the nature of the animal in a manner quite impossible in the case of inorganic appropriations, which lie outside the realm of variation and heredity, of selection and breeding.

§97. **Animal Services.** Man appropriates first the flesh of the animals, and then their special powers. When he has a good hunting-dog, he is virtually as well off as if he himself possessed the sense of smell, the keenness of sight, the speed, swimming capacity, and so on, of his animal. Man appropriates, in the domesticated animal, a sort of living tool or weapon which, within limits, can be shaped to his hand as are other implements. There are certain works of man whose accomplishment is dependent upon his disposal over animal forces much surpassing his own; the highest development of the nomadic stage is impossible in the absence of the horse, for without him the widely grazing herds cannot be held together and supervised. It is seldom that the whole manner of life of a people is altered as was Indian life by the importation of the horse.[15] On the other hand, Central African agriculture is hardly more than gardening because there is rarely power available to handle a tool more efficient than the hoe. Concentration of animal energy under his control has meant more for man's advancement than this age is wont to recognize.

This fact comes out still more clearly, perhaps, when the services of animals in transportation and communication are contemplated. Civilization being a matter not only of numbers but of contact as well,[16] it is evident that agencies promoting intercourse are of high import. Where there were no suitable domestic animals, communication and trade have always remained rudimen-

15 Bourdeau, *Forces de l'Industrie*, 97; Keller, *Soc. Evol.*, 158.
16 §26, above.

tary over stretches of country without navigable waters; thus in Australia, much of Africa, and the Americas, there existed among the aborigines but the feeblest of contacts. Contrast this with the extension of the interests of the Chinese Empire, across deserts and plateaus, almost to the borders of Europe, or the penetration of even the Sahara through the agency of the "ship of the desert." Caravans crossed and re-crossed the regions between India and Egypt, and formed an original factor of great moment in the development of trade, that characteristic forerunner of civilization and peace.[17] When one reflects that up to some hundred years ago domestic animals represented the only means of land transportation and communication, and then seeks to realize what results, in the promotion of culture, even these faulty interrelations have meant, he gets some perspective of the service to civilization rendered by animals under domestication. The fact is that, until man could bring what he wanted to himself, he had to move himself to it. Development of transportation, by enabling him to bring it to himself, promoted sedentary life, with its momentous sequels.[18]

Moreover, transportation-service has worked out into results quite inevitable, though not readily foreseen. It is in all ways likely that the draught-animal has often succeeded, and so freed to some degree, the draught-man and especially the draught-woman. In parts of Africa, where there are no beasts of burden—no roads, indeed, wide enough for such—man has long been the pack-animal, and there has been no alternative to extensive enslavement. An acute observer[19] has remarked that the quickest way to rid Africa of its eternal slave-system is to build roads and introduce locomotor forces, animals or steam; for this would cut the ground from under slavery. In far earlier ages it is likely that this African situation often appeared and that it was solved or ameliorated, though through no premeditation, by the shifting of burdens and drudgery over upon the animals.

17 Gregory, Keller, and Bishop, *Phys. and Comm. Geog.*, ch. XIII.
18 §31, above.
19 Fabri, *Deut. Kolonialpolitik*, 55; the author accredits Livingstone with the idea.

Dr. Harvey[20] remarks on the supercession of the human pack-animal in China. "Over most of the country of China there are no roads, and man is the pack-animal. For instance, in the city of Siang-tan, thirty miles above Changsha, there used to live a hundred thousand carrying coolies. They were wont to transport goods from Canton to Hankow overland through Changsha. The narrow road, with a fourteen-inch slab of granite in its middle, still exists but steam transportation from Canton via Shanghai has displaced the men."

§98*. Pastoral Society. The demands upon the power of intellectual adaptation connected with domestication and breeding have entailed for man a diversity of mental and institutional reactions and discipline, the results of which emerge in a distinctiveness of societal type. Any society which has specialized in herding or, more clearly still, in tillage, develops characteristic mores based upon its occupation, which sharply differentiate it from what went before.[21] The use of fire, being so universal, is, together with its results, a point of differentiation between human societies and others; the use of organic forces, being less general, forms, together with attendant mores and institutions, a point of differentiation as between types of human society. In a preceding connection[22] have been set down the broadest influences on population exercised by the advance to domestication. The further development of those influences means the closer characterization of the pastoral economy. That domestication advanced self-maintenance by the creation of a better and steadier food-supply is well recognized in the mores. Genuine pastoral peoples live and breathe in the atmosphere of their chief vocation.

Ratzel[23] devotes a good deal of space to the enthusiasm of the African pastoral races for their cattle. "These pastoral tribes, which in the Soudan reach right across Africa, and extend almost without a gap on the eastern highlands from the Dinkas on the Upper Nile to the Kaffirs at the southern point of Africa, with whom one must further reckon the Hereros in the West, and in a certain sense even the Hottentots, are one of the most important phenomena in the national life of Africa. Some of them despise every kind of agriculture; but even to those who do something in that way, it appears as a burdensome necessity. The herds form the centre—the centre of gravity—of the whole physical and mental existence. Among races who are pastoral and nothing else, the stock accounts for ninety-nine per cent of all conversation. . . . From their very earliest youth thought and eye are fed on the forms and colours of their animals. . . . As their life in general, so their knowledge in particular,

[20] Personally communicated.
[21] Keller, *Soc. Evol.*, 141 ff.   [22] §30, above.
[23] *Hist. Mankind*, II, 409 ff., 416; Ratzel, *Vkde.*, I, 57; Keller, *Hom. Soc.*, 30 ff.

here reaches its culmination." Cattle are for the negro the "basis of life, fountain of joy, measure of property, means of winning all other desirable things, above all women, and finally even money." He is unwilling to kill them, partly, perhaps, because sharing-customs would rob him of all but a small share in the ensuing feast. The cattle may even become, when thus cherished, a limitation; for he will not give them up to advance in civilization. He can be reduced to utter misery when this his one source of life and well-being is removed; the Dinka and Basuto were thus ruined. If the cattle thrive on good pasture, their owners are prone to be lazy; life is too easy. This was the case with the South Africans visited by Holub;[24] their qualities were narrowed down to their sole interest.

Ratzel's picture of the African herders may be supplemented by a few details. Of the Akamba we learn that "many of them died of starvation, leaving their livestock to their children, sooner than kill what would have saved their lives." They seldom kill for ordinary purposes, though they readily devour cattle and goats which have died a natural death. "Every kind of domesticated animal has a specific name according to its colour, sex, age, etc." Fines are levied in cattle, showing an economy based on beasts as ours on metallic money. Cows are much more valuable than bulls. Unquestionably the animals have some powerful religious qualities; all along occur cases of purification by use of the contents of the stomachs of goats and sheep, in which people tread or formally rub their feet.[25] "When listening to Masai talking to one another it would often appear as if many of the terms of relationship used were the same as names of cattle, sheep, goats, and donkeys. . . . This is chiefly due to the fact that whenever a woman is brought into the family by marriage it is customary for her husband's relations and their wives to give her an animal to show that she is recognized as a member of the family. The giver and the recipient ever afterwards call one another after the animal which has been given, to which the particle *pa-* is prefixed. Thus, a man gives his brother's wife or his paternal uncle's wife, or his paternal uncle's son's wife a cow, a calf, or a lamb, and the terms of address used by the two, instead of being *par-sidan* or *yeiyo*, as the case may be, are *pa-kiteñg, pa-ashe,* or *pa-supen;* a father-in-law gives his daughter-in-law a calf, and the two call one another *pa-ashe;* and a paternal uncle gives his nephew's wife a she-goat and calls her *pa-kine.*" The author[26] cites a number of other examples.

The mores form around the engrossing occupation as if crystallizing about a sort of core, and always reveal in their general conformation the outlines of this core or matrix around or out of which they grow. Nomadism, says Ratzel,[27] always shows the same features of society and of life, in both ancient and modern times; there is but a slight range of variety. And if the service of fire was to lower infant mortality, the eventual employment of milk as the food of the weaning-period must have been doubly effective

[24] *Capstadt,* II, 203; Paulitschke, *Nordost-Afr.,* II, 100.
[25] Tate, in JAI, XXXIV, 135, 136; Dundas, in JAI, XLV, 251, note; Hobley, *A-Kamba,* 78 ff.
[26] Hollis, in JAI, XL, 477-478.   [27] *Vkde.,* III, 4.

along the same line. Hence the pastoral stage is characterized, according to Lippert,[28] who regards the use of milk as a decisive factor in societal development, by a large increase of population, which ultimately outgrows the supporting power of its local environment and drifts away in folk-movements ranging in importance from the separation of family stocks one from another, as in the Biblical story of Abraham and Lot, to the irruption of whole hordes and to historic invasions.[29]

In the secondary societal mores, as well as in those of self-maintenance, a primarily pastoral people reveals its own characteristic stamp. The matrimonial and familial institutions of pastoral peoples afford a striking example of consistency of type in the mores. If the earliest matrimonial unions were based, like any other form of association, upon economic interests,[30] then any such thoroughgoing alteration of the terms of the struggle for existence as the cattle-raising stage introduced could not have failed to effect a marked change in marriage and the family.

The type of family-organization regularly accompanying the pastoral type of self-maintenance is strongly patriarchal. "The patriarchal system has reached its highest development among pastoral races; so that the introduction of cattle-breeding into the industrial life of mankind may well have played an important part in the extension of this system."[31] The most familiar illustrations of this correlation are those afforded by the old Hebrew and Greek societies. The "patriarchs" of the Old Testament were primarily herdsmen, and the Homeric heroes reckoned their wealth in cattle.[32] The "fanatically pastoral" races of Africa have been alluded to above.[33] It would seem fair to say that while the patriarchal system may be found among peoples who are not predominantly herders, it is seldom absent where they are; and that that system, in pronounced and typical form, is not likely to exist among tribes which have not yet attained to pastoral life, though it may persist among those who have passed into an agricultural

[28] *Kgchte.*, I, 478 ff., 490.

[29] For the climatic factor in these movements, see Huntington, *Pulse of Asia.*

[30] §§335, 337, below.   [31] Ratzel, *Hist. Mankind*, I, 117.

[32] Keller, *Hom. Soc.*, 34, 96-97; Seymour, *Homeric Age*, 360 ff.

[33] See Ratzel, *Hist. Mankind*, II, 407 ff., *passim.*

economy. It seems clear enough that there is some vital connection between the presence of herds of domestic animals and a certain pronounced phase in the evolution of self-perpetuation institutions; for this patriarchal system, here referred to as a whole, covers multitudinous details of relations between the sexes, between parents and children, and amongst blood-kin, which are to be reviewed in another place.[34]

Only one further consideration belongs here; and that is that cattle-raising seems to have been the factor which, because it so altered the economic status of the sexes, actually ushered in the patriarchal régime.[35] It is evident that woman's contribution was considerable upon the earliest stages,[36] where she collected vegetable food or even practised incipient tillage; where rude agriculture has occupied women while men were little more than hunters, the former have contributed an important element to livelihood, and the typical patriarchate has not developed. But with herding and nomadism man rises in the scale and woman sinks. He becomes independent of her contribution. Her economic efficiency could not but decline relatively to man's, for his winnings are now copious, sure, and of high quality. The mother-family[37] seems to be as much out of place among herdsmen as the father-family is characteristic of them. If this is the case, then the domestication of herds drew after it what has been characterized as the profoundest adjustment shown in the whole course of family-organization. No other conceivable event, upon those earlier stages, could have turned the tables so abruptly, by so radically altering the economic basis of the family-organization. Furthermore, as will appear in another place,[38] the patriarchal régime was of the deepest significance as a transition to later and historical tribal and state-organization. Here are, yet again, the infinite interlacings of mores and institutions; here are, in particular, consequences very remote and unpredictable, arising out of the appropriation of a certain form of energy out of nature.

§99*. **Animals in Religion.** There is still another series of

34 §§419 ff., below.
35 §386, below; Lippert, *Kgchte.*, II, 73 ff.
36 §67, above. 37 §§416, 421, below.
38 §§153, 185, 188, below; Lippert, *Kgchte.*, II, 505 ff.

societal consequences arising out of the relation of man to domesticated animals. Since the cult of primitive times lays hold of and permeates the whole structure of society, the animal-possessions of early man cannot but figure in his religion. In conformity with daimonistic beliefs,[39] the domestic as well as the wild animal's body was the food of the ghosts and of the gods, as it was, or had been, the food of the living. In Homeric times, meals were regularly sacrifices and most sacrifices were feasts.[40] The story of the reception accorded to the offerings of Cain and Abel[41] seems to indicate a preference for the pastoral product rather than the agricultural; and in many instances the animal as well as the grain or fruit of sacrifice belongs to a past time and has ceased to form part of the regular food-supply. In the French Congo, for instance, sheep and goats are kept for sacrificial purposes and for the payment of heavy blood-fines; they are rarely eaten as other animals are.[42] In accordance with the principle of cult-conservatism, it is to be expected that the superseded or "old" foods of a former age shall persist in the stereotyped cult-ritual;[43] in fact, it is largely from a study of that ritual that we are enabled to reconstruct conditions of the remote past and, in particular, to draw the inference that most if not all animals were originally domesticated as a food-supply.

In considering the position of animals in the cult itself, a start must be taken from the all-pervading fetishism of the primitive stage. At once it is found that a host of animals have been, in various places and times, regarded as possessed of spirits. Although not all such animals belonged to domesticated varieties, a number of the most important of them did. The fetish-character of an animal lay in the indwelling of some spirit which made the animal something more than itself; and when a beast had taken on this character, becoming thereby distinguished from other species and individuals, it demanded a treatment peculiar to itself or, rather, to the spirit within it. Once accepted, the fetish-idea led out into not a few important societal consequences. It is entirely likely that the fetish-quality attaching itself to wild animals or to

[39] §§206, 221, 228, 236, below.
[40] Keller, *Hom. Soc.*, 126 ff.
[41] *Gen.*, IV, 2-5.
[42] Kingsley, *Travels W. Afr.*, 451.
[43] §324, below.

those whose domestication had not gone very far, was a critical factor in drawing the attention of men to such animals, and so in securing their domestication and breeding. For the attention attracted to any animal, or plant, formed one of the conditions favorable to artificial selection.[44] What Lippert[45] calls "cult-selection" is seen in a number of cases and must have been present in others, as the beginning of domestication or as a powerful factor in furthering it. Thus the cult-motive should really be added to other incitements, resting upon economic necessity or vanity, which led to the full appropriation and artificialization of the animal forces in nature.

To develop the societal effects of animal-fetishism is a matter of detailed instance rather than of generality.[46] The case is not so simple as is that of fire, for fire is one where the animals are many and diverse. All animals are not fetishes nor are all members of a species sure to be. In general, where the species is one that either feeds upon the bodies of the dead, or is supposed to do so, the fetishism is species-wise; but where this is not the case, or where this criterion is no longer dominant, there must be some special reason why an individual animal is regarded as possessed. A holy species or genus is, for example, that of the serpents or flies, while the case of individual fetishism is that of an Apis-bull,[47] significantly marked, or the white horse. Again, while a whole species of dog, cat, or domestic fowl was often regarded as holy, yet even here there was a persisting distinction, as in the case of the Faust-dog,[48] the witch's coal-black cat, or the cock as distinguished from the hen. Though fowls in general have been utilized for divination, the crowing chanticleer was the preëminent spirit-watcher and the power that caused the sun to rise. The Goat figures in a Walpurgisnacht and the Dove in many a less unholy occasion. Most of the important aspects of animal-fetishism come out clearly in the remarkable history of the dog.[49]

The persuasion as to the spiritual quality of certain animals

[44] §96, above.   [45] *Kgchte.,* I, 484 ff., *passim.*
[46] Lippert, *Kgchte.,* I, 478 ff.; II, 390 ff., presents considerable detail illustrative of the topic.
[47] Herodotus, *Hist.,* IV, §5.
[48] Goethe, *Faust,* I, 1147 ff., 1238 ff., 1328 ff.
[49] *Case-Book,* §99.

permeated into the type and ceremonies of the cult, into its symbolism, and even into the ranks of its divinities.[50] There resulted what has been called "zoölatry." The term is misleading if it is not constantly borne in mind that the object of worship was not the animal as such, but the embodied spirit. It is readily seen that such complex beliefs must have reacted with great power upon the domestication and breeding, upon the utilization and treatment, and so, indeed, even upon the disposition itself of the fetish-animals. Further, herein lay the vindication of an attitude toward the animals which in any case differed much from that of the present day. The term "totemism"[51] alone should convey some idea of that attitude. Primitive man envied the animals their better natural equipment for the struggle for existence, bore their names as titles of honor, and even traced his ancestry from them; and if to this generally recognized superiority there were added qualities that represented deductions from the ghost-theory, certainly the place of the fetish-animals in the whole economy of primitive life must have been, and is by actual evidence demonstrated to have been, a very influential one.

[50] Spencer, *Prin. Soc.*, I, ch. XXII.   [51] §§256, 260, 261, below.

CHAPTER X

APPROPRIATION OF ENERGIES: MEN

§100. **Enslavement.** From the evidence at disposal it appears
that man hesitated as little to appropriate man as he did to utilize
plant or animal. He sought to secure his own interest in all cases;
if that interest was food, he practised cannibalism; if it was self-
gratification, he tortured his captives; and when it had become
somewhat more developed and refined, he enslaved the conquered.
We are setting aside for the time the first systematic form of
enforced labor, which might be called enslavement when viewed
from the appropriate angle,[1] namely, the coercion of woman by
man; for such mastery, combined as it is with the sex-relation,
belongs to marriage and the family rather than to slavery in the
specific sense of that term. With this reservation, the beginnings
of slavery are found to issue from group-conflict. Between groups
engaged in the struggle for existence there was bound to be a
strife of interests issuing in physical violence;[2] then those who
went into war must take the fate of war; and as a result some
disposition had to be made of the vanquished by the victors. They
might be eaten, sacrificed, tortured, or set to fight one another;
but in the course of time this disposition came to be enslavement,
or the appropriation of human forces or energies. Thus the "taming" of fire and the domestication of animals are followed by the
enslavement of man.[3]

This form of appropriation of energies out of nature is later
of development than the two already considered. For among the
conditions admitting of the existence of slavery on any scale deserving of the name and significant in its results for societal life,
is the presence of a relatively strong regulative organization, or
government. That is not demanded as a prerequisite for the appropriation of non-human energies. As enslavement amounts to
the substitution of an alien will for the will of the men whose

---

[1] §64, above. [2] Keller, *Soc. Evol.*, 56 ff.
[3] Nieboer, *Slavery;* Letourneau, *Esclavage;* Sumner, *Folkways,* ch. VI.
These books contain copious evidence.

energies are to be appropriated by other men, it demands incessant repression and coercion. Evidently, then, it calls for disciplined coöperation on the part of the dominant class, that is, for military and regulative organization. This development, depending as it does upon accumulations in the mores under the activity of societal selection, especially through war,[4] does not come at once in society's evolution. Even the Roman government in the time of the Republic had trouble in keeping its slaves subject. The reason why there was no slavery in the Middle Ages was because the feudal lord could not get the help of a state to maintain his authority.[5] Slavery cannot exist in the absence of a regulative power in society capable of imposing its will upon numbers of adults, and of maintaining that will in the face of resistance. The situation as respects government thus conditions the economic status.

Aside from this necessary condition for the development of slavery, another exists in the prior development of a more than rudimentary standard of living. This presupposes a stock of capital, which is the only real "demand for men."[6] It will be noted that the appropriation of human forces goes rather with the struggle to attain such a standard than with the mere struggle for existence. People who are really striving to keep alive are not in the way of keeping slaves.

"The simple wish to use the bodily powers of another person as a means of ministering to one's own ease or pleasure is doubtless the foundation of slavery and as old as human nature."[7] "All desire to increase material production for the sake of increasing material supply makes it necessary to win the services of others."[8]

The impelling vision of a higher standard of living did not come at first. Primitive life was full of dull hardship; grinding, weaving, rowing—even hunting—were drudgery. The savage wanted more and better things, but he wanted them only feebly and fitfully; had the primitive man not preferred leisure to labor, when immediate need was satisfied according to traditional standards, he might well have attained speedily to an elevated standard of liv-

---

4 §143, below; Sumner, *Coll. Ess.*, I, 30 ff.; Keller, *War to Peace*, ch. XIV.
5 Vinogradoff, *Villainage*, 152.
6 Sumner, *Coll. Ess.*, III, 109 ff., 143 ff.
7 Maine, *Anc. Law*, 164.   8 Gumplowicz, *Soc.*, 122.

ing. As it was, he forged ahead very slowly and with much back-slipping. With the domestication of animals certain of the most oppressive tasks were gradually and partially shifted from man to beast; nonetheless it took time before man came to realize the utility of animals for purposes other than the food-supply. It is doubtful whether domestication would have taken place at all generally and completely if its prime object, to furnish food, had not been thus intimately connected with the bald struggle for existence.

When, however, it came to keeping slaves, a more refined motive, involving much more insight into the conditions of life, and more foresight, was a prerequisite. Human beings have been kept in temporary slavery for the sake of sacrificing them; there was a deep satisfaction to vanity in holding enemies in servitude; but the evidence points to the desire for a labor-force as the salient incentive to enslavement. When human energies had been appropriated, the barrier of inertia had been, if not surmounted, at least circumvented; now the more protracted and arduous work could be done without sacrificing the leisure, and yet the loftier standard could be reached. And the attainment of one standard led to the emergence of higher ones; wants were elevated and visions of desirable satisfactions, hitherto unimagined, entered with the widening of horizons. It is easy to raise the standard of living when others must work or pay for it; modern as well as ancient history or pre-history shows this. The race has always done it that way, when occasion offered; and in this case conquest, resulting in social inequality, presented the opportunity. Captives could be forced to do what fellow group members would not do and could not be made to do without endangering the in-group, all members of which stood or fell together.[9]

Says Dundas[10] concerning African slavery: "Slavery is by no means known among all tribes, and from the fact that it is principally to be found in the territory which was formerly German East Africa, and where slave-raiding by Arabs and others was conducted on a much more extensive scale than in British East Africa, I conclude that actual slavery has been introduced in comparatively recent times. The savage African would rarely take male prisoners in war, for either the enemy escaped or was killed, consequently slaves captured in war were practically only women and children. But these as often as not became wives, concubines, and adoptive children."

[9] Gumplowicz, *Soc.*, 121.   [10] In JAI, LI, 263.

§101. Slavery and Hunting. It is clear that what lay behind enslavement was something less primitive than the impulses to fire-getting and animal-breeding. Slavery was an adjustment some-what farther along the road toward civilization. This appears also from a consideration of the status of slavery upon the several schematic stages of self-maintenance.[11] Wherever societies are classified on the basis of types of industrial organization, the other mores and, among them, the type of slavery are correlative with this basic form.

There is little place for slavery in the hunting economy; the man-woman differentiation is adequate, and there is, in any case, no settled regulative system capable of holding in subjection re-sisting bodies of men. The American Indian hunters generally either adopted conquered enemies, in which case the latter became virtually the equals of their conquerors,[12] or killed them. When the life of a hunting tribe is considered, it is evident that there are no particular tasks constituting a field for slave-labor. "In the absence of industrial activity, slaves are almost useless; and, in-deed, where game is scarce, are not worth their food."[13] Hunting is regarded as a noble and honorable occupation, in which the savage likes to excel; there is an element of adventure in it; it is not the sort of activity, hard though it may be, from which he would seek relief by turning it over to a conquered enemy. To do that would not minister to his vanity.

Hunting, further, is closely allied to war, and slaves could not be equipped for it without at the same time furnishing them with the arms which had just been taken away from them—without, that is, putting them again into the field. Nor could any control be exercised over slaves who were set to hunting, even if a rela-tively strong regulative organization existed. Evasion was a sim-ple matter. The only economic control in the hunting tribe is that of the women by the men, into which special elements enter. Even if the captives were set at woman's work—and they sometimes were, in order to heap indignities upon them—they could not be well controlled during the recurring absences of the men.

[11] §§28 ff., above.
[12] §§141, 188, below; Hewitt, "Adoption," in HAI, I, 15-16.
[13] Spencer, *Prin. Soc.*, III, §796.

In conformity with these considerations, we find Nieboer,[14] who has collected and classified a good body of instances, asserting that "hunters hardly
ever keep slaves; and when they do, slavery is of little moment." He cites
eighty-eight cases of tribes on the hunting stage, of which eighteen hold slaves
in some fashion; and believes that the few exceptional cases will show special
conditions. An exceptional case would be that of the poorest Mbayá Indian
of Paraguay with at least three or four slaves, to whom the roughest and most
unpleasant labor is assigned.[15] Fishing, however, is more favorable to slavery;
of the fishing tribes investigated by Nieboer, nearly half, while of the hunting
tribes only one-twelfth, hold slaves. These fishing tribes, largely of the northwest coast of North America, have fixed habitations, live in rather large
groups, and practise considerable industry and trade. Their hunting and fishing are on a large scale and admit of organized labor. They are somewhat
exceptional, even among fisher-folk. Reflection will reveal that for fishermen
several of the salient disqualifications for holding slaves, mentioned above in
connection with hunters, do not apply, at least in so determinative a degree.
To provide them with fish-hooks was not to equip them for renewing hostilities.

The present-day Asiatic Eskimo live in peace with the Chukchi; at certain
times they have lived in union with them, but on a war-footing against other
tribes "from whom they have got captives, namely, women who were made
slaves and wares in trade."[16] Among the Yukaghir of Siberia, "the slaves were
captives of war, and the position of women among them was better than that
of the men, who could belong neither to the class of warriors nor of hunters."
The only manly occupation open to them was fishing. "The slave stayed in the
house with the women, the old people, and the children, and did house-work
on equal terms with the women. In addition, however, he was allowed to do
such work as the fitting up of the sledges and nets, and to participate in fishing parties."[17] Of the Tlinkit slaves it is reported: "These wretched men and
women were the constant victims of cruelty. They were compelled to do all
kinds of menial work, such as getting wood, making fires, packing dead game,
providing fish, carrying water, paddling canoes and, in short, every species of
drudgery."[18] There is an estimate of the number of Tlinkit slaves which represents them as forming about one-third of the population; "the price of an
adult slave was about $500 in blankets; of a child, 50 blankets, about $150."[19]

It is the economic basis of slavery, as of other societal forms,
which is primordial. Had it not been for the existence of economic
conditions favoring or even demanding slavery, it could not have
existed to any degree; and when economic conditions have ceased
to call for slavery, it has fallen. It is very important to keep in
mind the economic background of a great societal institution.

[14] *Slavery,* 190-ff., 255 (quoted); 202, 203, 205, 207; summary on p. 255.
He is subjected to some criticism by McLeod, in AA, XXVII and in *Soc.
Forces,* IV.
[15] Koch, in *Globus,* LXXXI, 44.
[16] Rink, *Eskimoernes Herkomst,* 297.
[17] Czaplicka, *Aborig. Siberia,* 39.   [18] Jones, *Thlingets,* 116-117.
[19] Henshaw, "Slavery," in HAI, II, 598.

However, it is the matter of control over the slaves that has been seen to be the vital one, not only as a precondition, but all along the course; and slavery thus comes to be an issue of the regulative or political organization quite as much as of the economic— a consideration which clearly reveals the tendency of a factor originally economic to pervade the whole societal structure, and to set up actions and reactions as if it were a wholly independent, underived societal element.

Although it is not intended to treat in this place of more than the economic aspects of the system, we cannot pass by the occasion to draw attention to the interrelation of societal factors or to hint at the general effects of the adjustment. The sequels of the enslavement of men who, though in servitude, yet form part of the society, are bound to be more extensive, though less vital and intensive, than those consequent upon the appropriation of fire or of animal forces. Power of control appears, indeed, as the decisive and determining condition. Slaves have had the will of others substituted for their own; and they have always resisted this consummation. The limit of enslavement lies in the superiority of the coercive or dominating power—whether this inheres in actual force, or in formidable organization, or in the mores—over the sum of the resistance that can be offered. Hence, again, no slavery on the large scale can be looked for where general societal organization is not more highly developed.

§102*. Slavery and Herding. Among pastoral tribes there is no strong economic impulsion to the appropriation of human forces. Domestic animals engross attention and provide for needs. The forms of labor are not so different in quality from those of the hunting stage, and the life is migratory. Of the pastoral tribes he investigates, Nieboer[20] finds that about the same number hold slaves as do not hold them; and he thinks that where slavery exists it can be referred in part to special conditions, such as the existence of the slave-trade or the proximity of inferior races. He concludes that "the relation between capital and labour among pastoral tribes renders the economic use of slavery very small." On the pastoral stage even sex-domination means less of the imposi-

[20] *Slavery*, 262 ff., 289.

tion of heavy tasks than before, for the beasts take the burden-bearing off the shoulders of the women. Further, the duties connected with the care of cattle are especially honorable and are discharged with satisfaction. Cattle-possessors do not care to entrust their wealth to slaves any more than to women. If slaves are kept, out of the spoil of war, they are likely to be the women and children,[21] for the regulative organization is not strong enough to hold down numbers of grown men. According to Lippert,[22] while mother-descent was to be found to some extent upon the hunting stage and upon the agricultural, it was absent upon the pastoral; and mother-descent knew no property in men.

It is significant that upon the pastoral stage, and to a lesser degree upon the one preceding it, there occurs a subjection of group to group, which is not slavery at all in the strict sense of the word, but group-domination followed by exploitation.[23]

"When a victorious horde subjects a people that moves about over a fertile tillage-country, it will force the latter to cultivate the ground. It will bind them to the soil and, for the purpose of exploiting land and people, will even become sedentary among them, dividing itself up to suit the case." This is to be seen in the organization of European agricultural states up to modern times. The author quoted[24] thinks, however, that an environment of extended steppes and pasture-land coerces to a different societal organization: then the conquerors, dividing up the conquered according to the demands of the case, take them with them to transport the burdens, tend the cattle, and perform other labors.

This latter alternative is rather rare; in general the occupation of the exploited group is agriculture. On an ethnological map of Africa,[25] which shows also the distribution of occupations, the central part of the continent is seen to be inhabited by tillers, while the Sudan region, the inhabitable sections of the southern Sahara, and certain districts in southern Africa are occupied by pastoral tribes; then between the prevalently agricultural and the prevalently pastoral regions is a belt of country colored to indicate agricultural populations under the domination of pastoral nomads. This is a step in state-building, for it is a species of con-

[21] Homer, *Iliad*, IX, 592-594.
[22] *Kgchte.*, II, 275; cf. §§421, 422, below.
[23] Sumner, *Folkways*, §272.   [24] Gumplowicz, *Soc.*, 120-121.
[25] Ratzel, *Hist. of Mankind*, II, between pp. 336 and 337.

quest; it is, in effect, serfdom, where natural conditions bind the
men to the land. Ratzel[26] generalizes to the effect that from Timbuctoo to Mexico we find the strongest state-formations located
where a rich and fertile land peopled by husbandmen borders on
a steppe whose vigorous, warlike, and masterful people rule the
tillers. The determining condition in such cases is the opportunity
for control. Masters of the Beduin order—to take the extreme
type—visit subjected groups of oasis-dwellers periodically. They
cannot remain and control them and their labors; it is the natural conditions that keep the subjected group where it is, thus
lending a compulsion toward the formation of the compound land-
plus-man unit which, as we shall soon see, is characteristic of
slavery and serfdom on the agricultural stage.

Somewhat the same situation has existed in China. Repeatedly the stronger
barbarian hordes have broken in upon the tillers of the rich river-bottoms.
They have not made actual slaves of the tillers because the latter have always
been too numerous and cultured to become actual slaves; yet the Manchus
were nomadic and powerful masters and imposed the queue as a badge of
political servitude. So often have oppressive conquerors come into China from
the north that a proverb has developed: "Do not regard the cock which comes
from the south but fear the wolf from the north."[27]

§103. Slavery and Tillage. Preceding cases have foreshadowed
the fact that with the fuller utilization of land through tillage the
whole situation as respects slave-labor and slavery is altered from
what went before. Tillage is regarded as laborious, monotonous,
and uninteresting; where it is typical woman's work, it is thought
to be demeaning to man. Hunters and herders have generally held
it in contempt, especially since they have regarded it as the very
antithesis to the virile occupation of war—as, in fact, leading to a
non-militant, effeminate disposition. Since it was both arduous and
contemptible, it was a fit occupation for those who had been overcome in the field of nobler endeavor. Yet the utility of a more
developed tillage was self-evident; when a people had risen to
apprehend the higher standard of living that went with it, they
would not easily renounce it. Nieboer[28] finds that agriculture does
not necessarily lead to slavery, but that "the more agriculture is
developed, the more frequent slavery becomes." Among the "hunt-

26 *Vkde.*, III, 7; §§185, 187, below.
27 Communicated by Professor Harvey.   28 *Slavery*, 292 ff., 415 (quoted).

ing agriculturists" the old sex-division of labor is more common,
but with "agriculturists of the higher stages" slavery comes to
be the order of the day, while "commercial agricultural tribes are
far more likely to keep slaves than agricultural tribes among
which commerce holds a very subordinate place." These cases fore-
shadow the developing importance of slavery. Nor should it be
lost to sight that the system of agriculture, having developed the
mores of enslavement, renders the people who practise it more
tolerant of their own reduction to servitude. No one ever enslaved
the hunting or pastoral tribes of the earth with any success; the
typical slave-race has been the African. The African, however, has
been characteristically a tiller; and where he was not, he was not
enslaved. It was the Congo and Angola natives, those of the Slave
and Guinea Coasts and, later on, the peoples of Mozambique who
furnished the materials for the slave-trade; no one cared to try
to subdue the Zulu and Matabele, who proved so hard a proposition for the British forces, nor yet the "Fuzzy-wuzzy," with his
home in the Sudan, "a poor, benighted heathen, but a first-class
fighting man." It is perhaps altogether futile to derive race-
character from style of industrial organization, seeking to identify the one as cause and the other as effect; but the fact remains
that the qualities of the negro which made him a tractable slave
were, in addition to great bodily strength, docility, cheerfulness,
a short memory for sorrows and cruelties, an easily aroused grati-
tude for kindness, a lack of race-fellowship and of sympathy for
his kind, also traditional acquiescence in enslavement—and these
were the traits of the agricultural tribes and not of the unen-
slaved others.

Tillage must go on, then, and there must be a labor-force superior to that of women, under whom, as it seems, the crude beginnings had been made. No one would willingly put forth the effort
necessary; hence those must do it who could be coerced. These
were the members of the "others-group" who had been reduced as
a result of conflict. Formerly there had lain before such the alternative of death or adoption; now came the appropriation of their
physical energies, hitherto of little use to their conquerors. Here
is where the appropriation of human energies on a significant scale
appears, along with a new need arising in the process of societal

adaptation to environment. Here was a new variation of specialization in labor, a new form, that is, of an economy in the struggle for life and for a standard of living.[29] The need was a derived rather than a primordial one, and so the adjustment could not be so direct and natural as were the other forms of appropriation of energies out of nature.

There was, in developing tillage, in addition to the heavy labors of clearing and ground-breaking, also more hard drudgery to be done than women could accomplish. Presently there was at hand, however, a coercive organization competent to cope with the situation; a more settled economy had emerged; and the danger of rearming the vanquished by putting into their hands the tools of agriculture was not impressive. What had to be done was, in a word, to hold together a compound unit of land-plus-labor. Land had come, under tillage, to bear economic rent and so to form an element of private property;[30] it is significant that this development as respects land went along parallel with the enslavement, or reduction to property, of men. But land, in itself, has no value; its successful utilization has always depended upon the possibility of holding the man-land combination together.[31] Though, under the domination of group by group, it was sometimes so held by the very natural environment itself,[32] much more commonly, when slaves and masters formed together a single society, the coercion of a military system, passing into a regulative organization, became indispensable. In the course of time the tiller got rights by being legally attached to the land—*adscriptus glebæ;* serfdom arises from the civil need of forcing men to stay on land and till it when to do so is more of a burden than an advantage. The serf finally worked through into an independence of such attachment, when the economic and social situation had so evolved that he did not care to run away. Then he was held to the land by his own interest. Thus slavery worked out into a more evolved societal adjustment.

The motives leading to enslavement were all rooted firmly in self-interest. It was pleasant to impose hard labors—woman's

29 §§70, 71, above.   30 §§118, 124, below.
31 On "prairie-value," etc., §126, below.
32 §102, above.

work—upon a defeated adversary, and the ability to do so and the exaltation of lordship over out-groupers were a constant source of satisfaction. And yet out of these crude and unsavory beginnings came an advantage to society which we now find it hard to realize. Here were necessary tasks, labors the more inevitable as population grew and became more sedentary, preconditions as vital for that stage of population-increase as rapid transportation has later become; yet these tasks could scarcely have been done had it depended upon the volition of the men. It was to society's interest rather that they should be accomplished even under cruel compulsion than that they should not be done at all. It was more expedient for society that someone should work, even though he did so under the stress of pain or fear, than that work should not go on. Labor does not have to be free in order to constitute a basic support for civilization—any more than capital requires to be equally distributed in order to discharge its beneficent function.[33]

The presence of slaves in a society introduced an additional element of unlikeness and of inequality, with an attendant extension of specialization.[34] The introduction of a new and lowest social category tended to alter relatively to one another the positions of the other constituent elements of the society; thus, in the industrial organization, the humblest member of the in-group was raised above his former minimum station, when a substratum of the enslaved had been slipped under him.

Lugard[35] reproduces the view of an intelligent African regarding slavery: "Slavery you say is bad. I agree that it is bad, but slave-labour is to the interior of Africa what steam-power is to your country. In your great factories where steam is used, is all well with the employees? Is there not much misery and suffering? You admit there is. Well, if the angel of God came and saw the unhappiness of your factories and said: 'This must not continue— abolish steam,' would you think it a wise decree? Would you not think it wiser to find means of alleviating the suffering? And so it is with slavery. You cannot say abolish slavery all at once because in some cases it has caused much suffering." The author believes, with his native friend, that slavery was "a necessary step in social progress," superseding the earlier law of massacre and cannibalism.

[33] "No matter who owns the capital, capital works for everybody. Ford owns the flivver factory, but everybody owns the flivvers." Davis, *Iron Puddler*, 268.
[34] §70, above.   [35] *Brit. Trop. Afr.*, 365, 354-355.

§104*. **Slavery as an Adjustment.** Slavery was, then, in its day, an expedient adjustment, and an indispensable link in the evolutionary series along which the race was moving to the attainment of what it has eventually secured in the way of maintenance-organization. It was a distinct mitigation of war; in Australia, "slavery in any shape or form is unknown; between friend and foe there is no intermediate status."[36] Plainly, even from the standpoint of our own mores, it represented something less cruel and restrictive than what went before. That it involved oppression is true; but it gave discipline. It was in the school of oppression, of which enslavement was a salient feature, that the human race learned steady industry. They never faced it willingly; some forced it on others by superior power and discipline. This action fell in with the exigencies of the struggle for existence, which required greater production unless the society was to sink back into permanent wretchedness, as many societies did. The existing savages and barbarians are those who escaped this process. Though the societal organization, with force, rule, coercion, classes, slavery, served primarily selfishness, greed, and luxury, nevertheless it worked along the line of civilization, and at last all shared its fruits.

"In my opinion," writes Boggiani,[37] "for the natives of the Chaco, who live in primitive savagery little above the mode of animals, slavery amidst people of a superior race and of more advanced mores is an incalculable benefit; and I am convinced that to hinder it in such a case would be a capital error. They will never improve by their own initiative. It is therefore necessary to force them to come out of their brute-like condition and to awaken their intelligence, which is not wanting if they receive practical and energetic direction." It is easy enough to see this aspect of the case; and if one realizes that it is only one side of the story, no harm can be done. But preoccupation with enforced uplift of native-peoples may readily lead to inhumanity.[38] One of the most blunt of the German writers[39] on colonization argues as follows. The free negro is worthless and wholly improvident; he will not work. Slavery is ingrained in the population; to try to get rid of it by a stroke of the pen is as foolish as to hope to ban the potato-bug from Europe by proclamation. Every freed slave starts out at once to acquire slaves. Nevertheless the native system is mild. Emancipation is a most questionable policy, for freedom, to the negro, means liberty to do nothing. He needs a certain amount of compulsion. The

36 Jenness and Ballentyne, *D'Entrecasteaux,* 66.
37 *Caduvei,* 100.
38 Giesebrecht, *Behandlung d. Eingeb.;* Keller, *Colon.,* 580 ff.
39 Boshart, *Afr. Leben,* 210, 218-224.

best plan is to regulate the conditions of slavery, not seeking to uproot the institution. It is folly to allow the missionaries to teach the negro the equality of all men; he takes it to mean that he need not work if he does not want to. There are enough socialistic schemes for world-beatification at home in Germany; they should not be imported into the colonies. The negro is the only serviceable laborer in Africa and will remain so. He must be forced to work. Is this tyrannical, when the German has to spend some of the best years of his life in the barracks? No; it is a necessary evil, in one continent as in the other. Above all there should be no sudden emancipation; otherwise there will be an ugly sequel as was the case in Russia, the United States, Egypt, and Brazil.

"In reality, the primitive slave had a better standing, not on account of sentiment, but for practical reasons. The fundamental reason is economic. Ancient communities were based on natural husbandry, and so weak and insufficient was the concentration of society, that any complex organization of labour or exploitation of dependents could not be carried out. As every one was close to nature, the best way of using one's dependents was to fleece them, as it were, to take what they could provide in the easiest way. The master's demands as regards his servant were limited by considerations as to the latter's existence and health. There was not much choice in the matter, and the best thing to do was to settle serfs in their own homesteads and let them take part in cattle-breeding or the cultivation of the soil in much the same way as the master himself. The tributary form of slavery was therefore the natural one, especially among the Aryans who practised pastoral husbandry and primitive agriculture. It is hardly a paradox to say that slavery was intensified, up to a certain point, by the progress of civilization. . . . A remarkable exception occurs in the case of female slaves, whose value depended on sexual attraction, not on labour. The female slave—*cumhal*—was used by the Celts as a unit of currency. . . . Thus primitive law is far from manifesting any sharp contrasts between the social orders and from degrading slaves to the position of cattle or tools. The lower classes were dependent, but they were not devoid of personal rights and judicial protection. The root of this lies in the necessities of the economic situation to which customs and morals had to adapt themselves."[40]

Thus an institution of which we disapprove for ourselves, and to secure the destruction of which we have been willing to spend much, even of blood, was in its time a distinct advance in societal adjustment. The fact that it has come to be a maladaptation upon our more evolved stage of civilization should not blind us, as it blinded the compassionate Darwin,[41] to its evolutionary expediency. The replacement of the system by more expedient adjustments, or even the objection that it ran out into forms injurious

[40] Vinogradoff, *Hist. Jurispr.*, I, 259.

[41] See the interchange between Darwin and Morley over the "crime of slavery," in Darwin, *More Letters*, I, 326; summarized in Keller, *Soc. Evol.*, 251 ff.

to society, does not nullify the fact that it was, in its day, a variation in the mores which was well-nigh universally approved, preserved, and incorporated in the codes of nations. It is the agricultural stage that brought about the appropriation of human energies upon a scale at all comparable to the cases of appropriation reviewed in preceding chapters. We do not conceive it necessary to cite cases of slavery among tillers. The connection of slavery with tillage can be seen in an extreme but characteristic form at a later stage of evolution; the great development of servitude in modern times has appeared along with the plantation-system of tropical and subtropical agriculture, where an acclimatized labor-force was the necessary condition of success in production.[42]

The utility of the human forces appropriated by enslavement has been less lasting than that of the other energies derived out of nature. From the standpoint of the general interest of society slavery has not permanently paid and, in form at least, it has been singled out and removed by the action of societal selection. As an expedient it could not meet the competition of mechanical devices or of free labor. Human force, as of a relatively inferior order, has been replaced by other forces wherever it has been a matter of physical strength alone: the use of men as burden-bearers, as in Africa, has been the employment of the only expedient available; then the acquisition of other transportation facilities has rapidly replaced the human pack-animal. Similarly in the case of manual labor—in short, in all activities other than intellectual—man has been found to be relatively ineffective. The changes due to improvement of the industrial organization have worked out in the mores to a disparagement of slavery, and then to an abhorrence of it, on the part of the most civilized peoples.

"A report of the temporary slavery commission of the League of Nations . . . indicates that slavery is practically confined to the Mohammedan countries, but that in Latin American countries a system of peonage exists which is equal to slavery." The latter is practically debt-slavery and is not unrepresented in other parts of the world.[43]

Further, the efficiency of slave-labor, as compared with free labor, as the economists have long ago explained, is not great. If

[42] Keller, *Colon.,* index, *sub* "Slavery," "Slave-trade."
[43] N. Y. *Times,* Aug. 18, 1925.

the slave will not use his brains, as we are told he does not—if his mental as well as his bodily energies cannot be appropriated— then there is left only a relatively inferior animal. In comparison with machines, which are tireless bodies that include the material- ized brains of able men,[44] that animal is doubly inferior. And slave-labor, in comparison with that put forth voluntarily or even eagerly under the spur of ambition and individual initiative, has been unwilling, careless, wasteful, slothful, and generally ineffec- tive. Cairnes[45] sums up the economic defects of slave-labor: "it is given reluctantly; it is unskillful; it is wanting in versatility." Thus it is that slavery has come to be a maladaptation; and, like plural marriage and other superseded societal forms, it has been selected out, wherever some form of isolation from competition, as for instance, in the tropics, has not operated to prolong its persistence. It is a system that seems to be inconsonant with a high degree of culture. Upon such an advanced stage, "it is a kind of pitfall for civilization."[46] Mill[47] was one of the few who saw beforehand what it would have meant, if the South had suc- ceeded in maintaining a big republic based on slavery, to the pres- tige of democracy. Slavery as a feature of the maintenance-organi- zation was bound to mold the mores and institutions all along the line, and not alone for the South but for all those who had to deal with it. Mill also foresaw the length and bitterness of the struggle necessary to select out of the mores so basic and long- standing a usage.

When it was suggested that the way to destroy the slave-trade in Africa was by making roads, so that the human pack-animal, who alone could carry ivory and other products along the narrow foot-paths, would no longer be needed,[48] the idea was really to make slavery a maladjustment by changing the environing conditions. It was a far-sighted suggestion. An effective cotton- picking machine would have operated in much the same way in our southern states. However, any such attempt as road-building encounters a vast inertia. When the roads were made, the natives still solemnly marched in "goose-order" along the edges, in the good old ancestral way.[49] The rude and primitive mode of grinding corn, employed throughout the Mohammedan Sudan, "contributes more than may at first sight seem credible to perpetuate the immense demand for female slave labor. The very laborious process is performed by pounding the grain on a large stone, called murhaga, by means of a smaller stone held

[44] Keller, *Soc. Evol.*, 19. [45] *Slave Power*, 39.
[46] Sumner, *Folkways*, §313. [47] *Autobiog.*, 267.
[48] Fabri, *Deut. Kolonialpolitik*, 55. [49] Meinecke, *Deut. Kol.*, 16.

in the hand; it is the only method of grinding corn known to the majority of African nations, and is so slow that by the hardest day's work a woman is able to prepare only a sufficient quantity of meal for five or six men. A mill worked by oxen has been erected by the Government in Khartoom, not only for the use of the troops, but also to enable private individuals to have their corn ground at a moderate price; but in spite of this provision, the durra-corn is still pounded on the murhaga in all the houses; not a single resident takes advantage of the improved facility that is offered."[50]

Slavery was one of the rude compulsions toward the overcoming of human inertia. But it was a strong compulsion, causing some to work steadily and pile up capital for others, where without it labor had been intermittent and accumulations of capital small. Despite its rudeness, however, the primitive forms of servitude did not make such demands upon the slave as did the modern system which was formally discarded not so many years ago.[51] Up to the time when communication and transportation of a modern type were developed or introduced, there was no clean-cut distinction, of race, for instance, between masters and slaves; no absentee owners; no strong demand for products in a world market, which led to the incessant and heavy demands made upon the vital forces and health of slaves of a "lower" race, under overseers who felt only the increasing insistence upon speedier production of what could be turned into dividends. The treatment of slaves may be said, in general, to have varied in severity with the degree of remoteness between the owners and the owned. Primitive slavery was relatively easy-going and slaves were more nearly house-servants; slavery came to have its abhorrent features when it was practised by peoples of a relatively high civilization. It is by these features chiefly that we know it, in these decades not so long after its abolition. And the horrors of the slave-trade certainly equalled those of the slave-status. It resulted from a demand made upon human energies by plantation-agriculture.[52] The blame that any-one wishes to assign to enslavers cannot in justice be loaded upon the resourceless native slave-holder. He had his mildly alcoholic drink, and civilization brought him "fire-water"; he had his relatively mild and local servitude, and civilization conferred upon him a double-distilled corruption.

50 Schweinfurth, *Heart of Afr.*, II, 424-425.
51 Lugard, *Brit. Trop. Afr.*, chs. XVII, XVIII.
52 Keller, *Colon.*, 9 ff.

§105*. **Slavery for Debt and Crime.** Hitherto we have dealt with the appropriation of human energies under impulses of an elemental order; in addition, the societal system, in the course of its development, produces forms of enslavement which are adjustments to life-conditions of a less underived character. Debt-slavery is one of these. "In nearly every country, during the lower stages of civilization, the insolvent debtor, by becoming the property of his creditor, may be reduced to slavery."[53] The connection of debt-slavery with the more elemental conditions lies in the fact that a debtor has used another man's product and is bound to replace it;[54] he has destroyed or diverted a portion of the creditor's provision for maintenance and must place him where he was before, even at the expense of his own liberty. This idea of compensation is the one underlying the talion,[55] but the practice as regards debt is evidently of a derived nature. Strictly speaking, enslavement for debt cannot be primitive in the sense of direct appropriation of human energies. It is different from less derived forms of the institution in that it is an intra-group affair and in that the debt-slave enters servitude, or at any rate incurs the risk of so doing, through choice, and often his own choice. It is also, in theory at least, a temporary matter, though the conditions surrounding the debt-relation are such that there is great difficulty in emerging from it. Borrowing, it should be noted, is not of the type current in civilization, namely, an expedient in production; it is done in order to live or to enjoy.

For the slave-owner the difference between slaves captured in war and debt-slaves is the difference between labor-force got as booty by expenditure of energy and capital in raids or campaigns upon the out-group and labor-force at disposal by reason of expenditures securing life, protection, or privilege to the weak of the in-group. In the one case, the slaves, as members of the out-group, have no rights; in the other, as members of the in-group, they have possible avengers and so certain rights; and this, in the primitive code, makes no small difference. The underlying sense of the matter is the same in both cases, however; slavery always means the relation of the powerful and successful to the weak and

[53] Letourneau, *Prop.*, 352.   [54] Sumner, *Folkways*, §271.
[55] §177, below.

unsuccessful, of the confident to the diffident, of the superior to the inferior. It is a familiar fact that protection has regularly been secured in turbulent times through becoming a powerful man's "man"; in becoming a vassal or retainer, the inferior became virtually a slave. This was the price paid for life and security; in return for these the protector really appropriated the energies, including loyalty, of the protected. Similarly in the debt-relation, as we have seen in a preceding connection:[56] it was often incurred to secure the necessities of existence; it was a surrender of self-direction and will in return for food and shelter. Sometimes it was by way of recompense for injury done;[57] and, again, as the evidence will show, it was lightly entered upon in order to secure the means of self-indulgence.

Marsden[58] summarizes the status of the debt-slave as follows: "When a debtor is unable to pay what he owes, and has no relation or friends capable of doing it for him; or when the children of a deceased person do not find property enough to discharge the debts of their parent, they are forced to the state which is called *mengiring,* which simply means to follow or be dependent on, but here implies the becoming a species of bondslaves to the creditor, who allows them subsistence and clothing, but does not appropriate the produce of their labour to the diminution of their debt." Wilken[59] finds this state a modification of imprisonment, in stocks or otherwise, accompanied by tortures of various description, citing a number of peoples who have made such modification. Debt-slavery is very widespread in the Indian Archipelago; together with the bodily punishment which preceded, it is wholly a private affair, only a few tribes using public authority to bring it about or guarantee it. In deriving enslavement for debt from imprisonment and other forms of collecting from the debtor's body, this author refers to the wellknown incident in *The Merchant of Venice,* noting that it was in the mores of a former time to assess the value of the several members of the body; and he sees the collection of a debt by mutilation as a reversal of the usage of paying the victim of mutilation according to a sort of customary tariff. With this custom he aligns also the fact that the corpse of a deceased debtor was at the disposition of his creditor, who could hinder its interment, thus following his rights into the grave and even beyond it. In Timor no burial may take place before all the debts of the deceased are paid; the corpse is hermetically sealed in a casket and then preserved for a period, even up to ten years or more, thus retaining the soul from rest and also dishonoring it, until it shall have been released by repayment of its debt at the hand of some survivor. If a man cannot pay his debts, he must suffer for it not alone in the body but also in the soul. The usage existed even in ancient Egypt. The primitive man thus sets no small valuation upon his property.

56 §83, above.   57 Ratzel, *Vkde.,* I, 83.
58 *Sumatra,* 252.
59 In VG, II, 401-403; 399, note, 404, 405, 406-407.

Such directness and crudity are characteristic of primitive thinking and action; they have lasted on into relatively recent stretches of history; they yield, however, to expediency and are not pressed to material disadvantage in the face of altered conditions. The Nagas of India show a practical modification in the form of remission. Their loans "are usually given in paddy—must be repaid in the following year plus 100 per cent by way of interest. If the principal is repaid then, the interest remains as it is and does not increase, however much delayed payment may be, but if the principal is left unpaid or only paid in part, the whole sum outstanding redoubles itself during the following year and so goes on at 100 per cent compound interest till the whole of the principal is paid off, at which point the outstanding sum becomes stationary. Under this system a small debt rapidly assumes impossible proportions, and while the Semas were independent large claims, consisting mostly of interest, were probably compounded for, the creditor gladly forgoing part of his rights in order to get the remainder. . . . All Semas . . . recognise a definite and uniform custom of remission on debt paid off in full. This remission is 10 per cent of the whole payment due."[60]

The cases reveal the local details of debt-slavery as differing under varying conditions and show that the institution as a whole has had its utilities as a general adjustment in self-maintenance. They throw the strongest of light upon the vigor and persistence of the sense of property. If the debtor could no longer be coerced directly, he could be forced down into slavery and there coerced— a clever and expedient adjustment. A specific case of confusion ensuing upon the arbitrary removal of the system is revealed in the words of the chief of Chittagong, India,[61] who describes the general conditions of slavery, concluding as follows: "The above custom has prevailed time out of mind, and discontinuation of it would cause many unforeseen distresses, innumerable complaints on the part of the masters, and at the same time would not be satisfactory to the slaves, who, owing to usage, have no desire to live otherwise." Having paid such respects to the mores, he goes on to the matter of debt-slavery.

"Until lately the universal custom prevailed in the hills of having debtor slaves. Persons borrowed money from their chief, or some other well-to-do individual, and gave one of their children or a female relative to serve as menial until the debt should be paid or cancelled. This service took the place of interest money, but the creditor was bound to release the slave on repayment or tender of the sum borrowed. The condition of these so-called slaves differed very little from that of free people. They were treated as members of the creditor's family and never exposed to harsh usage. They could not be sold or transferred. Their position was far better than the galling bondage in which

60 Hutton, *Sema Nagas,* 160-161.
61 Letter to Warren Hastings, in Lewin, *S.E. India,* 85-86.

hill men were subsequently often legally held by the Bengallee mahajuns. Since the direct management of the hills has been taken in hand, upwards of 300 debtor slaves have been released, some at the request of relatives, who wished to get off paying their creditors, others simply because they were supposed to be slaves; many of the latter afterwards returned to their creditors to fulfill their engagements. The Chiefs and principal men, being immediately under the eye of the authority, were unable to retain a single menial in their houses, and the daily work of their houses suddenly fell upon their wives and daughters. In consequence of the measure debtor and creditor lost confidence in each other. The hill men no longer sought assistance from their chiefs, or sought it uselessly. They could neither read nor write Bengallee, the language of the courts, and even the ability to speak this language was uncommon. How then could they draw up the bond by which only a debt could be legalized, or become acquainted with or comply with the Procedure of Act 8, of 1859, according to which all suits for debt must be laid?"

White traders in Brazil have seized upon the device of debt-enslavement, press-gang fashion, in order to get work out of indolent natives.[62] The pressure thus brought to bear, being in consonance with the mores, is not felt to be in itself strange and unusual. Of course conscienceless traders and settlers have used the system freely to plunder the natives.

The industrial organization under slavery has a consistent stamp which results from the special type of division of labor in operation. This type is not based upon any "natural" system of differentiation of function, like that between the sexes, but upon coercion. Some have to do the drudgery, while others, freed from that, form a class of the privileged—privileged to do the more interesting things, or to do almost nothing at all. It is at bottom this enforced, fixed relation which Spencer[63] sought to define as status under militancy, as over against free contract where compulsion does not exist. Since the conquerors could choose their occupation, their choice naturally fell upon a continuance of those activities which gained for them their enviable station, that is, militant activities, or upon the derived function of organizing the coercion which they had imposed, that is, upon the regulative or governmental function. It would be easy to infer that any regulative system developed by a slave-keeping society could not but reveal derivations and correlations with a factor so salient as was slavery among the maintenance-mores; and such will be shown

62 Koch-Grünberg, in *Globus*, XC, 8.
63 *Prin. Soc.*, II, chs. XVII, XVIII; III, ch. XVII.

from the facts to be the case.[64] So that the consequences of the appropriation of human energies will be seen to have extended into the derived and apparently remote range of political phenomena.

As an illustration of the interrelation of the slavery-system and the regulative system, there may be singled out the use of enslavement as a punishment for crime. "The criminal fell under obligation of restitution of value to an individual or to the whole (chief)."[65] This form of slavery is possible only within a relatively well-integrated society; and it is also allied to debt-bondage. If non-payment of a debt is looked upon as a crime, then enslavement is its punishment; and there are fines on debtor-slaves which are paid for by protraction of their status. It can be lengthened out by a mean master who will fine the dependent for breakages and other little transgressions, so that his debt may even be increasing while he is a slave. Fines for breaking the *adat*, or code of precedents, are paid by the owner and charged up against the bondsman.[66] Slavery as a punishment for crime, though often merely a working-out of property-damages, is not, however, limited to any special type of misdemeanor.

§106. Societal Effects. Instances in several of the foregoing paragraphs must have suggested the wide influence of slavery upon all parts of the societal structure. It is to be noted, however, that slavery is not imposed for compensation of debt or for punishment where it is not already known as a direct expedient in self-maintenance. That is the primordial form and the others are derived. Given the conception of enslavement, the cases of slavery for debt or for crime have certainly witnessed to the keenness of the property-interest; to secure property, and also law and order, society seems to have snatched at the enslavement-expedient both as a sufficient punishment and as, at the same time, a means of compensation. In the latter respect it was superior to the spilling of blood and was preferred, on that account, to their own cultural advantage, by peoples who were quite indifferent to the taking of human life.

Along with the other manifestations of its pervasive influence

[64] §§164, 167, 186, below.   [65] Sumner, *Folkways*, §271.
[66] Schwaner, *Borneo*, I, 205-206.

in society, slavery strongly affected the family-organization. Foregoing cases have made this plain in several particulars. Perhaps the outstanding effect of slavery on the family lies in its alteration of the status of woman. "The evidence shows that in funeral immolations as elsewhere slavery relieved wives of some of the burdens of matrimony"; slaves were substituted for the widows.[67] Further, by the enslavement of men the women were freed from much of the drudgery that was their lot, and their social status was, in consequence, both elevated and lowered. They were no longer slaves in the fullness of the old sense, yet they must needs sacrifice some of the economic value which they had formerly possessed.

Here again slavery modifies the "natural" system of specialization of function between the sexes; and the introduction of slave-wives or consorts involves the whole question of exogamy. Since the impelling factors in this latter case are hardly classifiable under societal self-maintenance, they must be treated elsewhere and upon somewhat different principles.[68] Here is to be noted only that the introduction of slavery has profoundly modified the various forms of the organization for society's self-perpetuation: marriage and the family. The maintenance-organization is seen, again, to interpenetrate intimately with another major form of societal organization.

Slavery has had a less vital and more incidental connection with religion. Wherever it has existed in the mores, slavery has been sanctioned by ghost-fear and its derivatives; but there are not many ways in which religion has had any special part in its development. Slavery to the ghosts of daimons was much like slavery to men; and where children destined for sacrifice were kept as slaves till they grew up, there was a chance to try out a new variation, just as there was in the case of fetish-animals.

Among the Dyaks, at the death of a great man, debtor-slaves are bound to carved village-posts which stand for glory in head-hunting, and are tortured to death; captives taken on head-hunting expeditions are held as slaves and for human sacrifice on occasions. The souls of those whose heads are taken at the death of a rajah become his slaves in the next life. Slaves are regularly sacrificed at special festivals.[69] The Aztecs, as is well known, made raids for

---

[67] Main, *Relig. Chastity*, 23, note.   [68] §§355, 356, 380, below.
[69] Bock, *Borneo*, 9, 78, 92; Schwaner, *Borneo*, 195.

sacrificial victims, who, in the interim, were slaves. "Grave-escorts" of slaves have been common.[70]

All this is merely a projection of the conditions of ordinary human life at the time; along with other mores, slavery is reflected in the cult. Punishments for transgressions of the taboo sometimes took the form of slavery, probably in commutation of the death penalty.

Among the Sengirese of northern Celebes, when a particular region is in mourning for anyone, any person using a parasol, wearing ornaments, or otherwise breaking mourning-precedents, is made a slave. In the same place, "in the manipulation of sago and rice, quantities of the material are often left in an old prau [boat] in the woods until they are ready for consumption. If during this process a man passes by the prau, it is supposed that he takes away the spirit of the sago, or pradi, or what not, and if caught he is at once seized by the rajah, and he and his whole family become slaves." If a man dies who was wont to fish at a certain place, that place is made taboo to his spirit, and anyone who fishes there is made a slave of the family of the deceased.[71]

Thus enslavement was a religious as well as a secular punishment. It remained so in much more evolved stages of civilization; in seventeenth-century Japan, Christians who recanted were not punished but only kept under surveillance; while those who refused to recant, even under torture, were degraded to the condition of slaves or else put to death.[72] The alternatives laid before the Indians by the Spaniards, of conversion or enslavement, are well known.[73]

§107. Extensions and Correlations.

It has been noted that the failure of slave-labor lay in good part in the impossibility of appropriating much more than the physical energies of men. There should be some brief allusion here to the development of adjustments through which the mental energies also have been evoked. Some of them have been noticed under incentives to labor.[74] Many societal arrangements are adjustments to human wants and are so ordered as to appeal to them and to rouse energy in the effort to satisfy them. What the slave lacks is a chance to satisfy his wants; when he gets that, under the system of free labor which as the result of selection replaced enslavement and

---

[70] §§229, 294, 297, below.   [71] Hickson, in JAI, XVI, 142.
[72] Hearn, *Japan*, 353, 354.   [73] Keller, *Colon.*, 257 ff.
[74] §54, above; Keller, *Starting-Points*, 73 ff.

serfdom, his output of energy, especially of mental energy, is an asset to society incomparably more expedient than what went before. The stimulation of ambition, by the removal of limitations and repressions, taps hitherto unavailable reservoirs of human energy. The establishment of law, order, and rights sets human powers free. Prizes, badges, ribbons, uniforms, coronets, eulogies, offices, and publicity of all kinds appeal to vanity in its coarser and finer forms. And the instillation of ghost-fear has been to men like digitalis to a sluggish heart. By all these means latent human energy has been summoned into action; they are no more than mentioned, in the present connection, for their effects are general and perennial and will be in evidence all the way along. We do not wish to widen the scope of the discussion at this point.

Without entering upon the endless detail of technology in the industrial organization, we have now examined three types of appropriation of energies out of nature and have looked somewhat into their influence upon the various categories of societal forms. Appropriations are made from all parts of nature; we might have chosen many other, but perhaps less typical examples; for instance, the utilization of metals, of falling water, of plants brought under domestication. The last of these has a history quite the equal of that of animal-appropriation, and is readily seen to be responsible for the agricultural stage with all its characteristic mores and institutions. But we believe it unnecessary to multiply illustrations of the general principle and process that have been before us in foregoing pages.

It is both curious and significant that while slavery has virtually disappeared, and while the sphere of usefulness of domesticated animals is in many respects in the process of shrinkage, the range of appropriated inorganic energies has lost nothing, but has, on the contrary, gained incalculably both of itself and at the expense of the others. Consider the waning importance of the horse as a draft-animal in competition with the gas-engine. It would seem that the first and oldest type of appropriation was the winning one. There has been, as it were, a sort of rivalry between the three types that has determined which of them is most efficacious for the achievement of the objects unconsciously or purposefully in view in their appropriation, namely, greater efficiency in maintaining existence and raising the standard of living. That form of energy which, by learning its laws, could be most easily adapted to the satisfaction of human needs has had survival-value over the rest. Further, that form which could be made to perform the functions of the others, where a reverse process was impossible or more difficult, has survived over the others. There has never been much success attained in improvement of the slavery-process; breeds of slaves could not be produced like those of the domestic animals. A great deal has been done in the artificial selection of beasts; they have been made over after the desire of men. Yet the results reached with forces appropriated from the inanimate realm, by pure and applied science, have cleanly surpassed all others. It is true that these energies have always remained just what they were in the beginning, not being subject to artificial selection; but they have lent themselves to investigation, experimentation, and application as no others have. New powers, like electricity, have become available and new apparatus for utilizing mechanical and especially chemical energy has been copiously contrived.

If these contentions are sound, it seems that, given these three forms of appropriated energy, with adaptability to human uses as the criterion for determining, under automatic selection, their value and permanence, then the form of energy most readily adaptable by man tends to become ultimately the prevailing form used by him in his struggle for existence and for a standard of living. One might go so far as to say that there are several stages in energy-appropriation: the appropriation of inanimate energies; that of animal-powers, used in connection with the foregoing; that of human powers, used in connection with the other two; then, elimination of the last because of inability to modify them for the required purposes; partial elimination of animal-forces, because of the difficulty in modifying them to meet requirements; concentration upon inanimate energies, as the dominant element in maintenance, because of the relative ease of manipulating them and of the infinite power which knowledge of their nature can focus at the desired point.[75]

It is now in order to consider that which has been appropriated from the aspect of ownership of it, that is, of rights to it, and thus to review the mores and institutions which surround the relation between appropriated things and men. Though these issues draw farther away from "nature" than those which have just been considered, they are for that reason of no less vital import in the organization for societal self-maintenance.

[75] The foregoing correlations and inferences were suggested, while he was a student, by Professor R. H. Gabriel.

It is now of interest to consider that which has been represented
from the map of relationship of it, that is to of right itself, and thus
to represent the forces and their relations, which surround the relation
hence to represented things but even. Though their forces grow
fortress away from "fastness" their those which just been represented. They are but that reason of no less vital import in the
organization for aggregal self-maintenance...

CHAPTER XI

PROPERTY

§108. Root-ideas of Property. Appropriation from nature, whether of energies or materials, is necessary if life is to go on and the standard of living is to be raised. Then the material for self-provision, when it has been appropriated, becomes, as the etymology of the verb "appropriate" suggests, attached to some person or persons. It becomes "property." Property is material for self-provision, in the broad sense of the term, when it has been appropriated. It is not confined to items of capital. As the latter is energy stored against the struggle for existence, it is essentially a thing of the economic life. Property, however, serves self-provision in a wider sense, and thus breaks through the category of self-maintenance into other ranges of societal life; it may include a wife, an ornament, an amulet—things not exclusively of the economic life and sometimes, apparently, totally disconnected with it, though one and all serve self-provision in its broadest sense.

The etymology of the word "property" has been mentioned. A key to the essential meaning of a term is not seldom furnished by its etymology. Terms covering the property-conception, when they are from the Latin, echo the adjective *proprius: proprio, própio, propre, proper* (meaning *own*, as "my *proper* self," a *proper* name or noun); while Teutonic stems repeat the adjective corresponding to *proprius*, forming terms such as *Eigentum, eigendom, ejendom, egendom, owning.* Property is part of the proper or own self, or somehow attached or assimilated to or set apart for it. It is something that belongs to a person, as a key belongs to a door; something attached to him; and then, too, something which he has used. Probably the purest case is that of the Australian *churinga*, a stone or wooden slab dropped by the spirit of life as it enters a woman's body to form the child. To that child it becomes almost a part of himself; it could never be alienated.[1] The relation of property is one between a person and a thing, the thing being conceived to have a certain individuality

[1] §§248, 260, 261, 334, below.

and to be consecrated or devoted or hallowed to the person, as, for example, a grandfather's chair or cane. His personality clings to it even after his death; it is a sort of fetish.[2] Here we grasp the salient feature of individual appropriation: something of the individual's own life is in that which he has taken up and handled; it has thereby come into contact with his personality and by contagion has absorbed something of him. It may be a weapon or an amulet which is in almost constant touch with his body; then again the notion of reception of personality is attached to the tree a man has planted or the ground which he has sown.[3] "That which I have touched belongs to me; I put hand to it; it is mine. The property I hold is the expansion of my own person."

The author[4] just quoted goes on to illustrate: "In the old German law, he who found his cattle in the possession of another, placed his right hand above a relic, a fetish, and his left on the left ear of the animal, claiming it for himself." This looks like the closing of a circuit between the fetish and the possession by the body of the claimant. "A woman in marrying placed her hand in the hand of the husband in whose power and possession she remained. . . . Parry tells of the people of Baffin Bay that in every trade the tongue is passed over the object acquired; likewise the eastern Eskimo lick the objects they buy as they receive them. . . . In written contracts, hairs of the contractants are put in the seals: some portion of the body binds the person and so the will."

This will do for a general introduction to the relation of property to personality; it is important enough to deserve detailed examination. First, then, it is a commonplace of animism that the soul inheres in any severed part of the body, that is, in the exuviæ.[5] If the whole of the body of one who is deceased cannot be recovered for burial, a part will do; if anything, like hair or nail-clippings, which has once been a component of the body, can be laid hand upon, the possessor can work magic upon the person of whom it used to be a part.[6] Further, the bodies of ancestors, since they contain the same blood as their descendants, are almost like the exuviæ; all kinsmen are detached fragments of one life, that of the kin-group, which reaches from the earliest ancestor to the latest descendant-to-be. We may begin by illustrating the consequences of such beliefs in the matter of property.

[2] §§247, 248, 272, 300, 302, below.
[4] Oliveira Martins, *Quadro*, 114–115.
[6] §300, below.

[3] Letourneau, *Prop.*, 28, 72, 91.
[5] §§213, 249, 298, below.

The Maori attached the greatest importance to bloodshed and death, says Taylor;[7] they had no place in their theory for mere happening. When a man struck his head against a beam in a house so that the blood flowed, the house became his, and all his comrades were bound to help him seize it. If a canoe was dashed on shore and a man's life imperilled, he acquired title on the spot. A chief had a claim on the location where any of his relatives had been murdered or killed in battle. In all such cases the idea of vengeance and atonement enters. Each warrior had a peculiar right to a portion of the land of his tribe; "having the bones of his ancestors rest in certain portions of the land gave him a claim there; or the fact that his navel string had been cut there; or that his blood had been shed on it."[8] In Uganda, where the king is regarded as the owner of all the land, able to dispose of it as he sees fit, if a kin-group can prove they have had three generations buried there, the land, no matter where situated or how valuable, is theirs and the king cannot dislodge them.[9] Johnstone[10] speaks of a dispute concerning a boundary where "the one tribe indignantly demanded of the other that they should point to the graves of their fathers on the debatable ground." "If a man is killed by a crocodile, the rights of fishing in the waters where the accident took place pass from the owner to the son of the deceased."[11] "With regard to the burial customs generally, it may be said that a man who buries a debtor is responsible for his debt, and generally speaking the man who buries a person is also his heir. If a man buries his own brother the child of the deceased cannot demand the property."[12] "Should a dispute arise at any time concerning the land whereon an *iho* [navel-strand] is buried, as over a boundary, or over the *mana* [authority or ownership] of a person or gens over such land, then the fact of such *iho* being buried is as good as a Crown Grant, and, as it is a perishable object, the stones [buried with it] are sought, and accepted as a proof."[13] Again, "when the cord drops off, it is handed, as a rule, to the father, who ties it to a kola or coconut tree; this tree is the property of the child when it grows up."[14] The navel-cord is peculiarly a part of the person, as is sufficiently illustrated by its careful preservation and treatment.[15]

Close upon the property-interest that is created by connection with exuviæ comes that which results from contact with the person. Classic cases are those wherein the South African, having touched a drinking-cup with his lips, thereafter regarded it as his, and the experience with the Fuegian woman who tried to keep, as a matter of course, a vessel in which water had been given her.[16] Perhaps the most convincing instance of all is one quoted else-

[7] *Te Ika*, 358, 555.   [8] Tregear, in JAI, XIX, 106.

[9] Roscoe, in JAI, XXXII, 50-51.

[10] In JAI, XXXII, 264 (East Africa).

[11] Cummins, in JAI, XXXIV, 156 (Dinkas).

[12] Thomas, in JAI, XLVII, 185 (Ibo).

[13] Best, in JAI, XLIV, 151.   [14] Thomas, in JAI, LII, 252.

[15] §§249, 408, below.

[16] Fitzroy, *Adventure and Beagle*, I, 52. Fitzroy seems to regard the case as one of unsuccessful pilfering.

where,[17] in which the belief appears that a man can be worked
upon magically by getting possession of some piece of his property, in default of some of his exuviæ. Of particular efficacy is an
intimate belonging, like an old waist-cloth; one that has his
smell.[18] In Australia "it is not considered right or proper to use
anything that has belonged to another man"; property appears
to be charged, as it were, with the owner's personality or soul.
Possessions "might lie in the fork of a tree or on the ground for
ever and no one would touch them even if they were left to rot."
This is the reason why Australians can leave their stone utensils
lying about when they change camp and be assured of finding them
if they return at some distant time.[19] That which is attached to a
person's body is an observed extension of his person: his tools and
weapons mechanically lengthen his reach and coördinate his
muscles in higher combinations; his clothing is another epidermis
or coat of hair; his house is a larger clothing; his beasts are an
improvement upon his legs or other muscular powers, and even
upon his sense of smell; his canoe is a higher potence of the power
to swim.

Take clothing, for instance. If one can get a piece of a dead man's clothing
to bury, in case it is impossible to recover the body, that is much better than
nothing.[20] Among the Dinka, "articles of personal wear are regarded not as
property but as part of the person wearing them. Identification of the wearer
with the clothing in obscure processes of thought is common in the superstitions of almost any part of the world." The author quoted[21] elsewhere includes
ornaments specifically and also the skin on which each wife sleeps. Among
the Palaungs of Farther India, "when a child begins to walk, one of the first
things that it is taught is that it must never in fun put on the clothes of any
one else. If the clothes have never been worn by another person they do not
in any way influence the child, but garments that have been worn by others
influence the child or any one who wears them. If a man is addicted to telling
lies and some one wears his hat by mistake, that person may catch the lie-
telling infection. It is therefore important that children, at an early age,
should not play with the clothes of other people. This also applies to shoes.
. . . To pass under the clothing of another person is . . . a risky proceeding,
as although the good qualities of the owner of the clothes might descend on
the person passing beneath, the bad qualities also descending might outweigh
the influence of the good ones. Palaungs say, 'Although we can see the body
we cannot see the heart'; so it is good to be careful."[22] Among the Nagas, if

17 §300, below; Hardy and Elkington, *S. Seas*, 163.
18 Kingsley, *Travels W. Afr.*, 447.
19 Horne and Aiston, *Cent. Aust.*, 33.   20 §§213, 218, below.
21 O'Sullivan, in JAI, XL, 174.   22 Milne, *Eastern Clan*, 37-38, 48.

a man proves not to be ready for the grave which has been made for him, but recovers after unconsciousness, his own stool "is wrapped in a cloth and put in the grave in his stead. The stool is chosen as, like the bed, . . . it is so closely associated with its owner as to contain some part of his essence, as it were, in virtue of which it is absolutely genna [taboo] at any time to cut or burn a person's stool or bed, while it is very bad form to sit on the bed of a Sema chief unless invited by him to do so."[23] "It is a custom of our people," said an old Alaskan chief, when a Secretary of the Interior had been admonished that he was forgetting his furs, a fine bundle of them on which he had been invited to sit, "it is a custom of our people that what a visitor sits upon is his."[24] One is inclined to wonder whether due importance has been assigned to the study of the etymology of such words as "to possess."

Cases of this sort would seem to form an explanatory setting for such remarks as that negroes have a strong sense of possession but a defective notion of property; that they are more likely to keep what does not belong to them than to steal; that in this they act with "childish egotism."[25]

The word of an experienced observer[26] is as follows: "Ownership of property can never be forfeited but by voluntary relinquishing: such a thing as the lapse of a right or claim by any other means is unthinkable to the Bantu. To what extent this actually applies would be hard to say, for though, as a rule, the native recognizes that sale of anything includes a transfer of ownership, I have constantly found . . . that the vendor will maintain his right at any time to demand back a beast sold against refund of the purchase price, and so much support will he find that I suspect herein a trace of some original right. It is therefore natural that loss or theft of an article cannot deprive the rightful owner of his claim thereto. But it is very common for a reward to be given to the finder or person into whose possession it has passed. . . . Ordinarily, a man who finds anything and does not attempt to discover the owner, will be assumed to have stolen it."

As the conception of the relation of property shades off into what are called "symbolic" acts, its outlines become more vague and uncertain. There are, however, various usages in connection with appropriation and transfer of property which involve personal contact with the property. The hand, we have seen, is laid upon that of which one would take possession. In legal language a person is "seized" of land, and slaves are "manumitted" or "emancipated." There is the marriage *cum manu* and that *sine manu*.[27] The primitive way of arriving at a clear understanding was to

23 Hutton, *Sema Nagas*, 242-243.
24 N. Y. *Times*, September 28, 1924.
25 Ratzel, *Vkde.*, I, 144.   26 Dundas, C., in JAI, LI, 275, 276.
27 Ch. XLVII, below.

act out the situation, so as to appeal to the eye as well as to the ear;[28] then the acting was subject to interpretation when the real reason for its particular form had been forgotten. It might then be viewed as merely a form of courtesy.

Take a single case; we do not assert anything more concerning its interpretation than that it probably goes back to the same ideas about contact which were prominent in the case of property. The natives of the Loyalty Islands "have a peculiar mode of drinking which appears awkward to a European; they throw the head back, with the mouth open, hold the calabash up with both hands, and allow the water to run down the gullet; this is done to prevent the vessel touching their lips, as it would be considered unpolite for several persons to drink out of the same calabash. They sometimes roll up a long leaf in the form of a tube, insert one end into the calabash, and drink out of the other; when this plan is adopted the leaf is always changed when passed to a stranger."[28]

Not all the survivals are thus vague. Certain modern Jews have thought one's property near enough himself to share his luck. Miss Antin's[29] mother was desperately ill. "There were midnight prayers in the synagogue for my mother, and petitions at the graves of her parents; and one awful night when she was near death, three pious mothers who had never lost a child came to my mother's bedside and bought her, for a few kopecks, for their own, so that she might gain the protection of their luck, and so be saved." That purchase is no more explicable apart from the conception of property as an attachment or adherence to self than are the prayers at the graves of parents or the idea of luck as a possession explicable apart from an antecedent ghost-worship or a former belief in a familiar or luck-spirit.[30]

Thus a fundamental notion about property is found in attribution, that is, in the idea of the physical connection of the thing, x, with the man, A, a sort of physical adhesion of thing to person. Later on the adhesion comes to be less material and more spiritual. This notion of attribution is the common element in all the conceptions of "own," "hallowed," "sacred." It is a fundamental association of facts, not a product of reflection. It prevails still in uncivilized society, and our children sometimes express it. All feel the force of it when an object long used by a certain person acquires an attribution to that person which is distinctive, sym-

28 Ray, in JAI, XLVII, 277.   29 *Promised Land*, 138.
30 Chs. XXV, XXVI; §§244, 285, below.

bolical, even consecrated. One would hesitate to use it after his death. The identification of the thing with the person in these cases may illustrate to us, in the midst of our realistic and rationalistic ways of thinking, that primary notion which, for primitive man, grew out of the habitual connection of x with A. When this connection, formed through attribution, had been recognized in the mores, the right of property was present.

The idea of property comes, with more sophisticated peoples, to cover a variety of connotations. The following is a list of terms for property in the Indo-Germanic languages: (1) belonging to one's self; (2) what is on hand; (3) what one has; (4) the product of labor; gain; (5) thing won; (6) booty of the chase or fight; (7) thing granted; (8) thing hoarded or concealed; (9) abundance; (10) power; (11) thing gripped; (12) clothing; (13) possessions; (14) dominion; (15) subsistence; (16) good thing; (17) related to the gods or to fortune.[31] This list will be seen to cover a number of derived ideas of property and property-tenure later to be encountered.

In view of the belief that the next life is a projection of this one[32] the property-relation did not end with the death of the person. The deceased wanted everything in the next life that he wanted here; just those things which were most peculiar to him here could he least spare there. Hence his property was buried or burned with his corpse. Survivors feared to appropriate that which had belonged to the dead; it was left to him as sacred, holy, or "unclean." Only as self-provision becomes harder, or as time passes, do such practices of renunciation in favor of the dead become symbolical rather than real. In some of the Maori villages half of the houses belonged to the dead.[33] A man's dwelling, even in Rome, was private and holy to the house-gods or ancestral spirits. The earthly estates of the owners in the other life were administered for them; thus the kings of Egypt ruled the whole land for Ra.

The right of property was eternal in the sense of lasting as long as the ghost that held it lasted. The guarantee of the right fell not alone on the individuals but also on the group at large; the conception of group-solidarity in penalty[34] forced the society to give sanction to rights of property for the dead. It is only on a relatively advanced stage, for instance in the laws of Solon and

[31] Schrader, *Handelsgchte.*, 59.　　[32] §206, below.
[33] Taylor, *Te Ika*, 221.　　[34] §§176, 274, below.

of the Twelve Tables, that an even partially successful attempt is made to limit the property of those who no longer live. Efforts to reduce the mortmain are phenomena of modern history.[35]

§109. Appropriation Makes Property. The formation of this intimate and enduring relation of thing and person comes through appropriation, or taking to one's self. The man with some sort of property-attachment is no longer the mere human animal; he is something more, because there is added to his personality the increment of the weapon, the wife, the ornament, or the talisman. With this attachment, as with some physical addition to his person, he shows a new form of variation and is selected upon it. To clear up the nature of property, manifestly, there is need for an explanation far more comprehensive than one confined to the range of societal self-maintenance alone. The human interests which property serves are far wider than those emerging solely from the physical struggle for existence; and so the term self-provision, as being wider than self-maintenance, has been used in the preliminary definition. Since, however, the bulk of property falls within the self-maintenance range, the institution is treated under that general division of the subject.

The scope of property, as well as the earlier stages of its evolution, are overlooked by those who assert that nothing can be property which does not embody labor; that it is labor which establishes the essential right to property. Primitive property shows no such antecedent to be indispensable; several of its most important and most cherished forms are quite unelaborated. Such are many of the amulet-ornaments, for instance. They are simply taken to the self in a somewhat less intimate way than the food introduced into the body. Appropriation must precede any other of the processes by which property comes to be. No doubt the application of labor to the fashioning of an arm-shell out of refractory material[36] rendered the product more precious to its owner, so that he was more ready to resist its removal; doubtless, also, there are things appropriated which do not come to possess special value enough to constitute real defended property; nevertheless appro-

[35] Lippert, Kgchte., II, 237, 245, 171, 597; §§231, 234, 251, below.
[36] Seligmann, Melanesians, 520-521.

priation is the sort of general experimentation by which all advance to property begins. And property, resting upon this appropriation, itself the analogue of assimilation, is the earliest, chief, most inevitable, and most permanent interest of mankind.

Property is the thing capable of serving human interest, appropriated to persons who are to enjoy it. It is appropriated by reason of the interest it stimulates. Men are interested in that which, like property, will satisfy wants, present or prospective. Interest is a sensation of wants unsatisfied; it is therefore a feeling consequent upon imperfect adjustment, involving stress that is always pushing, because adjustment is never more than temporary, toward adaptation by way of the mores. Under this stress human beings develop their inherited nature, with all its needs and capacities, toward the highest possible grade, no matter how modest that may be, of fulfilment and excellence. Interest is a relation of humanity to environment by which the development of men's innate possibilities is awakened and sustained, and without which mankind could not exist, or could not attain to the measure of its possibilities. Herein is the sense of need. Interest may be instinctive and unreflective or rational and present to consciousness; and it is sure to show divergent forms. Hence what one person desires sufficiently to make it his property may be a thing of indifference to another; that is, the valuation set on the thing, which determines the tendency of the person to hold to it, may be wholly subjective, finding no corresponding response in the minds of others. A treatise on differential calculus is not property to a savage or a hod-carrier; neither is "interested" in it. An arm of a corpse, however desirable as property to the cannibal or to the medical student, is not to the majority of civilized people a goal of endeavor. An alleged splinter from the True Cross could not be property to a rationalist as to a fervent believer. Shells, fetishes, "medicines," relics, are property of high value to some, while it would not even occur to others to appropriate them. When, in a society, it comes to pass that there is no one whose interests can be served by an object hitherto prized, it ceases to be property.

Thus the type of things that constitute property depends upon the life-conditions of the society and upon expediency as related thereto. Societal adjustments bring in new sorts of possessions, unknown to previous ages. Far earlier than might be expected, rights and incorporeal things became property. The relations between men multiply and become more refined and complex; advantages in the struggle for existence arise from them and onerous obligations ensue upon them. One man stands to win; another to be burdened. A must render to B, or serve him; whether or not he has promised to do so, the mores of the society, enforcing certain views about relations within the societal organization, compel him to conform. In the Middle Ages the disciplinary coercion of the rulers over the ruled was carried so far that there was nothing that a man might want to do which his lord could not forbid him in order to exact from him a payment for license to do it. Such rights were property. Wives and children have been property; but now human beings, and also a large number of rights, have ceased to be owned by anyone. That means that the things that can be property change from time to time, both ways: that becomes property which formerly was not, and *vice versa*. The direction taken in the matter by group-interest is determined in the mores as these adapt themselves to the nature of the relation between society and its environment.

Those who have to do with native peoples sometimes find themselves embarrassed by the discovery that they and their uncivilized charges have been looking at the matter of property from two wholly different angles. Consider the misunderstandings about property in land which took place between the white man and the American Indian.[37] "In most parts of Africa direct taxation has taken the form of a hut tax. The hut was, of course, intended as the symbol of population, and there was no intention of claiming property in it, or of charging a rent for it. But the method was unfortunate, for as Miss Kingsley justly observed, the African assumes that 'the thing you pay any one a fee for is a thing which is not your own,' and that Government has confiscated his hut."[38]

§110. **Property a Monopoly.** Interests are the starting-point and motive of acts; but it is not possible for all to attain to the

[37] §117, below.
[38] Lugard, *Brit. Trop. Afr.*, 252; the expression by Miss Kingsley is in a letter to *The Spectator*, March 19, 1898.

satisfaction of them. All cannot appropriate at the same time, for the supply of satisfactions is limited; those who have appropriated hold their takings against the rest. These are facts, and there are forces behind them which are never to be escaped. The generic distinction of property is that it is held in adverse possession, that is, against all others; it is founded in monopoly and is monopoly. Every person born must occupy an emplacement on the earth's surface, from which he excludes every other. Though after death the body returns to the inorganic world, yet, so long as the soul is conceived still to live, it displaces all human beings from the portion of earth which covers its dust. So long as the grave is respected the soul continues its monopoly. In China this antagonism of the living and the dead, this competition for emplacement, has been carried so far that the building of railroads has been impeded or prevented by it; graves, however ancient, could not be disturbed, whether or not the track-laying has had to follow serpentine windings or stop altogether.

The emplacement-exclusion is not all; monopoly in property derives also from the fundamental fact that the same nutriment cannot go to the support of two existences, two separate bodies, at the same time. Two persons cannot eat the same root or fruit; one excludes the other, and one goes hungry. If there is but one protective amulet and two are in danger of ghostly assault, one goes unprotected. Man in society cannot eat a morsel without taking, appropriating, and monopolizing what God or nature has "given to all"; nothing can be "made" without appropriating raw materials. This monopoly-element runs through all grades; though when food is plentiful and mouths few, it has no practical importance, let the food-supply diminish or the mouths multiply, and it traverses a series of stages toward famine and starvation. To deny the existence of monopoly because there are cases in which it has no vital significance is evidently quite childish.

When it is asserted that greed and desire to plunder each other led men to seize whatever they could monopolize, the facts are misconstrued. When water was scarce, the monopoly was in nature, not of human creation, and men were forced into an antagonism of interest and of strife with regard to it. Salt, always eagerly desired, was found only in limited quantities in particular places.

He who took some left less for others. Appropriation of the salt and of the place of deposit was inevitable. Force in one form or another came into action; tribes fought for salt-wells and flint-deposits. Then the might of society came in to enforce the customs, with their differing modes and details, by which the appropriation was effectuated. Fetishes guaranteed property in crops, trees, stores of honey, and other desirables that had been appropriated; the appropriator secured the aid of a spirit, not as a sanction of an abstract right, but to help him defend his interest and safeguard his monopoly. Force was the consequence of the natural fact of monopoly; law, crystallizing out of the mores, was the sanction of society extended over some peaceable solution. It was this societal sanction that made the right of property.

These are the functions of force and law in the case; they did not create property, but marked out and sanctioned it in society's interest. Force and law have defined the relations of husband and wife, parent and child, as these have worked out in the mores, in just the same way. Property is a product of force only in the sense in which marriage, the state, rights, and justice are products of force. Whenever the monopoly-element comes into prominence, all have to make submission to force and law, only it is disguised. We should all like to live on the Avenue facing the Park, and do business opposite the Post Office. If we are not rich enough to do so, we yield to force and law and go off peaceably to live and do business where the monopoly is not felt. Five thousand of us would like to get into a theater with a capacity of three thousand, to see a first performance. By various methods, three-fifths of us get in and the rest submit to force and law and resign ourselves to stay away. Force and law do not make the case; they sanction the right. The case is made by the fact that human affairs are conditioned in time and place. The same conditions create property.

If two could use the same thing at the same time there would be no justification of property; no one would be assaulting or defending it, because it would not be in existence. Those who assail property all talk about equality, and they turn for illustration to things which are or seem to be present in superfluous amount. This is traditionally true of air and water; yet they are monopolized where there is not, or is sure soon not to be, a superfluous supply.

Rights to water, air, and sunlight are even now paid for; consider the relative costliness of outside apartments and staterooms, or southern exposure. The grades of limit on the supply are the grades of intensity of property. However careless people may be of what is in ample supply, they are not generous with that which is limited. This is true on any grade of civilization.

Though the Arawaks have the notion of private property, yet what any one possesses is so simple and easy to get that each borrows and lends without much care about the returning. No one has much stimulus to win wealth by industry and trade. Supplies for a year can be acquired by three or four months' labor in the field.[39]

At the other end of the scale from such possible insouciance, however, the property-interest is both widened to cover many things that make no appeal to the unsophisticated and sharpened in respect to everything that shows a declining supply relative to increasing numbers.

The keenness of the property-sense is clearly exhibited in the practices connected with the debt-relation.[40] Consider also the wild rage of the Matabele who could not understand the slaughter of their cattle, infected by the rinderpest, at the hand of the British government. The negroes saw merely a gratuitous outrage on their favorite property. This was one of the principal causes for the ensuing Matabele revolt.

§111. Property is Societal. Property in its essence implies antagonism between owner and non-owner; this antagonism is harmonized in the mores; property is therefore societal in nature. In no real sense did Crusoe own property until the man Friday had come. One could not affirm that anything was his when there was no one else from whose claim or use his could be distinguished. Property is the relation between a person and a thing, established in the mores of society, by which the dominion over the thing in the person secures to him the exclusive use and advantage of it, that is, the right to it. Adverse possession and prescription form the only right to property. Here again it is might, the power of the society behind the mores, that makes the right. Property is mine until someone takes it away from me by force which I cannot resist; or until someone else puts in a claim of priority of title under law which the mores, sanctioned by the authority of society,

[39] Von Martius, *Beiträge*, I, 92, 692.   [40] §105, above.

will support. There is no right to property, or to anything else, which depends upon anything "absolute," unconditioned by the exigencies of life, independent of public opinion as expressed in final instance in the mores. Property, law, rights, government, classes,[41] marriage, religion—all are born together and linked together. Among these, property, as the material provision for self-maintenance, is the first and broadest interest of man, the fountain of societal, usages and institutions; for these latter deduce their norm from it and get their sense by their relation to it.

There is an unshaken solidity about property which causes it to be selected as a sort of stabilizer for other human institutions. The passage of property in marriage guarantees the permanency of the relation;[42] and the state, as has been recognized in property-qualifications for the franchise, has been thought safer in the hands of those whose stake in law and order has rendered them more judicious. Merely as an equilibrator of society, property has shown a high survival-value.

Along with all the other institutions of society, property developed out of the mores. The primitive mores are nearly all rude and rough to us. They are so because they represent methods of action and feeling not so far removed from those of the brutes. In any case, one of the prime characters worked out in the struggle for existence and bequeathed as an instinct to all animals is that which leads them to make a monopoly of the means of self-provision. Man would be recreant to his origin if, on the primitive stage, he did otherwise. Hence to complain of property as a monopoly is like complaining of the force of gravitation. Property, being in the mores, is, along with them, a function of the sort of struggle for existence that is being, or has been in the recent past, carried on by the group in question; and thus, especially when finally crystallized into a settled institutional form, it must remain substantially untouched by theorizing and by utopian yearnings and scheming. Indirectly only can these elements, by assisting in the disintegration of the mores, manage to secure changes in the institutions.[43]

[41] §166, below.   [42] §341, below.
[43] Sumner, *Folkways,* §§61, 80.

"Property is always an inseparable attribute of the personality of man. . . . It is entirely allowable to start out from property as an arrangement which is hit upon for the use and benefit of men; which, therefore, because it assures advantages, must be supported, but which, if it should afford disadvantages, must be done away with. Property must be apprehended from an essentially broadened point of view. It is an institution that springs out of the essence of man; one which . . . forms the unshakable foundation of the race of man. What forms private property has to take remains on all sides an open question and belongs undoubtedly among the most debatable subjects of human interests; but the inner necessity of property stands beyond question, and to take away from private property as a human institution is to take no account of the life of man. Man without property ceases to be man."[44]

§112. **Property and the Socializing Forces.** Though, in the divergence of interests, that may become property in one place or time which is not such in another, there are still certain constant and fundamental interests which work out into motives for appropriation of materials for self-provision, and therefore make property. These interests are connected with self-maintenance, self-perpetuation, and self-gratification, and the driving impulses are the now familiar ones of hunger, love, vanity and the other sentiments classifiable with it, and ghost-fear.[45] These motives in all cases cross and intertwine. Says Lippert,[46] after citing cases: "The reader will divine how manifold and tangled is the web of motives which have shaped the institutions having to do with forms of property within the range of higher civilization"; and it would not be going too far to say that this complexity is clearly foreshadowed in the primitive forms. However, a broad fourfold classification of these can be made: the weapon which is the means of getting food or of self-defense; the wife who bears offspring while laboring as a complementary coöperating agent; the ornament that emphasizes individuality and ministers to pride; the amulet that wards off evil from supernatural sources—these are forms of property corresponding to the elemental socializing forces.

Unquestionably self-maintenance is fundamental; the needs that spur men on to it were present at the outset and could never have been intermitted for more than a negligible interval. Nevertheless there is reason to infer that supplies of sustenance or apparatus developed in the struggle for existence did not constitute, to the

---

[44] Samter, *Gesellschaftl. u. Privat-Eigenthum*, 3.
[45] §§11 ff., above. [46] *Kgchte.*, II, 530.

exclusion of other things, the first real property. It has been seen
that supplies, apparatus, or persons, accumulated under the stress
of the socializing forces just named, constitute capital;[47] the
present discussion is designed especially to show how the same
impulsions stress toward the formation of property that is not
strictly capital.

Primitive people cherish various things as property which, from
our point of view, do not minister either to self-maintenance or
self-perpetuation. There is the ornament, for instance. It takes
the unusual to attract the attention of the savage; he picks up
and attaches to his person, through vanity, any shell, stone,
feather, or other find that catches his eye. Any such odd object
may be the abode of a spirit whose aid in winning luck or avoiding
harm is appropriated by attachment. It is preserved as insurance
against the element of chance in life.[48] It becomes an amulet, is
tested out by experience, and is either kept or abandoned. In time
an amulet that is retained becomes attributed in a special manner
to its wearer: it marks or distinguishes him among his fellows; it
sets him off; it increases his personality. The power residing in it
commands respect and excites emulation. Fashion now takes hold
of the case, and a similar possession is indispensable to all who
want to be in the mode. Without this distinctive piece of property
one appears mean and ashamed.

Such an object, however originally appropriated, comes to possess the dual character of amulet and ornament. It distinguishes
its possessor; it is not like vulgar food or common clothing, which
any one can have; it marks out its owner, as a wonderful knife
or tattoo-marks may lend distinction to a schoolboy. It is a superior good which excites the envy of men and the admiration of
women. It nourishes pride and ostentation and confers a new
species of gratification over and beyond animal-satisfactions. It
becomes identified with the possessor, who may be described as the
man who has it, and may even get a name from it. "My ornaments,
you know," said a woman of the Sahara, "are a part of myself.
. . . We do not take off our ornaments because we must enjoy
them while we can. When we are dead, we shall have no good of

[47] §81, above. [48] §§194, 197, below.

them."[49] The person who appropriates an ornament attaches it to
his body to keep it from others and to have it always with him.
If the object is also a trophy, it serves to distinguish its wearer
in an even sharper degree, recalling as it does some glorious deed.

§113*. The Rôle of Vanity and of Ghost-Fear. A savage will
hold with greater tenacity to such an object of pride than he will
to one which is merely useful. It is the fashion of uncivilized man
to strive most for such items of luxury as the civilized man subordinates to the useful and necessary, if indeed he does not regard
them as hostile to the latter.[50] If vanity be considered apart from
ghost-fear, there is here a motive of greatest strength entering
to ensure the perpetual and exclusive relation of a thing to a person. To take it away from him rouses all his anger and calls out
all his power of resistance. Here is the birth of the right of property and of the distinction between mine and thine. It is no strange
thing that property is rooted in vanity; the whole life of the race
shows its highest and most sacred interests provided for or nursed
by its vanity; and in time they are often sacrificed to vanity. This
is yet another illustration of the fact that motives and consequences have no necessary relation between them.

Property may even be assembled with ostentatious self-destitution in view. There is one special and extreme example of prop-
erty-spending which casts strong light upon sentiments in the
primitive mind that spur efforts toward accumulation.

Among certain North American tribes there occurs periodically the so-called
"potlatch" or "potlache." "This is one of the most widespread and curious
customs on the northwest coast. It has its origins not only in the custom of the
exchange of gifts, but in securing the good-will of others by presents. To
procure a wife; to enter the ranks or obtain the influence of medicine men;
to become a great chief; to give social standing to one's children; to take on
oneself the name of a paternal ancestor; to build a house; to become a respected member of the community; to atone for a wrong done; to resent an
insult—property in some form or other must be sacrificed either by destroying
it, to show one's rage, grief, or disregard of wealth, or by giving it away to
obtain the good-will of others. The accumulation of property is a necessity in
these Indian communities in order to stand well in them, and wealth becomes
primarily the basis of social organization. In any case, however, the distribution is the final ceremony, and is conducted as follows: The guests all being
assembled, the goods are displayed about the walls and on poles and cords

49 Pommerol, *Sahariennes,* 71.   50 Lippert, *Kgchte.,* I, 364.

or piled up on the floor in a great mound. The host stands or sits arrayed in ceremonial attire, and presides over the affair with the ceremonial baton in his hand. The herald . . . announces the opening of the ceremony in a speech, extolling the liberality and prowess of the host, and calls a name, giving the present he is to receive. An attendant takes the present and deposits it in front of the person who is to receive it, where it remains until all are thus honored, the names being called out one by one. On the announcement of each name, the host solemnly nods his head and thumps on the floor with his baton. The whole ceremony forcibly reminds one, in a general way, of a Sunday-School Christmas-tree distribution. Formerly slaves were given away to the rich and powerful visitors, but to the poorer guests worn-out blankets, or even pieces or strips of blankets were and still are given, on the principle that to those who have shall be given."[51] Boas[52] goes into a lengthy description of the potlatch, with interpretations differing from those current preceding his investigations; in any case, it appears that "unwitting interference with the system by white men has wrought great injury to the Indians."[53]

The origin of the term potlatch is a Chinook verb meaning "to give." The giving is magnificent and even reckless. In 1877, a rich chief made a potlatch at which four thousand Indians were present. Often a person will save for years in order to give presents on such an occasion; and when one ceremony is over he will begin to save for the next. The writer now being quoted[54] was present, in 1876, at a potlatch that had been prepared for through many years, old women going in rags to fill trunks with calico to be given away. He estimates that 10,000 yards of calico were distributed by the women; then the men gave away money, blankets, and guns. Ten men gave an average of a little over three hundred dollars each. In 1900, an Alaskan chieftain distributed ten thousand dollars' worth of blankets, flour, tents, guns, and hymnbooks, and ended penniless, but with a name sure to be handed down gloriously.[55]

Dorsey[56] says that the Haida and Tlinkit give a potlatch every time a new and bigger labret is assumed; and elsewhere[57] it is stated that among the Sioux the motive to self-destitution is to have no property which would attract the spirits to make the owner unhappy by taking it away. Again potlatches are given to indicate respect for the dead.[58] The Eskimo have this practice and also force him who has gained in trade to make general gifts lest he be killed and his property distributed without regard to his family.[59] Reclus[60] cites the case of an Eskimo family on the Yukon who invited friends and gave away all their property, the accumulation of fifteen years. By this they gained "honor and consideration," accompanied by high esteem and deference in the community.

[51] Niblack, in USNM, 1888, 365-366.
[52] In USNM, 1895, 341-346, 353-356; McLeod, "A primitive clearing house," in Am. Econ. Rev., XV.
[53] McGee, in AA, X, 338.
[54] Eels, in Smithson. Rep., 1887, pt. I, 675 ff.
[55] N. Y. Times, Oct. 24, 1900.
[56] In PSM, LIII, 173.   [57] Dorsey, J., in BAE, XI, 374.
[58] Swanton, in BAE, XXVI, 434, 442, 449.
[59] Nelson, in BAE, XVIII, pt. I, 305, 365.
[60] Prim. Folk, 111.

Of the Tlinkits we read: "For vainglory they often destroy their own property. We have seen fine canoes demolished with an axe in a few moments of time; dishes, stoves and other household goods smashed by their proud owner, just that he might be considered a greater man than some other. In the days of slavery, owners of slaves vied with one another in the sacrifice of slaves. Slaves were property, and the owner who destroyed the most was considered the greatest man. Potlatches are given more for vainglory than for anything else. Public praise and honour are the objects in view. Because oolikan oil is a luxury, and costly, chiefs spatter their canoe sails with it to indicate that they are rich enough to waste the article. . . . Two women were quarreling. In a rage one of them said to the other, 'I'll shut you up!' at that she rushed unto her house, came out with both hands full of silver money and scattered it to the crowd that was watching the proceedings. This did shut the mouth of her opponent, as she could not do likewise. A man in an altercation shoved a chief's wife and she fell. The chief owned a number of slaves. As soon as the wronged woman informed her husband, he sought revenge by heaping a greater shame upon the man who gave the insult, accomplishing it by making a public sacrifice of some of his slaves. As the man who offered the insult had no slaves to sacrifice, he was thus put to everlasting shame. So now when natives quarrel it is a common thing for one to say to the other, 'Shut up! You might be like Mitkeen,' that is, have nothing to destroy in order to get even."[61]

Casuists may say that, as property was born in vanity which we now affect to despise, therefore property has lost its legitimacy. Much fine argument of this type is to be met with.[62] But, as every real student of society knows, there are plenty of societal structures that have been built upon a framework which has long since perished; they are like the arch which stands by itself after the keystone is in. It is a sufficient tribute to vanity, if it needs one, that it left such fruits behind it. Vanity made men work long and hard to save up capital to get ornament or to secure social position; it made them "hold still" and endure long enough to have the hair dressed or to be tattooed; it helped powerfully to elevate the standard of living; and it furthered, in general practice at least, the rudiments of several other social virtues. Rarified into pride, a "sense of honor," *noblesse oblige*, and other sentiments of a refined order, it has acted effectively throughout the mores. And if it is asserted that property began in violence, the reflection is at hand that it is, in that respect, in the same situation as the rest of the societal institutions.

Vanity, however, strong as it is as a driving sentiment toward the creation and persistence of property, yields precedence here

[61] Jones, *Thlingets*, 93, 95-96.   [62] §329, below.

to ghost-fear, that supreme disciplinary force of the earlier periods. The amulet-ornament in its quality of amulet was inalienably one with the person, his soul, and his ghost. All that is to be said later under the topic of daimonism will emphasize the importance of the religious motive to the appropriation and tenure of property. Lippert[63] thinks ghost-fear the oldest source of property because the things needed by the dead man were left to him without dispute as sacred and holy; they were his more exclusively than in life, for nobody dared use them. Things ordinarily held communally, notably land,[64] were thus set aside for the individual; his grave became his personal property in a very real sense. Whether this is a real "origin" of property or not is, for our purposes, rather a matter of indifference;[65] but there is no doubt that the supernatural connection lends extreme value to the amulet, charm, or talisman.

A peculiar object is appropriated by a person sometimes for no other reason than that it is supposed to be something more than a stick or stone; not because it has been worked by human hands but because it has a spiritual quality and is a fetish.[66] Representing as it does some sort of favorable relation with the spirits, the amulet is of unparalleled import to its owner. It is often selected or made at his birth by the shaman and becomes a life-long talisman.[67] The notions of sacred or own, of consecration and making one's own, are originally identical; it is only by a later differentiation that consecration has been connected with worship. Objects originally appropriated for actual use came to take on the fetishistic quality needful to attach them indissolubly to a person as proper to him alone. Of all primitive property the object with the talisman-quality is parted with most reluctantly. The owner's being is all concentrated in the possession of it and his existence may, in his own conviction, be staked in the defense of it. Hence the intensest passion is evoked by any encroachment.

Further, each amulet-ornament is, in the nature of the case, unique. No two are alike; no two are interchangeable. The amulet has a high utility to its wearer in the midst of the chances of life; the ornament or trophy is interwoven with the pride and prestige

---

[63] *Kgchte.*, II, 237.   [64] §117, below.   [65] §454, below.
[66] §247, below.   [67] Ranke, *Mensch*, II, 511.

of its owner. Hence this article of property is exclusive and individual; it pertains to its possessor only and distinguishes him as fortunate, powerful, secure, noble, heroic. Thus the amulet-ornament cannot be common property as a tool or weapon or even food can be; and accumulation, be it noted, is here possible.

Methods of taking possession of land bear instructive witness from a quite different angle to the connection, shown in the case of the amulet, of property with religion. A ship's party, migrating to Iceland, at its early settlement, selected a dwelling-place and then each one appropriated as much land as he wanted by carrying fire around it; this was called "hallowing the land to one's self."[68] The fire was brought with them, so that this method was religious in nature.[69] In the Landnamabok,[70] a man took land by lighting fires at the mouths of the rivers which bounded it or by shooting a burning arrow over a river into it, or simply by bringing fire into it. To take possession of a house, one rode about it with fire. Again a fiery arrow was shot down a valley, between two hills, to take possession of land. Similarly the Aztecs appropriated land by shooting arrows to the four cardinal points of the compass.[71] In Iceland the limit of land which a ship's company could take was that amount which they could surround by fires to be kept up all day at such distance apart that the fire could be seen by night and the smoke by day. The chief divided this among his companions. It appears that a woman might not handle the fire; whereas the man used it in taking land, she led an animal around her appropriation.[72] Many other such ceremonies in taking possession of land are found among the ancient Scandinavians.[73] There are said to be traces of a custom among the Druids of appropriating land by human sacrifice.[74] All such employment of solemn ceremonial in appropriating land witnesses to a high and positive notion of property.

Thus property is found to be rooted firmly in vanity and in what is now considered superstition, as well as in the elemental necessities of self-maintenance and self-perpetuation. With the case of property in mind, we pause to note an important generality: that the origin of an institution in force, superstition, injustice, vanity, or in any other source which is base or abominable according to our present ideas, has no bearing upon its validity now. Science itself began in superstition and was corrected out of

[68] Geijer, *Svensk. Hist.*, I, 117.
[69] Lippert, *Kgchte.*, I, 262; §§89 ff., above.
[70] *Landnáma-Bóc*, in Vigfusson and Powell's *Orig. Island.*, I, 149, 207; Dasent, *Burnt Njal*, XXXVII; Leo, *Island*, 410.
[71] Quiroga, *Cruz en Amér.*, 109.
[72] *Landnáma-Bóc*, I, 144, 207, 276; III, 7, 12; IV, 10; V, 1, 3, in Vigfusson and Powell's *Orig. Island.*, I, 200, 191; Leo, *Island*, 413.
[73] Gröndal, in *Annaler*, 1863, 90-98.
[74] Von Pflugk-Harttung, in *Trans. Roy. Hist. Soc.* (N.S.), VII, 62.

it. On the other hand, the fact that certain mores and institutions have, to our taste, an admirable or noble origin cannot give them excellence now if, as a fact, they do not possess and exhibit it. Moral judgments passed upon the motives that led to property, or to any other institution of society, are irrelevant and futile. The explanation of action as consequent upon the interests is all that is in order. The crucial question is as to whether the institutions, at a given time and in a given place, constitute expedient adjustments to life-conditions. Again, it will be found, in the cases of other mores and institutions as well as of those under review, that the primary motives of hunger, love, vanity, and ghost-fear are intertwined with one another, so that each of them has produced results on domains other than the one which belongs to it.

CHAPTER XII

FORMS OF PROPERTY

§114*. **Communal Property.** The cases cited hitherto probably convey the general impression that property in its simplest forms is private rather than shared or communal; that the appropriation was by the individual rather than by the community or society. Undoubtedly this was so; nevertheless among the most primitive examples of property there occur also instances of a communal stamp. Much has been made of them by parties who are intent upon proving the modern system of private property "unnatural" and iniquitous. The fact is that the mores show a series of relations of things to persons, ranging from what might be called non-property all the way through to the most strictly private possession. There is non-property or nobody's property; then there is the arrangement by which any individual—one at a time—has the use or usufruct of property that belongs, in a general way, to his group; there is undivided or periodically divided joint property; public property; corporate property; administrative control over property; eminent domain; reversion of private property to the group; and a number of other intermediate forms that shade into one another like the colors of the spectrum. Evidently there are here, as in all evolutionary products, no sharp distinctions but zones of transition; and the only possible classification, like that of human races, is one of types. A pure case of common property would be one in which a number of persons have the same and equal power and right over the same object; and such instances are hard to find. Excluding land for the time, let us scan some instances of property that approach the communal type.

It might be inferred that the first private property would be food, for that was certainly the first thing appropriated, in the most literal sense of the word, out of nature. Yet food is often regarded, on lower stages of civilization, as the common possession of the group, and even now we act as if on the theory that everyone has a right to sustenance; it is a disgrace to a modern community that anyone should starve within its confines while food enough for all is present, unequally distributed. A number of primitive peoples have extended sharing-customs; where there is anything at all to eat, all group-members have an equal right to it, and sometimes even aliens are admitted to an enlarged hospitality. Potential food, not yet appropriated, such as game, is really non-property; it is otherwise with gathered sustenance, or food in hand, the matter here in question.

The tribes of Australia divide the spoils of the chase or the vegetable collection of the women without any reference to the individuals who obtained it; "the North American Indians, the Peruvians, the Chittagong Hill Tribes, the Borneans, and the South Sea Islanders, all appear to have cultivated in common; and to have possessed common rights in the produce."[1] Rivers[2] goes extensively into the matter of communalism, in particular as regards Melanesia and Polynesia; in the former region he finds property vested, not in the family in the limited sense or in the clan, but in some form of the joint-family or kindred, and he thinks the same to be true of North America. It appears that indigenous objects are generally owned by the community while those introduced from without may be the property of individuals. "A good example of the difference is presented by the weapons of Ambrim, of which there are four: the spear, club, bow and arrow, and sling. The first two are common property, and a man will always say 'our spear' and 'our club,' but, on the other hand, the bow and arrow and sling are individually owned objects, and people said 'my bow and arrow' and 'my sling.' Associated with this usage was a definite tradition that the people had always had the spear and club, while the sling and bow and arrow had been introduced from a neighbouring island." If this is true, it would indicate that variations toward richer equipment for the battle of life are correlative with those leading to private property. Perhaps also there is a tendency for the products of individual enterprise and labor to be held in contravention to the communal system. Nevertheless the Melanesians are veritably dominated by the communalistic mood; Rivers was "continually impressed by little occurrences which indicate the strength and pervasiveness of these sentiments." He believes that there is "much evidence for an early state of communal ownership of land and of certain kinds of property" in both Melanesia and Africa, and that individual ownership in the former region came about as the result of foreign influence; further, that the indication is that, whereas now the owning community is a group of kin inside the clan or moiety, it was once the clan or larger division. Thus the type of communalism has been in the process of narrowing.

The same author reports communalism as pronounced in Polynesia. "I must be content to give you an example from my own experience. I was travelling on a boat with four inhabitants of Niue or Savage Island, and took the opportunity of inquiring into their social organization. At the end of the sitting they said they would like now to examine me about my customs, and, using my own concrete methods, one of the first questions was directed to discover

1 Roth, in JAI, XVI, 112.
2 *Soc. Org.*, 25, 106-107, 113-114, 108.

what I should do with a sovereign if I earned one. In response to my somewhat lame answers, they asked me point-blank whether I should share it with
my parents and brothers and sisters. When I replied that I would not usually,
and certainly not necessarily do so, and that it was not our general custom,
they found my reply so amusing that it was long before they left off laughing.
Their attitude towards my individualism was of exactly the same order as that
which we adopt towards such a custom as the couvade." Details of the Polynesian system have been collected by Williamson.[3] In one region "hospitality
made a single family of these large populations, and even united one island
to another. It was a vast community, where everyone had the right to take,
and nobody went to the trouble of bringing anything; it was not so much
hospitality as a general mendacity, authorized by the ideas of the country—
the right to live at the expense of others. Houses, food, animals, children, any
object whatever, although supposed to belong to special proprietors, were
really public property. If a man built a house for himself and his family, and
another wished to live there, he could do so by virtue of the rights of hospitality. He who was preparing his meal was obliged to share it with all those
who presented themselves, and if there were too many mouths for the food,
it was he who must wait. If a man had anything, and another person saw it,
it belonged to the latter, and must be offered to him with apologies for its
smallness, and the offer would never be refused. A father or mother had to
give up their children to anyone that asked for them. The missionaries had to
avoid opening some of their trunks in the presence of chiefs, not because they
feared open thefts, but because they would have been compromised by refusals.
It would have been said that they were violating the laws of the community,
in virtue of which the chiefs had a right to call their own all things that
belonged to the missionaries, whilst the latter were equally entitled to claim
ownership of anything that belonged to the chiefs." Examples are given in
profusion. Of the Marquesas this author says that they lived in "as near an
approach to communism as it was possible to conceive, the communistic principle being apparently carried into their marriage customs. If one of them
was smoking you only had to wait for a few minutes to see the pipe or
cigarette passed round the whole group. . . . There were no poor people,
properly speaking, among the Marquesans; all the inhabitants had a share in
the fruits which were so abundant there."

Among the African Bushmen, anyone who gets game conceals it, for all
would get a share; "everything is common property."[1] Even these unfortunate
children of the moment are trying to squirm out from under the system. "A
Herero never kills one of his cattle for meat; when an animal dies, no matter
how it came to its death, it is common property," for it is then food. The Madi
of the Upper Nile recognized no private ownership of beer.[5] The Russians
say of the Buryats that they have everything artel-fashion; if one of them
kills a lamb, all the neighbors go in with perfect freedom if they please, as to
a common meal. The Yakuts share meat when they slaughter and also dainties
such as vodka, sugar, and tobacco. They wondered that anyone could die where
there were rich people, evidently regarding such as a public resource; "Why,"
they asked, "does such an one not go to eat with his neighbors?" They re-

[3] *Cent. Polyn.*, III, 265, 295.
[4] Lichtenstein, *S. Afr.*, II, 43, 45, 48, 50, 60, 196, 198, 272.
[5] Ratzel, *Vkde.*, I, 332, 506.

garded it as a shame to trade with food. Anyone could enter and use a house. The land belonged to nobody and the herds were owned by the group. Similarly among the Crimean Tatars, who maintained patriarchal simplicity and equality of rich and poor, the laborer might enter the house of his employer and eat whatever was set out for the company.[6]

As regards food, "the hungry Indian had but to ask to receive, no matter how small the supply, or how dark the future prospect. It was not only his privilege to ask, it was his *right to demand*."[7] Of the Iroquois and Hurons it is said that "whenever one of them has something specially good to eat, he invites his friends and makes a feast. Indeed, they hardly ever eat alone. . . . No one can want food while there is corn anywhere in the town."[8] Among the Virginia Indians it was death to steal maize after it was gathered in.[9] Among the Omaha, "the offense of *wathihi*, that of scaring off game while the tribe was on the buffalo hunt, could take place only by a man slipping away and hunting for himself. By this act, while he might secure food for his own use, he imperiled the food supply of the entire tribe by frightening away the herd. Such a deed was punished by flogging. Soldiers were appointed by the chiefs to go to the offender's tent and administer this punishment. Should the man dare to resist their authority he was doubly flogged because of his second offense. Such a flogging sometimes caused death. Besides this flogging, the man's tent was destroyed, his horses and other property were confiscated, and his tent poles burned; in short, he was reduced to beggary."[10]

In his almost unique treatment of East African Laws, Sir Charles Dundas[11] frequently sets down comments and interpretations which are by no means local in their application. The following excerpts throw much light upon communalism, especially as it dwindles away, leaving only vestiges and reversions on particular occasions.

"It must always be remembered that in native society the individual is essentially a unit within the family and clan, both of which claim a certain interest, in that he serves to strengthen while his property augments the wealth of the family or clan. Therefore it happens that when a man becomes a convert and leaves his home to go and settle among strangers in a distant locality, the clan may step in and take possession of his property. This happens more commonly in the case of converts to Islam, who migrate to the coast, and are to all intents and purposes lost to the tribe. The practice has been misconstrued into a confiscation of property on account of change of religion, but the above will explain that it is really quite a different matter, and in fact from the point of view of tribal interests is justifiable and desirable." Again, "a man's right of ownership in respect to his property is so absolute that perhaps even the public authority has no sort of dominion over it, and much lack of authority is

[6] *Russ. Ethnog.* (Russ.), II, 69, 488; Sieroshevski-Sumner, in JAI, XXXI, 69, 70.

[7] Powell, in BAE, VII, 34.   [8] Hale, *Iroq. Rites,* 85.

[9] Bruce, *Va.,* I, 149.

[10] Fletcher and La Flesche, in BAE, XXVII, 215.

[11] In JAI, LI, 270-271; XLV, 291-292, 296.

thereby explicable. It seems, however, that the family and clan always have a certain right of control in the property of their members. If a man should recklessly expend his substance they would intervene, nor would they allow him to deprive them of this control by taking his stock out of the country. It must be considered that the wealth of each member makes up the wealth of the clan or family, and both may make demands on the individual, just as he may avail himself of their wealth. Such mutual assistance we have already remarked in discussing the mode of compensating for homicide. . . . Discussion with the elders will soon disclose the fact that there is no one who could deprive a man of his lawful inheritance, but on the other hand the clan and family can deprive the owner of the right to dispose of his property improperly." He cannot take his inheritance out of the country; "but if he remained in the country no one could deprive him of his inheritance, whatever his creed or manner of life might be."

There are numerous cases where the communal system is in decay. The Veddahs of Ceylon, for instance, show only one form of communal right, namely, the equal claim of each family to the honey of the rock-bee. They have in this connection, indeed, a sort of mutual liability: "if the collector of the honey has a mishap through the breaking of the rope, the man who fastened the rope up, who is always a very near relative of the collector, has to support the latter's family."[12]

When communalism is modified away, the resulting forms come to resemble practices with which all are familiar; as will later be noted, we still have and always shall have usages which are communalistic. What we have done is to eliminate such exhibitions of the system as have proved under selection to be inexpedient, while we adhere to such of its features as represent adjustment to our conditions. Of course, as the real reason for sharing drops away, the system is rationalized upon and all sorts of fanciful and sentimental interpretations are put upon it.

Jenness and Ballentyne[13] seem to think that sharing of food was due to religious motives. "A hungry man would naturally ask any one whom he saw eating to give him a little food. The person asked would hardly venture to refuse, even if he wished to, lest the other in his anger should secretly strike his shadow with a spear and cause his death." This sort of explanation is neither fanciful nor sentimental; anyone who has acquainted himself with primitive ideas about the soul and is familiar with the doctrines so widely harbored concerning the evil eye,[14] cannot for a moment doubt that religious elements enter into almost all the mores, and he sees at once the reasonableness of the above conjecture. It seems, however, that even a highly reputed specialist may indulge in rather thin speculation as regards this matter of sharing; thus Seligmann,[15] commenting upon the custom of ceremonial exchanges of food between villages that are on a friendly footing, writes: "It seems likely that it arose as a convenient way of disposing of surplus food,

[12] Sarasin, *Weddas*, 490.
[13] *D'Entrecasteaux*, 205.
[14] §§210, 265, below.
[15] *Melanesians*, 141-142.

it being assumed that the recipients would return the compliment, when they, in their turn, had more food than they could consume." The figure of the savage in anxiety that food should not be wasted is not a convincing one. Doubtless the truth of the matter lies in the subordinate clause. The author goes on to say that "as existing at the present day, it is a highly conventionalised affair," which means that it got automatically into the mores long ago when men are not likely to have had much concern over conservation of resources.

It is a long step from keen interpretations on the basis of real knowledge, or even from unfortunate and perhaps accidental slips on the part of noted students to foundationless and biassed guess-work. For the latter exercise communalism has furnished an unrivalled opportunity.

The case of food-sharing, or of regarding food as common property, is naturally reflected in systems of landholding; for the question of holding land in common or in severalty is at bottom a question of how sustenance shall be held. Land will be treated by itself; but before that is done, there is to be considered the fact that a number of things other than food or land may be shared or held in common. It is characteristic of primitive families and larger groups that they show a certain solidarity, whereby the individual merges into his clan or other association; it is responsible for him and all are their brothers' keepers.[16] Except for the most strictly personal possessions, there is little that the individual can own. Community of property and community of industry go together. What a man wins is turned into the common stock and divided. If he makes a kill of game, he must raise a shout which brings his fellows up to share it with him; and if he gets wages, he has to resort to evasions if he is to retain anything for himself. Perhaps the well-known aversion of herders to the killing of their cattle is a reflection of the tendency to evade sharing. In some cases it seems indisputable that there is a communalism in women and children; marriage and property are, in fact, so intertwined throughout their evolution that they cannot be separated without doing a certain violence to their intimate relationship; it is therefore not strange that if property is communally held, women, who are often a species of property, should be held in that way also. However, the case of women will be treated elsewhere,[17] for if marriage is property, it is property with a difference.

[16] §§151, 176, 178, 274, below.   [17] Chs. XLIII, L, LI, below.

The various shadings of communalism in things other than food
and land can be appreciated by a review of instances and in no
other way. In general, where the setting is communal, only the
very personal and unusual possessions are exempted from the
sharing-usage; and the number of things held in common varies
inversely with the size of the group. Sharing, which is quite extensive within the immediate family, dwindles as larger aggregations
are formed. That is natural enough and is seen in any society.
Interesting beyond the mere facts about sharing, however, is the
assessment of it as a policy. There is a fanciful thing referred to
as "primitive communism" which has been held up to later generations as a treasure once possessed by the race and now lost. The
conception of community of property furnished a fruitful topic
for mediæval ecclesiastics to elaborate upon; we shall see later on
what they succeeded in deducing out of what they took it to be.
More modern sentimentalists and theorists have also seized upon
communalism, which they have known mainly secondhand, and
have asserted it to be the ideal, unspoiled, natural system of the
primordial era of felicity. It has been a convenient weapon to
catch up in the defense of a selected thesis. Let us see what several
field-investigators have said about the system of sharing.

In Fiji, where definite communism flourishes, there is a custom
"whereby persons may take the property of others, to such an
extent that it has served as an effectual bar to the adoption of
European methods of trading. A Fijian who sets up as a trader is
liable to have his goods appropriated by anyone who comes into
his store, to such an extent as to make his success impossible."[18]
The Upper Congo native "works for a year, and at the end of his
term he receives his pay and returns to his farm, where in eight
cases out of ten his pay is taken from him by the eldest of his
family, or by the chief of his town, or by his master if he is a
slave. Knowing this beforehand, what incentive has he to industry?"[19] This case aligns the status of a family-member with that
of a slave.

Among the Kru, "where family organization is at its strictest, you can see
the anxiety of the individual Kruman to secure for himself a little portion of
his hard-earned wages and save it from the hands of his family elders. The

18 Rivers, *Soc. Org.*, 107.   19 Weeks, in JAI, XXXIX, 135.

Kruman's wages are paid to him, or changed by him, into cloths and sundry merchandise, and he is not paid off until the end of his turn of work. So he has to hurry up in order to appropriate to himself as much as he can in the boat that takes him back to his beloved 'We' country, and industriously make for himself garments out of as much of his cotton goods as he can; for even a man's family, even in Kru country, will not take away his shirt and trousers, but I am afraid there is precious little else that the Kruman can save from their rapacity."[20] When the Kru boy returns from a voyage, says another author,[21] there is a partition of his property among the whole family, leaving him only enough to buy a wife. By repeated voyages, each ending in this manner, he finally acquires a harem.

In Guinea, says Miss Kingsley,[22] the theory underlying the laws of property is "the conception that every person is a member of some family, and all the other members of the family are responsible for him and to him, and he to them; and every family is a member of some house, and all the other members of the house are responsible for and to the families of which it is composed. The natural tendency of this is for property to become joint property, family property, or to be absorbed into family property. . . . The good point about the African system is that it leaves no person uncared for; there are no unemployed starving poor, every individual is responsible for and to his fellow men and women who belong to the same community, and the naturally strong instinct of hospitality, joined with the knowledge that the stranger within the gates belongs to a whole set of people who will make palaver if anything happens to him, looks well after the safety of Negro land." The authoress, nevertheless, finds the Kru sharing-system, although it leaves no person uncared for, to be cumbersome, and favorable to the tracing of descent through the females, thus preventing the building up of great families. The mother-family is a primitive institution that cannot support the competition of the father-family;[23] and sharing seems to be, as other foregoing instances indicate, correlative with this non-surviving arrangement.

Sieroshevski[24] says that two-thirds of the much-sharing Yakuts suffer from hunger during some part of the year, and are constantly in peril from evil chance; their system is not a winning one. Of the Nairs of India we read: "The peculiarly civilised idea that success is the criterion of intrinsic merit, and that, consequently, failure by itself proves that it was deserved, is almost totally unheard of. . . . The fact that the individual members of a family have to pool their abilities and, to some extent, their personal incomes, prevents the sharp distinction between the rich and the poor which is so characteristic of societies organised on an individual basis." The joint-family system gives them "a great advantage. Their capital is strategically massed, so to say, and while the property of a family is joined together its credit is much more than it would be if it were divided between the various members." Intelligent Nairs "see the advantage of this position, and are loth to break up what is most certainly an effective economic organisation."[25] To this last clause should have been added, "upon their stage of evolution"; if they could

[20] Kingsley, *W. Afr. Studies*, 429.   [21] Bastian, *Afr. Reisen*, 250.
[22] *W. Afr. Studies*, 436.   [23] §§421, 422, below.
[24] Sieroshevski-Sumner, in JAI, XXXI, 67.
[25] Panikkar, in JAI, XLVIII, 287, 289.

have arrested the course of things, it might have remained indefinitely expedient.

Turner[26] enters quite fully and with some feeling into the Samoan situation; he says of the native that "the entire tribe or clan was his *bank*. Being connected with that particular tribe, either by birth or marriage, gave him a latent interest in all their property, and entitled him to go freely to any of his friends to ask for help in paying his house-builder. . . . The system of common interest in each other's property . . . is still clung to by the Samoans with great tenacity. They feel its advantages when they wish to raise a little. Not only a house, but also a canoe, a boat, a fine, a dowry, and everything else requiring an extra effort, is got up in the same way. They consider themselves at liberty to go and take up their abode anywhere among their friends, and remain without charge, as long as they please. And the same custom entitles them to beg and borrow from each other to any extent. . . . This communistic system is a sad hindrance to the industrious, and eats like a canker-worm at the roots of individual or national progress. No matter how hard a young man may be disposed to work, he cannot keep his earnings: all soon passes out of his hands into the common circulating currency of the clan to which all have a latent right. The only thing which reconciles one to bear with it until it gives place to the individual independence of more advanced civilisation, is the fact that, with such a state of things, no 'poor laws' are needed. The sick, the aged, the blind, the lame, and even the vagrant, has always a house and home, and food and raiment, as far as he considers he needs it. A stranger may, at first sight, think a Samoan one of the poorest of the poor, and yet he may live ten years with that Samoan and not be able to make him understand what *poverty* really is, in the European sense of the word. 'How is it?' he will always say. '*No food!* Has he no friends? *No house to live in!* Where *did* he grow? Are there no houses belonging to his friends? Have the people there no love for each other?' " In Raratonga "the constitutional unit was the family, and the family system gave a refuge to all and prevented pauperism; but this family communism also killed energy and enterprise, and while it lasted no material progress could be expected. Community of property was the general rule, though a member might cultivate for himself any particular portion, and keep the produce to his own use, *if he could.*"[27]

In the Caroline Islands "the communistic tendency of social conditions, which makes customary the 'olngith'—borrowing really, more exactly, begging, among neighbors as well as the moral compulsion to sell a part of the yield, are further causes whereby the planter can never be sufficiently supplied with tobacco. At the beginning of the new harvest there is a relative satisfaction of the need, but the supplies are soon divided among the non-productive part of the population and each time, before the harvest of the new tobacco, 'bosok,' namely 'need,' prevails."[28]

Powell,[29] who tells of the Indian "right to demand" from others the fruit of their toil, comments: "By reason of the custom, the poor hunter was virtually placed upon equality with the expert one, the lazy with the industrious, the improvident with the more provident." The more favorable aspects of the case are as follows. "The peculiar institutions prevailing in this respect gave

[26] *Samoa*, 158, 160, 161.

[27] Williamson, *Cent. Polyn.*, III, 287.

[28] Kubary, *Karolinen-Arch.*, 163, 164.   [29] In BAE, VII, 34.

to each tribe or clan a profound interest in the skill, ability and industry of each member. He was the most valuable person in the community who supplied it with the most of its necessities. For this reason the successful hunter or fisherman was always held in high honor, and the woman who gathered great store of seeds, fruits, or roots, or who cultivated a good corn-field, was one who commanded the respect and received the highest approbation of the people." Vanity as a stimulus to activity is here conceived to act as a sort of substitute for economic self-interest, the latter being weakened or eliminated by the sharing-process; whether the substitute can exert the stress of the original can be judged in part on general principles.

The Guiana Indians "have no interest in the accumulation of property, and therefore do not labor to obtain wealth. They live under the most perfect equality, and hence are not impelled to industry by that spirit of emulation which, in society, leads to great and unwearied exertion. Content with their simple means, they evince no desire to emulate the habits or the occupations of the colonists; but, on the contrary, seem to regard their toils and customs with a sense of pity or contempt. . . . But this perfect equality does not necessarily imply a state of socialism; far from it. They have not a community of goods, individual property being distinctly marked between them. But this property is so simple and so easily acquired that they are perpetually borrowing and lending without the least care about payment."[30] A case like this simply shows that communalism is not the only system that goes with slackness in the economic life. The practice, however, is about the same, only there is no duty or doctrine to systematize it. The instance is, as it were, one of pre-communalism. Says Darwin[31] of the Fuegians: "Even a piece of cloth given to one is torn to shreds and distributed, and no one individual becomes richer than another."

It will be noticed that comments included in the foregoing cases occasionally draw attention to the expediency of the sharing-system or alleviate a criticism of it by citing certain of its advantages. One competent observer[32] interprets a number of usages sometimes considered as communalistic as guards against quarreling; again, we are informed, with instances in point, that "the natives are remarkably honest . . . in their dealings one with another. Where property is held so much in common there is little inducement to steal."[33] Whether a moderate amount of theft is worse than universal mendicancy is not considered. The defects of any such system are commonly counterpoised by certain expediencies; otherwise it would not have endured long enough to form an object of investigation. The participation of the whole horde in the winnings of the individual has doubtless its expedient

30 Roth, in BAE, XXXVIII, 632.
31 *Voy. of Naturalist* (Hundred Book Series), 166.
32 Von den Steinen, *Zent. Bras.*, 491.
33 Jenness and Ballentyne, *D'Entrecasteaux*, 207.

aspect. It is like insurance; for the one who is fortunate today may have ill luck later on, and then he will be listening for the summoning shout of the hunter who has brought down a quarry as eagerly as any of the rest. Primitive life was full of hazards and could not be lived in independence of one's fellows. Nevertheless sharing is a hindrance to the development of enterprise and to the accumulation of capital; sharers are not likely to save. The early adjustments of mankind often crossed and neutralized one another;[34] which adjustment was most expedient at the time, or in the long run, can be judged only by patient study of the facts of evolution. No amount of speculation, meditation, or logic-building can take the place of that sovereign method.

It is significant to find that "there are facts pointing definitely to the close connexion between communal ownership and mother-right, on the one hand, and individual ownership and father-right on the other hand"; also that "in several parts of Melanesia there is definite evidence for the association of communal ownership with customs which point to the existence in the past of organized sexual communism, which is still present here and there in Melanesia."[35] Sharing-systems seem to be yoked up with forms of the mores which selection is bound to remove.

§115. **Land the Crucial Case.** Resentment against that adverse possession or monopoly which is the essential feature of property is regularly most strenuous in the case of land. Possession or use of land means, ultimately, the opportunity to maintain life. This obvious and elementary fact makes the mores about land-holding highly crucial at any time. It is clear that the mediæval ecclesiastics have filled the minds of many with false ideas as to the "law of nature" in this matter, by citing "God's will," by referring to land as a "gift of God," and by various dogmatic statements that took their origin in interpretations of Scripture that reflected nothing but the predisposition of the interpreter.

Gregory I declared:[36] "The earth is common to all and therefore produces its fruits for the common use of all"; and the Council of Vienna, in 1267, re-

[34] Lippert, *Kgchte.*, I, 247.
[35] Rivers, *Soc. Org.*, 114, 115, 116; see preceding citation from Miss Kingsley.
[36] *Regulæ Pastoralis Liber*, pars III, admonitio 22.

peated this. "God's will," says Ambrose,[37] "was that the possession of the earth and the enjoyment of its fruits should be common to all, but avarice has controlled the distribution of rights of possession." And Aquinas[38] follows: "By the law of Nature all things are common"—meaning by that law the ideal mode of life in a sinless state; with the "fall of man" came avarice, with distinctions of mine and thine. He says property is allowable, but avarice is to get more than one needs. Into the "Romance of the Rose"[39] is injected the sentiment that all ill came to earth with property: divisions with boundaries, strife, and the triumph of the strongest. From such premises it is easy to arrive at the sentiment that "every rich man is a thief or the heir of a thief."[40]

Over this whole subject broods the illusion of an original blissful state, or golden age in which the earth and its products belonged to all by "natural right," and when "avarice had not yet set up the distinction of mine and thine." There is, in such statements, no claim to scientific accuracy; they are revelations. Latterly some writers who rebel against the present system of private property have, with and without candor, seized upon stray cases of "primitive communism" in order to support, with a seeming scientific demonstration, the traditional belief in an original and natural state of plenty shared by all. It is solely with statements that lay claim to scientific verity, rather than with interpretations of revelation, that any useful issue can be joined. The dogmas of the churchmen do not come into the field of science at all, except as they can be shown to be the necessary products of their times, or to have had inevitable consequences in the life of society. There is no profit in arguing with revelation, or with the interpretation of revelation, as such; exercises of that sort belong to another discipline of a different type. The only interest here is to get at the truth about the existence and nature of communal property, particularly in land, not by any exercises in dialectics, but by a study of attested facts. And any conclusions respecting communal holdings in other things than land should be held in abeyance until cases are before us presenting the facts about joint land-tenure, with the underlying reasons for it. In what follows, the man-land ratio is evidently the basic consideration.

§116. Emplacement. The ultimate need for holding land is the

---

[37] Psalmum CXVIII, sermo VIII, §22.
[38] *Summa*, II, Q. 2, 66, 2, 118, Q. 55, 6, and *Summa Angelica*.
[39] I, 318.
[40] Cesar von Heisterbach, hom., III, 66.

necessity of ground-room—of a footing, a standing-ground, an emplacement. The need of an emplacement is in actuality a need of space rather than of land; it is only because the space must be on the ground, by reason of the action of gravitation, that this aspect of the matter concerns land at all. Here at the outset, however, is evidence of the inevitably monopolistic quality of property; for two bodies cannot occupy the same emplacement at the same time. Even if no idea of property in land exists, there must yet be exclusive areas, however small, occupied by individuals or groups; there must be dwelling-places, and even in the houses there must be individual sections of floor-space assignable to a person and his appropriations or personal accessories in the way of tools, weapons, or ornaments.

In general, among the tribes of Brazil, "if several families occupy the same building, each of them possesses especially, as property, that part in which it suspends its hammocks and kindles its fires." There is a lattice-frame attached to the proper part of wall or roof for the family-implements. Since the fire-place is essential for each constituent family, "the savage designates the size of the hut by giving the number of fire-places, just as is the custom with the North Americans."[41] The dwellings of certain Veddahs are caves. But "the case may appear that there are fewer caves than families which come together, and new mutual adjustments must occur. In consequence of this, a somewhat larger cave may be inhabited at the same time by two or three families, which, however, do not live mingled together with each other in the cave, but mark their division against their neighbors by means of twigs, bark, and the like."[42]

A house-site is a sort of family-emplacement. In one place in Melanesia, "the site on which a man's house stands descends to his sons, or failing these to his nearest male kinsman. Strictly speaking, a man's hereditary house site is the only place on which he may build a house, although as the site is generally bigger than the house, a married man will often build a house immediately behind his father's, if there be room on the hereditary house site."[43]

Everyone must occupy exclusively, for himself and his belongings, a part of the earth's surface. Facts bear witness to the constant realization of the significance of the emplacement of each soul on earth, so long as it is not outlawed or banished from society. The emplacement is a societal as well as a physical fact and by virtue of it relations between individuals arose; it is recognized in societal institutions. It is noteworthy that fire is often

41 Von Martius, *Beiträge*, I, 87; Morgan, in *Smithson. Contrib.*, XVII, 153, note.
42 Sarasin, *Weddas*, 477.   43 Seligmann, *Melanesians*, 90.

the typical feature of an emplacement.[44] The monopolized space is property under such guarantees as the mores provide; and, as in the cases cited, may be held group-wise.

As regards exclusiveness of emplacement, the tenure of the ghost in the grave is supreme; for it is guaranteed by a more than human sanction. Thus private property in land reaches, in the form of the grave, back to the remotest stages of human society of which there is knowledge. The ghost enforces his adverse possession by way of the supernatural. In many cases the custom is found of burying a man under his own fire-place, or elsewhere under his house; where else should he lie than where he has lived? Very often, also, the house was abandoned or pulled down over the grave;[45] the place was still the property of the deceased. Later the descendants lived on in the house, and the hearth was made sacred by the presence of the ancestral spirits; their sanction then extended to the whole house, in which they commanded peace, thus guarding the domicile from intrusion; and at length to the grounds about the house. From this usage arose the temple and temple-enclosure, over the grave of a great ancestor, hero, demigod, or deity.[46] There is thus some reason for asserting that the first permanently exclusive property in land was owned by the dead.

§117*. Land as a Maintenance-Area. The idea of emplacement may be expanded to cover an area within which an individual or a group secures self-maintenance.[47] This extension covers ground-space plus the nutriment derivable from it, that is, the ground plus the water and organic matter needful to sustain life. Of itself the ground, or dirt, is generally of no utility whatever except as it produces the means of self-maintenance; unless the earth itself is used for some purpose, as pottery-making, or unless it contains salt, flint, or other desirable substance, its surface provides no more than the stage upon which plants and animals rest or move and where they can be sought. The very fact that the latter are not anchored irrevocably to a particular spot renders

44 §90, above.   45 §§222, 223, below.
46 §§250, 251, below.
47 Lippert, Kgchte., I, 620; Spencer and Gillen, Nat. Tr. Cent. Aust., 590.

the possession of that location a matter of indifference as compared, say, with the place where minerals are deposited.[48]

If such considerations are taken into account, it becomes clear why the first property in land was so vaguely defined. It was not the land but the use of land that counted; the maintenance-range, rather than the standing-ground, engaged attention. It is very necessary to make this distinction between the appropriation of land itself and the appropriation of the plant and animal life to be found on a certain area. In the most general aspect of the matter, where land is plentiful and men and their needs few and slight, there can be no real property in land, communal or other. The sharpness of definition of this monopoly and the vigor with which it is defended must vary according to the competition in the field; the definiteness of tenure of property in land varies with the density of population of the whole district. The man-land ratio[49] is fundamentally determinative, here as elsewhere.

The emplacement must first be appropriated and held, or one would be "pushed off the earth"; then the range upon or out of which sustenance is to be obtained, that is, the collection-area or hunting-ground. There was generally in primitive times an emplacement for every one; hence a struggle to safeguard an individual emplacement-monopoly is only a sort of inevitable logical conception; and something the same may be said of a group-emplacement, though groups have been swept from the earth. On the contrary, there was not always enough food for every individual or for every group; and the earliest form of effort to get and retain possession of land was put forth in the direction of the hunting ground. There is no reason, however, why any one person in a group should wish to hunt on a particular, limited area only; what he wants is the right to hunt where the game is. Strictly speaking, he does not want the land but the game, and his "land-laws" are really game-laws.[50] Hence his interest is not the possession of the land itself, but the use of it.

With the uncertainty and shifting of the game, no special spot bears "rent" over another for the individual. The group it is

---

[48] Lugard's chapters (XIV, XV, XVI) on "Land Tenure and Transfer" are instructive upon the general subject, irrespective of their local application to British Tropical Africa.

[49] §2, above.   [50] Lippert, *Kgchte.*, I, 246 ff.

which must struggle to keep outsiders from utilizing its area; and within the group the land cannot well be other than common. That which would make an individual want to own some limited piece of land would be that he could get more from it than from other parts of the group's holdings. Where, as in fishing, there are favored spots, there appears a tendency to individual appropriation and tenure. Before such conditions rise, there could be nothing developed in the mores toward the distinction of my land and thine; it was the rough competition for the especially desirable area which led, in the interests of order, to the regulation of itself. It was the taboo against theft which secured private property in other things than land;[51] but the idea of stealing or encroaching on a piece of land could follow only upon its appropriation in consequence of its superiority.

It is plain already that communal property in maintenance-areas was the only possible tenure in primitive times, and the inference is at hand that it could not endure as societal life developed into greater complexity. Collective holding of land is a vague form of property, it may be; and some people object to "levelling or evaporating down the conception of property in land in this manner, that is, in robbing it of all its specific content."[52] Nevertheless this same vague form was the one out of which the more specific types developed and, whatever it may be called, it is with this un-individual appropriation of land that the evolution of property in it begins.

Ratzel,[53] generalizing about the Australians, says that they hold very stringent notions of tribal property in their districts as against all outsiders; permission is necessary to cross each others' territory. In Central Australia, "until the whites came the tribal boundaries were religiously kept, and it is sufficient for them that these are their lands and have been for generations; even men of the same totem do not enter without formal permission. This survives in the custom requiring a visitor to sit down at a distance from the boundary and wait to be invited to come in by the old men."[54] Often whites have provoked the Australians' hostility unawares by violating their conceptions of the right of property, which they hold with great tenacity. In Victoria, each of the tribes "had its own district or country—its extent, at least, and, in some instances its distinct boundaries, being well known to the neigh-

---

51 §272, below.   52 Hildebrand, *Recht,* I, 85.

53 *Vkde.,* II, 78.

54 Horne and Aiston, *Cent. Aust.,* 35; Spencer and Gillen, *Nat. Tr. Cent. Aust.,* 431.

boring tribes. The subdivision of the territory even went further than that; each family had its own locality. And to this day the older men can clearly point out the land which their fathers left them, and which they once called their own."[55]

Not to multiply instances, we turn to the American Indian for a few typical illustrations. Of the Omahas it is said that "each tribe claimed a certain extent of territory as its own, for purposes of occupancy, cultivation, hunting, and fishing. But the right of a tribe to sell its land was something unheard of."[56] The Indians of northern California everywhere had their tribal boundaries marked off with the greatest precision, these "being defined by certain creeks, cañons, boulders, conspicuous trees, springs, etc., each one of which objects has its own individual name. It is perilous for an Indian to be found outside of his tribal boundaries [in war-time] wherefore it stands him well in hand to make himself well acquainted with the same early in life."[57] Here is a case of the group-emplacement idea. This author goes on to say, concerning three of these tribes, that they have the coast partitioned off between them, with marked boundaries. The coast is owned by each tribe in common, not in severalty, and all gather the flotsam and jetsam. "Any attempt on the part of a neighboring band to appropriate any part of the treasures yielded them by Neptune and the Nereids, even to a piece of putrescent whale-blubber, is strenuously resisted, and leads to bloody contentions."

Property in land assumes the same general character along the northwest coast; and it is instructive to note that the water is treated like the land when similar opportunities for self-maintenance are offered by it. Here, however, even on the hunting stage, areas are common property of families rather than of all the tribesmen. "Throughout this region the coast line, streams, estuaries, and adjacent lakes are divided amongst the different families, the right of possession descending from one generation to another as personal property. The larger salmon streams are sometimes jointly owned by several families, or owned by one family and leased for a consideration to one or several others. Stranded marine animals, or other débris washed by the tide, belong to the family owning that portion of the shore line, the boundaries of possessions being definitely marked and respected accordingly. Nor is this boundary confined to the strip of coast, but extends well out to sea, carrying with it the right to shoot seals and gather birds' eggs on outlying rocks, hunt sea-otter, and to fish on well-known halibut or cod banks."[58]

Because of Grinnell's[59] standing as an authority on the Indian we cannot forbear reproducing at some length his views on Indian land-tenure. "There is nothing in an Indian's traditions or experience that enables him even to imagine the ownership of land by persons, although he regards personal property much as we do. His food, arms, and clothing, his horses and other live stock, are his to do what he pleases with: to sell, to give away, even to destroy. He may have rights in less tangible things. He may have the sole right in his tribe to carry some ceremonial object, to sing some sacred song, to tell some particular story. This is a property right that is respected by others and one that he may usually divest himself of by giving it away or by selling it. A man who belongs to a certain society, on leaving the society may sell his place in

[55] Smyth, *Vict.*, I, 41. [56] Dorsey, in BAE, III, 366.
[57] Powers, in *Contrib. N. Amer. Ethnol.*, III, 109, 66.
[58] Niblack, in USNM, 1888, 335. [59] In AA, IX, 1, 2, 3, 4, 6.

it to another, but such sale must be confirmed by the members of this society. These views and practices are closely analogous to those of civilized man. But with regard to the ownership of the soil the case is quite different. Many savages, but especially our own Indians, are absolutely unacquainted with the ideas held by the whites of property in land. They cannot conceive of the individual ownership of land; they think of their land as held by the tribe for those who shall come after them, who in turn may occupy it. . . . There was no individual ownership of land, but there was tribal ownership. In some cases a tribe occupied certain lands to the exclusion of all others. In other cases various tribes, friendly or allied, occupied or controlled certain territory from which they expelled other people who ventured on it. Again large tracts might be claimed—even though not permanently occupied or controlled—by half a dozen tribes and might serve as hunting grounds for them, where at any time hostile tribes might be encountered and where war might be a part of every hunt. In earlier times the lands bordering the Ohio river in Ohio, Indiana, and Kentucky, and later those along the Yellowstone and the Missouri, . . . and about the Three Forks of the Missouri, constituted in this way debatable ground."

In short, the Indian held land under characteristic conditions. "No Indian could understand the need or sense of expressing some of those conditions. Some of them the white man would have misunderstood if they had been expressed. The white man knew more than one way of having an individual and exclusive interest in the land. He was familiar with the idea of leases for years or for life; he was familiar with the estate in fee. His mind was imbued with the idea of exclusive tenancies running for years or lives, and of exclusive individual ownerships, running from generation to generation. But the Indian's savage mind knew no such thing as absolute ownership of land by individuals. According to his view neither the tribe nor any member of it has in any piece of land rights other than the right to occupy and use it, the individual for life in common with his fellows, the tribe forever, to the exclusion of unfriendly peoples. . . . This land cannot be sold by the individual or the tribe. The individuals now living on it may sometimes barter away their personal rights in it, but they cannot alienate the land, because the sole ownership of it is not in them. The tribe are tenants and in a sense trustees; and individuals can part only with the rights which they possess as members of the tribe, subject to the rights and duties of the tribe. . . . Until within comparatively recent times, all land sales and all treaties have been made by the Indians on the theory that they were passing over to the white people certain rights of occupancy—were lending them the use of the land. These rights in a general way were to live on the land, to pass over it, to cultivate it, to use its waters, the animals that lived on it, the birds that flew over it, and the fish in the streams; yet the Indians looked forward to a time at the end of the loan when the land should be returned to them, when nature would heal the scars made by the white man, when the animals and the birds would reestablish themselves and the fish would increase in the rivers."

We must not forget that "our notions of land ownership have developed through thousands of years. It seems to us now quite reasonable and expedient that one man should fence out others from his farm and that another should monopolize a lake and another a water power; but a primitive Indian can no more understand such private monopolies than an average American can understand how there could be a private monopoly of air or light."

These examples illustrate the sort of vague ownership of land found among tribes on an undeveloped stage of culture. They have a persuasion that a certain territory belongs to them all, either as a sort of group-emplacement or as a hunting-ground. The former conception is not essentially different from that of a state's territory; the latter involves a claim to the use of the land, in the sense of a right to appropriate its natural products and as distinguished from actual ownership of the soil. It is only because the supplies are on or in the ground that the land-question emerges at all. This can be seen the more clearly by contemplating aboriginal notions about property in game, as these come out in game-laws and otherwise. Many native peoples can no more entertain the white man's conceptions about property than a child can take in differential calculus; they have not grown up to them through the indispensable intervening stages. The native cannot understand the white man, and if the latter takes no pains to find out what is in the mind of the former, collisions are sure to result.

Certain Australian tribes do not understand that animals and plants can belong to one person more than to another; they are non-property. Smyth[60] quotes a native speaker: "Sometimes a party of natives come down from the hills, tired and hungry, and fall in with strange animals you call sheep; of course away flies the spear and presently they have a feast! Then you white men come and shoot the poor black fellows." And so with "the poor hungry women: they have always been accustomed to dig up every edible root, and when they come across a potato garden, of course, down goes the wanna [digger] and up comes the potato, which is at once put into the bag. Then you white men shoot at black fellows." This author cites also the periodic return to non-property in the case of a certain fruit (bunya-bunya); at the time of its maturity access is free to all, and the natives flock to the district to eat it. They do not dare to touch the animals of the region, since these belong to the local tribe, which allows the fruit to all because it is so abundant.

Eyre[61] quotes from a letter in part as follows: "In fact, as the country is occupied [by Europeans] chiefly for pastoral purposes, the difference between the Aboriginal and the European ideas of property in the soil is more imaginary than real, the native grass affording subsistence to the kangaroos of the natives, as well as to the wild cattle of the Europeans, and the only difference indeed being, that the former are not branded with a particular mark like the latter, and are somewhat wilder and more difficult to catch. Nay, as the European regards the intrusion of any other white man upon the *cattle-run,* of which European law and usage have made him the possessor, and gets it punished as a trespass, the Aborigines of the particular tribe inhabiting a particular district, regard the intrusion of any other tribe of Aborigines upon that district, for the purposes of kangaroo hunting, etc., as an intrusion to be

60 *Vict.,* II, 228-229, 218.   61 *Cent. Aust.,* II, 297 ff.

resisted and punished by force of arms." This case is illuminative on the transition between the hunting and pastoral stages;[62] the cattle-run is really a game-preserve.

The common family-property in New Guinea includes landed possessions, the right to fish in certain places and to hunt over certain areas, the stock of sago, and the big signal-drums. To illustrate diversity in the mores of ownership, the author[63] tells of Englishmen who were attacked by natives unexpectedly and who replied with shots intended only to frighten them. But a native was hit in the arm. "A regular fight, therefore. Who was in the right? The Englishmen, of course, as they were the attacked. The cause of all the strife was that they . . . had killed a boar. Captain Webster regarded this boar as belonging to no one, because it was wild, as appears from his own words: 'Having no brand or ear-mark of any sort' . . . But he did not know that the right to hunt in certain parts of the woods was an integral part of the Papuan family property." The native could not explain that even wild pigs could be owned. As a matter of fact, they are "communal property of the village-members. No one can freely dispose of such quarry, but it is eaten by all together. Such honor befalls likewise the grunters that are bought, even if only a few have contributed to the purchase. The purchaser or killer of a boar cannot even make disposition of the teeth to suit himself; the disposition of these too should inure to the benefit of the community."[64]

For three hundred and fifty miles the Ural River is fishing-ground, and there is no private property of individuals or of villages on it; it belongs to the community of 110,000 people. At the fishing-time all come to the banks, but they have to await the signal to begin, so that no one shall get ahead of the others.[65]

It is to be noted that even among hunters there automatically develop adjustments to secure economies and responsibility, and that such adjustments represent movement toward private holding. Among the Wood Crees and cognate tribes, "if the lands were not subdivided, the hunting of the finer kinds of fur-bearing animals would be constantly interfered with, the beaver houses broken down, and the beaver killed at all seasons, as it would be no one's special interest to protect them."[66] This expedient of subdivision is a step in the direction of private property and toward the enlistment of the personal interest and initiative which go with that system.

Interest in the use rather than the possession of land reappears on the pastoral stage. In the crudest form of animal-raising, it has been noted, the beasts are not far from forming a game-preserve; they are somehow marked for ownership and are thereafter sub-

[62] §30, above.
[63] Hagen, *Papua's,* 194-195; 252-253; 262.
[64] Krieger, *Neu-Guinea,* 196.   [65] Borodine, in PSM, XLIII, 772.
[66] Frere, "Discussion," in JAI, XII, 275; Ratzel, *Anthropogeog.,* I, 349.

ject to little control. Here is a sort of transition-phase from pure hunting toward the typical pastoral stage. The salient consideration is that, even when the animals are less wild and unrestrained, their owners are engrossed primarily in them; any land-question is accessory. What is wanted from the land is that it shall sustain the animals; that is all, here as on the hunting stage. Only here there is ownership of specific animals that the owners know where to find, of whose needs in the way of sustenance they are aware; so that instead of hunting the beasts in areas which they naturally frequent, the herder hunts land suitable to the beasts he is herding. In that sense certain regions are preferable to others, though scarcely more so than on the hunting stage; nor does the case apply to small sections of land or to the more than temporary use of areas for grazing-purposes.

Cattle-raising, like hunting, demands extensive rather than intensive use of ground; there is not enough difference in degree of intensiveness between the two to affect property-adjustments in the matter of land very noticeably. The mores call for nothing in the way of private holdings; and what is encountered is a common right to the use of shifting grazing-grounds. Among the comparatively few strictly pastoral peoples, those who are highly specialized show a consistent property-adjustment as to land; and where herding accompanies other occupations, it does not fail to evoke characteristic partial adjustments.

Where there is seasonal migration, on the order of the movements of the Hyperboreans,[67] the population is interested only in the periodic use of wide stretches of territory, and there can be no thought of holding it in severalty. Where there is less sweep of movement, pasture remains common long after cultivable land has ceased to be that. This is true even among advanced peoples and in spite of a tendency toward temporary and at length permanent private holdings; a survival of the practice remains in the word "common" as applied to park-areas in towns and cities. "So long as certain land is regarded as doomed for ever to be pasture-land and so long as every one knows how many beasts he may turn out on it, the question as to the ownership of the soil does not arise

[67] Ratzel, *Vkde.*, II, 720; Semple, *Geog. Env.*, 57.

and is not answered."[68] Such waste is not strictly non-property if encroachment upon rights of pasturage in it would be resisted; but, in any case and whatever the particular form of adverse possession is called, it is communal.

Temporary private tenure is illustrated in the case of the Herero; they hold land in common, but he who has first occupied a piece with his herd remains master of it as long as he pleases, and no other one will invade his right.[69] "The economic basis of Dinka society is the possession of cattle. The Dinkas are essentially a pastoral people. As we might expect, their currency is in cattle. The bride-price is paid in cattle. Quarrels are settled by the payment of cattle as fines or compensation. Raids are made for cattle. They have, indeed, other domestic animals, such as sheep and poultry; but these are of minor importance, and probably of modern introduction. Property, therefore, to a Dinka means cattle."[70] This is the usual idea of the nomad; then comes pressure of population and limitation of the grazing-grounds, forcing the property-concept, as it were, over to land.[71] "Among the Todas, property may be held by the clan, the family or the individual. . . . In general, land, the dairies of the chief villages, and some buffaloes may be said to be the property of the clan. The house, and probably also some villages, are the property of a family, and most buffaloes, household goods and ornaments are the property of the individual."[72] The conception of pasture-land as waste, and as no one's property, is brought out by Baden-Powell[73] in respect to the Hindu village. "In the ordinary village of Manu the individual cultivators . . . make use of the adjacent waste for grazing and wood-cutting, but do not claim it as theirs. . . . The waste area adjoining such a village was used for grazing, cutting fuel, etc., but the village cultivators never thought of it as their common property." "In nomadic Arabia there is no property, strictly so called, in desert pastures, but certain families and tribes hold the watering-places, without which the right of pasture is useless." This sort of monopoly "is broadly in accordance with old Arabian custom, but indeed with general Semitic custom, as appears from many passages of the Old Testament."[74]

The following case foreshadows the maladjustment into which the traditional treatment of pasture-land was bound to fall, as conditions of life approached the modern type. In Denmark, in the middle of the eighteenth century there was communal occupation of land, affecting pasture as well as plowed land. The right of pasture was owned in common, apparently as a survival of the ancient rights in the waste. All who owned these rights turned as many cattle as they chose upon the pasture. Attempts were made to rate the pasture and to specify the number of animals that each peasant might put on; but there was much cheating. Also different villages had rights on the same pasture. The woods were used for grazing-purposes; and sometimes the trees and grass had different owners. Also on the heath there were common rights of cutting furze, and in the swamps of cutting turf. The author shows at length the complicated mischief produced by this remarkable instance of

[68] Pollock and Maitland, *Eng. Law*, I, 608.
[69] Ratzel, *Vkde.*, I, 338.
[70] O'Sullivan, in JAI, XL, 173.
[71] Lugard, *Brit. Trop. Afr.*, 287.
[72] Rivers, *Todas*, 557.
[73] *Land Syst.*, I, 128, II, 224.
[74] Smith, *Relig. Sem.*, 104-105.

coöperation in land-ownership, and describes the practical difficulties encountered in trying to do away with all these practical inconveniences, by a reform-commission of 1757.[75]

The foregoing cases may serve to represent varying conditions arising in connection with a typical form of the industrial organization whose effects on land-tenure we are, for the moment, and in some connection with those of hunting, trying to isolate for purposes of exposition. It should now be clear enough that pastoral conditions raise no demand for that adaptation which we call property in land except on the broadest understanding of that term; certainly there is no reason for an adjustment in the mores looking toward the institution of private ownership. It seems to us scarcely justifiable, however, to call the area covered by the grazing herds non-property or no-man's-land. Although it is a shifting emplacement or food-area, yet while it is occupied it is defended, that is, appropriated as a monopoly, held in adverse possession. It satisfies our definition of property; and, since what is held is held by the group and used by all members, we prefer to retain for it the term communal property.

§118. Property in Tillage Land. The foregoing situation, as developed under hunting and herding, changes as a whole and radically with the development of agriculture; for that maintenance-occupation tends to center interest upon particular and small areas of land. At first this is for the time of crop-growing only, the land reverting to the category of communal property, or of non-property, when the harvest has been gathered. The very principle of private possession may here be seen in its embryo. It is not the land itself that is in question, but the use of the land over a period covering its productiveness. It is almost possible to say that the most primitive state of things on the agricultural stage is the absence of any notion of property in land, together with fluctuating practices as to the use of it, upon which almost any construction can be put. The property-idea may attach only to the product, as where the negro puts his mark upon a growing gourd which he thinks will be of use to him at maturity, much as a cowboy brands a calf, or as when a taboo is laid upon a bee's-nest

[75] Hansen, *Danskelandbrug.*

or a tree in the bearing season. However interpreted, this sort of thing leads straight toward the actual possession of the land.

The Hottentots of southwest Africa, who live in part on a kind of melon, parcel out the dunes in which it grows among the families, and thus secure care in collection.[76] "The only idea of landed property in East Africa seems to be that the tribe owns the district which it occupies. This right of occupation is assured by usage and is generally respected. . . . As far, however, as the individual is concerned there is no proprietorship of ground. . . . A transaction was impossible, it being contrary to custom to sell growing trees . . . it was as impossible to sell anything rooted in the earth, as the earth itself."[77] "The land for cultivating a field, like a site for a village or the bush for cutting firewood, is free to everybody to use as they like. Between the different settlements there are always stretches of uninhabited country, so that disputes between the different settlements cannot easily arise, and within such settlements they rarely occur; for one thing, of course, the population is so thin that there is plenty of land for everybody."[78] This last consideration is regularly determinative for land-tenure. "The population to the square mile being small, there is ample land for all, and hence land tenure does not exist; a man may cultivate in one place one season and in another place two miles away next season; that is to say, the fact of a man clearing a patch of ground one season gives him no particular rights to that same patch next season."[79]

Rivers[80] goes into considerable detail concerning the land-system of the Pacific island of Ambrim, thinking of no better way to illustrate ownership of a simple society. People of any kin-group might clear patches of uncultivated land which would in time become the property of the kin-group of the clearer; if that kin-group died out, its land became the property of the inclusive village as a whole; "it went out of cultivation and then shared the complete indifference of the people to the ownership of uncultivated land." There was "no appearance even of the individual ownership of land. It was the custom in this island to indicate the nature of the ownership of an object by means of the possessive pronoun. Where there was individual ownership a man would indicate the fact by the use of the personal pronoun, and would speak of 'my bow and arrow' or 'my armlet,' but . . . he would never speak of 'my land,' and would always say 'our land.' Moreover, this mode of speech was no empty form. A man might clear a piece of ground entirely by his own labour, and might plant and tend it without help from anyone, but any member of his *vantinbül* [kin-group] could nevertheless help himself to any of its produce without asking leave or informing the cultivator. Inhabitants of the village belonging to a *vantinbül* other than that of the cultivator might also take produce, but had to ask leave. Since such permission, however, was never refused, the communism extended in practice to the whole clan. For property of other kinds the case differed with the kind of object."

Of the Barito region in Borneo it is reported:[81] "In actuality there is no property protected by right and laws; neither the community nor its members possess such property. . . . That, with their tendency, consistent with their

76 Ratzel, *Vkde.*, I, 96.   77 Johnstone, in JAI, XXXII, 264.
78 Dundas, C., in JAI, XLIII, 500.
79 Dundas, K. R., in JAI, XLIII, 70.
80 *Soc. Org.*, 105-106.   81 Schwaner, *Borneo*, I, 169-170.

folk-character, to a wandering life, the conception of property in land could not have arisen, is easy to conceive. The place held for a time by a kampong [village], the surface on which the inhabitant has laid out his fields, is for so long the unassailable property of the community, or of its separate members, as use is made of it. But so soon as the kampong is abandoned and the fields are no longer cultivated, it stands free to any other community to take possession of them. Nevertheless the first planters of fruit-trees retain the right to come back yearly in order to harvest in the ripe fruits."

Von Martius[82] knows of no nomads of the Asiatic type, depending solely upon their herds, in the whole of South America; nearly all the tribes practise tillage in some degree, and the property-form shows an adjustment to its presence. "However widely spread over a certain area the families of a horde or a tribe may live, this area is regarded by every individual as property of the whole. This conception is clear and vital in the soul of the Indian." It is just like our conception of state-territory. "This clear conception of a definite property of the whole tribe is founded chiefly on the necessity that the tribe shall possess a certain range of forest as its exclusive hunting-ground. For while a few acres of cultivated land are enough to provide plant-food for a numerous community, a sufficient hunting-ground must extend over a much larger range. The undeveloped Indian form is the more noteworthy because in it is clearly to be recognized the transition from the true communal property of the people, tribe, or community to the true private property of the individual. . . . Each family is free to select and appropriate a family-holding inside the common area, but this holding then ceases to be a piece of the common land, that is, the usufruct of the horde recedes before the delimitation, and the private control of the family-members prevails here exclusively."

Tillage comes to mean an actual investment in a particular area of soil; a short-time investment, it is true, to begin with, consisting of the seed entrusted to the earth. When the seed is in, the soil that holds it is, so to speak, different dirt from that which is adjacent to it: it is impregnated; it has potentialities. The planted area takes on at once an added value; and it is no longer a matter of indifference as to who uses the area. Its usefulness is dependent upon the exclusion of those whose capital is not invested. The planted spot is land plus something else; more valuable than the adjoining land, it bears economic rent. The investment may be no more than the labor expended in preparation for the seed; it is an immemorial custom that the individual may make a portion of the waste his own by clearing it. The cleared land is then superior to the uncleared; if it were not tabooed to the individual in adverse possession, it would become an object of general competition; and if it were that, no one would risk his capital on it.

The degree of intensity and permanence of the monopoly thus

82 *Beiträge*, I, 81, 82, 83.

assured varies with the character of the tillage-operations. In the
crudest types of cultivation the monopoly lapses when the crop is
harvested; the planter may even leave the region after the seed
has been scattered, returning only when the harvest is at hand.[83]

A curious piece of information bearing upon the earliest phase of experimentation with planting was given by a Malay chief: a certain people "were originally in the habit of eating the fruits of the jungle in a small shelter built
upon the spot where they had been gathered, but on its being pointed out that
this practice resulted in a superfluous number of fruit-trees all growing in the
same spot, the whole tribe took to carrying their fruit to a little distance
before eating it, and afterwards removed during the fruit season to a fresh
spot every year, in order to spread the seeds over a wider region of the
country."[84]

As the investment becomes more extended, the assurance of private possession becomes the more necessary. Crops needing greater
care and calling for a longer-time investment demand a more
stable tenure of the land; and when an advance is made to the
culture of vines and trees, plots of ground must remain private
property in perpetuity, this involving the right of inheritance of
private holdings, for in some cases planting is done which will not
yield results till after the planter's death.

"Permanent occupation is essential to individual ownership, it is not essential to communal or tribal ownership. And as in human history the nomadic
life of the hunter, the herdsman and the migratory husbandman precedes the
settled life of the farmer under the more advanced systems of tillage, it seems
to follow that individual ownership of land has been developed later than
communal or tribal ownership, and that it cannot be recognized by law until
the ground is under permanent cultivation. In short, common lands are older
than private lands, and the transition from communal to private ownership
of the soil is associated with a greatly improved mode of tillage, which in its
turn, like all economic improvements, contributes powerfully to the general
advance of society."[85]

One of the most instructive facts in connection with property in
land is the inevitable collisions of the tillers and herders.[86] Nothing could afford better evidence as to the essentially novel attitude
toward land introduced by tillage than the recurrent antagonism
in the attitude of herder and cultivator toward the matter of land-
ownership. It is one of those inevitable conflicts attending adjust-

[83] Mason, *Invention*, 192; Semple, *Geog. Env.*, 57, 62.
[84] Skeat and Blagden, *Malay Penin.*, I, 338.
[85] Frazer, *Folk-lore in the Old Testament*, I, 452.
[86] §31, above.

ment with which we are familiar in the case of the cottage and factory forms of industry. This antagonism works out into derived forms in the general societal organization; it was that antagonism which led, in some cases, to the practice of re-locating the tillers from period to period, for changing the tillers about distributed the annoyance.[87]

§119*. Family-Holdings. Although the assignment of land in adverse possession was temporary and in favor of a group long before it could become permanent and in favor of an individual, yet, as such, it was a transition toward private property in land. Land was apportioned to families and kin-groups, and the individual was as fully identified with and as indistinguishable among his kin in this matter as in others.[88] That which was normally taken into account as a unit in the society was the family; the society itself was a kin-group, actual or fictitious, subdivided into smaller sections of those who were more closely and definitely related. Among primitive peoples, communalism on the basis of family or kin is the only regular type of land-communalism; it is only on higher levels of organization and differentiation that communal property in land can exist as the system of a larger aggregation, or can be altered into the form characteristic of civilized peoples, that of private holdings.[89] This is because the family is also the labor-element in the land-labor or man-land unit, which alone confers value on land;[90] and where the labor-constituent is of this order, ownership cannot be in severalty. If the labor-element includes the whole community, then ownership cannot be even family-wise. The right of eminent domain and the contentions concerning "the unearned increment" represent recognition of the common interest under the modern régime of private property in land.

The title to land begins with a limited kin-group and for a brief time; then there is a re-allotment. This time-limit is found inexpedient, as the intensiveness of cultivation and the cost of improvements increase, and the period of allotment extends toward the "forever" of the modern deed. Later on we shall see how the

---

[87] Hildebrand, *Recht*, I, 92.   [88] §§149, 178, 274, below.
[89] §§185, 187, below.   [90] §103, above.

group-wise allotment also becomes unsatisfactory. "As the common ancestry fades away into indistinctness, and the community gets to consider itself less an assemblage of blood-relations than a body of co-villagers, each household clings with increasing tenacity to the allotment which it has once obtained, and re-divisions of the land among the whole community, whether at fixed periods or at a death, become rarer and rarer, and at last cease altogether, or survive only as a tradition."[91]

Rivers[92] is willing to "lay it down as a definite proposition, that whenever we find the family (in the narrow sense) as the dominant feature of the social organization it is combined with the institution of individual property. . . . In all cases in which society is founded mainly or altogether on the family, property is owned by individuals." On the other hand, "in all . . . forms of the joint family we have a definite departure from individual ownership in the direction of communal ownership, the special feature of the communism being that common ownership is limited to a relatively small group bound together by close ties of genealogical relationship or kinship." The case "is complicated by the feature, which we have seen to produce complications of other kinds, that the clan-grouping is always, so far as we know, complicated by the co-existence of a family grouping of some kind." Then, too, the older system holds over; "in many societies where the institution of individual property is definite, there are nevertheless customs which show the existence of a group-interest in property at variance with individual rights." Out of such generalizations the idea cannot but be drawn that, as the system of landholding shrinks from a kin-group ownership to that of the family in the narrow sense, it is on its way to individual tenure. The more power and responsibility are focussed, the more can be made of both.

Primitive tribes often allot planting-grounds, as they do hunting-grounds, to families in order to get the advantage of care and zeal in their exploitation. But "a piece of ground cannot so easily be divided as can a herd, and this is particularly the case when the land in question is only a small area." In addition, when the allotment is but for a time, say a year, a division does not pay.

[91] Maine, *Early Inst.*, 188-189.   [92] *Soc. Org.*, 103-105.

"These were the reasons why they left the land undivided or pursued agriculture communally."[93]

"In West Africa there is not an acre of land that does not belong to someone who is trustee of it for a set of people who are themselves only lifetenants, the real owner being the tribe in its past, present, and future state, away into eternity at both ends."[94] This is mortmain carried to the utmost extreme; nobody living can ever deal freely with the land. While, however, there is by native law and custom no private property in land, yet "a family in occupation of land cannot be disturbed; and land so occupied only practically reverts to the community when it is abandoned or thrown out of cultivation. When once land has been allotted to a family, the usufruct belongs to that family for as long as it chooses to cultivate it; but the land cannot be sold by the occupiers or assigned to any third party."[95] "Property in land goes apparently by families, and is quite definitely owned. At first sight one would suppose that the fields of every village are owned in common, but this is not the case; the climate is so favorable, and the population through wars and slavery so low, that there is usually an abundance of food, and anyone who is hungry goes to the field and takes what he requires anywhere. But if there is a famine or scarcity, the rights of the different families are carefully maintained."[96] It is the pinch of necessity that leads to the assertion of rights which have lapsed while the pressure was off. Here again the status of the man-land ratio is determinative of the form of property-tenure and of the degree of "humanitarianism" or easy generosity.

Among the American Indians, all land whatever was held in common by the tribe, or, in a few cases, by the clan.[97] The tilled land was generally in a single mass; among the Iroquois often several hundred acres. To this the field-work gave claim; and as the woman did field-work, she had a special right to the land. Title depended upon continued use, but it could be sold or bequeathed.[98] Among the Creeks every village had a common, enclosed field which was divided into delimited pieces for the separate families. Horns announced the beginning of the field-labor, which was done in common; and of the harvest a certain part was set aside first of all for the common store, out of which the sachem supplied the needy.[99] Among the Omaha the land was an inalienable common possession of the whole tribe, but was divided among the separate families for cultivation. "Each head of a household held a possessory right to such a tract or tracts of land as the members of his family or household cultivated; and as long as the land was thus cultivated, his right to its enjoyment was recognized by the rest of the tribe. But he could not sell his part of the land."[100] The Brazilian Indians show the transition from communal to private property. It is by use continued through years that the family gets property in land.[101]

Allotment is mentioned often in the Old Testament,[102] sometimes metaphori-

[93] Ratzel, *Anthropogeog.*, I, 349; Hildebrand, *Recht.*, I, 100.

[94] Kingsley, *W. Afr. Studies*, 438.   [95] Ellis, *Ewe*, 217.

[96] Elliot, in JAI, XXIII, 82.   [97] Powell, in BAE, VII. 40.

[98] Ratzel, *Vkde.*, II, 627.   [99] Waitz, *Anthrop.*, III, 128.

[100] Dorsey, in BAE, III, 366.   [101] Von Martius, *Beiträge*, I, 83-87.

[102] Deut., X, 9; XII, 12; Joshua, XVII, 14, 15; XVIII, 11; Jer., XXXVII, 12; Micah, II, 5.

cally: "Thou maintainest my lot. The lines are fallen unto me in pleasant places; Yea, I have a goodly heritage."[103] These Biblical instances, says the writer[104] who cites them, "demonstrate plainly that, at a time when land had become in part a private possession, the Israelites still recognized common land along with it." An interesting survival remains in the custom of redemption. The nearest relative (*goel*), to whom a variety of obligations fall, has the duty, in case an Israelite is obliged to sell a piece of farming-land, of buying it of him, that it may not come into the hands of strangers. A striking case is where Jeremiah, in prison, is approached by a cousin who demands that he buy a certain field. Despite the complication of the situation the duty is accepted and accomplished.[105] "If thy brother be waxen poor, and sell some of his possession, then shall his kinsman that is next unto him come, and shall redeem that which his brother hath sold."[106]

§120*. Ownership by the Chief. "It is from family-property," says Oliveira Martins,[107] "that personal or allodial property developed, just as the family retired in favor of the state. . . . The land was disunited when the authority was dis-patriarchalized." It has been noted, here and there in the foregoing, that the family-property was administered by the family-head, or by the sachem or chief. It was necessary, obviously enough, that some one should have responsibility and power in the matter; and the organization was such that these fell to the patriarch. Such a form of ownership tends, however, in only one direction; even among backward tribes, "the ownership of a tract of land by a family has come, through being vested in an individual or the head of that family, to mean practically individual ownership."[108] In reality, ownership by the chief can readily be taken to mean that nobody else owns anything; it is a sort of Cæsarism as respects property. The cases include all sorts of possessions, but most consistently refer to land.

The chiefs were the first to get private landed property because the choice pieces were reserved for them. They set the fashion. Ownership by chiefs was in this respect, again, a step toward private property. Political power and wealth have been closely correlated from the beginning: "Whatever else a Chief is," says Maine,[109] "he is before all things a rich man"; again, "the possession of personal wealth is a condition of the maintenance of chief-

103 Psalms, XVI, 5, 6.   104 Buhl, *Israeliten*, 57, 58, 59.
105 Jer., XXXII, 6 ff.   106 Levit., XXV, 25.
107 *Quadro*, 103.   108 Niblack, in USNM, 1888, p. 335.
109 *Early Institutions*, 133, 134, 135.

tainship"; through the acquisition of such wealth the road was always open to it.[110] Conversely, if a man becomes chief he becomes rich. Though the chief is often, as we have seen, no more than the family-head, merely standing for the family, and in that capacity owning the land along with the rest of the family property, he is nevertheless in a position to draw power to himself. In most of our cases he has already done so and has no longer the sense of trusteeship.[111]

First as to the chief's ownership of property in general: in West Victoria, the stone ax is so scarce and valuable that it is generally the property of the chief of the tribe. He lends it for a consideration.[112] Among the Niam-Niam the weapons as a rule do not belong to the individuals carrying them, but are the property of the chief, who doles them out as needed.[113] The despotism of the African chiefs was largely sustained by their ownership of the herds which were the property and means of subsistence of the tribes. The acquisition of private property by their subjects, who earned wages from the whites, has broken this up.[114] Thus property in beasts, like property in land, had political and social effects; the real significance of that fact is that property in anything which for the time being is of commanding importance in the struggle for existence—horses, ships, merchandise, money, water—has characteristic political and social effects. It has made aristocracies.

So much by way of brief illustration of the chief's ownership of things in general; we now come to the specific case of land. "The land-tenure of Africa differs from that of Melanesia in a very striking respect. In Melanesia chiefs have no functions in relation to land. If they possess land they own it in the same way, and subject to the same communal usages as other persons, and, in one case at least, they are not even landowners, and only obtain land for their gardens by the grace of their subjects. Among the Bantu of Africa, on the other hand, the position of chiefs in this respect is very different. They hold the land and distribute it among their subjects, but they probably only act in this respect as the representatives of the people as a whole." Africa shows a common ownership or usufruct of land, which is never sold; the natives of certain parts can hardly conceive what is meant by sale of land. There is a native saying in Melanesia that "chiefs command people, not the land."[115]

Among the Bechuana, "the land laws are simple. The land belongs to the chief. He divides it among his head men, and they in turn among their people. There is no division of grazing land. The mealie fields are practically the property of their cultivators so long as they are tilled. . . . A chief can only legally assign untilled lands to new members of the tribe."[116] Among the Zulus all land belongs to the king, whose permission must be obtained to cultivate it.[117] In Dahomi nobody except the king can hold land, or property of

[110] §302, below.
[111] Cases of chief's ownership in Muntz, *Contact*.
[112] Dawson, *Aust. Aborig.*, 24.
[113] Burrows, in JAI, XXVIII, 42-43.
[114] Ratzel, *Vkde.*, I, 207.
[115] Rivers, *Soc. Org.*, 108-111.
[116] Conder, in JAI, XVI, 86.
[117] Ratzel, *Vkde.*, I, 248.

any other sort, "except by pure tolerance," and even then the king may confiscate it at will; "this theory is pushed so far that parents are held to have no right or claim to their children, who, like everything else, belong to the king, and are retained by the parents at the king's pleasure." In Ashanti all the land is viewed as inalienable crown-property. The Zulu monarch is a military autocrat, and Dahomi and Ashanti present extremes of despotic rule; probably a natural tendency to chief's ownership has been exaggerated in those cases; still, something the same situation as to land prevails throughout Fantiland.[118]

The Hindu rajahs "claim to be themselves landlords or owners of all the soil, and only recognize landholders as tenants, hereditary indeed, after holding for some generations."[119] The Lepcha chief loaned land to his subjects; "thus the individual had no motive for amassing property, as he could not expect to keep it. Perhaps this is the chief reason for the so-called 'laziness' of the Lepcha."[120] In China the Emperor was "considered to be the original grantor or lord of the soil."[121] The sacred chief, or *tuitonga* was considered to be the sole proprietor of the island of Tongatabu, the chiefs holding under him; but he could not displace a chief from his land. "The chiefs could, and often did, displace the peasants. The kings and chiefs reserved a portion of land for their own use for raising vegetables. . . . The feudal principle prevailed, the whole country belonging to the king . . . who regulated the disposal and tenure of lands, and the common orders being placed in a state of serfdom. Land was held in fief. . . . Here, as in Samoa, the idea of an out and out sale of land seems to have been unknown to the native mind prior to contact with the white men." The author[122] remarks upon "the inability to draw a defined line of distinction between the temporary and seasonal allocation by the head of a group to sub-groups or members of certain portions of the land of the group . . . and the more permanent allotment and division of the land of a group," and also "the difficulty of distinguishing with exactitude between things done by the head of the group solely in the interests and for the protection of the food supply of the group as a whole, and those his motives for which were . . . of a more personal character. The latter of these can hardly be separated entirely from the subject of tribute." Such difficulties are characteristic enough when it comes to the endeavor to classify customs which are in process of development.

In New Zealand "the land could belong either to an individual, or a family, or a whole tribe. . . . If such land is sold, the price is paid to the chief, who however distributes it to the several tribal members. And it is the same when a family is the owner; then every member of the family—the relationship being reckoned from the first, often mythical ancestor—gets his share of the price, reckoned according to the closeness of the relationship."[123] Here is a case where the chief retains only the ceremonial survival of ownership or headship of a group owning in common.

118 Ellis, *Ewe*, 216, 162; Ellis, *Tshi*, 298; Connolly, in JAI, XXVI, 146-147.
119 Baden-Powell, *Land Syst.*, I, 99, 129, 184, 230.
120 Waddell, *Himalayas*, 105-106.
121 Medhurst, in *Trans. China Br. Roy. Asiatic Soc.*, pt. IV, 31, note.
122 Williamson, *Cent. Polyn.*, III, 229 ff., 265-267, 320-321.
123 Waitz, *Anthr.*, VI, 228.

Doubtless the remark of Darwin[124] about the Fuegians has a general application. He says that they can never get on until some chief arises who is strong enough to compel them to hold an advantage they have once won, for example, domestication; as it is, if one of them gets something, as a piece of cloth, he cuts it up and shares with all the rest, so that no one becomes richer than another. The backward and lowly need a differentiation between rich and poor to help elevate them; the suggestion is implied that the prosperous can lower themselves by dispensing with such invidious distinctions. In the fourteenth century, when hops were introduced into Sweden, the only way to secure property-rights in them was to put them under the king's peace.[125] The power of the chief, and his ownership of goods and land as well, evidently secured expedient results and had survival-value.[126] Standing even so vaguely as he did for an approach to private property in land, the chief was in the coming line of adjustment. Perhaps this form of tenure did hamper initiative somewhat and make people lazy, as in the foregoing case of the Lepcha, but at least one person had an intensity of interest which, under full communalism, no one had.

Many of the preceding instances have verged toward the political conception of sovereignty; the more developed the people concerned, the more clearly do they show an approach to that conception. It is always needful to avoid confusion in this matter, especially so as the cases become complicated.

"The word *Dominium*," says Maitland,[127] "has to cover both proprietory rights and many kinds of political power; it stands for ownership, lordship, sovereignty, suzerainty. . . . Now if we are going to confuse sovereignty with ownership, *imperium* with *dominium*, political power with propriotary right, why then let our socialists and collectivists cease their striving and sing *Te Deum*. Already their ideal must be attained. Every inch of the soil of France, to name one instance, 'belongs' to the French Republic."

This warning, though it has reference chiefly to European conditions, is applicable in its degree to the instances before us. Doubtless in many mediæval cases the turbulence of the times led the weak, in return for protection, to "commend" their rights to the

124 Fitzroy, *Adventure and Beagle,* III, 235.
125 Lippert, *Kgchte.,* II, 599.   126 §§152, 155, 156, below.
127 *Domesday Book,* 334 ff.

strong; and then, when the strong appeared to own the land for the community, a case of collective property or of non-property was inferred,[128] whereas the antecedent state of things was not one of communalism but of individual holdings. The lord might stand as the owner only of the dues or taxes from the land, the land being conceived to have no owner. Not alone is the political evolution of the chief[129] rendered more understandable by spreading these economic conditions in the background, but also the religious ideas about God as the ultimate owner of all things—as in some sort the father of the family of which we are children and servants. "What we possess is no more than a *peculium* of which He lets us have the usufruct."[130] Thus a whole class of cases arises from doubt as to the line between jurisdiction over men and jurisdiction over land. Nevertheless the contention deserves reiteration that ownership by the chief, whatever its complexion, is one of the transitional forms toward modern private property in land. It is for that reason that it is given so much space here.

§121*. Personal Property. "The facts show us that in the rudest communities there is a private holding of useful movables maintained by each man to the best of his ability. A personal monopoly extends itself to such things as can readily be monopolized."[131] Men might stand and wrangle over common property till it rotted, as some seem to wish to do; then no one would get it, for such property does us no good until some one monopolizes it; thus only does it enlist the interest of the individual, spur on his initiative, urge him to its own preservation and improvement, and so come to be useful to all. Even upon a low stage of civilization these qualities of the individual have been cultivated, unconsciously or unpremeditatedly, as they have demonstrated their expediency. It is not at all difficult to assemble cases of personal property among backward peoples; in fact, the inference is that the first property of all was an attachment to the person.[132] There is no reason for citing numerous cases of personal property in things, for it is much the same all over the world and at any age.

[128] Baden-Powell, *Land Syst.*, I, 98, 186-190; II, 225.
[129] §§155, 158, below.   [130] Schmidt, *Soc. Civ.*, 261.
[131] Spencer, *Prin. Soc.*, I, §318.   [132] §108, above.

In Melanesia, "personal property consists in pigs, which are everywhere much valued; money, in whatever form it is found, canoes, weapons, and the various implements used in native life."[133] Among the Seminole Indians, holes in a log serve as mortars, and each woman owns a *hole*.[134] "In the Indian family, every belonging is personal; even little children have their own things. . . . To the man belong his weapons and implements, his own clothing, and his horses; to the woman the tent, the house-utensils, and her own horses."[135]

The question rises at once as to how the individual managed to keep his private property. There was no guarantee at the outset except force; what one could take and hold—hold down, sit upon, "possess," in the etymological sense—was his. As the variation in the direction of private possession got into the mores, however, private holding came to have a societal sanction and a religious one. What guaranteed it was the taboo; the very idea of "private" is that of "set aside for," or "sacred to," a person. The system went along with other expedient adjustments.

Thus in certain Melanesian islands there was a clear distinction between ancient hereditary cultivated ground which went to the sister's son and land recently reclaimed from the waste which was inherited by the children of the one who cleared it. Property in trees also went to a man's own children.[136] Among the Malays of Padang there was a distinction between what a man earned himself, by his own diligence, and inherited property. The former was private property, the latter a family-possession. On the communal basis the property of man and wife remained forever separate, in so far as it was composed of possessions brought into wedlock from the contributions of the families of the spouses; but what they earned together by joint effort they owned together and could pass on to their children in any way they pleased.[137] Again, in Easter Island, it was the chiefs who were exempted somewhat from the system of common landholding, while in Tikopia Island, though the coconuts belonged to all, the chiefs had most of them. "A man who had nothing to eat might go into someone else's field and no one would say anything to him";[138] the general system was thus communal; nevertheless, together with the development of a more efficient regulative organization appeared a partial departure from the sharing-system.

If private property went along with modifications of the system of inheritance from one based upon the mother-family toward arrangements characteristic of a more highly developed form; if it accompanied the emancipation of individual initiative to strive for the benefit of one's own offspring; if it was correlative

[133] Codrington, in JAI, XVIII, 312. [134] MacCauley, in BAE, V, 514.
[135] Fletcher, in *Globus*, LXXIII, 253. [136] Codrington, *Melanesians*, 63.
[137] Wilken, in VG, I, 316, 317.
[138] Williamson, *Cent. Polyn.*, III, 318, 319.

with the strengthening of the power of government; then it was in good company. Private property, along with these and other expedient adjustments in the mores, received religious sanction; it is evident that the property-taboo in this form represents one of the many indispensable contributions of religion to societal welfare.

The taboo, especially as connected with the personality-symbol and the fetish,[139] comes out clearly in the property-marks employed by many peoples to guarantee personal possession. These expedients run all the way from the vaguest to the most precise indications of ownership. It is not asserted that all such devices must be of a religious stamp; but many of them are, and the presumption as to most of the rest is justly entertainable. A survey of these property-marks amounts to a review of the forms taken by personal property.

One authority[140] holds that all peoples make use of marks to denote ideas, although they may have no writing; and that of the conventional marks that come to be known and recognized among them, one of the very first is the sign of the appropriation or ownership of property. A second writer[141] follows through many peoples the custom of marking property with a peculiar sign. He finds such marking, once believed to be a Teutonic device, more or less over the whole earth—on doors, beams, utensils, and even, corresponding to one's autograph, on documents. Such a sign is a man's "mark," and so his seal, reduced at present to the cross which an illiterate makes if he cannot sign his name; it has long been commonly known, and has had just as much force in the community as a signature. There are also the marks of merchants, modern trade-marks, and the monograms of artists. Personal marks appear among the ancient Greeks and Germans as identification-devices in lot-casting;[142] and also among present-day Kabyles and North German peasants. Of course the cases are more significant where an indication, which may or may not be a mark, is placed upon some object in nature, by way of securing its appropriation. There may be private and special marks, indicating

139 §§210, 248, 253, 301, 302, below.   140 Ratzel, *Vkde.*, I, 28.
141 Andree, *Eth. Parallelen*, 74, 78; §161, below.
142 Homer, *Iliad*, VII, 175, 183 ff.; Tacitus, *Germania*, X.

by whom the object has been appropriated or, more commonly, there may be general taboo-devices, simply warning everybody off; the following cases will illustrate both varieties. Each variety marks off private property. Sometimes the mark is of a type worthy of experts in personal identification.

In Queensland, "when a black proposes leaving camp for a few days, and is unwilling to take with him all his belongings, little enough though they are, he will go to some neighboring and not too much frequented spot, leave his impedimenta there, and on the surface around clear a circular space, upon an extra well-smoothed portion of which he will plant an imprint of his foot: this impress being well known to his mates, he can rest assured that the property will remain intact during his absence.[143] Again, a tree containing a "sugar-bag" or bee's-nest is marked by the finder, who thus protects it until he wants it; and any one who disregards the mark is under disapproval as a wrong-doer.[144] Von Pfeil[145] noticed similar signs in Melanesia: "It is plain that an invention which readily permits of the accumulation of property could not remain without reaction upon the people who succeeded in getting it." But he means general taboo-devices rather than specific personal symbols, and cites a case in which the religious character of the property-protection is evident. "At the time of the ripening of the coco-nuts, the owner winds the trunk of the tree with plaited work made of its leaves. This is for the purpose of hindering thieves from climbing the tree; for they think that the climber must necessarily touch the plait and through so doing be attacked by illness. Meanwhile, just in the one case in which the power of the evil spirits is made use of, does the effect fail; although in every small palm-grove the wound trunks can be seen, yet no man heeds them, and every skilful climber ascends with a spring, whose execution certainly presupposes much practice, above the plaited rope, and steals what he can." Sometimes the tongue of a fish is enclosed in the winding, which preserves the tree from robbers as long as it hangs to the trunk, for transgression of the taboo brings sickness and death. "In a case of unintentional infraction of the taboo, charmed water, which the setter of the taboo gives to the breaker, is regarded as a curative."[146] In New Georgia, "property is well recognized; every island of the great eastern lagoon, however small, has its owner. Groves of coconut trees are well protected by hopos [talismans], as are also taro patches. Hunting rights over opossums on a man's property are also protected by hopes."[147]

Among the Eskimo, to secure property in articles washed up by the sea it was necessary only to carry them up above high-water mark and put stones on them.[148] Sticks of drift-wood are marked with an adze. A claim to a barrel could be acquired simply by setting it up on end.[149] Certain Indian tribes "still have the custom of drawing upon the blade of a canoe or bull-boat paddle such designs as are worn by the chief and owner to suggest his personal habits." The marks are chiefly horse-shoes and crosses, representing

[143] Roth, *N.W. Cent. Queensland,* 133.
[144] Palmer, in JAI, XIII, 288; Smyth, *Vict.,* I, 145.
[145] *Südsee,* 115, 142.   [146] Krieger, *Neu-Guinea,* 187.
[147] Somerville, in JAI, XXVI, 404 ff.   [148] Cranz, *Grönland,* I, 218.
[149] Murdoch, in BAE, IX, 428.

ponies captured and *coups* in warfare. The squaws who chiefly use the boats "have need of this illustration of their husbands' prowess as a matter of social status, and it is also a matter of pride."[150] The tattoo-design worn by a land-owner, in California, served as a property-mark; "such marks were equivalent to the owner's name, and were known to the rest of the tribe."[151] Several tribes in South America have the custom that the family chief marks a certain figure upon the breasts of the women, upon the horses, and even upon the dogs. It is the mark of his ownership.[152]

§122*. **Property in Trees.** It is plain enough that primitive people practised the private holding of many kinds of property, that they marked and tabooed freely in the interest of the individual, and that such adverse possession was successfully guaranteed. Private property in things was thus an early development. Not so the private holding of land. It is toward the development of that form of property that we are working; and the usages concerning property in trees are transitional, for a tree may be, at the one extreme, no more than the structure which supports desirable objects, while at the other extreme it may be conceived to have such value in itself, as a product of the soil, that, in order to own it, the land beneath it must be owned. In general the advance from the former view to the latter is marked by a constantly increasing element of investment[153] in the tree. The bee-tree stands at one end of the scale and at the other, let us say, the olive-tree, which will bear fruit only after an extended period of care and cultivation. The former is a case of natural monopoly appropriated through the brief process of marking; the latter involves labor and utility extended through time; and the interval between the two shows interesting gradations.

"On one occasion, when exploring, and suffering severely from the want of food, . . . his [G. S. Lang's] black guide pointed to a bee passing over them, loaded, and evidently in straight flight for the hive. Mr. Lang told the native to follow it, and he did so; but when they reached the tree, the black had scarcely got off his horse when he remounted as if to go on again. Mr. Lang asked the reason for his action, when he pointed to a mark on the tree, evidently made by a stone tomahawk, and said that it belonged to 'N other one blackfellow,' and that he could not touch it—and at this time he was almost on the point of starvation." If two or more men have the right to hunt over a given territory, and one of them breaks off the tops of some grass-trees (thus forming a proper receptacle for the growth of grubs), by their laws the grubs become his property. The man who took the trouble to break off the

---

150 Mallery, in BAE, IV, 182.   151 Hoffman, *Writing*, 39.
152 Von Martius, *Beiträge*, I, 230-231.   153 §84, above.

tops was entitled to gather the grubs; but he acquired no right to the trees, and they could not, by his simply breaking the tops, become his property as a huge gum-tree might, or a parcel of land.[154]

In Fiji, "fruit-trees are often held by persons who do not own the land; but there is a curious distinction here. The property in this case is rather in the fruit than in the tree, and is therefore not considered to be in the land. You may take the fruit, but you must not cut down the tree without the land-owner's permission." Closer distinctions also appear: "He who has a tree on another man's land may cut it down and take it away; his axe does not touch the soil; but he may not dig the tree up by the roots, for his digging-stick would turn up the soil.[155]

The Kabyles show a division of property even as between the stories of a house; and with them "trees, notably olive-trees, can constitute an immovable property independent of the ground. . . . The owner or owners of the tree have the right, if it dies, to replace it twice . . . unless there is a stipulation to the contrary. Likewise they may take the shoots . . . which sprout out of the ground in a square of sixteen meters around the trunk as soon as they are in a condition to be transplanted. In some tribes the owner of the tree has no right to let the shoots come up. The owner of the soil has the right to cultivate up to the foot of the tree, on the condition that he shall not injure either the roots or the shoots. He must warn the owner of the tree at the time of the proclamation of harvest and give him the chance to do his picking and carry it away. If he has not completed his operations when the harvest, according to usage, ought to end, the owner of the soil can plow, whatever damage the owner of the fruits may experience. The proprietor of the trees . . . has the right of passage, either to cultivate the tree or to collect its fruit, at the time of the harvest proclamation."[156] In this region private property may extend even to the branch of an olive tree.[157]

"Property in individual trees is . . . everywhere recognised, and in the immediate vicinity of any village most . . . oak or alder trees belong to some particular individual, who has marked the tree as his own when it was small. . . . In fact, the attitude of mind which governs relations between the individuals and the community of any Naga village, the views as to *meum* and *tuum*, and what must, may, and may not be done, together with the absence of private life, is most vividly reminiscent of that which obtains among English schoolboys and regulates their unwritten codes. . . . Bamboos, like trees, are private property, belonging, as a rule, to the man who planted them and to his heirs, irrespective of the ownership of the land on which they are planted. It is quite common for a man to plant bamboos on someone else's land, and, if near a village, the owner of the land is not entitled to uproot even newly-planted bamboos if he did not forbid the planting before it took place, and must clear a fire line round them when jhuming his land."[158]

Cases parallel to the foregoing are widely distributed.[159] An instructive one is that of the Ojibways, who make great amounts of maple sugar. Each woman

[154] Smyth, *Vict.*, I, 146; II, 289.
[155] Codrington, *Melanesians*, 61, note (quoting Fison).
[156] Hanoteau et Letourneux, *Kabylie*, II, 230, 255.
[157] Letourneau, *Prop.*, 187.   [158] Hutton, *Sema Nagas*, 67-68.
[159] Clarke, "Right of Property in Trees on Land of Another, as an Ancient Institution," in JAI, XIX, 199-211.

head of a household had her own clump of trees and her sugar hut to which she always went, and which were inherited by mother-descent and totem.[160]

Instances of private property in trees show clearly enough that men do not take naturally to the expedient of private property in land in order to cover and include personal ownership of the products of the land. The finder and marker of the bee-tree cares nothing for the tree itself; the owner of the fruit has a somewhat more intimate interest in the tree; but neither of them thinks about appropriating the land. The following instance reveals the contrast in attitude toward land existing between the tree-owner and even the crudest agriculturist.

In the Solomon Islands, "any individual of the tribe appears to be able to select at will a piece of land from the forest, which he clears, fences in, and upon it rears his crop of yams or bananas. After the crops are taken off the land is allowed to relapse again to forest. When, however, a native plants coco-nuts, his property appears to be in the trees themselves, apart altogether from any idea of ownership in the land upon which they are planted."[161]

The occasions where the tree-owner is forced to take account of private property in land is where it is in the hands of cultivators who are limiting his freedom in some way. It is therefore doubtful whether tree-ownership by itself would ever have led to private property in land, although when once that conception is present, the cultivation of long-time crops, such as vines and trees, tends to strengthen it. The tree, since it is a different thing from a short-lived plant, occasions an almost unique set of mores in adaptation. The product of the wild tree is about like game, while that of the planted and cultivated one represents, one might say, the extreme of agriculture; the appropriation of the former demands little foresight, while the rearing of the latter calls for security of tenure in the relatively remote future. Further, the inheritance of tree-property seems to follow along with that of land redeemed from the waste or property won by other exhibitions of personal energy and initiative.

In Melanesia, "while land on which trees are planted passes, according to ancient custom, to the children of the sister, the trees which a man has planted on this land may be inherited by his own children; and it seems clear that this forms a social mechanism by which the separate ownership of trees and land

160 Hoffman, in BAE, XIV, pt. I, 288.
161 Woodford, *Head-Hunters*, 33.

has come about. I believe that these customs in general are the result of the blending of peoples, patrilineal immigrants having succeeded in transmitting their trees to their children, while the land itself has to follow the laws of matrilineal inheritance of the indigenous inhabitants."[162] Whether or not this last explanation on the basis of immigration be accepted, it remains evident that the separate inheritance of trees is correlative with conceptions of personal property that go with the father-family.

§123*. Personal Holdings in Land. If the communal holding of land after it had been tested out freely, as we have seen that it was, had not proved to be less expedient than the system of private property in land, the latter system could not have gained even a foothold in the societal organization. That the circumstances of primitive life often evoke a communal holding of land or leave it simply as non-property, exercising no stress at all in the direction of personal tenure, has been shown in the foregoing cases and discussion. It is evident that there was a prevailing system of private holdings in things other than land; and that land itself, where the chief held it for the community, and especially where tillage was developing, was, under very primitive conditions, slipping from the tenure of the many over to that of the one. Private property in land came in when people began to feel an interest in land. On the earlier stages they were engrossed wholly in what happened to be upon it. Before entering upon further generalities, however, there should be spread before us several typical primitive cases of private property in land.

An Australian, of New South Wales, we are told, owned a small island near Sydney Cove, which had been his father's and which he purposed giving to a particular friend. To this spot he seemed much attached; and he spoke of other persons who possessed this kind of hereditary property which they retained undisturbed.[163] "Every male has some portion of land, of which he can always point out the exact boundaries, heritable and alienable. . . . Landed property does not belong to a tribe or to several families but to a single male."[164] "A father divides his land during his life time, fairly apportioning it amongst his several sons, and at as early an age as fourteen or fifteen they can point out the portion which they are eventually to inherit."[165] Letourneau[166] presents other examples of this Australian form of land-owning.

"The constitution of the Papuan tribe, like that of the Australian horde, is radically democratic, but differs from it in being much less communistic.

[162] Rivers, *Soc. Org.*, 112. [163] Smyth, *Vict.*, I, 145-146.
[164] Eyre, *Cent. Aust.*, II, 297, 298.
[165] Grey, *Expeditions N.W. and W. Aust.*, II, 236.
[166] *Soc.*, 384.

Private property, in distinction from tribal possession, begins with the tillage of the soil, and this general principle applies to the fields, houses, and tools of the Papuans."[167] On the Maclay coast of New Guinea, every inch of land, every fish in the brook, every useful tree in the wood, has an owner.[168] In the Bank's Islands the town-land and the garden-grounds "are so far private property that the owner can be found for each piece." Cleared land passes to the children of the man who has cleared it; "the children divide it into separate lots, and do not in any way hold the property in common."[169] In Fiji, "land is considered personal property, and is equally divided at death among all the children, or, failing these, among immediate relatives, as are also the possessions of the deceased"; the town lots and arable lands are divided among landowners, while the forest-lands are held in common.[170]

"In Shoa and its southerly environs, people formerly cherished the axiom that all land is a common possession; but agriculture forced division."[171] Among the Galla the mountain-lands yielding gum and frankincense were held strictly in severalty.[172] In the Chin Hills of India, "fields are not worked in common; each man has his own fields and each cultivates his own patch; the fields are not fenced and no one hesitates to shoot strange cattle which stray into his fields."[173]

Lugard[174] says that "it is not easy to focus into a paragraph a general conception of African land tenure." One who has read his book is, however, quite ready to trust him to do as much justice to the effort as can be in reason expected. "The general principles would seem to be that the assignment of land to the individual is entrusted to tribal and family authorities, who, however, have no claim to ownership in it themselves; that every individual has a right to a share of the use of the land, and holds it in perpetuity, subject to the performance of tribal obligations, but may not alienate it; that these principles are held more tenaciously by the forest tribes than by those farther north, where, in some cases, it is the representative of the earth-god who assigns the land, in others an individual chief, while pastoral nomads are indifferent to questions of land ownership and value grazing rights only. The forest tribes jealously maintain that all unoccupied land belongs to some community or other, while the northern tribes are less insistent on such claims. All alike recognise the right of the conqueror to dispose of the land. The inevitable tendency to individual ownership is meanwhile constantly asserting itself, with the evolution of the tribe, and is fostered by pressure of population, by foreign example, and by the replacement of annual by permanent crops."

The focus of the above passage lies, for present purposes, in the last sentence; it might well have been italicized. What it signifies is that the private system of landholding goes with a general advance in culture and is the only one consistent with the mass movement of the mores in response to a pronounced alteration in the relation of men to land. Presumably the crucial criterion of

[167] Evans, in PSM, LII, 34.

[168] Ratzel, *Vkde.*, II, 282.

[169] Codrington, *Melanesians,* 63, 64.

[170] Fison, in JAI, X, 338.

[171] Paulitschke, *Nordost-Afr.,* I, 212.

[172] Ratzel, *Vkde.,* I, 431.

[173] Carey and Tuck, *Chin Hills,* I, 211.

[174] *Brit. Trop. Afr.,* 287.

private property in land, as indicated in several of the foregoing examples, is the lodgment of the power of sale in the hand of the individual.

The right to private property in land, in the special case of redeemed waste, is recognized by people very low in the scale of civilization, as well as by jurists of a higher stage. It both takes account of individual initiative and evokes that desirable thing.

In the words of Blackstone,[175] "Bodily labor bestowed upon anything, which before laid in common to all men, is universally allowed to give the fairest and most reasonable exclusive property therein." "A man who, of his own impulse, with his own labor, clears a piece of ownerless waste, wins this land and its product as free personal property. Such a right in severalty is recognized by most agricultural peoples along with communal rights; and in this way the chance is offered to peculiarly capable and active individuals to win a larger property and with it a larger power."[176]

This variation in the mores has existed, in general, wherever communalism in land has existed; and it has always provided an expedient outlet for the energies of individuals. It has been the solvent of the levelling-down influence of communalism, and has shown survival-value. It is a sort of forerunner of the settled system of land-holding in severalty.

"It is remarkable indeed how precisely alike in the Solomon Islands, the Banks Islands, and the New Hebrides, the character of property in land reclaimed from the bush asserts itself to be; and how the same effect has been produced of introducing or strengthening the tendency towards the succession of the son to his father's property, in place of the right of succession through the mother"; that is, instead of the nephews inheriting collectively, the children inherit.[177] "If a man reclaims a piece of bush land, it becomes his, and the different character of his property in it is shown by the difference in the right of succession to it."[178]

Wilken[179] presents a rather detailed account of the system of property in land in Celebes; his description, followed by certain of his generalizations, provides a perspective of the customs about waste land in the setting of the local system. Land in each district is of two chief forms: (a) lands that have never yet been cleared and are covered with heavy original growth, and (b) lands which have already been cultivated once, both those which are still actually in use and those which, for a longer or shorter time, are lying fallow. This latter category can be divided into: (1) lands actually in use; (2) lands that have lain fallow one or two years; (3) lands that have lain fallow four, five, or six years, and on which already a low growth has sprung up; (4) lands

---

[175] *Commentaries,* Bk. II, I, 5.   [176] Grosse, *Familie,* 136.
[177] §134, below.
[178] Codrington, *Melanesians,* 61, 63 ff.; Codrington, in JAI, XVIII, 312.
[179] "Landbezit," in VG, II, 356, 364, 368-369; Wilken, *Vkde.,* 429-430.

where this growth has already become high. Each variety of land has its own designation, and numerous details accompany the classification.

The regulations in the Minahasa district are as follows: "1. All lands belong in property to the district within whose legal boundaries they lie. There are absolutely no lands known to which one or another district cannot lay claim. 2. The lands which have never yet been cleared (*tierre vierge*) stand at the disposal of the members of the district, each of whom may, as he sees fit, gather the natural products in the bush situated on these lands, or clear a part of them in proportion to his strength. 3. Through the fact of clearing, the clearer or his lawful representative gets the exclusive right of usufruct over the clearing. The rights which the rest of the members of the district individually could make good over this land are thereby halted. The district retains over it, however, a covering property-right (*un domaine éminent*). 4. All the already cleared land, as well that which is still cultivated or lies fallow as that which, abandoned for a long time, has again become waste, thus belongs in inheritable possession to certain members of the district, either individually to single persons or communally to families. 5. Persons who do not belong to the district are excluded from all rights to land. However, the district can alienate lands to them temporarily for use. Over the land thus alienated for use they get no rights. They can attain to possession of the land only by getting themselves received as members of the district." By far the majority of tribes in the Indian Archipelago show a parallelism with or an approach to the above system.

Wilken generalizes the case of waste-occupation: it is usually true "that this similar and common right of the tribe, etc., to the land is regulated by the fact of first clearing, in so far, namely, that he who clears a piece of land gets a preferential right of use to it above his fellow-members, that he holds this right as long as he cultivates the land, that this right may go over to his heirs, and that it can be transferred to other persons, provided they are members of the same tribe; that when the clearer or his legal representatives abandon the clearing, the preferential right of use to it gained by clearing is lost after a certain time, and the land returns again to the community."

A review of the cases of property-tenure in the waste reveals an astonishing range of variation away from the system of communal holding. The man who has redeemed waste land is like the one who has hit the game first, acquired booty, or called something to life. He has a right to get back his capital and a reward for his enterprise and labor before the community can call upon him to share. He is not beholden to the chief for what he has won. He can hand down what he has gained to his own children where regularly inherited property goes to nephews; thus is a breach made in the ancient mother-descent. So long as he keeps up his interest in his acquisition, as indicated by cultivation, he is not to be interfered with. All of these privileges and immunities amount to a premium upon initiative and enterprise; the greater the number of cases reviewed the more types of reward appear. The case of property in the waste is therefore exceedingly enlightening as a transitional form toward settled private property in land; and the display of opportunity to ambition and effort which it exhibits is a forerunner of those stimuli, characteristic of the non-sharing system, which have assured it survival-value in the evolution of society.

§124. **Private Property in Land.** "What rights," it is asked,[180] "what privileges could individual proprietorship confer in a community of savages?" In answer to this query it may be recalled that foregoing cases reveal some reason for private holdings of land among savages, even apart from the grave: unshared tenure evoked economy in preserving game, for one thing; without assuring possession to individuals it became, in time, impossible to obtain from the land a sufficient supply of food. More generally, the call for individual ownership is raised by reason of an advance in organization; then private tenure, in turn, sustains a higher organization, one with a more developed specialization in function and with new societal organs. This is where an agricultural economy comes in, under which land is valuable not only for subsistence but also for profit. Then the land, bearing economic rent, becomes an object of competition, and a new phase of societal evolution is opened.

"The conception of property has a significance for the agriculturist quite different from that for the nomad. Instead of the tribal interest and communal tribal possession appear the local interest and private possession."[181] People soon begin to think territorial-wise instead of kin-wise, and the state is not far off.[182] "As soon as the land was fixed in the hands of the cultivator, civil liberty struck its roots in property; the condition of men improved; society became firmer; civilization took a new start."[183] "In the Middle Ages liberty and property are closely connected ideas."[184] At its first opportunity property begins to exercise its characteristic function of stabilizer.[185]

---

[180] Smyth, *Vict.*, I, 147.
[182] §§185, 186, 187, below.
[184] Maitland, *Select Pleas*, II, xx.

[181] Maurer, *Vkde.*, I, 144-145.
[183] Guerard, *Irminon*, I, 210.
[185] §341, below.

Land is not a product of labor and is not saved; it is a natural monopoly and therefore can be appropriated. If a man should appropriate a piece of land and should simply wait, without spending an atom of capital or a moment of labor upon it, population would increase until some one would desire to use that land to obtain means of subsistence from it, and would pay the appropriator to abandon his right to exclude all others from it. Such a payment is rent. The case is similar to that of any other monopoly; a monopoly is theoretically possible wherever the supply is limited and cannot be increased by applying labor and capital, but no monopoly is practically operative if the supply, though limited, is far in excess of the demand. In older countries, persons who have saved capital, attracted by the natural security, permanency, and advantage of property in land, exchange their capital with the appropriator for the exclusive right which he possesses over a certain plot. This does not make the land capital. The two men have only changed places. There is, as before, land and capital; the landholder has become a capitalist and the capitalist a landholder by exchange.

It is scarcity of valuable land in proportion to population—the land-man relation, again—that leads, through rent, to private property in land. Private holdings often occurred only near a river, or a settlement, or the center of a settlement. The increasing density of population has thus created conditions to which the system of private property in land has been an adjustment. Cities and city-systems have grown by reason of the same conditions that evoked property in land. Such increase of population means, in general, advance in the arts of civilization; thus the advance of civilization and that of private property in land are correlative. In fact, property in land is not so different from other property as has been asserted. Forms of property in food, amulets, chattels, canoes, houses, beasts, slaves, and land all differ from one another in details which depend upon the character of the things and the convenience of their use, but not otherwise. Different ways of holding land show divergences along the same line.

We may conclude our dealings with land-systems by quoting again from Lugard and citing several companion-pieces which set forth the series that culminates in private holding. Says Lugard:[186] "In the earliest stage the land and its produce is shared by the community as a whole; later the produce is the property of the family or individuals by whose toil it is won, and the control of the land becomes vested in the head of the family. When the tribal stage is reached, the control passes to the chief, who allots unoccupied lands at will, but is not justified in dispossessing any family or person who is using the land. Later still, especially when the pressure of population has given to the land an exchange value, the conception of proprietary rights in it emerges, and sale, mortgage, and lease of land, apart from its user, is recog-

[186] Brit. Trop. Afr., 280-281, 327.

nised. . . . In Africa every stage of this process of evolution may be encountered." The author goes on to say that Cecil Rhodes "firmly held to the view that social progress and development among the natives could best be promoted by individual holdings in land. . . . In conversation he frequently asserted his belief that individual possession of land was the key to the social elevation of the natives, and created self-respect."

Another expert on Africa[187] emphasizes the adjustment of the property-system to local conditions. "The laws as to Land Tenure among natives must necessarily vary according to the conditions under which the tribe settled, the area available to them, and the nature of the crops grown. As illustrating this it may be shown how one tribe follows two systems. The Atheraka . . . originally settled on the north bank of the Tana River, where their leader allotted land to each family. In the course of time the land did not suffice, and a portion of the tribe crossed to the other side of the river. Here land was plentiful, and consequently a division of lands was not necessary. Such is the tradition, and it is noteworthy that the Atheraka have no individual tenure on the south side of the river, while on the north side they have." With one exception, "the rule is everywhere, broadly speaking, that everyone has equal rights to forest, grazing, water, fuel, building material, and trees. Where individual tenure exists it is actually only in respect to the right to cultivate the land. In this respect the tribes under discussion may be classed as follows: —(1) Those among whom a perpetual title to ownership is admitted. (2) Those who only recognize a temporary right of occupation."

The same author illustrates how private property in land may revert to a communal type: "In speaking of land tenure, we must clearly distinguish between the land itself and the cultivated soil: the former is called *gethaka* or *terri* (earth) and the latter *mugunda* (field). The *mugunda* is rented from crop to crop and conveys no right whatsoever to the land; in fact, the owner may turn the tenant off at any time and even root up his crops. . . . The original purchaser is of course sole owner, but on his death the *gethaka* belongs to all his sons equally and is inherited by all sons from generation to generation. It is thus held as common property by the entire family, in which no member has a greater share than another. Here also the eldest son is designated as the sole owner, but only as representative or trustee of the family. . . . It is interesting to note that these three tribes present four different forms of land tenure—in Ukamba it is by right of acquisition, in Kikiyu by right of purchase, and in Theraka by right of distribution by a leader and of communal claim."

Hutton[188] relates the forms of landholding practised by the Nagas to the population-land relation: "Land that is the common land of a village, clan, or family cannot, of course, be sold by an individual, nor can an individual sell his share in any land. . . . Land questions in the Sema country are all very highly coloured by the extreme scarcity of land and the rapidly increasing inability of the population to support themselves on the land at their disposal, no other suitable means of livelihood existing. Land held in common by the whole community, though it probably still exists in one or two of the most eastern Sema villages, has long ceased to exist, at any rate in any appreciable quantity, and probably entirely, in the administered part of the Sema

[187] Dundas, C., in JAI, LI, 271; XLV, 298-299.
[188] *Sema Nagas*, 155-156.

country. All land is now privately owned, though, as a man's land may not be divided by his sons, but must await the second generation for division, much land is of necessity owned jointly by brothers or even cousins, the eldest allotting the land for yearly cultivation. It cannot pass to women by inheritance or gift."

Characteristic of the system of private holdings is the mortgage. This device, in so far as it is employed in the Indian Archipelago, has been made the subject of a special monograph by Wilken,[189] We need not go into the details of the matter. It bears upon the topic before us to note, however, that Wilken thinks the mortgage, in a general sense, is an original arrangement in the Archipelago; and especially that, in its most primitive form, it bore upon immovables and conferred only the privilege of use. It resulted from the inability of a man to pay back a loan or to raise a bride-price, pay a fine, or otherwise meet exceptional demands. Of course what he borrowed for such a purpose disappeared at once. Then the creditor saw a way of recouping himself for the indefinitely protracted absence of his capital. The debtor, if he owns a field, has something productive to lay hand on besides his own body, as in debt-slavery. The creditor can now collect by getting hold of the debtor's land and raising something on it. The highest form of this sort of transaction, the regular foreclosable mortgage, appears only among the Balinese.

It should now appear that the institution of property began in the facts of man's relations to his material environment and in his earliest notions about weal and woe on earth. Private property in land has come to be as the result of a constant automatic shifting, and not in obedience to baseless speculations about justice and equality, or to erroneous assertions about the facts of ethnography and history. It is now a part of the self-maintenance organization and, indeed, a phase of the societal division of labor. That some own the land is a fact of no profounder or more perilous significance than that some own the factories, others the stores, and others the ships. The contrary idea is a survival of feudal notions of the connection of land with jurisdiction and social preëminence. The constitutional proviso that private property shall not be taken for public use without compensation is the final guarantee of private property as a fully developed institution. It shows the relation between it and civil liberty. Taxation of A and B to get means to give something to C and D, or to do things speculatively alleged to be in the public interest, still remains as an abuse to be suspected and resisted. It is now flourishing under forms more or less disguised. It means that A's rights of property ought not to stand in our way when we have made up our minds what we will make him do for B.

[189] In VG, II, 444.

CHAPTER XIII

SOME GENERALITIES ON PROPERTY

§125. **Variation in Property-Forms.** The evidence now before us teaches us that we must not be led astray by the temptation inhering in classification to believe that exclusively private or exclusively common property ever existed. "A view that denies intermediate forms between private property and communal possession is one-sided."[1] Property rises, be it recalled, when two cannot use the same thing and the supply of things is limited. Some tribes automatically meet the case by sharing; others in other ways. The facts and forces in the field can never be escaped; and the method that secures the best adjustment to the situation as presented prevails. "To appropriate," says Oliveira Martins,[2] "is to create, to extract an object from the totality and to individualize it. In favor of whom? Of the man, of the family, of the nation? Of any one of these, according to the conditions and the occasion. Individual and collective property are not far enough apart to constitute dissevered forms or aspects of the same natural-social phenomenon." Society "moves between the two poles of individual property and collective property, in their more or less perfect form, and the exclusive theories of communism and of individualism do not go farther than abstractions and utopias."

With numbers of cases and some running comment now before us, we are ready to consider this larger generalization respecting the essential likeness of all property, in all ages and stages, as a form of adaptation in the mores. This may best be done by examining somewhat into the whole conception of property, but more particularly into that of property in land. For while there can be no denial of the assertion that the first property of all was individual and private, there has yet been a great deal of theorizing about "primitive communism," especially in land, in which it has been maintained, among other things, that land differs radically from other forms of property. And such a common-property system, held to be the "natural," not to say the divinely ordained

---

[1] Kowalewski, *Oekon. Entw.*, I, 79.   [2] *Quadro*, 78.

development, has been regarded also as a better arrangement, characteristic of the good old times of human innocence from which the race has retrograded.

Laveleye[3] (who wrote hastily on a very inadequate outfit, and spread highly incorrect opinions under a semblance of competent authority) holds, for example, that such a system is "an ideal which man once possessed, but has gradually lost, as egoism has prevailed, but it is an ideal which it is our duty to restore and establish"—as if the "nos-ism" of group-property, held against other groups, were any better than the "egoism" of personal property held against other persons. There is need here of positive and far-reaching correction.

Again, what has been read into the term "village-community" has been mischievous. If the word community meant here no more than it does when we speak of "the community," meaning the public, the undefined and unintegrated societal group, there would be no harm. It would then be roughly equivalent to "village" or "town." The "village-community," however, has been taken to mean a village with a communistic organization. It has become technical; and some writers have applied it in the colonial history of the Anglo-American colonies, where it imports error. It is clear enough from our cases that property is a varying conception in the mores, and that nobody had any "ideal" about it. So-called "primitive collectivism" is a figment of learned but uncritical imagination.

The notion of common property in land as a widespread and well-organized primitive system of land-tenure, produced by a rational coöperation of equal tribesmen, is largely due to the German scholars. They thought they found it in the statements of Cæsar and Tacitus about the Germans of their time. These statements are meager and obscure, conveying connotations not likely to have been present in German society. The reasons Cæsar gives for the German usages which he cites are evidently not German reasons; they are Roman guesses and speculations, and their standpoint is Roman; yet it is easy to see that they have entered into the minds of modern readers and commentators of Cæsar as if a part of his statement of facts. Under the influence of ethnocentrism, German writers have filled in the background and created a scene of primitive communalism that will not bear criticism.

Where there was really no property in land at all, scholars have imagined collective property and have carried back into it modern notions of "collectivism," in all their vagueness and variety. It remains to be proved that men have ever anywhere, on a primitive

3 *Propriété*, 282.

stage of life, established free and voluntary coöperation in land-culture with a democratic-republican organization of control; what has been so interpreted is really non-organization and absence of ideas. The case is parallel to that of alleged communalism in women, which was absence of positive order.[4] The idea of men coming together in free and voluntary union for common ends is unhistorical; they have come together without premeditation under pressure, from an apprehension of danger, an experience of suffering, and a need of common defense. Any other kind of union is modern and is due to intellectual development at the top of civilization. Even now, and among the most civilized and best educated, successful and enduring coöperation of the free and voluntary kind is possible only among a small number of individuals who are selected with a knowledge that they are congenial and have such confidence in one another's characters that they can trust each other.

"Community in land," says De Coulanges,[5] evidently with such "collectivism" in mind, "has not yet been historically proved in a single case in history." Cunow[6] tells us that the "alleged ideal-socialistic measures of the Incas of Peru existed long before the time of the Incas as a natural product of a primitive society built on kin-unions." It "was just like the aboriginal agrarian communism seen among the Indian-Aryans, Japanese, Germans, and Celts." He destroys the fiction of Peruvian communism, so often cited in support of doctrinaire pronouncements, without contributing to bolster up German communism—which, indeed, he did not intend to do.

§126. Fictions about Land. In a broad sense, land is one of the energies, like fire, organisms, and man, which are appropriated out of nature. Being thus appropriated, is it property like the others, or is it incapable of being property at all? It is a method of arguing about this matter, which seems to be considered weighty, to say that land is a gift of God, like air or water, and on that account cannot be made property. When we say that land, water, and air—and we might as well add fire, wind, falling water, and electricity—were given us by God, we mean simply that when the human race takes account of itself it finds itself here on earth in certain surroundings, circumstances, and conditions. We may say that God made these things and made us. That is a theological

---

[4] §343, below.   [5] Origin of Property, 149.
[6] Verf. d. Inkareichs, 7.

construction of the facts, not an antecedent truth which throws any light upon the facts. We must equally say that drought, inundation, tornadoes, destructive insects, pestilences, diseases, passions, and vices of men—things which handicap them in the struggle for existence—are gifts of God.

The ruling consideration must be for all the natural monopolies just what it has been for land, namely, the answer to this question: what institutions will encourage such exploitation of natural resources as will give society the most abundant and economical use and enjoyment of what they offer for self-realization? "The land," said the Omahas,[7] "is like water and wind . . . what *cannot be sold.*" Naturally so, at their degree of advancement. It is easy to see, however, that on an advanced stage of culture the appropriation even of the water of great seas, not to say the high seas, once free to all if anything was, has begun and will go on. Inventions like the submarine cable require it. We are living in the midst of a movement as to property in water which is running parallel to the historical development of property in land. And property in the air is doubtless yet to come.

In fact, as to air and light, they are property already when they are scarce. The price of land in a great city is really, to a great extent, the price of light and air. Corner-lots illustrate the point. The charge for light and airy rooms in a hotel or on a steamboat, to which allusion has already been made, is significant along the same line. When the streets are lined with buildings many stories high, it is readily seen that land cannot be used for emplacement and for light and air at the same time. When devices are adopted to throw air and light into buildings, the appropriation, property-form, and value of these necessaries of life will be on the same order as they now are in the case of water provided by city water-works. In the sunlight and in the phenomena of combustion, God gave light and heat, but if we want either where it is not, labor and capital are required to get it there. When it is produced or transported, it is appropriated and owned; it has value and bears rent. Monopolies of place and time are economically represented by cost of transportation and by credit respectively; they therefore enter into the same category with land and the rest.

[7] Dorsey, in BAE, III, 366.

Talent, God-given though it may be, requires education and training. There is even property in ideas; patents and copyrights are the devices for guaranteeing it. Such grants of monopoly secure for society the most energetic exploitation of the natural monopoly of talent and initiative. This case falls into exact parallelism with property in land. Where a patent expires, the device does not become common property, but non-property; ideas and devices never could be property except by the arbitrary exercise of societal power. Thus the argument against property in land from the alleged gratuitous gifts of God in land, air, water, and the rest, is based upon imperfect knowledge and inadequate analysis. It has no validity at all.

The allied conception of land as a "boon of nature"[8] is like the eighteenth-century notion of a "state of nature" or a "golden age." It is an idle and a foolish dream. With it must be rejected the fiction of "prairie value," for no such thing ever existed. The difficulty of clearing land has been noted by Bruce[9] for Virginia; and "it must have been a tremendously difficult piece of work to prepare the soil of Europe for planting, matted as it was with roots, and with the instruments of primitive times."[10] The prairie-value of such land would be a negative quantity. It would be a task for convicts working in chains to break up new land if it were not for the "unearned increment" which comes to the pioneer with settlement and civilization, and will be an advantage to his children. With the chance of an unearned increment goes also the hazard of an unearned decrement; and to confiscate the gains which are won by some from a favorable conjuncture, while leaving those who suffer from an unfavorable one to bear their own losses, is a policy scarcely squaring up with the most modest ideals of justice.

The "boon" of land cannot be "given back to the people," because they never had it. They did not take it when it lay free because nobody wanted it. The free land was a burden when its societal obligations were taken with it, and men had to be held to it as serfs. Wild land is only another name for the struggle

---

[8] See Sumner, on "The Boon of Nature" and "The Banquet of Life," in *Coll. Ess.*, II, 217 ff.; 233 ff.

[9] *Va.*, 196; §123, above.   [10] Schrader, *Aryans*, 289.

for existence in its concrete form. When the hard work is done and
the time for enjoying results has come, it is proposed to give the
land back to the people, that is, to force those who did the work,
or their assigns, to share with those who did not. The people can
still get their original boon in outlying parts; they want it within
a few miles of some population-center where it is beautifully cultivated or bears a high rent. It seems hard to understand that land
may not be property at all, just as the ocean is not; that six hundred and forty acres of land may have no more value than a
square mile of ocean; yet a square mile of Iowa land, two hundred
years ago, was no more property and worth no more than the
same area of tossing salt water, defined by latitude and longitude.

Many attempts were made in the sixteenth century to found settlements in
the present Atlantic States. All failed in misery and in famine. Jamestown
was in jeopardy of its existence for twenty-five years and Plymouth survived
only on the charity of the savages. If land is a boon, why was this? For no
landlords held the soil against the laborer. The English kings gave away tracts
of land of thousands of acres each; but not one of them was worth having;
the grantees sunk capital in attempts to settle and develop the grants. Why
was this, if prairie-value was present? Where the grantees thought they owned
empires, the property was not even zero; it was a minus quantity. To own it
was to be subject to burdens, expense, heavy labor, great risks of capital and
health, war with the elements, with disease, with wild beasts, and with aborigines. Hence a man needed to be paid for going on it. The unearned increment
and the hope of advantage to his posterity, from prior possession, were the
inducements.

It is a popular notion, further, that there should be no property in land because land is not "made." "Land," says Jenks,[11]
"cannot be multiplied and cannot be carried away." The assertion is rendered pointless by the reflection that no title to any
property is due to the fact that it is made. Even if this were not
so, yet land is made by human labor even more clearly than several
other recognized forms of property. Labor is necessary to bring
land into cultivation, and land which is ready for seed is "made"
in as full a sense as any product of handicraft. To make anything
a man must appropriate the materials; the alleged vice of robbing
others by appropriating the boon of nature lies at the root of all
property in chattels, from the flint knife to the watch, as it does
in the case of land. Likewise the crop that comes out of the ground

[11] *Law and Pol.*, 207.

is a new thing on earth, a product of human labor, and is made in an even fuller sense than an artifact in which the original material is the essential part. If there is any reason why a domesticated horse, a descendant of generations of domesticated horses, should be private property, there is the same reason why land, which has been tilled for generations, should be private property. No one can domesticate an animal unless he can take it and hold it for a period; and similarly no one can reduce land to cultivation unless it is appropriated and held through time.

It is practical conditions, not theories or metaphysical whimsies that determine men's arrangements about land. There was a stage when property in beasts was an innovation and an invasion of common rights previously existing; and the same may be said of trees and wild fruits. Living people in the United States have seen a great advance of private rights in respect to nuts, game, and fish. In view of these considerations it is an error to say that land cannot be property because it is not made or multiplied. Its two predominant uses are for emplacement and for the production of plants. We multiply the emplacement when we build several stories high; we multiply tillable land when, by applying labor and capital, we make an area produce a multiplied product.

§127. **Communalism.** The word "communism" is always likely to have a doctrine in it: an implication of what "ought" to be; an ideal; a therapeutic scheme for the future of society. Men "ought" to share with one another and to bless society in so doing. It often means "collectivism." Nowhere in our study do we find any primitive communism or socialism, or any other doctrine. Communalism, as we use the term, is distinguished from communism in that it covers purely practical arrangements—existing phenomena of the mores, objectively and automatically arrived at. When it is stated that in the Fiji Islands neither chief nor man is absolute owner of any land, that each possesses only a lifelong usufruct of it,[12] there is presented a case of real communalism; but it is not so by theory. There is plenty of communalism, in this sense of corporate ownership, at any period. In every state the population, in its civil totality, owns the land in some sense or

12 Fison, in JAI, X, 351.

other. We do not analyze it. How many people in Connecticut could tell whether, or in what sense or degree, all the citizens and inhabitants of Connecticut, of the "State" as the abstract unit of us all, own the land? If we ourselves cannot tell, then we may the more easily understand why uncivilized people accept usage and never analyze it to determine what is the nature or philosophy of their property in the territory from which they exclude all others.

When the land is said to be owned by the tribe, on the hunting or pastoral stage, the expression is misleading. It is derived from later ideas. In fact, such tribes never think of the land; to them it is only the emplacement. It means being here, that is, existing. Savage men do not reflect much more than animals; they think of the game, or the beasts, or the trees, or the water, or the honey. They have in mind what is, in their experience, the limiting condition of existence, or some luxury that gives spice to it. It is not until agriculture begins that land takes on such character.

Ratzel[13] utters a caution when he writes that there is no communistic nation, but that among nomadic people, living widely scattered, the notion of property is not equally developed on all sides. They cling tenaciously to their cattle, but care little for land. Many respect property when it is locked up, but if it lies free they regard it as anybody's. They are objective and practical, and do not philosophize.

Communalism, as corporate ownership, shows a variety in form which is due to the imperfect power of primitive people to grasp the corporate idea or to carry on a corporate institution. Hence what is called communalism fluctuates between the notions of everyman's land, no man's land, and lordship with serfdom.

Similarly where the land is said to belong to the chief, the arrangement may vary through a wide range. Is it a pure fiction of law, or really a living fact? Does the chief allot lands, and can he take them back at will upon any or upon specified occasions? Or is there a fiction here, used to get tribute for the crown—not for the king as an individual? Two usages found in this connection are significant: first, that all must pay the chief tribute from all game, booty, or product won (purveyance); second, that the chief grants to his officers, relatives, favorites, the tribute of a district, out of which the grantee gives a fraction to the chief in recognition. These two usages are due to circumstances of constant recurrence, and they suffice to sustain a whole series of institutions which lead from ownership of land by the chief of a wild tribe to a complete feudal system.

13 *Vkde.*, I, 85.

Certainly if property is in the form of a single object or chattel, it is hardly conceivable that a number should have the same and contemporaneous right to enjoy it. Although members of a club own its property communally, all cannot sit in the same chair or read the same magazine at the same time. They take turns, or divide time, or adopt other devices; nevertheless the result cannot but be inequality of advantage. The plate of food set on the boarding-house table may be viewed as common property, like the club-furniture; yet in either case practical enjoyment requires regulations of courtesy, precedent, and law in which any theoretical communism disappears. The varieties of communalism as a practical expedient are evidently endless.

We have an illustration close at hand in which to study these varieties and their relations with individual property. In one of our houses the furniture is nominally the property—certainly in the custody—of the head of the house. Much of it is for the use of all members of the household. Some of it is restricted from servants. Visitors admitted for a longer or shorter stay get the same privileges of use as members of the household. A guest has a room and its furniture allotted to him exclusively during his stay. Each member of the household has such an allotment permanently. Table-furniture, silver, heating-apparatus, and floor-coverings are in purely common use. The householder is the owner, as the lord of the manor owned the soil, behind the common usufruct. A chair, table, desk, musical instrument, picture, or book may be individual property—not absolutely forbidden to others than the individual owner, but usable by others only with permission or in a limited way or with due recognition of the owner's rights. It is noteworthy that the degree to which individual property is exclusive varies much in these cases. Clothing, drawing-instruments, a sewing-kit, school-books, toys, umbrellas, or canes may be purely individual property. A son's room furniture is regarded as his.

The historical phases of property are represented in this familiar case, and the transition of one form into another can be made out. Study of such cases will lead us to see that what have been regarded as cases of communalism are only such phases as convenience brings about; they are circumstantial, not intentional; they are not enacted.

Things are now owned collectively which were not so owned until modern times. It is incorrect to say that more and more things are being made into private property, with no recognition of movement in the other direction. Some public property, as parks, hospitals, museums, schools, libraries, is communal, and the type seems to be on the increase; and some is not, for example, that which is used by public departments in the public service. In the Middle Ages churches were about the only form of public property, and were communal; now, when owned by congregations, they are not. In modern states and municipalities there has been a great increase in the amount and variety of this kind of property. In practice, communalism is either controlled by usages and laws which reduce it to an entangled case of individual rights or it is ruled by a scramble. The evolution of communal into private property generally brought about simplification and reality.

§128. **Communalism as Insurance.** Communalism, says Starcke,[14] is a custom with the power of a custom; there is no idea of common possession. The usage is one which, like all others, has developed because it suited conditions; for property grew up by custom, without reflection, and never as a system which was regarded as "just." What one collects and appropriates is one's own, and there is in regard to it no call for communal tenure. One owns his spear and his hat and, on redeeming waste land, he owns that. "Communalism," he concludes, "is only the special union of individual, isolated spheres of interest"; for the individual has interests and powers that demand this form. Starcke would agree that property-forms are evolutionary adjustments in the mores; he sees the justification of communalism in the fact that it prevents the individual from taking his own insurance too much into his own hands.

This idea is well worth reflection. If we recall the reasons for living in human society at all,[15] we see the insurance-interest playing a significant part. No one can deny the presence of a levelling tendency in such association; the insurance attained calls for a constant series of small losses and of small gains, and by its prescriptions, which cause all to share in the advantages that may have been gained by one, it prevents the individual from either prospering beyond the common measure or suffering exceptionally. It is a sort of safe bet for small stakes. The most the group can do is to be sure that none of its members shall starve to death

[14] *Samvittighedslivet*, 229-235, 244-245, 252. Starcke uses the word "kommunisme," but he means by it what we call communalism, and we so translate it.

[15] §§6-8, above.

although all go hungry. It will not permit the individual to live for himself alone, to take his own risks and bear his own losses or keep his own gains, that is, to do his own insuring. When he brings down game, he must raise a shout and call the rest in to participation; and, on the other hand, if luck is not with him, he may answer the shout of someone else and fill his belly.

Where now this sort of group-solidarity has not yet permitted of the development of individuality, but clings to the old defensive mores of group-insurance, there is where communalism is at home. In its decline the communal system is acted upon by freed individual initiative, a solvent which secures its disintegration. Its displacement accompanies the development of capital.

Here should be recalled the cases of sharing previously cited.[16] Where the game, as soon as it is downed, is the property of all, the hunter who tries to retain his quarry is a thief or a sinner against the ghosts. Among the Eskimo, it will be recalled, distribution of game is general except at periods of plenty, when it is the housemates only who share in the catch; in other words, when conditions are very precarious, not even the house-group, much less the individual, is allowed to take its own insurance into its own hands. It is levelled down with the rest of the groups. A more favorable situation admits of the appearance of group-independence, and this is conceded at last to the individual. Says Morgan:[17] "The fact of the conjunction of several . . . families in a common household is of itself an admission that the family was too feeble an organization to face alone the hardships of life."

The extent of communalism seems therefore to vary with the difficulty of the struggle for existence and the competition of life. Where the struggle presses hard, the group, through its adapting mores, assures its existence by forcing all its members to insure. Here is compulsory insurance in its primordial form. If A's risk is small, or seems so to him in his state of rudimentary foresight, and he prefers not to pay the premium, he yet must do so in order that B and C—in short, the group as a whole, including himself in spite of his real or fancied immunity—may be insured. In the interest of all, he must not be allowed to take his own fate, much less that of others, lightly into his own hands. All of this is an unpremeditated development, in the mores. The pursuit of this principle might lead us on to examples from life no longer strictly primitive and somewhat altered in mode. It is always those who are not getting on who clamor for sharing. From our lists of cases it

16 §114, above.   17 *Anc. Soc.*, 453; §345, below.

is clear enough that the essence of communalism is group-solidarity as against individual independence, initiative, and opportunity.

Vinogradoff[18] writes: "In Serbia, Montenegro, Bosnia, Herzegovina, Dalmatia and Croatia, . . . where the population had constantly to fight for existence against the Turks, the Albanians, sometimes the Hungarians, and where the economic struggle was also no easy matter in the absence of good roads, political security and commercial credit, the stress of social organization was laid emphatically on the communal principle as against individual action. According to a Croatian proverb, a single man does not get food nor work. Another saying likens a man devoid of communal support to a man without an arm. As a result, all the provinces enumerated above were covered with Zadrugas, large families which had grown out of the narrow family. . . . Altogether the Joint Family presents an interesting example of the value of co-operative action, and of customary restrictions on the free play of individual self-determination." The author generalizes as follows.

"The most profound difference between modern and ancient organization consists in the fact that modern society starts from individuals and adjusts itself primarily to the claims of the individual, whereas ancient society starts from groups and subordinates individual interests to the claims of these groups. There are two general reasons for this state of things. To begin with, there is the weakness and insecurity of the single man in barbaric surroundings, which drives him to seek companionship and to place himself under protection at any price. It is only by close union that tribesmen can survive in the difficult struggle for life against outsiders. A single man would be a lost man." The author quotes Smith:[19] "It is only by mutual help, by avoiding intestine quarrels and subordinating individual interests to those of the kin, that, in the hard conditions of desert life, and in a state of constant war with outsiders, a tribe can hope to hold its own. . . . To get the full benefit of this mutual support, the group must not only fight together, but as far as possible move together." The second reason cited "may not perhaps be so clearly perceived by those who deal with these matters. In modern society the State has assumed the monopoly of political co-ordination. It is the State which rules, makes laws, and eventually enforces them by coercion. Such a State, as a wide and more or less abstract union, did not exist in ancient times. The commonwealth was not centred in one sovereign body towering immeasurably above single individuals and meting out to every one his portion of right. Therefore the necessary political elements which are never absent from any human society, were distributed among formations which we regard now from the point of view of private law: churches, local bodies, kindreds."[18]

§129. Communalism as a Maladjustment.

Few of our instances of sharing are taken from the lives of progressive peoples. Such a system, expedient enough in its day of smaller things, discourages qualities that have been essential to the development of higher civilization. In this respect it is like slavery: once an expe-

[18] Vinogradoff, *Hist. Jurispr.*, I, 268, 273, 299.
[19] *Kinship*, 37.

dient and selected variation, long a settled and useful institution, at length a maladaptation and a curse. Communalism levels all down to the same plane and pattern; it thus opposes that inequality of individual opportunity, action, and reward which is at the bottom of variation in the mores.[20] And variation is essential as the starting-point of new adjustment.

Krieger,[21] after describing the Papuan practice, remarks: "That such a communalism hinders advanced progress is only too clear. Under these circumstances, it is to no purpose for the Papuan to save or to strive to win riches; he must still surrender what he has to the rest, or, in the other case, he would be bewitched and killed out of hatred and envy. It is thus only natural that he prefers to give rather than to die; and so it appears no longer marvellous, even to us, when we hear that paid-off laborers, returned to their villages, remain hardly three days in happy monopoly of the goods they have earned with difficulty and hard labor during three years." The case of the Krumen and other instances of sharing cited here and there in the foregoing[22] will come to mind to reinforce this comment. Büttner[23] speaks of the communalism of the Hottentots and Herero: according to the custom of the former, one who has must give to anyone who has not till he himself has no more. This hampers progress. Among the Herero, before coin came in, a man had to share his purchases with a number of "good friends"; after it was introduced it was possible to rescue something for one's self. Evidently the advance to coin-money helped along the development of private property; thus do the mores reveal their "strain of consistency." In India, "community of property naturally tends to discourage individual activity, personal exertion, and independence of spirit. The expenditure of a large family thus united may be less than if divided into several separate families, but the aggregate income would be much larger, and the peace and comfort enjoyed by the latter plan would be incomparably greater."

Communalism is a plan, as it were, of increasing a fraction by lowering the denominator rather than by increasing the numerator; it is a negative expedient of caution and saving rather than a positive one of aggression and winning.

To resume the last quotation: "Misery, idleness, ignorance, and poverty follow from these laws; life is wasted in listless inactivity. Such a home is 'no true home, but rather a sort of family club, where all the male members of the household take their meals together. Employed or unemployed, active or indolent, he and his may live here and take their share with the rest so long as there is property enough, or employment enough, among them all to keep things going.' "[24] With such conditions goes shameless beggary; it is the strength of the private-property idea that causes begging to be disliked, thus influencing the mores of all. Maine[25] shows how this situation altered with the

[20] Keller, Soc. Evol., 51-52.
[21] Neu-Guinea, 196.
[22] §114, above.
[23] Walfischbai, 24, 91.
[24] Mateer, in JAI, XII, 301.
[25] Early Law, 358, 253, 264.

growth of wealth in modern India, and cites the case of Eastern European house-communities: "The reluctance to surrender individual gains is a sentiment observed to be gaining in force everywhere, and . . . it universally tends to bring about the dissolution of the communities. Doubtless it was always among the most potent of the influences which began to transform the old world of consanguinity into the new world of economical relation." The adventurous and energetic member of these house-communities always rebels against their communalism, just as the savage, in some of the foregoing cases, tries to keep to himself the products of his own toil. "He goes abroad and makes his fortune, and strenuously resists the demand of his relatives to bring it into the common account. Or perhaps he thinks that his share of the common stock would be more profitably employed by him as capital in a mercantile venture. In either case he becomes a dissatisfied member or a declared enemy of the brotherhood." Upon the stock procedure he evolves a variation upon which societal selection can work. The communal or sharing-system squanders economic and moral power—a decisive fact sure to make itself felt as the competition becomes more keen and complex.[26]

The course of change from communal to private property in land was by way of allotments for a time. This expedient was inconsistent with permanent improvements because the advantage of them could not be reaped, before a re-allotment took place, by the one who made them; the rights of those who wanted and of those who did not want a re-allotment conflicted. The system was also inconsistent with any form of production which required several seasons or years. It lasted on where no great improvements were made and where the utilities of the land tended to pass into the hands of different holders, resulting in great complexity and uneconomic conditions. This is illustrated in Danish experience at the end of the eighteenth century.[27] A modern case where the system of full private property was a need in order to do away with the abuses and difficulties of short-time tenures is that of the oyster-beds of Long Island Sound and Chesapeake Bay.[28]

"We see," writes Starcke,[29] "this community vanish when separate vocations start up and life becomes so variegated that individual differences in powers and inclination can make themselves effective." That is, differentiation of occupation breaks up communalism. The variable of special aptitude cannot forever be reduced to a constant or planed down to uniformity. In variety of vocation there is less chance to sense group-advantage and risk,

[26] Simkhovitch, *Feldgemeinschaft in Russland,* 579.

[27] Hansen, V. A., *Stavnbaands-Løsningen;* Hansen, P., *Landbrugs Historie.*

[28] Hadley, *Economics,* §144.   [29] *Samvittighedslivet,* 236, 237-239.

and the powerful takes his insurance on himself. Modification is gradual: first one's gains in work outside the family are his own and the rest that he has is common; then inherited property is communal while personally won property is at free disposition.

"Free property," Starcke resumes, "was the means which society found to make it possible for personal initiative to move unconstrainedly and to discover and use all possibilities there were to better life's material conditions. . . . Free possession fulfills all the demands which life, under shifting conjunctures and with new, unexpectedly arising possibilities for use of things, can make." There is no great advance in adjustment for which somebody does not suffer. A régime of inequality naturally pains those who are comfortable under communalism. "Individual property," says Von Hartmann[30] "creates more pain than pleasure, and . . . the complete suppression of private property seems to be the only means of doing away with the pain-producing inequality of possession. From the evolutionary point of view, on the contrary, increasing inequality or differentiation is the condition of social organization, without which civilization is unthinkable, and so property has its positive significance in the history of civilization precisely in the fact that it is the most essential means to social inequality."

In short, communalism was a phase of property-tenure which corresponded to a feebleness of individual initiative, and was sure to be modified away and to disappear as a type, where civilization had attained elevation, especially in the modern age whose very basis is the development of individual initiative and enterprise.

Men are faced, one might say, with an alternative neither branch of which is unalloyed with misery and pain. They may share whatever nature affords and for a time, perhaps, there is less misery. But there is little advance in the arts to take care of increase in numbers, and presently all who still live are dragging out a sort of minimal existence. On the other hand, each may seize what he can and use it to fight for himself. Some prosper sooner and others become miserable sooner than by the former plan. Nevertheless the arts develop and are socialized, and after a time all are sharing in the gains won by some. It is not the enterprising and powerful alone who gain by progress.[31] Civilization has actually run on the non-sharing course and, though superficially the grab-and-hold policy seems less attractive, there is no reason to think it a mistake. Between the attractions and repulsions of the two branches

30 *Phänom.*, 677-678.

31 Sumner, "Who Win by Progress?" in *Coll. Ess.*, III, 167 ff.; Davis, *Iron Puddler*, 268 ff.

of this alternative the opinions of social philosophers of all ages have wavered to and fro. It is possible to see here, as in all life, a choice between evils. Which is the lesser of the pair? Between two such vital and mutually exclusive lines of action, one of which, in its primitive form, has been superseded by the other during the evolution of civilization, the evolutionist has but one choice. His plan is to scrutinize the variations presented along the line that has prevailed under automatic selection and rationally to foster those which promise to be expedient in rising situations.

§130. Schemes and Doctrines. There was, in former ages, no conscious effort to devise a system which should have the effect of freeing individual initiative; hence the automatically developed form of communalism is to be sharply distinguished from modern schemes of levelling-down and equalization which are aimed squarely at the inequality that has been the race's salutary heritage. Primitive communalism lay in the mores, while modern schemes lie too often in discontent with the mores on the part of unsuccessful individuals—a discontent fostered by agitators with irrelevant motives.

To show that their schemes are realizable, these promoters yearningly recall the good, old, innocent times. The modern schemes are a phenomenon of societal evolution; but their case receives no legitimate support from reference to earlier conditions, alleged to be happier, under "primitive communism." Let Tylor, in his preface to Turner's *Samoa*,[32] recall the upshot of the communism practised in these Isles of the Blest: "Political theorists among us have been speculating about communism, but the Samoans, like other peoples near the same level of culture, have for ages been living it. Among them might be, and perhaps in some measure still may be seen practical common property, where each may freely borrow another's boat or tools or clothes, and live as long as he pleases freely in any house of a clansman. Here is a people who hear with wonder that among the white men the poor can be hungry and homeless. From this sorrow and disgrace the Samoans are free; but they pay dearly for this good in a social state where work is unprofitable and progress is checked because

32 P. xii.

the earnings of the industrious pass into the common property of workers and idlers." If communism comes again, it will be far from primitive and unsophisticated. Its supporters gain nothing real from a swift snatch at analogy. To set out with the honest idea of re-introducing primitive communism would be about as wise as to try to return to the crooked-stick plow or the Malay blow-gun. The advocacy of such folly is partly ignorant and innocent and partly specious and interested.

Exigencies of a later age have seemed, in the case of the Russian *mir*,[33] for example, to demand the development of adaptations which have resembled, often quite superficially, those of an antecedent stage of societal evolution. Emergencies have demanded, and are demanding, a surrender of private rights in favor of community rights. But each such case is a new one, deriving nothing of its urgency from the necessity of a return to the system of the antique world. That which caused primitive communalism cannot come again; necessity and interest have swept that form away forever. If it is to be succeeded by some superficially similar adjustment in the mores, that new form will be essentially as different from the primitive communal form as is the form of private property in this its day. Dean Inge[34] thinks that "the only conditions under which Communism can succeed were realized in the monasteries, and the monks are the only people of a Communistic regime going on for a long time. If you once allow the family, private ownership must come back. The family, private property and religion are the three strongest human instincts and Communism declares war against all three together." One may not agree with the terminology of this pronouncement, but there is much to reflect upon in its sentiments.

Among the doctrines that have been set afloat in popular and even in political discussion is the pronouncement that the right to enjoy material goods should be, not in him who has them, but in him who wants them. Such doctrines are all absurd when reduced to practice; for the existing institutional relation grew out of facts and expediency, and the new doctrines are anti-social. For example: A is a laborer seated by the roadside to eat his dinner. He opens his dinner-pail. He is the possessor of it. B is a tramp

[33] *Case-Book,* §119.   [34] N. Y. *Times,* May 2, 1925.

coming down the road who "wants" a dinner and has none. By the doctrine B has a better right to the dinner than A. If A surrenders it, then B is the possessor and A the wanter. Then A may demand the dinner back. Thus they may pass it to and fro until both starve to death. It is a jest to set up a societal right to property founded on need, for that means that some men have a right to have the struggle for existence carried on for them by others. Out of need no right can grow except against God or nature.

The institutions of society have not been evolved by lunatics, but by normal men who were doing their serious best to live under actual conditions and were being checked up at every turn on the hard facts of life. Therefore the usages they have set up respond to experience. We could have done no better under the circumstances. The doctrines naïvely or disingenuously proposed are phantasms; reduced to actuality they are absurd and, if they could be applied, would defeat the interests of mankind.

§131. Property-Forms as Evolutionary Adjustments.

It is plain enough, in view of our cases and attendant discussion, that property, like other societal arrangements, is in the mores; and that the mores about property are, like all the rest of the mores, in constant process of evolutionary adjustment.

> With the Siouan, "as among other barbarous peoples, the land was common to the tribe or other group occupying it, yet was defended against alien invasion; the ownership of movable property was a combination of communalism and individualism delicately adjusted to the needs and habits of the several tribes—in general, evanescent property, such as food and fuel, was shared in common (subject to carefully regulated individual claims) while permanent property, such as tipis, dogs, apparel, weapons, etc., was held by individuals. As among other tribes, the more strictly personal property was usually destroyed on the death of the owner."[35]

This case brings us back, in some degree, to the point at which we started with the topic of property: "the first private property was in objects forming, so to speak, part of the person, such as weapons and ornaments, made by the possessor himself, and . . . generally put into the grave with him."[36] Then those objects which, by their nature, cannot regularly be assimilated to personality,

[35] McGee, in BAE, XV, 177.   [36] Letourneau, *Prop.*, 365.

were the ones held, for a longer or shorter period, communally. It is by virtue of the amount of personality put into an object that it takes on the character of a private possession; and unless it can be private property, the personality is not likely to be put into it. Thus movables are said to be regularly private property while immovables, and especially land, are held in common. No such formula, however, can give more than a general summary or perspective of the cases, for these show the "delicate adjustment" of custom to life-needs and interests mentioned by the author just quoted.

The adaptation of the property-system to life-conditions can be illustrated indefinitely—it has been exemplified already in the cases presented. In the Anglo-American colonies, the tenure of land was at first imitated from the forms of English usage, which were manorial. It is instructive to notice how the attempts to set up manorial institutions all failed. Tenure moved inevitably toward the allodial type. The societal forces at work tended in that direction. Landlord, tenant, and laborer were all one. Land scarcely bore rent and was not the basis of social classification; it was purely an instrument for use in the struggle for existence. Its relation to the state was wholly utilitarian and realistic. There was no fiction in it. The owner could not see why he should pay taxes; he was a "sovereign" on his piece of land. He knew no difference between his title to his land, his horse, and his plow. No king or feudal lord ever held property in land in such a simple, direct, and absolute sense as that in which a colonist held it, or as a settler in a new country, under similar circumstances, holds it now.[37] It is a specific case of frontier-mores that is here encountered.[38]

Property is one of the most basic and enthralling interests of man. It is about such dominant interests that the mores form in blocks or accretions. These are then wrought upon by societal selection, generally in the form of the taboo, and chiselled into the shape suitable both to fit the life-conditions and also to form a consistent structure with all the other blocks of mores similarly surrounding other basic interests, such as that of sex. The blocks, when shaped into identifiable form are labelled as property, marriage, religion, and become institutions. The various forms taken by property or any other institution are found to fall into an evolutionary series. This does not mean that in any such case such a series was historically realized by any specific people. Human groups show endless variation; and the entire study of property demonstrates that the institution has been very unequally and

[37] Sumner, *Coll. Ess.*, III, 289 ff.   [38] Keller, *Soc. Evol.*, ch. IX.

inconsistently developed under the play of circumstance and interest. Such series, however, like those of animal-forms, have turned out to be highly illuminative for the understanding of earthly life.

In conformity, then, with the normal evolution of the folkways, there have come to exist certain selected societal customs surrounding the property-relation which are consistent with the rest of the mores of the society and sanctioned by the ghost-fear common to all societies. In conformity, again, with these social usages, mankind has held and handled property; and that was all the "right" they had.

§132. Property-Rights.

It is a "great mistake to think that the right of property is lightly held by uncivilized people among whom the amount of property is small."[39] It is as great a mistake as it would be now to think that a man who has saved a few dollars does not cling to them with as great tenacity as a millionaire to his millions.[40]

Amongst the Kaffirs the right to property is the most respected of all rights.[41] "No people carries to a higher pitch than the Kabyles the respect for property."[42] "All private property once secured is sacred, very sacred, in the African state-form."[43] The Veddahs have a strong sense of property.[44] Of the Arawak it is reported that the conception of private property is certainly quite sharp in his mind, "even though what he possesses is so simple, in most cases so easy to get, that he is always borrowing and lending without giving much care to returning or getting back."[45] And so on through a multitude of cases.

Such evidence could be enforced by a display of facts about punishments accorded to theft and views and customs surrounding the debt-relation.[46] Scrupulous honesty is reported of the Tungus, who "hold others' property almost more in respect than their own" and among whom "theft is as good as unknown; a thief is punished with blows by his fellow-tribesmen and is looked upon as dishonored and disgraced for his whole life."[47] The Veddah is inflexible in the matter of injury to his own property.[48] Among the Macusi Indians, property is holy and injury to it, except in war, is almost impossible. "Strifes over mine and thine are therefore in the highest degree rare." Little is heard of theft and robbery among the Brazilian Indians.[49] Sapper,[50] during twelve

[39] Ratzel, *Vkde.*, II, 35.
[40] Sumner, *Coll. Ess.*, II, 337.
[41] Letourneau, *Soc.*, 438.
[42] Hanoteau et Letourneux, *Kabylie*, II, 227.
[43] Kingsley, *W. Afr. Studies*, 429.
[44] Sarasin, *Weddas*, 489.
[45] Von Martius, *Beiträge*, I, 692.
[46] §§184, below, and 105, above.
[47] Hiekisch, *Tungusen*, 67.
[48] Sarasin, *Weddas*, 548, 488.
[49] Von Martius, *Beiträge*, I, 85-86.
[50] In *Globus*, LXXXVII, 131.

years of wandering life in Central America, never had anything stolen by the Indians.

All such cases speak clearly for the definiteness of conception of property-right. A good part of the regulative organization of society is employed in defining and guaranteeing property-rights. This applies with especial relevancy to private property in land; for its developed form calls for a well-knit state. When civil order is broken, property in land becomes insecure. "Disputes about landed property and unmovable goods in general are perhaps nowhere in the world more common than in the badly administered Empire of China."[51] If there is quarreling, anywhere, about land, that is not because there is in the notion of "holding" land anything absurd or which cannot be grasped;[52] it is because the definition, and therefore the guarantee of landed property depend on memory and require ceremonies, or public testimony before witnesses, or records, or monuments; and also either customs or enactments which are universally known, with administrative machinery to enforce them. Subdivision of interests in land and transfers of it add greatly to the need of a well-organized state, if property in land is to be made a fact. This is for the same reason that a firm societal organization is needed for property in slaves.[53]

The need of state-organization to support property in land rests upon the fact that transfers of land cannot be made like transfers of chattels, beasts, or even houses; land stays where it is and cannot be passed around. If it is occupied by father, son, and grandson in succession for centuries, there is little trouble; but when a holder wants to transfer, he must get a tangible expression of the abstract fact of ownership. The transfer does not change one sensible fact into another, like the delivery of a chattel from the hand of A into that of B. It changes one abstract relation into another. Hence the symbols employed to secure the semblance of concreteness: the transfer of a sod with a twig set in it, before witnesses or in a church. A record, a deed, the passing of a deed, show that the conveyance of land still requires methods that differ from those which suffice for the transfer of other property.

[51] De Groot, *Relig. Syst.*, I, 129.   [52] Gumplowicz, *Soc.*, 109.
[53] §100, above.

"To represent physically, symbolically, or fetishistically an act or a wish," writes Oliveira Martins,[54] "is a natural necessity of primitive man. In this circumstance is seen the psychological foundation of property, and its definition. To appropriate a thing is to refer it to ourselves, identify it with us, or introduce into it, as it were, our own soul, separating it from all that is alien to us. . . . Only thus, that is to say by way of symbols which represent fetishistically an abstraction, is it possible to change the appropriation [in the case of land] into a positive thing. Only by snatching from it a fragment, in order, in that piece, to *visualize*—only thus is it possible to invert the natural law which makes us slaves of the soil, and change us individually into masters of the land." All relations and transactions run to this form of envisagement. Nothing mental and metaphysical has sense otherwise.

The fact that it is difficult to hold on to crops in the soil causes a correlation between private property and agriculture; there must be secure public order or crops cannot be raised which require time for sowing and reaping and which the owner cannot always be on hand to protect. "The right of property," says Letourneau,[55] "is of such capital importance that every profound modification in the social structure necessarily reacts upon it and often is but the inevitable consequence of some novel manner of regarded ownership." Without order and control, property is sure to suffer disintegration. Tampering with property is one of the surest ways of promoting social disintegration. Lincoln,[56] addressing a deputation of working men, and having asserted that "the strongest bond of human sympathy outside the family relation, should be one uniting all working people, of all nations, and tongues, and kindreds," went on to remark: "Nor should this lead to a war upon property, or the owners of property. Property is the fruit of labor; property is desirable; is a positive good in the world. That some should be rich shows that others may become rich, and hence is just encouragement to industry and enterprise. Let not him who is homeless pull down the house of another, but let him work diligently and build one for himself, thus by example assuming that his own shall be safe from violence when built."

§133. Property and Law. The concept of property and the right of property, as well as the determination of what things may be property, arise in the mores. The protection of the relationship between a man and a thing, when experience had shown

---

[54] *Quadro,* 115, 116.   [55] *Prop.,* 22.
[56] Quoted in Stephenson, *Lincoln,* 340.

that it might be broken, was by taboo within the group. Hence it is clear that the juristic idea that property is created by law refers to the right of property, not to the conception of property. To say that property is a product of law is to ignore its origin, as well as that of law, in the mores. It is a mistaken inference from the contention that the state is needed to support property in land. Law is a customary rule of societal relations whose origin may be lost in antiquity, like the origin of the race itself; but it could have come from no other origin than the mores.[57] The idea that law makes property derives from the conception of the latter as a modern institution and, as such, belonging to the societal order and enforced by society through law. Legal considerations define the sphere of marriage[58] and the relations between parents and children, just as they do property-relations; yet no one will say that law makes marriage or parenthood.

In point of fact, property had a sanction which was long antecedent to law; before formal secular law existed religion guaranteed property.[59] Lippert[60] suggests that the right of property accrued first to the ghosts. Things needed by the dead man were left to him and became sacred and holy; they were his more exclusively than in life, for no one dared use them. The right of property is an incorporeal good. It is the definition given by society to the tenure, involving the distribution and transfer, of useful things. Though civilization regulates the exclusiveness of property and covers it with a veil of manners and morals, it is always a fact which may rise at any time into importance so great as to rend the veil and reveal the crude, stark truth again. The definition is in the mores, then in law; and society brings its force to bear to realize the definition. The right of property therefore varies from time to time and from one society to another.

These truths dispose of all highly theoretic views of property. There is no indication that primitive men theorized at all over the essence of property or began with a selected "concept" of it. People had things and resisted having them taken away; and society had to take cognizance, in the mores, of the situation. The institu-

---

[57] §§180, 181, below; Keller, "Law in Evolution," in *Yale Law Jour.*, XXVIII, 769 ff.

[58] Starcke, *Prim. Fam.*, 241. [59] De Greef, *Soc.*, II, 199-200.

[60] *Kgchte.*, II, 237.

tion of property, with right and law, grew out of the taboo against theft. Societal evolution, like organic, must have some concrete utility to work on; and there was no occasion for the definition of rights, or the making of formal laws, or the provision of a standing sanction by the force of society, until something was stolen, that is, alienated in a manner repugnant to the sense of the local code of behavior. When, however, rights are legally defined, other and cruder devices for securing interests can be relaxed. A man fortifies his house until "law," that is, the society, guarantees his rights to it and in it; he carries a sword until the state can defend his person; he shuts up wife and daughter until public law and order and definition of rights secure them to him. Property in rights is still more dependent on law. It would be quite rational to conclude that law made property, just as it would be to conclude that religion made marriage, if the simple evolutionary stages have not been studied and accorded their due weight.

All existing property is based ultimately upon the militaristic régime of conquest and contest and must return in the last analysis to the guarantee of force. This statement hardly needs demonstration. But property, once settled in the mores, has societal rather than physical force behind it; it is sanctioned by public opinion and conviction; inside the "in-group" it comes first to rest upon priority and prescription rather than immediately upon force. Prescription is the association between a person and a thing continued through a period of time; and when the time-element is lacking, priority of appropriation is recognized as deciding conflicting claims. Title to property from "making" a thing has never been recognized, although it has won great popular currency. "The Kaffir custom regarding the tenure of land forms no exception to Savigny's definition as quoted by Sir Henry Maine . . . that 'property is founded on adverse possession, ripened by prescription.' "[61]

This was always, at first, within the "in-group" or the peace-bond;[62] members of the "out-group" had no rights other than that of force, here any more than elsewhere. International law is still no more than a series of precedents. It was inside the group that

[61] Frere, in JAI, XII, 265.   [62] §§146, 151, below.

the mores were bound to oppose aggression and violence, for internal cohesion and peace were conditions of group-existence. Hence lapse of time in possession came to mean much the same thing as individual power to hold and defend. We still keep what we have because no adverse claim has as yet been established. This is the condition of priority which lawyers seek to establish by scrutinizing long series of property-transfers to get a clear title. The innocent receiver of stolen goods runs the risk of having an adverse prior claim established at short notice; on the other hand, lapse of time confirms actual possession, however attained, as in the outlawry of debts or through the declaration of the legal death of a too long absent claimant. Claims can be "jumped" only under conditions of lawlessness and disorder.

§134. Inheritance. The general idea behind inheritance is that what belongs to one goes at his death to those who belong to him. Thus communal property is, strictly speaking, not inherited at all; it remains the possession of the undying society, just as a national park is the enduring property of a nation. Since immovables are the characteristic form of common property, they are wont to remain undivided—this applying in particular to land —where movables are passed on to separate heirs. Real inheritance of property is alignable with succession to social position or office, and both are governed very largely by the prevailing system of descent.[63] Property follows the blood. If community of blood is reckoned through the mother, property is transmitted along the female line, and the heirs of a man are then his sister's children; if through the father, it is the man's own children who inherit from him; if through both mother and father, a mixed form results. Heirs are mostly male, for males regularly inherit while in many cases females may not; in fact, it is not infrequently found that women may not even own.[64] Naturally it is the older and stronger of the inheriting generation who are fitter to preserve the possessions, either as trustees for the group or as full owners; hence it is likely to be the eldest son or nephew, though this is not always the case, who becomes the heir-in-chief.

[63] §§156, 412 ff., below.
[64] Chs. L, LI, below; Morgan, *Anc. Soc.*, pt. IV.

These matters are but mentioned here in order to envisage them from the angle of the present chapter; they will come up in their detail when the subject of family-organization is reviewed. When one looks at them in perspective, he gets the impression that systems of descent might well have been developed solely to take care of property-interests. That is in truth one of their chief reasons for existence and perhaps the dominating one; the very deviations from exact lines of descent make for such an impression. Thus the nearest of kin may be passed over as an heir if he is a defective, for the property-interest is so enthralling that men can stick to no system the strict application of which would imperil that interest. The same is true as respects succession; the more distantly related efficient person, or the younger son, becomes chief if the heir-apparent has not gained the confidence of those whose interests are to be entrusted to him. The following cases are designed only to indicate the lines taken by inheritance, pending fuller discussion in another place.

In communal states, says Letourneau,[65] supporting his assertion with a number of cases, "when a man died, the community merely took back the share that had been his and assigned it to another." In East Africa, "owing to the fact that land is invariably public or family property, the question of inheritance of land hardly comes into question. On the other hand, inheritance of position such as a chiefship is not always regulated by the rules for inheritance of property."[66] In the East Indies the communal heritage which is left undivided consists of immovables, such as houses, lands, fishing-weirs, and also movables of great value, such as certain clothing, ornaments, and musical instruments. As a survival is found the custom of leaving a small plot of land in undivided inheritance, as a bond; to this all have equal claim. Under the mother-family, though the women are helped to some extent by the men, they must yet maintain themselves and the children; and to that end the common heritage serves; under the father-family woman herself may be property and so all that is hers is her husband's.[67]

In Southeast Papua, "when a man dies his land is inherited by his sisters' children, his brothers, and his sisters. His own children do not inherit, for they belong to their mother. The deceased's mother may plant on the land; also his father until he returns to his own village as a widower. When a woman dies her land goes to her children, her sisters, her brothers, her mother's brothers. The first-born has no larger share than the others. The share of a child is taken care of by an elder until he is fit to use it himself."[68] In Melanesia, among the Southern Massim, "the greater part, if not the whole, of a man's garden land passes to his sisters' children who, if all be married,

65 *Prop.*, 326-330.   66 Dundas, C., in JAI, LI, 270.
67 Wilken, in VG, I, 49; Wilken, *Vkde.*, 328-329.
68 Bromilow, in AAAS, 1909, 474.

divide it equally between them. . . . It was said that a portion of a dead man's land might sometimes pass to his maternal uncle or to his own mother, but it appeared that this only occurred when his sisters' children were young, and that his land would in due course revert to them. . . . There does not seem to be any very rigid precedence between a brother, sister, or sister's child. . . . A woman's garden property including her coconut trees is equally divided between her children. . . . If none of the dead woman's children are grown up, their maternal uncles and aunts would look after the garden property and feed the children, using the surplus food themselves."[69]

This author describes similar systems in other localities. In the island of Tubetube, "as regards inheritance two categories of personal property must be recognized. A man's drums, lime pots, lime spatulae and canoe or canoes would, it appeared, always pass to his sisters' children, . . . even if these were girls." In the event of a man having no such relatives, "his maternal uncle would take his canoe and other property, such as drums and fishing nets, and only after the death of the maternal uncle would the property revert to the dead man's own brothers and sisters. The second class includes such valuable property as arm-shells . . . which would in part go to a man's own children, and it seems that some of a dead man's pigs might sometimes pass to his children who would, however, not dare to eat these themselves. It seems that as much as half of a man's shell jewellery might pass to his own children, the remainder going to his sisters' children, but that presents of valuable jewellery made by a man to his own children at any time during his life would be remembered, and the items so given figure against the children after their father's death. There is also some reason to believe that a man might, when ill, express a desire that particular articles of jewellery should descend to his children, and his wishes would be respected." In Bartle Bay, "when a man dies a good deal of his personal property is used to pay for offices connected with his burial. . . . His coconut palms and fruit trees go to his sisters' children, but to a limited extent a man can intimate his desires as to the disposal of his property after death, and his wishes will be respected. . . . When a woman dies, her brother is more responsible for the children than their father. When the Mission took an infant . . . whose mother had died, it was the child's maternal uncle who came to us to make arrangements. . . . In olden days, the house in which a man died was usually shut up and left to rot, but if it were a new and a good house it might be used by the dead man's sisters' children, the difficulty being got over by closing up the old doorway and cutting a new one. If the house were shut up and left to rot, the site would be unoccupied for some time, but ultimately the dead man's sisters' children would build there."

In the D'Entrecasteaux Islands, "property, whether personal or real, except of course the land, descends in the first instance to the eldest son. He retains possession of it for a time, then hands on the more valuable—the inalienable—portion to his younger brother, and he in turn to the third son; finally it reverts to the son of the eldest brother and the process is repeated. But the rule is not invariable; a man may be passed over for some reason or other, if for example he suffers from epileptic fits; or a younger son may receive them before an elder brother if he should marry first or the elder brother be away. . . . It is the duty of the kinsmen to help and protect one another, so

[69] Seligmann, *Melanesians*, 521-525.

such a service is not rewarded by any payment. The daughters inherit nothing from their fathers, but it is usual for the brothers to give their sisters two or three coco-nut trees. They inherit, however, their mother's ornaments and fruit-trees, which are handed down from one to the other in the same way as the men's property, more irregularly, however, because what they inherit is usually of little value. . . . There is one other kind of property, a thing at least that can be bought and sold. The man who knows a ceremony and incantation for raising the wind, or for making yams grow big and thick, or the wild pig entangle itself in the net, occupies a very important place in the life of the district. . . . Let success attend a man's first efforts and his reputation is made; the district retains his services, and though no fixed stipend attaches to the post, a payment is usually made every time he is called upon, whether in a public or a private cause. From generation to generation the ceremony and song are handed down, the eldest son as a rule succeeding to his father's practice."[70]

Concerning this emerging primogeniture Rivers[71] writes: "The custom of junior right, in which the youngest son is the chief heir, of which our own custom of Borough English is an example, exists in many rude societies. In some cases it has a feature which suggests the origin of the practice. It is sometimes the rule that the youngest son inherits the house, while other kinds of property pass to his eldest brothers, or are shared by all. This practice seems to be the result of the custom by which the sons, as they marry, set up establishments of their own, so that, when the father dies, only the youngest son is still living at home." In East Africa often "an elder brother is designated as the heir when the sons are minors, but it must be explained that in the vernacular the word for heir is often used in the sense that such and such a one is the executor or trustee, and always it will be found that he has only trusteeship of the property during the minority of the children, it being considered that the mothers, as women, cannot have control of property, and in particular not of stock, which after all is the sum total almost of a native's property. . . . Among a polygamous people there arises not merely the question of inheritance between elder and younger brothers, but also between the elder and younger sons of several wives. Here the distribution of the portion due to the sons of each wife is generally determined during the lifetime of the father, for a man distributes his stock among his wives, and the sons of each wife inherit their mother's portion, or if, as is the practice in Ukamba, the sons marry any of the wives, they will take the portion allotted to the wives they marry. . . . The eldest son has a larger share than his full brothers. Thus the right of primogeniture is not to the eldest son of the father, but to the eldest son of the senior wife. It happens also that a father may put a curse on such and such cattle if taken by any but a particular son, and so compel the others by fear of taking them over." Ordinarily in East Africa "a man's property is inherited by his son, father, brother, or uncle, in this order. There is no division between these relations, one of them taking the whole of the property. Natives will often say that the eldest son inherits everything, but this is not so in actual fact. He will claim outstanding debts, and so long as the brothers live together he will be called the owner, in the sense that he is the representative of the family. The property is, however, divided among

[70] Jenness and Ballentyne, *D'Entrecasteaux,* 72-74.
[71] *Soc. Org.,* 116.

all the brothers, and legitimate or illegitimate children have the same rights as to inheritance. . . . The father's power to make a will may be said to be confined to bequeathing his property to his immediate heirs only, so that it is in practice only the distribution which he decides. Nevertheless, he may, for instance, entirely disinherit a disobedient son. . . . If the direct heir or heirs are minors, the property is taken charge of by the next heir. Because of this it is often said that the brother is the heir."[72]

Among the Ba-Yaka, property, "including wives and slaves, cannot be bequeathed by will, but is inherited, in the first instance, by the eldest brother, in default, by the eldest son of the eldest sister. If the deceased leaves no heir, his wives and goods pass into the possession of one of his slaves, who thus becomes a free man. Women cannot inherit." Again, among the Ba-Mbala, "a man's property is inherited by the eldest son of his eldest sister, or in default by his eldest brother; widows cannot inherit. No one can dispose of his property after his death by will, but he can, of course, give it away in his lifetime. Guardianship is known; the maternal uncle . . . acts in this capacity."[73] "The general rules on the death of a Suk are:—1. Exclusion of ascendants for descendants. 2. Exclusion of descendants in favour of collaterals, balanced by inclusion of descendants as far as property acquired by a deceased father other than by inheritance is concerned. 3. Exclusion of females. 4. Preference to primogeniture, balanced by a preference to male ultimogeniture on death of mother. 5. Specific deathbed bequests. Creditors of deceased recover from inheritors."[74]

Among the Singhpos of India, "the eldest inherits all the landed property and the titles; the youngest son gets the personal effects; the intermediary brothers being excluded from the succession." This is a combination of primo- and ultimogeniture.[75] Primogeniture is very common in the East Indies. "If the father dies intestate, and without declaring his intentions, the male children inherit, share and share alike, except that the house and pusaka (heirlooms, or effects on which, from various causes, superstitious value is placed) devolve invariably to the eldest. . . . When a man dies, his effects, in common course, descend to his male children in equal shares; but if one among them is remarkable for his abilities above the rest, though not the eldest, he usually obtains the largest proportion, and becomes the head of the . . . house; the others voluntarily yielding him the superiority."[76]

Once in a great while daughters inherit in preference to sons; among the Zuñi, "land, along with most other kinds of property, is owned by individuals and passes to the daughters in preference to the sons."[77] Our final case illustrates the two facts, first, that it is the son of the wife of status who inherits, and, second, that personal fitness is not left out of account; the people in question are ancient Scandinavians. "That child whose mother is bought with a mund is heritable if he come living into the light, and meat once in his mouth. . . . The man is not heritable that knoweth not whether the deep saddle shall

[72] Dundas, C., in JAI, LI, 267, 268, and notes; and in JAI, XLV, 294-295.
[73] Torday and Joyce, in JAI, XXXVI, 44; and in JAI, XXXV, 411.
[74] Barton, in JAI, LI, 99.
[75] Dalton, *Eth. Bengal,* 13; Letourneau, *Prop.,* 325.
[76] Wilken, in VG, II, 281; Marsden, *Sumatra,* 220, 244.
[77] Swanton, in HAI, II, 610.

be turned backward or forward on the horse or how it shall be turned, but if he have more understanding than that he shall have his share of the heritage."[78]

The foregoing examples incidentally cast some light upon the subject of bequest. In general among primitive peoples there is no room for personal choice; all matters are arranged, once and for all, by usage, and whimsical departure from traditional ways is not viewed with sympathy or toleration. There is a system by which people live; it has proved itself because they are alive and perhaps prosperous; who is the individual to presume to blast at such a rock of ages? Still, there are certain ways of circumventing some customs by recourse to others, as where the father has his way by cursing property which is not allocated as he wishes. Cursing is even said to be "the germ of will and the beginning of entail."[79] "One fundamental difference between the treatment of inheritance by tribal custom and by modern law consists in the fact that primitive organization leaves no room for the disposal of property by testament: volition is naturally supposed not to reach beyond the physical existence of the individual."[80] In general, if a man wants to dispose of his property in disaccord with the mores, he must do so before he dies. There is no such thing as a last will and testament, but there are the small beginnings of such; naturally they are in evidence only where private property is the prevailing system, which is yet another reason for viewing that system as an advance in adjustment over what went before.

The original homogeneity of society was broken up by narrowing the range of the right to inheritance and succession. Thus was produced a beneficent inequality. The administration of property turned into free disposition over it and then to private holding.[81]

When it is said that bequest and inheritance are the creation of law, the state, or civilization, those who say this assume some anterior state of communism or collectivism against which these creations were devised. In fact, antecedent to bequest and inheritance there existed one thing only, and a crude one: the absolute right of the individual to his property, not only in this world and

[78] Vigfusson and Powell, *Orig. Isl.*, I, 332.

[79] §277, of text and *Case-Book;* Hobley, in JAI, XLI, 406, 416-417, 419, 427-429.

[80] Vinogradoff, *Hist. Jurispr.*, I, 288; §234, below.

[81] Lippert, *Kgchte.*, II, 529.

time but in the next world and forever. He took it with him.
There is no comfort for the sentimental in this foray into primitive blessedness. Bequest and inheritance have been preserved in
the mores and law because of the societal advantage involved, such
advantage meaning the more efficient use of all available instrumentalities. It was one of the reasons for the slowness of gains
in uncivilization that capital was wasted when destroyed at the
grave of its owner. The only advantage of such waste lay in the
ensuing coercion upon survivors to win for themselves. This was
at an early stage. Where bequest and inheritance are customary,
production and thrift are stimulated and love of children is enlisted to further the welfare of society; to suppress them is yet
another stroke at individual initiative. The motive supporting
them is neither the greed of some individuals nor the servility of
others; it is the perception that when the talent and power of
each one are enlisted to the utmost, primarily for himself and his,
then each other one gains more as a participant in the societal
welfare than he could in any other way.

The individual never gets an amount of satisfaction exactly
equal to that of all others; what he has to consider is only whether
he gets more than he could in any other way that is practicable
and also consistent with permanent peace, order, and security.
This reflection ought to give him his motive for willingly defending
the property of those who have many times what he has. It should
make him wary of radical attempts at sharing-systems that involve the abolition of bequest and inheritance. The latter have
been, like private property, of immense advantage to the race and
should not lightly be moved aside on untenable assumptions as to
their nature and origin.

Says Von Hartmann:[82] "For those individuals who are already, from whatever causes, in possession of property, the suppression of the right of inheritance would be equivalent to a premium on the squandering and dissipation of
this property during their life-times. This would have unfortunate effects on
the character of these artificially created squanderers and of those who came
into personal touch with them—just as unfortunate as on the preservation of
material culture in general; for the latter must needs go down to destruction
if not only all the income, without remainder, but also the capital, over and
above, should, by being spent on temporary means of enjoyment, be withdrawn
from productive investment. The suppression of the right of inheritance ap-

[82] *Phänom.*, 683-684.

pears, therefore, as the most senseless and the most offensive to civilization of all the demands of the social democracy."

The abolition of bequest and inheritance would put a premium upon unproductive consumption. This would be antagonistic to the formation of capital, and would threaten societal welfare at its very basis.

§135. The Property Institution. The struggle for property is the struggle for liberty.[83] He who feels the constraint of his situation and desires to win command of it, which is liberty, finds that he can succeed only through property. The effort to get property stimulates the social virtues. Each soul has its outfit of inherited energy and capabilities, and its life-conditions. To carry out the process of self-realization or career-fulfilment, it must keep up its activities upon the environment and must draw therefrom corporeal and incorporeal goods necessary to the maintenance and growth of its physical and other powers. These relations to the environment are its interests. The contributory relations by which other souls and the society are bound, by the mores and institutions and through the organization of society, to minister to the self-realization of the soul in question, are its rights. Its counter-relations in the societal system, through which it is bound to minister to the self-realization of others and of the whole, are its duties. The corporeal and incorporeal goods which are drawn to it for its self-realization, under the mores and institutions of the place and time, sanctioned and secured by the power of the society, are its property.

The form of the institution is a taboo, a prohibition and a warding-off of all others from the things attributed to the one, by virtue of which those things are consecrated, devoted, hallowed to him. Since, in primitive society, religious sanction is always included in the taboo, the latter carries with it not only the force of the united living members of the society but also the terror of the ancestral spirits who will be enraged if the customs which they have esteemed and handed down are broken. The taboo is a negative; there has been no positive definition of property until modern times. The "sacredness" of an institution of such development is

[83] Oliveira Martins, *Quadro,* 121; Sumner, *Coll. Ess.,* II, 171 ff.

neither the superstitious notion of savages only, nor an inflated suggestion of civilized selfishness. Property is "sacred"—not to be lightly touched—because it is the actual and indispensable basis of the existence of men in society. The monopoly in property, the exclusion which is of its essence, is an expression of the fact that men are pressed against one another in the competition; and this has aroused antagonisms of interest. Then antagonisms have been composed, coöperation has ensued, and there have arisen all the mutual relations which constitute the societal system.

One of the first practical necessities inside a group was the prevention of quarrels over the possession of useful things, because internal strife meant weakness in the face of hostile neighbors. War-leaders imposed peace, and the sanctions of ghost-fear were brought to bear to secure it, the motive being military expediency. To do that, they had to decide and award, and the customs grew by precedent and usage into rights. The taboo was defined and developed into law. Hence law, government, rights, morals, peace, and order grew up around property as an internal interest, and war, superstition, and vanity reacted upon it to strengthen it. Men live in order to live, and property is the support of existence. A vast array of societal usages and institutions get their sense and significance directly from it, others from their alliance with it. To assail it is to assail existence.

If life is regarded as a pilgrimage whose value and significance are all due to its goal in the other world, then there are more important things than property here. Otherwise all human interests depend on property as their end-result, in order to use it again for another step. Poets, philosophers, sages, artists, literary men, scholars, and scientists have cultivated a proud pretence of superiority to property, as to a sordid thing, and of devotion to a "higher good." Certainly the sense of the products which they cultivate is that they all turn back again into the arena of life to enable men to get more satisfaction and growth out of earthly existence. It is possible for a man of any of these classes to make his pursuit an end in itself and to work solely for the joy of working and knowing; but if he does this, he puts himself on the level of the athlete, sportsman, miser, or voluptuary. Even then he cannot live or move, and cannot accomplish any of his purposes, without property. If he lives by his activity, and if he pursues it for the welfare of men, he will find that it all passes through the materialization of property at every recurrence of the action and reaction by which its achievements are won. It is true that the demands of the market are no criterion of what is worth producing on the intellectual domain; there is, in fact, no criterion which is good in advance. It is society which selects what it will have, demands it, and pays for it.

Though the society may be working up or down, the individual who goes against it, whether he be prophet or apostle, takes his risks. All intellectual goods have their sense in their bearing on the knowledge by which the struggle for existence is helped; but the people, not knowing what this knowledge is, cannot demand it in advance.

The pressure of distress and the emancipation which comes from conquering the conditions of distress—these are the two major alternating forms throughout the life of society. They hinge on property; upon the lack of it and the power to win it. A sufficient supply of corporeal and incorporeal goods, or wealth, is the essential prerequisite to all achievements of mankind. Wealth, however, cannot function, indeed cannot be formed, as a massive conglomerate; society has recognized the fact that the highest efficiency of goods is attained when they are the property of individuals and groups, distributed into definite relations to these holders to serve their interests. Only in later centuries have men reflected upon the property-institution and have adopted enactments which embody theories about it. Unless such theories are sound, because founded upon knowledge and correct analysis of the facts and acquaintance with the laws of society's life, it is evident that arbitrary enactments based upon them must produce both confusion and also the loss of all the slow, unconscious, unpremeditated, but substantial, gains of the age-long process.

Property is sacred as marriage is sacred, as government or religion are sacred. It is the great stabilizer and equilibrator of them all. This same sacredness, if one cares to call it that, is attached to private property. It is not to be handled lightly and airily by irresponsibles any more than is that parallel monopoly, the monogamic family. It has the dignity conferred by ages of inestimable service to men.

PART III

SELF-MAINTENANCE: REGULATIVE ORGANIZATION

CHAPTER XIV

ANTAGONISMS

§136. Regulation as Maintenance. Societal self-maintenance has been presented, thus far, as a process of adjustment to the natural environment. We have observed the manner in which men have organized the appropriation and tenure of natural supplies and energies. The transformation of materials and the utilization of forces derived from the inanimate and organic world have been seen to constitute a series of adjustments by society to its life-conditions. Even in the case of slavery, as that topic has been presented, the enslaved have been handled as an organic force, pretty much as animals were handled. But there is another angle from which all these matters should be viewed. There are to be considered the interrelations between the men as well as those between the men and the things—social connections as contrasted to, and also as correlative with, economic connections. There is, for instance, another aspect to slavery which might be called the political, as distinguished from the economic or industrial; for the human animals are after all men, and the relation between masters and slaves is social as no relation between men and beasts can be. Though slavery lies partly, and most primitively, within the industrial organization, it falls partly also within the regulative organization.

Men's relations are thus not confined to those existing between themselves and the natural environment, but include also contacts with the human or social environment; human beings have to get along with their like as well as with nature. This amounts to a necessity of mutual adjustment; that cannot take place, however, without regulation of men by men and the development of an organization for that regulation. Such a development is indispensable for any society that is to persist, for it is only by limitation of freedom and imposition of obligations that men can get on together. Any society, in order to continue to exist, must present a united front; and that can be done only under condition that law and order prevail within the society. Discipline is a vital necessity for stability.

From these preliminary considerations it follows that regulation is as indispensable for societal self-maintenance as is industry itself. There must be effective government of some sort, for anarchy means chaos and helplessness in the competition with other societies. The elements of control lie in the mores; all government roots in them and continues to exist only as it conforms to the public opinion that sanctions them. Yet the mores are not enough by themselves; there is need here of organization and institutional development, as there is in industry, property, religion, and marriage. This section of the science of society traces the evolution, out of the mores, of the regulative institution of society, that is, of government.

The prime function of regulation is to secure peace and order within a society; it insists ever upon internal peace, for the regulated society is always a peace-group.[1] Regulation discharges its function by reducing antagonisms between members, through reconciliation or demarkation of their spheres of interests and rights, and thus effecting antagonistic coöperation.[2] The successive enlargement of the peace-group, from the family to the nation or empire, has been the outstanding feature of political development.

A natural start for a review of this development is with the antagonisms, together with the crudest and least evolved methods of neutralizing them so as to arrive at peace and coöperation. Were it not for the existence of antagonisms there would be no need of a regulative organization. It is by ignoring them or imagining them absent that various utopian structures have been reared, and that men have been hoodwinked into believing that regulation is not a natural necessity but an arbitrary imposition by interested parties. Here again the romancers yearn back to the golden age of the free, highminded, unspoiled, uncontrolled, and noble savage, as evidence of what might be were it not for the fetters that men have had laid upon themselves. It needs but a slight acquaintance with the facts of primitive life to dispel such phantasms.

1 §§146, 151, below.   2 §§16, above and 462, below.

Antagonism is present as a condition of the struggle for existence and the competition of life; and its first manifestation is in the form of violence toward competitors. Where regulation is feeble, or where men are unrestrained by a traditional code, antagonisms issue readily into bloodshed; and although violence is exceptional within a regulated society, yet if the antagonisms are hot enough or irreconcilable, the sword is always the final arbiter. Any dispute can be settled summarily and once for all by the death of one of the disputants. Violence is effective as nothing else is. Only it is exceedingly costly and has been superseded in adjusting societies by measures which, even if less competent to secure speedy and final settlement, are less wasteful of human life and property and less perilous to society's existence.

When mankind first appears within the range of scientific observation, what is seen is a vast number of little peace-groups—families, clans, tribes—each of which is the scene of controlled or reconciled antagonisms between its constituent members. While within each there is peace, yet between these little societies there exist, as a rule, uncontrolled and unreconciled antagonisms; and the regular way of settling them, though not the only one, is the primal mode of violence. We are to take hold of the situation at this point, setting aside for the time the process by which the little peace-groups have been developed and fixing attention upon the antagonisms existing between them as they stand. This amounts to taking up the evolution of the peace-group in mid-course. So doing, one need not involve himself in the inferential, for attested cases lie before him. Having learned what they have to tell him, he can then infer more safely as to the formation of the earlier and simpler peace-groups. What he will notice all along is that, wherever violence appears in the evolutionary series, it is correlative with unregulation.

It hardly need be shown by citation that the peace-group which is highly organized possesses an advantage over its loosely integrated neighbors. We cite a pair of examples. "The Masai invasion had a very disintegrating effect on the older occupants of the area under consideration. A tribe with a coherent military organization suddenly appeared on the scene and raided tribe after tribe. In a few generations their prestige became so great that the very name of Masai almost caused a panic: not that the Masai were individually so much braver than the tribes they raided, but simply owing to the sudden nature of their attacks and the fact that they worked with a rude discipline under recognized leaders who had definite tactics. The fact too that the . . . warrior class was continually segregated in kraals, and always ready for war, proved a perpetual menace to their more peaceful neighbours. Thus it happens that we find many of the surrounding people have imitated the Masai war dress and even adopted Masai customs and rules of life." Thus do the mores of a conquering group spread along with the achievements of their bearers. A parallel instance is that of the League of the Iroquois.[3]

The case just cited has reference to offensive warfare; but a defensive organization has a survival value even greater than an almost purely offensive one, such as that of the Masai. "Two classes of warfare were recognized among the Omaha, defensive and aggressive. Each had its distinctive rites, its rank, and its duties in the tribal organization." In the Omaha word for "tribe" one can "get a hint of the growth and influence of defensive warfare. Self-protection naturally expanded toward the protection of one's family and to extend this protection to a group of families living near together was a logical progression and leading naturally to an appreciation of the necessity for permanency in the group to be protected. When therefore the thought expressed by the Omaha word for 'tribe' had taken hold of the people so strongly as to become the name of a community held together at the risk of life against outside aggressors, that community had ceased to be a congeries of people and had become a more or less stable association of persons among whom political ideas could take root." Thus it would appear that defensive warfare and an organization for group-protection led straight to a regulative system. Aggressive warfare had no such sequel. People vaguely realized this and referred it and its results to what stood in their minds for Providence. "The disintegrating tendencies of aggressive warfare, particularly the quarrels and schemes of ambitious men, were checked by the inculcation of the idea that war is allied to the cosmic forces and under their control."[4]

§137*. Group-Hostility. The members of the smallest and most primitive societies are found already prone to draw a sharp distinction between themselves and others, or between the persons constituting the "in-group" and those belonging to the "out-group." This is ethnocentrism, group-egoism, or "nos-ism."[5] The "we-group" and everything it does are right and good, while there is an abiding suspicion and contempt for the outsider or stranger. The distinction persists throughout the course of societal evolution and is the feature of social life seized upon as a key-note by Giddings,[6] in developing his "consciousness of kind." Another term for this approval of the familiar is "syngenism," meaning the sentiment resulting from being born and bred in proximity; and

[3] Hobley, *A-kamba*, 132; §188, below.
[4] Fletcher and LaFlesche, in BAE, XXVII, 402.
[5] Keller, *Soc. Evol.*, 57 ff.; §21, above.
[6] *Prin. Soc.*, 17-19.

it is acutely noted by the inventor[7] of this term that such a sentiment is acquired so early and imperceptibly that it appears to be
inborn and natural, or at least to belong to "second nature." If
second nature means the mores, the appearance is not deceptive;
but that there is a syngenetic "instinct" is not to be demonstrated.[8]

Hostility between groups is based upon a recognition of differences. These are sometimes physical, as in the case of race-an-
tagonism. More often they have to do with the mores; take the
representative instance of language, which has remained perhaps
the most distinctive of the mores. Language is so characteristic of
human groups that the very adjective descriptive of nationality
is employed as a noun meaning the national language. If we use
the term "English" alone, we refer to that most distinctively English thing, *the* English thing, namely, the English speech. We do
not mean by "französisch" the French religion, nor by "español"
the Spanish government. It is not necessary to say "la langue
française"; the adjective is enough, and the noun will be automatically understood or supplied in the adjective. If you want to recall a person you think of his most distinctive part—his face, not
his feet; similarly the stranger has always been identified chiefly
by his speech. If he cannot say "ich," or "thither," or "shib-
boleth," he is under suspicion of not being one of ours. To closer
observation there are revealed other and less immediately obvious
peculiarities in the mores of aliens—cannibalism, perhaps, or polygamy—which add to the sense of strangeness, uneasiness, and
suspicion; and the ground is sown for a crop of discord and hostility.

It is this sense of group-differences, with its sequel of suspicion
and enmity,[9] that engages attention at the outset of any survey
of antagonisms. Such a sentiment comes directly out of experiences incident to group-competition and is easily traceable to the
original man-land relation. It forms a sort of atmosphere within
which men live without being able to imagine anything different.
It is another of those zero-lines, like poverty, from which a start

[7] Gumplowicz, *Soc.*, 242 ff.; Lippert, *Kgchte.*, I, 479.
[8] §6, above.
[9] §9, above; Sumner, *Folkways*, §§13-16.

is made; and if the race has moved away from it, that has been the result of painful adjustment, not of natural endowment or divinely conferred blessedness. Ethnocentrism and group-hostility deserve renewed illustration in the present connection.

Nansen[10] quotes an Eskimo letter of 1756, written with European war-conditions in mind. The native cannot understand how it is that men of the same faith are hunting each other like seals and stealing from people they have never seen or known. Fighting about land seems to him sheer greed. He apostrophizes his own country. "How well it is that you are covered with ice and snow! How well it is that, if in your rocks there are gold and silver, for which the Christians are so greedy, it is covered with so much snow that they cannot get at it! Your unfruitfulness makes us happy and saves us from molestation." The writer was surprised that the Europeans had not learned better manners among the Eskimo and proposed to send medicine-men as missionaries to them.

"The Indian is extremely patriotic. He believes himself to be the result of a special creation by a partial deity, and holds that his is the one favored race. The names by which the different tribes distinguish themselves indicate their belief that as their race is the one favored race, so each tribe of the race is a little ahead of all the others. 'Men of men' is the literal meaning of one name; 'the only men' of another."[11] A Canadian Mohawk offers as the etymology of the term Iroquois, "I am the real man."[12] The Plains Indians have "the conscious feeling of the tribe as a unit or body"; the Mohave feel "that all members of the tribe are inherently and psychically different from all persons of other tribes." There is also "a sense of racial rather than of tribal separateness."[13] It is said of the Turks that "they have an inborn contempt for all that does not belong to their nation."[14] "Of the geography of our country these Chinamen [in Formosa] knew absolutely nothing. We were barbarians. We came from some poor village of our particular tribe outside civilization, civilization being solely within the dominion of the Celestial Emperor. All the rest of the world—if there were any poor remainder—was benighted, and but the home of 'barbarians,' not 'men.' "[15] This sense of superiority is exemplified by all "chosen people" and has been noticeable in the case of the modern Germans.[16] "We Germans," quoth Bismarck, "fear God and nobody else."

Correlative to such self-satisfaction is hostility to outsiders. In Australia, "strangers invariably look on each other as deadly enemies. Now-a-days, when accidentally brought together, they usually feign friendship; but, before the Whites interfered with native manners, no Black ever neglected to assassinate a stranger at the moment that he could do so without risk to himself. . . . The Australian Black, without exception, nurtures, one might almost say from the cradle to the grave, an intense hatred of every male at least of his race who is a stranger to him. The reason they themselves assign for what I

10 *Esk. Life*, 180.　　　　　11 Powell, in BAE, VII, 36.
12 Braut-Sero, in *Man,* 1901, 166-170. (Reported in AA, IV, 558.)
13 Kroeber, in AA, IV, 279.
14 Lepsius, *Briefe über Aegypten,* 72.
15 Pickering, *Formosa,* 136.　　　　16 Keller, *War to Peace,* ch. XI.

must term this diabolical feeling is, that all strangers are in league to take their lives by sorcery. The result of this belief is that, whenever they can, the Blacks in their wild state never neglect to massacre all male strangers who fall into their power. Females are ravished and often slain afterwards if they cannot be conveniently carried off." This belief of the Australians figures prominently among the causes of their wars.[17]

An aged Fijian is reported as saying: "Of old the islands of Maola and Mataku held no intercourse; if a man of one island went to the other, he was clubbed; but there were relationships between them. . . . If I wished to hold a ceremonial exchange . . . I saw my kinsmen of Maola and informed them first; if they approved, it was done." The author[18] reporting this goes on to say that it "is an example of the Fijian way of expressing as absolute a qualified statement. The sequel shows there was intercourse, only it was not a daily event, an enterprise without special reason. . . . Even at the present day a Fijian is not fond of travelling to places where he has no relatives." Another native, a woman, "thinks it is useful to know one's mother's pedigree, as visiting a place a man will thus know whose house to stay at, and thinks her son takes no interest in his mother's relatives because he is not given to travel." "I have heard Akamba say that they dislike all foreigners, but they hate each other. There are so many old scores left unpaid, so many know of cattle and women which were theirs being now in the hands of others; the man whose four sons were killed knows those who killed them or their relations, which is all one, and he will not easily forget his grievances. Villages which fifteen or twenty years ago were deadly enemies will not easily harmonize now, and hence it is that natives living quite close to each other remain perfect strangers, not necessarily because they have an old account to settle, but because from old habit the Mkamba has nothing to do with 'strangers.' I have known this to be the case with villages not half an hour apart. And being now unable to settle his old grievances, the Mkamba turns to litigation and perseveringly adheres to some old claim to foster his hostile inclinations. Thus despite Government and order the Akamba of Kitui continue to live as isolated as they can, caring nothing for the fate and fortune of most of their neighbours and utterly opposed to undertaking anything in common."[19] Among the Cheyennes, a stranger is an enemy; Grinnell[20] relates an incident in connection with the explanation to him, by an Indian, of the Crazy Dance ceremony: "White Frog, explaining these matters to me, made a prayer to all the spiritual powers, asking them to pardon him for revealing these things to an enemy, that is, a stranger—myself."

A modern instance of the tendency toward isolation by way of language may be added. Professor Manning[21] says there are two great factors in play as regards language. "The simple man, the common man, the man in the street, in whom there live local pride and local consciousness, the love of his home, his village and his country, presses for the development of his native tongue. He does not care for the outside world and is not troubled directly by the obstacles which he is thus putting in the way of international relations. On the other hand, all who are interested in bringing together the nations of the earth or

---

[17] Curr, *Aust. Race*, I, 64, 85-86.
[18] Hocart, in JAI, XLIII, 118.
[19] Dundas, C., in JAI, XLII, 485-486.
[20] *Cheyenne*, II, 288, note.
[21] In *Sewanee Rev.*, July-Sept., 1924.

who have anything to say to the people of the world other than in poetry or art,—the scientist, the man of affairs, the missionary, the teacher, all these are seeking a universal tongue, a tool which they can use practically and successfully everywhere in the world. Which side is to be the victor? If we may judge by the experience of three thousand years, the definite triumph of either side is still far in the future." The writer shows how people recognize at once, inevitably, any attempt to change their language; this they resent and, by clinging to it are led eventually to emphasize nationality by arms. "In a word, the linguistic problems presented by the modern world are far more complex and dangerous than might at first be thought. Everything which is included in culture in the broadest sense; nations past, present and to be; peace and war; friendship and hostility; are all included in the struggle which is being fought out as forms of speech seek to perpetuate themselves. Linguistic unrest, the developing of dialects and languages, has in itself a powerful political result which we are only half inclined to recognize." An elastic system of spelling eases this situation; but "if there were a phonetic system, how long would it be before different communities would take pride in employing their own pronunciations and spelling to the confusion of the English-speaking world and the serious embarrassment of the internal unity both of the British Empire and of America?"

Despoiling the alien is the gist of "the advice given by Moses to the Hebrews when coming out of the land of Egypt—namely, that they should borrow, with the fixed purpose of never giving them back again, the vessels of gold and silver and the precious raiment of the goodnatured Egyptians."[22] The salutation "Peace" was for a member of the religious peace-group; outsiders were to be despoiled.[23] An Arab robs enemies, friends, and neighbors, provided they are not in his tent.[24] Greek tradition tells of tribes that murdered strangers, and regards the practice, along with cannibalism, as belonging to typical savagery;[25] and Heracles is represented as going to Egypt and killing a king who massacred all strangers venturing into his country.[26] The Greek idea was that war did not merit the name unless it was between Greeks and strangers; later, with the spread of the Greek language to the East, the distinction between Greeks and barbarians faded.[27] In later times the Inquisition dealt with heretics as aliens, out of the fold.[28] Contempt for the member of the out-group and his mores runs down into petty persecution, as where the Connecticut parson, captured by the British in 1777, was forced to chew up the Continental money which he had on his person.[29] Historical writing of recent times exhibits the same group-hostility: laudation of the friend and belittling of the enemy.[30]

Thus ethnocentrism and group-hostility extend from a primitive type based upon crude criteria, and expressed in murder and robbery of the alien, to many and variegated modes characteristic

[22] Letourneau, *Prop.*, 209; Exod. XII, 3-36.

[23] Lippert, *Kgchte.*, II, 452.   [24] Burckhardt, *Bedouins*, 90.

[25] Keller, *Hom. Soc.*, 3-4.   [26] Diodorus, *Hist.*, bk. IV, ch. I.

[27] Burckhardt, *Griech. Kgchte.*, I, 327-328.

[28] Lippert, *Kgchte.*, II, 591.   [29] Moore, *Diary*, I, 414.

[30] Gumplowicz, *Rassenk.*, 250-252.

of civilized peoples, often based upon criteria equally crude, even
if expressed, in general, in less violent ways. All manifestations of
group-hostility lead to conflict of some sort; for the time being
interest is to be centered upon the crudest form of such collision,
namely, war. As we pursue our way through this topic, much light
will be thrown back upon the preliminary considerations of ethnocentrism and hostility to the out-group, and also forward upon
the nature and mode of origin of the peace-group in its several
and successive forms.

§138*. Incentives to War.[31] War lies in the competition of
life; and there is a heightened competition if the man-land ratio
is altered by the increase of the men.[32] This condition results in
what has been called economic "earth-hunger,"[33] and it is in evidence wherever population has come to press on land so that existing conditions appear insupportable and more supplies must be
had. Migration has often been the solution of such a situation;
portions of tribes have broken away from the main stock and have
occupied new land wrenched from its possessors by force. Migrations of greater or less volume, involving tribal jostlings and war,
do not require illustration; economic earth-hunger is a historic
phenomenon.

The disturbance of the population-land equilibrium has not
always led to the replacement of one people by another, much less
to actual conquests. Since it was less the land than the products of
land that satisfied the needs of a growing population, the plundering of others, without any migration or conquest, served to restore
the shaken equipoise. Hence an increasing population or what
amounts to the same thing, so far as the dislocation of the man-
land relation is concerned, a decrease in the food-supply, has not
seldom resulted in the development of a predatory organization.

Of a Himalaya tribe it is reported that "the smallest shrinkage in the food
supply brought on a famine, and then the only resource of the people was war
for the sake of plunder." Hence they were forced to become a robber tribe.[34]

31 Davie, *Evol. of War*, is a very full treatment, with copious illustration,
of this and subsequent topics.
32 §§2, 24, and ch. II, above.
33 Sumner, "Earth Hunger," in *Coll. Ess.*, II, 31 ff.
34 Conway, *Himalayas*, 251.

Scandinavia once became overpopulated upon the then existing stage of the arts and was forced to live on the rest of the world. Sea-rovers set out every spring, after a great sacrifice to insure victory. Unsuccessful years caused famine, revolt, and the sacrifice of the kings to the gods. The rovers often became immigrants, settling in outlying countries, and Scandinavia came to be known as the *officina gentium,* or laboratory of races.[35]

What happened in such cases is that the military rather than the industrial arts rose to support numbers and so became arts of maintenance. Thus war was a mode of getting a living parallel with industry. War for plunder is a method of appropriating what others' industry has produced. Gumplowicz[36] speaks of "the effort of each social community to make serviceable to itself every other social community that emerges within its horizon . . . which effort has its final origin in the self-maintenance of the first community." This is war for plunder, whether the booty is material objects or human beings. The property-incentive to war needs reiterated emphasis for, although obvious, it is often dissembled. War has repeatedly broken out over the possession of local supplies of necessary goods in nature, such as salt, flint, metals, or timber. If the holders can be dispossessed, all their advantages accrue to the dispossessor who succeeds to their monopoly. Then other groups fall under the temptation to assail that monopoly. Again, though less frequently, there is war for captives who may be used directly as food or set to work. Men want more product but hate more work; so they appropriate the energies of other human beings.[37]

To this offensive type of war for self-maintenance there is the corresponding defensive type. Self-defense is as essential a part of self-maintenance as eating, a parallel that may stand forth quite stark when it is realized that the booty sought is sometimes human flesh and the possession defended is one's own cells and tissues. Possessors have to defend what they have, whether it is property or their own lives. It is to be noted that the offensive and defensive types of war run one into the other; in the last great war all the combatants, the real aggressor vociferous among them, sought to clear themselves of the charge of aggression. "The best defensive is an offensive" is a saying significant of much.

[35] Geijer, *Svensk. Hist.,* I, 12.   [36] *Soc.,* 100.
[37] Ch. X, above.

The following cases are designed to illustrate war as a sort of industry through which the products of the labor of others, their property, and even their persons are appropriated by force. This is war for plunder in the broadest sense.[38]

War of this sort is but little represented in Australia, or in any other country where there is next to nothing to plunder. Abduction of women is, along with resentment of magical "bone-pointing,"[39] about the only cause of fighting. There is no object in accumulating spears, or tent-coverings, or dingo dogs, or anything else that might be taken from a defeated enemy. They would be only a burden to a wandering people without beasts of burden; and there is no special or luxurious property to exert temptation. The Australians and other very backward tribes are almost immune from war for booty. But in Melanesia war becomes a speculation in the accumulation of shell-money. Would-be plutocrats hire men to burn and plunder villages and bring in such money. Peace is granted for money, and the fighters get a share in the booty.[40] On Chatham Island there were not many fights except over the possession of the flesh of whales and other sea-animals; and they had a law that the first drop of blood ended the strife.[41] Of the Hottentots it is reported that "the causes for wars are here, as in the case of most other tribes that lack wider political viewpoints, almost solely infringements of the material interest of a tribe by its neighbors; that is, trespasses upon property in respect to cattle, pasturage or, even though only infrequently, women."[42] In South Africa the wars in the center of the country, where no slave-trade existed, have seldom been about anything else than cattle. So well known is this, that several tribes refuse to keep livestock so as not to tempt their enemies to come and steal. Nevertheless they have no objection to eating cattle when offered, and their country admits of being well stocked. Livingstone,[43] who reports these facts, had heard of but one war arising from another cause, where three brothers fought for the possession of a woman, and their tribe had remained divided ever since. In southwest Africa, "the regions about the watering places are naturally in extraordinary demand for purposes of settlement by the natives, especially in the more arid spaces, and have formed the cause for many a feud."[44] The Bantus in this region do not like to fight, and tribes leave between them, where possible, wide uninhabited stretches. If they come together because of restriction of land by drought or other cause, they fight and rob until the number of cattle is smaller and the former condition is restored.[45] This is a pretty example of the working of the man-land ratio. The militant Zulus, who allowed no marriage for warriors and practised infanticide, kept up their population by constantly raiding other tribes.[46] Here is a truly basic case of war for self-perpetuation.

These cases illustrate war for plunder. The other salient motive for fighting is the attainment of glory, which ranges war under

[38] Letourneau, *Guerre*, 29 ff.
[39] §§299, 300, below.
[40] Von Pfeil, *Südsee*, 126.
[41] Weiss, *Chatham Isl.*, 18-19.
[42] Fritsch, *Eingeb. S.-Afr.*, 323-324.
[43] *Mission. Travels*, I, 232, 233.
[44] Schmidt, *Deut. Kol.*, II, 206-207.
[45] Büttner, *Walfischbai*, 25.
[46] Ratzel, *Vkde.*, I, 264.

self-gratification.[47] Vanity is a powerful incitement to effort, and
it battens on prestige. "The individual's own desires and claims
on life, the ideals with which he is inspired, and the powers he
possesses to carry them out, determine his place in the social
scale."[48] The position of eminence accorded to the successful warrior is a reflection of the fears and hopes that have centered about
armed conflict in the minds of peoples whose existence and well-
being were always being set up as the stake of conflict. The field
of battle has for ages been the arena where glory could be most
speedily won. One has only to read the Old Testament, or Homer,
or the sagas of the North, to observe the incitement to war inherent in the possibility of winning renown. The mores are still shot
full of that incitement, and religion has long ago sanctioned it
with power. Christian hymns are often highly militant, though
their militancy is conventionalized. Only very slowly does the "religion of amity" succeed that of enmity.[49]

To list the rewards and gauds accorded by primitive peoples to
success in war would be an endless task. The chieftainship is
doubtless the greatest of these, for that office, as we shall see,[50]
derives predominantly out of war. This should not seem strange
to civilized eyes, for many modern wars, considerable or otherwise, have produced their kings and presidents. A few illustrations
of the glory-motive in war may stand for many.

In New Guinea a cause of strife among the natives is "the custom that a
youth, before he can chew sirih, that is, be counted as an adult, must have
'fetched a head.' "[51] Guise[52] numerates twelve badges of distinction for warriors, the standard being the number of lives taken. "The Sea Dyaks' history
likewise shows a growth of head-worship parallel to the increasing economic
importance of war. When they were mere agriculturists, fighting only among
one another over disputed ownership of land, they used to take the heads of
their enemies slain in these battles; but it was not until the Malays taught
them to grow rich by piracy that the passion for head-hunting became deeply
rooted, and that they went on expeditions for the avowed purpose of getting
heads."[53]
Among the Plains Indians, "to kill an enemy was good in so far as it reduced
the numbers of the hostile party, but otherwise the act was regarded as rela-

[47] §449, below.
[48] Starcke, *Samvittighedslivet*, 43-44.
[49] Spencer, *Study of Soc.*, 296-298.   [50] §§155 ff., below.
[51] Krieger, *Neu-Guinea*, 416; §§229, 365, below.
[52] In JAI, XXVIII, 213.
[53] Morris, in *Jour. Amer. Or. Soc., Sec. Hist. Relig.*, VII, 38.

tively unimportant. Likewise to scalp an enemy was not a notable feat and in no sense especially creditable. If scalped, the skin of the head was taken merely as a trophy, something to show, something to dance over—a good thing, but of no great importance; but to touch the enemy with something held in the hand, with the bare hand, or with any part of the body, was a proof of bravery . . . a feat which entitled the man or the boy who did it to the greatest credit. . . . The chief applause was won by the man who could first touch the fallen enemy. In Indian estimation the bravest act that could be performed was to count coup on—to touch or strike—a living, unhurt man and to leave him alive, and this was frequently done. . . . When hunting, it was not unusual for boys or young men, if they killed an animal, especially if it was a dangerous one, to rush up and count coup on it. . . . It was regarded as an evidence of bravery for a man to go into battle carrying no weapon that would do harm at a distance. It was more creditable to carry a lance than a bow and arrows; more creditable to carry a hatchet or a war-club than a lance; and the bravest thing of all was to go into a fight with nothing more than a whip, or a long twig—sometimes called a coup-stick. . . . The Cheyenne counted coup on an enemy three times; that is to say, three men might touch the body and receive credit, according to the order in which this was done. Subsequent coups received no credit. The Arapahoes touched four times. . . . I believe that the high esteem in which the act of touching the enemy is held is a survival of the old feeling that prevailed before the Indians had missiles and when, if they fought, they were obliged to do so hand-to-hand with clubs and sharpened sticks. Under such conditions only those who actually came to grips, so to speak, with the enemy could inflict injury and gain glory. After arrows came into use it may still have been thought a braver and finer thing to meet the enemy hand-to-hand than to kill him with an arrow at a distance. The general opinion that the act of scalping reflects credit on the warrior has no foundation . . . a scalp . . . was regarded as an emblem of victory and was a good thing to carry back to the village to rejoice and dance over but any part of an enemy's body might serve for this. Scalps were used to trim and fringe war clothing . . . and to tie to the horse's bridle in going to war. Usually the scalps taken were only a little larger than a silver dollar, but like any other piece of fresh skin they stretched greatly. Occasionally the whole skin of the head was taken."[54] Mason[55] views this matter from a slightly different angle: "A custom existed among the Plains Indians, when fighting, called 'giving the coup.' When a foe had been struck down in a fight, the scalp belongs to him who shall first strike the body with knife or tomahawk. This is the coup. If in a mêlée a warrior kills an enemy, he, in order to secure his proper recognition and reward, must rush at once on the prostrate body and strike his coup. Otherwise . . . the enemy being in full flight, a brave and skilful warrior who presses on adding victim to victim, returns to find his scalps at the girdles of laggards." There is an element here which really militates against the full effectiveness of war in favor of the glory-motive.

The Sioux chief Red Cloud stated that he had "counted coup" eighty times. "As war honors were public tokens of a man's courage and ability, they were regarded as his credentials; therefore when a man was called to any position or service, either social or tribal, custom required that before he entered on

---

[54] Grinnell, Cheyenne, II, 29-32, 36-37.   [55] Invention, 399.

his duties he should give his public record by counting his honors in order to show his fitness to receive the distinction offered him. Among some tribes, at the telling of each honor a blow was struck on a post or some other object, and this form of recital has become known by the composite term 'counting coup.' "[56] It is readily understandable that the fieriest young orator who was able to count but few coups could make little headway against a few unadorned words from an aged warrior whose deeds were known to all.

Of the incentives to war that are less general than the desire for plunder and for glory, a number center about woman; they might be aligned with the plunder-motive or are in reprisal for woman-stealing. Retaliation for real or fancied injury or humiliation bulks large among the motives to war; its most striking form is perhaps vengeance for manslaughter, intentional or not, out of which comes the blood-feud. Sometimes men fight merely, as it seems, to vary the monotony of life; again, it is for the sake of disciplining the young men. Genuine religious wars, for the sake of extending the sway of the faith, are absent or very rare among the uncivilized; their religions are pretty much alike and they feel no fanatical urge to universalize them. There are, however, various religious purposes represented among the causes of war, such as the securing of sacrificial victims or the avenging of injuries referred to magic. One modern incentive, namely, earth-hunger in the political sense, that is, the desire to build an empire through conquest of territory, is conspicuously absent among primitive peoples. It belongs to the era of state-formation.[57]

Important accessory causes of war in New Guinea are "jealousy, superstition, murderousness, and the women; especially in the south are the women frequently the direct inciters to conflict." If they want to have a feud fought out and the men are unwilling, they fall upon them like furies with stones and abuse. "Not seldom do trivial causes, often only an insignificant oral dispute, lead to war and bloodshed."[58] Again, the women are a very fruitful cause of war, apparently through their trading-methods. They visit inland tribes for the purpose of bartering fish for vegetables, and are very keen dealers. Then, again, a disappointed hunter or fisherman "turns over in his mind how to discover who would be likely to have bewitched his nets. He perhaps raises his eyes and sees a member of a neighboring friendly village on his way to pay a visit. It at once occurs to him that this man is the sorcerer, and watching an opportunity, he suddenly attacks and kills him. This man's life has the value of another man's life, and unless full compensation is made in the shape of boars' tusks, shell armlets, etc., his friends take the first opportunity of squaring the account by killing a man, or as many as they can. Thus a vendetta is

56 Mooney and Fletcher, in HAI, I, 354 and II, 914, respectively.
57 §187, below.   58 Krieger, *Neu-Guinea*, 320.

established that lasts years and years, until one day it strikes some chief that
it is time this state of affairs is ended, and he sends a message to his enemies
by a friendly native, suggesting a squaring up. A place is appointed; the
number of lives taken on each side is estimated, and the value of the balance
of lives taken by the stronger tribe is paid for."[59]

Life for life, by vendetta, is the aim in the New Hebrides. The natives of
Tanna are divided into two divisions at either end of the island, and these
divisions into districts and villages. If the latter fight one another, as they
often do, there is no cannibalism; but if the two big divisions go to war the
conflict is fierce and accompanied by cannibalism.[60] War is often undertaken
to frighten the enemy into paying shell-money; every life and wound has to
be paid for in that medium.[61]

In South Africa, "two chiefs of equal standing as paramount can never
meet. If they meet, one must salute the other, and this act would indicate the
superiority of the chief saluted. If there is no salutation, each chief's followers
fall to blows, and a struggle leading to inter-tribal war is the result." Omission
of certain formalities may readily lead to hostilities when these greetings are
identifying marks of friendliness. Take the matter of gift-giving which, as is
well known, easily passes into trade. "A gift is never recoverable, but it is customary with many tribes for a return gift to be given, and this may amount to
a claim, in that it would cease to be considered as a gift if no return were
made. Moreover, a gift is usually given as a form of greeting, and if no return
greeting were offered, this would be construed as a hostile act."[62] Considering
the above notions of the passage of an unreturned gift into a claim, it would
be almost a case of theft or at least of indebtedness.

A man named Van Zijl was a great "elephant-murderer" in Southwest
Africa. The Hottentots hated him and trumped up a case against him so that
he might be considered guilty of the murder of one of their chiefs; that is, they
showed that, as a consequence of Van Zijl's conduct there might have been a
combat in which, if it had become extended, the said chief might easily have
been wounded or killed. Therefore Van Zijl was guilty of taking the chief's
blood and must die. He escaped only through the firm attitude of the missionaries who threatened to leave at once if Van Zijl was killed and to keep others
from coming to the country.[63]

Letourneau[64] finds that the yellow races exhibit a complete gamut of war.
To some of the tribes it is unknown; others wage "juridic warfare," for the
sake of retaliation; there is war for cannibal purposes, for slaves and booty,
for glory, for "consolidated pillage," and for feudal and religious purposes.

Modern causes for war include many that have arisen by reason
of developed and complicated interrelations and outlook, unrepresented in simpler times, such as the desire for "a place in the sun."
Malignant journalism has fanned the flames of animosity. Doctrines have been set forth to cover motives that, unadorned, would

[59] Guise, in JAI, XXVIII, 212.
[61] Danks, in JAI, XVII, 314.
[63] Büttner, *Walfischbai*, 101.
[60] Gray, in AAAS, 1892, 648.
[62] Dundas, C., in JAI, LI, 276.
[64] *Guerre*, 243-245.

sound less worthy and elevated.[65] We do not undertake to treat of these.

If we seek to sum up the causes of war, we find that the militant impulses are the familiar socializing forces of hunger, love, vanity, and ghost-fear, and particularly the first and third of these, to which war for plunder and war for glory respectively correspond. War because of the abduction of women, though it is traditionally and also logically aligned with fighting over property, is unmistakably connected with marriage and the family; and so is war for blood-vengeance, rooting as it does in the conception of blood-unity and kin-group solidarity. And there are also the religious and political causes for war, which reveal its connection with religion, government, and the state. The fact that war has its relations to all these sets of institutions should not be lost sight of; for it is only by keeping such perspectives open that one apprehends the super-fact that the whole of societal life is a mesh of interlacing elements, separable and classifiable only by doing a certain necessary and temporary violence to the truth. If war is taken out for the time being, to be scrutinized by itself, the strands thus isolated must be allowed to slip back into their natural tangle before the perspective view of society's evolution and life can be taken.

§139*. Warlikeness. "In the eighteenth century it was assumed that the primitive state of mankind was one of Arcadian peace, joy, and contentment. In the nineteenth the assumption went over to the other extreme—that the primitive state was one of universal warfare. This, like the former notion, is a great exaggeration."[66] Those who evolved these ideas about primitive man did not trouble themselves to go beyond one or a few striking instances, sometimes of shaky authenticity, even when they did not deduce their contentions forthwith from inner consciousness, "the logic of the case," or some other figment of thin air. The proper course, if one is looking for the truth and not defending a thesis, is to go to the facts instead of inferring or meditating. So doing, one finds that there are very few peoples who do not quarrel and use violence and that these few are generally, if primitive, in such

---

[65] Sumner, *Coll. Ess.*, I, ch. I.   [66] Sumner, in *Coll. Ess.*, I, 3.

isolation that there is no one to fight or so poverty-stricken that they have nothing to tempt aggression. "The natives resemble children in many respects; their emotions lie close to the surface and are but little subjected to the discipline of self-control. The merest trifle will sometimes give rise to a serious brawl. They are especially sensitive on all questions relating to food. . . . Some question of food or of women lies at the root of most of their troubles."[67]

There is no "instinct of pugnacity." What there is is a set of life-conditions demanding adjustment. That demand has been felt in the form of the various incentives which have just been reviewed. Those who acted upon the incentives were more or less "warlike" and developed something in the way of a military organization. No other expedient in adjustment could stand in the face of a military organization at that time, and none has ever been able to do so since. The most peaceably disposed societies, however much they hate to do so, must take to arms for self-preservation in an environment of militarism. Peoples have always gone to war with various degrees of relish or repugnance; but such sentiments have been in their traditions and not in any inherited instinct, one way or the other.

Some peoples have been in the way of feeling fewer of the incentives to war, or of feeling them less intensely, than others. In general more of the incentives appeal more strongly to peoples who have developed some degree of culture, and those societies which have gone to war and prevailed are the ones that have got ahead in the world. For there is among primitive peoples no adjustment without selection, no selection without competition, and no prevalent form of competition except by violence. Where group-conflict has been persistent, the path of evolution is strewn with discarded codes. Conflict reveals the lurking and unsuspected weaknesses. It is probable that the salient and characteristic features of all prevailing codes represent the residue from such rude tests, involving the virtual extirpation of the losers, with the resultant elimination of many inexpedient codes.[68] However much one abhors war, in these days when there are other and more expedient forms

67 Jenness and Ballentyne, *D'Entrecasteaux*, 202.
68 Keller, *Soc. Evol.*, 63-64.

of competition, he must realize that it once had its points, just as slavery had, or despotism, or the stone axe.

Authentic cases of unwarlikeness, meaning by that cases of absence of militarism in the mores, are hard to find and are seldom pure. The following citations represent our total findings. It is to be noted, however, that just as primitive slavery was of a type considerably milder than one is likely to think, with the recently abolished modern system in mind, so is primitive warfare less destructive than the modern type. The conflict is generally brief and loose, casualties are often negligible, and not much use is made of the result. A savage would stand aghast before the wholesale slaughter of civilized warfare, and beside some of its methods his own are those of a gentleman. We begin with representative cases of unwarlikeness.

One African people is reported as being the most peaceful and orderly folk that one could think, doing all that is asked of them, and wishing only to be left alone.[69] During the whole period of his residence in the Bechuana country Livingstone[70] never saw unarmed men strike each other. "Their disputes are usually conducted with great volubility and noisy swearing, but they generally terminate by both parties bursting into a laugh." The Mrús of India are peaceable, timid, and simple; "in a dispute they do not fight, but call in an . . . exorcist, who takes the sense of the spirits in the matter."[71] A traditionally pacifistic people are the Veddahs of Ceylon. "The Veddahs carry on no warfare among themselves." In the seventeenth century it was reported of them: "They live so peacefully among themselves that strife among them is seldom heard of, and never war"; and, further: "The Veddahs have never taken the step from hunter to warrior. But there occur, at infrequent intervals, hot disputes about the boundaries of their hunting-grounds."[72] The Chinese had the theory that war was a disease, though they fought many and bloody ones. Their commercial interests led them to avoid wars where they could, even buying peace with money. Considering the ratio of population to land, their armed conflicts have been relatively few.[73] India, under the influence of its higher religions, could put up little resistance to the Mohammedans.[74] In Borneo, "bravery is the virtue *par excellence* of the Kayan, but to the Sea Dyak, with his larger interest in agriculture, the virtues of the settled life are equally important."[75]

Some of these latter examples reveal the natural antithesis of the militant and industrial types of mores, and are not primitive; but in Micronesia we discover in several small islands an extraordinary case of unwarlikeness. Of one people in the Caroline Archipelago it is said: "War is unknown, and real

[69] Freiherr, in *Globus*, LXXXVI, 77.   [70] *Travels*, II, 503.
[71] Lewin, *S. E. India*, 232.   [72] Sarasin, *Weddas*, 488, *cf.* 479.
[73] Letourneau, *Guerre*, 233 ff.; Schallmayer, *Vererbung*, 201.
[74] Ratzenhofer, *Soc. Erkennt.*, 193-194.
[75] Morris, in *Jour. Amer. Or. Soc., Sec. Hist. Relig.*, VII, 35.

weapons therefore are lacking." Again, "the people of Núkuóro always felt themselves to be more a family than a folk; they never needed to oppose an enemy, they knew no war, and the traditional Fijian invaders were fought with fish-spears."[76] Here was "the one land of the earth which might rightfully lay claim to the honorable name of a home of peace among mankind; there they neither knew war nor any means of exercising power over other men; the commands of their authorities were obeyed out of natural good-nature and innate impulse."[77] On the island of Yap war was a sort of athletic contest. Personal security is said to have been "without doubt greater than in Europe, since even weapons were almost wholly lacking."[78] Polynesian battles were often sets of duels.[79]

Ratzel[80] says that the North American races were of two types, peaceful and warlike. Of them all the isolated Eskimo are certainly the outstanding examples of unwarlikeness. "It is wonderful in what peace and unity they live with each other; for quarreling and strife, hatred and covetousness, are seldom heard of among them."[81] There is reported "a very marked trait of the Greenlanders which shows how sorrowful they are to do anything that might offend others. When a band nears an occupied shore to pitch their tents, they row slowly, and when they are a gun-shot from land, they come to a stand-still, holding with their oars, without speaking. If the newcomers are welcome, the people on land do the compliments, saying: 'Here are good locations for tents and a place where the woman's boat can lie; come and rest yourselves!' The settlers assist with the unloading of the boat and the bringing up of the baggage. At departure they do not help with the launching of the woman's boat nor work at the loading. If, on the contrary, the strangers are unwelcome, those standing on shore keep still, and then the newcomers row away with the greatest haste to another spot. . . . They refrain from everything which might publicly offend one another, such as abusive terms or fighting."[82]

It might appear from the cases cited above and in the *Case-Book* that a little of the poet inheres in several of the ethnographers. However that may be, these are all the instances at our disposal illustrative of the unwarlikeness of peoples who are, for the most part, primitive. The clearest of them merely indicate that men do not fight unless they have to. The picture is not wholly idyllic. It is true that the hostilities of such tribes seldom demand, to describe them, a term as strong as war. In some of the cases, the special reason for unwarlikeness appears, on the face of it, to be extreme isolation. It is probable that other peoples would be peaceful too if they were let alone; but the struggle for exist-

[76] Kubary, *Karolinen-Archip.*, 94; Kubary, *Núkuóro*, 20.
[77] Bastian, *Mikr. Colonien*, 4-5.
[78] Senfft, in *Globus*, XCI, 174; Kl. Nachr., in *Globus*, LXXXVII, 180.
[79] Letourneau, *Guerre*, 123.   [80] *Hist. Mankind*, II, 133.
[81] Nansen, *Esk. Life*, 104.
[82] Holm, *Ethnol. Skizze*, 129-130, 132.

ence does not allow of that in many instances. Even the Veddahs are ready for resistance if their hunting-grounds, that is, their potential food-supply, are in jeopardy. It is not so much that men like to fight, in the same way that they like to eat or sleep; when they resort to violence, it is generally for some reason that seems to them sufficient or compelling, however trivial or mistaken it may appear to us. If, however, the cases of unwarlikeness are few, and some of them uncertain, there is no doubt about either the quantity or quality of the evidence for warlikeness. This does not mean that savages fight all the time or that they are by nature, or "instinctively," pugnacious. War is the only way they know of relieving stresses and settling difficulties. Though civilized men have other agencies to resort to, and generally give them their chance, yet the final recourse, for them too, is violence. And we must seek to realize the glaring actuality of the fears and hopes, such as the fear of sorcery or the hope of propitiating the spirits by acquired heads, which impel the savages to war but which never enter into our own sets of causes and motives. We are as little likely to allow for such fears and hopes, unless we know about them, as the savage would be to understand a contest for "balance of power," or any other of our war-producing doctrines.

In New Guinea "for the most part every village has been at bitter hostility with its neighbor since ancient times, and so it comes about that nowhere is a single language, with wide branchings, spoken, but nearly every nest has its peculiar dialect. . . . On the island of Tamara, with an area of about five hundred hectares, five different tongues are spoken in five villages, one of which, according to the investigations of the missionaries, altogether lacks recognizable relationship with the rest." In some parts of New Guinea whole districts have been depopulated and entire tribes wiped out by raiders.[83] Letourneau[84] lists African cases where, because of continuous hostilities, there is no security. No one can hunt or till for fear of ambushes. There is always danger of assassination in sleep. Long wars bring famine and depopulation. Parallels from other parts of the world are cited. "The history of the African peoples has been, in the course of the millennia, undoubtedly a frightfully bloody one. Among savage communities that live in the darkness of superstition and in slavery, acknowledge only the might of the stronger, and without cessation war upon, subject, or oppress one another, it is indeed hardly thinkable that it was anything else. Even in the most recent history and in the present it is not otherwise."[85] "Every man is a warrior from his childhood, as

[83] Blum, *Neu-Guinea*, 23; Seligmann, in JAI, XXXIX, 261.
[84] *Guerre*, 66, 84, 92.   [85] Junker, *Afrika*, III, 292; II, 271.

the Baris are always at war."[86] The inhabitants of the Upper Welle District form five tribes who keep aloof from one another, each clinging tenaciously to its own rites and customs and living on terms of intermittent war and peace with its neighbors.[87]

In Northeast Africa "the sole field that they cultivate is the field of the dead." The whole life of the Somali and others is a permanent campaign; only he remains victor who can use his weapons promptly and skillfully. "Neither the development of spiritual nor that of physical strength guarantees life; he only possesses it to whom his lance has become staff, and his dagger mattock and spade. The picture of armed children and women, which the traveller encounters everywhere, impresses upon the landscapes of Africa's eastern horn a characteristic stamp. Even the construction of the weapons, the majority of which are designed for close fighting, indicates the never-ceasing feuds among the tribes themselves and a world in arms. To be unarmed (hubla) is regarded as the same thing as being naked." The author[88] cannot understand this situation, in so meager a country where all "alike possess and need little." The Berbers too, in an arid habitat, show a "state of eternal warfare existing among themselves. It is a case not only of tribe against tribe and family against family, but often of individual against individual."[89] With these cases should be compared that of the desert-dwelling Teda and others, cited at length elsewhere.[90]

The relation of men to their environment of fellow-men is evidently full of antagonisms, real and fancied, between sets of interests. Assuming a number of tribes, composed of smaller constituents (families or larger kinship-aggregations) which have reconciled their antagonisms and combined to form a tribal peace-group, these tribes are found to be always colliding in the matter of their interests, as they see them or sense them. The expedient for settling differences that is right at hand, for it is the method of the organic world, is violence. Doubtless some peoples take to war more readily than do others; some get to love it; but all, unless there are some who live in exceptional isolation or are spiritless, have to take recourse to the only expedient they know when the inevitable competition of life is upon them. They also have to remain in readiness to do so. If this is warlikeness, then most peoples on a low stage of culture are warlike; nevertheless the habitude is referable to circumstance rather than to an innate urge. It is interesting to note the survivals of warlikeness among peaceable peoples, as, for example, the Swiss who used to go to their assemblies with old fashioned sabers and rapiers, yet carried

[86] Baker, *Ismailïa*, 135 (edit. 1875).   [87] Burrows, in JAI, XXVIII, 40.
[88] Paulitschke, *Nordost-Afr.*, I, 109, 110.
[89] Harris, in JAI, XXVII, 64.   [90] §9, above.

their umbrellas along too.[91] Court-dress sometimes includes the sword; language is full of survivals out of war, such as "captain" of industry, "corporal's guard," "free-lance," and many metaphorical expressions that reveal war as something that has been much in people's experience. Religion makes large use of military terminology; there is even a salvation army. Inferences from such survivals truthfully portray the prevailing militancy of former times.

Perhaps enough evidence has been cited as to the "why" of war; the next question is concerning the "how." Peoples are forced into fighting by the circumstances of life. Being in the conflict, they carry it on in certain ways, that is, they exhibit various usages and rules of war. Though it is impossible to cover these exhaustively, they may be called before the mind by reviewing certain of their representative types.

§140*. War-Usages. Among uncivilized peoples there is little or no fixed differentiation between the fighters and the rest except upon the basis of sex and age. Even among the Aztecs, "with the exception of children, old people, infirm or crippled persons, and sometimes priests, every one had to go to war. . . . There was no standing army, the available force being composed of all the able-bodied men of the tribe of Mexico."[92] The army was the tribe in arms.

To this generalization the Zulus and the Dahomans would seem to offer exceptions were it not for the fact that European influence is demonstrable or to be inferred. The Zulus had a real military organization with universal male service and their army was said to be one of the most complete and stable ever exhibited by nature peoples. The warriors were not allowed to marry until they had passed the age of activity, and were subject to constant drill. It has been said that this people could have put a well-organized force of fifty thousand, possibly twice as many, into the field, half of whom were maintained, even in time of peace, on a war-footing. The soldiers were fed at the chief's expense. In time of war the women, boys, and captives drove the cattle after the army and did the cooking, water-carrying, and transportation of equipment and stores. Dahomi also had a standing army which was the basis of its military supremacy.[93] These exceptional cases simply show that the peoples in question were near enough to the natural development of an army

[91] Letourneau, *Polit.*, 416.   [92] Mason, *Invention*, 370.
[93] Ratzel, *Hist. Mankind,* II, 439 ff.; Frere, in JAI, XI, 332-333; MacDonald, in JAI, XIX, 286 ff.; Shooter, *Kafirs,* ch. X; Ellis, *Ewe,* 185 ff., 195 ff.

to be able to take over the idea and apply it. Certain half-civilized Asiatic conquerors had armies, but one looks for them in vain upon the lower stages of civilization.

This does not mean that there was no system in the primitive military organization. Savages all have the beginnings of organization in their chiefs and sub-chiefs. The war-leader could summon warriors to a campaign by sending a spear or some other token from village to village around the country, with an indication as to the place and time of meeting.[94] In particular, much stress was laid upon the drill; that it was partly pleasurable and, in some of its aspects, was like a dance, derogated in no manner from its efficacy. The boys began early to practise with weapons; this was largely play but there was serious purpose behind it. Tests of fortitude were contrived through which they had to pass before they could be full-fledged warriors.[95] Without going into needless detail it may be said that the war-training focussed upon discipline, obedience, and coöperation.

Bagehot[96] believes that "a diffused deficiency in a warlike power is the best attainable evidence that the pre-historic man did not possess that power," arguing as follows: "If one-armed people existed almost everywhere in every continent; if people were found in every intermediate stage, some with the mere germ of the second arm, some with the second arm half-grown, some with it nearly complete; we should then argue—'the first race cannot have had two arms, because men have always been fighting, and as two arms are a great advantage in fighting, one-armed and half-armed people would immediately have been killed off the earth; they never could have attained any numbers.' "
The Mandan boys engage in sham fights. "This mode of training generally lasts an hour or more in the morning, and is performed on an empty stomach, affording them a rigid and wholesome exercise, whilst they are instructed in the important science of war. Some five or six miles of ground are run over during these evolutions, giving suppleness to their limbs and strength to their muscles, which last and benefit them through life."[97] Of the drill of the Plains Indians, Col. Dodge[98] writes: "There seems to be no fixed system of tactics, each chief instructing according to his own peculiar ideas. There are no ranks, no units of command, but there are words or signals by which the same evolutions are repeatedly performed. The whole band will charge *en masse,* and without an order on a supposed position of the enemy. At a word it breaks and scatters like leaves before a storm; another signal, a portion wheels, masses, and dashes on a flank, to scatter at another signal. The plain is alive with circling, flying horsemen, now single, lying flat on the horse or hanging

[94] Roth, in JAI, XXII, 55.   [95] §§163, below.
[96] *Physics and Politics,* 123.
[97] Donaldson, in *Smithson. Rep.,* 1885, pt. II, 319.
[98] *Plains of the Great West,* 367-369.

to his side, as if to escape the shots of a pursuing enemy, and now joined together in a living mass of charging, yelling terror. The remarkable control of the chief is exercised by signals. Wonderful as it may seem, the orders are given on a bright day with a piece of looking-glass held in the hollow of the hand. In communicating at long distances their mode of telegraphing is equally remarkable. Both the signalling and telegraphing are modifications and extensions of their sign language. All are offspring of a necessity growing out of the constant wariness instant to a life of peculiar danger." The superstition which condemns every scalped warrior to annihilation is the primary cause of a drill peculiar to the Indians, namely, stooping from a horse going at full speed and picking up objects from the ground. At first, light objects are selected. These are exchanged for heavier and more bulky ones, until some individuals attain such wonderful proficiency as to pick up, while going at full speed, the body of a man and swing it across their horses. This is generally done by two men working in conjunction.

The drill of the Indians is a peculiarly perfected adjustment. Many other tribes show less developed forms. In Borneo, for instance, "the men vied with each other in wild leaps and shouts, springing high in the air and coming down on their knees, all the while battling with imaginary foes; slashing with their parongs and waving their shields in rhythmical time to the drone of the kaluri."[99]

Among the salient usages in war are practices designed to avoid ill-fortune or to secure supernatural aid. Taboos surround the warriors and especially are they prohibited from association with women.[100] They carry amulets and other protective devices and "medicines." Magical means include also what the portion of the tribe which remains behind in camp may contribute toward success; that is, in its way, just as important as anything else. It may be that the use of magic in agricultural operations comes to be a sort of substitute for industry and energy, thus throwing the whole situation into a wrong focus; but in military enterprises, if it does nothing else, it heightens morale. Men who believe that they are invulnerable and their weapons sure and deadly by reason of some medicine which their doctor has provided for smearing on both men and spears are endowed with a distinct advantage over those who have no such conviction. Many of these magical provisions will appear under later headings;[101] the following miscellany is given by way of present visualization.

"It is very important that the people staying at home during a war expedition observe certain rules of conduct, for their behaviour is by no means immaterial for the success of their fighting friends, whom, on the contrary, they

[99] Furness, *Head-Hunters,* 101.　　　　[100] §§388, 389, below.
[101] §§267, 281, 282, 300, below.

can help or injure from a distance. . . . The whole village must be silent, for otherwise the enemy will be warned prematurely (as if hearing the noise) and run away. Therefore the women at home only do the most necessary work. They also have to restrict themselves to certain kinds of food." They keep a sort of sabbath. This is sympathetic magic.[102]

In one African tribe, "a charm consists in scarifying the man all down his arms and breast and back, after which, it is believed, no sword will cut into his body. The great doctors have a powder which they put into water, which the warriors drink. On approaching the seat of war, the warriors assemble, when everyone is smeared on the face with a certain preparation and given medicine, and is licked by the *fundi*," or medicine-man.[103] In Borneo, "while the men are away at war, their fires are lighted on the stones or fire-places as if they were at home. The mats are spread and the fires kept up till late in the evening and lighted again at dawn, that the men may not be cold. The roofing of the house is opened before dawn, that the men may not lie too long and so fall into the hands of the enemy."[104] Again, before going out to battle "every peg whereon the pots had rested was with scrupulous care pulled up, and the embers scattered;—nothing brings worse luck to a war-party than the omission of this last duty in breaking camp."[105] It is reported of the Comanche Indians that, "going to war, they have no faith in their success, unless they pass a celebrated painted rock, where they appease the spirit of war (who resides there), by riding by it at full gallop, and sacrificing their best arrow by throwing it against the side of the ledge."[106]

"In Guatemala a woman and a female dog were sacrificed before every battle."[107] To get victory, or to obtain information about a battle already fought, the Caribs whipped two boys mercilessly over the whole body. "If the boys endured the pains, without letting a tear fall or a sigh be heard, the victory was certain. One of the boys was then laid in a hammock from which he must shoot at a mark fixed upon one of the roofs. As many enemies would be killed by the warriors as there were arrows to hit the mark."[108]

Among the New Zealanders, "a young chief on his first war party always received a special baptism, where he and his companions had to stand naked in the water and be sprinkled and charmed. Until he had passed through this ceremony and the bloodshedding, he was a nobody."[109] In the Hervey Islands, stone axes were buried on the eve of battle in some out-of-the-way place. The place of deposit was handed down by tradition.[110]

In the American Northwest, the ceremonial masks and head-dresses, generally of a pronounced religious significance, "would seem to have originated in the actual wearing of them in war. Much of the ceremonial display amongst these Indians has reference to prowess in combat, and it is an undoubted fact that, in the survival of many primitive implements of war we

[102] Landtmann, "Magic of the Papuans in Warfare," in JAI, XLVI, 329; §302, below.

[103] Dale, reported in PSM, XLIX, 860.

[104] Roth, in JAI, XXII, 56.   [105] Furness, *Head-Hunters*, 84.

[106] Donaldson, in *Smithson. Rep.*, 1885, pt. II, 326-327.

[107] Nadaillac, *Preh. Amer.*, 268.

[108] Schomburgk, *Brit.-Guiana*, II, 431.

[109] Tregear, in JAI, XIX, 110.   [110] Gill, in AAAS, 1892, 613.

have the origin of much of the dance and ceremonial paraphernalia peculiar to this region."[111]

Victory removes any taboo imposed to attain it; thus in an African tribe, "in case of victory the women greet the warriors with great joy, and shave, for the first time since their husbands went to war."[112]

It is noteworthy that savages do not fight as civilized men do, but in ways more suited to their looser organization. Their war is more like a series of duels than a conflict of masses. The Abyssinians look with contempt upon the "soldier-machines" of the white men, much preferring their own free-lance style.[113] Though the Indians have made good scouts, they have never taken to the style of fighting of the European invaders; in fact, the latter found it necessary to adopt the Indian open style as better adapted to local conditions. It is astonishing to realize that that style was re-introduced as a successful adjustment in the most recent of wars; for an advance in rank and file would have been disastrous. The Indian relied further upon surprises, sudden and furious dashes, and the demoralization consequent upon unearthly yells. "They never receive a charge, and very rarely meet one. When charged the portion immediately in front of the charging force breaks and melts into individual Indians, while the bands on either side close in to harass the flank and rear."[114] It is generally impossible for savages to prosecute a close siege, for in the absence of a developed commissary they have to live off the country. Even the Homeric Greeks were able to do no more than loosely invest the city of Troy.[115] In short, the military forces of uncivilization reveal a general imperfection of organization natural to their stage of evolution.

"Seldom or never did the Kaffirs go to meet their enemies in the open field when the two were equal in number, but under such circumstances avoided such ground as much as possible; for they carried on war by sudden dashes and especially by night-attacks upon single posts and isolated forts, by ambush in chasms in the rocks or in the bush, impenetrable for European soldiers."[116] Occasionally the natives are naïve in their methods. "The Khonds of a certain village could not be reasoned with, and it was thought best to proceed against

111 Niblack, in USNM, 1888, 268.
112 Dale, reported in PSM, XLIX, 860.
113 Letourneau, *Guerre,* 296.
114 Mason, *Invention,* 397, from Dodge, *Plains,* ch. XXV, and Dorsey, in BAE, III, 312 ff., where much detail is given.
115 Keller, *Hom. Soc.,* 296-297.   116 Fritsch, *Eingeb. S.-Afr.,* 50-51.

them with a strong force of Police. The Khonds fortified a pass in the way between the Police camp and their village, and had large stones nicely poised and ready to be rolled down the hill sides to discomfit their foes, who they supposed would attack the front; they neglected to protect the rear. The Police entered the village from the rear and the Khonds protested against the unfairness of the movement when they had taken such precautions for their front!"[117] Letourneau[118] cites many contrasting cases of preparation for hostilities in which nothing was done offhand and no possible advantage overlooked. Connections and alliances were arranged beforehand, emissaries sent to stir up old quarrels. Councils were held by the Indians and the agency of spies in disguise was not infrequent. Even the Law of Manu, in India, advised the king to organize a spy-system and to corrupt the officers of a foreign prince and foster their discontent. The king was to negotiate if weaker, but to go ahead energetically if stronger.

Here and there in what follows it will be noticed that primitive warfare is not very bloody. In the Indian Archipelago, for instance, there are seldom pitched battles in the open field. Where they do take place, they often degenerate into a sort of ordeal-duel; "the party which first has a member killed or wounded regards itself as beaten and retires." A number of examples follow. In Sumba the wars are "seldom very bloody. The hostile bands deploy armed with spear and shield upon open ground, in opposite ranks, and try to hit each other. The party that first has several wounded deems itself defeated, takes to flight, and pays the fine or compensation which is demanded, whereupon the making of peace is celebrated with great feasts."[119]

It has been stated that the warriors of a tribe are differentiated from the rest of the able-bodied almost solely on the basis of sex, and good reasons for woman's common exemption from military service have been cited.[120] Yet there are some few cases in which woman stands forth as an actual front-line combatant; and even where she is not that, she is by no means a negligible quantity. She is the commissary in so far as there is any; she is the pack-animal in default of any other. Her normal place is behind the line, where she attends the wounded fellow-tribesman and not infrequently gives the *coup de grâce* to the disabled enemy. She also strives to operate upon the morale of both the friendly and the hostile by a judicious mixture of encouragement, praise, taunts, ridicule, epithets, and insults. The men on her own side are especially sensitive to her opinion of them, and the general impression one gets from reading is that she is a mistress of jibes, flouts, sneers, and local allusion calculated to upset the poise of the enemy.

[117] Fawcett, in JASB, I, 240.
[118] *Guerre*, 47 ff., 150 ff., 371 ff., *et passim*.
[119] Wilken, in VG, II, 507-508, note.   [120] §58, above.

The Australian women of Victoria appear always to be active participants.[121] Roth[122] tells of certain individual women who, contrary to custom,
engaged in war. "Notwithstanding the ancient customs of the blacks, not to
permit the women to take any part in active war, these individuals could not
be restrained from joining in and sometimes leading the attack. One of these
persons, . . . a woman of one of the East Coast tribes, . . . planned and
executed nearly every outrage that was committed in the districts bordering
on the north and northwestern coast. In the days of their decay, she collected
the poor remnants of several tribes into one hostile band, of whom she was
the leader and chieftainess."

Regular forces of fighting women are found in several isolated instances.
They are usually referred to as Amazons, thus recalling legends of antiquity.
In Dahomi, "the female corps, to use the common expression, the Amazons,
was raised about 1729, when a body of women who had been armed and furnished with banners, merely as a stratagem to make the attacking force appear larger, behaved with such unexpected gallantry as to lead to a permanent
corps of women being embodied. Up to the reign of Gezo, who came to the
stool [throne] in 1818, the Amazon force was composed chiefly of criminals,
that is, criminals in the Dahomi sense of the word. Wives detected in adultery,
and termagants and scolds were drafted into its ranks; the great majority of
the women 'given to the king' by the provincial chiefs, i.e., sent to him as being
worthy of death for misdemeanors or crimes, were, instead of being sacrificed
at the Annual Custom, made women soldiers. Gezo, who largely made use of
the Amazons to keep his own subjects in check and to promote military rivalry,
increased and improved the force. He directed every head of a family to send
his daughters to Agbomi for inspection; the most suitable were enlisted, and
the corps thus placed on a new footing. This course was also followed by
Gelele, his successor, who had every girl brought to him before marriage, and
enrolled those who pleased him. The women of Dahomi, having for many generations past endured all the toil and performed all the hard labor of the
country, have, for the weaker sex, an exceptional physique, which enables them
to bear hardships and privations as well, if not better than the men; this fact
no doubt was an important factor in the causes which led to the formation
of the corps. By state policy the Amazons are considered the king's wives,
and cannot be touched without danger of death. They are sworn to celibacy,
a necessary restriction in the case of a female corps. . . . Nature, however,
will assert itself, and when Capt. Burton visited Agbomi, one hundred and
fifty Amazons were found to be pregnant and were brought to trial. Such
offenders are always put to death in secret within the palace, with cruelties
that are only whispered of outside. . . . The Amazons, in common with the
real wives of the king, never leave their quarters without being protected by
a bell, which is the signal for men to leave the road. The Amazons only meet
men when on the march or in the field; for when the two corps of the standing
army parade at the palace, the sexes are kept apart by pieces of bamboo laid
along the ground, which barrier no one may pass."[123]

In modern times, exceptional circumstances have resulted in the formation
of a Chinese and a Russian "Battalion of Death," in 1911-1912 and during the

---

[121] Smyth, *Vict.*, 156 ff.   [122] *Tasmania*, 89.

[123] Ellis, *Ewe*, 183-184; Markham, in JAI, XL, 82, cites a tribe of female
warriors on the Amazon.

late war, respectively, whose members fought as men do, but are reported to have armed themselves with poison against an outcome of defeat and capture which men do not have to fear.

The exceptional and traditional character of such instances needs no comment. Though, in general, the women have to assist the men in war, their aid has almost always been afforded in an accessory or supplementary capacity: women have been the transportation-agency in war, as they so often were in peaceful times; they have carried off and attended to the wounded; and they have provided the food. They often have peculiar rights and duties in connection with war, and incur special treatment at the hands of the combatants. To be especially noted is their not uncommon inviolability in war and their consequent availability for missions, trade, and peace-making.

"The New Caledonian women went to battle. They kept in the rear and attended to the commissariat. Whenever they saw one of the enemy fall it was their business to rush forward, pull the body to the rear and dress it for the oven."[124] In West Africa, "many of the head-men of hamlets and villages, when war has been declared, are accompanied by their wives and female slaves, who look after the commissariat and carry the baggage; and when a native army takes the field, the towns and villages are deserted by all save women, children, and old men. This system is also in vogue in Dahomi, but, in addition, there is a standing army, maintained by the king, and always ready for active service."[125] On the Loango Coast, the men have to get their wives' permission to go to war. If one will not give permission, she runs the risk of being burned as a witch, for it is laid to her door if her husband falls on the battle-field or is wounded.[126] "Tacitus wrote that the women went to battle, encouraging the soldiers and dressing their wounds."[127]

This book does not linger over the details of the war-organization any more than it did over that of industry; it illustrates them and passes on to their broader societal aspects. In so far as any war-usages are significant for general societal development they will appear in various connections as we go on. Interest attaches not so much to war itself as to what war does to bring about a regulative organization. It can be seen from the foregoing that war has imposed a strict drill and discipline; it has enforced obedience and orderliness; together with the subordination it demands, it has promoted inequalities and recognized sheer ability; it has classified societal membership. The apprehension of such

[124] Mason, *Woman's Share*, 238, 239.   [125] Ellis, *Ewe*, 182.
[126] Bastian, *Deut. Exped.*, I, 203.   [127] Mason, *Woman's Share*, 238, 239.

matters does not call for a minute survey of military instruments and methods any more than an understanding of the industrial organization calls for a rehearsal of the detail of basketry or pottery-making. There are, however, certain features of military evolution that are especially significant for general societal evolution and therefore demand a more thoroughgoing examination. Prominent among these are the rules of warfare.

§141*. Rules of War. Conventions covering the conduct of warfare, like the mores in general, had to be developed; they could not have been there at the outset. In their absence the man-hunt was like any other sort of chase; it had no choice of methods except that between the immediately effective and the immediately ineffective. Yet there are a good many peoples, even upon very low stages of culture, who have developed codes of warfare which limit the ruthlessness of the process and exert an ameliorative influence upon its crude harshness. It is about as difficult to realize the chivalric spirit exhibited by some primitive savages as to credit the primitive savagery revealed by certain nations whose claims to culture and even Christianity have been generally honored. To most people the savage, as they have casually read about him, is a plain fiend, and they are astonished to learn of his scrupulous attention to what would be considered among civilized nations to be a moral code.

We need to have a set of the facts before us, and shall begin with several cases of the absence of any code or rules of war, in which the stark struggle is unrelieved by pity, mercy, or any kind of chivalry. Especially is the foreigner the object of unbridled ferocity. In such cases, as Tylor[128] intimates, there is no difference between war and assassination; sneaking night-raids, ambushes, and attacks from behind are combined with prompt flight if any effective resistance is in sight.

The great object of the Dahomans "is to surprise the foe, and when they fail in this, they rarely succeed in capturing any place of note. In both of the corps of the standing army, but especially in that of the Amazons, the military spirit is strongly cultivated, and they are taught to disregard obstacles, dangers, wounds, and death itself. Hence they often display a ferocious courage which carries all before it. . . . The standing army fights with the ferocity

128 *Anth.*, 223.

and cruelty of savages who have been intoxicated with a craving for military glory; it fights to conquer and to kill. The general levy fights after the ordinary manner of untrained savages; that is, it avoids direct combats and unnecessary risks, and its object is plunder and profit."[129] The foreign wars of the Masai are managed in the most cruel way, but the inside or civil wars are less bloodthirsty.[130] Though wars between the three nations of the eastern horn of Africa are characterized by "outspoken cruelty," they are less bloody because they demand fewer human sacrifices; but where there is a chance of getting glory from the foreigner, ruthlessness is rife. They have a sort of prize-list in their killings, both of men and beasts. If a slave kills a man, he gets freedom; if more than one he acquires the right to be adopted; if a large number, he becomes notable and receives various privileges. To kill a buffalo is equivalent to murdering two enemies; a leopard is worth seven, a lion ten, and an elephant fifteen. An elephant is equivalent to a white man, who is, therefore, worth fifteen ordinary enemies.[131] An enlightened African chief complained of the irregularity of his enemies' methods: "These Machopas are mean, mean, mean. . . . They set their women out in the front ranks and in front of their villages, and when my brave soldiers rush up to steal the women, then the men rise up and shoot us down. O, but they are mean!"[132]

"To kill a baby in arms, or a woman, was accounted a greater feat than killing a man, as it implied having penetrated to the innermost recesses of an enemy's country, whereas a man might be killed anywhere by a successful ambush. I knew a man who had killed sixty women and children, when on one occasion he happened to come upon them after all the men had left the village on a hunting expedition. . . . A party of forty men of Mozema went over to Kohima, and were admitted by one of the *khels* [kin-groups] friendly to them, living next to the Puchatsuma quarter, into which they passed and killed all they could find, viz., one man, five women, and twenty young children. *The people of the other khels made no effort to interfere, but stood looking on.* . . . One of the onlookers told me that he never saw such fine sport (i.e., the killing of the children) for it was just like killing fowls."[133] "Amongst the Siyins the man who kills a woman and the baby at her breast is thought to have performed a finer feat than the man who has killed only one man, as two heads are better than one, even if those of babes."[134]

The instances of ferocity in war which remain in the recollections of many readers are connected with the torturing of captives by the American Indians. We need not go into the detail of such torture,[125] under which white victims begged for death. It was really a mode of self-gratification,[136] and both the torturers and the tortured understood it as such, the latter singing defiant death-songs and priding themselves on showing no sign of pain. But the Indians were not alone in the practice of torture; the Bushmen, between whom and the Hottentots there existed the mutual hatred of hunters and herdsmen,

129 Ellis, *Ewe*, 190.   130 Letourneau, *Guerre*, 92.
131 Paulitschke, *Nordost-Afr.*, I, 254, 263.
132 Reported in *Illust. Christian World,* March, 1897.
133 Godden, in JAI, XXVII, 13, note, 23, 24.
134 Carey and Tuck, *Chin Hills*, I, 167.
135 Finley, *Indians*, 79 ff.; Nadaillac, *Preh. Amer.*, 280.
136 §449, below.

tortured Hottentot prisoners, and big swords, set with sharks' teeth, were used by the Polynesians, not for battle, but for hacking captives to pieces.[137]

Many of the methods of primitive warfare seem to us cruel, unusual, and revolting—or did so prior to the late world-war in which they were completely outdone. One tribe in New Guinea set in the paths "small spikes of ironwood, about ten inches long, and steeped in the juice of some poisonous plant." These are to prevent the approach of enemies to their mountain retreat, and are imbedded so as to leave two or three inches of point, inclined at an angle of forty-five degrees and pointing toward the sea-coast. "These are placed in the native tracks a few feet apart, and are expertly hidden by twigs or leaves, but on any one walking upon them they penetrate right through the foot, being so finely pointed."[138] The Fans of Africa fix small poisoned spines along paths which their enemies are expected to take. They project from the ground just far enough to inflict a slight puncture. They have no idea of a *droit des gens* and regard any weapon as good enough provided it kills.[139] In India, among all the hill tribes, bamboo-spikes are stuck in the paths, especially during retreat, "precisely as among the inhabitants of New Guinea."[140]

The various forms of ruthlessness in warfare might be covered by the statement that any method is regarded as proper and right which secures the result desired. This was the sentiment of those who recently introduced flame-jets and poison-gas into modern warfare; it was not figured out beforehand that the latter was humane because it produced casualties rather than fatalities. Here, however, the point of real interest lies not in the unrestricted use of the first-best expedient but in the restriction upon such use which is found in practice, except among the very most backward of peoples. For war came to have its rules just as did hunting; war-laws and game-laws show, indeed, points of likeness. The use of poisoned arrows must once have been very common, even among the peoples from whom we derive our own civilization, as is attested by the etymology of the word "toxic," which is derived from the Greek term for "bow"; *toxicon pharmakon* was originally poison in which arrows were dipped.[141] Nevertheless, even in Homer's time, the employment of poison for such uses had almost passed away. It seems that unrestricted warfare has fallen short as an adjustment and has been selected away in greater or less degree, with the advance of civilization. It is parallel to the

[137] Hahn, in *Globus*, XVIII, 122; Ratzel, *Vkde.*, II, 157.
[138] Cayley-Webster, *New Guinea*, 214.
[139] Letourneau, *Guerre*, 68.
[140] Peal, in JAI, XXII, 252; Godden, in JAI, XXVII, 14.
[141] Tremearne, in JAI, XIV, 64; *Cent. Dict.*, *sub* "toxic."

renunciation of violence in favor of peaceful trade.[142] Now to be noticed are various cases of such restriction, which amount to instances of mildened or ameliorated strife and also of abbreviation of conflict.

All such expedients for making war less deadly are mores tending in the direction of peace between societies. Anything, in particular, which suspends the initiation of conflict, affords a chance, even though it be slight, of composing differences before resorting to violence. And there has gradually grown up a set of war-rules or war-mores which, while they may not deserve the name of chivalry, yet operate in the sense of giving the adversary a chance, or a fair field. Sometimes this is theoretic rather than practical, as where the Australians arm a white captive with spear and defensive staff, and set him up opposite their best spearsman, or as where the Indians' captive is set to run the gantlet. That there is a bare chance is undeniable, for prisoners have broken through the gantlet as they could not have broken away when chained to the torture-post. All such practices mitigate war. They are not mere empty sentiment, like much of mediæval chivalry, which tolerated all sorts of excesses when it came to the treatment of the unarmed masses. The sentiment and ideals of that chivalry were restricted in their field of application; their essentially grotesque character is burlesqued in Don Quixote. Primitive practices have the seriousness of tested expedients in a hard battle for life; they are not "chivalric" in the sentimental sense.

Instances of the declaration of war prior to attack, of the use of intermediaries, the prohibition of poisoned weapons, the negotiation of truces and other ameliorations, the enslavement of the vanquished, all witness to the tendency toward peace and challenge the sweeping statements concerning the essential belligerency of savages and their innate love of war. Often the conflict ceases as soon as several are killed or wounded, or when it can be shown that the losses are equal. Sometimes battles are reduced, as in the case of Menelaus and Paris, or David and Goliath, to duels between champions; the context of the former incident betrays weariness of war and a desire to avoid further loss and misery.[143]

---

142 §§76, 77, above.
143 Homer, *Iliad,* III, 84 ff.; §295, below.

Again, warfare is merely strife of words—boasting and mutual abuse, loud and relieving to the soul, but innocuous.

The Portuguese in India were able to make use of the native custom of sounding trumpets preparatory to attack; they took advantage of this habit without imitating it.[144] Of some of the wild tribes it is reported by an army officer: "I remember a challenge being conveyed by means of a piece of charred wood, a chilli, and a bullet tied together. This declaration of war was handed on from village to village, until it reached the one for which it was intended, where it was no sooner read than it was dispatched to me by a special messenger, who in turn brought with him a spear, a cloth, a fowl, and some eggs, the latter articles signifying their subordination and friendship to me, at whose hands they now begged for protection." The charred wood of the challenge was a threat of burning the village, and the chilli indicated the smarting, stinging nature of the punishment. Another challenge was "a piece of wood with a twisted bark collar at one end and a rope at the other, used for tying up dogs on the line of march," indicating that "a dog's treatment was in store for the unfortunate recipients of this truculent message."[145] A desire to lessen the evils of feud may be seen in the custom that "when the villagers are desirous of fighting, notice on the one side is invariably given; and . . . the date may be given, and a stand-up fight in the open agreed upon at a given place. In other cases, intimation is made to one village from another that its members from a certain time will be killed whenever an opportunity is found."[146]

In February, 1622, "when Tisquantum returned and the arrows were delivered, and the manner of the messenger's carriage related, he signified to the governor that to send the rattle-snake's skin in that manner imparted enmity—and that it was no better than a challenge."[147] This quotation recalls the familiar schoolbook story of the Indian declaration by arrows wrapped in rattle-snake skin, which was answered by the return of the skin filled with powder and shot.

The Caribs declared war by hurling arrows or javelins into the enemy country, or sticking them into the ground at the boundary. If the spear thus planted was later removed, there was nothing further to fear. "Here is repeated the ancient usage of the charred and bloody spear which the Romans used to cast into enemy territory as a declaration of war."[148]

The Romans resented the non-observance of the right behavior in war by the men of Veii, who went out to lay waste rather than "in the manner of just war." The Romans demanded reparation for injuries, and on refusal declared war for the thirtieth day from that day. The formula for declaring war was elaborate, solemn, and ceremonious, containing much alliteration, many obsolescent words, frequent repetitions of verbs of almost the same meaning. Then came the spear-casting.[149]

Among the poisoned weapons the chief are arrows, and among these the

---

[144] Whiteway, *Portuguese Power*, 27-28.

[145] Woodthorpe, in J A I, XI, 71.　　　[146] Godden, in J A I, XXVII, 13.

[147] Winslow, "New England," in *Mass. Hist. Coll.*, VIII, 240.

[148] Von Martius, *Beiträge*, I, 97; Livy, *Hist.*, I, 32; Vergil, *Æneid*, IX, 52, 53.

[149] Livy, *Hist.*, I, 15, 22, 32.

darts used in the blow-gun. These are so light and small—a few inches long and a small fraction of an inch in thickness—as to inflict but slight damage in themselves. They are commonly tipped with some deadly poison. The blow-gun is found in two main localities: in the Malay Archipelago and environs, and in tropical South America. The Borneans shoot darts to the distance of twenty yards with great rapidity as well as accuracy, but the lightness of the arrow prevents much extension of this range. "On a calm day the utmost range may be a hundred yards." "A Sakai clever in the use of it will put five darts out of six into a common playing card at fifty yards distance."[150] The poisons used are generally expressed from certain plants by secret and cere-monious processes, and are very quick-working and deadly, requiring only a few minutes to kill a man who has been even superficially scratched by the dart.

Markham[151] in his list of Amazon tribes cites many that are cannibalistic, many that are warlike, not a few that are peaceable, and a number that use poisoned arrows. Unregulated warfare is typical. It is not always clear that the poisoned weapons are used in war as well as in hunting; Letourneau[152] says that the American tribes which use the blow-gun and poisoned arrows ordinarily abstain from them in war, for they do not wish to exterminate each other. But it is probable that no such distinction was made at all generally, especially in warfare with utter aliens. Poisoning food or the wells is a strata-gem to be found here and there, as in Tibet; here a poison-ordeal finally ends a protracted feud. Two bowls of food are set out, and representatives of the two tribes eat. The tribe whose representative eats the poison is held to have been in the wrong.[153]

Such methods have dropped out of the mores of most advanced peoples; and some primitive tribes show a distaste for them. They are rare even in New Guinea. It is evident enough that the majority of the peoples who use ruthless methods on this order are backward in civilization, and that the practice has long been frowned upon by those who have developed any sense of interna-tional rights and law.

The negroes of the African Lakes region despise the bow; for it is the lower tribes of their neighborhood who use it and poisoned arrows. The Tuareg never poison their arrows, and stop fighting after several have been killed or wounded.[154] The Code of Manu prohibited the king from striking "with weapons concealed (in wood), nor with (such as are) barbed, poisoned, or the points of which are blazing with fire."[155] In Homer,[156] where the bow is held in some contempt as somewhat the weapon of a coward, Odysseus is repre-sented as trying to get poison for his arrows from a man in Ephyre, but the

150 Roth, *Sarawak,* II, 187; Hale, in JAI, XV, 289.
151 In JAI, XL, 73 ff.   152 *Guerre,* 533.
153 Reid, in *Cosmopolitan Mag.,* XXVIII, 448.
154 Letourneau, *Guerre,* 81, 261-262.   155 Buehler, *Manu,* VII, 90.
156 *Odyssey,* I, 260-263, IV, 242; Keller, *Hom. Soc.,* 60, 298; Sophocles, *Aias,* 1120 ff.; Schrader, *Aryans,* 226.

latter would not give it, "since, of course, he reverenced the ever-living gods." Tylor[157] mentions this case, which is the only one of poisoned weapons in Homer, along with others, as an instance of amelioration of war-methods.

In the treatment of the conquered, men begin with the same sort of ruthlessness. It appears "that savages in the lowest known scale make no slaves, but eat or sacrifice their captives, that tribes who have made some advance in the arts, even without becoming husbandmen, commence to make slaves of prisoners of war, and that agricultural tribes make slavery an institution."[158]

The ferocity of the ancient Hebrews in accord with Jahweh's orders,[159] has seldom been exceeded. "In the early days of the Dahomi kingdom, massacres such as might well rival those mentioned in the Old Testament, as taking place under similar circumstances, used to follow every successful contest."[160] Africa shows special devices for decapitating prisoners of war, "and a more ghastly spectacle could not possibly be seen anywhere."[161] In western Borneo, the methods of war are "extremely barbaric: all men, old women, and small children are killed and their heads carried along as trophies, while the young women, girls, and boys are doomed to slavery. All portable goods are seized and what can not be carried off is given over to the flames."[162] "Dyak warfare does not spare the men and rarely the women. Heads are more valuable than captives, but they do sometimes take the women and children prisoners and reduce them to slavery."[163] Ariovistus declared to Cæsar that "by right of war the conqueror was free to dispose of the conquered at his pleasure";[164] and both Greeks and Romans were not altogether above deliberate destruction of cities and ruthless massacres of entire populations. "The normal fate of the captive, which, among barbarians, had been death, was, in civilized antiquity, slavery; but many thousands were condemned to the gladiatorial shows, and the vanquished general was commonly slain in the Mamertine prison, while his conqueror ascended in triumph to the Capitol."[165] By way of striking contrast: "Never did conquerors go farther in tolerance and moderation toward the conquered than did the Arabs of Spain. From the tenth century Arabic was the common language of Mussulmans, Jews, and Christians. Mixed marriages were frequent, in spite of the opposition of the clergy."[166] It has been seen[167] that slavery once formed an adjustment taking the place of indiscriminate slaughter, one which has had its day of expediency and has now been superseded. Among many tribes there was also the device of tribal adoption. "The Angoni raided and made slaves in every direction, marrying

[157] *Anth.*, 221-222.   [158] Roth, in JAI, XVI, 127.
[159] Num., XXXI; Deut., III, 3-11; XX, 6-19; XXI, 8-17; Josh., VIII, 16-27; X, 40, 42; I Sam., XVIII, 17-25; Judges, IV, 10-20; Tiele-Gehrich, *Gchte. Relig.*, I, 277.
[160] Ellis, *Ewe*, 120.   [161] Lloyd, *Cannibal Country*, 350.
[162] Veth, *Borneo's Wester-Afdeeling*, II, 289.
[163] Roth, in JAI, XXII, 57.   [164] Cæsar, *Bell. Gall.*, I, 36.
[165] Lecky, *Europ. Morals*, II, 256-257.
[166] Renan, *Averroès*, 174.   [167] Ch. X, above.

the women captured, and keeping the men to help them fight. . . . All captured people and their offspring are admitted into the tribe and called Angoni, and now only the chiefs remain of pure Angoni blood, and only the old men can talk the language. . . . The Angoni have freely intermarried with the women of conquered tribes, and the offspring naturally learn to a great extent when young the language of the mother."[168] In the Congo, "the bodies of enemies are carried when possible from the field and eaten at a general feast. If the prisoners are not redeemed they become slaves, and while young ones may be amalgamated with their conquerors and eventually become part of the families of their owners, the elder ones who have their own tribal marks well defined take nothing but a servile position in the town of their new masters."[169] In these cases we see adoption as a sort of modification of existing slavery. In America, where the agricultural economy was much less developed, the natives were wont to replace their losses in battle by having their women select from among the prisoners substitutes for members of their families who had met their deaths. When an Osage war party took a captive, "anyone who had lost a child or who was without children could adopt the captive to fill the vacant place. After the ceremony the person became an Osage in all respects as one born in the tribe and was subject to the duties and requirements of the family into which he entered by a kind of new birth. . . . When all were assembled the captive was brought and placed in the back part of the lodge opposite the entrance, the seat of the stranger. Then the ritual used at the initiation and naming of a child born in the tribe was given. . . . The letting of blood symbolized that the captive lost the blood and kinship of the tribe into which he had been born. All trace of his former birth was removed by the washing away of the blood. . . . He was then given food by those who led the tribe in the hunt when the food supply was obtained. The new blood made by the Osage food was thus made Osage blood." It was further explained that the drama "means to represent the death of the captive not only to the people of his birth but to his past life, and his rebirth into the family of the Osage who saved him and 'made' him 'to live' by adopting him."[170]

Adoption was the alternative to burning and torture, and generally admitted the adopted into full rights,[171] though Parkman,[172] speaking of the fate of captives, says the Indians burned six and "adopted, or rather, enslaved the rest." "It was an Iroquois custom to use captives to assist their women in the labors of the field, in carrying burdens, and in doing general menial labor; but when a captive proved himself possessed of what, in their judgment, constituted manly qualities, then he was fully adopted and admitted to all the privileges of an Iroquois."[173] These people paid considerable attention to agriculture but had not yet developed genuine enslavement.[174]

Adoption as a system appears to be antecedent to slavery. It made an enemy at once into a friend. Hence the passage already quoted:[175] "Slavery in any shape or form is unknown; between friend and foe there is no intermediate

[168] Stigand, in JAI, XXXIX, 35, 36, 38.
[169] Weeks, in JAI, XL, 415.
[170] Fletcher and LaFlesche, in BAE, XXVII, 61-62.
[171] Hewitt, "Adoption," in HAI, I, 15-16.
[172] Old Régime, 24.
[173] Carr, in Smithson. Rep., 1891, 517.   [174] §188, below.
[175] Jenness and Ballentyne, D'Entrecasteaux, 66.

status," is still in point. Adoption provided no such intermediate status; it is, in fact, so far as higher political organization is concerned, an expedient distinctly inferior to enslavement.[176] The Iroquois, it will be noted, practised some trial-slavery prior to adoption, but the situation was evidently not ripe for such variations.

It is naturally impossible to follow the evolution of the rules in mitigation of war through the history of particular primitive tribes, for that history is not available; there is seldom even a short consecutive record. It is evident, nevertheless, that the tendency, beginning with very backward peoples, is toward variation away from utter unregulation and toward a selection that preserves such departures as more expedient adjustments. The passage of hostile relations into those of trade, together with the tendency of exchange to limit hostilities, has already been illustrated.[177] It cannot be thought that any conscious revulsion produced these results; they were unconsciously utilitarian, as the results of the evolutionary process generally are. Further evidence is afforded by the various operations connected with the making and maintenance of peace.

§142*. The Drift toward Peace. Peace-making after war takes many forms which may be briefly illustrated; they are largely ritual and symbolical, and regularly express a strong intent to keep the peace in future. That the intentions, which often seem to be entirely genuine, are no measure of the consequences, is to be expected. Men have to learn how to keep the peace; it has not been given to them, here or elsewhere, in the past or now, to accomplish such matters by the mere act of wishing. They must know how to realize their purposes by overcoming and neutralizing the war-producing factors. Peace-making seems usually to be attended by expressions of relief and special ceremonies of amity.

In Australia, "the renewal of friendly relations between tribes is always marked by a corroboree. When tribes corroboree, it is a gage of peace; and peace is, as far as I know, ratified in no other way. A quarrel between two associated tribes is usually brought to an end by an invitation to a fight, which almost certainly ends in a corroboree."[178] There is even a special ceremony the reason for which is that all the tribes in a district may meet and settle

176 §§186, 188, below.　　　　177 §76, above.
178 Curr, *Aust. Race*, I, 92.

any disputes that may have arisen since the last ceremony.[179] In New Guinea, "if they want to make peace, they send arrows into the hostile village or shoot them into the air in sight of the enemy or break them. Green twigs in the hands indicate the same intention."[180] Some of the Kaffirs divide the body of an enemy, after a victory, with the conquered, performing certain ceremonies over it; then the combatants may visit each other in peace.[181]

In northeast India peace was possible when both parties in a blood-feud had suffered equal loss; but "until each of the opposing parties had lost an equal number, peace was impossible."[182] Smoking—the "dance of the Calumet"—sealed a North American peace. A god guarded military pacts and punished infractions.[183] In the Northwest, hostages are given as a token of good faith. "These are obliged to eat with their left hands for a certain period, as they carried weapons in the right hand during combat. Each hostage has two companions of equal rank assigned to him by the tribe which holds him." On landing from the canoe in which he came, "the hostage threw himself flat on his back in the shallow water, according to the custom of the country, and continued in this posture till some of our people arrived who were sent to lift him up and conduct him." The treaties of peace were generally ratified by feasts and elaborate ceremonies often lasting many days.[184] Among two New England tribes the usual ceremonies for making peace were as follows: "(1) a marriage was contracted between a brave of the challenging people and a maiden of the challenged people. This was regarded as a type of perpetual future good will. (2) A feast lasting two months was celebrated nightly; and (3) games of ball, canoe and foot races and other sports were carried on. After such ceremonies were over no breach of a treaty is on record, not even a single murder."[185]

Herodotus[186] tells of two tribes who, after a treaty of peace, sealed it by mutually pricking their arms and sucking the drops of blood. This custom of instituting blood-brotherhood will be further illustrated presently. The Greek word for "treaty" means "pourings" or "drink-offerings." According to Livy,[187] when the Albans and Romans made peace, a pig was killed, as a sort of foundation-sacrifice,[188] with a stone, and the abortive attempt to settle the issues of the Trojan War included a similar sacrifice.[189]

It is not enough to wish for peace or to swear solemnly that it shall not be broken; there are certain practices, allied to those which mitigate war, which are well calculated to prevent hostilities from beginning. These are in the main taboos,[190] backed by ghost-fear, which effect the neutralization of certain times, places, and persons. Waste strips of land, uninhabited, though containing

[179] Howitt, in JAI, XX, 84.
[180] Krieger, *Neu-Guinea*, 324.
[181] Tyler, in *Ill. Afr.* for December, 1895.
[182] Godden, in JAI, XXVII, 40.
[183] Letourneau, *Guerre*, 160-161; Hewitt, "Calumet," in HAI, I, 191-195.
[184] Niblack, in USNM, 1888, 343.
[185] Leland and Prince, *Kulóskap*, 27.
[186] *Hist.*, I, 74.
[187] *Hist.*, I, 24.
[188] §297, below.
[189] Homer, *Iliad*, III, 260 ff.
[190] Ch. XXXI, below.

traces of destroyed villages, serve as "marches" between tribal territories.[191] There are instances where fighting is allowed only during certain hours of the day, days of the week or month, or months of the year. Forms of greeting serve to identify those who have friendly relations.[192] Women, children, and special function-aries are inviolable, and can be employed as ambassadors; children are even raised and trained to be tribal intermediaries. Roads may be neutralized and asylums provided; markets and festivals are tabooed to violence, and holy places and days are set apart for peace. The function of trade in the limitation of war can scarcely be overestimated.[193] Then there is the house-peace, woman-peace, temple-peace, god-peace, king's peace, and also safe-conduct for emissaries connected with any of these. All such usages represent extension of the peace-group; they are really incipient state-building. Beginning with the family, there is a series of constantly enlarging groups which prohibit violence inside as a condition of coherence and the presentation of a united front to the enemy.[194] Intermarrying South American tribes, we are told, always remain at peace with each other.[195] Inter-group arrangements for the mitigation of violence and unrestricted ferocity, however incom-plete they may be, are outreachings beyond narrower boundaries, which ultimately expand the cramped limits of the primitive peace-bond to include considerable portions of mankind.

"Plentiful food and peace," said the Omaha sages, "are necessary to the prosperity of the tribe"; and they spent anxious care in working for both. They did not simply orate; they inculcated all the traditional safeguards of which they knew. "The old Omaha men, who are the authority for the inter-pretations of tribal rites and customs contained in this memoir, have earnestly sought to impress upon the writers that peace and order within the tribe were of prime importance; without these it was declared neither the people nor the tribe as an organization could exist. War was secondary; its true function was protective—to guard the people from outside enemies. Aggressive warfare was to be discouraged; any gains made by it were more than offset by the troubles entailed. It was recognized that it was difficult to restrain young men; there-fore restrictions were thrown about predatory warfare, that all who went on

---

[191] Torday and Joyce, in JAI, XXXVII, 143.
[192] Dundas, C., in JAI, LI, 276.
[193] Lippert, *Kgchte.*, I, 459; a boy-intermediary appears in Homer, *Odys-sey*, XXI, 20-21.
[194] Keller, *War to Peace*, chs. VII, IX, X.
[195] Markham, in JAI, XL, 130.

the warpath should first secure permission, while the special honors accorded
to those whose brave acts were performed in defense of the tribe tended to
make war secondary to peace."[196]

There is a term "eirenicism," or "peace-ism," which is not pacifism but connotes a genuine reaction from war. It might be used
to cover such expedients in war-prevention. It is a bond of custom
or convention to limit militarism or to make gaps in it. It includes
the esoteric or in-group peace-bond and also the exoteric conventions, with the out-group, which are continually invading the
domain of militarism—beginning with peaceful access[197] to fire,
water, and supplies, passing through *commercium* and *connubium*,
and emerging in an emphasis upon the moral efforts of peace-pacts
and group-concurrence as contrasted with those of strife and war.

As the result of a preliminary adjudication of differences by
violence, or of some other antecedent, tribes are to be found over
the earth which have united with one another in a peace-bond.
Despite the legends which inveterately endeavor to link such a
league with the name of some mythical founder, it is not at all
probable that a savage could plan any such expedient.

The end of a movement, says Lippert,[198] is not its purpose; and he goes on to
show that the raw necessities of life are most easily got by organization. How
then can a relation between hostile and mutually suspicious tribes be founded?
Only, is the answer, by a rite appealing to what was to be an even higher
unity than that of blood, which was the only unity conceived of by the most
primitive people. This rite was religious and resulted in the various taboos on
places and times just alluded to: the temple-peace, peace of God, house-peace,
market-peace, church-peace, holiday-peace. Christianity is conceived of as the
universal unifier of mankind.

It is true that peace-bonds, whatever their real basis, are regularly sanctioned by religion. Exogamy and exchange lay nearer
the basis of things, however, and each of them meant the necessity
of stopping quarrels by treaties of intermarriage and trade.
Guest-friendship, often an adjunct to trade, has an astonishing
prevalence around the earth.[199] What are encountered are agreements between tribes, to which they have been gradually and automatically stressed in the course of adjustment, because living

[196] Fletcher and LaFlesche, in BAE, XXVII, 211-212.
[197] §76, above; Lippert, *Kgchte.*, I, 619-620.
[198] *Kgchte.*, II, 359, 360; I, 267, II, 26, 559.
[199] §§150, 151, below.

could be better accomplished under peace than under war. Mention and illustration of such agreements anticipates somewhat the subject-matter of the next chapter; they are transitional forms between antagonisms and associations.

For instance, there is in Borneo a peace-making "which is not a fraternisation, but only an agreement not to kill each other on unprovoked raids."[200] In northern Sumatra, the chief seeks to keep the peace by offering whatever satisfaction is possible. An interesting example of survival follows upon the success of his efforts, for the projected burning of houses by the injured party is carried out symbolically. A hut of light material is set on fire amidst the loud shouts of the avengers. Although each knows that the conflagration is a pure stage performance, they attach much importance to the fact that it has happened in earnest; for later it can be said to the inhabitants of surrounding communities: "Did you see the smoke rising from the house of X? Yes, we are no Nias slaves or Klings that we should allow ourselves to be injured without vengeance through genuine indemnification!"[201]

One of the most remarkable of the peace-bonds is that formed by the Iroquois and attributed to Hiawatha. We shall see more of the organization of the League of the Iroquois later on;[202] for now we are interested chiefly in its pacific aims. "It was the boast of the Iroquois that the great object of their confederacy was peace; to break up the spirit of perpetual warfare, which had wasted the red race from age to age. . . . The duty of living in harmony and peace, of avoiding evil speaking, of kindness to the orphan, of charity to the needy and of hospitality to all, would be among the prominent topics brought under consideration" in the exhortations at festivals.[203] "In pursuance of Hiawatha's original purpose, when the league was firmly established, envoys were sent to other tribes to urge them to join it, or at least to become allies. One of these embassies penetrated to the distant Cherokees, the hereditary enemies of the Iroquois nations. For some reason that does not appear, perhaps the natural suspicion or vindictive pride of that powerful community, this mission was a failure. Another, sent to the western Algonkins, had better success. A strict alliance was formed with the far-spread Ojibway tribes, and was maintained inviolate for at least two hundred years, until at last the influence of the French, with the sympathy of the Ojibways for the conquered Hurons, undid to some extent, though not entirely, this portion of Hiawatha's work. . . . The territory of the Iroquois, constantly extending as their united strength made itself felt, became the 'Great Asylum' of the Indian tribes." Fragments of tribes fled to them. The name of the league appears to mean "Great Peace." The Iroquois Book of Rites shows them as "a kindly and affectionate people, full of sympathy for their friends in distress, considerate of their women, tender to their children, anxious for peace." The Iroquois struck at the root of most Indian wars—individual murders, followed by revenge—by prohibiting wars for such cause between any of their cantons. "So effective was this provision of their constitution that for more than three cen-

[200] Furness, *Head-Hunters*, 128.
[201] Snouck-Hurgronje, *Atjèhers*, I, 81, 83.
[202] §188, below.
[203] Morgan, *League of Iroq.*, 91, 190.

turies this main cause of Indian wars was rendered innocuous, and the 'Great Peace' remained undisturbed." "Covenant chain," or "Chain of Friendship," was the Iroquois expression for the treaty of union. Their wampum belt had on it a line which was a "peace-path" from one tribe to another.[204]

Smaller peace-bonds were organized here and there, after destructive wars. Two New England tribes, at a general council, decided that "as long as the sun rises and sets, as long as the great lakes send their waters to the sea, so long should peace reign over the two tribes."[205] The chiefs of the Omahas, "being the civil and religious leaders of the people, cannot serve as captains or even as subordinate officers of a war party. . . . Their influence is exerted on the side of peace, and they try to save the lives of murderers. They conduct peace negotiations between contending tribes." War-parties are generally organized by individuals who drum up an expedition.[206] The doctrine of the Ghost-Dance Religion forbade war, and it created a tremendous and radical change in the whole spirit of savage life. The prophet's "teaching is accepted and his words obeyed by four-fifths of all the warlike predatory tribes of the mountains and the great plains. Only those who have known the deadly hatred that once animated Ute, Cheyenne, and Pawnee, one toward another, and are able to contrast it with their present spirit . . . can know what the ghost-dance religion has accomplished in bringing the savage into civilization. It is such a revolution as comes but once in the life of a race."[207]

In South America too there are powerful peoples who have gained ascendancy over their neighbors. "They smoothe over the strifes between the weaker, and are the guarantors of peace.[208]

There were two great federations in Gaul and fraternal alliances that were not broken save for weighty reasons. Even after a rupture, remembrance rendered war less bloody. These leagues were formed under peril of Roman domination, and Cæsar[209] worked one against the other to accomplish his ends.

If we put together what we have learned about the mitigation of war and the measures to prevent and limit it, we see that there has been a persistent drift toward peace. This becomes the clearer when one considers the progressive increase in the size of the peace-group. The degree to which war could be excluded at any time has always been a question of how large a body of people could become an in-group. Far back in the evolutionary series the family seems to have been the largest peace-group; then as civilization increased kin-associations took on greater scope. The clan or gens, composed of a number of families, and at length the tribe, composed of several clans or gentes, appear as peace-groups of a wider comprehensiveness. At length comes the nation, which might

[204] Hale, *Iroq. Rites,* 32 ff., 37, 68, 70.
[205] Leland and Prince, *Kulóskap,* 27.
[206] Dorsey, in BAE, III, 217, 315.
[207] Mooney, in BAE, XIV, 783. [208] Von Martius, *Beiträge,* I, 57.
[209] *Bell. Gall.,* I, ch. VII; Letourneau, *Guerre,* 491-493.

be figured as a super-peace-group including all the rest. The kinship-bond is lost somewhere along the evolutionary course and the territorial state emerges as the largest in-group known in human history.

For several centuries back the sentiment against war has been growing. Its tragedies have been recounted[210] and programs for its abolition have been formulated. They always look to the extension of the peace-group and take the form of leagues or associations of nations. They all provide for such reconciliation of conflicting interests as the smaller, national peace-group has succeeded in effecting between its constituent elements. They aim at that mutual understanding and acceptance of a common code which are characteristic of the smaller in-group; and those nations which are incapable of adhering to the code common to civilization are excluded until they demonstrate their capacity. An unparalleled impetus has been given to the effort to extend the peace-group by the late war which, involving as it did almost the whole civilized world in hostilities and all mankind in its consequences, has convinced serious men that civilization may not survive another general conflict. They are fain to echo the "Never again!" of the soldier. No one of the nations engaged in this war was eager to claim credit for starting it; not one admitted that it had deliberately planned and prepared for hostilities; on the contrary, one and all made haste to disavow such responsibility. Honest men who still call for swollen budgets for army and navy talk only of defense and peace at any (economic) price, for the admittedly enormous outlay is interpreted as an insurance premium—an evil, indeed, but preferable, under the necessity of choosing between two evils, to the hazard of war, with its crushing calamities. There is no quarrel between such persons and those who advocate the now functioning League of Nations as to the undesirability of war; they unite in decrying it and differ only as to the proper policy to adopt. The advocates of the League want to extend the peace-group and in-group, while the others, not believing that possible or advisable, wish to strengthen their own in-group against outsiders. The case will be worked out within the life-time

210 Grotius, *De Jure*, bk. III, ch. IV.

of many now living; but it is not going too far to contend that the trend of evolution is toward the extension of the peace-group.[211]

One of the most serious barriers to understanding between nations is language. Unconsciously men have surmounted it to some extent by adopting a "pidgin"-tongue or by conceding the use in international relations of one or more of the existing languages. There has been put forth a strenuous endeavor to construct some "universal language." Meanwhile the cinema has come in as a partial solvent of the difficulty by reason of its appeal to the eye instead of the ear; it breaks down the barriers that confront both the monolingual and the illiterate. A moment's reflection will reveal the menace to linguistic barriers from the rising importance of broadcasting devices.

§143. The Services of War. A modern advocate of war shows himself to be of the same ilk as a present-day defender of slavery; he is supporting an institution that is recognized by public opinion to be undesirable. Even slavery, however, was not always unpopular and a maladjustment; it performed unique services for civilization in its day. The same is true of war. As in the one case, so in the other, he who wants to know the truth must set aside his personal opinions of the institution in its modern phase and view it in the setting of its era of popularity and unquestioned competency. The fact deserves reiteration that war, now a last resort, was once the only recourse for the settlement of both important issues and those that merely seemed to be important. War, last resort or not, then or now, has always been effective; that point should not be allowed to escape. Something was actually accomplished by an undoubted display of energy. Often this was not what people set out to do; nevertheless, during the course of the conflict they have often lost sight of their original aims and have come to believe that they had got, in the end, what they were after.

It is manifest from foregoing evidence that primitive warfare was not so destructive of human life as one has often been given to understand. Battle-casualties were frequently insignificant— the loss of five in a fight "would mean a serious disaster"—[212] and non-combatants were generally spared. The relentless ferocity of the Old Testament warriors or their god should not color ideas of all savage warfare. What destructiveness there was resembled the

[211] Keller, *War to Peace*, chs. IX, X.
[212] Jenness and Ballentyne, *D'Entrecasteaux*, 85.

havoc wrought in nature by the struggle for existence. In fact, primitive warfare was not so bad a way of settling conflicts of interest as we, with the shattering tragedies of modern conflicts in mind, are wont to imagine. And it must be realized that the savage, with his distinctly lower valuation of human life and harboring no idea of its "sacredness," did not view slaughter with the revulsion and horror felt by civilized man. Nor was savage warfare counter-selective as the modern type is said to be.[213] All the males, not the selected physical types alone, were exposed to danger; and strength, speed, keenness of vision, and other superior qualities advantaged their possessors as they do not under the conditions of mass-fighting.

Doubtless the destruction of property was often thorough, but even so it could not approach the desolation wrought by a modern army. War was defensive of what had been gained as well as offensive; it was often only by fighting that encroachment could be prevented and peace secured. Says Livingstone,[214] who can certainly not be accused of lack of Christianity:

"The pugnacious spirit is one of the necessities of life. When people have little or none of it, they are subjected to indignity and loss. My own men walk into houses, where we pass the nights, without asking any leave, and steal cassava without shame. I have to threaten and thrash, to keep them honest, while if we are at a village where the natives are a little pugnacious they are as meek as sucking doves. The peace plan involves indignity and wrong."

For nature-peoples, at any rate, pacifism was a maladjustment. Well-being and enlightenment lead men to fight for peace;[215] it is never so much valued as under anarchy and barbarism, and the desire for it has regularly led to preparedness for war.

War, because it could stimulate enthusiasm, has contributed positively to the development of many things which we are accustomed to consider expedient and desirable. There is no question of the intense interest involved in it. Brinton[216] calls war "the most potent excitant known to all the faculties." It has laid hold of the emotions and has thus moved men, through their fears, their hopes, and their vanity, to strenuous activity. "A society needs to have a ferment in it; sometimes an enthusiastic delusion or an

---

213 Schallmayer, *Vererbung,* 111 ff.   214 *Last Journal,* 474.
215 Gumplowicz, *Soc.,* 126.   216 *Races,* 76.

adventurous folly answers the purpose."[217] Eagerness to win has put spur to ingenuity and war's necessity has been a prolific mother of invention. It has developed individual talent and has differentiated men according to their bravery, executive ability, and other qualities. It is therefore an agency that has revealed inequality and given to variations the chance to prove themselves. Then the results, both in the development of processes and of men, have been carried over into peace-times, constituting a perennial contribution of the arts of war to those of peace. Those who have come to the front in the testing-time of war, for instance the war-chief, have managed to hold their power when the war was over.[218] The more material contributions of war to peace are less discernible in primitive times because war was not so far removed from industry; the tool and the weapon were often one and the same implement. Upon later stages of evolution the contributions of war, when attention is once called to them, are so manifest as to need but brief illustration.[219] Over and over again men would have gone on putting up with inconvenience, incompleteness, and imperfection but for the fact that the need of defense forced them by a powerful motive toward better adjustments.

In history the military inventions have led the way and have been afterwards applied to industry. Chemical finds were made in the attempt to produce combinations which would be destructive in war; we owe some of our most useful substances to discoveries which were made in this effort. The skill of artisans has been developed in making weapons, and then that skill has been available for industry. The big machines which the ancients made were chiefly battering-rams, catapults, and other engines of war. The construction of these things familiarized men with mechanical devices which were capable of universal application. Gunpowder was discovered in the attempt to rediscover Greek fire; it was a grand invention in military art but we should never have had our canals, railroads, and other great works without such explosives. Again, we are indebted to the chemical experiments in search of military agents for our friction-matches. New England roads were much improved during the period when coast-wise traffic was imperilled by the British; inns multiplied, and shops of various artisans, such as blacksmiths and wheelwrights, appeared along the roads. "So that, besides liberty and independence, the United States will derive this advantage from the war, that commerce and population will be greatly increased, and that lands, which had long remained barren, have been so successfully cultivated, as to prevent them

217 Sumner, *Coll. Ess.*, I, 33. 218 §§155, 156, below.
219 Harbord, "The Army as a Career," in *Atl. Mo.*, CXXXII, 337-339.

from being again abandoned."[220] The newspapers[221] have recorded, since the late war, plenty of examples of the contribution of the arts of war to those of peace: we are told that poison-gas has medicinal qualities; that tear-gas assists in making arrests of desperate characters; that the aeroplane has become useful in locating schools of fish and forest-fires, as well as in sprinkling arsenate of lead over insect-infected areas; that tanks are employed to cut the way for roads; that the ground-telephone, or geophone, "can be effectively used to rescue entombed miners, locate mine fire areas, and reduce accidents through blasting"; that a fog-making apparatus, devised to render ships invisible to the enemy is now being adapted to keep frost away from fruit-trees and to kill such pests as grasshoppers; and so on. The "Army's Chemical Branch Has Turned Attention to Pursuits of Peace with Success" is announced in a headline. The Chief of the Chemical Warfare Service of the United States Army is reported as declaring, in the course of an address: "In 1915 on Flanders fields gas was used as a deadly weapon to mow down men by the thousands. Today instead of human lungs being the target, it is waging war on the germs. . . . If the future vindicates the indications of the present, and we have no cause for doubt, it is believed that this chlorine gas will save in peace more lives each year than gas destroyed in the entire World War."[222] The stress of war-necessity resulted in an improvement of flying-craft and of the tractor that years of peace might not have brought about, and then they were handed back to peace-times in their advanced state.

There is no doubt that war imposed discipline and put a premium on fortitude;[223] the loss of power to fight goes, as in the case of the later Romans, with civic degeneration. War intensifies societal organization; it develops political institutions and classes. And the more highly organized society has produced gains for all its members, including the oppressed and their posterity. War sets in relief the national bonds of unity by reconciling lesser interests in the interest of the whole; as in Holland, so elsewhere, "discord was the greatest among us, as a rule, in times of truce or peace."[224] Patriotism and sympathy for the rest of the in-group develop more fully under pressure. Oliveira Martins[225] goes so far as to say that "life is a strife; war is the living fountain from which the entire society is derived . . . it is certainly the origin of civil institutions." He thinks even religion came out of war. We take no such position, and feel that this author has exaggerated the selective function of war into a creative one; but there is no doubt that war powerfully influenced the structure of society by the

[220] Chastellux, *Travels in N. Amer.*, II, 55 note.
[221] N. Y. *Times*, June 20, July 1, Aug. 30, Nov. 12, 1923; Jan. 31, 1924.
[222] N. Y. *Times*, February 15, 1925.   [223] Tylor, *Anth.*, 226.
[224] Van Duyl, *Beschavingsgeschied.*, 190.
[225] *Raças*, II, 55, 59 ff.

introduction, following conquest, of ranks and classes and of higher organization in general. The development of slavery as a consequence of war set in motion the profoundest consequences. War dissolved whatever primitive equality there was, and introduced social inequality, discipline, and organization. The Eskimo are practically all equal, for they do not fight much; in South America, when the natives obtained the horse and could get at one another, fighting and the beginning of differentiation appeared. Where no one submits to anyone else in time of peace, war brings about, at least temporarily, a social gradation.[226] War is the greatest enemy of social equality; "it works among the tillers in the same direction and with the same force as among the hunters and herders."[227] Now this very recognition of inequality is an adjustment to the facts of life; it allows the fitter to get their deserts and stimulates individual initiative.

If there had been no war, it is quite probable that exogamy and the father-family, which constitute preconditions to further development,[228] would not have developed so widely; and war, as a phase of contact with others, was at least more favorable to the development of culture than was utter isolation. This can be seen in the Middle Ages, and in particular in the Crusades.[229] War and conquest, if they do not actually make the state, create more complex states and more comprehensive societies, and the larger combinations render possible enterprises of greater scope. Conflict stabilizes the societal forms and so is the source of political power.[230] It has fostered deliberation concerning group-interests involved and fathered deliberative assemblies.[231] It concentrates and solidifies the regulative organization, for cohesion within is indispensable to defense or offense. It is because the stresses of war have had so much to do with the evolution of the regulative organization that we prefer to come up to that topic by way of a review of war.

This is no panegyric of war; it is a recognition of the demonstrable services of a rough and crude instrumentality. There is

---

[226] Letourneau, *Polit.*, 55-63.   [227] Grosse, *Familie,* 137.

[228] Chs. XLV and LVI, below.

[229] Debacq, *Libéraux et Démagogues,* 44.

[230] Ratzenhofer, *Soc. Erkennt.*, 248.

[231] Spencer, *Prin. Soc.*, II, §§491, 493.

nothing gained in the way of enlightenment by emulating the much-defamed ostrich in this matter. Many an obsolescent practice has shown a similar effectiveness in its day. The services of armed conflict have been stated first; they long assured it survival-value; having them in mind, one can the more intelligently estimate the qualities which the substitutes for war must have shown, and must continue to show, in order to replace it to a considerable and increasing degree. When one realizes what power war has had, and what it has accomplished as the primordial factor in societal selection, he will not be taken in by sentimental projects designed, with excellent intentions but feeble understanding, to do away with the primitive instrumentality.

§144. **Militarism and Industrialism.** Protracted warfare breeds a state of mind and a set of mores and institutions that Spencer[232] summed up under the term militarism. Opposed to this type in his well-known analysis is the industrial type of society, or industrialism. The contrast between the two should be recalled partly to exhibit the results of warfare and partly by way of indicating the nature of the set of adjustments which has replaced violence and the militaristic system. The antagonisms between herding and tillage, and between war and trade, are prototypes of those existing between militarism and industrialism. Hunting is so like fighting that no vital inconsistency appears between them; and a good deal of fighting accompanies cattle-raising, which itself is the offspring of hunting. The first typical industrialism comes with agriculture, for here, as we have seen, the population takes on qualities and mores quite distinct from those of hunting and herding peoples; it is sedentary, industrious, peaceable, provident, perhaps softer of fiber and more under feminine influence, and less courageous; and it has developed characteristic institutions, such as slavery, private property in land, and the state.[233] As it presents nothing to offset the excitement of hunting or of nomadic life, it seems dull and base in comparison.[234] Agriculture is a considerable variant from the other types of self-maintenance and as

232 *Prin. Soc.,* II, pt. V, ch. XVII.
233 §§31, 103, 118, above, and 187, below.
234 Peschel, *Races,* 428.

such has its characteristic set of mores. It is more intolerant of war; and when industry and trade have developed upon it as a foundation, the antagonism increases. War declines when the booty is not worth the harm of interfering with industry and commerce.

"There are two classes of deities worshipped in Borneo which are, if I may be pardoned the colloquial expression, not on speaking terms with each other. They are the tutelary spirits of war and of agriculture. Tuppa, the harvest god of one tribe, is, they say, of so pure and gentle a nature that he cannot endure the fierce gods of war, and will come to no feast where they are invoked." War and rice-culture do not get on well together; "these two are more or less incompatible, requiring different manner of life, different laws and customs, different organization of society, and different personal qualifications. . . . The warpath leads to domination of the fighting men; agriculture to greater importance of the women, who do most of the farm work."[235] There is an element of insight in the remark of Mason[236] that "a great impediment to the present disarmament of Europe is the fact that the men would have to do woman's work when they laid down the musket."

There are many other antagonisms between the war-régime and that of peace. "Family happiness can be found only under sedentary and peaceful conditions. . . . Woman's conquests in peace—and they should in no case be underestimated—are lost by her in war."[237] The military organization of the Zulu altered the societal structure by suppressing more or less completely the patriarchal institutions of peace. "The unconditional support of the royal dignity came to be the sole object in life of the people. . . . The householders, accordingly, had not the position of fathers of families, but formed parts of certain army-divisions, regiments, or army-corps, which lived together under their leaders. Women were of course present, but they were only concubines, and if they bore children these were as a rule put to death. If certain regiments had repeatedly distinguished themselves, and if they were in advanced years, the king allowed them, as a mark of favor, to marry as a body. . . . But as soon as the pressure let up, mankind turned back, and wherever the arm of the king did not reach, the patriarchal family-system reëstablished itself."[238]

The influence of war and militarism will reveal itself repeatedly in any study of the evolution of government. Militarism and industrialism are really two philosophies and policies existing at the same time in the minds of the same men, by reason of their relations inside and outside their groups. There is one kind of right and one theory of property inside, namely, priority and prescription of appropriation, and another outside, which is force and

---

[235] Morris, in *Amer. Or. Soc., Sec. Hist. Relig.*, VII, 30, 31, 39; §389, below.
[236] *Woman's Share*, 238.   [237] Frobenius, *Masken*, 222.
[238] Fritsch, *Eingeb. S.-Afr.*, 135, 136-137.

conquest. These two are always inconsistent and are ever jostling one another. The ethics of militarism and industrialism have always been mixed. States that are eager to spend their revenue on industrial enterprises within the peace-group stop, turn back, and lavish huge sums upon armament against the chance of war. This contradiction will probably persist until, if ever, the peace-group is practically all-inclusive. There is no doubt that the size of peace-groups has greatly increased; once the blood-tie was the only peace-bond and the only suspension of militarism, and adoption was necessary for one not in the blood-bond to be entitled to participation in that of peace. Then came exogamy, slavery, free access, and trade, to bridge the gaps between the we-groups and the others-groups. Additional connections have developed with time, as we have seen, with the result of enlarging the areas of peace, law, order, guarantee of rights, and government as replacements for war, plunder, vendetta, and conquest; so that at length fewer and larger national peace-aggregations have taken the place of a multitude of small, tribal ones. Militarism, nevertheless, has been intense, costly, and destructive in the modern world; even China has seen organizations for "righteousness, harmony, and fists."[239] Apostles of preparedness deliver impassioned exhortations and are not without striking examples and arguments.

Militarism is the system of a warrior-society, or of any society in a warlike phase. One of its chief characteristics is concentration of power. Its organization approaches that of an army under an absolute commander. Functions that may have been distributed and diffused tend to run back into a single hand. State-initiative is expected. Courts become courts-martial. Aristocracy, hierarchy, prerogative, status, traditional authority, prescription, privilege, curtailment of liberty, patriotism, jingoism—all these appear and the type of life is feudal, romantic, poetical, chivalrous, and adventurous.

A German wine-merchant avers that war unfits men for work; in war, two or three months of intense endeavor and adventure are followed by months of inactivity.[240] Thereafter steady industry seems tame. "Until then [1861-1865], American rural life had been ultra-conservative and stationary. But marching and counter-marching for years over Southern battlefields made foot-loose sol-

[239] "Interview with the Chinese Minister," in N. Y. *Times* for May 31, 1900.
[240] Nolan, "Germany Revisited," in *Atl. Mo.*, CXXVII, 109.

diers of fortune out of thousands of farm boys, who otherwise would surely have contentedly followed the plough on the family acres."[241] Men have gone into war for adventure, to get a change of status, to shift responsibility, as well as for highminded purposes. Improvidence and fatalism have not seldom attended them on their return to civil life.

Militarism has a code of its own, with characteristic virtues and vices: code of honor, duel, blood-revenge, title by conquest, exaltation of courage and physical vigor, emphasis on classes and ranks, organization by discipline, tolerance of hardship, self-denial; and oppression, cruelty, sensuality, venality, and indifference to suffering have often supplied the darker side. It is part of militarism that the war-functions are held to be the nobler; in the past this has put women, except as breeders, and also their occupations, into an inferior position; in the most modern of wars, however, woman's part has been recognized as efficient and essential. Militarists have regularly scorned workers and traders; the churl who labored and the merchant were fair prey, to be robbed or restrained.

Industrialism is characterized by the constitutional or jural state, democracy, delegated powers, liberty, free competition, contract, individual initiative, rational coöperation, private judgment, personal responsibility, enactment, equal rights before the law. It is commonplace, placid, prosaic, often philistine, practical, and scientific. Its ear-marks are fidelity to contract, credit, recognition of law and title by appropriation and production, exaltation of equity, charity, executive ability, financial skill, enterprise, industrial leadership, justice, and rights. It abhors violence, robbery, irregular sex-relations, and lawlessness in general, aiming at highly organized industry, popular education, science, and art. Its vices are materialism, worship of wealth, luxury, softness, and pusillanimity. Industrialism can assert that "it is labor that ennobles." Its liberty is constitutional, as compared with the militaristic type, which is freedom from control; its punishments are less retaliatory than for expediency—to prevent social harm and to discipline the offender. The motive of industrialism is to get on with wealth-production; this is not ethical, but thus are ethics built.

In time of peace industrialism tries to subject the military

241 Van Wagenen, in *Atl. Mo.*, CXXVII, 596.

authorities to the civil; as the power of capital increases the payer gets more control and the army may become merely a hired corps of defenders. The police are that in a very real sense. From the most primitive times, and into the Middle Ages, the priest or medicine-man allied himself with the military power. The Protestant Reformation aimed in part at breaking this combination; it was an effort of industrialism, of the middle class, and of capital against birth and rank and it resulted in the exclusion of the clerics from civil power. Thus industrialism enforces its interests; yet the early twentieth century saw much of European industrial society forced to become military through and through; and the exploitation of outlying countries, such as Africa, has included a considerable element of militarism.[242]

Militarism, we are told, makes states, and it also assists in their evolution. The aim of state-authority is often to maintain itself as it is, and to suppress everything else or force it into conformity.[243] Those in power, who are often the old, instead of guiding toward inevitable readjustments, may merely gather themselves up at once to resist. This means that, in an aggravated case, war and revolution may be necessary. In the United States, with no big neighbors, industrialism has had exceptional freedom in working out the happiness and welfare of the people. Change has been attained without much revolution except of the political order. The conservative element has been weak and sometimes almost wanting, which has meant an occasional riot of unchecked variation. In general, however, we have been open to reform, without militarism, until our isolation was dissipated by the annihilation of distance and the extension of interests.

§145. War as an Evolutionary Factor. To one who has acquired the evolutionary point of view the virtual universality of war over long stages of societal development does not rouse dismal reflections as to the depravity of the race. It does not prove that man, seeing the better, chose the worse. Nor does it support such philosophical inferences as that "of all the ideas the idea of war is perhaps the only one which is innate in man"—the conclu-

---

[242] Jefferson, "Delusion of Militarism," in *Atl. Mo.*, CIII.
[243] Ratzenhofer, *Soc. Erkennt.*, 170.

sion being that war is likely to last forever.[244] In this latter case
is exemplified the common reference to "nature" of anything whose
origin is not revealed to meditation with folded hands. It is foolish to speak of war as an idea; it is a fact and a practice. The
writer quoted seems to be groping about after some "instinct of
combativeness." The evolutionist sees in the practical universality
of war a clear proof that it had once its utilities, just as daimonism and slavery and the mother-family had theirs. A number of
these utilities are now in the reader's mind. It should be clear
enough that the primitive man, for the reason that he fought, was
neither a degenerate, an obstinate and wrongheaded fool, nor a
knave. He saw nothing better to do, when he had reached the end
of his short list of alternatives, any more than we do when we
have reached the end of our somewhat longer list. His last resort
was nearer the head of his list than ours because his list was
shorter. It was often a list containing but one item. He did not
know that violence is a crude way of settling difficulties and by no
means always efficient; it has always seemed, indeed, to be getting
results even when it is later seen not to have done so.

If war had not been efficient to secure results that were in the
main expedient, it would have been replaced in favor of some other
variation in the mores. Not only, however, have almost if not quite
all peoples practised it, but in general the most civilized have
striven the most. It is they who have always been thus testing and
discarding their maladjustments. Where a people is in isolation
so as not to come into conflict with others, it regularly clings to
primitive mores that are represented only in the form of survivals
in the life of competing societies;[245] for selection has been but
feebly at work upon its code. It is said of Polynesia that "isolation condemned these islands to a state of immobility."[246] Out of
the armed conflict emerges a selection whereby old and effete
societal forms are eliminated. New forces are set free and the
process of development enters into its next phase. Internal societal
powers and capacities develop in periods of rest and routine, and

244 Barrot, *Phil. de l'hist.*, 32, quoted by Gumplowicz, *Soc. u. Pol.*, 97, §35
and note.
245 Keller, *Soc. Evol.*, 64; Anon., "Völker u. Politik," in *Pol.-Anth. Rev.*,
III, 403.
246 Oliveira Martins, *Raças*, I, xxxiii.

they need the winnowing-out and testing ensuing upon competition. War and revolution are modes of change, where resistances have accumulated which obstruct adjustment or make it impossible. Whatever cruelty or wastefulness there is about them is like the alleged cruelty or wastefulness of nature. In cases like the French Revolution it can be seen that war was the only remedy, for it alone could break down the resistances. In the case of Greece, Rome, Islam, and the Asiatic empires we see what happens when there are no forces of change present and strong enough to sweep aside inertia and resistance, so as to secure the needed readjustment or reform.

War is certainly effective enough. Whatever it may not be, it is at any rate a great force that cannot be set loose in the world without weighty consequences. It is not so hard to start, but once in motion it eludes control, like a boulder tipped over the crest of a sharp declivity, and it yields many unplanned results.[247] A modern war seldom brings about a speedy and clean-cut solution of the issue on which it was made; it does not reach a rational result in the sense of doing what is expected of it, and no more. Though it breaks the way for change, yet the old and the new often struggle on together in compromises, inconsistencies, antagonisms, and new collisions, for a long time afterwards. Supporters of conflicting views not seldom become more dogmatic and more tenacious of party shibboleths. In war and revolution, writes Thucydides,[248] parties become violent; words change meaning; prudence and moderation are scorned; frantic activity is the true manliness. Violent persons get an audience and the best party man is he who is bold without knowing why. The leaders use big phrases, such as the "equality of the masses" or the "wisdom of the aristocrats." All this looks irrational, and is so, except as the protagonists may be skilfully realizing their own personal ambitions. Few are thinking in terms of the society and seeking to promote its adjustments; only the exceptional statesman can rise to an intelligent perception of society's needs and to a rational program for society's adjustment. If society's fate had had to depend upon such

247 Keller, *War to Peace*, chs. III, IV; Sumner, "Purposes and Consequences," in *Coll. Ess.*, II, 67 ff.
248 *Hist.*, III, 82, 83.

rational action, its case would have been desperate from the outset. Modern issues are, of course, highly complicated; yet even where the savage's war-aims are confined solely to so simple and direct a program as that of "head-snapping," instead of to restoring the balance of power or propagating the faith, still the consequences of warlike activity cannot but spread beyond the range marked out in preliminary intentions.

War is forceful enough. The trouble with it is that it gets promptly out of hand and runs its own course. To start a war is like throwing society upon the mercies of some ruthless natural process concerning the nature of which men know very little. It is a sort of abdication of reason. There are occasions on which reason has had to yield place to something surer, deeper, and more primordial; but that was when it had failed after repeated effort, not before it had been tried at all.

The evolutionist knows that war, faulty as it is, like all the rest of human activities, is, like them, evoked in response to life-conditions; it is societal and not biological, and its persistence inheres in its comparative adequacy as an adjustment to the life-conditions encountered by society. Unless the evolutionary process is to be suspended or superseded, selection must be perennial; and it can take place only through conflict. There have also been issues in all ages which have demanded for their adjudication a conflict on the basis of physical violence. That the number of such issues has been reduced as civilization has increased supports the hope that further reduction toward zero is inevitable. Individuals do not any longer explain a mêlée by saying: "I thought that some outsider had taken my fire and gone off alive; that was why I became angry and did what I did"; or "I thought that some devil, a frightful demon, having eaten up my son-in-law, wanted to play the master in the house; that is why I got into the fight."[249] Nations do not plunge into war because a citizen of one is thought to have pointed a dead-man's bone at a citizen of the other.[250] It is true that previously unexampled causes for war have been added since primitive days;[251] these too, however, have been subject to

[249] Sieroshevski, *Yakuts* (Russ.), I, 571, note 2.
[250] §300, below.
[251] Woods and Baltzly, *Is War Diminishing?*

the reduction-process. War is effective, but it is costly. It is sometimes, even yet, worth the cost, for its woes may be less than the
miseries it eliminates. It is strong medicine.

The race has come, as a whole, not to want it—if, indeed, it
ever did want it—or, at any rate, where milder medicines will do,
to shrink from employing heroic measures. The trouble with war
is that while it may cure the disease, it is likely to kill the patient.
Once war was practically the only expedient available in most
cases; now it has become a last, repulsive recourse in case others
fail. It is treading the road over which have passed cannibalism,
human sacrifice, slavery, the mother-family, and many another less
prominent expedient in living. It is certainly tougher and more
durable than any of these, but it is emphatically not wanted by
mankind; and cases are rare indeed in history where public conviction has not had its way. Further, the trend of the automatic
process is against it; it has been displaced again and again in the
course of evolution and replaced by less costly expedients. Even
if it has had its good points, "the better is always the enemy of
the good." The war-ferment acts until it is replaced by one that is
more expedient. Unless the age-long current reverses itself, war is
headed for progressive diminution.

To hail war as a sovereign expedient in any age is to reveal a lack of historic sense; it is like an advocacy of slavery on the basis of what it undeniably
did for the primitive age. German writers, who have a weakness for the epic
period, have swept aside all the objections to modern war, while recognizing
them more or less perfunctorily, and with a worshipful enthusiasm have
exalted war and war-lords into an agency of "natural selection" in the race-
struggle: "the preparation of peoples for efficient war-making has formed,
and prospectively will continue to form, one of the most important means of
cultivating and educating mankind in all phases of the evolution of culture.
It has been natural selection by wars which has led the most advanced tribes,
step by step, out from among the savage primitive population of the earth
and to victory—tribes who precisely through their superiority had demonstrated their higher capacity for culture."[252] This is a mild pre-war statement
of the German doctrine. The unlovely implications and applications of that
creed appeared with startling clarity in the World War and were recognized
by the civilized nations as constituting a challenge to the international code
of conduct.[253] This attitude was characteristic of its sponsors in the field of
the social sciences; it is an awkward leap at an available analogy that may
be employed with some effect in justification of a selected national program,
and has led to the grotesque contention that Darwinism supports Prussianism.

[252] Von Hartmann, *Phänom.*, 669-670.
[253] Keller, *War to Peace*, ch. XII.

One author[254] has with some concern attempted to clear Darwin of the charge. There is here a confusion between two modes of evolution: the organic and the societal. "The struggle for existence is becoming a social phenomenon which underlies the conformity of the social process to law. . . . Association constricts the struggle for existence and removes it, so to speak, to the periphery of the social structure."[255]

War has not been eliminated to the degree attained in the case of slavery or cannibalism. That is not to be expected; for it is one of the major practices of mankind—not a detail of some larger organization, but an organization on its own account, parallel to those of industry, religion, or the family. It is vain to assert that it will last forever, for that is to assert that certain sets of life-conditions are eternal and that the final and most adequate settlement adjustment to them has been hit upon once and for all. It is quite as futile to hope to end war by merely passing resolutions against it or expressing pious sentiments. Most futile of all are dreams like Tolstoi's;[256] to become mystics is no solution of life's ills, much less of the special woe of war. There has always been a rude setback prepared for ineffectual hand-wringing and tearful exhortation in the fact of ineluctable crises. Even the man who knows and can tell what he knows is not sure of an audience when war is on or is near. There is an excitement over war-making, especially when conflict is once started, that sweeps people away from coolness of judgment; there is also a glamor about war and militarism, even in peace-times, which is supported if not begotten by tradition and romance—one which still clings to them, though perhaps with waning luster. It is yet bright enough, however, to constitute the basis of political appeal;[257] and the disconcerting fact is that many who cheer for militarism on June 24 will solemnly nod acquiescence to a Tolstoi's doctrine on July 10. Though war will doubtless be with us still for a long time, that it is not subject to selection and elimination, along with the rest of society's adjustments, is a contention not warranted by the facts or by reasonable inferences upon them.[258] Where there are advan-

[254] Nasmyth, *Social Progress and the Darwinian Theory.*

[255] Ratzenhofer, *Soc. Erkennt.,* 360, 361.

[256] "Bethink Yourselves," in N. Y. *Times,* July 10, 1904.

[257] "War the Keynote of Mr. Black's Speech [nominating Theodore Roosevelt for President]. Peace is a Child's Dream," in N. Y. *Times,* June 24, 1904.

[258] Keller, *War to Peace,* chs. V, VII; Keller, *Soc. Evol.,* 62 ff.

tages in life which are limited in amount, there men are brought into antagonism, and violence and war are not afar off. If some higher interest brings about compromise and peace, then on the level of this higher interest antagonism begins again. The vaguer and "higher" the interest, the less chance is there to effect a settlement, by war or otherwise; the question as to which state is to be the greatest and rule the world would mean war forever. But despite the fact that local conflicts inside an enveloping peace-group have always had the possibility of running out into violence, they have steadily tended to transform themselves into peaceful competition—commercial, industrial, political, or other—or, if not, their violence has been presently suppressed.[259]

War is one of society's ways of getting results, just as conflict is one of nature's ways. The fact is that society's destiny is being worked out by powers and forces that are not to be swayed about or neutralized by men's wishes or even enactments. Men want to act, not to think and know, and, as Webster[260] said on one occasion: "A strong conviction that something must be done is the parent of many bad measures." It is strange that in this field of societal relations, of all the most complicated and difficult, men think themselves competent to foresee and direct independently of such study as they would feel it necessary to give even to gardening. Real investigation into the nature and life of society is regarded as "academic"; one man's opinion is taken to be about as good as another's. Whereas no one would think of engaging in chemical experimentation without knowing about chemical laws or without direction from one who knows, in matters having to do with the destiny of human society the idea is to pitch in forthwith and do something. This means, in the case of collisions of national interests, to fall back on the old expedient of belligerency and begin to growl and brandish fists. It is easier to do that than to think the thing out and act rationally. And yet any candid man is forced to admit that there must be laws covering the evolution and life of society which can be discovered and taken into account, as the laws in the physical world have been, to the race's immense

[259] Keller, *Soc. Evol.*, 78 ff.; Keller, *War to Peace*, ch. VII; Simmel, in *Année Soc.*, I, 105.
[260] Quoted in Sumner, *Coll. Ess.*, III, 177.

advantage. To strive to learn these laws and operate in the light of them is the only course that deserves the name of rational. The laws and the forces go on, despite futile attempts to ignore them or to act in opposition to them, and it is they that determine, in their highly efficient, automatic manner, the destiny of society. It would be better for man if he fell in with these powers and forces, for they go forward unperturbed, in serene indifference to what he thinks or does not think.

It may be deemed a matter of immense regret that the affairs of men must go on in this way and not by intelligent perception of the case and its requirements; but much more hard study is required before the situation can be materially altered so that men will perceive the existence of law in the societal field, as in nature, and learn to adjust intelligently to the inevitable. It is only the verdict of science and history that can tell us, in the light of their perspectives, what war has really done. In that light its results seem rational as do those of any elemental automatic process. Then we can explain its operation and see that its course and results are in accord with law, and are inevitable. We shall at length be in a position to realize that, during the earlier stages of civilization, "in spite of the countless miseries which follow in its train, war has probably been the highest stimulus to racial progress";[261] but, along with that, to see that in most of the relations of modern life it is as flagrant an anachronism and maladjustment as witchcraft.

Once blood-letting was a sort of cure all in medicine, as it was for society's ills. Knowledge of the forces in the field has expanded, and with it discrimination in adjustment. Blood-letting of both kinds had its merits in its day and was regarded with general favor. Now public opinion is against it. Most people would agree that "a statesman who proposes war as an instrumentality admits his incompetency; a politician who makes use of war as a counter in the game of parties is a criminal."

"War is like other evils; it must be met where it is unavoidable, and such gain as can be got from it must be won. In the forum of reason and deliberation war never can be anything but a makeshift, to be regretted; it is the task of the statesman to find ra-

261 Brinton, *Races*, 76.

tional means to the same end. . . . We find that in the past as a matter of fact war has played a great part in the irrational nature-process by which things have come to pass. But the nature-processes are frightful; they contain no allowance for the feelings and interests of individuals. . . . The nature-elements never suffer and they never pity. If we are terrified at the nature-processes there is only one way to escape them; it is the way by which men have always evaded them to some extent; it is by knowledge, by rational methods, and by the arts." In the face of issues that lie in the immediate future "the only alternatives to force and bloodshed are more knowledge and more reason."[262]

[262] Sumner, in *Coll. Ess.*, I, 34, 35.

CHAPTER XV

ASSOCIATIONS

§146. Rudimentary Groups. It is impossible for any one who
looks the facts squarely in the face to escape the conclusion that
antagonisms of interest have always been among the life-conditions of mankind. Adjustment to the social environment of fellow-
men has always included the composition, reconciliation, and har-
monization of conflicting interests. The prime expedient worked
out automatically by societal evolution, in the face of this set of
life-conditions, has been coöperation between those whose interests
conflicted. We have called this expedient "antagonistic coöperation."[1] It has conquered an ever-widening territory, excluding and
replacing the more immediate and direct reaction of hostility and
violence. Association, having been evoked in rudimentary form in
response to life-conditions as encountered by the most primitive
men known,[2] appears in a variety of types to which the names
family, horde, clan, gens, phratry, deme, and others have been
given. Evidently the degree of association attained is indicated in
all cases by the size of the in-group or peace-group, and the quality of association by the intensity of the in-group organization.

In size the in-group runs all the way from the smallest aggregation to which the name "society" is by our definition applicable,
to the greatest modern nation, and in organization from the
loosest and vaguest of integration to the strictest and most definite. We shall begin with the smallest in-groups and work up to
the larger, noting their degree of organization, and then emerging
into a consideration of organization in and for itself. Though the
extension of the peace-group in numbers and over space is a very
important matter, it is the regulative system existing within it
which is the special object of study in this place. We are thus
focussing down from the survey of inter-group relations—war,
trade, and the rest—to that of intra-group organization, which is
government, with all that goes along with it. But the internal and
external relations of a peace-group always interlace and condi-

[1] §§16, above, and 462, below.   [2] §§6 ff., above.

tion one another, so that, even though the reader bears in mind
what has been found true about the latter, he will still need to recur
to them from time to time. This is, again, the usual situation in
the analysis of the institutions of society, if they are to be seen
living and not spread out cold and lifeless as on the dissecting-
table.

It is probable that life-conditions prior to the development of
the first germs of civilization caused mankind to be scattered in
tiny groups.[3] Says Ratzel:[4] "The most important step from barbarism to civilization is the emancipation of the individual from
the complete or occasional isolation which is inseparably connected with the lower stages of barbarism." "Civilization really
means simply the art of living in a community, or the checks and
counterchecks, the division of labor, and the conveniences that
arise from common action when a group of men live in close relation to each other. This will perhaps be objected to as including
all, or nearly all, mankind in its scope. Quite true; all civilization
is relative and not absolute."[5] Galton[6] cites a striking case of the
Damara cattle: though they have no affection for one another,
they are in apparent agony at even a momentary severance from
the herd; if an ox gets separated from the rest, "he strives with
all his might to get back again, and when he succeeds, he plunges
into its middle to bathe his whole body with the comfort of closest
companionship." Galton, who calls this a "centripetal instinct,"
is too wise to infer a human "gregarious instinct"; he utilizes the
parallel as follows: "I insist on a close resemblance in the particular circumstance, that many savages are so unamiable and morose
as to have hardly any object in associating together, besides that
of mutual support. If we look at the inhabitants of the very same
country as the oxen I have described, we shall find them congregated into multitudes of tribes, all more or less at war with one
another. We shall find that few of these tribes are very small, and
few very large, and that it is precisely those that are exceptionally
large or small whose condition is the least stable. A very small
tribe is sure to be overthrown, slaughtered, or driven into slavery
by its more powerful neighbor. A very large tribe falls to pieces

---

[3] Lippert, *Kgchte.*, I, 386; §9, above.   [4] *Vkde.*, I, 88.
[5] Petrie, in *Smithson. Rep.*, 1895, 591.   [6] *Human Faculty*, 71-73, 78.

through its own unwieldiness, because, by the nature of things, it must be either deficient in centralization or straitened in food, or both."

Here we have the very gist of the matter. The tendency is toward enlargement of the peace-group, and those that lag behind are destroyed or incorporated; and yet, on the stage of the arts attained, as respects the food-quest or regulative organization, the enlargement is strictly limited. Between such boundaries, set by some of the mores upon others and involving the necessity of consistency in the mores,[7] societal adjustments must live and have their being. They cannot attain to an ideal status at any time. "Care has been taken," says Goethe, "that the trees shall not grow up into the sky." Several examples of the rudimentary peace-group follow.[8]

The Australian horde is estimated as containing from forty to sixty souls; where there is a larger gathering it is for some special purpose. In some of the most barren regions the groups consist of a family of from six to nine.[9] The largest local group in one district consisted of forty souls upon one hundred square miles.[10] At Lake Victoria, on the Murray River, Eyre[11] once saw upwards of six hundred natives congregated, but again he passed through that neighborhood and scarcely saw an individual. The tribe does not generally "hunt, camp, and live in a body, but in small chance parties, which only meet occasionally. . . . Tribes in Australia vary much in the numbers of their members, probably from as low as five-and-twenty persons in desert country, to five hundred souls or more where food and water are plentiful. . . . Where food is plentiful, weapons and instruments are more elaborately finished, customs more artificial, and the mental energies and understandings more developed, than in poorer districts. In such localities, also, a tribe sees more of its neighbors; in other words, entertains more, and is more given to fighting."[12] In New Guinea are to be encountered petty family-groups, characterized by peace within.[13] Of one of the New Guinea peoples it is said that we see in them "one of the very oldest original forms of human society . . . a life without God, without princes, without authorities, without religion, but yet already with the germs of them all." Again, in another tribe, we observe "men of the stone age still at the present day on their neolithic culture-stage; we notice primordial prehistoric forms of state and society still in full bloom, and thanks to these primitive peoples who have been preserved to us by good fortune and miraculously, as it were, as an irreplaceable example, we can look back and form a living picture of the mental life of our ancestors of thousands and

---

[7] Sumner, *Folkways*, §5.   [8] §§9, 32, 146, above.
[9] Semon, in *Korr.-Blatt, Deut. Gesell. f. Anth.*, XXXIII, 4; Eyre, *Cent. Aust.*, I, 103, II, 212; Salvado, *Aust.*, 265.
[10] Spencer and Gillen, *Nat. Tr. Cent. Aust.*, 9.
[11] *Cent. Aust.*, II, 369.   [12] Curr, *Aust. Race*, I, 53, 66.
[13] Krieger, *Neu-Guinea*, 192.

thousands of years ago." Markets are almost their sole occasions for association, along with the Duk-Duk and other secret rites.[14]

Livingstone[15] speaks of a Bushwoman who "had fled from a party of her countrymen, and was now living far from all others with her husband." A well nigh hopeless environment imposes atomism upon the Bushmen, as well as a meager physique. "It has been observed that if a Bushman gets a good diet for two or three weeks he will fatten up round and smooth";[16] but his lack of sociability is in his mores and cannot be set aside. He has no settled dwelling-place, but spends the night in a cleft in the rocks, bends down a bush as shelter and protection, or hollows out a trench in the ground into which perhaps two adults and several children squeeze. Their small hordes scarcely unite them except for some special enterprise requiring strength; and such hordes keep at a distance from one another "since the smaller the number the easier is a supply of food procured." Even families have to break up to get food; if by chance they meet again, they stay together if they have provision or need to coöperate in some enterprise.[17]

The Abors of Assam exhibit two or three houses together at places scattered over the mountains. They quarrel, scatter, and cannot combine.[18] The Veddahs of Ceylon form, according to their family-connections, small and silent circles about their little fires.[19] Among the Tungus, "seldom are more than ten yurts [tents] seen together; commonly they are set up on open spaces near a water-supply."[20] The Kubus of Sumatra "live without men in authority and only in a small number of little hordes. Every family lives for itself."[21] The Patagonians, at mutual convenience, "all assemble in one place, but if food becomes scarce or quarrels happen, each party withdraws to its own territory. At such times one party will encroach on the hunting grounds of another and a battle is the consequence." There were about four hundred adults in one party, the women outnumbering the men three to one.[22] Of the Fuegians it is said that there are never more than a dozen together.[23]

From such rudimentary groups we now pass to societies of greater size and higher organization, realizing always that those two qualities must go forward together; for if the corporeal growth outruns the structural or institutional, the clan, gens, tribe, or confederacy will split into two or more fragments which continue to grow independently.

The course of development to be portrayed, here as elsewhere, is an advancing complexity of organization, representing adjustment to more complicated life-conditions, and running from the most rudimentary forms to that of the

---

[14] Hagen, *Papua's*, 220, 276, 278 (quoted).

[15] *Mission. Travels*, I, 72.   [16] Hahn, in *Globus*, XVIII, 85.

[17] Lichtenstein, *S. Afr.*, II, 46, 47, 48, 49, 194.

[18] Gomme, in JAI, XVII, 128.   [19] Schmidt, *Ceylon*, 87.

[20] Hiekisch, *Tungusen*, 75.

[21] Anon., "Kubus," in *Globus*, XXVI, 44.

[22] Fitzroy, *Adventure and Beagle*, II, 131.

[23] Ratzel, *Hist. Mankind*, II, 91.

state. There here appears the time-honored difference of opinion concerning the origin of cultural phenomena, whether they are locally developed in response to need and are similar over the earth because men and needs are similar (parallelism) or whether they are worked out in certain centers and thence carried by contagion or acculturation over wide areas. It is, of course, necessary to admit their original rise somewhere in response to life-conditions, so that either theory is evolutionary.

Rivers,[24] in the course of his studies of Melanesian society, came to assign much more importance to acculturation than to parallelism. He believes that most of the changes in social organization which have taken place in Melanesia "have been due to the influence of relatively small bodies of immigrants." Nevertheless he holds that there must be some considerable tincture of the evolutionary as opposed to the purely historical in any treatment of the subject. "Such changes must be slow and gradual; in other words, they must have those characters which we are accustomed to regard as belonging to evolution. . . . In spite of the change in standpoint which took place in the course of my study of the subject, the early evolutionary treatment holds good because it is only by a process such as we are accustomed to regard as evolutionary that it is possible for changes in social structure to come about." We believe firmly in the occurrence of wide parallelisms resulting from the tendency of the human mind, which we regard as essentially the same everywhere, to make adjustment to similar types of life-conditions along similar lines; but even if culture is conceived to be formed by contagion from without rather than by independent development from within, its reception must follow along lines of adjustment already laid down in the societal organization which is to take it over. Hence we have no quarrel with moderate and reasonable hard students like Rivers, who is a great observer. The famous saying of Darwin, that it is not errors in theory that are serious, but only those of observation, for the former can be corrected while the latter lead to endless repetitions of false data, is even more to the point in the social sciences than in the natural.

§147. Kinship and Proximity. The smallest society possible by our definition is the family, consisting of an adult male and female and their offspring; some of the most rudimentary associations are family-groups but little larger than this. Since we are not seeking origins, we need not infer as to the primordial form of association. In general, when men come first into the range of history and ethnography, they appear in societies which make a great deal of the blood-tie, as they understand it.[25] Many of them assert that they have derived their blood from a common ancestral source; even in cases where this seems to be a mere assumption, or where it is evidently untrue, or where community of blood has to be established artificially, they adhere tenaciously to the doctrine of blood-kinship. This is significant, and so is the etymology of the

[24] *Melan. Soc.*, II, 4-6.   [25] §§411, 412, below.

word "nation" (*nascor*). And it must be added that alliances with aliens are commonly cemented with some ceremony involving the establishment of community of blood. The thought of the race has centered so persistently about blood that it must once have bulked very large in primitive life.

Though the blood-tie is by far the most dominant bond, the simplest condition leading to association is propinquity in place. The society-idea in its primary form is "we" as distinguished from others. We who are here are one party; those over there are another. The degree to which propinquity may exist is determined by the condition of the man-land ratio as modified by the status of the arts of life. It should be realized, however, that in case of propinquity all will become akin to one another within a short time.

The Carib Indian constantly moved about the coast of South America from the Amazon to the Orinoco and Magdalena, and even over to the Antilles; "often it was impossible for him to find his own people again, and since women took part only in small numbers in these wandering and thieving expeditions, the . . . savage formed new unions where he could." The result was that "a mass of human beings, flowing together from the most diverse hordes and tribes, was regarded as a genetically homogeneous community, as a tribe or a people, because they were concordant in their manner of life."[26] Coöperation in predatory and other enterprises has often led to such an outcome.[27]

It is evident that unrelated proximity is a sort of theoretical antecedent stage deserving of little attention. Intermarriage and the blood-tie speedily supersede it, in any case. "The separate little hordes of Bushmen consist always of a single family. Sex feelings and instinctive love for children, or the habit of familiarity between relatives, are the sole bonds which hold them together at all."[28] This blood-tie is really indistinguishable from the bond of familiarity and habit which comes from propinquity or from the sympathy engendered by united defense against a common enemy. It is a concrete evidence of toleration and sympathy. Blood-tie is to us only a figure of speech for common heredity which we retain out of tradition just as we retain "sun-rise" or "sun-set," knowing the while, if we think of it at all, that it has no actuality.

[26] Von Martius, *Beiträge*, I, 377-378; 263.
[27] Keane, *Ethnol.*, 13.   [28] Lichtenstein, *S. Afr.*, II, 194.

It is impossible to get far away from the blood-tie when dealing with primitive conditions; some writers, however, prefer to begin with what they call a "horde," a term covering a loose, pre-familial group. The authority of Darwin[29] is invoked in opposition to the theory of original parental groups: "Some authors suppose that man primevally lived in single families; but at the present day though single families, or only two or three together, roam the solitude of some savage lands, they are always, so far as I can discover, friendly with other families inhabiting the same district." "It is this complex group, then, from which the history of man has to start"—that is, if we are to take things as they are, and not as they may be inferred to have been. The controversialist who thus presents the matter[30] goes on to say that "The family appears in history in its most archaic form, as the unit of the genealogic tribe. But the tribe, made up of these family units, is just then entering upon its career in the formation of nations—is, in fact, just on the threshold of modern history. And at the back of this union of families is that large body of custom . . . from which kinship-formed tribes were developed. Under whatever form of society this body of custom existed, there is no part of it which entitles us to use such a term as 'family' in connection with it. It was not a family unit in independence; it was not a group of family units bound by kinship ties." It is better to call it a horde. It is really a set of "temporary groups in local contact with each other."

Brown[31] uses the word "horde" (from a Tatar term meaning "camp") "to denote what is, in Australia, an extremely important and very well-marked social division. The horde, as it is found in the normal forms of Australian social organization, may be defined by the following characters:—(1) It consists of a number of persons who regularly live together in one camp and share a common life. (2) The horde is the primary land-owning group, each horde owning and occupying a certain area of country. (3) Each horde is independent and autonomous, and manages its own affairs by means of a camp-council, often directed by one head-man. (4) A child belongs to the horde of the father—i.e., descent is strictly in the male line. A woman, on marriage, joins and lives with the horde of the husband. (5) The horde acts as a unit in its relations with other hordes of the same or other tribes. . . . By a tribe I mean a collection of persons who speak what the natives themselves regard as one language, the name of the language and the name of the tribe being generally one and the same. . . . By a family I mean a social group consisting of a man with his wife or wives and such of their children (own or adopted) as are still dependent upon them—i.e., unmarried girls and uninitiated boys. The family is a well-marked social unit of great importance in Australian life."

According to Howitt and Fison,[32] who differ from Brown as to the prevailing line of descent, by horde is meant "a certain geographical section of an Australian community which occupies certain definite hunting grounds. Its members are of different totems. In fact, all the totems of the community may be represented in any given horde. Descent being through the mother as a

---

[29] *Descent of Man*, I, 84.

[30] Gomme, in JAI, XVII, 119, 121, 128.

[31] In JAI, XLVIII, 222-223.

[32] In JAI, XIV, 143; Mucke (*Horde u. Familie*, 40) presents no adequate definition.

general rule, the child is of its mother's totem, not of its father's. *But it belongs to the horde in which it was born.*"
Much has been made of this last fact, as indicative of the prevalence of the locality-tie over the blood-tie, but it does not seem to us so significant. Of course there are other bonds than those of kinship: community of speech, religion, and general customs and manner of life. The first bond, that of blood, "is natural, while in contrast to it all others are evolutional, that is, they arise out of social development. . . . The distinction here is only that we know the development of the latter and not of the former. . . . In reality there are no other social bonds than those of the primitive horde—the facts of propinquity, common blood, equality of material and intellectual needs, that is, equality of interests with reference to their satisfactions; and there are also no social contrasts which would not rest on the lack of one or the other of these common qualities mentioned."[33]

"After the establishment of sedentary life, territorial bonds become more important, but without wholly destroying those of relationship. Even in contemporary states which rest essentially upon the territory-principle, the power of the old principle of relationship is exhibited, though only in so far as citizenship is regularly obtained not through presence or residence in a state, but only through being the child of a citizen."[34]

While it is well to remain attentive to socializing factors other than that of blood, for they have come, in the modern world, almost completely to displace it, there is no occasion for an excursion into tenuous theorizing over the presence of such factors.[35] To our way of thinking, the kin-tie is the outstanding bond of association and the monandrous family[36] the basic unit of society. Under very primitive conditions, since kinship can be reckoned only very faultily and vaguely except for the mother-child relation,[37] it seems likely enough that proximity played a much more important rôle, relatively to the blood-tie, than it did upon subsequent stages of development up to relatively modern times. Survivals of a status where kinship seems not to be the dominating consideration doubtless appear, though their identification seems to us a rather uncertain matter. In any case, and whatever the origins may have been, there is a stretch of evolution that begins with preoccupation with the blood-tie and extends far enough to give us all we need for our present interest, which is the development of the regulative system.

---

[33] Gumplowicz, *Soc.*, 142-143.   [34] Ruppin, *Darwinismus*, 20.
[35] As in Mucke, *Horde u. Familie.* The theory of the horde is closely related with the inference as to primitive promiscuity. Westermarck (*Marriage,* I, chs. III-IX) assaults that inference.
[36] §345, below.   [37] §§411 ff. of the text.

The strength of the kinship-prepossession may be judged from the following cases. In East Africa, "when a man goes to settle in a new district he is required to pay a bull to the elders. This payment is not intended to purchase a right to the use of the land, but for the taking of the oath of *muma* between himself and the people, in which both swear to be loyal to each other. It may, however, be regarded as a purchase of title, in so far as without it the newcomer would not be admitted. Incidentally this oath explains in a great measure the extraordinary support that persons of one settlement give to each other against strangers, even though they may otherwise not be on good terms; it would, for instance, be a breach of loyalty to give evidence which would go against a neighbour in favour of one from another settlement." This sort of oath, unaccompanied by some ceremony establishing common blood, is rather an exception; whereas "a fictitious relationship is created by blood-brotherhood, which is held to be so close that children of blood-brothers cannot intermarry." Very likely the blood-brotherhood idea is behind practices where it is not specifically in evidence: "If a Mkamba kills a foreigner in Ukamba he must pay full bloodmoney to the Mkamba with whom the stranger lived, if he was an adopted son (i.e. if his host had bought him a wife), otherwise only four cows are paid, or two only if the stranger was not able-bodied. In Theraka and among the Ndia Kikuyu the life of a stranger must be compensated, even though he was staying with the one claiming only for one day. In Ukamba, Theraka, and Ndia, if a stranger kills anyone his host must under all circumstances pay full bloodmoney. Among other sections of the Akikuyu, bloodmoney for murder of, or by, a stranger can only be claimed if the stranger was fully adopted by the claimant, or if he had entered into blood-brotherhood with a member of the family. . . . When a Mkamba is called upon to give evidence in a dispute, or to speak his mind in regard to two men, he seems to take into consideration only one point, namely, which of the two lives nearest to him—the nearer to him a man lives the stronger will be his support of him against the other, and family and clannish feeling are extraordinarily strong in him."[38]

These cases seem to support the theory of proximity in space as a unifying bond; it is probable, however, that in most cases proximity means kinship, actual or potential, as several details in the above indicate. "A person with no family would soon become a slave, as a single individual without family could not stand alone. Some charge would be brought against him and being without family he would not be able to defend himself, and he would either be reduced to ordinary slavery or would have to attach himself to some other family and his estate would be taken by them."[39] Nothing is clearer than that primitive conditions do not permit of individualism. Maine[40] avers, doubtless too flatly, that "all ancient societies regarded themselves as having proceeded from one original stock, and even laboured under an incapacity for comprehending any reason except this for their holding together in political union. The history of political ideas begins, in fact, with the assumption that kinship in blood is the sole possible ground of community in political functions." He is supported, however, by Wilken,[41] who reports "by far the greatest number of

---

[38] Dundas, C., in JAI, XLV, 297, 301, 266-267; and in JAI, XLIII, 488.
[39] Weeks, in JAI, XXXIX, 426.   [40] *Anc. Law*, 128-129.
[41] In VG, I, 292-295.

the peoples of the Malay race as located in this phase of development." There are cases of transition, also, where the kinship-bonds and the territorial are peculiarly blended. "Without any doubt the territorial division is evoked by the stock-division, in that with the establishment of sedentary life each stock settled in a particular spot. Originally the members of the stock lived united in a single village"; then, with increase of population, the villages split up. The offshoots remained connected with the mother-village, all together constituting a district; thus was the land spontaneously divided on the basis of territory. The kinship-system was evidently the more primitive.

One further case may illustrate the persistence of the kinship-idea, in a segregated part of Europe. "In Montenegro, until recent times the word 'friend' had not an English meaning. You could not be the friend of a man to whom you were not in some way related. If you were not a friend you were, of course, a possible enemy. It is possibly on this account that blood relationships were traced to such great lengths. It undoubtedly made for peace, and a crowd of imaginary relationships were brought about by marriage, and classed as blood relations."[42]

§148. Composition of the Tribe. It is perhaps fair to say that the tribe is the first political body, as the tribal chief is the first political functionary, that stands out clearly enough to make study of it very profitable. Nevertheless the tribe is already complex, including families, clans, gentes, phratries, and other components. We must look somewhat into these. The most noticeable characteristic which they have in common is that they are kinship-organizations—a fact which invites us to contemplate, first of all, the connection of the organization for societal regulation with that for societal self-perpetuation. In truth, much that is to be said here about the family, clan, and the rest must be taken somewhat on faith, pending the closer study of these kin-groups under the section on self-perpetuation.[43] We shall find there that the family itself is an organization of authority and discipline; for no society, however small, can prosper without regulation. "There existed even in the most primitive state of things a natural organization of the society, because the regulation of the separate wills, over and under one another, corresponded to the necessary adjustment of the mutual relations of men to life-conditions."[44]

Whether association is limited to the family-form or extends beyond it is largely a question of the type of environment. In the case of animals, whether they shall live pair-wise or herd-wise is a

42 Durham, in JAI, XXXIX, 89.
43 §§352, 353, and chs. LV, LVI, LVII, below.
44 Ratzenhofer, *Soc. Erkennt.*, 293.

question of the mode of life and kind of food. Those beasts which individually need a large amount of food-domain are likely to separate into pairs.[45] These animal-ways have their analogues among human ways.

"For the mode of maintenance of herders the union of larger groups is not only superfluous, but decidedly disadvantageous. The herding economy calls for very extended space and relatively very few men. The men of a single big family are perfectly able to care for and use a stately herd. . . . But when the need of food allures the several families of a nomad tribe to dispersion, the need of protection forbids them to get too far away from their natural helpers, their blood-kin. A separate family is well able to pasture a large herd; but it is not strong enough to defend its wealth. The danger of being robbed always hangs over it; for to most nomads cattle-raiding is reckoned as just as pleasant and honorable an occupation as cattle-raising. We shall therefore see that the kin-organization is weakest among the most peaceful tribes of this type, while it has attained its strongest development where robbery and war form a permanent condition."[46]

In short, the size and complexity of societal organization depends upon conditions existing in the natural and societal environments and also in the type of adjustment attained in meeting these conditions. However, when a combination occurs which allows of and indeed enforces wider organization, it is characterized by the cleaving together of those who are blood-related, or believe themselves so to be.

In New Guinea there are no political units, but only village-groups held together by the bonds of blood-kinship and a common language. This allows of but limited combinations, for there is a new language every fifteen kilometres along the coast, and the interval is less in the interior. The only *lingua franca* is "pidgin-English." The factor of control is respect for old customs and precedents.[47] Fiji shows similar unions which are composed of the descendants of a bond of brothers, from each of whom is descended a minor division. The people of the several divisions "are theoretically of a common descent, though they are not always actually so."[48] There are social divisions in every village in Melanesia, the tie being blood or economic interests. Each of these classes has a division, with its own cooking-place and joint-house, where the men eat and hold assemblies, while the women and children eat in the huts.[49] This kin-tie is not always one of good feeling, however; Curr[50] assures us expressly that the kin-bond in Australia is not necessarily a friendship-bond. But the fact that it is persistently recognized bespeaks its inveterate character.

In South Africa there is a so-called "bywoner-system," whereby a young

[45] Lippert, *Kgchte.*, II, 6.   [46] Grosse, *Familie*, 124.
[47] Schmidt, *Deut. Kol.*, II, 335-336; "pidgin" is a corruption of "business."
[48] Fison, in JAI, X, 335.
[49] Ratzel, *Vkde.*, II, 278.   [50] *Aust. Race*, I, 69.

pair that has not the small outfit allowing of independent living, attaches itself to some property-owner in a sort of clientage. In western Cape Colony, however, where the family is not so split up, this system is less in vogue; "or it exists rather in modified form, in that the 'bywoners' are not strangers, but near relatives of the proprietor. A community is not seldom to be found which is composed only of members of a family. The grandfather—often the first settler—has the best house, while his sons, with their families, live near him in huts or tents. Uncles, aunts, and cousins dwell on neighboring farms—in short, bloodkinship rules everywhere."[51]

We shall see enough about joint-households, in another connection,[52] to emphasize this natural tendency of blood-kin to herd together. "Association is the soul and life of Kabylie. . . . The *thadoukeli* is an institution rather than a contract: it is the antique mold of the Kabyle family, it is the harmonious fusion of the principle of paternity with the immutable right of property, having for its base free consent and the respect for age-old traditions." This community furnishes the bride-price and receives it. The family is the true social unit, and the oldest man is its head.[53] Thus does the family-motive persist also in more highly developed societies; it is strong in China and Japan. "The individual is ready to give his life, in a majority of cases, for the family, the home, the ancestors. And the filial piety impelling such sacrifice becomes, by extension, the loyalty that will sacrifice even the family itself for the sake of the lord,—or, by yet further extension, the loyalty that prays . . . for seven successive lives to lay down on behalf of the sovereign."[54]

The tribes of East Greenland "regard it as their first social duty to stand by their house-mates and nearest relatives."[55] Morgan[56] shows through many pages that native American society was much more a combination resting on blood-relationship than a political one. The family maintains order, redresses wrongs, punishes crimes, and has a real police power.[57] Family-terms persisted to cover tribal relations: "if the deceased chief belonged to one of the three older nations, the duty of conducting the condoling ceremony which followed was performed by the younger nations, who mourned for him as for a father or an uncle. If he were a chief of one of the younger nations, the others lamented him as a son or nephew."[58] The Arawak tribe, like the Arab, was divisible into families; genealogy was reckoned through the mother and kept with extreme care. Endogamy within such a group was strictly forbidden.[59] Ten to sixty warriors with their families constituted a Botocudo society.[60]

The peculiar affair of the Arab tribe is war, that of the family blood-vengeance; the latter was a higher moral duty, when relatives had been killed, than war in tribal union. Family-feuds disintegrated tribes and produced social chaos. Islam, as a superior force, overriding and integrating by producing a new idea and a new jural principle, was a blessing.[61] The Swedish "atter" of the thirteenth century were groups united for common defense; they were kin-

51 "Kleine Nachr.", in *Globus*, XCII, 194-195.
52 §414, below.
53 Hanoteau et Letourneux, *Kabylie*, II, 4 ff.; 468 ff.
54 Hearn, *Japan*, 58.   55 Holm, *Ethnol. Skizze*, 43.
56 *Anc. Soc.*, 66 ff., 90 ff., 102 ff., 123 ff.
57 Hewitt, "Family," in HAI, I, 451.   58 Hale, *Iroq. Rites*, 59.
59 Schomburgk, *Brit.-Guiana*, II, 459.
60 Von Martius, *Beiträge*, I, 325.   61 Proksch, *Blutrache*, 29, 30.

groups bound to blood-vengeance, but also contract-bound for united help and defense.[62] The Teutonic "sib," an agrarian and military unit, was purely agnatic,[63] based, that is, upon kinship through the father.

These examples should help to set the family in its due place in the tribe or larger aggregation whose basis is no longer kinship. But the persistence of the blood-tie is not yet exhausted. There are the combinations known as clans, gentes, phratries, and classes, which form constituent elements of tribes and are still based with pertinacity upon kinship. Of these the clan and gens, as being better understood and more important for our present purposes, may be set aside for the moment while brief attention is accorded to the other tribal divisions.

There are, in many societies around the world, divisions larger than the clan or gens but included within the tribe; these are called phratries, moieties, classes, or divisions. Their chief function seems to be in connection with the regulation of marriage, for they are typically exogamous. This will come out in other sections of this book.[64] At this point we shall follow Rivers[65] chiefly, for he has given more systematic attention to these divisions, and also inspires more confidence, than any other writers of whom we know.

We may begin with his characterization of the tribe. "Although the food-gatherers wander about in family groups, peoples with moieties and clans are usually grouped together into larger units, called tribes. We are accustomed to speak of tribes only in connection with relatively simple societies. The tribe shades off into groups of a more complex kind, such as the nation, and its exact definition is not easy. It may, however, be described as follows: 'A tribe is a social group of a simple kind, the members of which speak a common dialect, have a single government, and act together for such common purposes as warfare.' A negative character is that it is not exogamous, that is to say, there are no rules compelling its members to marry into other similar groups. On the other hand, it is usually more or less endogamous: its members usually marry within the group, but not rigorously enough to make it possible to use the practice as an essential feature of the definition." That is to say, the tribe is not an organization having any special function with respect to marriage and descent; "the tribe is, in the main, a political rather than a domestic group, with a common speech as its main characteristic. The tribe corresponds largely to the much debated variety of social grouping known as the nation. It is probable that students of political science would be greatly helped in their attempts to reach an understanding concerning what they mean by a nation if they were to take the far simpler tribe as their pattern, and regarded as a nation the social group which, in large communities, has social functions similar to those of the tribe. One of the chief processes by which the nation has evolved from the tribe is that of federation."

[62] Montelius, *Sver. Hist.*, I, 461.   [63] Schrader, *Aryans*, 398.
[64] Chs. XLIV, XLV, LV, LVI, LVII, below.
[65] *Soc. Org.*, 31-33, 27, 28, 29, 30, 33; *Melan. Soc.*, II, 70, 557-558, 563, 564, *et passim*.

Now the first division within the tribe, so far as size is concerned, is the moiety. "It is found, especially in Melanesia, Australia, and North America, that many communities are divided into two distinct divisions, called *moieties*, which play a definite part in the life of the community, particularly in respect of the regulation of marriage. The dual system of Melanesia is usually associated with matrilineal descent, a person belonging to his or her mother's moiety. . . . Especially important is the strange feature that, though the chief purpose of the organization is the regulation that marriage shall always take place between members of the two moieties, these moieties are hostile to one another, and regard one another with dislike and suspicion, but I do not know of any cases of organized hostility between clans in Melanesia. In dual communities with matrilineal descent, a father and son will necessarily belong to different moieties, and will therefore be hostile to one another. . . . There is no evidence of hostility between the two moieties of the dual organization in America. Some kind of rivalry between them is common, and may be present when the dual character takes no part in the regulation of marriage, but it is purely ceremonial. . . . We know of only one case of an arrangement in Africa which can be classed with the dual organization." There are forms of social organization which resemble the genuine dual system and have been confused with it. "When a society consists of two classes, such as chiefs and commoners, it would be possible to speak of a dual organization, but unless they form an intermarrying system, as in Melanesia and among the Gallas, there is no point in classing the two together. Cases intermediate between the two, however, occur. . . .

"At the present time students of sociology are almost unanimous in ascribing the dual organisation of society to a process of fission whereby a single social group came to be divided into two moieties. The opposite opinion that the dual organisation came into being by a process of fusion has been put forward, but has few, if any, adherents. It has been my task in this book to show that many of the social institutions of Melanesia have come into being as the result of the interaction of peoples, and it will be quite in accordance with the rest of my argument that I should now attempt to show that the dual organisation may have had a similar origin. I have to inquire whether the fusion of two peoples is able to account for the chief features of this form of organisation as we now find it in Melanesia." The author goes on to cite such facts as that the dual system involves hostility between the moieties and ascription of different characters to their members; in one case, for instance, the people of one moiety "are reputed to be ignorant and unimportant, always quarreling and unable to manage their affairs properly," while those of the other "are capable of governing themselves and others, versed in social lore and living peaceably with one another. Such differences of character are just such as might be expected if the moieties were originally two peoples. A special feature of the dual organisation of Melanesia is that it is common to large groups of peoples who possess few other signs of social cohesion. The dual organisation acts as a link between peoples differing widely from one another in general culture and language. . . . The general character of the dual organisation of Melanesia is thus such as would be natural if it was the result of interaction between two peoples."

The extensive and detailed treatment of Rivers inspires confidence. Fox[66]

[66] In JAI, XLIX, 156.

adopts it as the most reasonable explanation of the organization found by him in San Cristoval, in the Solomon Islands: "The dual people seem in San Cristoval to have quite clear traditions of the origin of the two moieties in two distinct races, the one original and the other immigrants, the latter very distinct physically and mentally from the former. These traditional differences are similar to those recorded elsewhere in the New Hebrides, Banks Islands and the islands north-west of the Solomons, but seem to be even more definite here, and to give considerable support to Dr. Rivers' conclusions regarding the dual people, which are adopted here." Mathew,[67] reviewing the literature, differs from Howitt and Fison[68] and Spencer and Gillen,[69] noting that he himself, in 1889, developed his own "natural, kinship theory." The authors he criticizes hold that phratries were instituted by the arbitrary authority of leading men among the natives; his own idea is "that the two phratries represent two ancient, distinct races, which amalgamated to form the Australian race."

As between theories which call for the exercise in institution-forming of arbitrary authority by savages and those which rest upon automatic development over long periods, we can have no hesitation. Although we are rather indifferent to long inferences concerning origins, there seems to exist in this case good reason for reproducing Rivers's views.

As an illustration of dual organization not on the order of the type under review, consider that of the Omaha Indians: "Human conditions were projected upon nature, and male and female forces recognized. The Above was regarded as masculine, the Below feminine; so the sky was father, the earth mother. The heavenly bodies were conceived of as having sex; the sun was masculine, the moon feminine, consequently day was male and night female. The union of these two forces was regarded as necessary to the perpetuation of all living forms, and to man's life by maintaining his food supply. . . . Consonant with this manner of enforcing these cosmic and religious ideas, the tribe was composed of two grand divisions, one representing the Sky people, . . . the other, the Earth people. . . . Within each of these divisions were five gentes. While each gens had its designation, its rites, its place, its tabu and its personal names, all these distinctive marks were subordinate to the two grand divisions and membership in the gens became merged in membership in one of these divisions . . . These divisions were not phratries, as they were not based on ties of blood but on mythic ideas as to how creation came about and how life must be continued on the earth. . . . Of the marriages in existence among the Omaha twenty-five years ago, a good majority represented the union between members of gentes belonging to the two rather than to one of these grand divisions. And it is also important that, amid the wreckage of the ancient tribal organization at the present time, the practice of exogamy is still observed. In short, all the conditions seem to show that the custom is based on fundamental religious ideas. The duality in the tribal organization was further represented by the two principal chiefs. . . . There were also two tribal pipes, which were always kept together and were never separated in any ceremonial use." These chiefs and pipes were assigned one to each

[67] In JAI, XL, 165, 166.
[68] Howitt, S. E. Aust., 89, 90, 140, 143-144, 171-174.
[69] Nat. Tr. Cent. Aust., viii.

division.[70] The division on the male and female principle reminds one of the Chinese Yang and Yin.

Finally, to revert to Rivers,[71] who writes of the relation of the tribe with the moiety and clan, it is to be noted that "the tribe is the larger unit which comprehends the other two, either singly or together. That is to say, a tribe may be subdivided into clans with no moieties; it may be divided into moieties with no clans of any sort, though this rarely, if ever, happens; and it may have both clans and moieties. From the historical point of view there seems to be no doubt that the earliest form of grouping is that of moieties and clans, each moiety being divided up into smaller groups. As has been said, the chief function of the moiety is the regulation of marriage: the clan fills governmental and other rôles in the life of the community, while, at the same time, playing its part, in some societies, in the regulation of marriage. The clan has its council, and certain members of each clan sit on the council of the tribe, or whatever the larger grouping may be. In this the clan differs profoundly from the moiety, which has no political functions whatever, so far as is known."

As present interest lies almost wholly in political functions and their development, there has perhaps been no occasion to enter into the matter of dual organization; but it is in the picture and an apprehension of its presence will be seen to be not altogether without utility.

§149*. The Clan. There is some disadvantage, when considering the kin-groups that go to make up the tribe, in not having as a background the evolution of marriage and the family.[72] Such dislocations of sequence are unavoidable in any selected order of treatment; there is nothing to do except to sketch in roughly that which is indispensable, referring forward for a fuller treatment. The tribe may be considered as composed of three types of constituents of decreasing generality: the dual division, the clan, and the family. In societal regulation the first and last are of comparatively small account; if it is desirable to see how government came about, the body to fix attention upon is the clan. Rivers[73] cites a committee-definition of the clan, as follows: "An exogamous division of a tribe the members of which are held to be related to one another by some tie, it may be belief in descent from a common ancestor, common possession of a totem, or habitation of a com-

[70] Fletcher and LaFlesche, in BAE, XXVII, 134-137 (the date is 1907).
[71] *Soc. Org.*, 33.   [72] Part V, below.
[73] *Soc. Org.*, 19, 20, 21; Brown, in JAI, XLIII, 159; and in JAI, XLVIII, 223-224.

mon territory"; and he adds a prominent feature to this definition: "It is a characteristic example of a unilateral mode of
grouping, so that a person belongs to the clan of his father or to
the clan of his mother; and his fellow-clansmen are primarily
related to him either through his father or through his mother,
though intermarriage may lead to relationship to the clans of
both parents." There is some advantage in having separate terms
for matrilineal and patrilineal clans; chiefly by American writers
the term "clan" has been reserved for the former, while the latter
has been called a "gens"; where the latter is used without comment
in what follows it means a patrilineal kin-group.

It can readily be seen that confusion is imminent in this terminology; and
to make it worse confounded, the American Morgan[74] is found using "gens"
to mean a matrilineal group; to him it covers "a body of consanguinei descended from the same common ancestor, distinguished by a gentile name,
and bound together by affinities of blood"; originating in three conceptions:
"the bond of kin, a pure lineage through descent in the female line, and non-
intermarriage in the gens."

From Rivers's definition of the clan it appears that two of the
three bonds that unite its members are those of kinship. The first
explains itself; the second needs a word of clarification, in anticipation of a later review of totemism.[75] "One of the most frequent,
almost certainly the most frequent, form of the clan is one in
which all its members believe in their relationship to a species of
objects, animal, plant, or inanimate, called totems, of which animal totems are by far the most frequent."[76] This belief may extend
to a conviction that all group-members have descended from the
totem, or from some man or woman somehow closely connected
with it. There is here a very strong element of kinship, whatever
the local complexion of the belief, so that we do not hesitate to
class the tie thus formed as essentially one of blood. There remain
the cases in which there is no totemic bond, "where the essential
tie between the members seems to be habitation of a common territory." Whether or not there may be a forgotten kinship-relation
in the background somewhere, such instances imply a recognition
of the territorial bond which bulks so large in succeeding stages.
The provision of exogamy, whereby the totem must be "crossed,"

[74] *Anc. Soc.*, 62, 63.   [75] §§260-261, below.
[76] Rivers, *Soc. Org.*, 21-22.

is characteristic of the clan; indeed, the fact deserves repetition that these intra-tribal divisions sometimes appear to find their reason for existence in serving as a basis for the taboo on the union of kin. If that were wholly true, the treatment of the clan would belong altogether under the topic of exogamy.[77] It is not true; Morgan[78] says of the gentile organization that it "opens to us one of the oldest and most widely prevalent institutions of mankind. It furnished the nearly universal plan of government of ancient society, Asiatic, European, African, American, and Australian. It was the instrumentality by means of which society was organized and held together. Commencing in savagery, and continuing through . . . barbarism, it remained until the establishment of political society, which did not occur until after civilization had commenced." "The clan plays an important part in the political constitution of the community at large. For, throughout the world, each clan has its own council, composed of the older generation of males, which transacts all its business. The clan usually has the right to elect its own chiefs, when it has any, and depose them, without regard to the council of the larger unit of which it forms a part."[79] The clan is evidently an organ of regulation, not merely a kinship-group. In it lies the control of ceremonial, marriage, descent, property, religion, offices, fines, bloodfeud, and even of the trivialities of life. What is to be kept in mind is that clans are peace-groups affording wider protection to life and property than the more restricted family. Inside the enlarged association a tribunal prevents revenge and retaliation, and the unruly suffer death or exile as punishment for the violation of public peace and order. The judges are all those who would have to share the duty of revenge, in case a member got into trouble; only later are specialized experts differentiated.[80] Clans show a marked solidarity, whereby all are responsible for each and each is therefore interested in controlling as well as defending the other. Gradually, it will be noted, under the influence of local and territorial interests, the kinship-organization tends to give way, having become a maladjustment, especially if numbers greatly increase; but it persists survivalistically for a long time. This tendency

[77] Ch. LXIV, below.
[79] Rivers, *Soc. Org.*, 27.

[78] *Anc. Soc.*, 69.
[80] Lippert, *Kgchte.*, II, 586.

away from the kinship-tie and toward the territorial bond will be seen to be characteristic of the late-developing state-organization, and then these tentatives among very backward peoples will be recalled with some astonishment. Among savages it sometimes carries with it a change from the female line of descent to the male, which itself points in the direction of the state. "In general, it may be said that wherever we are given the kindred as a unit of society, we find that one of its chief manifestations is *projection on the land.* . . . Viewed from the historical point of view, the clans begin by being combinations of kinsmen, and end by being territorial communities. It is on this basis only that neighbors can be considered as claiming a share in property or succession."[81] The further characterization of the clan is left to the cases, of which a considerable number are cited in order to bring out details into which the main body of the text does not go.

In Australia there exist both social organization and local organization. As for the former, "the tribe is generally divided into two or more exogamous intermarrying classes distinguished by titles (badges) which are certainly in some cases, possibly in all, the names of animals. As a general rule each class is again divided into smaller segments also distinguished by animal names. These we may call *totems.*" In the matter of local organization, "the tribe is also made up of a number of clans or local groups, each of which has a local position in some part of the tribal territory. . . . Each clan is made up of individuals of many or all the classes and totems; hence, while the clan has perpetual succession through males, and its local name remains constantly the same, the class and totem names of its members, being transmitted through females, change with each generation. In other words, the sons occupy their fathers' hunting grounds, but they inherit their mothers' names, and therewith the right to certain women for wives—if they can get them. Thus we see that the social organization permeates the local. It rules in many cases the assemblies and ceremonial of the tribe; it regulates marriage, descent, and relationship; it orders blood-feud, it prescribes the rites of hospitality, and it even determines the sides to be taken at the ball-play. Nevertheless the tendency of the local organization is directly hostile to the social—that is to say, it tends to modification and to change of its rules. It tends to create local interests which may clash with the general, it facilitates reparation, and we shall see that in the end it becomes paramount, discarding uterine succession and establishing itself as the local clan with descent through the father, and even perhaps with hereditary chieftainship. . . . The local organization is hostile to the social;—not consciously so, in the minds of the natives, but from the very nature of things. In fact, it is the earliest germ of the State. Its tendency is to modify and contract the range of the social organization, to usurp its authority, to bring about descent through males, to arrange society on its own basis,

81 Vinogradoff, *Hist. Jurispr.,* I, 324.

and finally to make itself paramount." Mother-descent belongs to the social organization, and does not touch the local; the son is, and remains, under the father's authority and in his horde.

This conflict between social and local organization is of high significance. The author[82] continues: "According to the general Australian custom the children belong to the horde of the father, and as the totem on this stage of social development is nothing but a name for the horde, the children adopt their father's totem. As with the Kurnai, *paternal* right reigns in every respect. Some tribes show a remarkable difference in this respect. They too consist of a number of hordes of a politically perfect autonomic character, and here too the children belong to the horde of the father. The totem, however, is inherited by the children from their *mother,* it is a mark of family, not of horde, a mark left by the mother upon her progeny, similar to our custom of inheriting the father's name." "The son is of the father's horde, but of the mother's totem— of the local division to which the father belongs, but of the mother's social division."[83] Thus are the blood-tie and that of locality in conflict and compromise. Game, and even trees, are taken to be somehow related to members of the several classes of the social organization. "When a man desires to perform some magical act, he must use for it only objects which are of the same class as himself, and when he dies he is laid on a stage made of the branches and covered with the leafy boughs of a tree of his class. Among all the natural objects of his class, there is some one which is nearer to him than any other. He bears its name, and it is his totem."[84]

Brown[85] mentions two facts about the Australian clan, one illustrative of the looseness of its organization and the other exhibiting the possibility of the clan extending to meet another like organization in a sort of confederation. "During the greater part of the year the members of the clan—that is the male members, with their wives and unmarried children—would be found living together in their own country. A camp would be formed in a suitable spot and occupied for a few weeks. This camp would be the temporary headquarters of the clan. As a rule the men and women would go out during the day in search of food and return before nightfall. When food was scarce they might scatter in small parties over the clan's hunting and fishing grounds, and such parties might be away from the main camp for several days at a time." The other citation from Brown is to the effect that two clans, not immediate neighbors, might have the same totem and be regarded as related. They are regarded as brothers and sisters together, may not intermarry, and do not fight each other. The same is the case where two clans have adjoining territory; here there is a tendency for each clan to claim the totems of the other. They might almost be regarded as subdivisions of the same clan, though the natives deem them separate units. Each of two clans thus connected maintained a separate camp and had exclusive rights of ownership over its own territory. This latter case affords hints as to the process of clan-amalgamation as the result of proximity; thus the territorial adjacency might eventually lead to a fiction of kinship.

In San Cristoval, in the Solomon Islands, there is a universal belief that the people of each clan are descended from their totem, which is usually a

---

[82] Semon, *Aust. Bush,* 229.
[83] Howitt and Fison, in JAI, XII, 33; and in JAI, XIV, 142, 144.
[84] Howitt, *S. E. Aust.,* 113.   [85] In JAI, XLVIII, 231-232.

bird. "The totem bird is treated with great respect, neither killed nor eaten, and was apparently once sacrificed to. There are two interrogative pronouns in the Arosi language, one used exclusively for persons and the other for everything else; *a tei* for persons, *taha* for things; but if you enquire about a man's clan it is common to use the former, *A tei burunga mu?* Who is your clan? and the bird is given . . .; and *burunga,* one of the words for clan, means also remote ancestor, and is used by Christian natives for Adam and Eve. . . . Formerly the clans were strictly exogamous, and though marriages within the clan took place, at the least a heavy fine had to be paid by the offender. . . . A member of a clan can always appeal to all the other members of his clan for help and protection and can never be destitute. Wherever he goes in Arosi he will find clansmen who will give him hospitality. . . . The real importance of the clans socially lies in their regulation of marriage, since membership of the clan makes a man the relative of all the other members, and all clansmen have definite duties and privileges as regards one another. Property in land is held by the clan. . . . When a boy or girl wishes to marry, the consent of all the members of their clans living in the village or near it must be obtained. This is not an easy matter: personal prejudices play an important part; one member of the clan, standing out for a higher payment, may stop the marriage; and the practical result at the present time is that marriages take place late, although the young men wish to marry and there are marriageable girls, if only the consent of the elders could be obtained. The members of the clan have very real power in this way and exercise it constantly. . . . The sense of solidarity possessed by the clan is well shown by the following incident which came under my notice. A member of the Araha clan had a young son whose death was caused in a fortnight by one of those virulent ulcers which occasionally attack the natives. Another member of Araha had committed adultery about a month previously, and this was held to be the cause of the boy's death."[86]

There is one feature about a man's membership in a social division that strikes strangely upon the ear, namely, that it is not for this life alone, but forever, so far as savages can be said to conceive of eternity. "There is one extremely important feature of the beliefs about reincarnation, and however opinions differ about the other details, this feature is stated and affirmed by all the informants; namely, that the social division, the clan and subclan of the individual, is preserved through all his transformations. The *baloma,* in the nether world, belongs to the same subclan as the man before death; and the reincarnation moves also strictly within the boundaries of the subclan." Thus the "persistence of kinship ties throughout the cycle is decidedly a belief illustrating the strength of the social division, the finality of belonging to a social group Conversely, the belief must strengthen those ties."[87]

In East Africa, "homicide seems to be the only offence affecting not only one individual. A man who has committed such an offence goes to all his clansmen and begs contributions toward the bloodmoney; this is done to the present day, and to refuse such assistance is regarded as shameful, and as equivalent to a denial of kinship. . . . The greater part of the bloodmoney is subscribed by the clan, but not in the form of a loan. For while the clansmen pay at one time, in the reverse case, when one of that clan is killed, they receive a share

[86] Fox, in JAI, XLIX, 101, 103, 104, 105.
[87] Malinowski, in JAI, XLVI, 406.

of the bloodmoney; in fact the claimant by no means retains the whole of the amount paid."[88] Hobley[89] says that the genealogies of the Nilotic tribes and sub-tribes or clans in Kavirondo show how they got their names; for there is no doubt that in olden times the chiefs were far more powerful than now, and a vigorous chief with a large number of wives could have descendants enough to form the beginning of quite a considerable clan." Sometimes an Akamba clan will decide that a certain man of bad character ought to be punished. "During the night his village is surrounded by a party of men, all of his clan, and a guard is placed on the door of his hut while others seize one of his oxen and slay it. If the offence is very serious, even a cow or more than one may be killed. If there are no cattle the party will kill a number of sheep and goats. The culprit is then dragged forth from his hut and beaten with fists, clubs, and anything handy and thrown down and trampled on. His wives will also be brought out and slapped and scratched; the children are not harmed." The Masai clans and families are disappearing, and this despite the fact that the marriage-laws are profoundly affected by the various restrictions connected with kin-grouping; "it is the existence of these barriers which probably prevents these divisions from being completely blotted out by the geographical grouping."[90]

Among the Hopi Indians the traditional account of village-development states that "families drifted to the site of the pueblo from different directions, and as they arrived certain sections of the village were assigned to them for their homes; these sections their descendants still occupy. By mutual consent each clan was allotted certain tracts of land in the plain for their farms, and these land holdings still remain in the clans. While the clans were living together, a community of interest developed and intermarriage broke down the limitation of sacerdotal societies to clans. Certain emergencies arose when clans were forced to act together. These influences resulted in an amalgamation of clans, and a new organization was effected. The clan languages were fused into a common speech, and a coalescence of the different arts and customs also occurred. The new organization retained much that was good in each of the component clans. The ritual developed along the same lines, but the religious sentiment being more conservative, the clan units have remained more apparent in the rites than elsewhere."[91] We shall wish to recall this case as an illustration of amalgamation of separate kinship-groups into a single political body. "The clans themselves were not fixed units; new ones were born and old ones died, as children of one sex or the other predominated. The creation of clans was a continuous process." Here is a clear case of automatic selection, and the instance goes farther, for even the forms of the houses are modified by the uncontrollable element of sex-proportion. "Thus, in the Corn clan of Tusayan, under favorable conditions there grew up subclans claiming connection with the root, stem, leaves, blossom, pollen, etc. In time the relations of clans and subclans became extremely complex; hence the aggregation into larger units or phratries. The clan is a great artificial family, and when it comprises many girls it must necessarily grow. Such is also the case with the individual family, for as the men who are adopted into it by marriage take up their quarters in the family home and children are born to them more space is required. But additional rooms, which are still the family property,

[88] Dundas, C., in JAI, XLV, 267.   [89] In JAI, XXXIII, 332.
[90] Hobley, A-Kamba, 80, 119, 121.   [91] Fewkes, in BAE, XIX, 1006.

must be built in the family quarter, and by a long-established rule they must be built adjoining and connected with those already occupied. Therefore in each village there are constant changes in the plan; new rooms are added here, old rooms abandoned there."[92]

Two sterling authorities[93] on Australasian institutions have seen profit in comparing primitive forms with those of the Greeks. In Athenian society there were two great organizations, one based originally on locality and the other on birth. "The demotic is the local organization; the phratrial is the social. The demes were in a political organization, artificially and arbitrarily constructed in the first instance, but they were originally arranged on the basis of locality. But no deme coincided with any phratria, or with any subdivision of a phratria. The members of the one organization were scattered among the divisions of the other. . . . Athens and Australia furnish clear distinctions between phrators and demotes—between the social and the local. They also give a clear and instructive distinction between the nature of the offense against the former and that against the latter. One is a breach of morality 'doing despite to the gods'; the other is a civil wrong 'defrauding his deme of its lawful gains.' The latter is a case for the law courts; the former one for the phratriac tribunals. . . . At Athens a child became a member of its father's phratria at birth, or as soon as it had been presented at the ancestral altar and accepted by the phrators. Such was not the case in the demotic organization. There the son became a member of his father's deme, but was not formally admitted until he had served a long period of probation. He was not qualified to look for a wife until he was 18, had passed 2 years in the gymnasia, was armed in the presence of the assembly, and registered in his deme. Even then he had to serve 2 years on the frontier before taking his place in the assembly. Thus the qualification for a born citizen to enter the demotic organization was proof that he was qualified to take his place in the community, and contribute to its defense. The Australian usage is very similar. In tribes having uterine descent a child at birth becomes a member of the social division to which its mother belongs. In all tribes known to the writers a boy is by birth one of his father's horde, but cannot exercise either his totemic or local privileges until the men of the community, assembled in their local organization, formally admit him." In Athens the bride was presented to the phratry-mates of her husband, which is a sign that the phratries were originally connubial unions. The Roman *curiae* were the same.[94]

It is clear that the kinship-idea strongly permeates the tribe inasmuch as it is the salient feature of tribal components. However, "the tribe is not merely a group of clans," for "its constitution becomes profoundly modified by the gradual substitution of patriarchal for matriarchal rights."[95] The male line issues at length in a control not based any longer upon kinship. The tribe is not the original form, but an ethnically composite social product; it shows a mastery of class over class, and therein is the prototype

[92] Mindeleff, in BAE, XIX, pt. II, 647.
[93] Howitt and Fison, in JAI, XIV, 147, 154, 162.
[94] Lippert, *Kgchte.*, II, 135.　　　　[95] Keane, *Ethnology,* 9.

of the state. "The most important people of antiquity came forward in their beginnings as composites of tribes united for conquest and mastery."[96] When one advances from these lesser kinship-organizations to the tribe, he is passing, in reality, from the blood-tie to a wider, political bond. The persistence of the former becomes survivalistic, for instance in the tribal marks which insure safety to the individual through fear of tribal vengeance. Though such marks or scars may be indicative of a merely artificial blood-kinship, or "blood-brotherhood," they point back unmistakably to the recognition of genuine consanguinity.[97] A few instances of tribal organization may serve to enforce the fact of transition from the idea of the blood-bond toward that of a political body.

Among the Australians what Howitt[98] calls "tribe" means "a number of people who occupy a definite tract of country, who recognise a common relationship and have a common speech, or dialects of the same. The tribes-people recognise some common bond which distinguishes them from other tribes, usually a tribal name, which may be their word for 'man.' . . . But while individual tribes are thus distinguished from others, there are numerous cases in which the word for 'man' is common to the languages of a considerable number of more or less nearly related tribes, indicating a larger aggregate. . . . A distinction is drawn by tribes between themselves and aliens by some term applied to the latter, either of contempt or fear . . . such as tiger-snakes, because, as I have heard them say, 'they come sneaking about to kill us.' " This author uses the words clan and horde to indicate respectively tribal subdivisions with descent in the male and in the female line—an illustration of the fact that terminology is not standardized.

The kinship-idea persists in the Yakut sib, which is a man-descent group modified by territorial circumstances; that is, its size is controlled by the number of cattle or horses which can be supported on the natural meadows on which they live. Here is the man-land ratio once more. The sib is constituted of patrilineal households, each living separately, and is the real group for all purposes.[99] Thus may a tribe, when limited in growth, remain practically a kin-group. In India, on the other hand, aliens might gain easy admission to tribes, and as soon as a man had permanently joined, he "became a participator in good and ill. Then, having shown his worth, he was given a vested interest in the tribal welfare by acquiring a portion of the tribal lands . . . and his admission was sealed with blood by women from the tribe being given to him or his sons in marriage. . . . The process is easy to follow: Admission to participation in common blood-feud; then admission to participation in the tribal law; and lastly admission to kinship with the tribe." From whatever point a start is made, the final and intimate bond is that of blood. A

96 Gumplowicz, *Rassenk.*, 194 ff.
97 Lippert, *Kgchte.*, I, 387 ff.; §297, below.
98 *S. E. Aust.*, 41, 43; Palmer, in JAI, XIII, 302; Howitt, in JAI, XIII, 335.
99 Sieroshevski, *Yakuts* (Russ.), 517.

whole tribe may be converted to Hinduism without abandoning the tribal name, and while retaining its totemistic exogamous subdivisions.[100]

In Polynesian social life the tribe or community preponderates over the family more than almost anywhere else;[101] Pereiro[102] speaks of a civil constitution, "in which the tribe or community constitutes the true family, ignoring the importance that we concede, in civilized countries, to the natural family."

Seebohm[103] writes of the Welsh: "The ruling principle underlying the structure of tribal society was that of blood relationship among the free tribesmen. No one who did not belong to a kindred could be a member of the tribe, which was, in fact, a bundle of Welsh kindreds."

Thus does the tribe betray, in its organization, the nature and relation of the component parts by the union of which it is formed. Association can develop only to a certain limited degree under the kinship-group, however relationship is reckoned. When men are brought into local contact and held there, the situation demands an organization of greater potency and comprehensiveness. True as this is, it should not be overlooked that community of blood was long the only bond, and that the kinship-idea continues to color social relations long after it ceases to be the basis to which they are referred.

Although the mere size of an association may preclude the continued availability of the blood-tie, the way in which that bond is reckoned has also had its disintegrating influence upon the kingroup. When relationship is traced in both lines, presently the compounding of names renders the system unworkable. All sorts of maladjustments and complexities arise.

"So soon as it is admitted that the bond of blood, the bond which groups men together for the purpose of blood-feud and of *wergeld*, ties the child both to his father's brother and to his mother's brother, a system of mutually exclusive clans is impossible, unless indeed each clan is strictly endogamous. There is a foray; grandfather, father, and son are slain; the *wer* must be paid. The *wer* of the grandfather must be paid to one set of persons; the *wer* of the father to a different set; the *wer* of the son to yet a third set. If kinship be traced only through males or only through females, then we may have permanent and mutually exclusive units; we may picture the nation as a tree, the clans as branches; if a twig grows out of one branch, it cannot grow out of another. In the other case each individual is himself the trunk of the *arbor consanguinitatis,*" or tree of relationship.[104]

[100] Risley, *Ethnog. India,* I, 63, 165.
[101] Ratzel, *Vkde.,* II, 101.
[102] *Ponapé,* 119.
[103] *Tribal Syst. of Wales,* 54.
[104] Pollock and Maitland, *Eng. Law,* II, 238.

By whatever means disintegrated, the kin-group system loses its efficacy as an adjustment and merges gradually into a system better suitable to altered conditions, living on within it to discharge such services as it is capable of performing. The family remains vigorous within the larger political aggregation; but the effective life of the constituent kin-groups is about over.

Dundas,[105] after reviewing the African forms, concludes that the foundation of the governmental system "is the family, and groups of families loosely connected by custom and religion, and in some cases by the physical features of the country in which they live." He then goes on to comment upon the fact that all these matters belong, as we should put it, in the mores. "Such ties as there are must, however, be regarded as voluntarily submitted to, there being no central authority to whom all submit. Disintegrated as such a form of society appears, it is yet based on a certain system, which not having strength to maintain itself must have been powerfully supported by custom. We can therefore imagine that in former times custom must have possessed a force amounting to necessity, which it is difficult to form an idea of at the present day. It is certain that present-day disregard for custom would break up any community based upon it."

§150*. Blood-Brotherhood. An application of the common-blood idea in relation to the out-group remains to be noted. So deeply ingrained in the mores is the conviction that close human relationship means blood-relationship that the exchange of blood between those who are establishing friendship is a relatively common ceremony. If two men draw and mix their blood, by drinking it or otherwise, what they are doing is establishing a peace-relation between them such as existed traditionally between people of the same blood. Adoption into a peace-group is sometimes attended by this ceremony or by one of its survivalistic forms. Symbols that appear in connection with marriage are reasonably interpretable in the same sense, and the cult-bond is intimately connected with blood-ceremonies.[106] The whole idea is to form a close relationship; the closest that is known is kinship under the blood-tie; and so the blood-tie is created by blood-mixture. Even property roots in blood-effusion.[107] Perhaps it is actually believed that such mixture establishes community of blood, for the savages cannot know much about the physiology of the matter; in any case they act as if they held that belief.[108] Throughout primitive life

105 In JAI, XLV, 249. 106 §§213, 297, 298, 371, 426, below.
107 §108, above. 108 §411, below.

appears a veritable preoccupation with blood, and there can be no doubt as to the genuineness of the convictions underlying the various blood-ceremonies.

Under this topic of brotherhood we shall first illustrate the ceremonies creative of community of blood, and then go on to consider other practices, such as guest-friendship, which extend association beyond the kin-group. The ground will then be cleared for the study of the larger, political peace-group, the tribe or nation.

The Australians are prone to blood-letting,[108] which they perform by cutting with a stone or, if procurable, a glass-flake. "Every adult native has a series of little lumps marking the course of the veins on the forearm which indicate the places where he has cut himself for the purpose of drawing blood. . . . The drawing and also the drinking of blood on certain special occasions is associated with the idea that those who take part in the ceremony are thereby bound together in friendship and obliged to assist one another. At the same time it renders treachery impossible." The men taking part in an avenging expedition "assembled together, and, after each one had been touched with the girdle made from the hair of the man whose death they were going out to avenge, they drew blood . . . and sprinkled it over one another. Sometimes, for the same purpose, blood is drawn from the arm and drunk, and on rare occasions a man, declining thus to pledge himself, will have his mouth forced open and blood poured into it."[109] If an avenging party were going into a certain locality, "and they had with them in camp a man of that locality, he would be forced to drink blood with them, and, having done so, would be bound not to aid his friends by warning." Being so forced "would have just the same influence as if the drinking had been a voluntary one. . . . Blood-drinking is associated with special meetings of reconciliation which sometimes take place between two groups who have been on bad terms with one another without actually coming to a fight. . . . If the offending group be willing, which they are almost sure to be, then the meeting is held, and at the beginning each party drinks the blood of its own members, and a more or less sham fight takes place with boomerangs, no one being hurt."[110]

Blood-friendship carried with it claims as of true relatives. In New Guinea, when a certain missionary died, his native blood-friends "took, in accord with their custom all his personal property, watch, knife, clothes, etc., into their possession and divided them among them. . . . The missionaries who had hurried from the coast were at first astonished and enraged, since they did not know the custom, and took the things away from those who had them. The latter gave up everything quite goodnaturedly, but were now, in turn, very much amazed and said: 'You whites must have then quite other customs than we have.' "[111]

The South African ceremony for cementing friendship is accomplished thus: "The hands of the parties are joined; small incisions are made on the clasped hands, on the pits of the stomachs of each, and on the right cheeks and fore-

[109] Spencer and Gillen, *North. Tr. Cent. Aust.*, 596, 598.
[110] Spencer and Gillen, *Nat. Tr. Cent. Aust.*, 461, 462.
[111] Hagen, *Papua's*, 262.

heads. A small quantity of blood is taken off from these points in both parties by means of a stalk of grass. The blood from one person is put into a pot of beer, and that of the second into another; each then drinks the other's blood, and they are supposed to become perpetual friends or relations. During the drinking of the beer, some of the party continue beating the ground with short clubs, and utter sentences by way of ratifying the treaty. The men belonging to each then finish the beer. The principals in the performance of 'Kasendi' are henceforth considered blood-relations, and are bound to disclose to each other any impending evil. If one of these men should resolve to attack the Balonda, the other would be under obligation to give warning to escape, and so on the other side. They now gave each other the most valuable gifts they had to bestow."[112] In some cases the exchange of blood has come, survivalistically, to be an exchange of some substitute, for instance, of a mouthful of liquor.[113]

In East Africa the method by which Europeans have established close and dependable relations with native chiefs is through mutual sucking of blood.[114] Blood-friendship ceremonies also seal the peace between two tribes. A representative of each sits one at each end of a mat, and an old man between them, armed with a sword, declares the sacredness of the blood-bond and warns them that if they break it they will perish by the sword. A kid is slaughtered between them. Each slightly roasts a bit of the liver and sprinkles it with the blood of the other, each having lightly wounded the other. They eat the liver. Stuhlmann,[115] whom we are quoting, tells of the establishment of blood-friendship between himself and an African chief. The latter took out of a little straw box a coffee-berry in the shell, broke it, and gave the author one of the halves. Each ate one, after sprinkling it with blood drawn from above the heart. Each reached out his half to the other on the palm of his hand, to be taken by the other's lips. The ceremony ended with a handshake. In Madagascar blood taken from the breast or side is mixed with other ingredients and stirred up with a spear-point before the swallowing and the imprecations.[116]

In one case saliva seems to have taken the rôle of the blood: "Lokomagul, on behalf of his people, and I, on behalf of my own, each seized in our right hands a round stone. Upon the stones we liberally expectorated. Each then passed his stone to his following, who did likewise. We then exchanged stones; and each, holding the stone in his right hand, with his left dug a small hole in the soil, meanwhile uttering words of supposed magic import. In these holes we finally placed the stones, and covered them with sand. We then grasped hands, and assured each other that we were the best friends possible."[117]

Blood-ceremonies of this order are typical of Africa, but they are represented elsewhere in the world, and not in survival-form alone. In India the friendship-forming ritual includes exchange of rupees and scarves, and the candidates "daub each other between the eyebrows with the paste made of rice and curds which is used in the marriage ceremony. The effect of the union is that the friends are reckoned as brothers, and intermarriage between the two families is prohibited for several . . . generations." Severe punishments, such as exclusion from caste, slavery, or even death are visited upon breach

[112] Livingstone, *Mission. Travels*, 525.   [113] Volkens, *Kilimandscharo*, 157.
[114] Schmidt, *Deut. Kol.*, I, 29; Abbott, in USNM, 1891, 395.
[115] *Mit Emin*, 24, 162.   [116] Sibree, *Great Afr. Isl.*, 223.
[117] Chanler, *Jungle and Desert*, 305.

of this rule.[118] In Borneo the actual blood-ceremony is carried out in a manner parallel to the African, with the incision, collection of drops of blood, imprecations, and final drinking.[119]

Our collections of cases show no blood-brotherhood ceremonies among the American Indians parallel to those of the Africans and Malays. Chambers, in his romance, *The Hidden Children*,[120] causes a Mohican sagamore to perform the rite with a white man—"an alliance of implicit trust and mutual confidence which only death could end."

Xenophon[121] mentions the dipping of spears in the blood of a victim in making an agreement. The Arabs are reported by Herodotus[122] to contract the brotherhood-relation by exchange of blood. In Scandinavia swearing friendship was accompanied by letting "blood run together in the footprint," that is the footprint was filled with the blood of the two prospective brothers, mixed.[123]

It is not at all improbable that the pledging of friendship, or the drinking of healths in wine, is a survival of the ancient ceremonial of pledging in blood.[124] According to the historically conscientious Sienkiewicz,[125] the Polish nobles and the Tatar murzas were wont to pledge brotherhood by dipping their weapons in the blood of an animal, spilled into a shield; and water was sometimes poured on the spear-heads. It is risky to assert that such a practice, taken by itself, is a survival of blood-mixing; but the consensus of many cases, as is proved by the unparalleled collections of Frazer, in his *Golden Bough*, though no one of them by itself is conclusive, forms an accumulation of impression difficult to resist. And in the matter before us, as in so many others, the explanation on the basis of survivalism is incomparably more satisfying than unverifiable imaginings or reference forthwith to "symbolism."[126]

We may pass rather rapidly in review certain other brotherhood-ceremonies which cannot readily, or even with cunning, be traced back to the artificial creation of a blood-bond. They are, however, practised to the same intent, namely, the extension of peace and friendship. They are socializing. Guest-friendship, hospitality, and, in general, the handling of the stranger as other than an enemy, are productive of the extension of the peace-bond.

[118] Risley, *Ethnog. India*, I, 202.   [119] Schwaner, *Borneo*, I, 214-215.
[120] P. 139.   [121] *Anab.*, II, 2.
[122] *Hist.*, III, 8.
[123] Vigfusson and Powell, *Corp. Poet. Bor.*, I, 423-424; *Saxo Gram.*, bk. I.
[124] Lippert, *Kgchte.*, I, 482; II, 333 ff.
[125] *Pan Michael*, 164.   [126] §456, below.

A Papuan chief split a large leaf in two lengthwise, gave one half to Finsch[127] and bound the other to the mast of his canoe. "I too had mine bound to the mast, which plainly gave pleasure to the people." The Herero of southwest Africa have a brotherhood-relation where the associates have their wives in common. A brother can lay claim to anything that is his brother's, and when the claim extends to the wife, the system is productive of great mischief. Mutual hospitality and gift-giving are duties devolving upon brothers.[128]

Foregoing cases should be recalled which exhibit the responsibility of a host for his guest; they seem to be not altogether referable to pure hospitality-customs, but to rest upon some lurking impression of kin-duty. "In dealing with an alien it would not be considered wrong to rob, beat, abuse, or even murder him, unless he had come on a visit, for trade or other purposes, to someone in the town. He would then be under the protection of his host, and would receive his hospitality and hence the hospitality of the town and neighbourhood. The host would have a *casus belli* against anyone who molested his guest. . . . For a canoe of strangers from neighbouring towns or districts to approach a town unannounced by drum or song was regarded as an act of war. If their coming were peaceful, why were they afraid to drum and sing? I have seen a crew of such a canoe badly handled for omitting these courtesies, and but for our presence some of the travellers would have been speared."[129] This case illustrates the suspicion that exists between savage tribes, as well as the several means which are in use for mitigating group-hostility. They all approach in their various degrees the establishment of blood-ties, which are the final and indisputable evidences of belonging together in a peace-group.

Often before a fight, in Africa as in the Greece of Homer's time,[130] two opponents might exchange lances, thus joining irrevocable brotherhood; an enemy can be saved by covering him with a cloak and exchanging guns with him; and a man surprised by enemies can put himself under the protection of one of them and become instantly safe and inviolable. This custom is like that of the Homeric suppliant.[131] The *anaia* of the Kabyles is a protection accorded to one or more persons by an individual, a village, a tribe, or any other association. The protected person is taken into a sort of solidarity with the protecting agent. Violation of the *anaia* is one of the deepest of injuries; if one village violates it with another, it must make humiliating and grave reparation—sometimes the guilty villagers leave their village and the injured ones come in and destroy a certain number of houses. "To the institution of the *anaia* there cannot be denied a character of true grandeur. It is an original form of mutual assistance pushed to self-abnegation, and the heroic acts which it inspires do the greatest honor to the Kabyle people."[132]

Oaths of friendship occur in India which, yet again, recall the "sacred oaths" of the Homeric Greeks.[133] A goat was stretched before the head chief who stood over it with a sword, "and taking a mouthful of liquor from a cup

[127] *Samoafahrten*, 295.
[128] Fritsch, *Eingeb. S.-Afr.*, 227; Holub, *S. Afr.*, II, 136 ff., 142.
[129] Weeks, in JAI, XXXIX, 446.
[130] Homer, *Iliad*, VI, 215-236.   [131] Keller, *Hom. Soc.*, 301.
[132] Hanoteau et Letourneux, *Kabylie*, II, 61-63; Letourneau, *Guerre*, 267, 268, 269.
[133] Keller, *Hom. Soc.*, 175-179 (where full references are given).

which was handed to him, he blew it first over me, then over the Chiefs, and a third mouthful upon the goat." After an invocation and the plucking and scattering of some of the goat's hairs, he severed its head. "The warm blood from his weapon was afterwards smeared upon the feet and foreheads of all who took part in the ceremony, with a muttered formula, indicating that anyone who was false or acted contrary to the object for the attainment of which the sacrifice was offered, could be slain without fault by his coadjutors."[134] "A young Palaung sometimes swears an eternal friendship with another man, not only for the present life, but also for all their future existences. They make their promises over a bowl of water and then each drinks his share."[135] That this may be a survival of blood-drinking seems quite self-evident.

The spirit of brotherly association, helpfulness, and mutual support, the child of the clan-system and the village-autonomy, under which régime the people of the Middle Kingdom live, is everywhere in evidence in China.[136] In Borneo, "if two men who have been at a deadly feud, meet in a house, they refuse to cast their eyes upon each other till a fowl has been killed and the blood sprinkled over them." It is said that "enemies can neither eat nor drink in company, without desiring a reconciliation."[137] "Every Kanaka," writes Dana,[138] referring to the Sandwich Islanders in California in the thirties of the last century, "has one particular friend whom he considers himself bound to do everything for, and with whom he has a sort of contract,—an alliance offensive and defensive,—and for whom he will often make the greatest sacrifices." Of a Kanaka who had adopted the author as a friend, Dana says: "I do not believe I could have wanted anything which he had, that he would not have given me."

"Among the Siouan peoples the individual brotherhood of the David-Jonathan or Damon-Pythias type was characteristically developed."[139] Among the Seminoles, "two young men agree to be life friends, 'more than brothers,' confiding without reserve each in the other and protecting each the other from all harm."[140] Where two persons belong to the same gild-like association they may not marry, for members of such associations regard each other as the closest blood-friends.[141] Von den Steinen[142] swore friendship with one of the natives according to the local custom, that is by exchanging names. The native struck him six or seven times on the back, pronouncing his own name each time. Then he blew on the breast of the white man, and pronounced his own name in each of his ears. The white man had to duplicate this performance with his own name. After that all the people called the white man by the name of the native. Even the Fuegians form certain kinds of friendships, involving mutual exchanges and presents, and the painting of faces and bodies after a certain manner. Thus they speak of aunts, uncles, brothers, sisters, cousins, nieces, and nephews who are so only through the friendship established; and according to the name they take they are expected to act.[143]

"Among the Arabs every stranger whom one meets in the desert is a natural enemy, and has no protection against violence except his own strong hand

[134] Lewin, *S. E. India*, 228.
[135] Milne, *Eastern Clan*, 216.
[136] De Groot, *Kongsiwezen*, 110, 113.
[137] Roth, *Sarawak*, II, 204.
[138] *Two Years before the Mast*, 160.
[139] McGee, in BAE, XV, 178.
[140] MacCauley, in BAE, V, 508.
[141] Von Martius, *Beiträge*, I, 116-117.
[142] *Zent. Bras.*, 125.
[143] Bridges, in *A Voice for S. Amer.*, XIII, 201.

or the fear that his tribe will avenge him if his blood be spilt. But if I have eaten the smallest morsel of food with a man, I have nothing further to fear from him; 'there is salt between us,' and he is bound not only to do me no harm, but to help and defend me as if I were his brother. . . . . The bond of union is conceived in a very realistic way, and strictly speaking lasts no longer than the food may be supposed to remain in my system. . . . . The bond of salt is not dependent on the actual use of mineral salt with the food by which the bond is constituted. Milk, for example, will serve the purpose." The protection extended to a guest lasts usually three days and a third, or two nights and a day, after his departure.[144]

Ceremonies for entering into close friendship occurred in ancient Scandinavia; and the Slavonian ritual contained a ceremony to bless the union of two men or two women as friends. If two Slavic people of different sex swear brotherhood, they may not marry. Among the Croats there is a custom of "chosen sisters," where two women join in friendship through marriage and death.[145]

Wilken,[146] makes a good deal of the practice of eating and drinking together in ceremonies involving the establishment of close relations of any sort. The Bataks slaughter a carabao when they make an alliance, and the eating of it together goes often with the drinking of each other's blood. At the conclusion of peace there is a common meal, with exchange of betel. In the Archipelago, as elsewhere among primitive peoples, crimes were regarded as committed not against the state but against individuals; then the evil-doer is reconciled with the community by a common meal; thus is the broken peace restored, the deed wiped out, and the land purified. "It is well known that men can enter an alliance with the ghosts as well as with men, that is, can make peace, by offering them a meal and themselves taking part in it." Such a sacrifice is a form of communion. "All association is, in primitive societies, blood-association. To such an association one may belong otherwise than by birth; through food and drink, at every turn, new blood is acquired. Those who eat out of the same dish and drink out of the same cup renew their blood from the same source and inject the same blood into their veins. A stranger, even an enemy, who shares our meal, even against our will, becomes

144 Smith, *Relig. Sem.*, 269 ff.

145 Kålund, in *Aarbøger,* 1870, 290 ff.; Grote, *Greece,* II, 87, note; Rhamm, in *Globus,* LXXXII, 189, 190; Tetzner, "Kroaten," in *Globus,* LXXXV, 40.

146 In VG, I, 536 ff., 608. Wilken's editor remarks (VG, IV, 194, note) that Wilken came to lay somewhat less stress upon the common meal than he had done; his extreme views, if they were such, are not represented in our excerpts. See his "Oorsprong der offers," in VG, IV, 161 ff.; §284, below.

thus, at least temporarily, of our flesh and blood, and is taken into the association to which we belong by virtue of our flesh and blood." Thus the eating together when alliances are made or peace established becomes quite explicable. It is not hard to see why the same ceremony accompanies the wedding, when the woman is taken into the family of the man; and there is more to it, for the wedding is often the occasion of a reconciliation after real or feigned violence. Betel and tobacco play a large part in such ceremonies in the East Indies; groom and bride often chew betel or smoke a cigarette together.

Fit to be ranked along with the brotherhoods and sworn friendships is the practice of guest-friendship. This is really an extreme form of hospitality. There are a good many tribes up and down the earth that treat strangers well, apparently in part because the stranger gratifies their curiosity by telling them of the outside world. Again, this hospitality is merely formal, representing a sort of lull in the prevailing hostility.

Of the Namaquas it is reported: "Like many other nomads, they welcome the stranger with a show of hospitality, but once beyond their district he is regarded as lawful prey."[147] Similarly among the Arabs: among themselves they are bound by relationship and the holiness of blood, while any conferring of rights and duties outside is in the hand of Allah. He guards the arrangements "whereby the natural circle of association experiences an extension and completion that inures above all to the benefit of the client and the guest." But the guest's claim to inviolability ends at the tent door, or at any rate with the third day.[148]

Peoples who dwell in proximity to one another differ markedly in their attitude toward aliens. Thus in Formosa "some southern tribes are very hospitable, while the northerners have been declared by many disgusted visitors to be 'about the most inhospitable people on God's earth.' "[149] It must not be thought that backward tribes are by nature sociable and hospitable, for such qualities are the product of evolution and there is plenty of hostility to strangers among isolated peoples. For instance, the Tarahumari of Mexico are not exactly hospitable. In their houses or caves there is no room for a stranger. To get on well with them one must, on arrival, sit patiently at thirty to fifty yards' distance from the house, until the head of the family is pleased to come out, which will not be before fifteen minutes. An utter stranger may have to wait two hours. They say that only the dogs enter a house at once. A Tarahumari who is visiting even his best friend is never, unless the weather is exceptionally bad, invited to remain over night. He goes off and sleeps under a tree or big stone. If he is an Indian, food is given him.[150]

[147] Keane, *Afr.*, II, 185.　　　　[148] Wellhausen, *Skizzen*, III, 190.
[149] Wirth, in AA, X, 365.
[150] Lumholtz, in *Int. Cong. Anthrop.*, 1893, 106.

Such cases of non-sociability warn us that the primitive state of man was as little characterized by universal love of fellow-men as it was by any other of the appealing qualities imagined by the partially informed. The fact is that if men have come to tolerate and even to like and welcome strangers, this has been brought about by something else than nature or herd-instincts or other original endowment. It is readily enough seen that a policy of hospitality must result in such advantages as are conferred by exogamy, trade, and other associative factors as distinguished from the outcome of a system of isolation and hostility. Without entering upon the various minor degrees of friendly treatment of strangers, we may as well concentrate upon some examples leading up to its most striking exhibition, in the form of guest-friendship, to which allusion has been made.

The Biotos of New Guinea have two houses, one at each end of their village, for visitors. "This provision for the stranger within their gates is a general custom in every Papuan village. Despite this form of hospitality, however, the Bioto people are not very amicable."[151] Here, as in a number of other cases, hospitality seems to be formal rather than heart-felt. The feeling for guests seems to be warmer in the thinly settled parts of Cameroons, or where there are not many Europeans.[152] In West Africa "a stranger is entertained hospitably. He is provided with a house and food for two weeks, or as much longer as he may wish to stay. On departing he is given a present. His host and the village headman are bound to protect him from any prosecution while he is their guest, even if he be really guilty."[153] Nachtigal[154] threatened in vain to leave one region where he had been badly treated, and the natives did not oppose his representations, but with sly reluctance agreed with them, for such a plan would be to their advantage: if they got him out of their dwelling-place and they were no longer bound by the duties of guest-friendship, they could give free rein to their impulses. Here the rights of the guest and the duties of the host were evidently highly formal affairs.

"Not to be a guest, or to have no guests, is to the Somali as to the Galla an almost unlivable situation. . . . A stranger cannot exist among them unless he is willing to be a guest or offers guest-friendship. If one is once taken into the society, for instance of the Somali, he is formally regarded as a child of the tribe. The southern Somali . . . spits into his right hand and rubs it on the forehead of the stranger . . . as a sign that he has become a native." He gets all the rights of a tribesman. The guest "is entertained and receives a gift at parting which corresponds in size to the intimacy of the friendship and the value of the visit." The inland Somal is not merely suspicious of, but hostile to the white man; but if he likes some European enough to throw grain upon him as he enters the house, "then there is nothing further to worry about, for this ancient Arabian custom gives to guest-friendship the real consecration

151 Pratt, *New Guinea*, 83.   152 Meinecke, *Deut. Kol.*, 30.
153 Nassau, *W. Afr.*, 17.   154 *Sahara*, I, 276.

and secures the inviolability of the stranger." Some natives of influence even exact high payment for the protection their friendship accords, as a safe-conduct, to a traveller.[155]

Among the Tungus, "relying upon the guest-friendship of their countrymen, individuals often set out on long journeys without taking even the slightest provision of means of livelihood." The Tungus, we are told, are always honest and do not suspect one another.[156] The Khonds of Bengal rival the Beduins in hospitality. So famous are they for this quality that the story is told that at a certain feast, a quarrel arising, the whole clan was cut to pieces. The fugitives, pursued to the utmost limit, finally returned to the homes that had once been theirs and knocked for admission. This was granted and friends and enemies dwelt together.[157] "The laws of guest-friendship rule among the Ossetes as strictly as among the rest of the peoples of the Caucasus. The guest-friend . . . stands for his guest with his goods and blood. The murder or wounding of the guest-friend represents the same injury as that of a relative, and evokes therefore the avenging of blood. The guest-right is so holy that if, for example, an Ossete had received an unknown guest in his house and it turned out from further talk that he was a blood-enemy on whom he must take blood-vengeance, yet he would entertain him thereafter as before and say to him at departure outside the peace-tabooed village: 'From now on take care, for I am thy enemy!' "[158]

Years ago a white man in Yap was discharged by his employer and, since no other of his race offered him shelter, he went, at the invitation of a native, to live with him without cost. The native had hidden him as far as possible. After some time the native was asked about it by a recently arrived European. He was frightened at the publicity and asked him not to spread it farther, "because it must have been painful for his guest."[159] The hostility between Eskimo tribes "did not hinder their seeming to stand on the best footing with each other, when they met, for guest-freedom is for them a necessary duty."[160] "A symbol that appears among all Brazilian savages is that the master of the house, and if it is occupied by several, all of these, receive the stranger while lying in their hammocks. As soon as they see anyone coming to their huts they hurry to lie down; and this often happens with all the rest of the family also, so that the one who enters is the only one standing until a place is offered him by the fire or in a separate hammock, which they hang up opposite that of the guest-friend. Without doubt the Indian means by this to announce his undis-puted right of house and of protection. . . . If the stranger, commonly by a silent sign, has been invited to take part in the meal, and if the house-father goes so far as to hand him his burning cigar, then guest-friendship is formally guaranteed and it is never broken."[161]

§151. Group-Solidarity. Doubtless the mother-child relation reveals association in its very lowest terms; and upon that relation is built the conception of kinship. The blood-bond is both the

[155] Paulitschke, *Nordost-Afr.*, I, 246.
[156] Hiekisch, *Tungusen*, 67. [157] Reclus, *Prim. Folk*, 260.
[158] Von Haxthausen, *Transkaukasia*, II, 32-33.
[159] Senfft, in *Globus*, XCI, 139. [160] Holm, *Ethnol. Skizze*, 45.
[161] Von Martius, *Beiträge*, I, 96, 97.

most ancient and also the most persistent of society-forming ties;
for within the kin-group there are peace, harmony, and coöperation, as contrasted with hostility to all that which, being outside,
is assumed to be threatening to existence. The clan is a peace-
group, for its members may not fight each other.[162]

"By the rules of early society, if I slay my kinsman, whether voluntarily or
involuntarily, the act is murder, and is punished by expulsion from the kin
[thus was Cain expelled]; if my kinsman is slain by an outsider I and every
other member of my kin are bound to avenge his death by killing the manslayer or some member of his kin. It is obvious that under such a system there
can be no inviolable fellowship except between men of the same blood. For the
duty of blood revenge is paramount, and every other obligation is dissolved
as soon as it comes into conflict with the claims of blood. I cannot bind myself
absolutely to a man, even for a temporary purpose, unless during the time of
our engagement he is put into a kinsman's place. And this is as much as to say
that a stranger cannot become bound to me, unless at the same time he becomes bound to all my kinsmen in exactly the same way. Such is, in fact, the
law of the desert; when any member of a clan receives an outsider through
the bond of salt, the whole clan is bound by his act, and must, while the
engagement lasts, receive the stranger as one of themselves."[163]

This bond of kinship is so preëminent in power and scope that
other ties tend to pass into kinship with amalgamation of groups
somehow brought into propinquity.[164] Take the case of conquest,
where two groups fall into conflict and one overcomes the other;
then the ensuing relation is one of dominion.[165] Conquest extends
the peace-group while producing inequality within it; but the
classes thus differentiated as dominant and subject tend to amalgamate by intermarriage and to regard themselves as kin, if not in
demonstrable fact, at least through some eponymous ancestor.
Another proximity-producing factor, traditionally associated with
connubium, is commercium. Trade brings peoples into each other's
presence, and mutual interests lead both to toleration and to the
formation of matrimonial alliances; for any regular and continued
association is accompanied by mutual acquaintance with and
transfer of the mores, beginning with language. In short, group-
bonds are formed by the action of those same socializing forces[166]
whose method of operation has been sketched above. It should be
noted that kin-groups may increase in size so that parts of them

162 Bancroft, *Nat. Races*, I, 109.   163 Smith, *Relig. Sem.*, 272-273.
164 §167, below.
165 Ratzenhofer, *Soc. Erkennt.*, 245.   166 §§11 ff., above.

may fall into competition for food or other necessities, and that then the ensuing hostility may be overcome by association for a larger common interest, through antagonistic coöperation; further, that when the gain of combination ceases, the association breaks up. The topic of socialization need not be re-canvassed here, even though it is approached from a different angle; but it may be further illustrated by the odd case of a group-bond formed by common criminality and by a more thorough review of such a bond as knit by the cult.

Crime may constitute a common interest of men, leading not alone to gangs of males associated in antisocial activities, but even to criminal societies in the sense of term "society" as here adopted.[167] Though bands of thieves or other criminals are no unheard-of phenomenon within a society, in some parts of the world there are outcast and criminal tribes who are held together as a body not only in the pursuit of a common enterprise, but also because they have a bond of fellowship in the fear and contempt felt for them by other peoples. Of such a tribe in India, which has been somewhat reclaimed, it is doubted "whether their hereditary predatory instincts have been really overcome, and it is an open question whether adults are ever reformed, though for a time they may refrain from crime."[168]

A contrasting interest about which association is wont wellnigh universally to take place is a common cult. Spencer[169] has something to say about the effectiveness of the cult-bond. In its simpler forms, it evolves naturally as a sort of necessary corollary to the blood-tie. The cult-group is composed primarily of those who have a common duty and obligation to a certain ghost or spirit, who is often an ancestor. Failure in this cult-obligation is sin, bringing woe on the whole group; and then it becomes a crime, for a penalty is enforced upon the guilty party and law arises; and crime is the violation of law. Though the law is developed on grounds of societal welfare, that welfare depends upon the spirits.

The sign of the cult-bond, so often also the mark of the bloodtie, is the result of blood-letting which establishes union with the

[167] §3, above.
[168] Meade, in JASB, I, 274 ff.; Gunthorpe, in JASB, I, 158 ff.
[169] *Prin. Soc.*, III, pt. VI, ch. IX.

spirit through exuvial sacrifice.[170] All who have the same mark are associated as cult-comrades, though the mutilation itself may be relegated into the background as an ornament or by some ornamental attachment, as in the case of tattoo or of a ring in a flesh-perforation. Up to our times ear-rings have been worn as signs of vows taken in illness to renounce certain things or actions; and then they have been interpreted as curative agencies. Gilds have prescribed the wearing of ear-rings as signs of devotion to a saint. This is a sort of rite-bond. The cult-union made law as wide as the realm of the god, whereas before it was limited to the kin-group. Large political aggregations have been built upon a cult-bond and have been held together by it. Christianity and Islam sought, on the basis of a new god-idea, to realize an old ideal of unity of cult-area and authority.[171] At a relatively high stage of culture, spiritual affinities are closer than those of blood; Christ said that his religion should divide families. Religion is undoubtedly a social bond; but it is not originally formative; the conclusion that religion built up society, as if it had been antecedent to society, is all untrue.[172]

The Papuan village-unit is held together by religion as well as by language and general interests; a secret cult is a closer tie than any political or family bond.[173] Speaking of the cow-places, or *kotlas,* of the Bechuanas, Starcke[174] remarks: "The religious ideas of these cow-places, as centers for the mystical ideas of each separate circle, and their use as the burial place for the dead patriarch, to the exclusion of all others, present facts from which it is not difficult to explain the Aryan worship of ancestors, the worship of the hearth, the Lares and Penates." In India a basis of classification, which may not be ethnological, brings together all Mohammedans "whose ancestors were converted from Hinduism and who are now engaged in, or derive their maintenance from, the cultivation of land or the pasturing of cattle."[175] Thus the cult-likeness goes along with that of economic life. The northern Arapaho Indians had a sort of ark; on the occasion of every grand gathering, the sacred pipe occupied a special large tipi [tent] in the center of the circle, and the taking down of this tipi by the medicine keeper was the signal to the rest of the camp to prepare to move."[176]

It is well known how the name of Jahweh brought heterogeneous Israelitish

170 §§229, 298, below.

171 Lippert, *Kgchte.,* II, 339, 345, 462.

172 Evans, in PSM, XLV, 83, 84; Tarde, *Opposition univ.,* quoted in *Année Soc.,* I, 115.

173 Krieger, *Neu-Guinea,* 192; Hagen, *Papua's,* 270.

174 *Prim. Fam.,* 101.   175 Risley, *Ethnog. Ind.,* I, 78.

176 Mooney, in BAE, XIV, 956.

elements into closest union with one another, for instance in war, and inspired them to enthusiasm.[177] Among the Arabs, "the god and his worshippers are wont to eat and drink together, and by this token their fellowship is declared and sealed." Generally, in eating together, "the meal is sacrificial, so that it is not at once clear that two men are bound to each other merely by partaking of the same dish, unless the deity is taken in as a third party to the covenant. The value of the Arabian evidence is that it supplies proof that the bond of food is valid of itself, that religion may be called in to confirm and strengthen it, but that the essence of the thing lies in the physical act of eating together."[178] Among the Greeks, what were doubtless originally kin-groups became cult-associations worshipping some hero and taking their name from him. The fiction of an ancestral cult was firmly held, and all were regarded as descendants of the eponymous hero.[179]

Lippert[180] has gone into this matter of the cult-bond rather exhaustively. One of the kings of Egypt devoted all men to Ptah, saying that he had put on them that god's hot brand, that is, the letter or name of the god. Slaves were presented to the domestic ghost-god; the Jews bored their ears to unite them to the house.[118] India is full of re-birth by rites into cult-caste; the Buddhists, opposing bloodshed, sanctified the cult-bond by sacrificing the hair in the form of tonsure. Parsees must enter the cult-bond at fifteen years of age, assuming a girdle with tassels which were shaken at evil spirits. In Greece the mysteries were cult-unions. There were numberless free associations which the Judaistic state religion would not tolerate and which were impossible at Rome because the gens was so strong. The aim of the mysteries was to escape sin, guilt, and the consequent ills of life, and also the burden of rites for protection against ghosts and for assurance in the matter of the next life. This idea led to the adoption of all promising rites, and so smoothed the way for the reception of Christianity. There was a sort of baptism at initiation into the Greek mysteries. The idea of brotherhood was prominent. In Rome, the fifteen year old boy laid aside the *bulla*, a fetish-charm of the house-genius, and was presented to the state gods. There were no free associations, but functionaries of the state saw the rites duly performed; the people were present but were not participants. Roman Christianity took over this form. In the north of Europe there was an Odin-bond, with Odin-marks at entrance, and devil-unions with blood-letting; the latter is a prototype of the witch-unions and witch-marks of a later time. The old rites turned into witchcraft and appear in the witch-processes.

In Montenegro "mere sentiment has not . . . stability enough to form a binding tie between man and man." If a reconciliation has been effected, "it is common to give it stability by insisting that the heads of the contending houses shall become spiritually related to one another."[182]

In contradistinction to the strict cult-bond appear the remarkable culture-ties under the Arabic domination in Spain, in the eleventh century. Here was "a tolerance of which modern times can scarcely offer us an example. Christians, Jews, Mussulmans spoke the same language, sang the same poetic lays, participated in the same literary and scientific studies. All the barriers that

[177] Kautzsch, "Relig. Israel," in Hastings's *Dict. Bible*, 635.
[178] Smith, *Relig. Sem.*, 271.   [179] Rohde, *Psyche,* I, 167 ff.
[180] *Kgchte.*, II, 345 ff.; §§279, 295, of text and *Case-Book.*
[181] *Numbers*, XV, 38.   [182] Maine, *Early Law*, 259.

separate men had fallen; all labored with one accord on the work of a common civilization. The mosques of Cordova, where students were counted by thousands, became active centers of philosophical and scientific studies."[183]

It remains to convey some idea of the solidarity of groups formed in one manner or another as illustrated in the foregoing paragraphs. The individual counts for little by himself; he merges almost indistinguishably into the family, clan, tribe, or other association. Only as a member of one of these does he exist; to be expelled from his peace-group is equivalent to being placed in an unprotected situation, with every man's hand against him. He must "belong" somewhere, and have avengers of his blood behind him, if he is to have any rights, even that to life. And he pays for the protection and immunities afforded by his group by having his liberties curtailed.[184] Being but an insignificant part of a whole, he must remain subject to control, especially since, however insignificant he may be—or perhaps for the very reason of his indistinguishability—the penalty for whatever wrong he does to outsiders is visited upon the group as a whole or upon any single member of it. This fact leads the members of groups to constitute themselves each other's keepers. It follows from such a situation as this that primitive society cannot be correctly conceived of in terms of the individuals who compose it. It is because all throw their lots in with that of the society at large, not conceiving of the possibility of any other course, that the latter can pursue its connected and consistent development.

In Australia all the members of the same clan are united in solidarity. They take part in war as one man, and their great object is to protect, defend, and revenge their blood-kin. If they cannot get the man suspected of having perpetrated an injury, they take any of his clan.[185] "A man's own kin are bound to stand by him even though he be altogether in the wrong. . . . If one member of a family is injured, all the family know it at once. If kinsmen are living at a distance, they are informed as soon as possible of the occurrence."[186] In Bechuanaland the law as to theft is very practical. "The whole village is responsible. The head man must assist the person robbed, and the responsibility can only be evaded by proving that the spoor (for it is generally a case of horse, cattle, or wagon theft) extends beyond the village lands to those of another village. Thus the whole tribe becomes interested in detecting the thief."[187]

The Kabyle çof is "an association for mutual assistance in defense and

---

[183] Renan, *Averroès*, 4.
[185] Letourneau, *Guerre*, 29, 30.
[187] Conder, in JAI, XVI, 86.

[184] §7, above.
[186] Danks, in JAI, XVII, 313.

attack, for all the eventualities of life." Its motto is "Aid your own, whether they are wrong or right." If one *çof* ceases to offer efficacious support to a member, he passes on to another. But to whatever one he belongs, its honor and interests become his passion; for it "he neglects his business, ruptures family ties, so sacred to him, and voluntarily exposes himself to death. . . . If one of his fellow-members is to be supported, the Kabyle will lie for him with impudence, will bear false witness, and the fear of hell, for all that very lively, will not cause him to flinch before the most solemn oaths. If he changes sides, he will put the same ardor into the service of his adversaries of the day before. The *çof*, on its side, never abandons its adherents. If one of them dies for the cause, his children are adopted, fed, and maintained at common cost. If he is only in danger, if his interests are threatened, if he has a wrong to avenge, aid of all sorts will come to him, without solicitation. He is assured in advance of the spontaneous, ardent, and devoted support of his co-associates."[188] Such a group is evidently an effective mutual-aid society.

"In 1873 a Chinese was accused and convicted of having broken open the grave of a relative of the Imperial family, in order to rob the coffin of certain gold, silver, and jade ornaments which had been buried in it. The entire family of the criminal, consisting of four generations, from a man more than ninety years of age to a female infant only a few months old, was exterminated. Thus eleven persons suffered death for the offence of one. And there was no evidence to show that any of them were parties to, or were even aware of his crime."[189] In Japan "even now to take a wife from another province is condemned by local opinion (it was forbidden in feudal times): one is still expected to live, work, and marry in the place where one has been born,—though, in certain cases, and with the public approval of one's own people, adoption into another community is tolerated."[190] In fighting, "the Dyak warriors gather round their Chiefs, and defend them bravely. Relatives often congregate together and help to defend each other. When one of them is killed, rather than allow the enemy to take his head, they decapitate him themselves, and bring his head back."[191]

Among the Eskimo, "stealing from people of the same village or tribe is regarded as wrong. The thief is made ashamed by being talked to in the kashim [council-place] when all the people are present, and in this way is frequently forced to restore the articles he has taken."[192]

Smith[193] finds evidence "sufficient to remove the last doubt as to the proposition that all sacrifice was originally clan sacrifice, and at the same time it puts the slaughter of a victim in a new light, by classing it among the acts which, in primitive society, are illegal to an individual, and can only be justified when the whole clan shares the responsibility of the deed." There is a "similarity between the ritual of sacrifice and of the execution of a tribesman. In both cases it is required that, as far as possible, every member of the kindred should be not only a consenting party but a partaker in the act, so that whatever responsibility it involves may be equally distributed over the whole clan. This is the meaning of the ancient Hebrew form of execution, where the culprit is stoned by the whole congregation."

In the Salic Law it is provided that no one may migrate into any village

[188] Hanoteau et Letourneux, *Kabylie*, II, 11, 12, 13.
[189] Smith, *Chinese Char.*, 234. [190] Hearn, *Japan*, 110.
[191] Gomes, *Sea Dyaks*, 83.
[192] Nelson, in BAE, XVIII, pt. I, 293. [193] *Relig. Sem.*, 284-285.

if any one there objects.[194] In Ireland it was a terrible thing to be a "broken man," or outlaw, for that meant a fugitive, outcast, or despised hireling. Such were ever striving to slip into some tribe or another. During the few centuries of widespread disturbance that followed in the West the fall of the Roman Empire, isolation was for the individual equivalent to death; the only person left to depend on himself was the vagrant, always despised, often hunted down.[195] This state of things in Europe doubtless reproduces the general situation in primitive days. The Middle Ages showed even a "tacit guarantee for the trading debts of one's fellow townsmen."[196] In New England, "if any robbery fall out in travell, between persons of diverse States, the offended State sends for Justice. If no Justice be granted and recompence made, they grant out a kind of Letter of Mart to take satisfaction themselves, yet they are carefull not to exceed in taking from others, beyond the proportion of their own losse."[197]

Such cases illustrate from different angles the group-solidarity which has been and will be evidenced so often in this book. The group holds together in self-maintenance, especially where communalism shows itself.[198] The family-system evinces joint-economy and the strong sense of solidarity of blood-kin. We have just seen what the kin-group means, in war and in peace, to peoples who know no developed political bond. Religious solidarity is illustrated in the cult-bond, the control exercised by the taboo, and particularly in the penalization of sin. So-called endocannibalism,[199] where dead fellow-tribesmen are eaten, has its revelation of the solidarity of the whole group-membership, living and dead. Redemption and covenant take in the group as a whole.[200] The various provisions concerning marriage show the solidarity of the interests of all community-members; ever must the interests of all be reckoned with in the case of any particular union. The tests of fitness for marriage and the publicity accorded to the wedding indicate that no union is formed unto itself alone.[201]

This feeling of solidarity will be seen manifesting itself in the development of the political organization; in fact, it is strongly present in the original, deep-seated, and universal sentiment of ethnocentrism.[202] The contrast between the in-group and the out-

[194] Clement, *Sal. Fr.*, 204.
[195] Maine, *Early Inst.*, 173-174, 153 ff.
[196] Maitland, "Select Pleas," in *Selden Soc.*, II, 135.
[197] Roger Williams, in *Coll. R. I. Hist. Soc.*, I, 76-77.
[198] §§127, 128, above.   [199] Steinmetz, *Endokannibalismus.*
[200] Ch. XXXI, §§274, 290, 292, 295, below.
[201] §§340, 341, 347, 365, 369, below.   [202] Keller, *Soc. Evol.*, 58 ff.

group rests upon the conception of peace and unity within as against the aggression to be expected from without. Jevons[203] speaks of the restriction against the shedding of kindred blood, "on which not merely the morality but the very existence of the clan depended . . . the mere fact of a clan's survival in the struggle for existence is proof conclusive that the restriction was obeyed." To that end religion lent a powerful sanction. "In a word, from the beginning, offences against the community are felt not only as immoral but also as sins." This sentiment of solidarity forms a basis for the primitive group-organization and, indeed, for any organization. It is lost to some degree in evolved societies that no longer make much of the kin-tie or that of proximity; but it will be found reappearing in derived forms throughout the course of political evolution.

[203] *Hist. Relig.*, 110, 112.

CHAPTER XVI

GOVERNMENT

§152. Regulation. The relentless spur of the struggle for existence ever drove men along the road of civilization; but not without an accompanying coercion exerted by the societal organization which gave order and method to the march. Anarchy as a system is a dream; where there is a state of things deserving the name, it is a maladjustment accompanied by human misery, and is speedily resolved into a régime of control—normally the more severe owing to the lapse into unregulation that has preceded. Regulation is one of the very life-necessities of society. As soon as there is any association at all, there must be authority. Although the final and fundamental authority lies in the public opinion that guarantees the mores, that all-powerful regulative force needs agencies for its expression, and those agencies are always forthcoming. The family is an association of authority, and so are the clan and gens; there could never have been a genuine matriarchy, or gynæcocracy—a real rule by women[1]—but there was a patriarchy, or androcracy. Government of some sort has been necessary almost from the outset, and that has meant that power of regulation has been lodged in the hands of certain human beings, generally men.

The basic function of government has been the securing of coördination; of peace and order within the range of its authority. It is readily enough seen that such coördination constitutes an advantage in the struggle for existence; the society possessing it is better adjusted to its life-conditions than the one that has it not. To secure the coördination it is not sufficient, however, to rely upon the natural impulses of group-members, for there is too much variation in them and too many antagonisms between them; the vision of the constituent individuals and groups must be surmounted by a super-vision over them all. Coöperation is too strongly tinged by the element of antagonism to pursue its course in the absence of a coördinating agency. While individuals can see their own interests, or what they take to be such, plainly enough,

[1] §§417, 420-422, below.

they do not readily appreciate those of others, much less the interests of society as a whole. These will be taken care of in the end by rude and violent selection; but any device which can effect such selection without the need of flying to extremities and fighting it out constitutes an adjustment with high survival-value. It is expedient, that is to say, that a society shall be a peace-group. Here is the prime reason for government. Some individuals are set apart and freed from the ordinary vocations of men which submerge them in the pursuit of petty and personal interests; and these individuals specialize in coördination just as the priests specialize in religion. The ordinary man cannot learn all the religious ritual while pursuing the engrossing task of self-maintenance; nor can he acquire the knowledge or ascend to get the perspective of individual and factional antagonisms that must be composed in order to secure peace and order.

No one but an *a priori* theorizer would wish to assert that peoples have been moved by such rational considerations to establish government and authorities. The reason that such arrangements embody is the rationality of any product of evolution that represents expedient adjustment; it is analyzed out of the act and after the act, not injected beforehand, any more than in the case of the hive-bee's cell. The man took on authority in the family, not because he was elected after rational reflection over his eligibility but because he was stronger. Strength seized authority, and then it turned out that, with strength in authority, the adjustment of a society to its life-conditions was favored and promoted. The variation survived selection and became traditional. When it had long been an accomplished thing, then, and then only, was its essential reasonableness revealed to reflection. Government is a development out of the mores, attaining its title, as covering a group of mores, just as did marriage or property; and the terms monarchy, aristocracy, and the rest are, just as are monogamy or polytheism, labels covering characteristic sets of mores.

§153*. Embryonic Government. If anyone wants to define anarchy, not as an absolute but as a relative absence of government, he can find a number of instances of what he is pleased to call anarchic society. Some travellers, in their amazement at the lack of functionaries or of organs of regulation commonly taken to be essential to control, have reported that certain tribes had no government at all. Sometimes, however, they have gone on, in succeeding pages, to enlarge upon the powers of the medicine-man in the control of conduct. Regulation is there, whether or not it is called government. It might as well be realized at once that there was no separation of church and state in the early days, and that temporal and spiritual power, like ecclesiastical and secular law, were inseparably intertwined. There are, however, a number of cases of government in its infancy; these are important, for they reveal the lowest terms of a complex institution.

Before embarking upon the cases, it should be understood that the development we are now approaching is one in which the local organization overcomes the social, meaning by the latter the organization based upon the blood-tie. The conflict of the two has been observed in certain Australian cases cited by Howitt,[2] who says that the local organization is the germ of the state. Contiguity, the principle of territory or of the state, replaces consanguinity which does not necessarily involve proximity; naturally enough, however, many of the cases reveal the persistence of the kindred-tie within the territorial. For the time we do not wish to consider the state, but gradually to work up to that conception; the tribe is a transitional stage in the series from family to state and nation, and a review of tribal government is indispensable to an understanding of more evolved and complicated forms. We come now to the cases where the territorial organization appears in embryonic state.

It is reported that "Australian languages have no name for 'chieftain.'"[3] In Tasmania, "the aborigines were without any chiefs, properly so called, without laws, or any form of regular government."[4] Papuan tribes "have no chief who speaks with authority and whose orders have to be obeyed. The tribe is split up into small villages and the village into families, and the head of each family is more or less on an equality."[5]

Of the Bushmen it is written that "the whole manner of life forbids a compact governmental organization. Even if at times a number of families have united into a larger horde, and in the Kalahari even today are still unified in little villages, yet this is no more than a chance association which is not regu-

2 §149, above.
3 Peschel, *Races*, 334; Ratzel, *Vkde.*, II, 78, 79.
4 Roth, *Tasmania*, 70.   5 Abel, *New Guinea*, 37.

lated by special laws. Perhaps one of the inhabitants, on account of greater renown, is regarded as 'captain,' but this is merely nominal, for a real leadership does not appear." They have really no social organization, and the Hottentots are in like situation, never having been able to unite their forces in a common resistance.[6] Junker[7] speaks of the splitting up of African peoples into numberless tribes and families, which stand mostly in enmity with one another, so that "there were recounted to me dozens of names for small, restricted areas." African tribes are subject to sudden consolidations followed by lapses into small constituent elements.

The old Yukagirs knew no authority, and the chiefs now existing were enforced upon them by the Russians.[8] Among the Hyperboreans the civil organization is of the lowest. There is no rule except a moral influence and authority of the oldest and wisest.[9] The Kirghiz have no government or general organization; what they have is strictly of the family and patriarchal. Similarly of certain Gypsy peoples of Russia: they never had any form of government, but the whole tribe was formed of families. The head of the family was the ruler of it.[10]

In Assam it is said that "united action by one village is an impossibility." Formerly they had had chiefs of a sort, with small powers, but "all transactions of importance were settled, not by these nominal chiefs, but by an assemblage of the aged warriors of the village; such an assembly would decide on the setting out on a predatory inroad, or on taking revenge on another village. A council of elders administered fines for thefts and other petty crimes." But later disintegration produced a state of affairs where if one village declined in population, "the larger villages at once insisted on annual tribute being paid to them, or otherwise they plundered and ruined it." With one tribe "might is right, and this is the only form of law—or rather the absence of all law—heretofore recognized among them." Theoretically, "every man is his own master, and avenges his own quarrel."[11] Of these Assamese tribes the common feature "is their organisation into exogamous subdivisions. . . . Village fights with village, exogamous subdivision fights with its immediate neighbour, but there is practically no tribal combination among the hill people." Only where environmental conditions are particularly favorable is there anything resembling tribal or national feeling; otherwise habitat seems to make little difference.[12] Again, of the Kuki-Lushai, while "in some of these communities individuals by their skill in war and the chase came to the front and attracted members of other families to their hamlets and became the founders of lines of chiefs," in other cases "the communities remained democratic, in fact the whole race is very democratic, and now that fear of their enemies no longer compels them to live in large villages, they show a great tendency to revert to the ancient system of consanguineous hamlets."[13] The Nature-Veddahs do not possess chiefs and never have; "never did they give to another of their

---

[6] Fritsch, *Eingeb. S.-Afr.*, 444; Ratzel, *Vkde.*, I, 57, 87, 109.

[7] *Afr.*, III, 63; Ratzel, *Vkde.*, I, 492.

[8] Von Stenin, in *Globus*, LXXVI, 167.

[9] Ratzel, *Vkde.*, II, 770.

[10] *Russ. Ethnog.* (Russ.), II, 158; I, 464.

[11] Godden, in JAI, XXVII, 24, 25.

[12] Hodson, in JAI, XXXVI, 93.

[13] Shakespear, in JAI, XXXIX, 372.

race any power over themselves. On the other hand it is the rule that either the oldest or the most intelligent man of a clan or a subclan wins a certain influence over his next neighbors; to him in the first instance falls the task of dividing the honey of the rock-bees among the members of the clan . . . Further, he seems to be able to exercise a conciliating influence in certain boundary-disputes. . . . He has to be the spokesman in contacts with strangers." His influence is really very slight. He could not be paid for his people's services and left to divide it among them; each individual had to be paid by the Europeans for what he did.[14] The Kiutse of Farther India "live in a condition of complete anarchy. There are among them neither tribal nor village chiefs; everyone acts rather according to his own pleasure."[15]

"Among certain peoples of the Archipelago, who have remained outside of European or alien influence, one cannot speak, on the whole, of any real government. Sociology teaches that man must have lived at the outset without any government, and that there was no question of a real regulative system—a central government. Each family stood alone, under the supervision of the oldest. Thus must it have been also in the Indian Archipelago." Some of the Dyaks and other tribes illustrate this condition, though in time of danger they choose the bravest warrior, who may be a young man, as leader; such a man is strictly obeyed but his power seldom outlasts the strife. However, in some cases, as with the Dyaks, a man who has been leader several times retains influence in time of peace.[16] In the house-group, which is composed of kindred, the father is the supreme head.[17] In Timorlaut the people "know no superiors." They have a sort of head-man, but he has no more voice than the others. The old men's opinion has some weight with the younger ones, but "the general voice is the law of the village community."[18]

In the Gilbert Islands, and elsewhere in Micronesia, war, disorder, and a sort of fist-law ruled which gave prominence to the strongest and most daring. Chiefs enjoyed little power or respect—not much if any more than old men. There existed a kind of "republican condition." This was true of all the islands visited by the author;[19] there were "only high people and lower."

In East Greenland the oldest man functions as head of the house when he is a good hunter, or has been such, and has sons who are good hunters. "In one case the oldest man had authority over the rest, though he was too old to go in the kayak or on the hunt. But earlier he had been very efficient and his two sons were excellent hunters."[20] Among the Central Eskimo, "if the distance between the winter and the summer settlement is very great or when any particular knowledge is required to find out the haunts of game, there is a kind of chief in the settlement whose acknowledged authority is, however, very limited. He is called the pimain (i.e., he who knows everything best). . . . His authority is virtually limited to the right of deciding on the proper time to shift the huts from one place to the other, but the families are not obliged to follow him. At some places it seems to be considered proper to ask the pimain before moving to another settlement and leaving the rest of the tribe.

[14] Sarasin, *Weddas*, 486.
[15] Reise d. Prinz. Heinrich, in *Globus*, LXXII, 187.
[16] Wilken, *Vkde.*, 337, 338, 339; Perelaer, *Dajaks*, 135, 137.
[17] Schwaner, *Borneo*, I, 229.   [18] Forbes, in JAI, XIII, 21.
[19] Finsch, *Ethnol. Erfahr.*, III, 28, 29.
[20] Holm, *Ethnol. Skizze*, 43.

He may ask some men to go deer hunting, others to go sealing, but there is not the slightest obligation to obey his orders."[21]

These are cases of government in its germ-form. Numbers of small aggregations, chiefly kin-groups, live under a simple and unorganized public opinion which has not yet developed agencies of any definiteness for its expression and enforcement. Only the old, the natural repositories of the mores and traditions, exercise an influence referable to their experience and knowledge of precedent; and it might be remarked here that they continue to retain prestige under higher organization, as the names "elders," "senators," "gerontes," indicate. Rivers[22] makes much of a "gerontocracy," to which he refers, with varying degrees of plausibility, a number of curious Melanesian usages. This power of the elders calls for further illustration.

"We know little about the exact nature or mode of functioning of the group of elders, but there is little doubt that it is not a body formally constituted, or marked off from the rest of the society by any sharply marked line. In Melanesia its membership probably depends in many cases on the power of malignant magic, which the old men are believed to possess, while still more definite is the part taken by graded organizations usually . . . called secret societies. . . . Owing either to their position in these societies, or to the belief in their magical powers, the old men may have almost unlimited authority."[23] In Australia, "seniority runs through the whole of the aboriginal systems. It is maintained by the old men, who always retain some rite or ceremony which is not made known to the juniors." The rite is often trifling but is for all that a fearsome monopoly. As for the younger man, "whatever the old men ordered he had to do. . . . It is absolutely useless putting a half-caste, let alone a pure aborigine, over the natives unless, according to their laws and rites, he is a headman. He cannot give orders, he can only take them, except some white man is in evidence to uphold his authority."[24] Among certain Bushmen, "tribal organization does not exist, but there is a little clan organization. A few of these clans or families may combine in the face of danger, but the combination soon comes to an end as soon as the danger is past. They never seem to feel the need of unity. Each family goes its own way, and the father is a despot as long as he can maintain his position."[25]

Sir Charles Dundas[26] portrays the East African situation in his usual masterly way: he remarks that so-called chiefs were only war-leaders. "In connection with the elders of the place the head of every family village rules the people who belong to him in accordance with the old customs and usages of the

21 Boas, in BAE, VI, 581.
22 *Melan. Soc.*, II, ch. XVII; §428, below.
23 Rivers, *Soc. Org.*, 166-167.
24 Horne and Aiston, *Cent. Aust.*, 12-13.
25 Dornan, in JAI, XLVII, 53.
26 In JAI, XLV, 237-239, 248-249, 250, 257-258; and in JAI, LI, 219-220.

country." The war-leader, "far from being a chief, was merely a warrior himself, and as such was subordinate to every elder at home. . . . After the most careful enquiry and consideration of what is still in evidence, I feel convinced that these tribes had no heads or leaders who could be dignified with the name of chief. . . . I will not say that there were no individuals more prominent than others: some were respected for their wisdom or wealth; medicine men gained a certain importance in proportion to their real or supposed abilities. . . . Even particular charms could command obedience. Between fear and submission there is little distinction among primitive men, and the supernatural was always that which inspired fear. So smiths and hunters were dreaded for their peculiar supernatural powers, the evil eye or even the anger of an old woman could bring disaster, and thus a number of superstitious fears might intimidate each one, and their very multitude debarred any one of them from rising supreme above the rest. The conception of a chief as a functionary essential to the welfare of the tribe had not become familiar to the people, and therefore the office of such an authority formed no part of the tribal organization." The author goes on to say that "it has often appeared as if the older a man becomes, the greater his importance, but this is so only within certain limits." There are ways of preventing, at least in theory, the reins of government falling into the hands of dotards. Further, the systems of grades and ranks renders it impossible for those who are young and flighty to participate in administration. The elders generally debated in council whether special circumstances did not warrant departure from recognized customs, that is, they considered variations in policy. "Had this not been so, custom would have stagnated and become sterile." The fact is that "custom, law and religion were all in the hands of the elders . . . in practice there was no distinction between those who legislated, judged, or acted as priests for the people—there were only various duties vested in the fathers of the people, and nothing could supersede their standing." There were both advantages and drawbacks to such a system, which was essentially patriarchal. "On the one hand the people never experienced the tyranny of an ignorant despot, but, on the other hand, they never enjoyed the power that such a despot might give the tribe, nor the discipline which in the long run is necessary to internal peace. In times of famine and disorder there was no one to check the liberties taken by anyone: there was no combination to enforce the law, and, when peace was restored, no one to redress the wrongs committed. The lack of discipline is perhaps one of the most deplorable results." This situation makes conditions of rule by a superior race a matter of some difficulty; the British could not deal with village elders, numerous and scattered as they were; they had to appoint chiefs. The latter, however, did not enjoy much authority; for the people continued to look to their elders and "failed to comprehend the idea of a chief. They asked themselves what authority the chief could have: was he father to every one of them, was he aged, and therefore wiser than the assembly of elders, or did he know the customs of the tribe better than they? Neither young nor old understood this innovation, but when the elders were reinstated in their councils matters became more comprehensible. On the other hand, so soon as they regained their natural authority, supported by ourselves, the newly-appointed chief's position became more problematic than ever, and gave decisive proof that in the original organization there was no place for him. Government through the elders alone is also not entirely without its problems. Rooted in their time-honoured customs and ideas, they are incapable of following the course of modern conditions. The younger generation, debarred from military occupation and training, is becoming a loose rabble, destitute of the sense of veneration which is necessary to patriarchal control. The elders are unable to manage them, but they are of course incapable of understanding the real cause of this degeneration, and of perceiving that more rigorous discipline must take the place of their former training." Apparently the curse of an elder, formerly one of his chief weapons, is no longer of avail. He used to curse the disobedient, and the imprecation could be removed only by submission and petition for forgiveness. The whole difficulty is that the community "is founded on mutual relationship, and not on executive authority, and by consequence there is no actual judiciary."

It is noteworthy, as illustrating the position and duty of the elder, that among the Akamba, "some elders have big herds of cattle, sheep, and goats which are used entirely for the purpose of wives, for the payment of blood money, and for redeeming from the Akikuyu any female relatives who may have been left among them as hostages in time of famine."[27]

The Kalmuks combine related families, each living in its own tent, into a larger group, with an elder at the head; such groups are compounded and re-compounded until an administrative or strategic group, on the order of a clan, is formed. These clans are again compounded and re-compounded until they form a tribe. All the way up, the ruler is an elder. "The tribal elder is in modern times almost independent of any control in the exercise of his office; for the council of clan elders, which was formerly invested with the power of regulating his authority, has practically lost all significance. Still, the old patriarchal tradition prevents exercise of an unlimited despotism by the tribal chief over people who are of the same tribe or clan as himself; he may, however, be as despotic as he will towards the class of slaves."[28] In this case may be seen the development of a real chief out of an elder, together with a species of survivalistic restraint upon the former by reason of his origin in the latter.

In Samoa the chief of a village "had no hereditary right to retain his position; the heads of families comprising the village district could at any time unite and take it from him, and give it to his brother or uncle, or some other member of the chief family, who would, they thought, act more in accordance with their wishes." The author,[29] after citing numerous data showing the relationship between village-heads and chiefs, concludes that Samoa might almost be called a family-state. "I say that it is impossible for any one to study Samoan history and ethnography without being conscious that the whole atmosphere of the social and political life and ideas of the people was one of family relationship rather than geographical proximity."

Respect for experience and wisdom is a primordial sentiment fathered by the actual exigencies of life. This is one of the reasons why one finds such influence as there is in the hands of family-heads and other natural leaders of consanguineous associations; and the other main reason is because the tribe is still composed of

27 Tate, in JAI, XXXIV, 137.   28 Czaplicka, *Aborig. Siberia*, 64.
29 Williamson, *Cent. Polyn.*, I, 46; II, 18, 36.

unamalgamated bodies as its constituents, and has not yet, so to speak, developed an identity of its own, with officers deriving their powers from genuinely tribal sources. Here the social element of kinship has hardly begun to be annulled by the development of the local element of contiguity.

The terms "republican" and "democratic" have been loosely used to designate the political atomism of these embryonic governments. Letourneau, in several of his long list of books, classifies certain tribes as "republican." There is no more than the most superficial resemblance between the lack of government which they exemplify and the modern state to which the terms "republic" and "democracy"[30] legitimately apply. The confusion here is similar to that existing at the beginning of this century in the minds of a good many pro-Boer enthusiasts who chose to regard England as the enemy of enlightenment because she was obliged to fight our "sister-republics" in South Africa and who wanted to align "Oom Paul" Krüger, since he bore the title of "president," with George Washington.

That one or two of the above cases are instances of retrogression should not annoy any one who has attained the evolutionary point of view; for they are adjustments, whatever went before them or whatever came, or is to come, after.[31] Such an instance as that of Gaul in the ninth and tenth centuries is quite in point. Anarchy and war prevailed, roads ceased to exist, and there was no trade; pirates were masters of the Mediterranean and the ocean, and ran up the rivers to commit depredations. Civilization broke down; the social organization was contracted; authority collapsed. All the little groups drew together around a castle or monastery and were at war with one another, while brigands roamed through them all.[32] Such a case is one of genuine anarchy that must be built up again into regulation on the basis of law, order, and government. It is essentially similar to the primitive cases, though it is undoubtedly, from our standpoint, a regressive phenomenon.[33] The islanders of Tristan da Cunha "have no Government, no court, no jail, no serious crime, only the most primitive of implements, and no trade except with ships that chance to call. . . . Their organization is a simple patriarchal one, in which the family is the unit and the eldest man rules the family. At times they have thought they needed a ruler and have chosen one from among themselves, but always they have given up the notion and removed the chieftain from office."[34]

§154. Tribal Government.

Out of rudimentary regulative systems there emerges at length, by gradual stages, government by a chief or king. Maine,[35] whose background included an intensive study of classical society, with little or no ethnography, asserted that the chieftainship developed out of the *patria potestas* of the

---

[30] Sumner, *Coll. Ess.*, III, 223 ff., 243 ff.
[31] §455, below.   [32] Pigeonneau, *Commerce*, I, 88.
[33] Keller, "Soc. Evol.," in Lull and Others, *Evol. of Man*, 127-128.
[34] Price, "Loneliest Islanders," in N. Y. *Times*, April 26, 1925.
[35] *Anc. Law*, 138; *Early Inst.*, 117; §419, below.

man-family head. The patriarch of a family or enlarged kin-group undoubtedly has most of the powers of a kinglet and exercises them over an association of persons in number not inferior to the membership of some tribes; further, this derivation has the logical attraction of making a direct connection between the family organization and the political, and of explaining with equal plausibility the persistence of patriarchal terminology—for example, where the king is called the "father of his people"—in tribal and state-government. Nevertheless Maine's derivation is too simple; though it may cover the classical situation, it will not do as a generalization of ethnographical evidence. The chieftainship, like all other societal forms, goes back not to one single source but to several. Like the god, the chief may as well have been a hero as an ancestor;[36] the great warrior has always had his opportunity to consolidate political power.

When tribes had not yet arrived at a degree of development where they could understand the idea of chieftainship, they were ruled by elders, who were family-heads; and while one of these might have prestige over the others and be a sort of *primus inter pares*, the whole situation was still envisaged from the traditional standpoint of the kin-group and there was no real political system. Here is a stage of development that may not be leaped over in deriving the chief from the family-head; apart from conquest, which primitive peoples do not accomplish, the only way to increase the extent of the peace-group is by a confederation of kin-groups, each with its own head-man or elder. These elders counsel together, but no one of them has, by virtue of his office, any executive power over the rest. The enlargement of the peace-group means that eventually power must be concentrated; that process, however, is not readily adopted, for it entails sacrifice of liberty. A real chieftainship is something to which mankind has had to work up gradually.

"It is in connexion with the tribe that the subject of authority becomes of special importance, and takes a form which justifies us in speaking of government. In tribal societies we can discern, at first sight, three main varieties of government: one in which authority is vested in one or two persons, giving us the institution of chieftainship or kingship, single or dual, the powers of which may, or may not, be limited by some kind of council; a second, in which

[36] §240, below.

authority is vested in a council; and a third, in which authority is in the hands
of the few, who may be either a body of hereditary nobility, or may attain
their prominent position by age or wealth. When we learn to know these various forms of government in simple societies, we find, in many cases, a state
of affairs in which such words as 'chief' and 'government' mean something
very different from that which they ordinarily bear." The author quoted[37]
believes that the chieftainship came in relatively late; in fact, his whole scheme
of social organization rests in good part upon that conviction.

The broad fact about regulation is that power and responsibility have to be concentrated. There must be organization, with
direction of the concentrated energy, if there is to be achievement.
This necessary adjustment to the nature of things was practised
long before it was even dimly understood; it is really another exhibition of specialization of function, like that which existed between
the sexes or that which set the medicine-man apart to attend to
his magical operations while the rest supported him.[38] When the
religious ritual became too complicated for the ordinary man to
be able to learn its detail, there had to be priests who made the
ritual their business, to the exclusion of all else; and when, with
the growth of societies, the matter of regulation outgrew its simplest stages, there must needs be similar specialists who concentrated upon regulation alone. Peace-groups, like wars, could not
be run by debating-societies; and while no primitive epigrammatist
ever struck off the situation in a neat phrase—in fact, no one sized
it up at all—yet automatic selection brought it about that such
societies as came to practise the concentration of power and responsibility were served by it to their advantage in their struggle
for existence and competition of life.

Different clans, gentes, or other kin-groups came into proximity through growth of population or otherwise. The fact that
each of them had its blood-bond, within itself, was not enough;
contiguity and the resulting need of regulation called for control
of a wider scope than the existing agencies were capable of providing. It cannot be assumed for the earlier stages that there has been
a conquest and that it has been consolidated by the conquering
family or clan so that the head of the latter has become the chief
of a compounded society. The tribe may, indeed, regard itself as

[37] Rivers, *Soc. Org.*, 160; Rivers, *Melan. Soc.*, II, 589.
[38] §§313, 320, below.

composed of descendants of a common ancestor, and yet such distant relationship can afford no basis for unanimity in the selection of a chief. Sometimes the head of the most numerous and important of several contiguous kin-groups may enjoy a chief-like prestige; and there are, as the examples will show, obvious attempts to stretch the traditional system to cover enlarged conditions; but, in general, before a re-adjustment is successfully consummated, the old type of regulation is already obsolescent and life-conditions have been altered enough to call for new variation and selection. The new adjustment is, to use Howitt's phraseology again, the supersession of the social or kinship régime by the local or territorial. In such case the chief's eligibility must be based less upon his blood-connections than upon his general fitness as compared with the rest of the persons present: upon his physical and mental qualifications as a governor.

"The Clan has a natural leader; the league of clans has none—it is an artificial body, though nearness of blood and similarity of worship must have had something to do with its formation. The leader of the Clan is the man who, on the principles of heredity, represents the eponymous ancestor of the clan. The natural authority of a league of clans would appear to be the chiefs of the component clans. Such a body apparently tends to form itself. But it is one of the least disputed conclusions of human experience that an army controlled by a group of leaders has no chance against an equal army controlled by a single leader. And so the league of clans produces the war chief, who may, perhaps, borrow the old Clan title of king, but whose proper designation among Teutonic peoples is 'heretoch' or host leader. This is the true character of the leaders of the Teutonic invasions. Childeric and Clovis, Alaric and Ataulph, Gundioc and Gondobad, Hengst and Horsa, are war chiefs."[39]

Such qualifications have never been altogether ignored. They could not be, for they are both basic and final. At a pinch they have always asserted themselves, whatever the situation as respects titular headship. Under the matriarchal régime it was the men who came to the front when there was fighting to do; and if the patriarch was old and feeble it was some younger man who took the reins, in actuality if not in name. It requires no prolonged reflection to see that all history from the very outset could not but have shown this recognition of general qualities of leadership; for in comparison with strength of body, mind, and person-

[39] Jenks, *Law and Pol.*, 74.

ality, the particular kinship-relations of a leader must ultimately sink into the background.

It is necessary to concentrate power and responsibility; yet the power is lent, not given; and it cannot be accepted apart from accountability to public opinion. The ultimate power exists in diffused form in the group-membership and no group, however obsequious to its head, ever surrenders its authority completely; nor is any tyrant, however ruthless, definitively freed from accountability. A chief may seem to have all of the rights and none of the duties; some peoples have been so despot-ridden that they seem to have no further will of their own; but in the long run, as is demonstrated by revolutions and assassinations, no individual or group can hope to enjoy irresponsibility in the wielding of power. Chiefs are delegates of power, not original holders, and the power may at any time be taken back. They may be forced to take office against their frenzied resistance and they may be deposed or told to "go to sleep," that is, to remove themselves by suicide. Tribes often seem to give authority grudgingly or with a string attached by which it can be recovered; they seem to wish to give it and yet to hate to see it go. Their action looks like what it really is, a tentative variation. Any impression of rationality conveyed by it is a misapprehension of the play of interests operating in short perspective. Further, when power is lent, it is generally hedged about with limitations and checks. The occasional case of apparently unlimited despotism should not be allowed to set the tone of the picture.

Before going forward to the chieftainship we wish to cite several passages illustrative of typical aspects of tribal government. First, there is some detail of the collision between the well-organized, raiding Masai referred to above[40] and the surrounding disorganized tribes. "The Akamba do not appear to have ever had recognized chiefs, but rather leaders, who in time of war ruled supreme as did the Dictators of Rome. Naturally, however, such a man would always command considerable influence and no doubt his authority bound the people more or less together." It is characteristic of African political evolution that men of this sort have risen from time to time and consolidated what have even been called "empires"; but there has been no continuity in the shape of lines of powerful chiefs and so the situation has reverted to the antecedent chaos. The author quoted[41] cites a case in point. After the death of their powerful chief, Kivoi, "the Akamba seem all to have drifted apart without any

[40] §136, above.
[41] Dundas, C., in JAI, XLIII, 483-485; Büttner, *Walfischbai*, 40-41.

leaders or chiefs and a deplorable state of affairs resulted. If they came to Kitui originally to escape the Masai they found no better luck here, for the Masai raided them continuously, robbing enormous quantities of stock. . . . It is not surprising that the Masai found the Akamba an easy prey at this time, for there was not only a total lack of combination among them but uninterrupted bloodshed among themselves, so much so that the Akamba now declare that none of their enemies killed half the number that were killed among each other." Said one of them: "We used to go to fight the Meru and Galla and came back with cattle, but when it came to dividing these, the people began to fight and often more died than were killed by the enemy. Other times the cattle would be fairly divided, but afterwards others claimed more and collected to rob a few." By all this disorganization the raiders profited. "In those days a man is said never to have left his village to go far alone, no one could go a few miles without encountering others who were looking for someone to rob or slay, and hence it is that the average native of Kitui knows nothing of the country except in his immediate neighbourhood." Where the Masai did not raid, conditions were even worse, for there was no external pressure to force what little cohesion was possible. "Nothing helped the Masai but the extraordinary divisions among their victims, it seems, in fact, to have gone so far that in many cases one village was inwardly pleased to hear of the annihilation of a neighbouring village, seeing in this an old score paid off."

Williamson[42] summarizes the Samoan system as follows; he calls it "graduated social, local, self-government": "(1) The smallest unit was the domestic family household governed by one of its members, who was its official head, the bearer of the name of the family, in consultation more or less with other members. (2) The village was a collection of related domestic families, forming a consanguine family. Its affairs were managed by the village *fono* [council-meeting], the persons taking part in which were the official heads—owners of the names—of the constituent domestic families. At the head of this *fono* was the official head of one of these domestic families, who would also be the official head—owner of the name—of the consanguine family which constituted the village. (3) The village district was a collection of related villages, and may, perhaps, be regarded as an enlarged consanguine family. Its affairs were managed by the *fono* of the village district. The persons taking part in this were, apparently, the official heads of the constituent domestic families of the constituent villages. Only one of these would, however, be entitled to speak on behalf of each village, this one being, as I gather, commonly, though apparently not necessarily, the official head of the village. At the head of this *fono* was the official head of one of these villages, who would also be the official head—owner of the name—of the enlarged consanguine family which constituted the village district. (4) The district was a collection of related village districts. Its affairs were managed by the *fono* of the district. The persons taking part in this were, apparently, the official heads of the constituent villages of the constituent village districts. Only one of these would, however, be entitled to speak on behalf of each village district, this one being, as I gather, commonly, though apparently not necessarily, the official head of the village district. At the head of this *fono* was the official head of one of these village districts, who would also be the official head—owner of the name—of the social group which constituted the district." The author cites many exam-

42 Williamson, *Cent. Polyn.*, II, 6-7; III, chs. XXXVI, XXXVII; I, 85-87.

ples of his several units. He has a chapter on elective appointments to family names and titles in which he tries to identify the electing agencies, concluding that members of consanguine families elect the family-head, and that there was a sort of electoral college of family-heads which chose the chiefs, the selection being limited in a number of the islands to persons of royal, sacred blood. He has also a chapter on deposition of the chief.

While citing from this author, we might include his mention of a curious "division of the country into two parties, the strong and the weak," a custom prevailing in several parts of Polynesia. This was the result of the overrunning of a district by invaders, the conquerors exercising the right of pillage and oppression over the vanquished which was usual in Polynesia. This lasted until the tide of fortune was turned by another war. Meanwhile there was a system of "administration and opposition."

The Omaha had a Council of Seven to manage their affairs. The Seven deliberated at length, a matter being passed round and round the circle until they reached an unanimous agreement. "No one person would dare to take the responsibility of the act. All must accept it and then carry it through as one man. The unity of decision was regarded as having a supernatural power and authority." Old men explained that the members of the council had been made chiefs by the Sacred Tribal Pipes which were from the Great Spirit; hence when the chiefs had smoked over a matter and decided, their decision was that of the Spirit. Here evidently is a case of religious sanction to a body whose original character might have been that of kin-group heads. "Among the duties of the Council of Seven besides that of maintaining peace and order within the tribe were making peace with other tribes, securing allies, determining the time of the annual buffalo hunt, and confirming the man who was to act as leader, on whom rested the responsibility of that important movement. While on the hunt the Seven Chiefs were in a sense subordinate to the leader, their duties being advisory rather than governing in character; they were always regarded, however, as directly responsible" to the Spirit for the welfare of the tribe. They appointed officers, called "soldiers" to carry out their commands; to preserve order during the annual hunt, the office expiring with the hunt. "Men who had once filled the office of 'soldier' were apt to be called on to assist the council in the preservation of order within the tribe. . . . There were no other governing chiefs in the tribe besides those of the council. No gens had a chief possessing authority over it, nor was there any council of a gens, nor could a gens act by itself."[43] Noteworthy here is the ancient pitfall of government, the requirement of unanimous consent of a consultative body to any action; and also the slipping of authority from a multiple power, in the face of a crisis such as the annual accumulation of a food-supply, into the hands of an individual.

§155*. The Chieftainship. It is with the appearance of a genuine chieftainship that government begins to take on recognizable outlines. The diffused power of an unorganized group must be sharply focussed at a point before it can accomplish much that is positive. Sporadic concentrations have undoubtedly occurred

[43] Fletcher and LaFlesche, in BAE, XXVII, 208-211.

from the beginning of life in society. To grant to one man a monopoly of power and responsibility might seem like flying forthwith to an extreme. It is not. It is taking recourse to the only workable expedient. "A genuine nature-people can be ruled only by a personality, never by an idea."[44] Here is again a case of fastening upon what may be rude and coarse, like retaliation, but strong. Division of counsel, especially in the face of peril, is disastrous; dictatorship and unity of command have been the final expedients from long before the day of Cincinnatus down to that of Foch. It is in time of peril that chiefs are made or, if they already exist, have reposed in them a power which they have not wielded before and which is often taken back immediately the crisis-time is over. War is perhaps the greatest chief-maker, which means that it is the crucial test not of individuals alone, but of systems. It shows the weaknesses of accepted men and of traditional organization. It tends to replace both by something stronger and more efficient: with abler men—abler, at any rate, to get definite results—and a more intense organization. Legitimate hatred of war, as of slavery, must not be allowed to obscure a correct estimate of its actual accomplishments in the evolution of society; and prominent among those achievements will be found the preferment of the chieftainship.

Periods of storm and stress and of peril throw superior human powers into relief. If the struggle for existence taught men anything, it inspired respect for strength and efficiency; in a crisis-time men are always ready to commend themselves to one who demonstrates those qualities. War always produces its leaders, and if it is protracted they are winnowed out until some commanding figure remains. Such a leader retains his authority, gets used to it, and increases it. The chiefs of warlike tribes regularly exert greater powers than those of peaceful ones. Further, the war-chief holds over into short intervals and then into longer stretches of peace and, after a time, attains the right to appoint his successor. General efficiency, not military success alone, comes to be expected of him; he adjudges the intra-group issues. It is necessary to realize, however, that he may have to make gradual way against clan-authorities and other heads of kin-groups already in

44 Holub, *Capstadt*, I, 383.

existence before he comes into the center of the scene; for many tribes have regular peace-chiefs on the order of the Indian sachem. These are likely to be elders who hold their positions because of their age and imputed wisdom rather than their vigor and who are the product of kin-organization rather than of pressing circumstance. They may belong to the mother-family régime rather than to that of the father-family, while the war-chief, overriding or ignoring the local form of descent, has not infrequently appointed his son as his successor, thus establishing the male line.

"In the Indies more than in Europe, the outcome of a war depends largely on a single man, who through high station or remarkable character or mental power, dominates the will of a whole people; so that, this single man being removed, the whole defense miscarries and the power of the Indian peoples breaks up." Examples are given.[45] Widely in the Archipelago "general army-commanders were chosen only in case of a war; but these retained in peace-time too some power, and gradually it became the rule to regard the person who had been appointed to be leader in war as permanent chief in peace-time." But such a chief was not unlimited in power.[46] Among the unwarlike tribes there was little difference between the chief and his most humble follower; but the piratic peoples had a more compact organization, and "found it necessary to have each war-canoe under a chief whose word should be law, and the whole fleet of both tribes under a common leader."[47] Again, "the warriors on going into battle are not commanded by a previously appointed chief. The individual men at first follow their kampong[village]-chief. After the beginning of the battle the man who most distinguishes himself by valor and perseverance is chosen for command, without regard to his social rank. All follow him, attacking the foe in a disorderly manner."[48] Here is a sort of rude test in action.

In Samoa the chief is ascendant in time of war, although he is of little importance on ordinary occasions, when he mingles freely with his followers and works at any of their occupations.[49] In some of the Pacific Islands the "chief" is generally an old man—"the oldest man of the oldest family of the tribe is the political head"; the people are devoted to trade, and, in a special case of war, such an old man is not displaced, but may be chosen to lead several tribes.[50] They do not fight enough, apparently, to need a younger and more vigorous leader.

Among the American Indians are found chiefs of two grades: the sachems and the common chiefs, the former office hereditary in the gens (clan), the latter a reward of personal merit and non-hereditary. The sachems were peace-chiefs and could not go out to war as such; the others were usually the superior class in ability. The sachem was a gentile, the war-chief a tribal officer. Among the Iroquois the sachem, or peace-ruler, succeeds by nephew-descent.

[45] Knoop, in *De Gids*, 1860, II, 218-219.
[46] Wilken, *Vkde.*, 337 ff.
[47] Morris, "Sea Dyaks," in *Jour. Am. Or. Soc.*, XXV, 237 (second half).
[48] Roth, *Sarawak*, II, clxxvii. [49] Ella, in AAAS, 1892, 631.
[50] Finsch, *Ethnol. Erfahr.*, III, 304.

He is the reconciler and judge, keeping peace by persuasion and influence. But the chief is a war-lord, chosen for his qualities, not his blood, and is the sachem's right-hand man.[51] Among the Siouan Indians, too, war brought out the natural leader. "The government was autocratic, largely by military leaders sometimes (particularly in peace) advised by the elders and priests; the leadership was determined primarily by ability—prowess in war and the chase and wisdom in the council—and was thus hereditary only a little further than characteristics were inherited; indeed, excepting slight recognition of the divinity that doth hedge about a king, the leaders were practically self-chosen, arising gradually to the level determined by their abilities. The germ of theocracy was fairly developed, and apparently burgeoned vigorously during each period of peace, only to be checked and withered during the ensueing war when the shamans and their craft were forced into the background."[52] The Pomo Indians "designate their two chiefs as the war-chief (arrow-man) and peace-chief (shell-man), the war-chief becoming the peace-chief when he grows too decrepit to conduct them to battle. The peace-chief is a kind of *censor morum* [arbiter of the mores], adjusts disputes, delivers moral homilies on certain anniversary occasions, performs marriage ceremonies, so far as they extend, and watches over the conduct of his people, and especially over that of the . . . young squaws. Even the war-chief is obedient to him at home, and in fact that functionary is of secondary importance, since the Pomo are an eminently peaceable people."[53]

In Guiana "the settlements of the members of a tribe consist for the most part of six to ten houses over which a common chief is set, whose importance, however, is recognized to its full extent only during strife that has arisen with other tribes. Power and influence is founded here not alone upon dignity and station; it is determined according to the degree of bodily strength and spirit of initiative."[54] Among the West Tupis, "the patriarchal power is for each larger union of families in the hands of a hereditary chief; but in peace-time he has only the right of counsel, while in war he commands." Of another tribe it is stated that "their military organization begins already in peace-time, for every male capable of bearing arms is obligated to participation in war by a notch in a piece of wood that is sent about. The chief has during war the power of life and death over the individual."[55] In Paraguay, "each horde has a chief who has much to say in war but almost nothing in peace, though he sometimes sends the men out to hunt or fish. The several hordes are named after the man who is chief for the time being. . . . The son follows the father in authority."[56] The chiefs of the more warlike tribes have much more power than those of the less warlike. If there is no natural male successor, they resort to election.[57] Of the Araucanians it is reported that "to correctly understand the tribal relations and administrative system of these people, it is necessary to sharply distinguish between their national life in times of peace, and the changes which are effected in time of hostilities. In their ordinary

51 Morgan, *Anc. Soc.,* 71-72 and ff.; Loskiel, *Mission,* 173; Lippert, *Kgchte.,* II, 79, 522.
52 McGee, in BAE, XV, 188.
53 Powers, in *Contrib. N. Amer. Ethnol.,* III, 157.
54 Schomburgk, *Brit.-Guiana,* I, 169.
55 Von Martius, *Beiträge,* I, 218, 391.
56 Koch, in *Globus,* LXXVIII, 219.   57 Koch, in *Globus,* LXXXI, 105.

peaceful life they have no form of general government. There are no general laws, no supreme authority, no taxes, no courts of justice. . . . But in time of war all was changed. The tribes formed a kind of confederation, the cacique or ulmen became the authoritative head of the tribe. Over each nine ulmen was an apo-ulmen and over each five apo-ulmen was a toqui. The council of all the ulmen and toquis determined the plan of the campaign and elected the toqui, who should have supreme command."[58] Here the integration of war extends throughout the tribal system, but the enhancement of the chief's power is the salient feature.

"The most striking feature in Caesar's account is that there is no common tribal authority in time of peace, though within the regional clans themselves, disputes are settled by the chieftains. As soon, however, as war breaks out, a common authority is elected for the whole tribe, and this representative (*magistratus*) of the union wields power over life and death."[59]

War evidently exerts a powerful influence over the establishment and development of the chieftainship, as it does in general over the integration of government. In the competition of groups not only does the efficient competitor come to recognition, but also, within the associations that come into conflict, there is a special chance for individual qualities to show themselves as they might not in an undisturbed condition of group-isolation. The same is true, as several instances have indicated, in the case of the hunt. Anyone who has demonstrated superiorities in public life, who has done something tangible for societal welfare, is likely to win prestige and power, even though the crisis is not so acute as in war-times.

"About 150 years ago a man of the Kilindi tribe gained renown chiefly by his skill in exterminating the wild pig which devastated the fields of the Washambaa, and was eventually invited to rule the tribe. In course of time the kingdom of Vuga was established." Like many African kingdoms it broke up before long, "until, at the present day, the Washambaa are divided into such a number of petty headmanships that they bear the appearance of a tribe which has never attained any real unity."[60] Cook[61] brings out the fact that the dominating personality wins the power. A certain foreigner in Easter Island, "who is guide, philosopher, and friend to these people, unites in his person (and being a giant in stature, he can well contain them) the duties of referee, arbiter, judge. They entertain the greatest respect for him; evince the utmost affection; look up to him as their master; go to him with all their troubles; refer to him all their disputes and grievances. His word is law, and his decisions final and undisputed." A parallel case has been noted among the Apache: "a remarkable example of individual adaptability, as well as aptness, can be seen in one of the Apache at San Carlos. For many years the

58 La Fetra, "Araucanians," in *Ill. Christian World,* Nov., 1896.
59 Vinogradoff, *Hist. Jurispr.,* I, 345.   60 Dundas, C., in JAI, LI, 218.
61 In USNM, 1897, I, 719; Geiseler, *Oster-Inseln,* 6.

man has been wholly blind (from ophthalmia), but he walks about alone, rides a horse, and even a broncho, has built himself an adobe house, and shoes his horse alone. The man is less than 40 years of age, and for his intelligence was chosen as one of the judges of the tribe."[62] Hill-Tout[63] speaks of a man who "acquired the chieftaincy by excelling all others in 'potlatching.' " He had a magical box that was always being filled with potlatch-treasures of all kinds. Another man, with the help of his father-in-law, gave many potlatches and became a chief. The author gives genealogies from which it appears "that the chieftaincy was practically hereditary, although theoretically within the grasp of any member of the tribe who could outdo the ruling chief in potlatching."

The converse of cases such as these is that the chief, once appointed, was obliged to maintain his ascendancy by continuing to perform the sort of services that raised him to his eminence; if not, he was likely to be deposed in favor of some other who would succeed him as he succeeded his predecessor. This will appear from later examples.

Thus did the pressure of life enforce upon primitive societies a recognition of real efficiency. There is also a variety of efficiency which might be regarded, at first sight, as unreal, existing only in the minds of a superstitious people; an indication of it appears in the foregoing case of the man with the magic box. This introduces an aspect of the chieftainship which has not been accorded proper attention, namely, that it is not infrequently a religious office. Cases occur where there seems to be an original companion-agency alongside the chief in the person of the medicine-man. Again, the chief himself is the head fetish-man. In some parts of the world there are two chiefs, one secular and one sacerdotal. There is usually, however, nothing to keep the two offices separate; temporal and spiritual power, on the contrary, tend to coalesce. If there is rivalry between the chief and medicine-man it is settled in such manner as not to admit of two competing agencies of control operating to thwart one another. Rivalry is generally resolved into the ascendancy of one person. The tests of government, upon the primitive stage, are rather evident and decisive; the savages know what they are getting, or think they are getting, from their rulers, for their demands are tangible and objective or else they are satisfied by traditional religious tests. They often like a tyrant because of his force and ruthlessness, for these inspire confidence; he is just what they need and want.[64] Obvious tests are generally

[62] Hrdlička, in BAE, *Bulletin* XXXIV, 155.
[63] In JAI, XXXIV, 22, 23, 25; §113, above.
[64] Letourneau, *Morale*, 159.

at hand by meeting which the man of parts gets or retains power. Such being the case, it matters little whether he rises out of the military force, the council, or the priesthood. The religious function of the chief, as in some cases all-important and in many others scarcely secondary to the political, demands illustration.

Rivers,[65] who emphasizes this aspect of the chieftainship, concludes that "in many parts of the world, the institution called chieftainship or kingship is unaccompanied by the exertion of real authority or of political functions such as we associate with government in our own country, at any rate, so far as the administration of justice is concerned. The divine right of kings, and the religious aspect of kingship, which long survived, if they do not still survive, in our own society, form the essence of the chieftainship of such regions as Melanesia and Polynesia, as well as of many parts of Africa and America." The author regards the Eddystone Island chief as a type: "It was only in connexion with the more ceremonial or religious aspects of warfare that the 'chief' was important, and this gives the clue to his special position, for it was in the ordering of ceremonial, and in the arrangement of the feasts which formed important features of this ceremonial, that he was especially prominent. This aspect of a chief's function was well exemplified by the chief with whom we had most to do in Eddystone. Though his proper name was Rembo, we found that he was habitually called Kikere, or bad, and we were told that he was definitely regarded as a bad chief. We expected to hear tales of his injustice or cruelty, of his arbitrary ways of government or of the severity of the punishments he inflicted, but in place of these we heard only the complaint that he gave few feasts, and these lacking in quality. The social function which stood out prominently in the people's minds was the arrangement and provision of feasts. . . . When we pass from Melanesia to Polynesia we find that the sacred character of the chief or king is so pronounced that it seems to be impracticable for him to exert such of his functions as would bring him into contact with the common people, so that another kind of chief, especially associated with war, is associated with him, producing the dual chieftainship characteristic of many parts of Polynesia." Examples follow; then the author educes the case of the Mikado of Japan as a parallel instance. "When a king becomes so sacred that none of his subjects may look at him, the exertion of any kind of social function becomes difficult; and it is probable that the seclusion which for several centuries was the fate of the Mikado of Japan was the direct result of his having acquired a character so sacred that the functions of government essential to the welfare of such a state as Japan had to be exerted by members of another, and more worldly, family." It would appear that one of the ways of separating the primitive church and state was to set the church off by itself in a splendid desuetude.

The author quoted passes on to consider the chieftainship in other parts of the world. Africa is rather difficult, for the secular chief has in many tribes very great powers; that he is also the rain-maker probably means that he has absorbed religious functions. "In North America, despite many superficial differences, the position of the chief appears not to have been very different from that of Melanesia."

[65] *Soc. Org.*, 165, 161-163, 164.

It seems to us that Rivers has somewhat exaggerated the thesis with which he seems to start, and that his special studies in Melanesia and Polynesia have colored his view of the rest of the world. His insistence, however, upon the religious nature of the chief is entirely in point and deserves all the attention accorded to it here.

"The king was a kind of link or intermediary between the gods and the community, and his first duty was to secure by divine favour the welfare of the people under his care. His merit as a kingly ruler depended on the degree of his fortune in representing the people before the gods. One of the most fortunate kings of Norway was Halfdan, the Black. The importance which the people attached to his good fortune was shown by the fact that when he died, his body was actually cut up, and every district of his kingdom tried to obtain a portion of it. The converse aspect is presented by the story of Olaf Traetelgya, a powerful ruler and a great colonizer, who at the end of his reign was pursued by ill luck: his sacrifices did not find favour with the gods. There was nothing for it, but to remove this source of offence, and to take some other ruler who was more pleasing in the sight of the gods. Olaf was therefore summarily dispatched, not on account of any wilful fault of his, but simply because he did not possess the necessary quality of kingly fortune."[66]

The priestly character of the king has been copiously illustrated by Frazer in *The Golden Bough*. There is no question whatever concerning the presence of the religious element;[67] but we cannot assign it the weight which Rivers gives it.

A more definite idea of what the chieftainship is may be obtained by running over a list of his actual functions. Williamson,[68] writing of Central Polynesia, the home of the religious chief, catalogues the powers of the ruler as follows: religious, administrative, parliamentary, consultative, military, diplomatic, judicial, and personal. There is no question but that he united in his person powers which had before been diffused and which later on came to be delegated. To some advantage he may be regarded as a sort of narrowed channel or node through which currents of power ran; from original dispersion they came, especially under stress, to be concentrated for a time, later to escape confines, then again to be assembled. If stress became unintermittent, these powers remained tied up together so as to be grasped by a single hand and retained by a dynasty; but, even so, they had to be delegated, and were ultimately differentiated, distributed, and developed into the complex organization of the state.

Only a copious selection of representative cases can reveal the

---

[66] Vinogradoff, *Hist. Jurispr.*, I, 352.
[67] §§243, 272, below.   [68] *Cent. Polyn.*, III, 99.

functions of the chieftainship in their detail; they may, however, be roughly classified on lines somewhat different from those adopted by Williamson. Whether the chief is or is not possessed of magical powers, he is a prominent figure in tribal economic life. He directs hunting, fishing, pastoral migrations, planting, harvesting, and trading. He is the economic representative of his people, being often the trader-in-chief; if an outsider wishes to deal with a tribe, whether in the matter of commerce or in order to procure a supply of labor, he must operate through the chief. In many tribes the chief is regarded as the owner of the land; he is, in any case, trustee and manager of tribal property.[69] In war, he is often the actual leader, fighting at the head of the tribe; and where he is too old or too holy to do that, he plans campaigns or creates morale by his incantations and medicines. His relation to religion has already been emphasized. In a number of cases he assigns wives, manages marriages, confirms inheritance, and otherwise makes his influence felt at many junctures of family life. Even the pleasures of the people are much under his direction. In short, he is found supervising, not infrequently in minute detail, the whole of tribal life.

When it comes to the more purely governmental functions, the chief is the guardian of the mores. He keeps order and represses internal strife. He safeguards the peace of the group, thus maintaining its character as a peace-group. In so doing, he operates largely through the laying of taboos. It cannot be said that he makes laws; what he does is to hold people to the code. Naturally this involves passing judgment upon divergences from usage. He is by no means the only arbiter, as will presently be seen, but he is found applying the ordeal and imposing punishments, often as the executive of a council; sometimes it is his duty to inflict the penalties in person. In a general way it might be said that he is the agency in emergencies, while in the ordinary, untroubled course of events he takes much advice and is not seldom no more than the mouthpiece of a multiple agency that moves more ponderously. In the end he is, of course, the replaceable organ of public opinion, for the public will is the soil out of which all power grows. In whatever he does he is obliged to adhere to tradition and

[69] §120, above.

to be successful; otherwise he is set aside or his people move off to some neighboring chieftain, leaving him alone in his glory. He is tested when he becomes chief, sometimes with severe torture, and is not allowed to slip down into sloth and ineffectiveness. On the other hand, when his position is assured, he is treated with the utmost respect and sometimes with an exaggeration of servility revolting to civilized standards; this is especially the case if he is a redoubtable sorcerer or is believed to be divine. When he has attained that status, the fear in which he is held exempts him from much control, although a failure to exhibit the powers with which he is credited, particularly when much depends upon his ability— say to make rain or to insure luck in various enterprises—may encompass his utter downfall.

There is no question that those who have a chief prize him. In Samoa, "at one time they had been ten years without a king, and so anxious were they to have some protecting substitute, that they fixed upon a large O'a tree . . . and made it the representative of a king, and an asylum for the thief or the homicide when pursued by the injured in hot haste for vengeance."[70] These people wanted a resumption of the guarantees of law and order. What happens in an interregnum may be judged by the experience of the Baganda:

"Directly the drum announces the death of the king the markets and public places are deserted; people hurry with their wares into every conceivable hiding place, whilst the lawless run riot, robbing and plundering everywhere; chiefs and peasants alike rapidly arm, and adopt the national mourning dress of tattered bark cloths, and a girdle of withered banana leaves; retainers crowd to their respective chiefs, robbing and plundering as they go; chiefs set guards over their enclosures and then hasten off to the royal enclosure to hear who is to be the king's successor."[71]

It is evident enough that the chief discharges a function of vital importance where conditions like these ensue at the withdrawal of his hand. In the face of such services to society it seems rather like quibbling to maintain that he does not govern, because his powers do not exactly coincide with those which a formal governing agency in a more sophisticated society exhibits. We turn now to a survey of representative cases, which will fill out the conception of the chieftainship in all needed detail.

[70] Turner, *Samoa*, 65.   [71] Roscoe, in JAI, XXXII, 44.

In southern Australia there is a "recognized form of government acknowledged by heads or chiefs. These chiefs make, with the consent of the tribe, alliances, peace, friendships or war, send ambassadors, and on very important occasions send embassadresses to treat with the neighboring tribes; great apparent kindness is shown to them and no offer of treachery when on a mission."[72] Semon[73] generalizes somewhat, as follows. Ordinarily the old people exercise a sort of authority, but it is limited to certain matters, chiefly to the initiation of marriageable youths and girls. Most of the tribes choose a kind of chief, a prominent warrior, hunter, or sorcerer whose advice has especial weight and who leads in common enterprises. Obedience is voluntary; and the leader is not suffered to make laws for the community or to dictate to the individual. A chief of influence and power is quite exceptional among Australians; one is mentioned whose courage, cleverness, and eloquence procured him an influence extending over thirty miles; but this is the only case of its kind. Such power does not devolve on the chief's posterity, for his children are in no way superior to others in the tribe. Semon goes on to consider the more developed chieftainship of the Papuans: "One may well speak of 'chiefs' among the Papuans, since we find in many villages men of considerable renown who play a leading part and exercise great influence. Still, the power they possess is due rather to the people's voluntary submission to their frequently-tested cleverness and experience than to any official or lawful claim to this prominent position. Thus in many villages we find, instead of one acknowledged chief, a number of prominent and leading personages. A valiant spirit, cleverness and experience, and with all this, a supposed gift of sorcery,—these are the qualities which gave one Papuan an influence over his fellows; hereditary power is found nowhere." These people have few laws, no important social contrasts beyond those of wealth and talent. Wrongs are at once redressed by force, man against man, or by kin. They are distrustful, timorous, and disintegrated.[74]

Melanesian chiefs keep order, direct common enterprises and industries, represent their tribes with strangers, preside at sacrifices, and lead in war. They can impose fines and generally possess the power of life and death. "The chief has with him young men who have attached themselves to him and carry out his commands," but he "has not more properly in or dominion over land than any other man." His retainers are part of his power, and they grow great and wealthy with him; but he possesses also a sort of familiar spirit or genius that counts for a great deal. "Public opinion supported him in his claim for a general obedience, besides the dread universally felt of the *tindalo* power behind him. Thus if he imposed a fine, it was paid because his authority to impose it was recognized, and because it was firmly believed that he could bring calamity and sickness upon those who resisted him; as soon as any considerable number of his people began to disbelieve in his *tindalo* his power to fine was shaken." This is a recognition of his fetish-character; he maintained his position by his character and success and lost it by weakness and failure; the ascription of his power to his familiar spirit, or genius, was the primitive way of looking at the matter. To the natives "the real ground on which the power of a chief rests is that of belief in the *mana* he possesses, with which also the

[72] Gason, quoted in JAI, XXIV, 173.
[73] *Aust. Bush,* 226, 346; Evans, in PSM, LII, 30, 34.
[74] Krieger, *Neu-Guinea,* 318, *et passim.*

wealth he has inherited with it, and all his successive life are connected. . . . The power to impose a fine was an active one; a chief forbids under penalty of a fine, which is a form of taboo. . . . Thus Takua imposed a heavy fine on the man who had proposed to marry within the prohibited degrees, and the offender had to hire an advocate to state his case discreetly, apologize, and beg off part of the fine." Offenders are dunned for their fines by women and boys, and if they refuse to pay, the chief sends his retainers to destroy and carry off their property. Thus does the chief guard the code of his group and in doing so receive the support of public opinion. "It is evident that a chief of sense, energy and good feeling, will use his power on the whole to the great advantage of the people; but a bad use of a chief's power is naturally common, in oppression, seizing land and property, increasing his stock of heads, and gaining a terrible reputation."[75]

In the New Hebrides the chieftainship is gained by successive steps, each won by the slaughter of pigs. All the chiefs are old. A chief's son may start higher up.[76] In the Torres Strait region, "the existence of chieftainship, either hereditary or acquired, has in no instance of which I am aware been clearly proved; yet in each community there are certain individuals who exercise an influence over the others which Europeans are apt to mistake for real authority. These so-called chiefs are generally elderly men, who from prowess in war, force of character, or acknowledged sagacity, are allowed to take the lead in everything relating to the tribe. In Torres Strait such people are generally the owners of large canoes and several wives; and in the northern islands, of groves of cocoa-nut trees, yam grounds, and other wealth."[77]

Even among very backward people there seems to be a feeling that a man who is going to have power reposed in him must be tested. When there are to be new chiefs, "those responsible for them pay them constant visits, ask them impossible questions, and then, in the pidgin-English they talk out here, 'larn them plenty sense' by thrashing them most unmercifully."[78]

In the Andaman Islands neither head-chief nor sub-chiefs have unlimited power; that of the former "is exercised mainly in organizing meetings between the various communities belonging to his tribe, and in exerting influence in all questions affecting the welfare of his followers. It is the chief alone . . . who directs the movements of a party while on hunting or fishing expeditions, or when migrating."[79]

Ratzel[80] has collected much information upon the African chieftainship. Families in South Africa come together in some accidental way, form a village, and call the most influential person among them "captain." African rulers are regarded with superstitious reverence. "There is in their practice something which reminds us of the old theory of divine right. The natives do not understand how a community, however limited in number, can manage its own affairs without a head." The author says they have a talent to obey which they acquire in the family; hence here is the place for despotism, and despots are the best rulers for Africans. A despot holds them together and enables them to act. But chiefs have very little personal pomp; their advantages consist in many wives, unlimited beer and tobacco for themselves and their courts, and a

[75] Codrington, *Melanesians*, 47, 52, 53, 57, 58.
[76] Leggatt, in AAAS, 1892, 698.   [77] Haddon, in JAI, XIX, 330.
[78] Cator, *Head-Hunters*, 199.   [79] Man, in JAI, XII, 108.
[80] *Vkde.*, I, 73, 157, 162, 163, 165, 262, 294, 305, 430, 476, 566, 601, 603.

stock of guns and ammunition. They have somewhat bigger houses, and troops of attendants. Among the Kaffirs the cruelties of chiefs made only the smallest impression upon their subjects; breach of custom, or weakness, overthrew a chief far quicker than the most arbitrary slaughter. It would be a total mistake to suppose that the cruelty and blood-thirstiness of the king of Dahomi cost him the affection and allegiance of his subjects. They acquiesce in it, on the contrary, as perfectly proper. If power is exhibited and success attained, the means are not much criticized; and there is no thought given to that sacredness of human life which bulks so largely in western civilization.

Kaffir chiefs hold their people together in time of peace by having the members of influential families in the several communities live for weeks at a time in "the big place," that is, the capital. They are the guests of the chief and are provided with all the necessities of life free; they form his personal following and add to the glamor of the court. Raids upon the neighborhood provide concubines for the guests. Among the Herero, "personal character sometimes gives to one or another a greater importance, and then more subjects stream to the notable leader, while a weak and unpopular chief sees his fall off. . . . The rulers of the Herero must for this reason be more than ordinarily careful not to rouse the public opinion of his subjects against him, and therefore they tend less toward despotism."[81]

Among the Hudson Bay Eskimo "there is no such person as chief; yet there is a recognized leader who is influenced by another, and this last is the conjurer or medicine man. These two persons determine among themselves what shall be done."[82] Among certain Indians "to preserve his popularity, a chief must give away all his property, and he is consequently always the poorest man in the band; but he takes care to distribute his possessions to his own kindred or to the rich, from whom he might draw in times of need. . . . Power is tacitly committed to the leading chief, to be held so long as he governs to general satisfaction, subject, however, to the advice of the soldiers. Age, debility, or any other natural defect, or incapacity to act, advise, or command, would lead a chief to resign in favor of a younger man. When war is deemed necessary, any chief, soldier, or brave warrior has the privilege of raising and leading a war party, provided he can get followers. The powers of a warrior and civil chief may be united in one person. . . . The leading chief may and often does lead the whole band to war; in fact it devolves on him to lead any general expedition."[83] Among the Menomini, "the leading chief, in time of peace, was not invested with any extraordinary powers. All matters of importance had to be settled by the tribe in general council."[84] The chief of the Natchez tribe was called the Great Sun and was first among the priests. "He acknowledged no superior but the sun, from which he pretended to derive his origin."[85]

The following instance is instructive as to the possibilities opened by the chieftainship to an unscrupulous man. "Blackbird was an ambitious man, who loved power and was unscrupulous as to how he obtained it. The traders found him a pliant tool. They fostered his ambitions, supplied him with goods and reaped a rich harvest in trade. From them he learned the use of poisons, particularly arsenic. If an Indian opposed him or stood in the way of his designs,

[81] Fritsch, *Eingeb. S.-Afr.*, 95, 228. [82] Turner, in BAE, XI, 193.
[83] Dorsey, in BAE, XV, 224. [84] Hoffman, in BAE, XIV, 43.
[85] Carr, in *Smithson. Rep.*, 1891, 539.

sickness and death overtook the man and Blackbird would claim that he had lost his life through supernatural agencies as a punishment for attempting to thwart his chief. Because of these occurrences Blackbird was feared. He exercised considerable power and adopted the airs of a despot. Before he died, however, the secret of his poisonings became known and the fact led to the loss of much of his power."[86]

In the North the best hunter is the leader. "There is no other kind of 'leaders' in any of the tribes—no councils and no election to such prominence by vote or heredity. Leadership is a survival of the fittest, and he who gains the distinction earns it."[87] "Each household is in itself a subordinate government. The head of it, through heredity, wealth, ability, or otherwise, simply is recognized as a petty chief in the village. The head chief merely overshadows in the extent of his influence the petty chiefs. Often reverses of fortune turn the tables, and some decline in influence while others rise. Often the alliance of the medicine men is gained by purchase or by the sacrifice of private property, and the chiefs and shamans combine to uphold each other in the respect and fear of the community. Many bitter feuds grow out of the rivalries of households and gentes in the struggle for power and influence in the tribe."[88]

In the California tribes, "the origin of government is something like this: Let it be supposed that there is a secession and a village establishes an independent existence. A large, round dance-house is built, and the prominent men entertain their friends in it in a succession of feasts. . . . They make presents to their followers according to their wealth. . . . Always at these gatherings there is a great deal of petty bickering and quarreling. The more earnest and grave old men of the tribe notice these matters; they observe the aspirant whose personal influence is most successful in keeping order among the young fellows. He is finally pitched on as leader."[89] Here we have a sort of test of all candidates.

Among the Guiana Indians, "the qualifications of a chief are put to the test, not only for making the necessary preparations, etc., in time of war, but in time of peace, for giving intelligent instructions for fishing, hunting, and cassava planting." Sometimes he must keep the paths clear from one village to another. "He also exercises authority and exacts obedience in his arrangements for the daily routine of the settlement. His rights and his duties are very much alike throughout the tribes." A number of examples are cited. "On any scarcity of provisions or prevalence of sickness all the branches of the family flock to the dwelling of the chief and live at his expense without the least doubt of a welcome. . . . It thus happens that the property of a chieftain is often consumed and he is forced, with his family to go and reside with other relations and friends, at whose expense he lives until the cassava fields yield their next crop."[90]

The Germans, we are told, appointed kings for their nobility of birth, and leaders for their valor.[91] In Iceland there was a sacerdotal chief of a tribe or gens, who passed into the secular station as time went on. He was a kin-official rather than a territorial one. The priests had the power of naming

[86] Fletcher and LaFlesche, in BAE, XXVII, 82.
[87] Whitney, in *Harper's Mag.*, XCII, 502.
[88] Niblack, in USNM, 1888, 251.
[89] Powers, in *Contrib. N. Amer. Ethnol.*, III, 319.
[90] Roth, in BAE, XXXVIII, 575.   [91] Tacitus, *Germ.*, VII.

judges and they promulgated the acts of the Althing or general council. In the saga-period we find a transition from personal and property-relations to political relations.[92] Chadwick[93] makes much of the fact that "in the North . . . priestly duties seem everywhere to be combined with temporal power. The temporal chief is both judge and sacrificial priest." His article is full of specific illustrations. The Druids exercised a powerful influence upon the Gallic regulative organization, influenced and decided the choice of magistrates, were rich and despotic, and held the people in subjection.[94]

"When Englishmen like Edmund Spenser first began to put their observations of Ireland into writing at the end of the sixteenth century, there was one Irish practice of which they spoke with the keenest indignation. This was what they called the 'cuttings' and 'cosherings' of the Irish chiefs, that is, their periodical circuits among their tenantry for the purpose of feasting with their company at the tenants' expense." But a ruler's peregrinations are not all for purposes of plundering: he had to get his living some way, and then too he travelled on official business. "The more barbarous King of communities spread over a wide territory was constantly moving about it; or, if he did not, he too perished, as the Kings called the *rois fainéants* of the Franks. . . . King John passes for an effeminate sovereign, but no commercial traveller of our day, employed by a pushing house of business, was ever, I believe, so incessantly in movement, and for so many successive years, with all the help of railways."[95]

The qualities of the native chieftain may be inferred from the experience of European powers in providing substitutes for him. Many of the best-intentioned and humane governors of colonial possessions have failed because they were, under the circumstances of the case, no less than maladjustments. The colonial literature of the Germans, in so far as it deals with the management of natives, reiterates the policy of "sternness with justice"; and the fact that they failed in practice to realize their theories does not invalidate the sense of their conclusions.[96] Worcester[97] dilates upon the unparalleled success, among Spanish governors of the Moro Islands, of General Arolas. He was "just, but absolutely merciless"; his every threat was carried out to the letter. In addition, he bore a charmed life, and the natives' imagination was captured by him, so that they called him "Papa." He had a mania for clean streets, and his insistence upon this hobby, incomprehensible to the natives, led them to say that he even forbade the

---

[92] *Saga Library*, I, XXVIII.
[93] In *Folk-Lore*, XI, 268 ff., 284 (quoted).
[94] Von Pflugk-Harttung, in *Trans. Roy. Hist. Soc.*, VII, 55 ff.
[95] Maine, *Early Law*, 179, 183.
[96] Keller, *Colon.*, 578 ff. (where references to sources are given).
[97] *Philippine Isl.*, 170, 190.

trees to shed their leaves on the roads. His weak predecessors and successors were always in trouble, while his incumbency was marked by a certain cheerful orderliness.

§156*. Succession and Distinction. The general character of the chieftainship has now been reviewed. It has appeared already that the office is not always or even regularly inherited, though it undoubtedly tends to be, and though there are instances where, even among backward tribes, it is passed down on lines of descent. Even in such circumstances, however, the succession is often checked up on the criterion of demonstrated ability, for if the natural heir is regarded as incompetent he is passed over. The strong man not seldom sweeps aside traditional rules, especially at crisis-times, and founds a new line of rulers. He may be really elected to office. Thus the system of choice prevails to temper succession by kinship; and where inheritance by kin is recognized it is almost always reckoned in the male line. The chieftainship goes only exceptionally to a woman. Further, though the succession of the oldest son is the natural usage where the system is patriarchal, primogeniture is by no means firmly established. An astonishing system is that which causes the title of chief to pass from a father to his child immediately upon the birth of the latter.

In the East Indies, Wilken[98] sees the situation as follows. The general rule for the Archipelago is that a rajah heads the tribe, with an under-chief for each settlement. "The chiefs owe their dignity to the will of the people. At first they were military leaders who were originally chosen for one definite campaign, as is still the case with the Dyaks, and later for their life-time. After their decease another must always be chosen as head, in which choice there was naturally complete freedom. Hereditary office was therefore unknown at the outset. This is still the case with several peoples of the Archipelago. Yet the kingship, there too, is already on the way to become hereditary. Among certain tribes, for instance the Mentawei Islanders, the choice is wholly free and so the office can go over to this or that man, no matter who. And yet the oldest son comes in for attention first of all in the election. . . . Other tribes go a step farther still; the kingship, though elective, is already hereditary. The choice must take place from the persons who stand nearest the deceased in descent; and the rule is in force that there must be no departure from the election of the nearest blood-relation, except for sufficient reason. It is therefore not so much a real election as a consideration as to whether objections exist to the successor indicated by birth undertaking the position." Among the Bataks, if the deceased king leaves no sons, that one of his brothers

[98] *Vkde.*, 340 ff.; 342-343 (quoted).

is likely to succeed who has the former king's wife—a situation recalling certain passages in the Odyssey.[99] In Borneo, "on the death of a chief the dignity passes to his first-born son; if, however, this son is not fit for the post by reason of physical or moral defects, then the rank is claimed by some other man eminent for ability and wealth, but in such case it is usually a member of the family of the defunct, whom his fellow villagers like to see made chief."[100]

In Polynesia there is an extreme view as to the inheritance by the son of a father's dignity and position. The firstborn son receives immediately after his birth the name and dignity of his father and from that time outranks his father, the latter exercising all authority in the son's name. On account of this vexatious arrangement, some of the nobles would recognize no children, that they might not have anyone above themselves.[101] Williamson[102] discusses this arrangement quite at length. "Whatever might be the age of the king, his influence in the state, or the political aspect of affairs in reference to other tribes, as soon as a son was born, the monarch became a subject, the infant was at once proclaimed the sovereign of the people, the royal name was conferred on him, and his father was the first to do him homage by saluting his feet and declaring him king. The herald of the nation was then despatched round the island with the flag of the infant king, and the young sovereign's name was proclaimed in every district. . . . Every affair, however, of importance to the internal welfare of the nation, or its foreign relations, continued to be transacted by the father, and those whom he had formerly associated with him as his counsellors; but every edict was issued in the name and on behalf of the young ruler; the father only acted as regent for his son." Royal insignia, homage, lands, and even income were all transferred immediately to the child. The same custom was followed by noble families. It is suggested that the idea was to secure to the son undisputed succession to the father; the former was thus firmly fixed in the government before the father's death. Only occasionally and for reasons of evident unfitness was the first son passed over. The author connects the usage with the sanctity of royalty; the god takes up his residence within the child immediately after birth, thus transferring the sanctity which formerly the father had had; then the title follows, being inseparable from the sanctity. More easily understandable is the custom of the Samoan chief who, knowing himself about to die, breathes on his son, saying, "Receive the succession of my office, with all the wisdom necessary for fulfilling it"; the Samoans believed that it was necessary for powers to be transmitted and that the dying man could yield them to whomsoever he pleased. The same idea was current in Tahiti.

This author thinks that succession might have been hereditary in the sense that the new chief must be selected from a royal family, while it was elective in that there was some choice between members of that family. Also that in Tonga there was a kind of electoral college composed of the principal chiefs who decided upon the succession to the secular kingship.

The dignity of the secular head in Núkuóro descends to his children, without regard to sex, the choice of the individual residing in the father's hands.

[99] Keller, *Hom. Soc.*, 225, 240, 242, 243.
[100] Roth, *Sarawak*, II, clxvii.
[101] Ratzel, *Vkde.*, II, 181; Starcke, *Prim. Fam.*, 89.
[102] *Cent. Polyn.*, III, 195-196, 219-220, 222-223, 189-192.

If there are no children, a brother or sister succeeds, or even someone outside the family. The head at the time of this report was a woman without sons, and she had not yet decided whether to select her successor from her sisters or her daughters.[103] In Yap the oldest son follows the father; if the boy is young he has an adviser of high rank or a regent in the person of his father's brother.[104] A genuine dynastic kingdom is rare in the South Seas; one of them was founded by a powerful native conqueror and it stands in contrast to the "republican" régime of many tribes.[105] On Easter Island the government was an arbitrary, hereditary monarchy. The king had sub-chiefs of various districts under him, but their fighting did not affect him. There was no great homage shown the king, and there were no taxes or laws, but certain customs defined rights and duties.[106] The Maori chieftainship was hereditary; but it was elective for the war-leader. "Of course there was no election by ballot, it was generally almost an understood thing as to the leader—the *prestige* would decide without saying. The chieftainship passed to sons first; failing these, then to brothers and sisters; then to half-brothers and sisters; then to uncles and aunts."[107]

"When the Indian system of consanguinity is considered, it will be found that all the male members of a gens were either brothers to each other, own or collateral, uncles or nephews, own or collateral, or collateral grandfathers and grandsons. This will explain the succession of the office of sachem which passed from brother to brother, or from uncle to nephew, and very rarely from grandfather to grandson. The choice, which was by free suffrage of both males and females of adult age, usually fell upon a brother of the deceased sachem, or upon one of the sons of a sister; an own brother, or the son of an own sister being most likely to be preferred. As between several brothers, own and collateral, on the one hand, and the sons of several sisters, own and collateral, on the other, there was no priority of right, for the reason that all the male members of the gens [clan] were equally eligible. To make a choice between them was the function of the elective principle."[108] It is said of the Indians that "the nobility of service, resting on choice, is of later origin than the hereditary chiefs."[109] When an Indian chief died, "his position was claimed, as a general rule, by his son, or some kinsman, as a hereditary right; but oftener, perhaps, the succession was in the female line. In some instances, when this right fell to one who was judged unworthy to possess it, the tribe chose their own chiefs. As instances of this kind, Brant of the Mohawks, and Tomah of the Menominees, were placed in that position, for their superior wisdom and valor."[110] The Shingu chief's dignity is hereditary, descending to a son, or if there is none, to a sister's son. In one case a girl only remained; and the brother of the widow became temporary chief, until the girl should marry, when her husband would be chief.[111]

Succession to the chieftainship presents many points of likeness to inheritance of property.[112] The office may revert, so to speak,

[103] Kubary, *Núkuóro*, 16 ff.
[104] Senfft, in *Globus*, XCI, 172.
[105] Finsch, *Ethnol. Erfahr.*, III, 28.
[106] Thomson, in USNM, 1889, 472.
[107] Tregear, in JAI, XIX, 113.
[108] Morgan, *Anc. Soc.*, 72.
[109] Waitz, *Anthrop.*, III, 123.
[110] Hoffman, in BAE, XIV, 43.
[111] Von den Steinen, *Zent. Bras.*, 331.
[112] §§134, above, and 411, 412, 422, below.

to the community which will choose anew out of its membership;
or it may even descend in the female as well as the male line. The
tendency is strong to follow locally accepted lines of relationship
as if political power were a sort of possession; nevertheless the
societal interest is strong and obvious enough to offer to the lodgment of power in weak hands a resistance that does not appear in
the case of property. If the family sometimes takes measures to
keep its possessions in the control of the mature and strong, the
tribe certainly dares not be behindhand in safeguarding its larger
and more vital interests by retaining its original right of choice
in the matter of its rulers. This is one of the salient reasons for
the modification of hereditary succession, even where it has become
firmly established.

One of the elements that make for the preservation of a ruling
line is the conviction that the royal blood carries superhuman
qualities. That the chief is spiritually endowed is a common belief
and it is evidenced in the conduct of his subjects toward him. It
has been noted that the chiefs of not a few savage tribes receive
but little consideration and are endowed with but slight powers
except in time of war. That is when the chieftainship is in the
process of becoming. And all crisis-times are not war-times.
Drought, for example, calls as loudly for a display of magic as
the aggression of enemies does for military prowess. All forms of
the state, says Ratzel,[113] have a more or less express tendency
toward theocracy; the power of the chief is often increased by a
monopoly of commerce, but still more by the might of sorcery.
Prostitution for royalty occurs and offspring are dedicated to
kings.[114] It is when the ruler has become a fetish-man,[115] that the
most exaggerated respect is accorded him. "His person is considered, if we may express it so, as the dynamical center of the
universe, from which lines of force radiate to all quarters of the
heaven; so that any motion of his—the turning of his head, the
lifting of his hand—instantaneously affects and may seriously disturb some part of nature. . . . The greatest care must therefore
be taken of and by him; and his whole life, down to its minutest

113 *Vkde.,* I, 90.
114 Main, *Relig. Chastity,* chs. XXIII, XXXI.
115 §257, below.

details, must be so regulated that no act of his, voluntary or involuntary, may disarrange or upset the established order of nature." Frazer,[116] from whom this quotation is taken, devotes many chapters to the king, illustrating copiously not only the honors accorded him by reason of his fetish-quality but also the taboos and regulation, amounting to an intolerable system, under which he must exist by reason of his exalted position. Though these phenomena generally belong to the developed kingship, they appear now and then in more primitive conditions. Several cases have been noted, for instance the one where the king must never sleep lying down; and representative instances may be added to sharpen the conception of his exaltation in both its privileged and its vexatious aspects.

In Africa all sorts of subservience are exacted in order to exalt the chief. Livingstone[117] tells of a kinglet who, on departing, "mounted on the shoulders of his spokesman, as the most dignified mode of retiring. The spokesman being a slender man, and the chief six feet tall, and stout in proportion, there would have been a break-down, had he not been accustomed to it." For any offense against the Zulu king the offender, with his family and all his property, is "eaten up"—that is, absolutely destroyed. The charge of sorcery is a state-machine for such confiscation.[118] The men who carry water for a certain south-central African chief are armed. "If any one careens against them and spills the water, the offender is killed." This chief never walks, but is always carried. When an elephant is killed the tusks are brought to him and he picks out the finer of them for himself.[119] In West Africa "the person of the king is sacred, and if he drink in public, every one must turn the head so as not to see him, while some of the court women hold up a cloth before him as a screen. He never eats in public, and the people pretend to believe that he neither eats nor sleeps. It is criminal to say the contrary.[120] In Angola there were three favorites who surrounded the petty chief at an audience and gathered up his expectorations from the ground in order to cast them outside.[121] Loango chiefs might not cross certain rivers or sleep on an island, a ship, or in any place surrounded by water. One of the kings might not leave his house except by night, and might not look upon the sea or a horse or a white man. Only his successor-apparent and three elders could have intercourse with him, with their backs turned toward him. In Uganda the court ceremonial is heavy and arduous. The mass of the people may not approach the king except under very special circumstances. The great dignitaries surround him.[122]

Even the savage Teda show extreme respect for the aristocracy of blood and the chief.[123] The servility demanded is often precautionary. If a man

[116] Golden Bough, I, 109-110; §§232, 259, 272, below.
[117] Mission. Travels, 517-518.   [118] Ratzel, Vkde., I, 266.
[119] Glave, in Cent. Mag., XXX, 923.   [120] Ellis, Ewe, 162-163.
[121] Serpa Pinto, Africa, I, 142.   [122] Ratzel, Vkde., I, 604, 471.
[123] Nachtigal, Sahara, I, 330.

removes all his clothes and approaches the chief flat on his breast, he cannot constitute much of a danger to him. Death must not be mentioned before certain African kings, nor may anyone come within twenty paces of the throne. An old woman transmits messages, and even she goes on all fours. The people seem to get pleasure out of being servile, and even sacrifice their lives at a coronation. They believe their kings to be immortal and omnipotent, and the kings share the belief; one of them announced that he must have certain tribute or there would be endless tempests.[124] A mistake in etiquette toward the chief is severely punished and in Uganda the offender may be slain on the spot.[125] "Where royalty is concerned the murderer is rigorously hunted out, and if the man escapes, one of his clan is put to death. No one may shed royal blood on any account, not even when ordered by the king to slay one of the royal house; royalty may only be starved or burned to death."[126]

In Madagascar there are tribes "who pay extraordinary respect to their chiefs, and from this fact everything relating to them is a thing kept specially for them, and is not allowed to be mixed up with what belongs to the mass of the people. The chief's houses, although there is very little difference between them and those of the people generally, are like something sacred or set apart in a special manner, so that no one can ever enter them at will, but only after having asked and obtained leave of the chief, or after being summoned by him. And again, after having entered, no one can push himself forward north of the hearth, or stand idly about, but must sit quietly and respectfully south of the hearth. And in the same manner also the things in the house are set apart, for the drinking-tin, the spoons, the plates, etc., cannot be handled or put to the lips; for if any one drinks from them, the hand must be held to the mouth, and the water then poured into it from above. The chief's bedstead cannot be used by any person except one who is also a chief. . . . Not only are *things* thus kept . . . for special use by their chiefs, but many *words* are also set apart for them, both the names for certain things and other words as well."[127]

In Polynesia, "a practice is reported from some of the islands of adopting, in connection with the chiefs, or certain head chiefs, a special form of language, or method of speech, or form of address, and the interest of it, as affecting the question of the sanctity of chiefs, is that a similar practice was adopted in speaking to and of the gods. . . . In Samoa there was a chief's language, used exclusively when speaking to a chief, whether he were addressed by another chief of a rank inferior to his own, or by a person of low rank. It was never used by a chief when speaking of himself; and persons of high rank, when addressing others, and talking of themselves, always used ordinary language." Examples are given. "The Samoans had a distinct dialect for courtly intercourse, and always, in their politeness, addressed strangers in royal speech." As for the supernatural powers of the chief, "the 'king' of Tutuila . . . had always to look downwards, as his glance, if it fell upon trees and animals and other things, would cause them to die. There is here no suggestion of any process of causing things to flourish, and it is rather a matter of the infectious taboo produced by indirect contact with a great chief."[128] The funeral of a Maori chief, in October, 1894, was an imposing

---

[124] Letourneau, *Morale*, 198 ff.   [125] Macdonald, in JAI, XXII, 119.
[126] Roscoe, in JAI, XXXII, 50.
[127] Sibree, *Great Afr. Isl.*, 222-223; §223, below.
[128] Williamson, *Cent. Polyn.*, III, 89, 90, 321.

sight. There was much firing of guns and exploding of dynamite around the grave before the funeral and at it. This was, of course, to frighten away any evil influences. "The death of a great chief was associated in Maori ideas . . . with convulsions of nature, portentous phenomena that accompanied the dissolution of the *wairua's* earthly frame, the quaking of the solid land, the lightning flashing above the tribal burial hills, and the thunder rolling along the mountain peaks." No one knows the location of this chief's remains; they are not where they were supposed to be, but have been spirited away, to "ensure perfect security for the sacred bones of the dead." The natives feared the unscrupulous white men, some of whom wanted the tattooed head of the old king for a museum.[129] In the presence of such godlike rulers it is no wonder that ordinary persons must speak only in whispers.[130] In New Zealand, also, "a chief's ornaments and other possessions become taboo by touching his holy body; and he must have his own sacred fire to sit by, lest some inferior may have used it, or used some of his fire to light another on which food was cooked."[131]

In Peru, to look the king in the face was a capital crime; all eyes were lowered; and in Mexico all who met the royal cortège lowered their eyes.[132] Brazilian savages exhibited a servility that would do credit to Africa; if the chief was about to expectorate those near him would hold out their hands to receive the spittle.[133]

Doubtless some of these obsequious practices are precautionary, but the great majority of them are evidently fetishistic. The chief or king is no mere man; he is the abode of some spirit and must be treated with the deference due his dignity as such. Part of the spiritual quality or personality of chiefs goes into the insignia they bear; all are familiar with the crown, ring, and scepter, and there are many others, some of which are listed elsewhere.[134]

Of the bull-roarer, an instrument for religious use, it is said that in West Africa it "represents the active embodiment of the civil power, the local police, the mysterious head or idol of the Civil Government; it is interpreted as the executive of the State where it is practiced, deified."[135] Most of the royal insignia were, in reality, exuvial fetishes derived from the living or dead fetish-

129 Cowan, *Maoris,* ch. XXXII, and 351, 352, 355, 353 (quoted), 356.

130 Becke, *Pacific Tales,* 21.

131 Tregear, in JAI, XIX, 106, 107.

132 Bancroft, *Nat. Races,* II, 178, 180-181.

133 Southey, *Brazil,* I, 127.

134 §248, below; Kropf, *Kaffir-Engl. Dict.,* 146; Holub, *Capstadt,* II, 81; Ellis, *Ewe,* 166, 167, 178; Rohlfs, in *Mitth. J. Perthes' Geog. Anst.,* Ergänzsheft 25, 15; Holtzmann, *Ind. Sagen,* II, 344; Nadaillac, *Preh. Amer.,* 308, 419, note; Quiroga, in *Globus,* LXXII, 160; Justi, *Persien,* 179.

135 Batty, *Yoruba* (discussion), in JAI, XIX, 163; §§163, above, and 254, below.

man. Lippert[136] goes quite extensively into this matter of royal fetishism and we shall follow him briefly in his contentions, without seeking to reproduce his instances. The exuvial fetishes connected with royalty are, he holds, mainly objects once attached to the person of a former sovereign, those buried with his corpse, and, in general, those into which the power of the dead has gone over. Many of them are forms of the staff and cup, with their derivatives. Authority passes with such objects, for example with the mantle or diadem; by virtue of them it is the now divine ruler whose spirit still rules. Occasionally the mummified body of the deceased king, or some part of the body preserved as a relic, gives the right to succession. A figure of the sun as a state-jewel upon whose possession succession depends is a more developed type. A Hindu king might strengthen his rule by having a relic of Buddha in his scepter.

The king himself is possessed of a spirit and is a fetish. He is the "image" of the sun or some other ancestral god, into which that deity enters, or he is spoken of as the son of the sun or of some other god. Where the Tahiti chief rules only in the name of his son, that son has been possessed of the kingly ancestral spirit at birth; he has one more divine ancestor than his father—namely, that same father—and is so much the higher. The inexpediency involved in such a system is lost to sight in the holiness of it; for religious advantage is regarded as transcendent over all other. The spirit enters the fetish-ruler by coronation or anointing. In Mexico he had to promise beforehand that the sun and rain should be held to their functions; being raised to the fetish-quality he received power to control them and it became also his duty to do so. A good bit of the court-etiquette and servility of savage peoples is merely worship and cult.

Since the government is so enlaced with religious ideas, the king is a sort of Messiah or Son of God. The religious ideas of people under a monarchical system are inevitably colored by, and themselves color, the regulative system and political ideas; the kingdom of heaven is a pattern for earthly empires. Government and the cult are separated when the latter has become so highly de-

---

[136] *Kgchte.*, II, 384, 385, 386, 441, 462, 463, 466, 467, 470, 479, 481, 484, 492, 493, 500, 503, 562, 565, 579.

veloped as to take all the time of its functionaries. It is clear that the king is the stronger for preserving his religious connections; in Tibet, in the seventeenth century, a civil king concealed for sixteen years the death of the Lama and ruled in his name. The Mikado had to sit crowned for several hours daily to secure safety to the land; thus a country has, in its ruler, a god dwelling in it and protecting it. This god or godlike being could cure disease; the English kings touched for scrofula, the "king's evil," up to the accession of the House of Hanover. There were endless fights in Scandinavia over the "king," because they wanted a ruler who would be a fetish and not govern.

Further, this royal god sanctioned peace within his group. Trade, tribunal, and united cult were inseparable and required assemblies at set times and places. These places and times were especially tabooed under the king's peace, and became sanctuaries, refuges, and asylums. The king's peace formed a territorial peace-bond wider than that based upon kinship, and the right of life and death for a whole territory was reserved to the king's tribunals. The notion of the "divinity that doth hedge a king," or which abides in him, is one for the full development of which it is necessary to go somewhat beyond the primitive stage.

Says a king of Egypt: "I am born of the loins, created from the egg, of the Deity. The divine procreation is in me. All hail to him. I have not acted without his knowing. He ordained that I shall act."[137] "From the Babylonian point of view there could be no legitimate king in Babylon unless he had been appointed to his rule by Marduk, patron god and real ruler of the city." When Marduk was carried off his restoration was all-important for the stability of the throne. The Persian king was bathed in the heavenly glow, a symbol of God's grace, "which, however, descended only upon persons of royal blood."[138] We might illustrate by examples from much later ages. "In the sixteenth century our lawyers will use mystical language of the king. At times they will seem bent on elaborating a creed of royalty which shall take no shame if set beside the Athanasian symbol. The king has a body corporate in a body natural and a body natural in a body corporate."[139]

In 1923, the life of the Prince Regent of Japan was attempted by a young man. The assailant was hung and his whole family went into a "humiliation retirement." "Because of the particularly heinous nature of the crime in the eyes of the Japanese, who consider the Imperial family of Divine descent, the youth's immediate kin withdrew from all ordinary contacts with the world."

[137] *Records of the Past,* II, 91.
[138] Justi, *Persien,* 40-41; Rogers, *Babylonia,* I, 406.
[139] Pollock and Maitland, *Eng. Law,* I, 495.

His father "was a member of the Diet and of honorable lineage. He resigned office, withdrew to the ancestral home, ordered the great front gates locked and the blinds drawn, and he died of grief soon thereafter. The family since has remained in close seclusion," which has been terminated at length by the order of the Prince himself.[140]

It is obvious that the notion of the divine descent of kings tended to keep the succession within that kin-group which reckoned its descent from deified rulers. Thus the king had a divine right to his position. "The ascription of a divine right to kings, independent of the wishes of the people, has been one of the most enduring and most potent of superstitions, and it has even now not wholly vanished from the world."[141] These words were written some years ago. Since then the divinity of kings has received some hard knocks. If the king was responsible to God alone, as the Germans and Russians averred of their Kaisers and Tzars, then he could do no punishable wrong. Common-sense revolted against this. Some time ago youthful royalty had its whipping-boys while adult majesty possessed vicarious sufferers in its responsible ministers; but then came the time when regicides dared to raise their hands against God's anointed. Recently the two most notable of European survivals of the fetish-ruler have not been preserved by their divinity from deposition, followed in one case by assassination and in the other by a world's contempt.

In the numerous examples of the chieftainship that have been cited it has not appeared that that dignity has been with any outstanding consistency accorded to mere wealth. Primitive peoples are, it is true, plutocratic;[142] they afford no exception to the general rule that wealth and social position go together. There are cases which seem to indicate that riches and the chieftainship are correlative.

In Melanesia, for example, where the chiefs generally have very little actual authority, they have lost what they had in contact with Europeans, for "influence rests only upon the possession of greater quantities of dewarra" (shell-money).[143] A case of the actual attainment of power is where, in 1815, a man made himself chief of the Basuto by exchanging his oxen for women whom he presented to his poor subjects to win their adhesion. All their daughters were his for further operations.[144] In the Niger region the head of a village is

140 N. Y. *Times*, July 1, 1926.
142 §166, below.
144 Fritsch, *Eingeb. S.-Afr.*, I, 483.
141 Lecky, *Morals*, II, 268-269.
143 Von Pfeil, *Südsee*, 77.

generally either an old man or a man who has the most worldly goods. One of these tribes has a head-chief, "but the richest man is the most looked up to."[145] In Borneo, "wealth is not so much the accumulation of cash, as the possession of gongs, brass guns, and jars; and if a chief is deprived of his wealth, he is also deprived of his power, and the people losing faith in him look out for another who owns 'thousands.' "[146]

The case of the Alaskan Eskimo illustrates the confusion in the minds of the whites between the chieftainship and general plutocratic influence. "There is no limit to the amount of property which an individual, at least the head of a family, may accumulate. . . . This has given rise to a regular wealthy and aristocratic class, who are not sufficiently distinct from the poorer people to refuse to associate on any terms but those of social equality. The men of this class are the umialiks, a word appearing in many forms on the coast of Western America and often supposed to mean 'chief.' " The word, meaning "wealthy," is "an explanation of the position of these men and not a translation of a title." These umialiks have been "more thrifty and intelligent, better traders, and usually better hunters, as well as physically stronger and more daring"; they acquire influence and respect from these reasons, as well as from their wealth, but "appear to have absolutely no authority outside of their own families."[147]

These cases, illustrating the usual and normal respect for the successful in the economic life, as well as the low estimate accorded to failures, do not, however, lend much countenance to the derivation of the chieftainship from economic success as a primary cause. Until the regulative system had advanced far enough to evolve the chief, it is doubtful whether anyone could accumulate and then hold riches enough to gain the position. And where the chief is wealthy it is often debatable as to whether that is the cause or the consequence of his elevation. Among most semi-civilized peoples doubtless the kingship is what Telemachus says of it: "speedily one's house grows rich"[148]—that is, wealth is a consequence, not a cause. On the earlier stages, affluence seems not to be an essential prerequisite and in many cases it is not a consequence. Whatever his sources of income, the chief has duties of generosity and hospitality, as well as responsibility for the support of his warriors, which often leave him a poor man in the end. There seems sometimes to be an elaborate provision for the disbursement of what he has or gets, with no arrangements about stipend. He is not at all in the strategic position of the medicine-man.[149] In short, the chieftainship seems to be a recognition of family-connections and

145 Granville and Roth, in JAI, XXVIII, 117.
146 Roth, *Sarawak*, II, 233.   147 Murdoch, in BAE, IX, 429.
148 Homer, *Odyssey*, I, 390-393.   149 §320, below.

of personal qualities rather than of wealth. It seems to go back
to kin-headship and to military and religious leadership as its
main roots and to administrative competence for its justification.

What the chief gets in the form of revenue comes in the way of
gifts, fines, confiscations, labor by his subjects, and in other simple and obvious forms. It is of no use to him to own the land, least
of all to own it by a fiction. He must have serviceable man-power
to put upon it.[150] He can only lend it out in fief, unless he can
compel service; and then the fief-holder's method of evasion, to
become "free," is to keep the land and elude or refuse the services.
Spencer[151] has developed the subject of revenue with copious illustration; a few examples should carry the point.

"The African is not peculiar in disliking taxes, but as soon as any degree
of tribal cohesion is reached, the obligation to pay tribute to the head chief—
generally in the form of slaves, concubines, food, and unpaid labour—is recognised. As the tribe advances in organisation, and its rulers become more
powerful and luxurious . . . the demands become increasingly heavy. . . .
Only among the most primitive peoples, where the authority of a paramount
chief has not yet emerged, do we find an entire absence of taxation, for there
is no authority to demand or enforce it. Such communities regard the payment
of tribute as the token of acknowledgment of a Suzerain, with the consequent
obligation to refrain from murders and robberies. Provided that it is not
collected by alien native tax-gatherers, and is not unduly onerous, they do not
appear to resent its imposition. . . . Refusal to pay it is usually a formal
and deliberate prelude to an outbreak of lawlessness."[152] "Among certain
tribes the finder of ivory has to surrender one or both tusks to the chief. So
amongst the Wasumbwa, where any article of considerable value found belongs to the chief; in Usove all ivory belongs to the chief, whether found or
hunted. In Ubena the same is the rule, and elephant could be hunted only
under permission of the chief; in Usumbwa the chief claimed one tusk. In
Unyamwesi all ivory belongs to the chief, who rewards the man who brings it
to him."[153]

In West Africa, "there is no taxation and no state revenue, properly speaking. The sub-chiefs and head-men subsist on the fees, bribes, and presents they
receive from those under their control, and in their turn contribute to the
wants of the district chiefs, who, finally, subscribe to those of the king."[154]
Road-tolls are collected by a strangely clad functionary armed with a whip.[155]

In Fantiland all must contribute something vaguely defined in recognition
of the chieftaincy, and the chief can call for special contributions in case of a

[150] Gumplowicz, *Soc.*, 129-130; §§103, 126, above.
[151] *Prin. Soc.*, II, §542.
[152] Lugard, *Brit. Trop. Afr.*, 231, 232.
[153] Dundas, C., in JAI, LI, 276.
[154] Ellis, *Ewe*, 162; Ratzel, *Vkde.*, III, 140, 143.
[155] Frobenius, *Masken*, 153, 154.

journey or a death, or to defray "legal expenses."[156] On the Loango coast, "when a prince enters a village, it is nominally his privilege to demand all that appeals to him, and generally these pests are in a position to give their words emphasis" through their attendants, a set of boys who have been renounced by their uncles and are very trustworthy.[157] Johnston[158] tells of how a certain traveller's only chance of reaching Europe was by dint of lavish presents to a sulky chief, who finally let him pass to the coast. In Madagascar the people had to render the first fruits of all crops, especially of rice, the chief one; a certain quantity of rice in the husk; manual labor in preparing the royal rice-fields, making roads, erecting public buildings, and similar undertakings. "The lands are not held on the feudal condition of serving in war, nor are they subdivided among the vassals of the more powerful chiefs; but every Hova subject (unless he be a slave or incapacitated by disease or infirmity) is obliged to serve in the standing army, such service being by a recent edict limited to a term of five years."[159] This report is dated 1882.

In India, "generally speaking, the universal plan of taking revenue was by taking a share of the actual grain heap on the threshing-floor."[160] In the Chin Hills "the chiefs are lords of the soil within their boundaries, and if any aliens wish to enter their territory and work the land, they must pay the chief thereof the customary tithes. Besides the tithes which he receives as lord of the soil, the chief receives tribute from tribes, villages, or families which he has conquered. . . . Tribute usually takes the form of *mithun* (cross between common cow and wild bison bull) and other cattle. Tithes not only include a certain proportion of the grain crop, but also a portion of the increase of live stock, such as one out of a litter of pigs, two puppies yearly, and very occasionally mithun." In some parts tithes include, in addition, "a hind-leg of every animal killed at a feast and a hind and front leg of every wild animal shot or trapped."[161]

Almost everywhere in the Malay Archipelago the chiefs have a right to the aid of their subjects in the care of their estates. Among the Bataks the chief had a right to three days' labor in the year, in the planting, weeding, and reaping of rice. Chiefs receive also part of the fines imposed.[162] In Borneo a certain share of all money-fines accrued to the chief; he received a regular payment of rice from the fields, and also a share in all booty, whether or not he had been present during a raid.[163] "Rebuke the company of the spearman . . . until every one submit himself with pieces of silver"[164] is interpreted as tribute to the ruler. Among the Arabs the prince must entertain the guest, feed the poor, and care for the widow and orphan. He received the fourth part of booty taken. This did not mean that he had won it in war, or could use it to suit himself; "but the tribe therewith created a sort of state-treasure which only indeed because of the lack of juristic persons lay in the hands of

[156] Connolly, in JAI, XXVI, 147.

[157] Bastian, *Deut. Exped.*, I, 195-196.   [158] *Uganda*, II, 228.

[159] Parker, in JAI, XII, 277.   [160] Baden-Powell, *Brit. Ind.*, I, 97.

[161] Carey and Tuck, *Chin Hills*, I, 201.

[162] Wilken, *Vkde.*, 343-345; Hagedorn, "Sultan of Jolo," in *Century Mag.*, LX, No. 1.

[163] Schwaner, *Borneo*, I, 172.   [164] Psalms, LXVIII, 30.

physical persons. Thus it was the source from which flowed to the prince the means of fulfilling his social duties."[165]

Of course such duties, and other exceptional ones, lasted on, or were invented, throughout history. The needy or grasping king could think out ever new sources of revenue, as, for instance, where "the King of France shall have two-thirds of the wrecks which shall befall on the shores of the Garonne and the Tarn, and that the other third shall belong to the abbots and monks of Moissac." Reversions and benefices accrued at the death of a vassal, and the heir must have investiture and pay "relief."[166]

There are occasional instances of what might be called a public treasure as contrasted with mere contributions to the chief. Of the Florida Indians it is reported that "previous to their carrying off their crops from the field, there is a large crib or granary, erected in the plantation, which is called the King's crib; and to this each family[-head] carries and deposits a certain quantity, according to his ability or inclination, or none at all if he so chooses; this in appearance seems a tribute or revenue to the mico [chief], but in fact is designed for another purpose, *i.e.*, that of a public treasury, supplied by a few and voluntary contributions, and to which every citizen has the right of a free and equal access, when his own private stores are consumed, to serve as a surplus to fly to for succor, to assist neighboring towns, whose crops may have failed, accommodate strangers or travelers, afford provisions or supplies when they go forth on hostile expeditions, and for all other exigencies of the State. . . . The Huron-Iroquois also had a public treasury, which contained wampum, Indian corn, slaves, fresh and dried meat, and, in fact, anything else that might serve to defray the public expenses."[167]

In general, savages are not mulcted by their chiefs and are not discontented even if they seem to be ill-treated in the matter of requisitions or otherwise. They grow up into the local system, and know no other with which to compare it so as to realize that they are downtrodden and oppressed. If they are badly treated according to their own ideas they will generally resist or move over under some other chief's jurisdiction. This is rather rare; the fact is that there is a sort of unreflective, traditional sentiment that the law and order secured even by a bloody and greedy despot are worth the cost and are to be preferred to anarchy and disorder.

If society means security, says Starcke,[168] then a good member is one whose presence increases security and whose absence diminishes it. In primitive society this means often a violent man, that is, one who possesses positive qualities. If the chief is such, the harm he does is overlooked. It is a question between use and abuse of power, where the use is so needed that the abuse sinks into insignificance. Hence almost anything is endured from a demonstrated warrior.

[165] Proksch, *Blutrache*, 7-9.   [166] Letourneau, *Prop.*, 312-313.
[167] Carr, in *Smithson. Rep.*, 1891, 527, note.
[168] *Samvittighedslivet*, 167-170.

If the ruler is strong and keeps order he is likely to be secure and even popular, for savages appreciate and worship strength. The powerful chief may, naturally enough, take recourse to means designed to strengthen his hold upon his subjects, such as retaining their children at court, ostensibly to educate them but really as hostages, or requiring vassals to pass a portion of their time in his neighborhood where he can watch them.[169] Of course no such devices can definitively check the expression of public opinion; he may kill all his relatives to rid himself of rivals, and then be overthrown by a palace-revolution. At some point servility turns into rebellion if he flouts what the people feel to be their rights. For a long time, it may be, a miserable and oppressed group will cringe and hug the small comfort and favors which they get the tighter the less those are; but if its spirit is not wholly broken a people will react eventually, and the more violently because of pent-up feelings.

It seems clear enough by this time that there is not much profit in debating whether the chieftainship did or did not come out of the *patria potestas* of the father-family.[170] There is no doubt that, whereas all social forms find some of their deepest roots in the family, the derivation may be a long one and quite indirect. One author[171] finds that the origin of property is bound up with the formation of the family; that the power of the chief grows with the increase of the family; and that "usually the same stage of the chieftainship is found conjoined with the same stage of property." He thinks it is the family that creates both the property-forms and those of the chieftainship. Such a parallel development of two of the most important of human institutions is yet another example of consistency in the mores. In their adjustment the mores move forward in rank, not in file, though that rank may not be without its irregularities due to a pushing forward in some places and a lagging back in others. Necessity is the sergeant who spurs on the stragglers and enforces an orderliness and consistency that make for survival and success.

[169] Letourneau, *Polit.*, 117, 135-136.
[170] Maine, *Early Law*, 239, 242; *Anc. Law*, 136; *Early Hist.*, 117; Starcke, *Prim. Fam.*, 276 ff.
[171] Mucke, *Horde*, 292.

§157*. **Women as Rulers.** Much has been made by chroniclers and historians of female chiefs and "queens"; and travellers have fastened upon cases of woman-rulers and given them the prominence accorded to the exceptional. Theorists have developed out of these cases a system which they have called gynæcocracy or metrocracy or matriarchate. It is a fact that relationship has been widely reckoned in the female line and that there has existed as a consequence, in a number of parts of the earth, what deserves the name of the mother-family. In that type of kinship-organization the women played a rôle of exceptional importance. Naturally the mother-family is not under review in the present connection;[172] and the matriarchate is really only a negative thing. The patriarchate is father-power, that is, positive dominion and property over human beings, involving differentiation and subjection. The matriarchate at its strongest is not so much woman-power as the absence of man's rule. There may be a "queen" at home in peace and under an industrial régime; but a chosen man is ruler in the hunt and in war.[173] Since in the present connection we have to do only with actual cases of female rulers of tribes, it is safe to begin with the statement that seldom indeed has a woman attained the chieftainship except by inheriting it. Women have taken only a secondary part in war[174] and have not been prominent in those activities success in which has elevated men to the chieftainship. They have exercised considerable influence upon government, generally in indirect ways, but have attained the highest political power only when the way to it had already been opened by male relatives as predecessors.

Though they are relatively few, the cases of woman-rulers should be examined, since the exception ought always to be scrutinized for the sake of the light it throws on the normal and usual.

Two cases of female chiefs are reported from New Guinea.[175] Ratzel[176] concludes that although women are badly treated by the Africans, yet they do not hold them in contempt, as is shown by the number of queens and medicine-

172 §§415 ff., 421, 422, below.
173 Lippert, *Kgchte.*, II, 40, where cases are given.
174 Chs. V and VI, above, and §§384, 386, 387, 391, below.
175 Finsch, *Ethnol. Erfahr.*, II, 298; Cayley-Webster, *New Guinea,* 211.
176 *Vkde.*, I, 153.

women. Livingstone[177] mentions several cases of South African female rulers. Women are preferred as regents by the Zambesi tribes because they are less cruel, and the succession may go to either sex.[178] "In his journeyings in the Zambesi country, Africa, Capt. A. St. H. Gibbons found an ancient and interesting custom prevailing . . . of investing the eldest surviving sister of the ruling king with the prerogatives of a queen without whose advice and sanction her brother can not give effect to any important measure in the government of the state. In minor local matters she in her own district reigns supreme, holds the power of life and death over her subjects, and is at liberty to wed or depose a husband at will. The present Makwai, or queen, from whom six husbands have been removed in ways not natural, is described by the author as having a mixed character, being unscrupulous and very polite."[179] This same princess had her minister and capital and adjudged cases, presiding at the council of chiefs.[180]

In the old Congo kingdom, "the princesses formerly possessed great prerogative; they could choose their husbands to suit themselves out of the great men of the realm and such a man, who had to prepare himself for his elevation by several months of seclusion, became her will-less slave." He must never see another woman, or he and she would be put to death, and so in his perambulations he is preceded by a tom-tom, which puts all the women to flight. In the Congo the husband of the king's sister is forced to follow her as a slave into the spirit-world. Again, the queen will have a "harem" of husbands, who are kept in a constant condition of enslavement and humiliation.[181] The queen's husband has no voice in the government.[182]

In Polynesia, "there is no doubt that in most, at all events, of the islands women were qualified to succeed, and that the line of succession could pass through women; and I could have collected a number of examples from the traditions and history which indicate that they did so, though as a rule the successors have been men."[183]

Perhaps, while upon the topic of woman-rule, we might as well add a few words concerning woman's share in the lesser powers of government. The subject of her public functions will appear elsewhere,[184] and it will be seen that her influence is exercised rather through the men of her kin than directly. Starcke[185] says with some justice that primitive woman "begins by being what the bard afterward became; she retains a faithful remembrance of traditions, and she stimulates the sluggish when they are slow to admit

[177] Mission. Travels, 104, 239, 295, 298, 541; Ratzel, Vkde., I, 309; Main, Relig. Chastity, ch. XIX.
[178] Holub, Süd. Afr., II, 186.   [179] Quotation in PSM, LI, 453.
[180] "Bertrands Reise," in Globus, LXXIV, 40.
[181] Bastian, Afr. Reisen, 173-174, 181; Bastian, Deut. Exped., I, 217.
[182] Serpa Pinto, Africa, I, 240.
[183] Williamson, Cent. Polyn., III, 395.
[184] §384, below; Cope, in PSM, XXXIII, 721-730.
[185] Prim. Fam., 64.

the claims of a bloody revenge." Female influence of this sort is entirely consistent with the imposition of drudgery upon women,[186] and because of it women are by no means to be ignored in the regulative system. They have their own weapons of ridicule, petty persecution, and shrill clamor, and where they are not actually accorded political or semi-political functions, they are yet to be reckoned with.

The only exception to the general oppression of the Australian women is the West Australian custom of making an old woman titular grandmother of the tribe, which gives her a prominent position and qualifies her to reconcile strife, separate fighters, and call to war.[187] Livingstone[188] saw about a hundred women present at a council in South Africa. "During the intervals between speeches these ladies burst forth into a sort of plaintive ditty; but it was impossible to make out whether this was in praise of Shinte [the chief], or of themselves. This was the first time the writer had ever seen females present in a public assembly. In the south, women are never permitted to enter the kotla," or assembly-place. In every town of the Yorubas there was a "mistress of the street" to whom were referred all disputes between women.[189] A Dyak rajah is reported as holding an assembly in which women participated.[190] In the Pelew Islands, the chief does nothing without the assent of the oldest women of the clan, secured in council; their advice was sought in regard to both internal and external affairs.[191] As elsewhere mentioned,[192] the women of the Caroline Islands have a political influence based upon their function as cultivators of the taro. In the Marianas Islands women could speak in council;[193] while in the Friendly Islands the discoverers found a woman above the chief ruler, honored by him as all others honored him, but without governing powers.[194] Among the Seneca Indians the women had great power. They could "knock off the horns" from the head of a chief and send him back to the ranks of the warriors. The original nomination of the chief was their prerogative.[195] They had a council of their own, and subjects presented by them were discussed in the great council. There were even female chiefs.[196]

Bastian[197] sums up the political position of women as follows: "In general, in developed state-relations which call for a vigorous and unintermittent activity, woman, just on account of her sex-peculiarity, will recede in comparison with man, whereas in the

[186] Morgan, in *Contrib. N. Amer. Ethnol.*, IV, 122.
[187] Ratzel, *Vkde.*, II, 67. [188] *Mission. Travels*, 816.
[189] Ellis, *Yoruba*, 167. [190] Bock, *Borneo*, 21.
[191] Kubary, *Pelauer*, I, 39. [192] §387, below.
[193] Waitz, *Anthrop.*, V, 107.
[194] Lippert, *Kgchte.*, II, 50 (from Hawkesworth's *Reisen*, V, 217).
[195] Morgan, *Anc. Soc.*, 455; Morgan, in *Contrib. N. Amer. Ethnol.*, IV, 66; Schoolcraft, *Ind.*, III, 196.
[196] Parkman, *Old Régime*, 30. [197] *Afr. Reisen*, 178.

simpler situations, when once the lowest stage of the nomadic hunter's life has been passed, both stand upon about the same level." Though we do not fully concur with this statement, it reflects, at any rate, the consequences of inevitable sex-differences. It should be added that when one sex does nearly all the hunting and fighting, and out of these occupations derives not only the possession of weapons but also the power of regular coöperation, drill, and discipline, it is but natural that the regulation of the society's public affairs should devolve pretty exclusively upon it. The decisive test of any regulative system is war; this has always been the case, and it has exercised a selection in favor of man-rule. Woman's sphere has been the family and her political influence has been, for the most part, exercised indirectly through the male members of the family.

§158. Monarchy. From a survey of the various aspects of the chieftainship it appears that, though power tends to pass into a single hand as a condition of its being exercised consistently and with some approach to special knowledge and perspective, yet, except in a critical situation, it is conceded reluctantly and with reservations. It is not so easy to become socialized and disciplined. Also, besides being more or less tentatively accorded and relatively unstable, authority is undifferentiated. The chief attends to nearly all forms of regulation and even controls religious life to some extent. He is the guardian of the mores in most of their phases, the executive of public opinion in many fields. It is to be recalled that his position is often a very difficult and laborious one, and that he by no means enjoys unlimited rights with no corresponding duties.

To realize the strain of the office, one must reflect not only upon the variety of the chief's functions, but also upon the fact that his mind undoubtedly feels as a severe weight what would seem to us, perhaps, a slight burden. It is hard for him to think things out and make decisions and yet he has to do that to some extent—to a greater degree, at least, than the common man with limited responsibility. His position is not one of unalloyed privilege. In his degree he is in "the fierce light that beats upon a throne"; interests center in his actions and even his godhood does not render him immune from criticism. It is not civilized peoples alone who readily shift blame upon the government. One finds himself harboring some sympathy for the savage chief, as for a sort of adult child called upon to face situations, simple as they may seem to us, which make heavy demands upon his powers, tire him out, and use him up. His great resource is tradition, which covers most cases and relieves him of even his rudimentary thought-taking about them; still there are enough left to keep what wits he has at a tension.

A further point which has emerged from the cases is that there is always going on, in the earlier stages at least, a sort of selection of the chief for quality. Failures are not tolerated. Even if the king is a god, he must be a preserver; and if he cannot preserve he must make room for one who can.[198] He is sometimes a spiritless, cloistered recluse, bereft of all power, in which case authority is wielded by those who are willing to forego the name and dignity. He may be killed when he grows old and feeble. The most resolute efforts have been made not to be elected to the office. Frazer[199] has developed all these aspects of the kingship, with copious illustration. "Ceremonial refusal," found in various parts of the world, is interpreted as "a ceremonial socializing of responsibility," whereby the people who press the election upon the chief are made co-responsible with him.[200] A visitation of popular displeasure is always a possibility to be guarded against. Evidently the factor of selection is at work in this range; it could hardly be otherwise where so much depends upon a single functionary in the midst of a struggle for very existence. Even where hereditary succession is regularly recognized, there are, as has been seen, ways of averting a palpable misfit. And presently to be encountered are certain developments which operate to control the chief in his possible erratic or capricious moods.

Indeed, it is quite debatable whether genuine monarchy—the rule of one individual—has ever been seen on earth. Such terms as autocrat, despot, unlimited monarch, have been employed to designate the relative freedom of some ruler from control; under special

---

[198] On what a chief should be, see Maine, *Early Hist.*, 134.
[199] *Golden Bough*, I, 115 ff., 216 ff.
[200] Van Gennep, in *Archiv. f. Religsw.*, X, 1-10.

circumstances, instances have occurred in which there has been lodged in the hands of an individual an amount of so-called irresponsible power so formidable that only a superlative or a universal would seem capable of describing it. Such cases, however, have been relatively rare. The distinction is between degrees of answerability in the exercise of power rather than between responsibility and its utter absence; between degrees of delegation of authority by the society, which alone possesses it, than between society's retention of such authority and total divestment of it. The question is always as to how sharply power needs to be focussed in order to realize a higher expediency in its application. It has been discovered, by experience, that the force of society can be most efficiently applied by delegating power to individuals rather generously and then setting up checks against its abuse.

§159*. **Checks on Monarchy.** It has been seen that few primitive peoples have conferred full power upon an individual, except in time of peril, without some reluctance; and that when the power has been accorded, responsibility has gone along with it. It is true that some chiefs and kings have come to be as nearly absolute and irresponsible as could well be imagined; even so, however, there are limits beyond which it is not safe for them to go. The precautionary etiquette of some native courts reveals an apprehension of the fact that popular patience is capable of being strained to the breaking-point. The final power always rests in the people and in their public opinion. Of course the public opinion of any society is not the sum of the opinions of its individual members—not even the algebraic sum of pros and cons. Quality and proportionate weight also come in. The opinion of one who is able to sway the opinions of others might be said to be the sum of the opinions which he can sway, plus his own. In general the play of individual interests is such that large numbers will resist departure from a situation in which most people's interests are, or are thought to be, satisfactorily served. A single will may not be capriciously imposed upon even a worshipful people if they feel that their interests are being ignored or opposed. Probably the man who has had the highest degree of autocratic power in history was Napoleon. Other absolute rulers have been bound by custom, tradition, strong ministers, and conditions; and they have not had a quick civil reaction such as he had. Yet Napoleon went down like the rest.

To oppose public opinion is, in general, to go contrary to the code of mores. The monarch's function is, as Homer[201] puts it, to defend the traditional rules and precedents—the *themistes*, *dikē*, or mores—which have been handed over to him by the high god himself. If he does wrong according to that code, punishment comes upon the people at large, as in the case of the Homeric plague, and public opinion forces him to correct himself. Though religious conceptions surround the whole matter, the underlying popular sentiment is unmistakable. So does the supernatural influence surround and enforce discipline and royal inviolability, as where the goddess restrains Achilles from an assault on the king; for the dignity of the ruler is the dignity of the society itself.[202]

Aside from tyrannicide and deposition as checks upon absolutism, there was also the practice of desertion, several times alluded to in what has gone before. An African chief could not harbor the illusion that he was popular if some day he found himself nearly alone. This method seems strange to us, for in these latter days the people stay and make the ruler migrate. The prospect of any one of these drastic consequences to unpopular action has been a deterrent to the abuse of power. It is hardly proper to use the word revolution in connection with primitive regulation. There is no real change of government, but merely the ejection of a person. In more highly evolved systems of regulation a whole system may be upset and a new one adopted. This often involves ejection, but there is something more fundamental to it. People get into power who, refusing to listen to the opinion of large minorities or even of majorities, allege "reason of state," and refuse to explain or to "show the books." The only answer to the reason of state is to oust the authorities, get at the books, and see for one's self. A real revolution is a mass-movement beyond the capacity of savages, involving change of policies and general rearrangements. It is hardly proper to designate the petty personal shifts and revolts

201 *Iliad*, II, 206; IX, 97-102; *Odyssey*, XIX, 111.
202 Homer, *Iliad*, I, 1 ff.; Keller, *Hom. Soc.*, 147-148, 258-259.

of primitive people, with no subsequent change of any consequence in policy or principle, as revolutions.

In New Caledonia and the Loyalty Islands, chiefs are hereditary and more despotic than, for instance, in Samoa. A tribe cannot depose its chief, but if he is unendurable, it goes off and leaves him, joins another group, or stays in exile.[203] It is the custom among the Kaffirs under no circumstances to give up a fugitive, whatever the reason for his flight, and "in this strictly maintained custom lies the most effective bridle to the despotism of the chief. A too severe, cruel ruler sees the number of his subjects melt away under his hands when they, in order at least to save their lives, flee to neighboring and better leaders." Sometimes the whole village goes off in the night, leaving the chief alone. This is about all they can do, for the chief's attendants fall upon the recalcitrant and "eat them up," that is, kill all their cattle and destroy their property, reducing them to a beggary where they can no longer resist authority.[204] One East African chief "oppressed the people greatly. He robbed them of their best milk cattle, and it is related of him that, when he heard of any specially fine beast, he would go to the owner's village and remaining there would refuse all meat and drink, until the man fearing lest his chief should die in his own village, gave up the cow to him. So the people wearied of Kitai's oppression, and one by one they crossed over the Nzaea into Loreko, until he was finally left with scarcely any people to rule over."[205]

In the highly militaristic Zulu state, escape from which by migration was virtually impossible, the king did about as he pleased.[206] The powerful kings of Uganda "maintained a certain civilisation and a considerable amount of law and order in the territories which they governed. But they put no limits to their lust and cruelty. The precincts of their courts were constantly stained with human blood, execution for perfectly trifling offences being a daily occurrence. Stanley relates how Mutesa [father of Mwanga], in the earlier years of his reign, when excited by banana wine and irritable from one cause and another, would slake his wrath by rushing in amongst his women and slashing them right and left with a spear. . . . The Negro worships force, and has a sneaking admiration for bloodshed. The kings of Uganda came to be regarded at last as almost god-like, and the attitude of their courtiers towards them was slavish to the last degree. Mwanga might have been a Stuart for his debaucheries, his cruelties, and utter faithlessness to those to whom he had passed his word. Perhaps he might still have been king had not his vicious propensities taken a turn which disgusted even his negro people, and made them fear that his precept and example spreading widely among his imitative subjects might result in the disappearance in time of the Uganda race."[207]

Among the Kukis, in India, "it sometimes happens that a chief fails to govern his clan with a firm hand or is so overbearing that he is deserted by his people, who fly to another village and to the protection of a more lenient ruler."[208] Revolutions are by no means seldom among the American Indians,

[203] Ella, in AAAS, 1892, 634.
[204] Fritsch, *Eingeb. S.-Afr.*, 93, 97; Starcke, *Prim. Fam.*, 58.
[205] Dundas, K. R., in JAI, XLIII, 22.
[206] Macdonald, in JAI, XX, 113.   [207] Johnston, *Uganda*, II, 684-685.
[208] Carey and Tuck, *Chin Hills*, I, 3.

especially since contact with the whites. Thus Red Cloud headed the opposition to the chiefs who had yielded to the whites the right to build a road through Montana. The under-chiefs strive with each other to control a greater number of families, and one who succeeds becomes a rival of the head-chief. All chiefs are subject to the danger of desertion by their subjects, who may go over to another tribe if they intend to stay there. Sometimes such desertion is *en masse;* in 1867 some of the Sioux wanted to help the Cheyennes, who were at war with the United States, but their chief, Spotted Tail, resisted. Twenty or more families went off in the night, against his orders, to assist the Cheyennes.[209] If the Shingu Indians are discontented with a chief they move off to another place and leave him.[210]

It is a long way from such cases to the teaching of the right of revolution, deposition of the emperor, and even of tyrannicide, as in China—a doctrine that was officially and generally recognized and based upon the conception that the people came first, the empire second, and the prince third.[211] Similarly in Japan the chief "is elected to enforce the public will, not to impose his own,— to serve the common interests, not to serve his own,—to maintain and confirm custom, not to break with it. Thus, though appointed chief, he is only the public servant, and the least free man in his native place."[212]

Aside from the original limitation of the power conferred upon him and the check put upon him by prospect of assassination, deposition, or desertion, the chief was controlled by certain informal or formal bodies of persons who were representative of public opinion. There were the elders, for example, who were the repositories of custom and tradition, and without whose sanction the chief might not proceed with confidence.[213] These counsellors dealt largely in proverbs, which are crystallizations of folk-wisdom, tested generation after generation, and always understandable and popular.

"The Yorubas have an extraordinary number of proverbial sayings, and regard a knowledge of them as a proof of great wisdom, whence the saying, 'A counsellor who understands proverbs soon sets matters right.' They are in constant use, and another saying runs, 'A proverb is the horse of conversation. When the conversation droops a proverb revives it. Proverbs and conversation follow each other.' "[214]

In many cases the aged headed the constituent elements of the tribe, the families, clans, or gentes; and the chief, whether or not he were one of them, must secure their adherence and support.

[209] Ratzel, *Vkde.*, II, 633.
[210] Von den Steinen, *Zent. Bras.*, 331.
[211] Schallmayer, *Vererbung*, 204.   [212] Hearn, *Japan*, 103.
[213] Many cases in Letourneau, *Morale*, and *Politique*.
[214] Ellis, *Yoruba*, 218.

Again, there was a regular council of the elders bearing a name such as *gerousia* or *senate*, indicative of its composition. Whether or not they constituted a formal body, the older men and often the women as well exerted a distinctly restrictive influence upon the chief or king. A council, whether or not it is composed of the aged, is found at the side of many primitive rulers, not only in war but also in peace; and there are a number of cases where, in addition, the chief must report to a popular assembly, often including the whole body of fellow-tribesmen. They can express their sentiments by silence, uproar, or grunts, even though they are inarticulate; and the canny chief is an expert in interpreting and adjusting himself to their verdict. Naturally the beginnings of such agencies are highly informal, but they are there on very early stages of political evolution, even antedating the chieftainship. In fact, it must have taken some sort of a body to select the chief in the first place, in so far as he did not simply impose himself by superior strength; and the council or assembly might thus be taken to have been the conferring body, later, subsequently to the choice of an executive, transformed into an advisory and restrictive agency.

In Australia, variations in policy "may perhaps have been locally introduced by some strong man acting in conjunction with the older men of his own group. This is discussed amongst the various leading men when they meet together, and then, if the innovation gains the support of other leaders, it will be adopted and will gradually come to be recognized as the right thing. At the same time it must be clearly understood that, in the tribes with which we are dealing, there is nothing in the form of a definite 'meeting,' in our sense of the term, such as has been described in the case of various Australian tribes, at which different members of the tribe, one after another, address the assembled natives."215 In some regions the tribal council is a formally constituted and exclusive body. It "breaks up peacefully, but quarrels sometimes follow it, although the camp is not allowed to know the real cause of disagreement, for the secrets of the council are always kept as sacredly as those of a Masonic lodge. The greatest cruelties are threatened to any one of the council who should divulge its secrets, which are many. I have never heard the younger men or the women drop a word which could convey the idea that anything had been communicated to them."216 The Dieri afford a very good instance of what is known as the "great council" of an Australian tribe. Its general council consists of all the fully initiated men, and within it is the great council, composed of all men of venerable age, or eminent because of some physical or mental

215 Spencer and Gillen, *North. Tr. Cent. Aust.*, 29.
216 Howitt, in JAI, XX, 69 (quoting Gason).

superiority—combined with their years. "It includes, therefore, the extremely aged men, the heads of totems, . . . the principal warriors, the great orators, the powerful wizards; and the most eminent man of them all becomes the headman of this council." The great council holds its meetings in secret, and death is the penalty for revelation. It decides the times for the great ceremonial meetings, including initiations and rain-producing ceremonies; it allots accessory husbands and wives to each other; it sends out embassies, declares war, and proclaims peace; it tries offenses against tribal welfare and the moral code, especially cases of incest. It deals with crimes and moral offenses, that is those against both the local and the social organizations.[217] In these cases we see the chieftainship in the process of becoming rather than in existence and under control.

"The highest power, the *suprema lex*—for in the Papuan state traditional usage (the Malay *adat*) ranks as that—rests in the whole commonalty, in the assembly of the people; all is settled by the mass-counsel and mass-vote of the male population. . . . If, for example, two brothers beat each other, the strife is not composed by the family-head, who rules only in a limited degree, but it comes before the general forum. Therefore it is easily understandable that oratory is highly valued."[218]

What is meant by the constitutional authorities which are supposed to limit the power of an African despot may be seen in the case of the ruler Sepopo who caused one after another of the members of the great council to be put to death. The little council was evidently a sort of beer and tobacco society. The great names given to officers were only for pomp. The king had a monopoly of the administration of justice and of the office of sorcerer.[219] In Ashanti the king is by no means absolute but is always controlled to some degree by the chiefs. He may not make war or peace alone, nor enter into negotiations or treaties affecting the interests of the whole tribe without the chiefs' consent. It is the chiefs of the first rank who, with the king in council, rule the tribe. The king is a chief of the first rank; there are a number of such chiefs over districts, and one of them is, in addition, the tribal king. The government is really an aristocracy rather than a personal despotism and the district-chiefs, though feudatories of the king, preserve a semi-independence. The populace has no voice whatever in the affairs of the tribe. Rule rests mainly on terror, and the chief strength of the king is his power to take life at any time.[220] Again, the sovereignty among the Yorubas is hereditary in one family, but the successor is elected by the council. Blood-descent is a qualification for election. "The council of elders, besides electing a king, controls his actions, and, should he show any disposition to make himself independent of it, invites him to 'go to sleep,' by sending him a present of parrots' eggs."[221] The king of Benin was assisted in governing by four principal officers, three of them civil. These officers and the Ju-Ju men were the real governors of the country, the king being little more than a puppet in their hands.[222]

The Unyamwesi are split up into little divisions each with a chief and sub-chiefs who form the nobility, and with village head-men under these. Around

[217] Howitt and Fison, in JAI, XIV, 153, notes.
[218] Hagen, *Papua's*, 227.   [219] Ratzel, *Vkde.*, I, 374.
[220] Ellis, *Tshi*, 274-275; Ellis, *Ewe*, 161.
[221] Ellis, *Yoruba*, 164.
[222] Kingsley, *W. Afr. Studies*, 450.

the chief are elders who greatly restrain him, especially as to war and peace.[223] Again, while the chiefs seem to have absolute power over the lives and property of their subjects, there are many customs that control them; and before any important move, a council of chief men is held.[224] "Strong chiefs handle their counsellors as puppets, weaklings must submit to their decision."[225] Again, a number of the aristocracy always accompany the chief to keep him from getting drunk or smoking, lest he should, under intoxication, perpetrate cruelties. He has four great counsellors. There is a popular assembly whose functions are vague. The Somal chiefs are limited by a sort of council of heads of families.[226] "Among all three of the big tribes of northeast Africa the arrangement obtains of considering the affairs of the tribe in assemblies, larger and smaller. . . . The speakers comport themselves with the highest parliamentary dignity," the listeners applauding or contradicting loudly. In some cases the chief calls the assembly only when he badly needs help in some unforeseen contingency; in others there is a dignified parliament which handles political and judicial questions.[227]

Williamson[228] enters upon a very detailed study of all the local systems of government of Central Polynesia and, in so doing, pays much attention to the various councils that surround the chief. A selection of his instances will be found in the *Case-Book*. Perhaps the following passage will serve as a sort of summary of many detailed descriptions. "I think we must conclude that, notwithstanding the great powers possessed by the chiefs in certain districts, the general and combined effect of the evidence, taken as a whole, is to indicate that their administrative and parliamentary power . . . was often curtailed largely by the necessity of acting in accordance with the views of their subjects, expressed in private discussion with their immediate advisers, and at the *fono*," or assembly. "The general impression left upon my mind by the study of the history of Samoa is that the great chiefs were interested mainly in themselves and their dynasties, their dignity, power and glory. The matters in which they seem to have exerted themselves mainly were such things as struggles for power with other great chiefs, the fortification of their own power by means of diplomacy and advantageous matrimonial alliances, insults or wrongs against themselves or their families by other great chiefs, and the military operations which these struggles for power and the vindication of their dignity would involve."

Powell's[229] account of Wyandot government gives especial attention to the council and to the important part played by women in tribal regulation. "The civil government inheres in a system of councils and chiefs. In each gens [clan] there is a council, composed of four women. . . . These four women councillors select a chief of the gens from its male members—that is, from their brothers and sons. This gentile chief is the head of the gentile council. The council of the tribe is composed of the aggregated gentile councils. The tribal council, therefore, is composed one-fifth of men and four-fifths of women. The sachem of the tribe, or tribal chief, is chosen by the chiefs of the gentes. There is sometimes a grand council of the gens, composed of the councillors of the gens

[223] Stuhlmann, *Mit Emin*, 91.   [224] Abbott, in USNM, 1891, 388.
[225] Volkens, *Kilimandscharo*, 249.   [226] Ratzel, *Vkde.*, I, 564, 431.
[227] Paulitschke, *Nordost-Afr.*, II, 130, 131.
[228] *Cent. Polyn.*, III, 108, 109-110. The *fono* is fully treated in II, 441-482.
[229] In BAE, I, 61 ff.

proper and all the heads of the households [women] and leading men—brothers and sons. There is also a grand council of the tribe, composed of the council of the tribe proper and the heads of households of the tribe, and all the leading men of the tribe. . . . The four women councillors of the gens are chosen by the heads of households, themselves being women. There is no formal election, but frequent discussion is had over the matter from time to time, in which a sentiment grows up within the gens and throughout the tribe that, in the event of the death of any councillor, a certain person will take her place. In this manner there is usually one, two, or more potential councillors in each gens, who are expected to attend all the meetings of the council, though they take no part in the deliberations and have no vote. When a woman is installed as a councillor, a feast is prepared by the gens to which she belongs, and to this feast all the members of the tribe are invited. The woman is painted and dressed in her best attire, and the sachem of the tribe places upon her head the gentile chaplet of feathers, and announces to the assembled guests that the woman has been chosen a councillor. . . . The gentile chief is chosen by the council women after consultation with the other women and men of the gens. Often the gentile chief is a potential chief through a period of probation. During this time he attends the meetings of the council, but takes no part in the deliberations and has no vote. At his installation, the council women invest him with an elaborately ornamented tunic, place upon his head a chaplet of feathers, and paint the gentile totem upon his face. . . . The sachem of the tribe is selected by the men belonging to the council of the tribe. The management of military affairs inheres in the military council and chief. The military council is composed of all the able-bodied men of the tribe; the military chief is chosen by the council from the Porcupine gens. Each gentile chief is responsible for the military training of the youth under his authority. There are usually one or more potential military chiefs, who are the close companions and assistants of the chief in times of war and, in case of the death of the chief, take his place in the order of seniority."

It may be recalled that Rivers,[230] regarding the chief as predominantly a religious functionary, thought that the chieftainship had "little or nothing to do with government." He asks himself how, then, the business of regulation is conducted, and seems to refer it quite largely to the council. "I have already mentioned that, in many societies possessing the institution of chieftainship, the power of the chief is limited, or he is assisted by some kind of council, and that, at any rate in some cases, this council exerts such functions of government as are obvious. In other societies a council may perform functions in connexion with justice or other branches of government. In these societies anything of the nature of chieftainship may be absent, or one member of the council may merely be more important than the rest. All gradations are found between a council of this kind, formally constituted, and perhaps consisting of persons representing different groups of the society, to one of a kind so indefinite that it can hardly be called a council." The author cites examples of the types to which he refers.

Thus while the need of coördination and concentration of a people's power led inevitably to the lodgment of control in a single

[230] *Soc. Org.*, 166.

hand, yet it was just as inevitable that the single hand—or head, or character—could not be safely trusted to exercise control uncontrolled. The checks that surrounded and limited the potential autocrat represent the action of the same automatic play of group-interests which elevated him to his eminence. All through the evolution of government there are alternations wherein power is now conferred upon one or a few and now taken back, according as the interests of the whole in whose hands power ultimately resides are felt to be better conserved by the one action or the other. Like all government, monarchy is an adjustment of society to its life-conditions, and the particular privileges accorded to or withheld from the monarch depend in the end upon conduciveness to societal persistence and welfare. In general the concentration of power in the single hand was the successful variation; crude, unadorned, and perilous as it was, it was the only obvious thing to do, just as was personal retaliation in case of injury, and recourse to it was taken about as unreflectingly as to association itself.

No one rose to propose that the strong man should be given control because of the obvious need of coördination and concentration, of peace and order. If some primitive genius had harbored vague conceptions of such abstractions, he could not have expressed them, for language, belonging as it does to the mores, can portray only that which exists in the minds of many. Command crept into the competent hand because of its objectively recognized competency. It was there before any reflection over the situation occurred. Its presence was recognized by the fact of following the natural leader: the old and wise, the strong and brave. In one sense the group appointed its chief; in another the gods appointed him by the endowments, referable in that age only to the supernatural, which he showed. It is not so foolish, granted the primitive habit of explaining the otherwise inexplicable by reference to the ghosts and spirits,[231] to regard the chief as a divinely chosen fetish-man.

Sometimes the monarch consolidated his power so that, like fire, which is "a good servant but a bad master," he escaped control and ranged about as a devastating element; but this could not last on indefinitely. If this variation in the direction of regulation be-

[231] §§195, 208, 257, below.

came destructive of the society and could not be checked, the society was extinguished, and the variation along with it. Commonly, however, the play of interests resulted in control; the monarchy was kept within bounds proper to the persistence of the society; the crude but strong expedient was refined into something that took its place and performed its function in the organization of control without overgrowing and incorporating the whole. Succeeding a time when nearly all government was in the single hand, differentiation inevitably appeared and this and that function were subtracted and set apart in the hands of others. The formal governmental organization, despite the fundamental regulative function of public opinion, unquestionably started with the chieftainship. Then there was something that had been knocked into rough shape, as it were, by heavy blows, and which was now capable of indefinite refinement under processes somewhat subtler, perhaps, though of the same evolutionary order, as those of its origination.

§160. **Administration.** In a very true sense it may be said of the chief that his people are given into his hands. His responsibility is heavy and his duties are illimitable. He cannot possibly attend to them all, and there grow up inevitably about him agencies to which he delegates political functions. Members of his family are associated in government with him and officers who are not relatives are appointed on demonstration of merit or loyalty. This tends, especially if such positions become hereditary, to form, surrounding the monarch, a nobility which becomes a governing class under him and may easily come to exercise control over him. There are also minor agencies of government, such as those of police and espionage, which represent delegations of duties and power. Commonly it is the secret societies, not seldom mere tools of the chief, which, as the next chapter will show, attend to the local ordering of conduct. All such specialization of regulative function, into the petty details of which it is not profitable to go, represents advancing organization. It also affords an arena for endless conflicts and mutual adjustments between the evolving agencies of control by which the character of the regulative organization as a whole is at length profoundly modified. Executive, legislative, and judicial functions, once virtually united in the chief, are differentiated and come into competition; then, if they can be brought into coöperation, organization advances farther in complexity and effectiveness.

The following representative cases may afford a sufficient illustration of the sub-agencies of primitive administration.

In West Africa there are, in one case, seven principal officers of the kingdom. The offices are not hereditary and the king appoints any one he thinks fit. Inferiors must salute them with bent knees and the clapping of hands. There are also a host of female palace-officials, parallel to the male ones outside, but their authority does not extend beyond the court. The inmates of the palace are all women or eunuchs, and the women take precedence of corresponding outside male officials, "apparently in consequence of the state fiction that all the women of the court, including the Amazons, are the wives of the king. The female officials are called the 'mothers' of the corresponding male functionaries, and everybody of note must have a 'mother' in the palace to represent him or his interests. There is thus an 'English mother' for English visitors, and every European nation that frequents or used to frequent Whydah is similarly represented. 'Mother,' it may be mentioned, is the official designation of an Amazon."[232] In Loango there is a strictly organized hereditary nobility, governing districts, and besides this an official nobility of members of the royal family, meritorious officers, and faithful vassals.[233] In East Africa, districts have each two heads, a so-called cattle-chief and a people-chief. "The king forms the apex of both hierarchies, and to him nominally belongs the ownership of all the lands and herds. All these people form the nobility of Ruanda."[234] Uganda is one of the best organized of African kingdoms; Johnston[235] refers this in good part to the introduction of Hamitic culture and to a long line of astute monarchs. But there is a well-defined old nobility which is powerful against the king. They are hereditary land-owners and seem to belong to a nation of conquerors. Each family gives the king a wife and when his successor is chosen each favors the son of its own "queen." This leads to wars. In a neighboring region the king is the first in the land but the government is mild and the chiefs and leading persons live almost undisturbed.[236]

The Galla have a sort of family-succession, whereby the representatives of the several families in strictly regulated succession rule for forty years. This system stimulates general interest in political affairs. The family-members who are chosen to attend to the state-business are called land-fathers.[237] In Madagascar the king is surrounded by an aristocracy which exerts great influence upon the government, since the ministers are chosen out of it. The aristocracy also furnishes a public opinion to which the king listens. Then the general body of nobles acts as representatives of the people. Still the king remains the fountain of laws, punishments, and honors, and is also the owner of every-

[232] Ellis, *Ewe*, 165, 166.   [233] Ratzel, *Vkde.*, I, 599.
[234] Kandt, in *Globus*, LXXXVI, 213.   [235] *Uganda*, II, 636.
[236] Stuhlmann, *Mit Emin*, 189, 242.
[237] Paulitschke, *Nordost-Afr.*, II, 114, 115.

thing; persons, property, time, labor, skill, and invention all belong to him. The Madagascans may not leave the island, under penalty of lifelong forced labor. The punishment for many offences against the state is enslavement by the king.[238]

In India there was much granting of revenue, or of estates or tracts of country to favorites or as recompense for services to be rendered. A great number of assignments of revenue grew into landlord-tenures.[239] Among nearly all the peoples of the Malay Archipelago there are the following authorities: the chief of the mother-village and all its colonies, the chiefs of these colonies, and the family-heads, who have no dominion but only a sort of protectorate. The village and its offshoots form a state with a rajah over it, and the village-heads are subject to him. "These heads act in agreement with the elders of the families."[240] Among the greater Malay states, the chiefs appear as the real governing agencies, while the rajah or sultan is their agent. "Therefore in most cases the political constitution appears to be in a transition stage from the patriarchal form to a confederated aristocracy moderated by representative elements." There are hereditary aristocracies and an aristocracy of property. If the chief is a supreme ruler, the aristocrats are the court-officers.[241] In Samoa each island has several political districts, and in each several tribes with many primary and secondary chiefs. Some districts have a head-chief or king. In the council the genealogy of those who wish to speak is recounted, and all the rest yield to the highest. Quarrels result over precedence and rank.[242] In the Pelew Islands the man second to the king is the war-leader and supervisor of all public and community works, "a genuine major-domus, who even here in the Pacific Ocean has often played a rôle similar to that of the Taikun in Japan or the mayor of the palace of the Merovingians in the Frankish kingdom." He sits opposite the king in the council of princes, and both of them have their adherents among the lesser princes.[243] In some cases the ruler of a widely scattered island "empire" seems to hold it tributary because the capital-island is a holy place for all the islanders.[244]

Spies and police appear here and there as appointees of the king or chief.[245] In Dahomi each petty chief tyrannizes over his district. The chiefs and priests are too strong for the king, and he cannot antagonize both. He has spies over the chiefs and they over their sub-chiefs all the way down. No one dares to murmur, and there is distrust everywhere.[246] In the Congo region, "an interesting relic of former development is found in the Kabinda class of people, . . . a set of masked and disguised men, who have license to steal anything that they can lay their hands on without disclosing their identity, and who may kill any one who succeeds in identifying them. They were formerly appointed as secret agents of the king to gather information, and to accuse powerful masters who were unjust to their inferiors."[247] Masked men are employed as police in many African communities. They maintain a sort of

[238] Ratzel, *Vkde.*, II, 515.

[239] Baden-Powell, *Land Syst. Brit. Ind.*, I, 98, 99, 130, 149, 189, 190, 230; II, 225.

[240] Wilken, *Vkde.*, 340, 341.　　　　[241] Ratzel, *Vkde.*, II, 442.

[242] Ella, *Samoa*, in AAAS, 1892, 629, 632.

[243] Semper, *Palau-Ins.*, 36.　　　　[244] Senfft, in *Globus*, XCI, 173.

[245] §184, below.

[246] Ellis, *Ewe*, 198.　　　　[247] Phillips, in JAI, XVII, 229.

curfew and enforce orders with clubs. They beat noisy children. Some of them are also toll-collectors. "But only when they are in 'uniform' does this fullness of power attach to them."[248]

"Among the Teton Sioux the interior police of a village is confided to two or three officers who are named by the chief for the purpose of preserving order, and remain in power some days, at least till the chief appoints a successor; they seem to be a sort of constable or sentinel, since they are always on the watch to keep tranquillity during the day and guarding the camp in the night." They have special insignia of raven-skins. "Among the Omahas on all occasions of public rejoicings, festivals, dances, or general hunts, a certain number of resolute warriors are previously appointed to preserve order and keep the peace. In token of their office they paint themselves entirely black, usually wear the crow, and arm themselves with a whip or war-club with which they punish on the spot those who misbehave, and are at once both judges and executioners."[249] The policemen or guards "form an important body among the Asiniboin as they do among the other Siouan tribes. These soldiers, who are chosen from the band on account of their bravery, are from 25 to 45 years of age, steady, resolute, and respected; and in them is vested the power of executing the decisions of the council. In a camp of 200 lodges these soldiers would number from 50 to 60 men; their lodge is pitched in the center of the camp and is occupied by some of them all the time, though the whole body is called together only when the chief wishes a public meeting or when their hunting regulations are to be decided. In their lodge all tribal and intertribal business is transacted, and all strangers, both white men and Indians, are domiciled. The young men, women, and children are not allowed to enter the soldiers' lodge during the time that tribal matters are being considered, and, indeed, they are seldom, if ever, seen there. All the choicest parts of meat and the tongues of animals killed in hunting are reserved for the soldiers' lodge, and are furnished by the young men from time to time. A tax is levied on the camp for the tobacco smoked there, which is no small quantity, and the women are obliged to furnish wood and water daily. This lodge corresponds in some degree to the two sacred lodges of the Hañga gens of the Omaha."[250] So too, "the government of the hunt was intrusted to the Pawnee soldiers," men of middle age, who acted under the chiefs but into whose hands the hunt and its guidance were practically given.[251] Among the Arapaho, "if any person violated the tribal code or failed to attend a general dance or council, a party [one order of the "Warrior" society] . . . was sent to kill his dogs, destroy his tipi, or in extreme cases to shoot his ponies. On hunting expeditions it was their business to keep the party together and see that no one killed a buffalo until the proper ceremonies had been performed and the order was given by the chief. They were regarded as the representatives of the law and were never resisted in performing their duty or inflicting punishment."[252]

It is evident that discipline, by whatsoever agency imposed, has reigned widely among the most primitive peoples. Though religion was the most powerful disciplinary factor of all,[253] the secular

248 Frobenius, *Masken*, 151, 153, 154.
249 Mallery, in BAE, X, 419, 420.
250 Dorsey, in BAE, XV, 224.
251 Grinnell, *Folk Tales*, 274.
252 Mooney, in BAE, XIV, 988.
253 §§328, 330, below.

regulative system was not lax. In the next chapter there will be presented a kind of union of the two, which, though but slightly represented in modern societies, has been widespread and important among savage and partly civilized peoples. Then we shall have finished, for the most part, with the agencies of regulation and can go on to such matters as the definition and safeguarding of rights through the evolution of law.

The conclusion of this chapter returns to the maintenance of peace and order through discipline. All promptness of response to laws and administrative behests is due to societal discipline. In the end, it should always be borne in mind, a people disciplines itself; if it does not do that, either informally or through regulative organization, it cannot maintain itself in competition with rivals who do.

The severe treatment of youths in Australia,[254] with restrictions as to food and other matters, takes the place of governmental discipline. They are disciplined so that the old men are able to exercise uncoördinated control over them, and keep them down like women. Says Curr:[255] "the constraining power in such cases is not government, whether by chief or council, but education: that the Black is educated from infancy in the belief that departure from the customs of his tribe is inevitably followed by one at least of many evils, such as becoming early grey, ophthalmia, skin eruptions, or sickness; but, above all, that it exposes the offender to the danger of death from sorcery." To break up the sway of tradition and custom is to plunge people whose lives are regulated by them into chaos. One South African chief, under Christian influence, dismissed his wives. The consequence was that he made enemies of all their relatives and the discipline in his tribe was entirely loosened. The English once deposed the despotic chief Cetewayo; then the sub-chiefs began to quarrel, and to restore order it was necessary to reinstate the cruel but efficient tyrant.[256] "Dyaks make splendid soldiers and the best of friends, as they are faithful and trustworthy, but once their enemy I would rather not meet them. Held in with an iron hand they are very valuable, but the sight of blood intoxicates them, and when they are let go they are worse than wild beasts." In civilized countries the Dyak custom of all living together would mean endless rows; "but all the time we were living with these head-hunters we were struck with their gentleness and the extraordinary peacefulness of their home-life."[257] In Japan "the coercion was not exercised only from without; it was really maintained from within. The discipline of the race was self-imposed. The people had gradually created their own social conditions, and therefore the legisla-

254 §163, below.
256 Ratzel, *Vkde.*, I, 294, 242.
255 *Aust. Race*, I, 54-55.
257 Cator, *Head-Hunters*, 26, 102.

tion conserving those conditions, and they believed that legislation the best possible."[258]

"The greatest thing Mohammed did, the secret of the power of Islam, lay in the firm discipline, in the unconditioned obedience, which he was able to infuse in his followers. The common prayer, to be performed five times a day, where the leader in the prayer stands in front of a community drawn up in close ranks behind him, and where each of his movements is imitated with military precision by all the hundreds of the faithful gathered in the mosque, took the place, at that time, with the Moslems, that the drill-ground now occupies: a school where the people learned to assemble, go through mass-movements, and follow command."[259]

Through many examples we have now seen mankind reaching toward a coördination and organization capable of guaranteeing peace and order. In the agencies developed we have noted the germs and the partial workings-out of a political system. At every step there has been felt an elemental strain toward adjustment of means to ends, whereby power has been unreflectingly conferred and then taken back or distributed differently; but always there has been a steady insistence upon discipline. This is the great need of men living in society, and government is one of the major methods for meeting it.

In the highly civilized state there are many institutions which provide for the coöperation of citizens to "make easier for one another the adjustment of acts to ends." Such a development "facilitates the making of adjustments by each, increases the totality of the adjustments made, and serves to render the lives of all more complete."[260] This is the function of institutions, among them that of government. "An institution consists of a concept (idea, notion, doctrine, interest) and a structure. The structure is a framework, or apparatus, or perhaps only a number of functionaries set to co-operate in prescribed ways at a certain conjuncture. The structure holds the concept and furnishes instrumentalities for bringing it into the world of facts and action in a way to serve the interests of men in society."[261] In civilized societies the "concept" referred to is generally interpreted as an abstract doctrine upon which the institution in question is formed. In uncivilization, however, the abstract conception is absent and only the automatically evolved apparatus and set of functionaries are

[258] Hearn, *Japan*, 199.
[260] Spencer, *Prin. Ethics*, I, 19.
[259] Von Kremer, *Kgchte.*, I, 10.
[261] Sumner, *Folkways*, §61.

in evidence. At most the concept-part of the institution is an interest that is sensed rather than consciously realized. The contention
should be clear and cannot, in any case, be over-enforced that
there was nothing abstract and wrought out by deep reflection
about early government. The abstract conception is the product
of synthesis, perspective, and reflection. There are in primitive life
no political and social doctrines such as political philosophers, far
from the hard facts, have enunciated; there is only a mass of
tradition.[262] In considering primitive regulation it must constantly
be borne in mind that it is automatically evolved and is objective
rather than planned and doctrinal. What is wanted is peace and
order within, and what is found by experience to conduce to these
indispensables is preserved and transmitted.

[262] Lippert, *Kgchte.*, II, 4.

CHAPTER XVII

FRATERNITIES AND USAGES AT MATURITY

§161*. Secret Societies. To one who is making a first acquaintance with primitive life it is astonishing to discover how generally over the earth men have banded themselves together in secret organizations. Casual inspection of such societies creates the general impression that they are religious in nature. Undoubtedly they reveal a religious aspect; any important primitive institution is sure to do that; nevertheless there is no question, upon deeper study of these organizations, that they discharge a distinctly regulative function. Almost universally also they effect sex-separation. Indeed, the more one reflects over the matter the surer he becomes that the secret societies themselves are adjustments for political and social regulation rather than responses merely to the imaginary environment of ghosts and spirits. Therefore they are treated here as part of the regulative system instead of being reserved to go under the topic of religion. Although some of the cases presently to come will show little or nothing of the regulative function, yet all the examples of this type of organization are brought together in this place because the great majority of them seem to belong here. Societies of the purely religious type, if there are any, will be readily distinguished; and the presence of the religious element in so many of them will enforce anew the permeation of the societal structure by that element.

If the more exclusive secret society appears as an adjustment in regulation, the so-called men's club, in which membership of mature males is general and the religious element negligible, must certainly belong to that type of organization. And while the still less exclusive maturity-usages which surround the initiation of the youth into manhood reveal a strong religious tinge, there can be no doubt that they too serve in the main distinctly secular needs; they afford a discipline and an education into the local code which have profound results on conduct. These contentions will be fully illustrated as we go on through this chapter, and the more specific social services of the fraternities, of men's and women's clubs, and of the puberty-practices will appear.[1]

We may begin with a summary of a survey by Rivers,[2] who has given special attention to the Melanesian types of social organization without, however, confining himself wholly to them. He objects somewhat to the inclusive name of "secret societies," inasmuch as there are many associations which, though not secret, yet have features in common with those which are. Such a feature is the process of initiation. These societies are almost always for the male sex alone, though in North America and, to a less extent, Africa, women are sometimes freely admitted. Where men only are members, there is a strong likeness to the so-called men's houses, where all the men, or it may be the bachelors only, dwell or sleep. Frequently these associations form a hierarchy in which the members differ in status and gradually rise in rank, each grade being entered by initiation. In such case, since each grade has its own fire, the place taken by that element in the ceremonial of the organization witnesses again to the religious character both of the fire and of the organization—a character plainly visible also in the masks, which often represent ghosts of ancestors as the bull-roarer and other sound-producing instruments represent ghostly voices. The initiation frequently symbolizes death and re-birth; the initiate is mourned for as if he were dead, and the fact that he gets a new name thereafter and is supposed to have forgotten all that occurred prior to initiation indicates that he is another person from the one that appeared as a candidate. The connection with political life is marked; thus, "wherever these organizations are found in Melanesia, there is nothing which can properly be called chieftainship, the place of the chiefs being taken by men of high rank in the organization"; still, such men are often regarded as chiefs, in which case their office is not hereditary but is attained by a process of successive initiations. That means that the chiefs must be old men; hence the "gerontocracy." The economic importance of these associations appears chiefly in the complex system of payments accompanying successive initiations. "The whole organization thus forms a highly complicated meshwork of incomings and outgoings which involve vested interests of a very varied kind." A man spends money to get a higher rank so that he can thereafter receive payments from later climbers. In some places where societies of this order exist, almost the only function of money is in connection with them; the words for shell-money and other varieties of tokens denote sacredness. Further, the societies stand for individual property against prevailing systems of communal holding, for society-members have a mark which consecrates their ownership. That the initiations provide a test for membership in society, and also some education, will appear in a later connection. About the only kind of social function which the societies do not discharge is the regulation of marriage.

Now the above summary has reference chiefly to Melanesian conditions; but

[1] There are two outstanding studies of the associations now under review: Webster's *Primitive Secret Societies* and Frobenius's *Die Masken und Geheimbünde Afrikas;* of scarcely less importance is Schurtz's *Altersklassen und Männerbünde.* These books belong to that class of able and conscientious special studies upon which any general science of society must depend; they are rich in illustration beyond the possibilities of any general treatise.

[2] *Soc. Org.,* 121-136, *passim.*

"there is hardly a feature of the associations of Melanesia which is not reproduced in one or other of the societies of Africa, though there are African features which are not much represented in Melanesia; for instance, the Africans make more of gilds, especially that of the smiths, and more commonly include circumcision among the initiation ordeals. American societies are divergent from the types prevalent among the black races; they are military and convivial, and often connected with health and therapeutics." There is a close resemblance also between the Greek mysteries and the African and Melanesian societies.

"We are met by the striking fact that secret organizations having features of ritual which bear a close resemblance to one another are found in three widely separated regions, one consisting of Melanesia, New Guinea, and Eastern Indonesia; a second in Africa and especially in West Africa; and a third in one region of North America. We have here a very interesting case of a problem which is now especially engaging the attention of ethnologists, namely, whether such close resemblances as are found in these three widely separated regions have come into existence independently, or whether they belong to one culture which at some time or other was widely diffused over the earth, and has only persisted in these three regions." In this case, as in a number of others, the authors of this book, while realizing the important part played by acculturation or contagion, lean to the theory of independent origin. This is no place to enter upon the general case; we wish merely to say that map-reading, if accompanied with some realization of distances and barriers to communication, ought to dispose of many assertions as to the spread of usages and institutions; and that the explanation offered as to the possible agencies of dissemination, say, between Egypt and Australia, have never seemed to us more than remotely possible.

Rivers concludes his summary with two theories of origin: first that secret societies "arose as a means of practising religious rites which had been forbidden by rulers. . . . In each case the societies embody an early religious cult which has been thrust into the background by rulers, who had either brought a new religion into there from elsewhere, or had adopted a new religion." This last sentence refers to parts of Melanesia. "A different view, for which I am responsible, was put forward especially to explain the nature of the organizations in Melanesia. It is that Melanesian secret societies embody the religious cults of immigrants who, coming in small numbers among an alien people, practised their religion in secret, and only gradually admitted the indigenous people to participation in their rites." In this book we are more or less indifferent to inferential origins; nevertheless we are of the opinion that neither the acculturation-theory nor that which makes of the societies typically religious formations is satisfactory; it seems to us that what explains the secret societies cannot be something apart from that which accounts for the other associations similar to them, but non-secret. We see in the associations, secret or not, closely or loosely organized, agencies developed independently in widely separated regions as adjustments within the regulative organization. Their undeniable religious characteristics are of the profoundest import in securing and consolidating the authority necessary to this function.

In the usual review of cases calculated to render concrete and to illustrate the general statements prefatory to any topic, we are always presenting the body of facts from which those statements have been derived. In the present instance we shall begin with the more distinctly religious types and aspects of the secret society. It is understood that we adopt Rivers's summary except as dissent has been indicated.

One of the most notable of the primitive secret societies is the so-called "Duk-Duk" of New Britain. Von Pfeil[3] thinks that "probably we make no mistake in believing that originally the 'Duk-Duk' was nothing but a form expressive of the tendency of the Kanakas to seclusion in the doing of reverence to departed ancestors. Several persons banded together and put on masks in order thereby to inspire fear in all those who wanted to push in somewhat curiously as uninvited witnesses of mourning-ceremonies. . . . The material instinct was not lacking in the Kanaka to make use of this circumstance, and so only such members were taken in as could pay well for the honor that fell to them." It was utilized also to keep the women under control. "Because they work more diligently than the men, they soon win possessions; and, since there is no legal way for the men to get their substance away from them, the 'Duk-Duk' was employed as an excellent means to prevent the women's wealth from exceeding a moderate limit. . . . If by chance a woman had been unfortunate enough to see the 'Duk-Duk,' that is, the bearer of this mask, she had to pay a fine in dewarra" (shell-money). Then too the male outsiders were made similarly tributary, and were beaten if they could not pay. "It is only human that individuals, at first, perhaps, members of the 'Duk-Duk,' later others also, tried to make the developed power of the union serviceable to their private ends. At the beginning the 'Duk-Duk' probably extorted contributions only from the enemies of its members, later from those also whose foes paid to have it done, so that as a result the 'Duk-Duk' was gradually transformed into a court—not in the sense, of course, that it determined right and wrong by its verdict but in the sense that, through the power that it possessed, it forced quarreling parties to peace." Then the man who had the right to summon the society together probably retained the power for successors from his own family. "We see, then, among a wholly savage, uncivilized people a remarkable example of protection for spiritual property and a definitely established hereditary succession. . . . Members of the Duk-Duk celebrate certain feasts of a very mysterious character; it is not clear how they are connected with the Duk-Duk, how they originated, or what they portend."

This explanation of Von Pfeil's, which is as good as any, illustrates how the secret society, though it began in religion, works out into control of social life. Some of the following cases will not show so evident a regulative function.

Codrington[4] devotes a good deal of attention to the Melanesian societies. "There is certainly nothing more characteristic of Melanesian life than the presence of Societies which celebrate Mysteries strictly concealed from the uninitiated and from all females. A dress, with a mask or hat, disguises the members if they appear in open day; they have strange cries and sounds by

[3] *Südsee,* 159 ff.; Von Pfeil, in JAI, XXVII, 184 ff.; Platz, *Australien,* 248; Finsch, *Ethnol. Erfahr.,* I, 115.

[4] *Melanesians,* 69 ff.

which they make their presence known when they are unseen. In some cases
. . . they make a public show of a piece of the handiwork of the ghosts with
whom it is pretended that they have been associating." The author names the
Duk-Duk of New Britain and several other similar organizations. "It is remarkable also that, so far as I have been able to ascertain, there is nothing
or very little that is obscene, or more objectionable from a moral point of
view than imposture. . . . In some places the neophytes had to endure hardships or even tortures. . . . The property of the uninitiated was plundered,
and themselves beaten and oppressed when the mysteries were at work; all
order and industry were upset. At the same time hideous and obscene orgies
were absent; a native convert to Christianity might go into his lodge and find
nothing there to offend him that he did not find in the village; an European
visitor might go in and find nothing more mysterious to be revealed to him
than the hats and dresses and the appliances for producing the unearthly
sounds."

Rivers,[5] naturally enough, substantiates through those parts of his *Melanesian Society* which deal with secret associations the conclusions summarized
above. He attempts to show the geographical distribution of the institution
and holds that "secret societies are found in those regions of Melanesia which
are relatively backward in culture and possess the most archaic form of social
organisation, while within the region where they flourish there is a certain
degree of correlation between the degree of development of the societies and
the general advance of culture." He states that, in the matter of the awe-
inspiring sounds or ghost-voices produced by society members, it is the most
important of the associations which produce the loudest and most complicated
effects. He describes all grades of initiation-ceremonial and notes that not
only the ceremonial but even the name of the societies is connected with the
idea of death; in becoming a member of a society the initiate is becoming a
tamate, or ghost. He illustrates the power of a member to protect his property
from other persons in the community. He cites copious detail to support his
contention as to the immigrant nature of the secret cults, a feature essential
to his general explanation of Melanesian society.

Africa is a classic ground of the secret society. First we shall follow Frobenius[6] in his survey. The common features of the societies are, first, that the
neophytes are taken into the bush for months, or even for two or three years;
again, that they are supposed to have died and risen again as new men; that
they adopt a new and special language; that they must abstain from some
specified food, and that the ceremonies show some connection with the ancestors. One of the societies of twice-born opens its ranks to new candidates only
when a cripple or some other monstrosity is born. The initiated go about for
weeks and months dumb, covering the lips with the hand; "for their past life
is completely forgotten and memory comes back only gradually." Very regularly circumcision is practised. The youths are subjected to ordeals, brought
into a death-like state, and buried in the temple. "When they are awakened to
life again, they have lost memory of everything past, even of their parents
. . . and cannot recall their own names any longer. Therefore they are given
new names according to the titles or gifts to which they have ascended." The

[5] *Melan. Soc.,* II, 205-207, 208-209, 210, 213, 215, 589.
[6] *Masken,* especially 49 ff., 60, 62, 75, 76, 78, 84, 85, 94, 95, 102 ff., 118, 167,
224, 243.

medicine-man manages this death and resurrection; "if all goes well, this ostensible sudden death often becomes a sort of hysteria." The dead are supposed to molder away to one bone—a sort of "resurrection-bone"[7]—from which, by magic, the person is again evolved. The new creations do not know the world any more and cannot even eat, but have to have some one to chew for them. They want everything they see, "and woe to the one who refuses them." They may strike and kill with impunity. "They know no better," the people say. There is much sensuality connected with their proceedings. Again, "every boy of from fourteen to eighteen years is initiated into all the mysteries connected with this great spirit. The novitiate lasts a year and more and the novices during this time must subject themselves to a rather hard treatment which apparently is thought to make a lasting impression upon their physical and spiritual natures and to restrain them from blabbing the secrets of the order." Each must take a vow, which remains binding for life, to refrain from a certain food or drink. When a notable man dies, the members of the local society appear in a fury the next night and seize upon the property of the villagers without distinction; "the chief aim today is said to be the keeping of the women and children in the desired subjection." Some of the societies practise an extended cannibalism. Also there are oath-takings which are confirmed by burning a human being alive and the breaking of which brings death. The neophyte is sometimes baptized by complete immersion and sometimes tattooed; he is qualified only if he can prove that he has accomplished several atrocities. In the secret societies, especially during the initiation-season and during certain meetings, theft is allowed and practised, that is, the right of property is suspended for the society-members; initiates are taught to thieve. Some societies veritably terrorize their communities.

The Ibo are a great artisan-tribe, their smiths being met in every village round about, and wherever a smith goes he carries with him the knowledge of a local art of writing, called *nsibidi*. "The system of writing is really the property of a secret society, the *nsidibi* society, into which men are regularly initiated after undergoing a period of preparation. Some of the signs of the *nsibidi* are known to outsiders, but the vast majority are known only to the initiated. To the uninitiated they are mysterious and therefore magical, capable of doing harm because of the 'medicine' that may have been used in making them. . . . The early missionaries maintained that they had no knowledge of writing. They knew the word *nsibidi* and applied it correctly enough to the cuts made on calabashes, native pianos, etc., unaware that many of these signs had significance. Again they were aware that there was an elaborate system of acted signs by which people held communication, but they had not discovered that this language of signs had been reduced to writing. . . . I do not think that there has been any development towards an alphabet, nor, had it been left to itself, would there ever have been any such development. . . . As regards the nature of the writing, it is pictographic pure and simple. Is a man a stranger who has no place in a town, then he is represented as standing on only one foot."[8] This quotation is rich in suggestion; first to be noted is the peculiar character of the smith; then the apparent development of writing from property-marks; again the invention of an art at the hand of a religious

[7] White, *Sci. and Theol.*, II, 52.
[8] MacGregor, in JAI, XXXIX, 209-210.

fraternity; and finally the magic that is thought to inhere in the inexplicable power of transferring thoughts by means of tallies.[9]

More highly civilized societies have their secret organizations, for instance those of the Arabs;[10] and that they last down into high civilization is a fact known to all. One of the historic cases was the Augustan brotherhood at Rome, founded by Augustus, and including twenty-one "companions" chosen by lot from the principal men of the state, to keep up the worship of Augustus and the Julian gens.[11] In later antiquity the mysteries played an important part in the life of their time.[12]

The secret societies thus far considered have been of a prevailingly religious stamp and their objects have been typically religious. To be especially noted are the ceremonies of re-birth; the special languages, secrets, and signs; the taboos laid upon the neophytes; the utilization of baptism, circumcision, means for producing hallucinations, and "medicines" of various description; and the reversions to the ancient mores of cannibalism and general unrestriction as regards theft and murder. There was a series of initiations to higher grades and even an induction of the dead. All this is highly religious; nevertheless there have been occasional indications that the societies discharge also a regulative function. It has been noted, in particular, that they often seek to control the women, whom they regularly exclude from membership, or all outsiders, by terrorism, confiscation, or fines. It is a rare case where the religious society, even that of the shamans, does not exercise certain public functions which are classifiable under government, at least in a broad sense.

We are glad to find ourselves in agreement with Webster[10] as to this matter of the essentially regulative function of the societies. "To outside observation the judicial and political duties of the secret societies appeared as their most striking feature. . . . They punish crimes and act as public executioners, serve as night police, collect debts, protect private property, and, where they extend over a wide area, help to maintain tribal amity. When the Melanesian organizations . . . first came into view it was noticed with interest how similar were their functions as judge, policeman, and hangman, to those of the African societies, a similarity which some have ventured to explain by an hypothesis of prehistoric diffusion across a continent now sunk beneath the waters of the Indian Ocean. In view of the well authenticated instances of precisely the

9 §§72, 121, above, and ch. XXXVII and §§313, 320, 321, below.

10 D'Estournelles de Constant, in *Rev. Deux Mondes,* LXXIV, 100 ff.

11 Tacitus, *Annals,* I, 54.

12 Cumont, *Mithra;* Wobbermin, *Mysterienwesen;* §§279, 286, of the text and *Case-Book.*

13 In JAI, XLI, 482-484.

same duties, assumed by some secret societies in America, at points as far removed as Tierra del Fuego, Brazil, and California, a theory of diffusion seems, at least, in this instance, distinctly less plausible than a theory of independent origin. I see in these organizations, so widespread throughout the aboriginal world, one of the most remarkable efforts early man has made to establish, under conditions otherwise anarchical, some semblance of settled government. . . . There can be little doubt that this legal function is or has been incidental to their main business of initiating young men into manhood. Under their direction the candidates are removed from defiling contact with women, subjected to various ordeals, instructed in all matters of religion, morality, and traditional lore, provided with a new name, a new language, and new privileges—in a word, made men. . . . There is . . . another aspect of primitive secret societies, very prominent in the American fraternities, but hitherto not sufficiently emphasized in the discussion of related organizations in other parts of the world. I refer to their dramatic and magico-religious ceremonies."

In the examples which are now to be cited, the regulative function will be stressed and the perennial effectiveness of an affectation of mystery will be abundantly illustrated. The control exercised over women will be seen to attain considerable strictness and to constitute one of the adjustments made by society to the basic life-condition of human bi-sexuality. It will be noted also that the society both controls and disciplines the young, and in many cases affords them the only education they get outside that of association with parents and fellows—in fact, the only formal and systematic teaching there is. They learn in particular to keep secrets under oath. It will also appear that the secret societies, while in some instances they stand for lawlessness, disorder, the suspension of the regular taboos, and even revolution, generally represent a force influential to secure orderliness and even come to discharge a judicial and police function. When the chief is strong and the government despotic, the secret societies are likely to be revolutionary; again, they are often of the type of the vigilance-organizations that spring up on the frontiers of civilization and take the regulation of society into their own hands, where without them there would be an approach to chaos; and, yet again, they become the agencies through which the chief rules or they are accessory and friendly to his rule, constituting a sort of aristocracy that assists in the control of the unorganized common people.

With these preliminary suggestions as to the bearing of the following cases, the latter may be allowed to instruct us as to the various methods by which the secret societies discharge their regulative function. But the reader should not fail to note that they cater also to individual interest and ambition; they assist their members in self-maintenance and general self-realization. A man is of no consequence unless he belongs, and he will run into lifelong debt to acquire membership. And in them appears the germ, and in some cases rather more than the germ, of plutocracy. They are recognized as a societal agency by the fact that initiates are fed at the community's expense and that their periodic festivals are public affairs. The religious element still persists, but the function discharged is by no means a purely religious one. These organizations often support the chief and are his agency for espionage; they specialize in collecting debts, under terrorism, and so help the merchants, who pay well for the service; they discipline the unpopular and constitute a tribunal to keep the peace; they are not seldom charitable agencies that force contributions for the needy; their badges insure a good reception to one who travels; their "cloisters" are often sanctuaries and refuges; and, finally, they are not seldom the centers of secret opposition to foreign influence and domination. In some of the following cases local societies which have already figured in our lists in their religious aspect will reappear as genuine organs of regulation.

The many secret brotherhoods of the Melanesians, "in place of a wider state-union, bind the settlements over very large stretches one to the other." They are like the formation of brotherhoods on the large scale.[14] Some of these Melanesian societies give dances for fun where they used to give them in honor of the spirits; old members derive considerable income from the payments of initiates.[15] The members of one of these societies, called "The Ghosts," indulge in much license. "When they choose to go abroad to collect provision for one of their feasts, the women and uninitiated are obliged to keep away from their paths. The warning voice of the *Tamante* is heard and the country is shut up. There is also a considerable power in these societies to keep order." To do this the taboo is freely employed. "In islands where there is no political or tribal organization, position in the *Suqe* and the *Tamante* makes the 'Great man,' whose authority is respected and maintains order."[16]

The Duk-Duk society, described already as a religious organization, has its political function in maintaining the authority of the chiefs or of a minority; it is a secret society and a civil institution both at once. The society is represented by a masked individual, called "The Duk-Duk," who arrives from the sea in a canoe, is inviolable, collects fines, lays penalties (which may go so far

14 Hagen, *Papua's*, 276; §150, above.
15 Ratzel, *Vkde.*, II, 278.   16 Codrington, in JAI, X, 287.

as death or house-burning), and is said to assemble material for cannibal feasts of the initiated. The members have secret signs and meet for feasts from which the uninitiated are excluded under penalty of death.[17] Really the Duk-Duk is a judge, constable, and executioner, appointed by the chief. An injured person pays duk-duk to get redress; and the society's representative demands satisfaction of the accused, burning his house or killing him if he refuses. Women and children will die, it is believed, if they see the Duk-Duk. Young men are initiated at a cost of a hundred fathoms of shell-money, and until they can collect and pay this they must avoid the Duk-Duk in his periodic perambulations. No one may resist or disobey him, for the chief would have such a rebel killed.[18]

One authority[19] states of the Duk-Duk society that "many hundred years ago it was invented by a celebrated chief here, as a form of native police. At the outset, men who had misbehaved themselves in the principal village, and were consequently debarred from getting food there, used to cover themselves with leaves, worked into weird and strange shapes, and repair to neighboring villages, and on their terrifying the people to such an extent, they willingly gave them food in order to get rid of them. This costume proved so successful in working upon the fears and superstitions of the natives that eventually the chiefs arrogated to themselves the right of clothing a kind of police in this manner, and any of their enemies were thus hunted down by the Duk-Duk who could and did kill any one with impunity." If this explanation and derivation are correct, we find here a striking case of variation and selection. To judge from the flogging of young men by the Duk-Duk and the belief that the old men summoned and prompted the masked figure, it would seem that the ceremony was an assertion of power by the old men over the young. The author goes on to say that "any woman looking upon the Duk-Duk was immediately put to death, and even to the present day upon the faintest sign of the approach of this dreadful apparition the women all fly in terror and bury themselves in the densest jungle possible."

In the Zambesi region there is a kind of free-masonry. "Some of them have on their chest three cuts. When they were asked what was the reason of it they generally refused to answer; but after gaining their confidence they confessed that they belonged to something like a secret society, and they said, 'I can go through all the valleys inhabited by Korannas and by Griquas, and wherever I go, when I open my coat and show these three cuts, I am sure to be well received.' "[20] In cases like this it is evident that we encounter a type of international union, or extended and organized brotherhood, which must have had important political bearings. The cuts in all such cases are reasonably interpretable as survivals of blood-letting or blood-mixing.

The home of the African secret society is in West Africa, as the collections of Frobenius demonstrate. Some added aspects of the activity of the Egbo and other societies mentioned by him are recorded by other writers. Miss Kingsley[21] says that high grades in the Egbo cost up to a thousand or fifteen-hundred English pounds, but that they are worth it to great traders in debt-collecting; "as the Egbo methods of delivering its orders to pay up consist in

[17] Ratzel, *Vkde.*, II, 281.   [18] Andree, *Ethnog. Parallelen*, 136.
[19] Cayley-Webster, *New Guinea*, 267-268.
[20] Holub, in JAI, X, 7; Holub, *S. Afr.*, I, 115.
[21] *Travels W. Afr.*, 532.

placing Egbo at a man's doorway, and until it removes itself from that doorway the man dare not venture outside his house, it is most successful. Of course the higher a man is in Egbo rank, the greater his power and security, for lower grades cannot proceed against higher ones. Indeed, when a man meets the paraphernalia of a higher grade of Egbo than that to which he belongs, he has to act as if he were lame, and limp along past it humbly, as if the sight of it had taken all the strength out of him, and, needless to remark, higher grade debtors flip their fingers at lower grade creditors." The plutocratic aspects of this arrangement are self-evident. "The Ogboni Society really holds the reins of government, and kings themselves are obliged to submit to its decrees. The members are popularly believed to possess a secret from which they derive their power, but their only secret appears to be that of a powerful and unscrupulous organization, each member of which is bound to assist every other, while all are bound to carry out, and if necessary enforce, the decrees of the body. Each town and village has its Ogboni 'lodge,' and the members recognise each other by conventional signs and passwords. At their meetings, which are held with a great affectation of mystery, they deliberate upon all matters which interest the tribe or community. The decisions of the Ogboni are final, and nothing of importance can be done without their consent." In some tribes they have less power and are "little more than public executioners. . . . It seems probable that the society was originally intended for the initiation to manhood of youths who had arrived at puberty . . . and that its civil and judicial functions are later usurpations."[22]

The Porroh society of Sierra Leone is of two kinds, religious and political. None but the circumcised are admitted to the Porroh. The candidate must live in the Porroh bush for a time, in strict seclusion, especially from the sight of women; during this time he is said to be eaten by the Porroh spirit. After initiation he receives a fraternity-name and is released. The political Porroh is more select and is used for arranging the affairs of the tribes, settling disputes and making laws. Wars are sometimes stopped by its arbitration, though it is used for bad purposes also. Its representatives are always held sacred like the ambassadors or heralds of civilized countries.[23] Karutz[24] calls it a Vehm-society, or vigilance-band, with extensive judicial and executive power. Its agents are masked warriors. He thinks there is no religious motive, but that it is a purely social arrangement. Then there is a Tasso society whose leaders are much respected and are really the heads of the Porrohs. "If a Tasso dies, he is buried in the forest; no woman may see a dead Tasso, and therefore the women must hide themselves till the burial is over." Porroh "is the ruling vital influence in native life, and these screens and huts and other to us meaningless sticks and stones, are to them all signs of this far-reaching power."[25] Frobenius[26] waxes quite cloquent over this society: "The ideal of a government for the West African conditions is the Purra. For us it is the more important, because in it, in spite of the fact that it is the noblest flower of African state-rule and association-building, there are retained in beautiful clearness all the

22 Ellis, *Yoruba*, 93-95.
23 Griffith, "Sierra Leone," in JAI, XVI, 309.
24 Maskenkunde, in *Globus*, LXXIX, 367, 368.
25 Cator, *Head-Hunters*, 187; Anon., "Ceremony of the Tasso," in *Illust. Afr.* for March, 1896.
26 *Masken*, 232.

features of its evolution; education, spiritualization, spirit-rule, masking, and the rest."

Voluntary associations, not of an exclusively religious character, have flourished among most American Indian tribes and are still found among those least affected by contact with civilization. Powell called them cult-societies; their members are designated by special paintings and marks entirely distinct from clan- or gens-marks and personal names—to the confusion of many travellers. "The translated names of some of these societies among the Sioux are 'Brave Night Hearts,' 'Owl Feathers,' and 'Wolves and Foxes.' They control tribes in internal affairs and strongly influence their policy in external relations, and may be regarded as the substitute both for regular soldiery and for police. It is necessary that a young man proposing to be a warrior should be initiated into some of these societies. But in distinguishing them from the purely shamanistic orders it must not be understood that their ceremonies and ties are independent of the cult of religion, or that they disregard it, for this among Indians would be impossible. . . . The bands, unions, or associations are found among the Blackfeet as well as all the other American tribes. They have a certain name, fixed rules and laws, as well as their peculiar songs and dances, and serve, in part to preserve order in the camp, on the march, in the hunting parties, etc. Seven such bands or unions among the Blackfeet were mentioned to me. They are the following: (1) The band of the mosquitos. This union has no police business to do, but consists of young people, many of whom are only 8 or 10 years of age. There are also some young men among them and sometimes even a couple of old men, in order to see to the observance of the laws and regulations. This union performs wild, youthful pranks; they run about the camp whenever they please; pinch, nip, and scratch men, women, and children in order to give annoyance like the mosquitos. The young people begin with this union and then gradually rise higher through the others. As the badge of their band they wear an eagle's claw fastened around the wrist with a leather strap. They have also a particular mode of painting themselves, like every other band, and their peculiar songs and dance. (2) The dogs. Its badge is not known to me; it consists of young married men, and the number is not limited. (3) The prairie dogs. This is a police union, which receives married men; its badge is a long hooked stick wound round with otter skin, with knots of white skin at intervals, and a couple of eagle's feathers hanging from each of them. (4) Those who carry the raven. Its badge is a long staff covered with red cloth, to which black ravens' feathers in a long thick row are fastened from one end to the other. They contribute to the preservation of order and the police. (5) The buffalo, with thin horns. When they dance they wear horns on their caps. If disorders take place they must help the soldiers, who mark out the camp and then take the first place. (6) The soldiers. They are the most distinguished warriors, who exercise the police, especially in the camp and on the march; in public deliberations they have the casting vote whether, for instance, they shall hunt, change their abode, make war or conclude peace, etc. They carry as their badge a wooden club the breadth of a hand, with hoofs of the buffalo cow hanging to the handle. They are sometimes 40 or 50 men in number. (7) The buffalo bulls. They form the first, that is, the most distinguished, of all the unions, and are the highest in rank. They carry in their hand a medicine badge, hung with buffalo hoofs, which they rattle when they dance to their peculiar song. They are too old to attend to the police, having passed through all the unions, and are considered as having retired from office. In their medicine dance they wear on their head a cap made of the long fore-lock and mane of the buffalo bull, which hangs down to a considerable length."[27]

"A thorough study of Nagualism leads to the conclusion that it was not merely a survival of fragments of heathenism, perhaps mingled with Christian teachings, but that it was a powerful organization, secret, widely extended, having members from the cultured as well as the lower classes, bound together by mysterious rites, powers, and doctrines; but more than all by a common hatred of the whites and a determination to annihilate them, their religion, their government,—in short everything which they had introduced."[28]

In mediæval and modern times there have been cases enough of secret societies whose masked members have taken the law into their own hands; such were the German *Vehmgerichte* and *Knabenschaften;* the vigilance-society and posse on the frontier, with their "lynch-law"; the American Ku Klux Klan of the Reconstruction period and its astonishing resurrection in recent times.[29] The various secret societies and fraternities of the present do not seem strange, for we are used to them; but it is surprising to encounter for the first time the fact that the veriest savages have such organizations, and often in an even more pretentious and ridiculous form than those with which we are familiar. This astonishment would perhaps be more rational if it were reversed and we were amazed at ourselves.

Although women are excluded from most of these societies, there are a few which include both sexes and more than a few which are composed entirely of women.

The Melanesian women are completely excluded from the men's society but have something of the sort among themselves. They admit to grades through payment, grow rich, and help their husbands to advancement in rank.[30] Similarly in Africa, where the women have secrets of medicine, keep a sort of vestal fire burning during their ceremonies, detect thieves, discover the secrets of enemies, and protect wives against hard treatment by their husbands. These societies are feared by the men and are regarded as very useful to the tribe. Again, the women perform the sacrifices to the memorial ancestral stones.[31] The West African Njembe is a woman's society, with a high initiation-fee. It threatens recalcitrants with the employment of fetish-medicines. Formerly it was considered an honor to be chosen to it; now, to perpetuate itself, it com-

[27] Mallery, in BAE, X, 528, 529.   [28] Brinton, *Nagualism,* 61.

[29] Kohler, *Strafrecht;* Andree, *Ethnog. Parallelen,* 134; Cutler, *Lynch Law;* "Kl. Nachr.," in *Globus,* LXXXVII, 211.

[30] Codrington, *Melanesians,* 110.

[31] Frobenius, *Masken,* 65, 120, 130, 131, 137; Ratzel, *Vkde.,* I, 599.

pels young women to enter it, especially if they have made derogatory remarks about it. The initiation becomes, then, a sort of punishment. They dance in a nude state in the jungle and their accompanying songs are vile. They pretend to detect thieves, to direct women in pregnancy, and otherwise to be useful. "The object of the institution originally, no doubt, was to protect the females from harsh treatment on the part of their husbands." The entire process of initiation and life in the society so terrorizes the novices and beats down their will that even those who were forced into it against their wish most inviolably preserve its secrets and express themselves as pleased with their experiences. One of the songs has as a refrain: "Look at the sun," and the candidate must do so, however blinding it is. Most of the "rules," which may be invented for any occasion, "are purposely hard in order to make the candidate suffer, and as part of the process of breaking her will, and ensuring secrecy by a reign of terror. . . . A girl who in ordinary times would be afraid to go out into the forest alone at night, will, under the Njembe initiation, go out in storm and rain to see that the fire is not extinguished. . . . It is remarkable how well the secrets of the society are kept. No one has ever been induced to reveal them. Those who have left the society and have become Christians do not tell. Foreigners have again and again tried to bribe, but in vain. Traders and others have tried to induce their native wives to reveal; but these women, obedient to any extent on all other matters, maintain a stubborn silence. . . . It is really a school in which to learn the fine art of using insults and curses which will be utilized outside the society, upon other persons on occasions of real anger."[32]

Another African woman's society is described as "an absolutely harmless one, with no political importance of any kind. Every girl, some time between the ages of eight and eighteen, has to go for two or three months into the bush, where she stays with a lot of other girls under the charge of one or two matrons, whose business it is to prepare them for their future lives as wives and mothers of families, by teaching them a certain amount of natural law and whatever in the way of medicine and other things is thought necessary for a well-brought-up black girl to know. They are initiated with a small more or less painful rite, and whitewashed all over, but most of the time is spent in dancing."[33] It is evident that we have here a sort of schooling for life-duties.

In the Pelew Islands the woman's society is viewed by the men's as a recognized corporation. "It seems as if in actuality the need of a certain representation in the state, felt by the women and recognized by the men, has brought into being these women's societies and has won for them the manifold prerogatives which they without question possess. . . . In short, the women's societies take a place in the state which fully corresponds to that of the men's societies in respect to the rights accruing to them, and the most powerful prince would never dare to oppose such a women's organization. . . . A single man, even the king, is powerless against any such association."[34]

The medicine-societies of the Indians, as has been seen, sometimes admitted both sexes.[35] "There are thirteen secret orders in Zuñi, in many of which women and children are conspicuous, besides the purely mythologic order of the Kok-ko. All boys are initiated into this order, while but few girls enter it.

[32] Nassau, *Fetichism*, 249-250, 252, 253, 254; Bastian, *Deut. Exped.*, II, 24.
[33] Cator, *Head-Hunters*, 192-193.   [34] Semper, *Palau-Ins.*, 72, 73.
[35] Beckwith, in *Smithson. Rep.*, 1886, pt. I, 248; Hoffman, *Writing*, 171.

It is optional with a girl; she must never marry if she joins the Kok-ko, and she is not requested to enter this order until she has arrived at such age as to fully understand its grave responsibilities and requirements."[36]

From the sense of many of the cases cited it seems that the men have needed more than mere bodily strength or military discipline in order to manage the women. Apparently many tribesmen have had to develop a special secret disciplinary organization to that end. Then the women have, occasionally, matched organization against organization. Upon the difficulties of sex-adjustment much light is shed by a review of the men's organizations, of both the secret and the non-secret types. To the latter, the clubs, we shall presently come. It is evident also that all forms of the secret society are in some degree educational. A girl who has not spent a period of "study" in some such organization is not regarded as well brought up and capable of becoming a proper wife.[37] Often every boy must belong to one or another of the local societies; and in this association with the older men he gets what education there is, short of a special course in preparation for the career of shaman.

These are some of the social services of the societies. As for their political function, it is now clear that they discharge a distinct one, though it may seem dubious in its expediency and may appear to consist really of license for the society-members and discipline for the outsiders. But it is necessary to take these societal forms as they are found, without letting a comparison with our own more evolved system cause us to censure them or depreciate them unduly. The comparison should be, not with a modern system, but with nothing. All the arms of primitive government are crude, rough, and dashed with clumsy, inexpedient, and irrelevant elements. Only gradually can these be purged away by selection and replaced by more refined adjustments. The chief question is as to whether there is power present, to be refined and better directed; and the secret societies certainly embody that.

§162*. Clubs. Besides the secret societies primitive life shows many associations where the element of secrecy is small or wholly absent and which seem to be of a distinctly secular type. It is not

---

[36] Stevenson, in BAE, V, 540.   [37] §§162, 344, below.

at all unlikely that the secret societies came out of these by a process of focussing and discrimination. In any case the so-called clubs or men's houses or bachelors' houses—in some cases, the women's or maidens' houses—are a much less exclusive, differentiated, and developed product than the secret societies. They are generally for all the men in the tribe and are exclusive only of women, children, and slaves or other aliens; or they include all the unmarried youths. They are to the secret societies somewhat as common and public schools are to private and exclusive ones. It is sometimes hard to say whether the organization in question is a secret society or a club; some of the cases listed, after considerable reflection, under the one category may seem to belong to the other. This is natural enough in classification and lends plausibility to the idea that the two types are genetically connected. Any further generalizations are better put off until the cases are before us, except that it should be noted that these clubs generally separate the sexes and so emphasize again the conception of sex-difference brought out most strikingly, perhaps, in the sex-taboo.[38]

The men's houses in New Guinea are common property of the family and all the men, married and unmarried, sleep in them. This "seems to be a measure of security against nocturnal attacks, since they take all their weapons into the house. Here too hang the shields and here lies the big drum. The ornaments for the dance are also preserved here. . . . At the same time it serves as a hostelry for stranger guests." Among some tribes it is taking the place of a cult-temple. As soon as the boy, at the age of four, gets his girdle, "he already belongs to public life; he moves away from his mother into the family men's house, where he sleeps until his marriage."[39] These houses are large and highly decorated, often have idols in them, and are used for the festivals. All of them, and most of their contents, are strictly tabooed to females and may not be entered by them. These houses are also work-shops, "for there are objects, for instance the big drums, which women may not see even in their construction."[40]

In every village on the Solomon Islands there is at least one so-called "tamboo-house," generally the longest building in the settlement and tabooed under penalty of death to all women; it is used publicly and belongs to the community.[41] The same is the case in New Ireland; "this club-house stood quite in the open, and I saw women pass at some distance, only in bent posture, almost crawling."[42] In the New Hebrides there is a "house for clubs" where men eat and drink kava unseen by females and where councils and festi-

[38] §§273, 388, 389, below.   [39] Hagen, *Papua's,* 200, 234.
[40] Finsch, *Ethnol. Erfahr.,* II, 57, 58; Finsch, *Samoafahrten,* 47.
[41] Elton, in JAI, XVII, 97.
[42] Finsch, *Ethnol. Erfahr.,* I, 130, 131.

vals take place.[43] Even where, as in the Torres Strait Islands, clans occupy a large and long house together, the men have a big room at one end for themselves.[44]

In South Africa the kraal is sacred and is a sort of men's house. Women who marry into the village may not enter it, out of respect for their departed fathers-in-law who are considered heads of the village and kraal.[45] West Africa has its "palaver-houses" but they do not count so much in view of the swarm of secret societies. Serpa Pinto[46] found in Angola that every community had a sort of "kiosk for conversation." This is like the "mosque or sort of community-house, which also serves for the sojourn of strangers," as found in southern Cochin-China.[47] There are joint-houses for the upper classes in Polynesia, but for the free men and the unfree these houses appear to be phalansteries for the purpose of the organization of labor and of services for the community as a whole. The duty of entering them has been designated as a kind of universal military service.[48] Sometimes these houses are used only by bachelors for living quarters, but the segregation of the young unmarried men is not so sharp as in our next list of examples. In general such a house is "the official dwelling of the chief, the hostelry for strangers, the sleeping-house for the unmarried men, and at the same time a store-house for the most important possession of a seafaring people that must be thinking every moment of flight —the boats." "Every man's club has its own 'bay,' a big assembly-house in which the members sleep nights and gather for common ends in the daytime, and generally a war-canoe whose crew it forms"; and there is also an assembly-house for the chiefs and generally one or two others for visits of strangers. The big assembly-houses are tabooed to women all over Polynesia.[49]

Williamson[50] writes at length of the *marae*, a sort of assembly-hall, as a social center. "Broadly speaking, the *marae* were sacred structures, in the formation of which stones were as a rule used largely, specially associated with the gods or with the spirits of the dead, where religious rites and ceremonies were performed, in or near some of which the bodies of the dead were exposed, or the bodies or parts of the remains were interred, and in or near which councils were held. . . . The *marae* would become standing evidence of family relationship and family rank. A chief's claim to rank of blood would be vindicated by his possession, as head of a social group, of the *marae* of that group, or, if he was not head of the group, his right of entering into it; the height of his rank would be based upon that of the group that owned the *marae*, and this again would depend, in the case of an offshoot *marae*, upon the rank of the larger parent group, from whose *marae* the other *marae* was derived. . . . De Bovis is speaking of a royal *marae* when he says it was a sort of family property, and the king often commanded there by right of his being the head of the race. . . . Two or three families, in other islands, or other parts of the same island, might have equal rights in the *marae*, and would go there religiously at certain periods; and sometimes there would be a great concourse

---

[43] Gray, in AAAS, 1892, 648.

[44] Thilenius, in *Globus*, LXXXI, 332.

[45] Kropf, *Kaffir-Eng. Dict.*, 148-149. [46] *Africa*, I, 82.

[47] Niemann, in *Bijd.*, 1895, 340. [48] Ratzel, *Vkde.*, II, 189.

[49] Kubary, *Karolinen-Archip.*, 47; Kubary, *Beiträge*, I, 64; Finsch, *Ethnol. Erfahr.*, III, 6, 7.

[50] *Cent. Polyn.*, II, 60-67, 75-76.

of people, often coming from scattered different islands, at the *marae* meeting there, and keeping up their common origin. If these princes, of common origin, were at war with one another, hostilities would be suspended on certain days, and the enemies would meet in this same *marae,* without any fear of one of them profiting by the circumstance. So also a canoe landing at the *marae* was respected; and even if it was met by superior forces in the open sea, it would be allowed to continue its course, on proof that it was going there. . . . The social significance of a *marae* lay in its character as representing a family; . . . and the social position of a man depended on the *marae* inside which he possessed a stone for a seat. In founding a *marae* the builder transplanted this stone of his to the new *marae,* thus making known the connection with the old *marae,* as well as the new one's dependence on it. In the *marae* there was a row of stones which indicated the seats of the families belonging to it, and were most important, as they formed, as it were, the ancestral tables of these people. . . . The *marae* was a walled enclosure, with an altar sacred to some god; but it represented, more than anything else, the family. The god was a secondary affair, and even the right to human sacrifices had little to do with the rank of the *marae.* To the Tahitians, the family and its antiquity alone were seriously interesting. An aristocratic society, their religious arrangements were rigorously aristocratic and a man's social position depended upon his having a stone to sit upon within the *marae* enclosure. This was the reason why the chief of Raiatea in 1774 asked Cook the name of his *marae;* for a man without a *marae* could be no chief, and Cook was regarded as a great chief; so he gave the name of his London parish. . . . The ownership by a chief of a *marae* was a title deed to the ancestral headship of the social group as chief of which he held it; and if that *marae* was an old one, long possessed by the group in the names of its chiefs, his ownership was a visible sign of his long lineage. . . .

"The information on the question now under discussion obtained from islands other than those of the Society group, is only very fragmentary. . . . It is stated that the chiefs—heads of families—sat on stones, and that *ariki* of other districts *also had special seats.* This implies that the seats of all the chiefs were 'special,' and I think we may gather that the meaning is that each chief had his own stone seat, and if so there can be no doubt that it would be the ancestral seat of his family that had been occupied by his predecessors." The author cites copious evidence throughout.

In the Pelew Islands, the king and the war-chief each heads a following with which he lives in a "bay"; the members spend the nights and a good part of the days there. Much more numerous clubs of this pattern surround the lesser chiefs; they are like our regiments, "for in fact there rules here a universal protective service than which none more extensive and reaching deeper into all social relations can well be conceived. . . . From the fifth or sixth year on all boys are forced to enter such a club and to take part in the wars and the public works ordered by the government. But in them the free and the unfree are not strictly separated from one another, even if the former always have precedence, first as freemen but also because it is out of their number that the real princes are taken, in part according to laws of inheritance, in part by election." In general each club of thirty-five to forty men, on the average, is comprised of those of about equal age. "The public works of the men's clubs are of the following description: (1) service in war, on land as by water;

(2) compulsory labor on occasion of the celebration of all public festivals without distinction." These are manifold, including those given to distinguished visitors, in connection with embassies, victories, burials, or with the idea of warding off sickness or other calamity. To such entertainments and to religious festivals "the men are forced to furnish a part of the necessary food and presents; (3) the erection of the houses, in which the clubs live; (4) the sewing of sails for their war-craft; (5) the catching of certain fish." In general these services are those discharged for the club or the government. The atlas-bone of the dugong, or sea-cow, is employed as an order of merit, conferred by the king only, who can also take it away from one in disfavor. "The putting on of the order, like its removal, is a cruel procedure; with force the hand is squeezed through the narrow opening, and in so doing a finger is often lost and the skin is always torn. The order may not be bought; it is acquired by the state, in return for much trepang, from seamen who now and then bring it in from the Philippines." Princes and freemen of standing can attain this distinction, but never the common warriors or the women.[51]

It is not always easy to distinguish the general men's houses from the specific bachelors' lodges. The former are more in the nature of a society with permanent membership, while the latter show a shifting personnel and resemble a school, forming an instrument of control over youths up to the age of marriage. The men's house is sometimes little more than a rendezvous for the guardians of the settlement and a place for storing weapons, boats, religious paraphernalia, and other community-property. It is the guest-house and may be considered as the center or capitol of the community. The bachelors' house will be seen to share in some of these public utilities, but is, on the whole, more limited and special in its functions. Though the two types run together, there is some profit in recognizing their differences; in particular, the bachelors' house bears more directly upon premarital relations. For into these quarters abducted girls are often introduced, though sometimes they go voluntarily or in adherence to custom, to collect presents against their later marriage. This, amounting to a species of prostitution, does not hinder the subsequent marriage of the girls. But it is quite evident that this custom has other elements in it than mere sensuality. Primitive peoples are not always thinking of sex-gratification. There are social, not to speak of economic, considerations.[52] There may be here a set of survivals of unregulated sex-relations; nevertheless, in this case

[51] Semper, *Palau-Ins.*, 36, 37, 72, note, 114, note.
[52] §§344, 364, 366, below.

as in that of the quarters for young men, the educational element, however crude, is unmistakably in evidence. In rather rare cases there are houses common to both sexes. These afford a sort of co-education, if the term may be used. And somewhat more commonly there are separate and special maidens' barracks corresponding to those of the young men.

In New Guinea the boys at puberty take up their abode in the bachelors' club-house where also strangers are entertained. They are under the supervision of an elderly man. "No woman is ever permitted to enter, and its object is to promote chastity and prevent too rapid an increase of population by illegitimate offspring."[53] In New Britain, where the Duk-Duk secret society flourishes, there are no large assembly-houses, as in New Guinea, but quarters are provided for unmarried men.[54] The "morong" of Assam, which is paralleled in Formosa, among the African Masai, in the Solomon Islands, New Britain, New Guinea, Borneo, in other parts of India, and throughout Indonesia, is a sort of communal barracks for the young and unmarried—occasionally for both sexes. It is regarded by Peal,[55] who describes it, as a possible relic of pre-marriage communism. There are in a village eight or ten barracks for young men and four or five for young women, the latter being under the supervision of an old woman and tabooed to married women. The former are often guard-houses, located "at the entrance to the villages, and those on guard keep tally of those who leave and return." Morals begin at marriage and thereafter infidelity is rare. The head-hunting peoples do not allow the young men to be tattooed until they have taken the head, hands, and feet of a member of another tribe, and women are despised till they are tattooed. "More or less the 'Morongs' of various kinds epitomize the racial customs and traditions, and also the social conditions of the past. They seem to concentrate the past to a focus in the present which we can leisurely examine, and a conspicuous feature is the general and marked antipathy to the 'married woman,' as an innovation [representing a departure from the looser relations of the good old times]; the tabu of the 'Morong' is directed *against her*. Whether captured or not she is the slave, and not the mistress of the situation. In fact, she is universally treated as an *interloper*. . . . The largest Morongs have from 50 to 60 grown men attached to them, while the others have 40 to 45 men. Every group of 30 or 40 houses has its *own* Morong, as a sort of parish courthouse."

On the island of Yap, in each of the great club-houses are kept three or four girls, who go through rites paralleled by the system of the Krumen of the African Gold Coast. "The natives say it is an ordeal or preliminary trial to fit them for the cares and burden of maternity." Such girls are thought no less of for their experiences; they are from outside the tribe, generally purchased slaves, though sometimes captured. This practice "is certainly a surprising coincidence with the Yoshiwara of Japan." The girls are richly en-

[53] Evans, in PSM, LII, 34 ff.; "Miscellanea," in JAI, XXI, 201.
[54] Finsch, *Ethnol. Erfahr.*, I, 100.
[55] In JAI, XXII, 244, 248, 254, 259; §344, below.

dowed with gifts when they leave, and their parents profit largely.[56] The Pelew Islands system is the most complete. Enterprising and patriotic women enter the "bay," or club-house of another community, as "armengols," to attain, in return for their action, a "bay" for their own communities. This makes for friendly inter-community relations, and involves an only temporary social humiliation for the women. They are treated well and learn the political habitudes and usages. In their own home they gain in dignity, "for the 'armengol' period is recognized as a period of education." The practice is customary and not at all an expression of sensuality. An insult to an "armengol" is an insult to the club. Some of these women represent tribute from a conquered village. Women of a female club sometimes get up excursions to go out as "armengols"; this sets money in circulation. In fact, the whole enterprise is more or less an economic affair.[57]

Semper[58] enters somewhat into the personal aspects of this matter, and represents an older woman comforting a younger who was weeping over the infidelity of her husband, by recounting her own experiences and rebellions. She said that "all men were equally bad in this respect—or really they did quite right, for the women themselves were quite often enough the first cause of the unfaithfulness of the men; and so long as they did not completely dissolve the relations of the lawfully wedded women to the unmarried girls living in the 'bay'—the 'armengols'—it would ever so remain. She should only think how she herself had been an 'armengol' . . . for several months, and that the free, unrestrained life that she led as such had been very pleasant—quite especially also the attendance on the part of the married women. So long as these must still bring the 'armengol' in the 'bay' her daily food, there would always be girls ready to pass several months in the 'bay'—the more readily since, at their return to their parents' village, they brought back a great deal of money and also did not have to wait long for a husband. In fact, to many women life in the 'bay' was so pleasant that they ran away from their husbands to enter such a life again. To interfere with all this, moreover, was forbidden by the old honorable custom, and if they did not wish any longer to bring food to the 'bay' for the 'armengols,' the men would have no service any longer either; for the proper wife might never show before the world that she lived in such confidential relations with her husband; that would be 'mugul,' and if once this word ceased to have power among them, then surely the whole of Pelew would go to destruction." There is much in this story that is instructive concerning conjugal mores, and much shrewd observation and wisdom is displayed. And the author adds to it the report of another conversation in defense of the local custom. "Such is the custom in Pelew, Doctor. It is not wrong; on the contrary we women have all once run off in that way. And it is a pretty custom; only so do we get to see something of the other islands. Our young girls here at Nasiass used to go to Eimelig; those from Argeutel, Orocoll, and Ardelollec went to Corŏre, those from Corŏre to Rallap. Then they remain three months in the 'bays,' learn there to serve the men and be obedient to them, and when they return they bring along to their parents a pretty sum

[56] Christian, *Caroline Isl.*, 290-291; Senfft, in *Globus*, XCI, 149; "Kl. Nachr.," in *Globus*, LXXVIII, 150.

[57] Kubary, *Karolinen-Arch.*, 226, 244, 245; Kubary, *Beiträge*, I, 52-53, 91.

[58] *Palau-Ins.*, 65, 66, 324.

of money. . . . Now the young girls when they are grown must go into a 'bay.' That is our 'makesang' [sacred social duty]. When a young fellow comes to the right age he must go somewhere and none of the young girls ought then to remain behind; if one does so anyhow, her parents scold her and she doesn't find a husband so readily either, for everywhere in the community she has the name of a clumsy and dull girl, who is worth nothing as a wife. But the others, when they come home, marry quickly."

So much for the various clubs and their features. They contribute a very characteristic and widespread adjustment to conditions of sex and age and also secure a considerable amount of regulation of conduct and of training and discipline. Even though less intensively organized than are the secret societies, they tend to keep before the minds of their mature members, and also to impress vividly upon the young, the traditional ways of managing social and political affairs which the wisdom of the past has found expedient. The clubs have a distinctly political tinge; that they are virtually confined to the sex that does the governing and are effective in preserving and consolidating its political prerogatives is significant of their function.

§163*. Initiation. It has been noted that all these societies have some sort of initiation-ceremonies. The highly special ones connected with the exclusive secret societies may be passed over without comment or description; for these are simply variations on the theme of the regular puberty-ceremonies, with specific features corresponding to their special character, shamanistic or other. The initiation into manhood, the recognition of the attainment of a distinct age-grade which is at the same time a distinct sex-grade, is the fundamental type of initiation. Where there are men's houses, it coincides with entrance into them and may be taken as a special introduction into the *bay*, or *morong*, or whatever else the men's or bachelors' associations may be called. More broadly, the initiation at puberty represents the coming of age which makes a man, or at any rate a youth, out of a child. The puberty-ceremonies celebrate the arrival of a new responsible member of the community; if he is not yet quite that, he is soon going to be; and it is at any rate time to school him toward his duties and to render him capable of carrying on when his elders are gone. Initiation is, in a very true sense, the testing of manhood and, in so far as it is practised on females, of womanhood.[59]

It cannot be thought that savages have the capacity to look far ahead into the needs of their society and deliberately to plan a course in citizen-making; they have in their heads only the conviction that their own social habitudes and traditions are conducive to welfare and that departure from them by anyone is perilous to all; and they know that, as Homer[60] puts it, "the minds of young men are unstable, but the old man from his wide experience plans the best." Nestor, the typical Homeric sage, lived to see two generations pass away "and he ruled with those of the third generation." Primitive peoples had their code of mores and an abiding intention to cleave to it; both automatically and deliberately they inculcated what they were convinced was good and moral and they sought to combat departures, whether purposeful or unwitting, from the code. Before a person became a full-fledged member of society it was essential, in their minds, that he should be both tested and instructed.

Initiation was then, in its broadest sense, the vestibule through which a youth entered, not into this or that special association, but into the society in which he was to pass his life. It was a selective process, practised by the society at large upon its potential membership, and was doubtless long antecedent to special rites of admittance to this or that intra-tribal association. A number of peoples which have no secret societies or clubs to speak of, for example the Australians, are very thorough on puberty-rites. The similarities of the puberty tests and ceremonies to the initiations into the secret societies and clubs are such as exist between members of a genetic series; it would seem that all the initiations to minor associations included within a tribe are merely developments and specializations of the basic initiation into the tribe itself. If this is the case, it would perhaps be more logical to begin with puberty-ceremonies and work up to the exclusive societies; still there are advantages in viewing the series the other end on.

One more general consideration should be mentioned before re-

---

[59] §365, below.

[60] *Iliad*, III, 298-301; I, 247 ff.; *Odyssey*, III, 244; Keller, *Hom. Soc.*, 177, 290.

viewing the cases: the typical initiation shows a distinctly religious cast. Puberty is the time when the tribal marks are cut upon the body, marks which signify membership in a bond that reaches beyond death; for the tribe consists not only of those who live but also of the unnumbered ancestors who are now spirits. It seems altogether probable that tribal marks are derivable ultimately from "cutting for the dead" and exuvial sacrifice.[61] In any case, the puberty-ceremonies, like all others that mark the crises of life, are solemnized by the presence and inmixture of the ghosts and gods.

In general though not always, the initiation of a boy into the societal bond takes place, or at any rate begins, with his arrival at puberty. It is evident that the attainment or imminence of sexual maturity is the salient fact that fixes the date. The youths are approaching the period when they can take part in society's self-perpetuation. Puberty is also the time of alterations in size, strength, and other corporeal and also mental characteristics which fit the youth to take his part in society's self-maintenance. These two activities of society are the basic essentials to its persistence; even unreflecting savages act as if they were aware of that fact. They are not, for their minds are incapable of comprehending such abstractions. What they do is to follow their codes very faithfully; and these codes did not merely happen but are tested adjustments to life-conditions and often exhibit a surpassing expediency. The practical utility of the puberty-ceremonies will come out from an inspection of the cases.

Many of the most important functions of men in Australia are conditional upon an initiation to which women are not admitted and which contributes to make them seem inferior.[62] The ceremonies vary through the continent; among the Central tribes "they are more elaborate and spread over a long series of years, the first taking place at about the age of ten or twelve, whilst the final and most impressive one is not passed through until about the age of twenty-five or thirty. In the Arunta and Ilpirra tribes the ceremonies are four in number: (1) Painting and throwing the boy up into the air. (2) Circumcision or Lartna. (3) Subincision or Ariltha. (4) The Engwura or fire ceremony." At the first of these the boys are told by tribal fathers and elder brothers that in future they must not associate with the women and girls, but go to the camp of the men. Up to this time they have gone out with the women in search of vegetable food and smaller animals; now they begin to accompany the men

61 §§221, 224, 229, 298, below; Lippert, *Kgchte.*, I, 389, 397.
62 Ratzel, *Vkde.*, II, 67.

in the hunting of bigger game. At the time of the operations the youth is supposed by the women and the uninitiated boys to have been taken away into the bush by a spirit whose voice is the bull-roarer. "This belief is fundamentally the same as that found in all Australian tribes." All sorts of inexplicable taboos surround these rites; for example, between the presentation of the fire-stick and until Lartna has been performed, the future mother-in-law of the boy is tabu to his tribal mother, who presents the fire-stick. While the lad who is between Lartna and Ariltha (period of five or six weeks) is out in the bush, "the men go and visit him occasionally, and at such times he has to undergo a painful rite called Koperta kakuma, or head-biting. . . . The men who are to do the biting . . . are usually from two to five in number. . . . Their duty is to bite the scalp as hard as they can, until the blood flows freely, the patient often howling with pain. . . . The object, they say, is to make the hair grow strongly, and at times the chin is also bitten."[63] The blood from the operations, which are performed with a stone knife, is allowed to trickle down into a hole in the ground which is later filled with earth. Afterwards the boy is shown the more sacred totemic ceremonies and is warned that he is now a man and not a boy, and must have nothing to do with other men's wives or he will fall dead. After a beating by his sisters he may take a wife and take his place among the initiated men in their camp. The final ceremony involves more beating and the scarring of his back and neck. "The scars left behind when the wounds heal up enable a man who has passed through the ceremony to be distinguished at a glance." The marks have mythical signification, and no man will stand or sit, if avoidable, with his back turned to the women and children. A number of other injunctions, many of them apparently wholly irrational, are put upon the initiated. Among those which control his social relations are the following. (1) That he must obey his elders and not quarrel with them. (2) That he must not eat certain foods, but must provide food for individuals who stand in a certain relationship to him. (3) That he must not attempt to interfere with women who have been allotted to other men, or belong to groups with the individuals of which it is not lawful for him to have marital relations. (4) That he must on no account reveal any of the secret matters connected with the totems to the women and children." Evidently these injunctions display considerable wisdom as to the conditions of law and order. The fire-ceremony, where the initiates had to ward off a shower of burning branches with a shield of leaves and then lie down upon a fire covered with green leaves, seems to have been a test of the endurance of the young men, who were at the same time taught the past history of the tribe. "The heat of the fire was very considerable. Professor Spencer knelt on the heap to try it, but could not endure it, even with thick trousers on."[64]

"It must always be remembered that the feelings of the person operated on are not considered in any way. It does not seem to matter to the old men how much they hurt the other fellow, and the young men consider it a disgrace to show any feeling; but by the time a boy is sufficiently initiated to be called a young man he is very subdued, and does not recover until he has assisted in the initiation of other boys."[65]

[63] Spencer and Gillen, *Nat. Tr. Cent. Aust.*, 212 ff., 246, note, 250, 251.

[64] Spencer and Gillen, *North. Tr. Cent. Aust.*, 334, 342, 502; "Miscellanea," in JAI, XXVII, 134.

[65] Horne and Aiston, *Cent. Aust.*, 95.

"To the Papuan young man, initiation is all-important. On the performance of the instructions he received as an initiate the social and moral welfare of his tribe depends; as an individual he is only a unit of his tribe, but as such he must always conduct himself in all things for the highest interests of his tribe. The knowledge he acquired when an initiate must ever be to him a sacred possession, and not be imparted to the uninitiated. . . . To divulge the mysteries . . . to any female of the tribe, *i.e.*, to let it be known among the women that the whining of the bull-roarers is not the cry of a god but the work of a man, is to bring upon the indiscreet the curse of *tiparu,* which is equivalent to death, and any woman found anywhere near the place where the feast of *tiparu* is being celebrated is taken and made the common property of all the men assembled there; to be released, later, with the warning that if she divulges what has taken place, to any female, she will be put to death."[66] The initiates are especially segregated from the eyes of the women who are of age to have sexual intercourse, whereas no harm would come to them if seen by a little girl or an old woman; it is said that the boy's growth would be checked unless this precaution were taken. This looks like a preventative of illicit sex-relations. The initiates have an easy and irresponsible life, playing most of the time; what they learn during the novitiate is less deliberately taught than picked up by seeing what goes on in the men's house, the hub of village life, and by listening to their seniors, especially to those charged with bringing them their food and carrying them hither and thither on their shoulders. Such an attendant receives some gift from the father of his charge; he is more of a nurse than an instructor.[67] Haddon[68] remarks upon the likeness between the initiation-ceremony and that at marriage; describes many such ceremonies, emphasizing the educative element in them; notes that the bull-roarer is thought to devour the novices and bring them back to life again, when they get new names; and points out the purificatory practice of steaming the initiates. It appears then that initiation is like both the funeral and the wedding; little wonder that it is assimilated to the latter, for it signalizes marriageability, and a boy who is marriageable is not long in becoming a husband.

At each stage of initiation the candidate is tested; "when the elders are convinced that the novice has absorbed the spirit of unselfishness to such an extent that his future behaviour will promote communal welfare, he is permitted to qualify for the final stage of initiation—a ceremony investing him with the homicidal insignia. In order to qualify he must kill a man of another tribe. The investiture with the homicidal decoration gives a boy the proudest moment of his life. Seated on a throne of crossed spears, he listens to the deeds of valour of the brave men of the tribe, and in the presence of the whole tribe receives the homicidal decoration with compliments and words of encouragement. Then he becomes an adult member, and for the first time is entitled to ask the hand of a woman in marriage. In this case we see that the suppression of homicide not only prevents a male from becoming an adult member of his tribe but also disallows marriage. . . . If homicide be an essential link binding together the social and religious fabric of a community, the suppression of homicide is likely to result in the collapse of the whole structure unless something equally capable of perpetuating tribal welfare is substituted to fill

[66] Holmes, in JAI, XXXII, 418, 425.
[67] Williams, in JAI, LIII, 369, 370.
[68] In JAI, L, 243, 249 ff., 255, 257, 270, 275.

the void. . . . As a result of the discussion, candidates for initiation were permitted to qualify by killing a wild boar instead of a man. This was communicated to me, and I was invited to attend the initiation ceremony, which proceeded through its final stages, in no way hampered by the substitution of boar-killing for man-killing. It was also decided that as the homicidal decoration could no longer be won with honour, on account of the abolition of intertribal warfare, it would be withdrawn from the final qualification, though fathers, if they wished, could transfer to their sons their own decorations for bravery."[69] The initiation-ceremonies are an occasion of great license.[70]

"It is quite clear that ideas concerning death are closely associated with the *Tamate* societies. Not only does the word *tamate* mean 'ghost' or 'dead man' but in the ceremony of initiation there is evidence of the representation of death and return to life. Thus, the beating of the novice and the destruction of his house during initiation is very suggestive of a ceremonial death, and so is the wailing of his female relatives when the candidate leaves them. . . . The seclusion again and the feasts during its progress and on its termination, have a very suggestive resemblance to the common Melanesian custom of holding a feast every five or ten days after death up till the hundredth day. Just as the feast after a hundred days of seclusion is especially important, so often is the feast on the hundredth day after death. The absence of washing and the taboo on touching the sleeping-place of the initiate may also be interpreted in this way. It seems as if there is during his seclusion a kind of ceremonial make-believe that the initiate is dead, though at the same time he has to carry out the duties of feeding the members." The author[71] illustrates in detail the several other functions of the societies as recounted in a former quotation, namely, the conferring of social rank, the distribution of wealth (though the mere acquisition of wealth for its own sake is probably wholly foreign to the ideas of the people—it is a means to further advance), the enforcement of property-right, and the rest. There is a strange element of reversion in these ceremonies. "Just as there is reason to believe that at certain festivals the most fundamental laws regulating the relations of the sexes are not merely broken but that an excessive degree of relaxation is allowed or enjoined, so may it be that we have on the occasions when the *Tamate* destroy property in a wholesale way a general relaxation of the laws regulating the protection of property in which the *Tamate* societies normally take so prominent a place."

The conclusion reached by Rivers is as follows: "It is clear that the *Sukwe* and *Tamate* societies are not merely associations to awaken and then to satisfy curiosity or to terrorize those who do not belong to them, but have a very definite and useful function in the community. They are closely concerned in the respect for property and in the maintenance of social order. At the same time they give the people an absorbing interest which . . . is shared by the whole population. The ordeals and trials of patience perhaps seem to present a less desirable side but even these have their merits and have probably contributed to form that habit of restraint and respect for authority which is so strongly developed in the people. To quote the words of a missionary who has observed the operations of the *Sukwe*, 'I could not help feeling that the existence of the *Suqe* does much to foster the virtues which go to make up the

[69] Chinnery, in JAI, XLIX, 37, 39-40, 280.
[70] Chalmers, in JAI, XXXIII, 124.
[71] Rivers, *Melan. Soc.*, I, 127-128, 139-143.

successful citizen and man of business and maintain the vigour of the community. To be a successful Melanesian citizen [*i.e.,* one high in the *Suqe*] means that a man must have unlimited patience, indomitable perseverance, excellent health, and a strong physique to enable him to recover from the perpetual succession of losses of which he runs the risk.'" "The Gulf Papuan believes implicitly in the survival of the fittest. Personal desires, likes and dislikes, everything there is, or can be, must be subordinated to the pursuit of obtaining the fittest. This idea is innate in him, it is fostered by his guardians when he is a child, it is inculcated in his initiation, it is dominant in him until he dies."[72]

"Woe to the initiate who should reveal to anyone the affairs of Mboïo! . . . There might happen to him what befel a woman named Boumba. That woman, less credulous than the rest, refused to give a chicken to Mboïo, saying that Mboïo was nothing. The same evening they searched for her in vain. It was said that Mboïo had carried her off; the truth is that the disciples of Mboïo had killed her! Since that time they swear only by 'Mouna Boumba.' The black who takes oath does it in these terms: 'What I say is true, as true as that Boumba was carried off by Mboïo.' . . . One of these tests consists in passing naked through a long trench dug in the sand, filled with thorns, and covered over with earth. It is conceivable in what a state and how torn a young man is when he emerges."[73] Barton[74] cites the following points as suggestive of new birth: "there is a ceremonial cleansing before and after the ceremonies; the initiate is fed as a child on pap and gradually taught to use his hands, and fed by an almost maternal sponsor; the initiate wears a large oxhide, a woman's garment, to cover himself entirely as a child in ventro; the initiate is taught to recognise the doll-like representation of common objects by the promptings of his sponsor, as a mother might teach her child; finally expiation is done for past misdeeds and the initiate enters upon a new life with a clean sheet." The same author notes elsewhere that the initiate's *mama,* or maternal uncle, pours rancid butter on his head and body, the *mama* being the functionary also who extracts his lower incisors and pierces his ears. He is beaten upon the head, body, and especially the pubes with nettles, which causes an intolerable temporary rash. He is asked whether he has had connection with a married woman, and must answer truly. But the central fact of the ceremony is circumcision. He is cuffed at any signs of cowardice; booming noises of bull-roarers frighten him; then his face is beaten with the nettles, the rash closing his eyes. "The ceremonies seem to indicate a return to a prenatal condition by the mother's skirt being worn over the body, a test of fortitude when the 'anæsthetic' is administered, and a test of integrity and secrecy in the matter of sexual relations with married women." The initiate is under various taboos. The ceremony lasts about six months, after which there is a period of twenty to twenty-five days during which the youth speaks to no woman; then he has connection with a girl or woman. If she is unwilling he may, by tribal custom, use force, but may never marry her or have connection again. There is a curious permission for a barren woman to be present at the ceremony, which includes circumcision or incision, in order that she may become fruitful. At a subsequent ceremony, marking entrance into elderhood as distinguished from manhood, the candidate must sit on stinging nettles; also a

[72] Holmes, in JAI, XXXII, 423.   [73] Trilles, *Fân,* 52, 460.
[74] In JAI, LI, 95; and in JAI, LIII, 52-68, *passim.*

sharp blade of grass, wet with salt, is drawn down his cheeks and breast, leaving a scar. It may be added that girls are subjected to something similar in the way of an operation, during which a childless man may be present. Such a female initiate must then entice a youth, though she may repulse him and run away to her husband. During her seclusion she is taught wifely duties by the old women. There are circumcision-age-grades for both sexes, members of which give each other nicknames, playful designations, probably, for a set of young people of about the same age at the time of circumcision.

Hobley[75] mentions a ceremony called "to be born again" which precedes eligibility for circumcision; the child has to go and lie alongside its mother in bed and cry out like a newly born infant. "The occurrence of these two ceremonies, connected as they are, cannot help but strike one as being in a lower civilization the genesis of the idea of the sacraments of baptism and confirmation, and in fact some of the missionaries it is said do not scruple to explain the two Christian doctrines mentioned by reference to the two pagan ones, and state that with the help of this key the natives at once grasp the idea of their doctrines."

The Indians, says Lawson,[76] had "one most abominable custom amongst them, which they call husquenawing their young men. . . . You must know, that most commonly, once a year, at farthest, once in two years, these people take up so many of their young men as they think are able to undergo it, and husquenaugh them, which is to make them obedient and respective to their superiors, and, as they say, it is the same to them as it is to us to send our children to school to be taught good breeding and letters. This house of correction is a large, strong cabin, made on purpose for the reception of the young men and boys, that have not passed the graduation already; and it is always at Christmas that they husquenaugh their youth, which is by bringing them into this house and keeping them dark all the time, where they more than half starve them. Besides, they give them pellitory bark, and several intoxicating plants, that make them go raving mad as ever were any people in the world; and you may hear them make the most dismal and hellish cries and howlings that ever human creatures expressed; all which continues about five or six weeks, and the little meat they eat, is the nastiest, loathsome stuff, and mixt with all manner of filth it is possible to get. After the time is expired, they are brought out of the cabin, which never is in the town, but always a distance off, and guarded by a jailor or two, who watch by turn. Now when they first come out, they are as poor as ever any creatures were; for you must know several die under this diabolical purgation. Moreover, they either really are, or pretend to be, dumb, and do not speak for several days; I think twenty or thirty, and look so ghastly, and are so changed, that it is next to an impossibility to know them again, although you was never so well acquainted with them before. I would fain have gone into the mad house, and have seen them in their time of purgatory, but the king would not suffer it, because, he told me they would do me or any other white man an injury, that ventured in amongst them, so I desisted. . . . Now the savages say that if it was not for this, they could never keep their youth in subjection, besides that it hardens them ever after to the fatigues of war, hunting, and all manner of hardship, which their way of living exposes them to. Besides, they add, that it carries off those infirm weak bodies, that would have been only a burden and disgrace

[75] In JAI, XL, 440-441.   [76] Hist. Carolina, 380-382.

to their nation, and saves the victuals and clothing for better people that would have been expended on such useless creatures."

The extreme of initiation is that practised by the Mandan Sioux, "for the purpose of conducting all the young men of the tribe, as they annually arrive to the age of manhood, through an ordeal of privation and torture, which, while it is supposed to harden their muscles and prepare them for extreme endurance, enables the chiefs who are spectators to the scene, to decide upon their comparative bodily strength and ability to endure the extreme privations and sufferings that often fall to the lots of Indian warriors." Some of these tests are "too terrible and too revolting to be seen or to be told, were it not an essential part of a whole, which will be new to the civilized world, and therefore worth their knowing." Donaldson,[77] who thus introduces the subject, devotes many pages to the details of the ceremonies, and accompanies them with reproductions of the drawings of George Catlin. The *Case-Book* presents a condensation from Catlin's account (1832).

The Nez-Percés subject their young men to the torture of being tied to a stake by a deer-tendon passed under the tendons on the back of the left hand. "The sun-dance is performed when a warrior is initiated into the band of braves, and one of the ceremonial rites consists in testing the lad's endurance by this horrible torture. If he can go on until the tendon breaks, or until he falls fainting to the ground, when some friend kindly severs any little shred yet unbroken, the lad, after passing the night alone and fasting in his tent, is admitted to be a brave. . . . The poor benighted savage could see no safety in meeting the unfeeling medium of the existing forces about him but to become as nearly unfeeling himself as possible, and thereby in some small measure be able to stand the hard strokes of terrible forces ever against him. The sun-dance is undoubtedly his method of 'solving the problem of the universe.' "[78] In these sun-dances the initiate may be forced to face the glare of sun from its rising to its setting.

Among the Omahas, "when a child was born it was not regarded as a member of its gens or of the tribe but simply as a living being coming forth into the universe, whose advent must be ceremonially announced in order to assure it an accepted place among the already existing forms." There had to be a ceremony of introducing the child into the tribe. "Through this ceremony the child passed out of that stage in its life wherein it was hardly distinguished from all other living forms into its place as distinctively a human being, a member of its birth gens, and through this to a recognized place in the tribe. As it went forth its baby name was thrown away, its feet were clad in new moccasins made after the manner of the tribe, and its *nikie* name . . . was proclaimed to all nature and to the assembled people." The authors[79] describe the attendant ceremonial in some detail.

Before attempting to gather up the general aspects of the ini-

---

[77] In *Smithson. Rep.*, 1885, pt. II, 352 ff.; Mathews, in USNM, 1890, 606 ff. Catlin's accounts are in his *Letters and Notes on the Manners, Customs, and Condition of the North American Indians* (London, 1841), I, 155 ff.; and in his *O-Kee-Pa* (London, 1867).

[78] Gorton, in *Pop. Sci. News*, XXVII, 17; Dorsey, in BAE, XI, 450 ff. Bibliography of the various types of sun-dance in Webster, *Secret Soc.*, 216, 217.

[79] Fletcher and LaFlesche, in BAE, XXVII, 115-117.

tiation-practices, it is necessary to note that, while they apply chiefly to the young men, they are also carried out in a number of cases in connection with the coming to maturity of the girls.

The maturity-ceremonies for girls are, in Australia, parallel to those for boys, but not so severe. There is, among the Dieri, a sort of communalization for the occasion.[80] In New Guinea, girls must go into seclusion for a period reaching to two years, not leaving the house in that time. Then there is a festival and they are exhibited in their glory of tattoo for all the young men to observe. "The girls enjoy on this day the greatest freedom and have the right to choose their swains," by handing them betel-nuts. There is a taboo on certain foods for the initiates and an operation corresponding to circumcision. A girl but indifferently tattooed has no attraction in the eyes of the young men.[81] Some of these ceremonies are like a "bride-show,"[82] where the girl is displayed, after her period of seclusion, in the midst of (often borrowed) magnificence. It is her "coming-out." This is so in southern Alaska; "a girl being thus launched forth into the social life of the community became eligible for marriage. In the general idea we see the beginnings of similar customs with which we are familiar in our own more complex social organization."[83] Parallel to the flogging of the boys, among certain Amazon tribes, is the fasting and fumigation of the girls: "to try the fortitude of their maidens they hang them in a net to the roof of a hut, exposed to continual smoke, where they fast as long as they can possibly bear it."[84] In Brazil the maturity-ceremony for girls is universal, and includes seclusion, fasting, fumigation, blood-letting, and scarring. Many girls fall a sacrifice to the treatment received. They are often beaten to insensibility, and while the rest feast, may only lick off the instruments of chastisement dipped in the food. If the victim endures, she may eat everything and is declared marriageable. "After her return from her first bath she must place herself for the night upon a stool or stone, where she is scourged by her mother with thin rods, without daring to emit a cry of pain that could awaken the sleepers in the hut—a circumstance that could have only peril for her future well-being." The flogging is repeated once, the next month.[85] In Paraguay the puberty-ceremony for girls includes feasting, but the girl must during the time refrain from certain foods.[86]

If we seek to sum up the sense of the usages at maturity, we find them issuing in injunctions as to conduct, enforced and sharpened by recourse to more or less impressive ceremonial. These injunctions have very largely to do with keeping the peace: obeying the elders and letting other men's wives alone. The fact that the pu-

---

[80] Spencer and Gillen, *Nat. Tr. Cent. Aust.*, 269; Howitt, in JAI, XX, 87.
[81] Krieger, *Neu-Guinea*, 296-297; Hagen, *Papua's*, 238; Guise, in JAI, XXVIII, 215.
[82] §361, below.   [83] Niblack, in USNM, 1888, 371.
[84] Markham, in JAI, XXIV, 280.
[85] Von Martius, *Beiträge*, I, 111, 390, 402, 428, 510-511, 599, 644; Spix and Martius, *Brasilien*, 1187.
[86] Koch, in *Globus*, LXXXI, 45.

berty-ceremonies have so much to do with sex enforces the recognition of that biological fact as one of the major life-conditions. In any case, with their taboos and ordeals, they are highly disciplinary; and if the accompanying instruction is heeded, the initiates will refrain from many forms of lawlessness and disorder. It will also be noted that there are various grades of belonging to a community: the child belongs, as a negligible factor; the women are an integral part of the tribe, but are not, as it were, officially recognized; the boys receive official recognition, though it is not full and complete; the men themselves must often go on from grade to grade. Perhaps the chiefs alone may be thought to be the finished political product.

Viewed as an instrumentality for educating the young to tribal membership, this set of associations might be said to begin its functions with the boy, let us say, who frequents the men's house out of curiosity and remembers and imitates what he sees and hears. Then at puberty he begins to undergo a sort of elementary schooling, culminating with initiation, in the formation of character and habits calculated to make him a good defender against outsiders and a precedent-following member of the in-group; for such is to be his function and destiny in life. He learns to perform and to endure according to the local code and to know and respect the mores. Initiation admits him to the general men's association where he learns, from a position of some perspective and detachment, as well as of preference and power, how to assist in the formulation, assessment, and manipulation of tribal opinion. Advancing to associations of deeper secrecy, he penetrates farther behind the scenes of tribal regulation, and as he rises through the grades of his fraternity he attains enlarged experience along with increasing maturity until he graduates into the council of elders or other repository of group-power. It would be difficult to devise for youths on the savage stage a more adequate schooling for life as it is to be lived. Here is to be seen, at any rate, the only systematic education, outside the family and beyond earliest years, that the nature-man ever had.

Anyone who reads the accounts of primitive initiations without prejudice is impressed with the seriousness of spirit in which they are performed. Why should they not be, including as they do a rehearsal of the three great crises in any human being's life: birth, marriage, and death? What is done is not horse-play; it is ritual and is carried out with reverence and solemnity. In all religious ritual there is a characteristic element of survival; the license permitted in the matters of sex-relations and of property is nothing but that. It is analogous to the "expiation for marriage,"[87] where relaxation takes place briefly just at the time of entrance upon a life-long régime of repression under strict taboo. The fact is that the proceedings of the period are sacramental, as one of the authors just quoted has suggested; and sacraments are traditionally surrounded by an insulation of conventionalization which makes holy that which would not be tolerated in the everyday life. There is power in these ceremonies, so that the barren woman and the childless man may profit by witnessing them; they are highly fecundating in the life of the society. That the initiates are taught to kill and steal from outsiders belongs to the stock training of any primitive people, as witness the admonitions of the Hebrew god; and one should be as little shocked by the cases of relaxation as by adjurations to prey upon the out-group. Rather should he note the significant fact that where the property-monopoly is infringed upon, there also are the marriage-monopoly and the sex-taboo suspended. There are very few reports, none that we know of from competent observers, which do not emphasize the soundly educational function of initiation. What is taught is not what we should teach, but it is what is needed for the stage of development in question; it is what makes the man-as-he-should-be in the setting of his tribal life.

One of the results of these educational practices is a selection whereby, under the eyes of the authorities, there is a winnowing-out of the most promising human material, together with a rejection of the least promising, so that the basis of a social classification and gradation is laid. Even modern education is still to some degree selective.[88] It is still expected that the new and young member of an established association will keep still for awhile and listen to his elders, only gradually rising through periods of acquisition and test to candidacy for leadership. Savages are

[87] §§343, 344, below.   [88] Sumner, *Folkways*, ch. XIX.

simply cruder and more direct than we are in the detail of their methods. Perhaps they clinch more of their ceremonies by eating-orgies than do civilized men; for, despite the fact that most celebrations of the latter still include that detail, it is usually refined into something less than the attainment of pure repletion.

In their organizations of various degrees of secrecy men early learned the application of two sweeping principles which of course they were unable to analyze. The first of these is that what is unknown is taken to be great. The mystery with which the initiated surrounded themselves, whether they were the inner circle of an exclusive secret society or merely the men of the tribe as distinguished from the inconsiderable women and children, conferred prestige and power. Many a modern association has won standing for itself and has succeeded in exercising wide control over uncritical minds by maintaining a portentous gravity and inscrutability together with an imposing ritual. Although a display of the terrorizing element has never been amiss, still the common recourse, for the generation of mystery, has been to that reservoir of all mystery, religion. Masks, secret languages, strange oath-takings, and, above all, pregnant silence have been the stock in trade of powerful secret organizations in all ages. And they have not alone sought to pique curiosity; they have also worked upon ignorance and superstition as, for example, when the Ku Klux Klan of a former generation made use of the ghost-beliefs of the negroes. The dark and reiterated threats to the initiate who should reveal secrets, supported by the knowledge of the swift fate of those who did, witness to the savage appreciation of this source of prestige.

Second, secret organizations have always appealed to the compelling sentiment of vanity. It is in large part their secrecy which has enabled them to do this. To be distinguished from the rest in physical strength or wealth has always tickled vanity; but to be one of an exclusive group—a person of whom outsiders stand in awe because of his conversance with superhuman mysteries, such as death and re-birth—must have been to experience sublime sensations of superiority. No outsiders in primitive times ever profanely flouted membership in the secret societies; all wanted to get in and were willing to go to any lengths in order to do so. It was a humiliation of the most tragic sort to fail in the puberty-test and remain outside with the women and children; the novices veritably longed for the torture-time and went through it in a species of ecstatic exaltation. They were nothing till it was over, and they ardently desired to be something.

There is no doubt that it was economically advantageous to belong to the secret society, the club, or the body of maturity-tested men; membership in any of these associations was an asset in self-maintenance. Further, since marriage could but rarely take place till after initiation, the impulse toward self-perpetuation spurred young men on to withstand and to acquire a new status. Membership likewise conferred a favored relation with the ancestral spirits and the gods and therefore an insurance against life's ills not enjoyed by the outsider. These economic, domestic, and religious motives were probably less engrossing than vanity, and they have not persisted so unmistakably into the present, it may be; but they certainly did not detract from the stress that drove men to all expedients in order to identify themselves with the various exclusive organizations.

The prestige of these organizations thus flowed from various sources, chiefly vanity and mystery; the stock socializing forces[89] combined to enhance it; and that their power was very great lies in the nature of the case. Where all eligible outsiders were so eager to get in, those who were in could set their own conditions. All the strong men were in and they held the inexplicable secrets. Here was power; and that it should be used in regulation of the affairs of the society at large was inevitable. Doubtless many antisocial acts have been done in their own interest by secret societies unaccountable or but imperfectly responsible to any authority but themselves; even when there are constituted authorities outside a secret organization, the latter is well equipped for evasion of control by them; yet on the primitive stage, where peace and order are immediate necessities for self-preservation, such instrumentalities as the secret societies, clubs, and bands of initiates were bound, in the long run, to be employed for the maintenance of these indispensables. This seems to us the main conclusion to be

[89] §11, above.

drawn from the study of the cases. Whatever their origin and whatever functions their aftertypes may have discharged, these associations stand forth in the earlier stages of their evolution as agencies of societal regulation.

CHAPTER XVIII

CLASSES AND RIGHTS

§164*. Social Distinctions. The social distinctions hitherto considered have been those which, arising inside the peace-group, are based upon sex, age, blood, and personal qualities as exhibited under tests of various sorts: one sex only has been regularly accorded political power; age has prevailed over youth; there has been a distinction between the high family and the low; and a chance has always existed for the exhibition of individual fortitude, endurance, intelligence, and other distinguishing characteristics. The existence of the last-named criteria has meant that within society certain social strata have formed which were not based upon the biological conditions of sex, age, and birth. This differentiation has been capable of further development; it has been possible, for instance, for distinctions to be drawn on the basis of wealth. That there are scattered throughout the primitive societal organization active germs of plutocracy has appeared incidentally but frequently in the cases cited. Nevertheless the exigencies of savage life are such as to call for the primary virtues of physical strength, bravery, and the rest rather than for the power of mere possessions. Only as peace and order become so firmly established as not to demand constant safeguarding does the distinction by wealth have a chance to establish itself in unshaken permanence. Property must first be firmly guaranteed or violence may sweep away personal or family-wealth before it has an opportunity to consolidate its social power. Wealth is not like superior personal qualities; it is an attachment and can be severed, so that its possessor drops into nothingness.

As has been noted, all these distinctions have evolved within a society as intra-group phenomena. It is now necessary to go beyond them, for in considering the subject of social classes it is required to include strata that are not a product of intra-group differentiation. The internally developed classes do not at any time cease to exist but go forward in their course; only there are added to them certain other strata which are introduced from without. The chief of these is the slave-class. The addition of this differentiation is comparatively late, calling as it does for a relatively strong regulative system and an advanced stage of industrial organization.[1] We have considered slavery as a whole while examining its economic aspects and, although what has been so recently covered need not be rehearsed, in the ensuing development of the class-system its presence and characteristic effects must be borne ever in mind.

Upon various criteria, then, social distinctions have arisen even among the most primitive of men. Their presence has determined both the character of the society that must be regulated and also the type of regulation evolved and imposed; classes have had to be governed, and they have themselves taken their characteristic share, ranging from an apparent monopoly to no part at all, in that system of control.

The qualifications for social position inhering in sex, age, and parentage need no further elaboration; but it is not always realized that even among primitive peoples talent, fighting-power, energy, enterprise, organizing and executive capacity, power to learn, to pray—in short, any distinctive superiority—has had its chance. It is significant that the mere ability to labor, that is, to get products out of nature, has never led to social prestige; stolid plodders in the ranks, who have never done the world's work or achieved social results except as they have followed leaders, have attained no distinctions. It has taken the variations or mutations of special ability, energy, and ambition to start off the process of evolution. Inequality has been the necessary precondition to advancing societal adjustment and it has always been recognized; for society to have done anything else would have been to reduce all to the same flats of mediocrity, and that would have resulted in stagnation. Society (to personify social law in that term as by "Nature" we personify natural law) pursued its own massive interests by letting the socially fit attain their reward. Careers have always been open to talent; enterprise exhibited in the food-quest or in war or in the acquisition of property has had its reward; eminence in magic and religion has been acquired by study and inventiveness. All this has come out in the case of the chief

1 §§101-104, above.

and will appear in that of the medicine-man;[2] and a review of the societies, clubs, and initiations has taught that these have operated to secure an incessant selection in favor of ability. That the selection has been made at times upon the basis of criteria which we should not consider to be proper does not invalidate the general sense of that selection.

Rivers[3] finds the typical example of class to rest upon kinship with a chief. "Wherever we find the institution of hereditary chieftainship or kingship, we find also that all the relatives of the chief or king have a privileged position. They are distinguished from other members of the society by special honorific names or prefixes, and have customs peculiar to themselves. The most convenient term for such a group is 'noble,' and this term may also be used for those who have a similar privileged position, even though they are not related to the chief or king. Such a group forms the most characteristic example of a class. . . . In the Hawaiian Islands the highest kind of noble is one who is the offspring of a union between own brother and sister of the noble class, whose parents were again own brother and sister." This effort to keep the noble blood untainted will be encountered in considering so-called "royal incest."[4] Again, "in the case of the priesthood we have a definite form of social grouping, in which certain members of the community form a group marked off from the rest by social functions connected with religion." There is a "distinction between religion and magic, between the priest, whose social functions are to bring men into relation with the gods or other higher powers, on the one hand, and the sorcerer whose social, or perhaps more correctly, antisocial function it is to bring disease and death upon members of the community. In many cases there is a sharp distinction between the two, but intermediate gradations are numerous." Here we have two sets of classes emanating respectively from the two outstanding functionaries in primitive society. Other classes form about other nuclei than the political and the religious; there are those which rest upon differentiation in economic function and in wealth; but in the early stages of society's evolution they are

2 §§312, 320, below.
3 *Soc. Org.*, 143-144, 145-146; §232, below.
4 §348, below.

less strikingly represented. There will now be passed in review some representative instances of class-stratification, not including except incidentally cases of enslavement.

Finsch[5] mentions the Papuan inhabitants of a rich island who are "the patricians of Astrolabe Bay," who often had to fight to retain their position. In Melanesia, there are many stages of rank, all of which have to be purchased. In the Banks Islands there are eighteen steps and "ovens," the latter term having reference to the initiatory feasts. The degrees have their particular emblems and often special costumes; the highest stages are very rarely reached. Within the Melanesian settlement, "the higher the house-mound, the higher its occupant's rank," and the expression "their house-mound is high" means that a family is of lofty social position.[6] In the New Hebrides there are four classes, and no one of them may eat with the others or cook at the same fire. To rise a degree a man sets up a carved and painted fern-tree, kills from two to ten pigs, and assumes a new name.[7]

In Bechuanaland society may be said to consist of four grades beneath the chief. "The rich men—sons of chiefs or counsellors—generally of the chief's family, live in the native towns and possess herds of oxen, mealie fields cultivated by their retainers, and wagons driven by their servants. Beneath them comes the agricultural population, also living in the town, engaging in trade and in native manufacture. The herdsmen, who keep the herds at the cattle posts, are again a lower class, and the poorest are the . . . nomadic hunters . . . considered in the light of serfs of the chief," and in many ways similar to the Bushmen.[8]

On the Gold Coast there is, at the top of the "Houses," the king, who may, strangely enough, be a slave; the free relatives of the king if he is free or the free members of the family for which he is trustee; the free petty people, clients of the house and protected by it; the slave "trade-boys"; the slave "pull-away boys" and plantation-hands. The best point about the system, says Miss Kingsley,[9] is that the poorest boy who paddles an oil-canoe may become king. "A House, in native parlance, meant a number of petty chiefs congregated together for mutual protection, owning allegiance generally to the richest and most intelligent one amongst them, whom they called their father, and the Europeans called a chief. A House could be formed as Oko Jumbo formed his. He was a bought slave, yet by superior intelligence and industry, he amassed, in early life, great wealth, was able to buy numerous slaves, some of whom showed similar aptitude to himself, to whom he showed the same encouragement that his master had shown him, and allowed them to trade on their own account. These men in their turn bought slaves, and allowed them similar privileges. This kind of evolution went on with uninterrupted success until Oko Jumbo, after 20 years' trading, found himself at the head of five or six hundred slaves; for, according to country law, all the slaves bought by his favored slaves (now become petty chiefs or head boys) belonged to him as he belonged to Manilla Pepple (the King); but owing to his accumulated riches and

5 *Samoafahrten,* 81.
6 Codrington, *Melanesians,* 103-105, 48 note.
7 Leggatt, in AAAS, 1892, 705, 706.   8 Conder, in JAI, XVI, 89.
9 *W. Afr. Studies,* 426, 427, 522, 523.

numerous followers he was beginning to take rank as a chief and head of a House. One must not think that the assistance given by an owner of slaves to here and there one is all pure philanthropy; it is nothing of the kind, for every hundred pounds' worth of trade the slave does on his own account nowadays means 25 pounds into the coffers of his master." In Benin, "the sign of nobility and also of office was a coral necklace placed round the recipient's neck by the king himself, sometimes with great solemnity, at a festival called the coral feast: to lose this necklace was death. Coral was highly valued, and a man's rank seems to have been in proportion to the amount he was allowed to crowd upon his person."[10]

In the East Indies the villagers' equality was broken by the hereditary chieftainship; around the ruler developed a class of nobility, who are called by terms meaning "rich man." The author[11] cites examples from many parts of the Archipelago. A burgher-class appears in the Javanese *dessa* or village; these are almost a separate people, and even among them there exists a distinction equivalent to a class-distinction, between the aristocracy of wealth and the poor. "Almost nowhere is found the idyllic equality of which some dream." There are the slaves and pawns at the bottom and the aristocracy of fortunate and preferred families above. In Celebes there are the highest nobility and then a lesser rank, including the war-leaders; the common free people, the heads of whose kin-groups have a voice in the assembly, and the slaves. For offenses there is a tariff which shows the class-rating: the killing of a male slave, female slave, free man, free woman, and nobleman rate in the proportion of 20, 30, 30, 40, and 80.[12]

The Polynesians are socially divided into something approximating castes, with a great deal of ceremonial between them which educates them in false pretense. In Tonga there are the following classes: royal family, chiefs, landowners, servants of nobles, common people. Many handicrafts are heritable and honorable. Barbers, cooks, and field-hands are in the lowest stratum. The Polynesian ranks are divided off by means of the taboo more sharply than they are elsewhere by a stringent caste-system; they are distinguished as having a share or no share in the divine things. There is an intense aristocracy. For the lowest classes death is the end, while the higher enter into or remain in permanent relations to the gods. The ranks of chief, freeman, and slave are universal throughout Polynesia, and the nobility hold the offices of the state. The highly developed despotism of Polynesia rested more upon the pressure of classes and castes than on the preponderant will of an individual. This is why despotism has such deep influence. Good judges ascribe to despotism the effects that the people despised life, that their industry and enterprise were broken, that they were indifferent to the future, that it was hard for them to go over to freer relationships—all of which induced rapid decline.[13]

Among the Natchez Indians the established distinctions were as follows: "The Suns, relatives of the Great Sun, held the highest rank; next came the Nobles; after them the Honorables; and last of all the common people, who were very much despised."[14] "All the tribes of the Pacific Coast are divided

---

[10] Read and Dalton, in JAI, XXVII, 368.
[11] Wilken, *Vkde.*, 396-398, 406, 418 ff.; Wilken, in VG, I, 460.
[12] Riedel, in Bijd., XXXV, 82; Ratzel, *Vkde.*, II, 452.
[13] Ratzel, *Vkde.*, II, 121, 193, 194, 197.
[14] Yarrow, in BAE, I, 189.

into a nobility, common people, and slaves. . . . The individuals personating the ancestors form the nobility of the tribe. The number of noblemen is therefore fixed. They are not equal in rank, but range in the manner in which their ancestors were supposed to range."[15] In Brazilian tribes there are found two classes or castes: free warriors and nobility. "These nobler and more powerful families jealously maintain a sort of primacy among the people, preferably by marriage of their members with one another."[16] In Paraguay there are three classes: hereditary chiefs or nobility, warriors or common people, and slaves. The nobility cover the family or kin of the chief and inherit in the female line, so that the child of a noble woman by a commoner or even a slave is noble.[17]

It is not necessary to follow social stratification into its more developed phases. It is said of the Greeks and Romans that they speak only of the higher classes; "the life of the poorer strata of the population, which is only a struggle to win the most essential necessaries of life, remains the same in all ages in its external phenomena."[18] It is significant that even the graves that are preserved are those of the better-placed classes, the simpler tombs of the lower having disappeared.[19]

§165*. Caste. The extreme of social classification is found in the caste, and the classic land of caste is India. The Portuguese, who were the first to trade directly with India used the word "casta," meaning "race," to denote the infinite number of classes into which Indian society was divided.[20] "The Sanskrit word for caste is *varna*, that is, 'colour'; and this shows how their distinction of high and low caste arose."[21] Whatever its origin, in practice "caste is merely a name for a trade or occupation, and the sole tangible effect of the Brahminical theory is that it creates a religious sanction for what is really a primitive and natural distribution of classes."[22] That which makes caste so powerful and inescapable is this religious sanction and the many taboos that go with it. It is contended that "castes have their place only in a finished and strongly-knit state. Only in this case can the necessary control be practised and the right and effective rules in case of an infringement of the institution be adopted."[23]

"Two of the special features of the caste-system of India . . . are its highly organized character, and the association of endogamy with occupation. Another feature is that the castes, thus segregated from one another by endogamy and occupation, are arranged in a hierarchical series, with the more or less

[15] Boas, in USNM, 1895, 338-339. [16] Von Martius, *Beiträge*, I, 72.
[17] Koch, in *Globus*, LXXXI, 44.
[18] Guhl and Koner, *Gr. and Rom.*, 236.
[19] Worsaae, *Nordens Forhist.*, 75.
[20] Monier-Williams, *Brāhmanism*, 452. [21] Tylor, *Anth.*, 69.
[22] Maine, *Vill. Comm.*, 57. [23] Geiger, *Ostiran. Kult.*, 486, note.

sacred caste of the Brahmins at their head. Still another feature is that this hierarchical arrangement is associated with rules of avoidance of various kinds, and also with regulations of other kinds concerning the relations to one another of the different castes. These rules are especially definite in relation to food. . . . Another group of rules of avoidance apply to personal contact. These rules have been especially developed in Malabar, where the order of precedence receives a quantitative character in terms of distance which members of various castes must keep from a Brahmin." Examples are given. "The four main features of the caste-system are, therefore, endogamy, hereditary occupation, hierarchical character, and rules of avoidance between different members of the hierarchy, especially in relation to food and contact. . . . Another noteworthy feature of the caste-system is that most of the larger bodies, such as the Brahmins, which are usually regarded as castes, are really groups of castes, and these groups may be very numerous. . . . One feature of the caste-system which may be mentioned is that it is continually growing by the inclusion within it of tribes which once stood without the system." The author notes that the caste-system affords an exception to the usual result when the political and religious systems come into collision. "One of the outstanding features of the history of human society is the frequent occurrence, at one stage or another, of a struggle between the ecclesiastical and civil powers, between the political and religious forms of social grouping. In advanced civilizations other than that of India, the civil power has in general gained the mastery; but caste seems to provide a case where this mastery has fallen to the religious side, a grouping primarily religious having acquired functions which elsewhere fall to the lot of groups of a political order."[24]

"When the creator made man and divided them into four colors, then he assigned to each the conduct that should be proper to him: to the Brahmans the care of sacrifice; to the Kshatriyas the duty of fighting; to the Vaisyas unresting diligence; to the Sudras subjection.[25] Here we have the priestly, the military, the industrial, and the slave classes. The first must study and teach; the second protect; the third tend to the beasts, till the earth, trade, and lend money; the fourth serve the other three. Significantly enough, while in a marriage of persons of equal caste the hands are joined, if a Kshatriya woman marry a man of higher caste she must take hold of an arrow, while a Vaisya bride must hold to a goad, and a Sudra to the hem of the man's garment. The man in each case takes hold of the other end of the arrow, goad, or hem and recites texts as in the case of a marriage between equal castes.[26] The occupational nature of the castes is evident.

It is impossible to rehearse the minute regulations of the system, but some of them may be summarized as follows: "It has for infancy, pupilage, and manhood its ordained methods of sucking, sipping, drinking, and eating; of washing, anointing; of clothing and ornamenting the body; of sitting, rising, reclining; of moving, visiting, travelling; of speaking, reading, listening, and reciting; and of meditating, singing, working, and fighting. It has its laws for social and religious rights, privileges and occupations; for education, duty, religious service; for errors, sins, transgressions; for intercommunion, avoidance, and excommunication; for defilement and purification; for fines and

[24] Rivers, *Soc. Org.*, 152-154, 156.
[25] Holtzmann, *Ind. Sagen*, I, 181 (from the Mahabharata).
[26] Bühler, *Manu*, III, 43, 44, and note 44.

other punishments. It unfolds the ways of committing what it calls sins, accumulating sin, and of putting away sin; of acquiring, dispensing, and losing merit. It treats of inheritance, conveyance, possession, and dispossession of property; and of bargains, gains, loss, and ruin. It deals with death, burial, and burning; and with commemoration, assistance, and injury after death. . . . The authority of caste rests partly on written laws, partly on legendary fables and narratives, partly on the injunctions of instructors and priests, partly on custom and usage, and partly on the caprice and convenience of its votaries." Most of the castes have peculiar marks which those initiated have to wear, but one is common. "The great index of Hinduism is the tuft of hair on the crown of the head which is left there on the performance of the sacrament of tonsure, on the first and third year after birth in the case of the three great classes of the Hindus." By this tuft, according to the popular notion, the wearer is raised to heaven. 'Each caste has its *dal*, or committee, presided over by its dalapati, or president, to whose judgment the members are bound to submit; and when any violation of the rules of the caste are reported against a member, the dal considers the matter, and, if it is proved, sentence is pronounced; and this punishment must either be endured, or the delinquent is put out of the caste, *i.e.*, the members 'boycott' him. They will neither visit nor eat with him; nor will they allow their sons to intermarry with his family. The punishment of this social ostracism is most severe. . . . The Hindu community found that by outcasteing those who had been bold enough to go to England to qualify for good positions in their own country, they were casting off the men who were throwing the brightest lustre upon their nation, and therefore a way was soon made by which they could be retained. With the exception of a very few of the more orthodox dals, Hindus may do almost anything they wish except receive Christian baptism. . . . In India every man is, more or less, religious; and even when his moral life may be bad, his observance of caste rules and religious rites and ceremonies is generally most strict. Men who can scarcely count beyond twenty, and know not the letters of the alphabet, would die rather than eat food which had been prepared by men of lower caste, unless it had been sanctified by being offered to an idol; and would kill their daughters rather than endure the disgrace of having unmarried girls at home beyond twelve or thirteen years of age. Every year thousands perish of disease that might recover if they would take proper nourishment, and drink the medicine that science prescribes, but which they imagine their religion forbids them to touch. . . . To eat rice with a man is to acknowledge equality of caste."[27]

Some class-divisions are cruder and less evolved; the Saoras say that "all Saoras are one" but they recognize as occupational divisions cultivators, weavers of coarse cloths, basket-makers, and iron-workers. A girl of the first class marrying into one of the others, or a girl of any one of the last three marrying into the first, will not, after marriage, eat the flesh of cows or bullocks.[28] Of one wandering tribe of potters it is reported that if a member does anything but make mud figures of men and animals he is dismissed from the caste, and readmitted only by "feasting and kissing the toe of a Brahmin."[29] It is thought by some that the Brahmans throughout India are of two classes:

[27] Wilkins, *Hinduism*, 125-126, 160-162, 299-300, 468.

[28] Fawcett, in JASB, I, 223.   [29] Gunthorpe, in JASB, I, 411.

"more ancient settlers and aboriginal superior natives raised, as tradition generally asserts, to this rank."[30]

Ceylon really belongs with India in this matter of caste, but the system was not so extreme or rigid under Buddhism as under Brahmanism. Yet it could happen that a Singhalese "still almost a boy, could stab to the heart an older sister because she, against the caste-taboo, was about to contract matrimony before the registry with an honorable man of somewhat lower caste; as the murderer a few weeks later mounted the scaffold, he still loudly acclaimed his own deed, through which he had saved the honor of his family."[31]

Class-distinctions elsewhere in the world have approached the extremes of India. For instance, among the Guanches, aboriginal inhabitants of the Canary Islands, there were several castes; alliance with the royal family, bravery, and fortune were the titles to nobility.[32] "Class distinctions were closely preserved in Teneriffe, and there were clearly specialized occupations corresponding to them. Nobles were farmers and the owners of flocks; potters dwelt in the hillside caves; tailors cut skin garments with stone knives; carpenters were characterized as *limpios en su traje* [clean of costume]; cleaners and embalmers of dead bodies and also butchers constituted the scum of society. Even criminals objected to associating with these last in prison, therefore their misdemeanors were tried at once and punished immediately by whipping in the court of justice. A follower of this trade could make known his wants only by pointing to the articles required, for his touch carried pollution—an ostracism which is continued to this day in a somewhat modified degree. Executioners were likewise execrated here as on the other islands. . . . Besides the chiefs there was a governing assembly of not fewer than 100 nor more than 200 warriors who preserved the religious rites and secrets. When five or six had died, successors were chosen from among men who had never contracted alliance with inferiors, and these were confirmed by the *faycan* [priest]. The aspirant to nobility must be the descendant of a noble, the possessor of flocks, and physically able to carry arms. On the day appointed, he appeared before the warriors with his hair flowing over his shoulders. The *faycan* said: 'All you who hear me, I conjure you in the name of God, to declare if you have ever seen such and such a one, the son of such and such a one, enter into a slaughter house to take or to kill goats, if you have seen him prepare his repast with his own hands, commit rapine in time of peace, or show disloyalty or insolence in word or action, especially toward women,' If no one condemned the young man, the *faycan* cut his hair over his ears and a little above his shoulders, and armed him with a javelin; his beard was allowed to grow and he was noble. If anyone testified against him, his hair was shaved and he became plebeian for life."[33]

One authority[34] regards "castes as a luxury which only rich lands can permit themselves. Only in lands like India and Egypt are castes definitely indicated. . . . Both lands are extremely fruitful and rich in products, so that the cultivator raises upon a

[30] Mateer, in JAI, XII, 298.   [31] Schmidt, *Ceylon,* 263 ff.
[32] De Bethencourt, *Canarien,* 127, note 3.
[33] Cook, in AA, II, 486, 487-488.
[34] Spiegel, *Erân. Alterthumsk.,* III, 546-547.

comparatively small area all that he needs for himself and his; therefore he can give of his superfluity to such as render him other services. But the two countries named have also a very mild climate and thereby it becomes possible to their inhabitants to content themselves with little, for housing and clothing are provided at small cost, while the dwellers in a less favored country must spend large sums upon precisely these things. This ease of life is the precondition upon which, to our way of thinking, the rise of castes depends." Another writer[35] concludes that "race-difference was the first big distinction. When the Aryans pressed down victoriously into the country of the Indus and Ganges, there they assumed position as 'first,' as 'twice-born,' in sharp contrast to the conquered, the 'black-skinned,' the 'goat-nosed.' " Then the Dravidians took over the system from their conquerors, with all its rules about caste-separation in marrying and in eating and its unmerciful expulsion for their infringement. "With such sharp caste-compulsion naturally the development of each individual suffers and a general national consciousness cannot evolve; the high sentiment of belonging to a common, great people is denied to the Hindu."

The caste-system is crumbling under contact with the outside world "and a slow dissolution of it is unmistakably on its way." Rules are broken, as where Brahmans take up agriculture, government service, or trade. Those of high caste are accepting service from low caste persons whose touch is profane to an orthodox Brahman. Unavoidable contact occurs at railway-restaurants and theaters. Infractions are treated capriciously; they may be passed over or they may be used for malicious persecution. Hindu youths go to England and America to learn arts or engineering and to acquire other desirable forms of education, to qualify for civil service and professions, or to learn and introduce processes. Most Hindu castes refuse as yet to break over the old prohibitions, but fine and lay penance on those who go.[36] "The original institution of industrial castes marked a period of social progress, inasmuch as it allowed of a division of work for the common benefit, but in

[35] Schmidt, *Ceylon*, 263 ff.
[36] Gehring, *Süd-Indien*, 58; Nathubhai, in JASB, VI, 353; Collins, *The Moonstone*.

the course of time, through the ascendancy of the agricultural and warrior castes, and the alliance with them of the sacerdotal class, the industrial castes fell into a state of decadence and servitude, from which they are now beginning to emerge, much as the industrial classes did in Europe in the Middle Ages."[37] There are always those who defend such a system; and they have doubtless caught part of the reason for its long persistence under past conditions.

One writer[38] protests against talking of the odiousness of the caste-system, "when it alone has abolished the hateful distinction between rich and poor, the high and low in position, which so characterizes the class distinctions in Europe and has substituted instead the national and professional spirit and assigned the highest rank to learning and piety coupled with the practice of austerities, which take the sting out of the jealousy against the Brahmins, who were rightly the spiritual and intellectual leaders of India, and who should continue as leaders in the altering conditions of the age if the Indian civilization and nationalities are to be preserved. The elasticity and yet solidity of the caste system are . . . scarcely suspected; its high spiritual aim in making everyone proud of his work in life is ignored, and the literature (in a wide sense of the term) ennobling the lowest handicrafts has yet to be brought to notice before Europe will understand how alone the social problems and the questions connected with the general education of the masses can be solved, if the collapse of Western civilization is to be avoided."

Connected loosely with the contempt for a lower caste is the attitude toward pariah races. Perhaps, as suggested above, the origin of caste lay in the relation between conquerors and the despised vanquished who belonged to another race and color. The combination of fear and contempt felt for aboriginal races such as the negritos will be met with under the topic of religion;[39] it must not be lost to sight that the caste-system is shot through with religious notions.

In India itself "there are often traces of conquests by separate races more aboriginal than the Aryan. In village communities in the Deccan, for instance, outcast races are never on one uniform level of inferiority. There are grades of outcasts as well as of the 'twice born.' One grade may not live, or eat with, still less intermarry with the others—the caste which removes skins and buries the dead ox may not intermarry with that which twists the skin into well-ropes, or makes the skin into leather, or the leather into shoes. It seems reasonable to think that each caste marks a separate conquest of some aboriginal tribe, each tribe having had its separate work assigned to it in the organization of the village community."[40]

[37] Dymock, in JASB, II, 15.
[39] §257, below.
[38] Leitner, in JASB, I, 194, 195.
[40] Frere, in JAI, XI, 315.

Elsewhere in the world there are outcast or pariah or accursed groups.
There are the Pygmy Batwa, who are either sedentary potters or nomadic
hunters living in the forest primeval.[41] "Prognathous, long-upper-lipped, short-
legged Negroes" appear in pariah-like condition in Uganda, "dwelling on the
outskirts of native villages, almost destitute of any arts or human accomplishments, living to a great extent on the raw flesh of such creatures as they shot
with arrows or trapped in the forest, and also subsisting partially on wild
honey and bee-grubs."[42] Accursed races in India include tribes of nomadic
robbers.[43] Pariah people in Japan are supposed not to belong to the Japanese
race. "Various tribes of these outcasts followed occupations in the monopoly
of which they were legally confirmed: they were well-diggers, garden-sweepers,
straw-workers, sandal-makers, according to local privileges. One class was
employed officially in the capacity of torturers and executioners; another was
employed as night-watchmen; a third as grave-makers. But most of the Éta
followed the business of tanners and leather-dressers. . . . As professional
singers they were tolerated; but they were forbidden to enter any house—so
they could perform their music or sing their songs only in the street, or in a
garden. Any occupations other than their hereditary callings were strictly
forbidden to them. Between the lowest of the commercial classes and the Éta,
the barrier was impassable as any created by caste-tradition in India; and
never was Ghetto more separated from the rest of a European city by walls
and gates, than an Éta settlement from the rest of a Japanese town by social
prejudice. . . . Besides the Éta proper, there were pariahs called *hinin*,—a
name signifying 'not-human-beings.' Under this appellation were included professional mendicants, wandering minstrels, actors, certain classes of prostitutes, and persons outlawed by society. The *hinin* had their own chiefs, and
their own laws. Any person expelled from a Japanese community might join
the *hinin;* but that signified good-by to the rest of humanity. The Government
was too shrewd to persecute the *hinin*. Their gipsy-existence saved a world of
trouble." Outcasts include also the descendants of Christian converts of the
sixteenth century who were not killed in the seventeenth century persecution.
As late as 1870 they were still held in a kind of ghetto under police surveillance.[44]

Anyone who is not liked is a "child of Ham"; so the Indians were regarded
in 1763.[45] Religious sects have charged each other with monstrous and bloody
secret rites. Accursed races are a common phenomenon, not only among savages, but in the European Middle Ages. Consider the mediæval Jew.[46]

§166*. Plutocracy. In preceding connections it has been seen
that social power and rank have been distributed upon the basis
of sex, age, blood, various personal qualities, occupation, and

[41] Kandt, in *Globus,* LXXXVI, 213.
[42] Johnston, *Uganda,* II, 511, 512; Ratzel, *Hist. Mankind,* II, 494.
[43] Meade, "Moghiahs," in JASB, I, 275.
[44] Hearn, *Japan,* 272-273, 274; Humbert, *Japan,* 287.
[45] Hildreth, *Hist.,* II, 505.
[46] Anon., "Parias," in *Polit.-Anth. Rev.,* I, 981; Lacroix, *Middle Ages,*
434 ff.; Pigeonneau, *Commerce,* I, 104, 127, 350.

other criteria. Incidentally it has appeared that wealth was correlative with social position and political influence; that correlation has not yet been stressed. Among primitive peoples wealth is perhaps more likely to be a result of power than power of wealth; it is unprofitable to try to fix upon precise distinctions of cause and effect in the matter. It might be reiterated that until a man can hold what he has as a monopoly, by virtue of societal taboos which restrain others from taking it away, he cannot very well utilize it to acquire social standing.[47] In a number of cases a high position is won by a person of small possessions by reason of his parentage or bravery or efficiency; in not a few the chief himself is poor when he becomes chief; and in some he stays poor, whatever his income, because of the requirements of hospitality and generosity. It is therefore not correct to say even that wealth and political power are indissolubly connected. Yet the instances where a man has to buy himself whatever social position he gets, for instance membership in a secret society, or where he can retain his status only by repeated gifts, or where he descends into slavery by reason of debt, are already before us in sufficient number to demonstrate the power of wealth in the primitive system.

Plutocracy is the social prestige, dignity, honor, precedence, or authority that is conceded to men in society because they possess wealth. An accumulation of ornaments, amulets, and other forms of property enables its owner to get a wife and an establishment to start with; then to win friends, the favor of the great, the envy of the lowly. Thus the great become greater and the small smaller. The chief, even though at first merely the war-leader, needs resources; and he steals, plunders, levies, takes taxes or tribute, exacts fines as penalties, and receives gifts in return for the conferring of immunity or positive social prerogative.[48] Plutocracy has been held in check by aristocracy of birth, though the aristocrats do not normally renounce their opportunity of becoming rich; and in its modern phase it has used democracy to ruin aristocracy. Democracy, as the power of the day, threatens capital which, on the defensive, reaches out toward plutocracy.[49]

[47] §155, above.
[48] Schurz, in *Deut. Geog. Blätter*, XX.
[49] Sumner, "Democ. and Plutoc.," in *Coll. Ess.*, II, 283 ff.

Only the germs of such complexities engage attention here, for our inquiry centers upon the question as to how far the possession of wealth has been effective to secure social power upon the more primitive stages. It will be found, among other things, that those who yearn back toward the days of "primitive innocence" or "the good old times" can find about as little justification for their dreams here as anywhere else. Dr. Johnson[50] was stating a universal when he remarked that money "confounds subordination, by over-powering the distinctions of rank and birth, and weakens authority by supplying powers of resistance or expedients for escape."

In Melanesia "poverty is a sin and property lends distinction . . . if any-one wants to marry without, however, being in possession of the required purchase-price, his chief makes the necessary advance while the young hus-band is obliged, until he can repay it, to do certain labors for his creditor, even entering into a certain relation with the latter as with an owner. In this manner the chief gains not only high interest for capital advanced but also influence over his debtors and, through them, over the village-members as a whole." These Papuans are mercenary to a degree. "Only with resistance does the Kanaka separate himself from his money. . . . Every and each thing is cheap beside shell-money. Every movable possession, wife and daughters, are purchasable for dewarra; every transgression can be atoned for by it; he will-ingly commits any crime if only the amount of dewarra in prospect seems to him sufficient. . . . If at the death of a rich man much dewarra has been divided by the heir, he has the right to proclaim a great taboo. During three months the receivers of [the divided] dewarra may not destroy anything, not even break off a branch or turn over earth. Thus they may not participate in gardening or harvesting but must have these labors done by others. After the expiration of the appointed time for the taboo each one on whom it rested must buy himself free, so that the original divider of dewarra [the heir] attains in the end a restitution of his outlay."[51]

In general in Melanesia social advancement is bought with shell-money. The monied man has power because his debtors are under his thumb, and by his privilege of imposing a loan he can hold rising men under.[52] Again, a father of a circumcized youth must celebrate by a feast for his friends; but this expense prevents the children of the poor from being circumcized—and the term "uncircumcized" is equivalent to "lout."[53] In New Britain there are mil-lionaires among the naked savages, "and each bestirs himself to become one, for as with us riches create distinction and a certain power. Dewarra is much more potent than money with us. With dewarra one can . . . attain every-thing: atone for adultery, blood-guilt, and murder; feuds are mostly composed with dewarra and in it is paid the war-indemnity of the defeated party. . . . For the murder of a common man usually fifty strings (about a hundred marks) are paid; without dewarra no one can get a wife. Older boys therefore

50 Quoted from "Tour in the Western Islands," in Garnier, *Brit. Peas.*, 71.
51 Von Pfeil, *Südsee*, 30, 33, 68-69, 81.
52 Codrington, *Melanesians*, 327.   53 Andree, *Ethnog. Parallelen*, 197.

are already eagerly saving for their future mates whose price, according to the rank of their parents, amounts to fifty to a hundred strings and more. . . . Dewarra is, like securities with us, subject to fluctuations in value and, what is still more surprising, is an object of usury. The noble 'savages' already understand, that is, about lending dewarra at interest, which best illustrates the significance of it. The value of the dewarra has, moreover, suffered no kind of diminution by reason of the imported articles of exchange."[54] In the New Hebrides the departed rank in the spirit-world according to the number of pigs they bring with them.[55]

"The ideal of the Kaffir, the object for which he has enthusiasm and which he likes best to sing about in his songs, are his oxen, that is, his most valuable possession.[56] The Herero starve themselves rather than kill any of their cattle,[57] acting like misers with their coins. "Sons who leave the paternal roof to pursue riches are one of the commonest phenomena in the life of the natives."[58] Among the herders of southeast Africa the man who has no cattle belongs to the lower class, however much grain he has; for only cattle will buy anything beyond what supplies immediate wants. Only he who has cattle can woo a wife, offer sacrifices, heal diseases, or attend funerals.[59]

In West Africa, wealth can be substituted at a funeral for a human victim, but "without slaves, wives, and funds, how can the dead soul you care for speak with the weight of testimony of men as to its resting place or position?" The wealth a dead man brings with him determines the sort of baby into which he is to be reincarnated. If a man has some wealth, he is subject to extortion and persecution; if much, to the envy and cupidity of the chief. "There is nothing that ensures a man an unblemished character in West Africa except the possession of sufficient power to make it risky for people to cast slurs."[60] This is the reverse side to the possession of wealth held without sufficient guarantees.

Indians of Labrador are thrown into direst confusion by the owl, and "hastily suspend some unworn garment, that the bird, perceiving it, may thus know that the people are not so poor" as the spirit he represents may think; for that spirit only annoys people who are too poor to have extra garments.[61] Of wampum Lawson[62] writes: "This is the money with which you may buy skins, furs, slaves, or anything the Indians have; it being the mammon (as our money is to us) that entices and persuades them to do anything and part with everything they possess except their children for slaves. As for their wives, they are often sold, and their daughters violated for it. With this they buy off murders; and whatsoever a man can do that is ill, this wampum will quit him of and make him, in their opinion, good and virtuous, though never so black before." The Missouri tribesman purchased his advance in the groups of men classed by age.[63] In the East some tribes fall into three classes, corresponding to the aristocracy, middle class, and poor of civilized nations: the first are the richest, the last the poorest.[64] The Indians of the Northwest

[54] Finsch, *Ethnol. Erfahr.*, I, 94, 95.
[55] Leggatt, in AAAS, 1892, 701.
[56] Fritsch, *Eingeb. S.-Afr.*, 50.
[57] Büttner, *Walfischbai*, 22.
[58] Haarhoff, *Bantu-Stämme*, 26.
[59] Ratzel, *Hist. Mankind*, II, 414.
[60] Kingsley, *W. Afr. Studies*, 146; *Travels W. Afr.*, 491, 497.
[61] Turner, in BAE, XI, 273.
[62] *Hist. Carolina*, 316-317.
[63] Ratzel, *Hist. Mankind*, II, 134.
[64] Kirby, in *Smithson. Rep.*, 1864, 418.

allowed all crimes, offenses, and improprieties to be bought off by money; the Russians were able to ransom even slaves destined for sacrifice. A woman who earned the greatest number of blankets or the most money by prostitution won admiration for herself and a high social position for her husband.[65] A recent name of honor adopted by one tribe, as a substitute for their former designation, is "The Rich Ones."[66]

The tribes that practise the potlatch accord great social influence to the wealthy who make distributions at festivals. "Wealth is here just as important as in any civilized community." Distinctions in houses, dress, and the rest are sedulously emphasized. "All ranks of their aristocracy are to be reached by especial generosity"; and the cost of initiation into the religious secret societies keeps out all but the wealthy. In California the chieftainship is hereditary only if the son has also inherited his predecessor's wealth; a richer man may readily be set in the place of a poorer chief.[67] "Probably there are no other Indians in California so avaricious as those of Del Norte County. Money makes the chief among them, and he is entitled to that honor who possesses the most *al-li-ko-chik*. No matter how high may be the intellectual and moral worthiness of the reigning chief, let the lowest vagabond of the tribe win his money from him in a game of 'guessing the sticks' (now a game of cards), and retain it a certain number of days, and he practically succeeds to the chieftainship. Even a child is not named for life until it has grown old enough to assert its nameworthiness by winning or otherwise acquiring money. An old Indian often accumulates great stores of shell-money, which he hoards up with a miserliness equal to anything recorded of his pale brethren; when on his death bed, he makes a nuncupative [or oral] will, and solemnly enjoins upon his relatives to see that his riches are divided according to his bequest. Takhokolli, the tatterdemalion chief of the Tataten, refused even to count ten in his language unless paid for it."[68]

The Avesta holds that "he who has property is far above him who has none."[69] The distinction between poor and rich is accentuated in Homer.[70] Generosity with one's wealth is the admirable thing among the Arabs, and accumulation is the constant object in life.[71] In the Scandinavian Valhalla the shades take rank according to the wealth they bring with them; this doctrine was a cause for the Viking raids. The getting of gold was about as strong a motive as love of fighting. It was not well to go to Odin poor. Gold is represented in the sagas as the cause of greed and evil; consider the Nibelungen story. In early Norse history there were fines for failing to attend the Althing, with disfranchisement for those who could not pay.[72] The old Irish had to provide against men becoming rich by frequent marriages.[73] Among some of the Slavs "'godhood' and 'wealth' are originally logically one and the same thing."[74]

The debt-relation is readily transmuted into the social range. Two hundred years ago "the people of rural Connecticut, being generally indebted to the

[65] Niblack, in USNM, 1888, 240, 347.   [66] Boas, in USNM, 1895, 333.

[67] Bancroft, *Nat. Races,* I, 123, 132, 160, 183, 191, 194, 211, 347, 348.

[68] Powers, in *Contrib. N. Amer. Ethnol.,* III, 66, 67.

[69] Müller, *Sacred Books of East,* IV; *Zend-Avesta,* I, 46.

[70] Keller, *Hom. Soc.,* 97.   [71] Burckhardt, *Bedouin,* 39, 104.

[72] Geijer, *Svensk. Hist.,* 82; Finsen, in *Annaler,* 1849, 170.

[73] Gomme, *Village Life,* 205.   [74] Krauss, *Sreća,* 37.

country traders, deferred much to them, and often stood speechless in a store until asked what they wanted."[75]

There is no point in carrying the illustration of plutocracy down into history. To be noted here is that wealth has been a factor of great significance, though not an original one like bodily strength, in the formation of social classes and in the distribution of political power and influence. If it can secure social standing not only in this life but in the life to come, it is no wonder that men struggle for it both zealously and ruthlessly. The foregoing examples reinforce those cited in a former connection[76] in demonstrating the power of capital in societal life. In whatever particulars it benefits a man, it still works out into prestige and so into prerogative. One may purchase rank or office directly, or he may be elevated to a position of power because men owe him money or because he has, so to speak, "retained" spiritual agencies by liberal sacrifice. Inequality is confirmed after security of private property-tenure has been evolved and accumulation has become possible; equality exists, if at all, at zero.

Nevertheless, as some examples have shown, there develops a feeling that a man can become too rich for the good of the community; and there is often a plain antagonism between political authority and the threatening influence of the wealthy. The rich may be persecuted as were the Jews in the not very distant past. The chief is often in a position to increase his own holdings by using his official power against the prosperous. Not infrequently will the wealthy man hide his possessions or dissimulate his fortune in self-protection.

"A native trader of Porto Novo, named Todjinu, whose wealth had excited the avarice of the king, was compelled to undergo the ordeal (of being thrown into the water), and, being an unusually powerful man, was able to struggle to the shore. The priests and the king were naturally dissatisfied with this result, and a little later Todjinu was again compelled to submit to the ordeal to clear himself from a trumped-up charge of treason; this time the priests caused him first to drink a potion they had prepared, and he was drowned without a struggle. This was what was required: the *vodu* had killed him, he was consequently guilty, and his property was confiscated. The accused is ordinarily taken to the middle of the creek in a canoe, and then thrown into the water. If he should be drowned, the body is exposed next day on a raft near the bank, it being placed there, say the priests, by the god. . . . In

[75] Weeden, *New England,* I, 411.   [76] §§80, 81, 83, above.

Dahomi it is dangerous to make any show of affluence, for before long some pretext for a palaver will be surely found, and the injudicious person who has paraded his wealth will find his property confiscated and himself reduced to poverty, if indeed he should escape being sold as a slave. . . . To facilitate extortion, arbitrary regulations are suddenly made and published in the capital . . . and officers despatched to all parts of the kingdom to seize and fine people for breaches of them. In vain a man might urge that he had heard nothing of the new regulations, and that they had never been proclaimed in his district, for ignorance of the law is no defence. One favorite mode is for the king to send a messenger to one of the trading establishments . . . to buy for him a particular kind of cotton goods. According to law, that is, the king's will, by the very fact of this purchase having been made for the king, an embargo is laid upon all cotton goods of the same pattern or kind, and no one may buy or wear such. Usually a kind much in vogue is selected, and as the establishment of the embargo is never proclaimed, numbers of people render themselves liable to fine or confiscation by continuing to wear cloths of that description."77 "When a West African kinglet decides that a chief is getting too rich, and hence too powerful, he calls his more immediate supporters together, and they discuss the means that are to be used to compass the doomed one's fall. If he be a man of mettle, with many sub-chiefs and aspiring trade boys, the system resorted to is to trump up charges against him of breaches of agreement as to prices paid by him or his people in the Ibo markets for produce, and fine him heavily. If he pays without murmuring, they let him alone for a time; but very soon another case is brought up against him. . . . After repetition of this sort of thing, the doomed one would refuse to pay, then the king would come down on him for disregarding the orders of himself and his chiefs; fine would follow fine, until the man lost his head and did some rash act which assisted his enemies to more certainly bring about his ruin. Or he gathers all his wives and children about him, together with his most trusted followers and slaves, and any of his family who are willing to follow him into the next world, lays a double tier of kegs of gunpowder on the floor of the principal room in his dwelling-house and knocks in the heads of the top tier of kegs. Placing all his people on this funeral pile, he seats himself in the middle with a fire-stick in his hand, then sends a message to the king and chiefs to come and fetch the fines they have imposed on him. The king and chiefs generally are shrewd enough to guess the meaning of this, and took good care not to go too near, stopping at a convenient distance to parley with him by means of messengers. The victim, finding that there was no chance of destroying his persecutors, would plunge the fire-stick into the nearest keg, and the next moment all were blown to pieces."78 "If a woman by diligence and industry arrives at a position of well-being that distinguishes her among her neighbors, she is accused of doing business with the help of the *fetissero*, and must subject herself then to the ordeal of *cassa*-eating."79 "Woe unto those that join house unto house, that lay field unto field, till there be no place, that ye may be placed alone in the midst of the earth."80

This sort of attitude toward the well-to-do needs little illustration, for resentment and envy of the "Haves" will always be with the "Have-nots," even

77 Ellis, *Ewe,* 85-86, 170-171.
78 Kingsley, *W. Afr. Studies,* 494, 495.
79 Bastian, *Deut. Exped.,* I, 159.   80 Isaiah, V, 8.

when the latter are paying adulation to the former. There is often considerable sense in the form taken by this antagonism. Weissenberg[81] mentions a Russian-Jewish practice which he says has had an undeservedly bad reputation. "If anyone belonging to a propertied family dies, only then can they go forward to the burial when the family has guaranteed a certain contribution for purposes of general welfare. The size of the contribution is fixed by the community and is in inverse proportion to the humanitarianism of the deceased or the survivors: the better the reputation of the family, the less is commonly demanded. If a rich *paterfamilias* dies, who all his life has done nothing for the community, he is not buried for less than several thousand rubles. But it would be false to call this reckoning with the dead an extortion; for the motives to such action are actually of the most praiseworthy nature. It is a sort of self-defense on the part of a community that is left to itself in respect to its social and cultural arrangements. For there, where the government does not concern itself with a certain block of population and leaves it to itself, a prosperous progress for that section is possible only if the rich concern themselves with its well-being. If they do not do that, they sin against the community, and guilt demands atonement. Unfortunately the Jewish community can now punish their antisocial and antinational members only after death, and justice demands the assertion that only seldom is the prerogative in this respect abused."

To a sketch of the social effects of wealth there may be added a word about poverty. As has been noted elsewhere, poverty, being present as an original factor, does not need to be explained. It is wealth that needs the explanation. Among primitive peoples beggar-classes seldom appear. Of the Kaffirs we are told that "few mendicants are found among the natives."[82] In one part of Tibet "there were no evidences of severe poverty, and not one beggar was seen."[83] Probably among the primitive folk there are fewer defectives because the weakly perish early under the unrelieved conditions of the struggle for existence. Furthermore, up till later times production remained personal and direct, even though pursued family-wise, and there was no unemployment-problem. It is only upon the more developed stages, as in China, that mendicancy becomes a profession, and is even recognized as such by the state.[84]

"Beggars swarm, and gifts to them are of the nature of an insurance. In the cities the beggars are organized into powerful guilds, more powerful, in fact, than any that can be raised against them, since they have nothing to lose and nothing to fear. If a shopkeeper should refuse a donation to a stalwart beggar, after due waiting and beseeching, he would be liable to an invasion by a famished horde, who would make his life a burden and prevent any business

[81] In *Globus*, XCI, 360.   [82] Tyler, in *Illust. Afr.*, Dec., 1895.
[83] Bishop, *Tibetans*, 97.
[84] De Groot, *Kongsiwezen*, 108-109, note.

until their demands should be satisfied. This is well understood, and beggars and shopkeepers act accordingly."[85]

There is not much room for this sort of thing among the savages. A man can become a slave, or he can attach himself as a sort of retainer to the powerful; but to be a free man and a beggar is pretty much out of the question. The case is not unlike that of prostitution: there are really scarcely any professional prostitutes; woman's destiny is to be married, and the premarital license, or wife-lending, or even the sojourn of girls in the men's houses is quite different from prostitution as we understand it. Religious mendicancy and temple-harlotry are probably the closest approaches to what we consider as beggary and prostitution. The circumstances of primitive life do not allow of the specialized development of these occupations.

There are measures for relieving those who are losing out in the struggle, even among the savages. Sharing or communalism[86] is one of them; hospitality another. Then there are some special arrangements that deserve illustration.

The Indians sometimes had storehouses for the relief of the needy; there was a "begging dance" that was staged by the Indians of the Plains, and the Cherokees had something like it.[87] The Sacs and Foxes had a ceremony known as "Smoking Horses" by which those who had no horses got them. Catlin[88] describes the scene. "The Foxes, who were making up a war-party to go against the Sioux, and had not suitable horses enough by twenty, had sent word to the Sacs the day before (according to an ancient custom) that they were coming on that day, at a certain hour, to *smoke* that number of horses, and they must not fail to have them ready. On that day and at the hour the twenty young men who were beggers for horses were on the spot, and seated themselves on the ground in a circle, where they went to smoking. The villagers flocked around them in a dense crowd, and soon after appeared on the prairie, at half a mile distance, an equal number of young men of the Sac tribe, who had agreed each to give a horse, and who were then galloping them about at full speed, and gradually, as they went around in a circuit, coming in nearer to the center, until they were at last close around the ring of young fellows seated on the ground. Whilst dashing about thus, each one, with a heavy whip in his hand, as he came within reach of the group on the ground, selected the one to whom he decided to present his horse, and, as he passed him, gave him the most tremendous cut with his lash over his naked shoulders; and as he darted around again he plied the whip as before, and again and again with a violent crack, until the blood could be seen trickling down over his naked

[85] Smith, *Chinese Char.*, 191.   [86] §§114, 128, above.
[87] Carr, in *Smithson. Rep.*, 1891, 527; Bancroft, *Nat. Races*, II, 597.
[88] Quoted by Donaldson, in *Smithson. Rep.*, 1885, pt. II, 323.

shoulders, upon which he instantly dismounted and placed the bridle and whip in his hands, saying, 'Here, you are a beggar; I present you a horse, but you will carry my mark on your back.' In this manner they were all in a little time whipped up, and each had a good horse to ride home and into battle. His necessity was such that he could afford to take the stripes and the scars as the price of the horse, and the giver could afford to make the present for the satisfaction of putting his mark upon the other, and of boasting of his liberality, which he has always a right to do when going into the dance, or on other important occasions."

The fact is that the family, clan, gens, and even tribe show a group-solidarity, possible on the primitive, uncomplicated stage, by which "a proletariat and pauperism are rendered as good as incapable of existence.[89] Despite this fact, it would be wrong to conclude that universal altruism and mutual aid prevailed among the "unspoiled sons of nature." The savages are practical-minded and realize that a fault is a fault, even in a poor man. And while the poor may not be allowed to perish, there is no cult of the weak;[90] the contempt felt for poverty is the obverse of the respect for wealth. It was a sharp challenge to tradition when it was taught that the rich man had small chance in the life beyond while the poor were to be transported to Abraham's bosom. Savages are seldom secure and prosperous enough to be humanitarian.

§167. Class-Evolution. In the foregoing sketch of social stratification and of the distribution of power and influence that go with class-distinction, the effect of war and conquest has been touched upon only incidentally. Since the argument has held pretty closely to intra-group development, there is yet to be considered that which has appealed to a good many students of the subject as the prime factor in class-formation. No doubt can exist that the contrast between victorious masters and conquered aliens is more thoroughgoing than any social distinction between original group-members. It is quite likely, though the data cannot always be assembled to prove it, that a good many of the class- and caste-distinctions already reviewed have taken their origin in some perhaps forgotten conquest. Slavery was such a mighty lever for cultural achievement that it led to the conviction that possession was the key to all organization. No other way was seen of subjecting

[89] De Groot, *Kongsiwezen,* 107.
[90] Starcke, *Samvittighedslivet,* 267-268.

one man's will to that of another. The army and war furnished about the only case of discipline without possession. Free submission for a common end is modern.[91] Says Letourneau:[92] "It would appear that it was slavery which first of all gave birth to classes, castes, and inequality of goods." This is an exaggeration due probably to immersion in the multitude of cases that point back to war, conquest, and enslavement as the antecedents of social differentiation; the instances cited in this chapter, and in the section on debt-slavery,[93] ought to have demonstrated that here as elsewhere in the study of societal evolution it is risky to universalize.

Let us now, setting aside intra-group differentiation of social strata, confine attention to the introduction of alien elements into a society and to the resulting class-stratification. There is a great difference between an inferior class which by tradition or training accepts its subjection as necessary and right and one which submits rebelliously. The subject-classes formed upon the basis of sex, age, personal qualities, or wealth have been of the former type; it took conquest to bring in the latter. The result of a conquest accompanied by enslavement, which, as has been contended, can come only relatively late in societal evolution, is to add to whatever social stratification formerly existed in the conquering group a substratum of aliens. The sentiment of "belonging together" or "syngenism," plus the allied sentiment of ethnocentrism, causes the conquerors and conquered to stand to each other in relations of hostility; for the conquered, as aliens, show a set of mores which their masters can regard only with dislike and contempt. Ethnocentrism fastens upon such often trivial differences as that of language and views them with both superciliousness and suspicion. Whatever the stratification of the conquering group, it feels itself a unit as against the subjected aliens, just as it did during the period of strife preceding the conquest.

The syngenetic sentiment is based upon the perception of likenesses existing among the membership of the group displaying it. These are listed by Gumplowicz[94] as follows: community of blood

---

91 Lippert, *Kgchte.*, II, 116.   92 *Prop.*, 59.

93 §§83, 105, above.

94 *Rassenk.*, 205 ff., 240-263; pt. V; *Soc.*, 178.

through unhindered intermarriage; community of language;[95] community of religion, together with customs and usages closely connected with it; community of culture and education; community of material interests. Men fall into hesitation, uncertainty, and vacillation where any of the associative elements uniting them with their own group are broken up; hence the phenomenon of the parvenu. A community is stronger if bound by all these at once though severally they can lead to union. In general the size and extent of a group stands in inverse relation with the number of common syngenetic factors in it.[96] Suppose, now, that one group reduces another to servitude and the two grand classes of masters and slaves are formed; then, hating each other, they nevertheless draw together by what has been called amalgamation. This is accomplished by the elimination of those differences upon which ethnocentrism insists.

Gumplowicz[97] catalogues also the factors making for unification and amalgamation; it is understood that their effectiveness depends upon the length of time they are in operation, whether temporarily, for a life-time, or through generations. The material factors are contiguity, familiarity, and blood-kinship, the last being the most powerful. Then there are what he calls the economic factors: class (noble, burgher, peasant, clergy, etc.), possessions (rural, urban, etc.), and vocation (landowners, manufacturers, merchants, artisans, etc.). The larger "moral" factors are language, religion, science, art, and "chance fate" (emigration, etc.). There is a certain parallelism in class-development which is expressed with some exaggeration by Lapouge[98] who asserts that in different historical periods, over the whole earth, racial differences between classes of the same people are far greater than those existing between the analogous class-strata of different peoples. He adds that between different classes of the same people there may be greater racial differences than between different peoples.

Language-differences first fall as a sacrifice to the process of amalgamation. Later are surmounted the much more stubborn barriers of religion, together with other distinguishing usages and customs; and when they are gone the way is pretty well open. Last of all comes intermarriage, which means the end of the blood-barrier; this is often long-delayed through caste-exclusiveness.

The Angoni, a section of the Zulus that migrated toward the north, all become gradually assimilated to the surrounding populations. Intermarrying with the women of the country they preserve their speech, dress, and usages for

[95] Lippert, Kgchte., I, 162-163.   [96] Keller, Soc. Evol., 80.
[97] Soc., 145-146.   [98] In Pol.-Anth. Rev., III, 220, 228.

the first generation in a slightly modified form, although the language of daily intercourse is that of the mothers. Then this class becomes the aristocracy of the whole nation, which henceforth comprises a great part of the aborigines ruled by a privileged caste of Zulu origin, perpetuated almost entirely among themselves.[99] In Sparta, the helot-class got a chance to rise during the Peloponnesian War; all who had distinguished themselves were to be freed and recompensed. Two thousand responded to the call; but the class-system was too strong to allow of amalgamation. They were taken to the temple and freed, it is true; but then they were all killed.[100] In Rome, starting with patricians and plebeians, the process of amalgamation was carried out. "Thanks to the tribunes . . . the people went forward to more and more equality; they obtained successively the abolition of the prohibition relative to marriage between the orders, the right to occupy offices called curule, *i.e.*, the quæstorship and censorship, then half of the consulship, and finally the dictatorship." Thus the linguistic and religious barriers fell first and they gained more rights, culminating in that of intermarriage.[101] In Holland the immigrants from the region of Antwerp in the second generation married Dutch women and took up Dutch mores. They came thus to feel at home. The antagonism between natives and immigrants was almost gone in the course of one generation, and the latter regarded Holland not as a refuge but as a fatherland.[102] Such assimilation has been marked in America.

For the first steps in amalgamation of races, thinks Gumplowicz, peaceful means do not suffice, because there is too much natural repugnance against those of alien blood and code of mores; but when once the masters and their subjects come into proximity the process of amalgamation goes on very "slyly" through political adjustments. By "slyly" he means what we mean by "automatically"; and his "amalgamation" of conflicting races is, in our way of putting it, the extension of the peace-group; only we think that extension is brought about not by war and conquest alone but through exogamy, trade, and several lesser factors as well. It has always seemed to us that Gumplowicz, living as he did in the former Austro-Hungarian Empire, was led by the hard facts of personal experience and observation to lay a too exclusive emphasis upon the race-struggle.

The class-struggle is, for one who holds such views, the lineal descendant of the race-struggle: the *Klassenkampf* follows the *Rassenkampf*. There is a strong element of truth in this contention, for the classes are doubtless often the relics of successive

---

[99] Codrington, "Angoniland," in *Geog. Jr.*, XI, 512.

[100] Thucydides, *Hist.*, IV, 80.　　　　　[101] Letourneau, *Polit.*, 378.

[102] Van Rees, *Staathuishoudkunde*, II, 87.

conquests between which periods of amalgamation have intervened. In any case, the class-struggle is a commonplace.

Summarizing Gumplowicz's[103] contentions we find that the masters are always in the minority. They make up for lack of numbers by the closeness of the bond which unites them, and the resulting organization and discipline. The minority always applies the strategical principle: "March separately and strike unitedly." The masses always lack union and organization, as a result partly of their numbers, partly of their indolence. The only exception is in the time of revolution when the tables are turned, but in the normal state of things in a civilized state each social group strives for the recognition and establishment of whatever it has won, through rights. Every right becomes the basis of a new struggle, for the wants and desires go on constantly expanding. Each group is bent upon the defense of its interests and upon self-aggrandizement, just as one state aggrandizes itself at the expense of another. Each group uses the means it possesses. The priests refuse to perform the worship unless they are granted concessions; the nobles exclude others from important offices; the masters in the gilds insist upon a proof of competency; laborers make use of strikes; manufacturers have a protective tariff. The group as a whole is infallible in the selection of these means, whatever mistakes the individual may make. This seems to be nonsense, yet it is proved by fact. The society possesses a demonic wisdom and the infallibility of a natural law.

Subscribing to most of these contentions, we extend them somewhat. Classes are formed within a society by interests and mode of life; they are based upon the kin-sentiment, upon the results of conquest, upon wealth, trade-relations, and other distinguishing and uniting factors. There are kings, nobles, ecclesiastics, merchants, peasants, slaves. All politics is the struggle of these classes for social power, and all history the story of the vicissitudes of this struggle. "Principles" of various sorts are only the instrumentalities, the battle-cries, in this struggle; and with them go dogmas to justify the "right to rule." "Social problems always appeal to classes; in the daily life of society individual meets individual, whereas in struggles involving the societal organization it is necessarily class that meets class."[104]

There are always groups within a society which, whatever their origin, maintain an interminable competition.[105] Competition does not stop when violence is ruled out; it is only in the utopias of dreamers that it is eliminated. It can never cease, and this is well; for only with the realization of utopia would the race have no

103 *Soc.*, 147.
104 Starcke, *Samvittighedslivet*, 223.
105 The rest of this topic is an adaptation of Keller, *Soc. Evol.*, 82-87.

further need of the spur of necessity and of the stress which, through the ages, have made us move toward what we have become. This competition within the state is no longer a struggle for existence, either of the individual or of the group; there are societal institutions and international codes whose business it is to interfere in the struggle short of that point. That mere existence is somehow assured is taken to be a fundamental fact; the struggle is not for existence but for a certain quality of existence; not for life, but for a standard of living. This struggle, in its separate cases that of the individual or family, is carried on in practice in some sort of wider association. There is an unending series of identifications of the individual or family interest with the interest of this or that group, be it gild, union, sect, party, class, or other. The class is perhaps the most typical and least special of these groupings of people with interests in common; it is also an elemental one. The interest of competing classes is, at bottom, a better standard of living—in the direct line of their class-mores, but idealized somewhat. There is a body of wants, common to all and there is a coöperative effort to obtain satisfaction of these wants.

The right of claim to such satisfactions is the object of the struggle. We have a right to a thing when fellow-competitors who want it cannot or will not prevent us from gaining or keeping it. To avoid a beastlike encounter it is a condition that the rest hold off and let us have it. Such a right has to be established in some way; it must be enforced by law or otherwise against fellow-competitors for satisfactions desired by many but not sufficient to supply all. Rights cannot exist where there are no fellow-competitors between whom claims to satisfaction are apportioned. The beginning of all rights or claims must have lain in force, or in the fear of its exercise. Even the rights of an infant are enforced by the might of the reproductive instinct projected at last analysis into mother-love. Those who could take and hold had the claim and the rest perforce submitted. Competitors would not of their own volition hold off from the appropriation of satisfactions; fear of some kind was the disciplinary factor, here as elsewhere. Rights were guaranteed and supported by appeals to that of which people were afraid: physical force, the power of authorities, of public opinion, of the ghosts and spirits that sanctioned the mores. Classes have always struggled to get one or more of these forms of power on their side, to enforce their rights against others. Until they secured one of them they had no rights at all; where slaves, for example, had none of these supports, they were without rights.

One of these forms of power has been singled out in history as the most obvious means of securing rights and the most evident sanction of them; this is political power. Organizations to secure such rights, not to mention bickerings about them, are mainly political in nature or soon become so. The privilege of making laws is the objective. There is a widespread conviction that laws once inscribed on the statute-books somehow acquire a power to alter the conditions of life as desired; and this in the face of archives teeming with legislation that has been dead-letter from the start or was promptly repealed because of adverse effects. And yet the fact remains that the governing class, if there is such, can exercise a certain selection in the mores.

A class is really definable only upon the basis of its mores; the code is the class. Terms like "bourgeoisie" denote a standard of behavior, a set of ideals, in short a standard of living which is in the mores. Its code is the truly distinctive thing about a class. If, now, a class gets political power, it can conserve and further realize its mores; and, since it is the powerful who are imitated, can very likely transmit its code to a wider social clientage. The class, on the other hand, which has no political rights has no chance to do this. Thus there is in the class-conflict for political power a selection in the mores through their bearers. Probably the importance of this variety of selection is easily exaggerated, because it is an obvious form. It operates among primitive peoples in rather marked degree, in cases, for instance, where the secret societies dominate the tribal life. Certainly it is evident that all rights are not legal rights secured by control over legislation, and that legislation alone cannot confer rights.

§168. Rights.[106] The regulation of this class-struggle is the internal function of government. It reduces to the delimitation of spheres of rights. Rights are not easy to define, either for a gov-

[106] Sumner, *Coll. Ess.*, II, 79 ff.; Corbin, in *Yale Law Jr.*, XXXIII, 501 ff.

ernment or for a treatise-writer. The conception of rights is thoroughly confused with those of equality and liberty. The ensuing treatment of these three topics is bound to be of a general nature, less supported by specific instances than is the case with most of the topics in this book. The very existence of rights, since they cannot be the same for all, implies inequality, yet equality may be aimed at in their definition and distribution; and they both confer and limit freedom. If, however, their ultimate reason for existence is sought, it becomes evident that whether they do or do not promote equality or liberty, their enforcement makes for peace, security, and order. Where there are almost no recognized rights, as among certain very backward tribes,[107] there exist violence, insecurity, suspicion, and disorder. Rights go with a regulative system, whether that is well-organized or not, and their stability varies with that of the agencies for societal control. Rights are in the mores before they are in law. They are the conventional adjustments by which the competition of life is regulated, the specifications of the relations between man and man, between class and class, or between the whole of society and any one of its constituent individuals or groups, which at a given time and place are accepted as normal and just. When enacted they are, in later stages of societal evolution, deduced rationally (or such is the attempt) from the nature of the relations of men and the way in which men's conflicting interests can be compromised or made to fit into one another.

The public code deals, in the interest of the society, with self-preservation and self-aggrandizement, especially in relation to the pursuit of gain and the relations of the sexes—that is, with self-maintenance and self-perpetuation. It sets conditions within which gain may be lawfully pursued: conditions necessary to prevent strife, oppression, and discord-producing relations in general. It marks out spheres of rights. Especially does sex-appetite require control; for individual passion unrestrained would seek immediate ends irrespective of the effects upon others, and that is not for the welfare of society. "The progress of our race depends on a complete organization of work and functions which is inconceivable without strict observance of the rights of others."[108] When

107 §9, above.   108 Peschel, *Races*, 298.

the public code concedes rights, it accords what is a monopoly, in so far as it is possessed by one person or group to the exclusion of all others. If an individual or class has a right to something when all the rest will or must hold off and let him or them have that thing, then the right of the one has as its correlative the duty of each and all the rest to keep off. This is what society makes them do.

Nothing is more important in connection with rights than this truth that each right has a duty corresponding to it. Between two persons, each right of A corresponds to a duty of B, and it generally exists by virtue of some right of B correlative with a corresponding duty of A. The duty of each is correlative both to the rights he has and to the rights of the other. If one starts out with a firm grip upon this correlation, he can often clarify his mind as to the validity of some asserted right, say to a higher education, by seeking at once for the correlative duty and finding upon whom it descends. He may discover that he himself is the "forgotten man"[109] whose duty it is going to be to pay for rights which he is urged to help get for someone else.

An evolutionist intent upon the nature of rights wants to see them beginning and growing. Arising out of the facts of human life, they are necessary adjustments, being the rules of the game in the competition between men. They can never, therefore, be absolute; in history they are seen changing to meet newly arising situations. They are thus evolutionary. Civil rights and those under martial law differ widely; rights are of quite another complexion in the industrial society from what they are in the militaristic. Nor can a system of rights be transferred bodily from one society to another.

In the former German colonies the right was accorded a white man to make a native woman his lawful wife. "But the black woman, because her entrance, in possession of rights, into the society of the whites constitutes a serious danger to the latter, must live and move outside it. We are therefore in duty bound to establish the regulation that rights in marriage between black and white may not be the same, that there may not be accorded to the colored woman the legal rights accruing from marriage with the white man."[110]

[109] Sumner, *Coll. Ess.*, I, 247; IV, 465 ff.
[110] Anon., "Rassefrage und Ehefreiheit in den Kolonien," in *Umschau*, XI, 257.

When rights have once been distributed by the automatic process of societal evolution, any sudden tampering with the system is likely to throw the society into confusion. This consideration should be in the minds of all those who are in a position to alter the incidence of rights among backward races.

Sir Charles Dundas[111] utters the following warning: "The introduction of our laws does not merely bring obligations, but it gives rights, and it is this that weighs so heavily in the balance. Take, for instance, the young native. Under normal conditions he would be entirely subject to his father and under parental control all his life. Of a sudden he is released from these restraints and becomes equal in every way to his elders. In Roman law we see that the emancipation of the son from the father's control was only gradually relaxed through centuries, but can we judge of the state of Rome had this been effected by one single act of law in early times? So also the native woman is naturally at all ages a minor, nor can it be said that her mental development assigns any other status to her. But European government steps in, and she has the same rights and duties as her father or husband. If she wishes to leave her parental village and attach herself to strangers, or if she goes to the towns and there leads a loose life, she is a free agent, and may follow her own inclinations. This sudden grant of rights falls like a thunder-bolt into the midst of native society. All precedent and custom are cast aside, and the controllers of society are disabled. Based as the law and organization of the tribe are on parental control, the ruin of this quickly spreads, and undermines the fabric of tribal constitution. We may bolster it up with laws, but we have robbed it of its foundation; for if the son is no longer subject to his father, no longer are the sons of the tribe subservient to the elders, since the family is but the miniature of the tribe. Thus, perhaps, no state of society is so frail before civilized rule as that peculiar to these tribes."

An obligation, paradoxical as it may seem, may turn into something to which men cling as a right. Hunting, for instance, as a prerogative of the European noble class, is not older than the sixteenth century. Earlier than that it was free or was a duty obligatory upon the noble class, in order to keep the vermin down, and where this was very burdensome the lord even got a fee for doing it. The whole case depended on whether hunting was an advantage and pleasure or a burden and task.[112] Rights always conflict, crowd each other, and shift about, as do the interests which they bound and moderate. They are a product of society's evolution, winnowed out through long ages of selection; although some of them seem to be conferred upon members of society as such, all of them have had to be won and held, like other monopolies which advantage their possessors in the battle of life.

[111] In JAI, XLV, 305.   [112] D'Avenel, *Hist. Écon.*, 219.

§169. Rights and Might. It takes force to establish any such monopoly and force to maintain it. Behind every right lies might. It is a pity that the confusion of right in the sense of claim or title and right as the opposite of wrong is so inevitable. Many a title or claim has been conceded and held which not even the holder has regarded as rightful and which others have denounced as a wrong. If it is said that every title or prerogative is backed up by power, doubtless there will be little exception taken; but if it is asserted that every right has might behind it, someone whose ear retains a jingle, and who confuses that aptitude with the capacity for taking thought, is going to charge the asserter with the sentiment that "might makes right." Might makes a right; whether that right is or is not rightful, just, fair, good, seemly, or proper, is quite another matter, for it involves a moral judgment. As a perturbing element in thinking, not because it enters into the present argument, the aforesaid jingle demands brief attention.

The proposition about might making right is a jointed and compound affair, consisting of two linked contentions. The first is that might makes what is; and the second is that what is is right. Only sentimentalists would dispute the first—people who deny that force ever accomplishes anything whereas nothing is accomplished without it; and as for the second, no evolutionist at any rate could subscribe to it. He believes that whatever has survived rigorous and unintermittent selection and has been widely retained—slavery or magic, for instance—has been expedient and adjudged to be right in its day, even though that day has long passed; at the same time he knows full well that both in nature and in society there are new variations as well as survivals that are not now and for us, as adjustments, expedient or right at all. Men get used to what is and assume it to be morally right. Society's "great gift is security,"[113] and the traditional seems to be secure where the new is problematical. Infanticide, killing the old, human sacrifice, polygamy have all been considered rightful in their time. Not so long ago manual labor was thought shameful, and trade and personal service, for instance that of a physician, were deemed degrading. Thus the notion of the rightful is in flux and is altered as situations change. And so force or might, in

113 Starcke, *Samvittighedslivet,* 171-173.

making what is, may make wrong as well as right and also may create right which, after a time, turns into wrong.

Appeal to history vindicates societal forms which are now rejected: slavery, war, monarchical absolutism, monasticism. Their reasonableness in their day appears upon inspection; all, taking into account their antecedents and the necessities of the case, were legitimate and explicable. This is always the case with evolutionary products. On the other hand, men have cherished many political and social ideas which do not correspond to historic truth—about rights of men, equal rights, rule of the people, state of nature, social compact, humanitarianism, and so on. If any part of these conceptions is historically true, the relations and details of it make it false; "history tells us that the conception of rights common to all the public is a modern one."[114] Nevertheless—and this is the wonder of the matter—these unsound conceptions have been used to get results that were expedient.

The more one studies the evolution of societal, including political, institutions, the more evident does it become that men's ideas of rights, liberty, justice, and the rest are only, as it were, statements of the position which certain relations of man to man and of man to society occupy in the horizon of our whole societal system; and that within another such system all the bearings are different. The horizon is the traditional economic situation, together with current economic doctrine, religion, and philosophy. The political aspect of rights corresponds to the questions: What do you want to do? What can you do despite others' opposition? What do others want to do? Can you stop them?

According to Gumplowicz,[115] the correlative of every right being a duty, wherever the right ends the duty begins. The duty is a recognition of the right of another, *i.e.*, of the ruled, who has had no rights. Every right must be limited, for pure self-will could not be a right. But then came the notion of right (*versus* wrong), which grew inevitably in the course of time out of rights, together with habit produced by living under rights, and the idea of rights became "inborn" in men. The property-owning middle class first seized upon the logic of rights. They set up the notion of universal human rights, with equality and liberty, and appeared to fight for the masses as well as for themselves. They flattered the masses and obtained their help. It now came their turn to become entangled in the logic of rights, for they had educated the masses and started the ideas amongst them. So the struggle of the Fourth

---

[114] Pollock, *Land Laws*, 16.   [115] *Soc.*, 153.

Estate for emancipation begins, although the falsehood and vanity of the ideas become more and more evident. But the emancipation cannot last. The ideas break up in contact with reality. The state, in its intricacy and complexity, cannot endure the form of rights which prevailed in the primitive horde, for now the social groups have that same kind of equality of rights with each other which the individuals had in the horde. Then follows a correction of these consequences of the jural notions, and might once more takes the place of rights, to predominate over a society weary of revolution. Thus in the social conflict we have the cycle of development, from the freedom and equality of the anarchical horde, through force and inequality, through right and law, to the freedom and equality of a revolution, then to the anarchy which dissolves the state, and then from this impossible state of things back to force and the rule of reaction, until a new development begins over again. One may be skeptical about equality of rights in the primitive horde, but the sense of the cycle is not thereby injured.

Might guarantees all rights, whatever the moral judgment passed upon them. Gumplowicz[116] sees this so vividly that he asserts there are no rights prior to the development of the state; rights are "the norm which fixed inequality" within the state; there are no equal rights for all but "each and every right is an ordering of inequality." If by "state," this author meant "society," we could subscribe to his dictum; but we contend that a regulative system highly enough developed to deserve the name of state is not necessary for the birth of rights. The most primitive of peoples recognize them, though they are in customary, not enacted form.

The Australians "respected each other's rights. The person who first struck a kangaroo—whether boy or man, and whether the animal was killed or not by the stroke—was held to have captured him, and, when taken, the animal was his property. And then he had to divide the kangaroo into portions if any of those with whom he had covenanted, as regards kangaroo flesh, were present; and the division was always fairly made."[117] The rise of rights out of custom is unmistakable in the Congo region; "if a trader perform a friendly service a few times for a native, it becomes looked on as a custom, and is forthwith expected as a right."[118]

It would strain the term "state" to apply it to such peoples or to a number of others who have very definite systems of customary rights, to property,[119] for example. The might behind rights under such circumstances is the diffuse public opinion that backs up all

---

[116] *Soc.*, 191, 119-120.   [117] Smyth, *Vict.*, I, xxxiv.
[118] Phillips, in JAI, XVII, 219.
[119] §§110, 111, 132, 133, above, and 380, 381, below.

the mores; for the rights are in the code and are matters of precedent and tradition.

There is not much point in trying to go back of the mores in a search for the ultimate guarantee of rights. There may have been a time when the strong individual took from the weaker whatever appealed to him but what we find in the actual cases is that both strong and weak are equalized before the incomparably greater power of society; and if one is found preying on the other it is because he is allowed to do so. Of course if the societal organization falls to pieces, it can no longer define and sanction rights and brute force prevails; at any time if the rights existing in the mores are not recognized, all that is left is the so-called "right of the stronger." It is the society through its code rather than the state through its specifically regulative agencies that guarantees rights. Mere precedent is sufficiently powerful; it is followed because nothing different is imagined.[120] Let a single case recall this fact.

"Having given a little Ciamocco a sugar-cane to eat, he, instead of keeping it for himself, with the greatest good grace and disinterest gave it to his little master who was present. The latter, as if the thing were owed to him, took it and carried it off without even thinking of giving part to the poor little slave who, however, did not venture to exhibit the least sign of vexation. I gave him another and urged him to eat it quickly. He took it and ate a small piece with evident pleasure; then he ran off, again carrying the rest to his master."[121]

The power of precedent and tradition is further strengthened, as many enacted laws of the state are not, by the sanction of religion. It is this guarantee which secures implicit obedience to the automatically developed rules about rights—to those tacit and unreflective recognitions and agreements of primitive peoples which precede all formulated law. Where behind secular law there lies the power of the regulative organization, behind the mores looms the tremendous sanction of ghost-fear and the supernatural. The general case is treated elsewhere.[122]

Religion "sanctions the expressed and the tacit agreements upon which intergroup rights rest." Among the Arabs these "tacit obligations and engagements rise, for instance, when any one touches the rope of my tent, or takes my child in his arms, or eats of my bread; then no one else save Allah can be the guarantor. Solemn agreements are concluded and sworn to at the holy

120 Sumner, *Folkways*, §80.　　　121 Boggiani, *Caduvei*, 105.
122 §§14, 18, above, and 201, 268, 269, below.

places; in that lies the original guarantee of the gods. In cases where the cult-act has become a mere formality, the thought of Allah as guarantor lies much nearer." On this stage, rights and morals are scarcely distinguished, "but over the general morality also watches the eye of Allah. The thought of him stands in the way when one wants to do something wrong. He does not stress toward the good, but he restrains from the evil."[123] "Among the Fulah the belief is deeply rooted that the heathen is without rights against them, and that fighting him is a behest of the Mohammedan religion; and on the other hand the heathen is so accustomed to his rightless situation that he views each change of relations at first with the utmost misgiving."[124]

It can be seen that rights may exist and enjoy the strongest of guarantee in the absence of anything really deserving the name of state-organization and entirely apart from enacted statutes. That in more developed societies the state is the guarantor of rights need not be much elaborated at this point. Where the state is weak, blood-revenge and private wars emerge to dissolve the peace-group; a man fortifies his house, wears arms, locks up his goods, fences his fields. If the state were perfect there would be no need of safes and locks; even in its present imperfection we need no longer fortify our houses or carry arms. The state takes all this over from the individual and assumes responsibility for law and order. When citizens petition for the right to carry weapons it is evidence that the state is not living up to its responsibilities in suppressing disorder and crime.

§170. Rights and the Peace-Group. Rights are phenomena of the peace-group; the alien has none until he is in some respect included within its bond.

"A fairly sharp distinction is made between the public and the private foe, the *hostis* and the *inimicus*. Within the district, often too within a number of districts, especially those which adjoin one another, quarrels were settled by the system of compensation or placation, and the normal relations were of the most peaceful and friendly character. But the public enemy had no rights; he could be put to death at sight with impunity."[125]

Rights began in the family and were developed in the more comprehensive associations. The peace-group becomes such by proscribing violence within its bounds, and it does that by defining rights and enforcing their observance. To stop quarreling there

[123] Wellhausen, *Skizzen*, III, 190, 191.
[124] Marquardsen, in *Globus*, XCII, 200.
[125] Jenness and Ballentyne, *D'Entrecasteaux*, 82.

must be precedent, tradition, and rules. Authority resides in the guardians of these; the elders, chiefs, and medicine-men. There develops the idea of rights, as well as of what is rightful; the right of property, for example, is the custom, usage, or traditional convention by which appropriation is put outside of force. Whatever is done about the owning of things must be done peaceably or not at all; for the interest of the society, which calls for peace and order, is paramount over all personal wants, impulses, and dissatisfactions. The individual is peremptorily invited to put up with the rules and keep still; to stay in quietly or to get out—and to get out has meant out of life, even when it was mere banishment, for every man's hand was against the outlaw, who had no rights because he belonged to no might-exerting group. The only way to offer radical resistance to the apportionment of rights by authorities is to assemble enough like-minded malcontents, stage a revolution, and supplant those authorities by others, that is, to destroy the peace-group and start over again. The prospect of such a resistance may accomplish the purpose without a resort to the extreme of breaking the peace.

It is within the peace-group then that rights are established. All share as group-members in the benefits of the household-peace, church-peace, market-peace, and king's-peace; all are relieved by the defining of rights from the menace in internal relations of the violence, bloodshed, and robbery which prevail between groups. This does not by any means signify that all have equal rights all along the line. Members of a society have only that degree of protection which the stage of ideas in the society approves. The child has few rights in barbarism; he is owned and his owner has the rights; he is not even a member of the community until he has been initiated or otherwise admitted.[126] The rights of women differ markedly from those of men. The rights of subject classes are defined only by inference when the powers of rulers are defined; where the latter end the former begin. Under general covering provisions as to peace and orderliness the rights follow power as the duties attend upon weakness. First the preponderating interests of society are satisfied, and then come grades of inequality as between status-groups unequally endowed with power.

126 Lippert, *Kgchte.*, II, 585; §163, above.

These status-rights apply to classes and are struggled for by classes through the effort to acquire power to realize interests. Thus inequality leads to rights as a definition and limit of authority, and there is nothing abstract or theoretic about their parcelling-out; they represent the distribution of power in a society at a time, as determined with respect to status by institutions and laws. The right to vote is an attribute of power in the political organization held by persons having a prescribed status; by individuals of a certain sex, age, amount of property, place in the social scale, and so on. It may be claimed by those who have not the status, for instance women, as a natural right due to everybody; and yet the women would not claim it for the children or for idiots. Powers and rights are always being re-distributed in society; and there can be no enduring harmony, rest, and equilibrium in the distribution. Once rights and duties went by status; now we rationalize about them and determine them in good part by contract. Contract-rights are taken to be mutually conceded between equals. The regulative system acts upon general rules, views, and theories; nevertheless rights always remain connected with power and the power can be struggled for. Rights are the prize of the class-struggle within the peace-group; members of sub-groups are straining after the next positive advantage in the task of living, after the realization of the next step in ministering to the common interests that make them a class. This often takes the form of a struggle to regain what prerogatives they think they once had—natural rights, rights of man—before they were taken away, as is alleged, and withheld by the more privileged.

Classes and groups contend within the peace-group for power. A subject class, emancipated and endowed with political rights, proceeds to rule and oppress as it can. At whatever point, at any time, the boundaries of group-powers meet and exclude each other, there is the definition of group-rights. The civil authority fixes this limit. To deal out decisions which prove expedient and wise, that is, which upon experience are admitted to be conducive to peace and social prosperity, is regarded with reason as a high and holy function; it is no wonder that the laws have been referred to the gods and that the state has been exalted into something of a supernatural entity. In one of the oldest religious-political documents of the Moslems, who had to reconcile fiercely contending parties, the community is erected into an infallible fetish; "it is not permitted to believe that the people as a whole can make a mistake."[127] *Vox populi vox dei.* This does not mean, however, that the rulings of the authorities are never challenged.

Mixture, or at least contact of races, succeeding a conquest or more peaceably, leads to discoveries of differences which "stimulate thought and produce coherence. Resistance and attack are alike provocative of definition. The conqueror wishes to enforce his customs upon his new subjects. He must needs explain what they are. The conquered demand the retention of their ancient practices. . . . Law is the expression of order and settled rule; but it is also true that the law came because of offences, *i.e.,* because of variations from existing rule. It is to law-breakers, paradox as it may seem, that the progress of law is due; for what we call Progress is simply the attempt of the individual to extend his freedom of action beyond those bounds which have hitherto been deemed inexorable. The criminal and the reformer are alike law-breakers. The criminal is the man who endeavors to return to a state of things which society has once practiced, but has condemned as the result of experience. The murderer, the thief, the bigamist, are unfortunate survivals from a bygone age. The reformer is the man who advocates what society has hitherto deemed unlawful, because it has not been tried."[128]

Here is the factor of variation at work, exploring in different directions in the effort to realize interests not subserved by the code as it is. Life-conditions change or they present themselves under altered aspects to individuals and groups within a society; then adjustments formerly satisfactory, or at least not intolerably unsatisfactory, become maladjustments under which numbers of individuals chafe. If only a few are dissatisfied with their rights and duties, they are suppressed; but if there are more and more who concur and make common cause, the struggle is on and the malcontent groups reach out for power to alter the rights and duties to their better satisfaction. The rights they win are the social recognition by which whole classes obtain the establishment and security of the fruits of the victories which they have won over other classes, each one striving all the time to aggrandize itself at the expense of the others or to make no concessions to them which it can help. No one has given more systematic atten-

<hr />

[127] Von Kremer, *Kgchte.,* I, 394-395.　　[128] Jenks, *Law and Pol.,* 11 ff.

tion to this class-struggle for rights than Gumplowicz,[129] and an abstract of his views may serve to sum up the subject. Though he is thinking in the main of modern class-struggles within a modern state, his generalizations have a wide application to class-struggles for rights within any peace-group. It must be remembered, however, that modern competition is of a more conscious type, and is less hampered by religious and other respect for tradition and authority than is the case among less sophisticated peoples.

At the end of a war the weaker give in. They submit to the superior power and accept the lot which comes to them. Then follow peace and permanence, which are the elements of order. Enduring peaceful order produces habits, customs, and rights. Such are the rule of the man over his wife, that of the father over his children, and, as regards the enjoyment of the fruits of property, that of the possessor over the non-possessor. It is therefore as great an error to regard rights as an equal distribution as it would be to believe that there could ever be equal rights for all. Rights exist only in the civil order of the state, and the civil order is the regulation of inequality. Rights are the standards by which the inequality is fixed. Hence rights are the form of the civil order. There is no right which is not the expression of an inequality, because all rights are compromises between unequal social elements.

Gumplowicz thinks that primitive peoples have morals and not rights. As it seems to us, he is not very sure of his ground when he undertakes to state the case as respects backward peoples. He is usually thinking of legal rights; that is why he asserts that there can be no rights except in the state—that every right is a bit of the state and contains a particle of the state-dominion. Man has only the choice between the state, with its unfreedom and inequality, and anarchy, which raises to the highest possible power the evils that are incidental and unavoidable in the state without any of the advantages of the state. Rights are devices for maintaining peace and order and if they fail to do it the state sacrifices them. Might is always turning into rights. The ruling classes, in establishing civil order, find themselves driven to transform their might into a right to get a moral foundation for their authority. The collision of heterogeneous racial elements creates a race-struggle which is continued after a conquest by a class-struggle for rights and limited by them. With the development of a middle class, the power of capital and property enters in a systematic manner. The ruling class gives no services in the class-interrelations. It gives treasures which have been received as feudal dues, or animals and game, which are a monopoly of the rulers, or products of the ground produced by the laborers; or it gives rights by means of which the services of the laborers are turned over to the middle class. Such are the monopoly of trade in certain objects of necessity, markets, and so on. The middle class, assured of property-rights, accumulates wealth and advances by its power.

In view of the foregoing considerations respecting rights, it

[129] *Soc.*, 119, 131, 148, 180, 190, 191; also *Rassenk.*, *passim*, and *Staatsidee*, 86, 112.

becomes pertinent to ask whether a man who finds his life-conditions hard has a right to call on other people to ameliorate them for him; that is, whether it is a task incumbent on the state to use its force to make somebody else work and pay to assist that man's struggle for existence. Such a question carries its own answer if the nature and evolution of rights have been apprehended. Around such matters as rights, when men began to rationalize and philosophize over them, there have clustered all sorts of whimsical notions which are the product of revolt against existing prerogatives and of various personal sentiments and speculations. There is, for instance, the fanciful idea of "natural rights."

§171. "Natural Rights."[130] When among primitive people or primitively thinking people a right has been in existence so long that nobody knows its origin, it, like all other such mysteries, is referred to the supernatural. Thus are morals referred to religion, or laws to some god's injunction. And when crude daimonism has yielded to sophistication, another explanation is offered of which it may be said that, in comparison with its predecessor, "the more it is different, the more it is the same." The mystery is referred to "Nature." In the case of rights, those which have existed so long that nobody knows where they come from are called "natural rights." Rights like that to life seem, in the popular sense, to be claims or prerogatives to which each one of us is born—and this despite the fact that every day many persons are losing their lives by preventable causes. There is no idea of referring to a right established at a known time by known persons as natural; the use of the term "natural" is simply a dissimulation of ignorance. It is a pretentious way of saying: I do not know. To announce that a right is natural is no more than repeating, in other words, that it exists. There is no need of investigation; consciousness is interrogated to find out what the natural rights are and then the rest is a development by logic and dialectics upon the basis of the major premise thus materialized out of the void.

Mill[131] speaks of the "chapter in which Bentham passed judgment on the common modes of reasoning in morals and legislation, deduced from phrases

130 Sumner, *Coll. Ess.*, index *sub* "Natural Rights."
131 *Autobiog.*, 64-65.

like 'law of nature,' 'right reason,' 'the moral sense,' 'natural rectitude,' and the like, and characterized them as dogmatism in disguise, imposing its sentiments on others under cover of sounding expressions which convey no reason for the sentiment, but set up the sentiment as its own reason." "There is nothing like acute deductive reasoning," says George Eliot,[132] "for keeping a man in the dark; it might be called the technique of the intellect, and the concentration of the mind upon it corresponds to that predominance of technical skill in art which ends in degradation of the artist's function, unless new inspiration and invention come to guide it."

It would have been a blessing to the race if those who have believed in natural rights should have contented themselves with the African definition: "Natural rights are born with us, about which nothing is said."[133] An amount of chatter has been engendered in developing the idea that a lifetime of application would not suffice to cover.

It is true that any right which grows up and becomes established is natural in the sense that it fits the case and satisfies the natural necessities of the situation.[134] If all adjustments are natural, then the adjustments known as rights are natural. In such cases "natural" means "in accord with law." Science comes limping after the ordered facts and shows that there is an orderly development in the universe; then men call such development "natural." This, though, is not at all what the exponents of "natural" rights have had in mind; science and its methods are no part of their preoccupation.

One editorial writer objects very decidedly to exterminating an Alaskan seal-herd in order to obviate international disputes. "It would be a very inhuman business to kill the seals merely for the sake of destroying them. They have natural rights which we are in decency bound to respect"—by killing them a few at a time instead of wholesale, apparently. Another gentleman objects to killing the English sparrows, for they too have a "right to life." The Russian mujiks stage a revolution and get their natural rights which have been withheld, especially that of liberty. Then they notice some fish in a pound at one end of a lake and hasten to raise the gates and free them. The fish cannot bestir themselves in revolution to regain their lost right to liberty, so the fortunate creatures who can must get it for them.[135] Cardinal Manning[136] asserts "that the obligation to feed the hungry springs from the natural right of every man to life and to the food necessary for the sustenance of

132 Essay on "The Influence of Rationalism."
133 Jung, in Sybel's *Ztsft.*, XLII, 65.
134 Gumplowicz, *Soc.*, 197; Keller, *Soc. Evol.*, 55.
135 N. Y. *Times*, Dec. 13, 1897; New Haven *Journal-Courier*, Dec. 21, 1916.
136 In *Fortnightly Rev.*, XLIII (n.s.), 154.

life. So strict is this natural right that it prevails over all positive laws of property. Necessity has no law and a *starving man has a natural right to his neighbor's bread."*

Perhaps these examples are enough to illustrate that essentially crude and naïve notion of natural rights, which would be amusing if it were not so mischievous. And yet the notion is a part of our western history, with accountable origin, and has discharged the usual function of a doctrine in societal evolution.

In the Middle Ages every man was someone else's man up to the Pope; and he was God's man; the individual was wedged tight in a social order bound by hierarchical and corporate bonds. All social relations were the result of the relations of different persons in this hierarchical scheme. Nothing could be accounted for unless it could be referred to a fief, benefice, or charter. Rights were franchises and privileges granted by the powerful, so that if a given man had been accorded none he had none. And so the rightless man, slave or serf, represented the starting-point, and the assumed anterior state was one of no rights or of slavery. In the Middle Ages there was no notion of rights as descriptions of the normal and just relations of man to man or man to the state. There were franchises and privileges, that is, things exceptional that enabled one to do what not all could do or to avoid burdens which others must incur. The time was consequently full of stresses and strains as the effect of these artificial interferences was distributed through society. It was worse than modern competition. The privileged regularly abused their privileges and it was necessary to fight privilege with privilege. The unprivileged classes had to bond together and coalesce in order to get privilege; there was so much oppression that combination became the feature of the time. When the state grew up, taking jurisdiction over all and disregarding the manors, the equality of all under the state was a natural inference. This is reason; but, says Gumplowicz,[137] it is pure imagination that man is a free being, and a still greater delusion that he is a reasonable being, if we mean by that that he is guided in his actions by reason and not by blind impulse.

With the opening of the modern era there came a revolt against this system. The Renaissance, the Reformation, the Discoveries, with changes in the economic system, especially in connection with advances in communications and commerce, all tended to break up the mediæval mores. No one thought out the reasons for the revolt. People felt deeply and the movement was in the air. The revolt needed a watchword or doctrine, deductions from which would suffice for a philosophical framework of a society in which the members came together as equals and got their relations from mutual consent or "social contract." The necessary doctrine was obtained by reversing the notion as to the assumed antecedent state of man, and insisting upon the "rights of man." To support this doctrine there was a "return to nature" and the protagonists of the new major premise, especially Rousseau,[138] created out of their fevered imaginations the natural state of man as it must have been in order to justify the doctrine called for to cover new aspirations and outlooks. There was no idea of finding out just what the state of primitive man actually was, by

[137] *Soc.,* 191.   [138] "Inégalité," in *Works,* I, 245.

examination of evidence and induction; that was not the point. The point was, not to find out how things had actually been but how they "must" have been, in order to serve the interest in hand. We need not go into the ridiculous *a priori* constructions of the "natural man"; it is enough to say that the "free and noble savage" never existed on sea or land. Whether he did or did not was totally irrelevant to the purpose of the reconstructors. If the unexpressed major premise of the Middle Ages was that men are, anterior to society, in slavery and destitution of rights and that social authority and institutions gave them all the rights they have, then the mediæval guess struck much nearer the truth than did the doctrine developed to cover revolt against the mediæval system—and this despite the fact that that system had become a maladjustment. The character of a doctrine created *ad hoc,* caught up to justify a set of feelings in the presence of such a maladjustment, evidently has no rational relation to the qualities of the system which it opposes or supports.

The revolt against mediævalism is a part of history and the doctrine is "true" in so far as it served as a factor in the new adjustment; but the ideas —that all men are equal and that there are natural rights—are all as fanciful as is the imaginative reconstruction of the original state of man. There was never any "social compact" whereby men got together and deliberately organized society; and yet all advanced modern states are politically and civilly organized as if the social compact doctrine were true; that is, they are organized in the modern in contrast to the mediæval way. We are told that the doctrine of natural rights, which any informed man sees to be in disaccord with the facts, has been an original factor in making history. It has not made history any more than a watchword wins a battle. It has furnished the vivid splash of color that could arrest the undiscriminating eye. Men in general are not convinced by historical and legal argumentation. Dogmatic statements have far more effect. "Natural rights" has been the exaggerated slogan of a campaign, like the "cross of gold" in our wrangle in 1896 over hard and soft money; but what was behind it, not what was in it, did the history-making. The idea was to form a philosophy of natural rights as against rights accorded by human superiors, by threading them all on some one formula as a cord or deriving them from some great first principle. Thus from being an exaggerated correction of maladjustment they were made into an assumption from which to spin new deductions. The doctrine of natural rights, or "higher law," or "unwritten law" is a means for evading and getting behind the existing law, which is historical and holds the field; the citizen, instead of being simply bound to obey, finds here a standing-ground from which to criticize and undermine the precedent, tradition, or statute. The reflective dogma, brought forth as a standard with which to assess the facts which occur by routine and tradition, becomes a criticism and a solvent. Natural law and natural right were the solvents by which the theory of feudal privilege and royal absolutism were dissipated. Hence the "power of ideas." It is all a part of the automatic process of selection; and the present case is sufficiently instructive to merit all the attention it can get.

There is then first the historical revolt, and then the philosophical and political speculation about what is "natural," which is the result of the revolt and which germinates and produces a host of corollaries or deductions. It is a reformatory, revolutionary, and destructive force. And finally the term "natural" comes to cover the primordial notions which underlie government in a jural state and are not open to dispute or change. Then things are on another basis and the actual revolution is accomplished; but the elusive phrases are still with us and their use and application are arbitrary and subjective. Our courts have recognized the actualities that the critics of the mediæval system were contending for, which seems to some to mean that they have made the "natural" rights legal ones, thereby admitting their actuality. Thus an essential fallacy in a covering doctrine seems to have been confirmed when in point of fact it is merely that definite readjustments in actual rights have come to pass. "Rights grow, not out of theories, but out of facts."[139]

Whatever may be proclaimed in declarations and constitutions, no regulative system that deserves the name ever operates upon the natural-rights doctrine. It is a flourish or an impressionistic piece of mythology that does very well to emphasize one attitude as against another; in practice it would speedily run out into absurdities like those about the seals, sparrows, and fish. Consider the right to leisure, to be born, to have children. The last is the result of a natural function and the question of prerogative resolves itself into whether one has a right to discharge that function. Some go further and say that every one has not only a right but a duty to do that.[140] If there are children, someone must carry the burden of them; but has anyone a natural right to bear a burden or, if that is not asserted, to make someone else bear it? It is proclaimed "that society is under obligation to assure work for each individual";[141] then everyone has a right to work. There is a doctrine that the right of property is with those who need it, not with those who have it; one recalls the dictum of Cardinal Manning, cited a few pages back. The doctrine that man has a natural right to what he needs to support existence means that the beggar has a right to the dinner which a laborer has provided for himself and which he is about to eat.[142] Behind this doctrine lies the very widespread and understandable hankering "to nibble at all good things." Does this nibbling also belong to the eternal rights of man?

Correlative to all rights, as has been noted, are duties. If the Have-nots have rights to things, then upon the Haves devolves the duty of providing. Against whom could the natural rights to life, liberty, and happiness be good? A right must have might behind

139 Lippert, Kgchte., II, 8.
140 Bebel, Die Frau u. der Socialismus, 76-77; §339, below.
141 Tikhomirov, Russia, 110.   142 §§127, 129, above.

it; then how may these natural rights be enforced—against God or Nature? It is absurd to talk of God's duties or Nature's. And what becomes of others' rights when one's own are enforced against them; or are natural rights simply one's own desires irrespective of those of others? If natural rights are valid claims against the state or against other men—which is the same thing—then they are property. If that is so, not only does a son of a man who has things inherit from him but every one who is born inherits a specific share in the products of the past. Certain societies recognize some such claims, for instance to education; but where they do that they are acting in their own interest, not trying to secure any form of natural justice.

That natural rights are our own rights as against those of others because we are by nature superior, is a doctrine which had to be demolished by a World War. Although those who held it meant to uphold it by force, they were nevertheless shocked that the rest of the nations could not see their right. This has been the attitude of the civilized man toward the savage for long ages; the notions about equality and rights to liberty did not refer to the blacks, even in the mind of Jefferson.

One author[143] thinks that the doctrine of natural rights has persisted in the minds of ethnographers long after it was given up in Europe; and that it has led them to assign such weight to the factor of race—their own race— in society's evolution. "Only through the events in East Asia has the doctrine of natural rights become untenable in the field of ethnography, for there the white race, which was regarded as culturally most highly endowed, met the yellow race which had been held of little account and in that meeting the Japanese have demonstrated that they are culturally superior to the Russians." That is the way to get "natural rights"—by the exhibition of superior military power. After the Japanese proved that they could fight and kill with the best, Japan became a Great Power and entered the concourse of civilization.

The fact is that the idea of natural rights is somehow connected with the hoary fancy of an original innocent state of man and the "good old times" of natural felicity. That myth is so ingrained in the race that it crops out in unexpected places. Science shows that the state of nature is generally a state of destitution.[144] There is no endowment; no goods, either material or immaterial, are furnished gratis; they have to be struggled for and therein lies the

[143] Goldstein, in *Globus*, XC, 332. [144] §49, above.

force that develops civilization. There is no "boon of nature" or "banquet of life."[145] If all are originally equal, they are equal in misery—equal at zero or not far above it. The only endowment with which mankind came into the world was existence itself; but this, after all, is an identical proposition. It says nothing more than this, that if a man is born, he is, and he will be and may be as long as he can be. Of course the primordial man naturally endowed with rights is a fiction, and the natural-rights doctrine deals with him as the Middle Ages did with a fictitious world. The philosophy evolved spun a new set of political cobwebs out of the assumed nature of man as other philosophies did out of the assumed will of God or of assumed "justice."[146]

A natural right to liberty might be taken to mean that no man born may be prevented by any other man or men from earning property, winning education, prolonging life, pursuing happiness, and the rest, if he can. This gives him only an unimpeded opportunity to acquire things, not at all recognizing his right to them irrespective of his own exertion; it is therefore a much more reasonable matter than a claim to satisfactions based purely upon the desire for them. But there is really no such thing as an unimpeded opportunity for men living together in society. If one is taxed, or taken as a soldier, or restricted by law in his pursuit of happiness, as he often is according to his own idea of it, then, unless he realizes that his rights are societal arrangements and not natural products, he feels that they have been impaired in the matter of freedom.

§172. The Right to Life. The right which is most solemnly declared to be natural is the right to life.[147] If one concentrates upon that right, he will find it a type of all the rest; and a review of it will lead him naturally to the conception of legal rights. The rest of the discussion about rights will center upon the right to life.

If a right is no right unless it is enforceable against something or somebody, how then enforce a "natural" right to life? An un-

---

145 Sumner, *Coll. Ess.*, II, 217 ff., 222 ff., 233 ff.
146 Gumplowicz, *Staatsidee*, 35.
147 What follows under this paragraph and the two following is quoted from Keller, "Right to Life," in *Unpop. Rev.*, VII, 290 ff.

armed man meets a tiger in the jungle. No natural right to life will save him. His right is a minus quantity if both man and beast are as nature fashioned them; the tiger's, however, is positive— at any rate he is going to live. This recalls the consideration that right must have might behind it. The man, meeting the tiger, has an enforceable right to life measured exactly by the degree of his superiority in might over the beast. It becomes positive to man if he can kill or drive away the antagonist; but that can be only if he has fire, let us say, or an express rifle.

If the same thing were not true of the relations of man and man, on the lowest stages of human development known, what has just been said would be irrelevant. Enemies had no rights at all, except those which they gained over one another by force; least of all were their lives "sacred." And even within a peace-group there were to be found only acquired rights, guaranteed by a might which was generally that of the group. What emerges from the actual cases is that some—not all—had one or more of the so-called natural rights, which they had got and held in some way; and that those who had not the rights did not sense any loss, or even lack, of natural privilege. Slaves and women were not always chafing under a natural urge toward the recovery of what nature had given them, to be "inalienably" theirs. They lived life as it fell to them and were not nearly so drenched in self-pity as we, projecting our ideas into their situation, and in our sympathy, have been wont to think.

The form of a right in favor of anyone is a prohibition upon the rest from taking something from him; and, as life goes, there must be power behind this prohibition or it does not work, in which event there is no right. Enemies, we repeat, had no acknowledged rights; and "enemy" meant anyone outside our own group: the stranger, the *hostis*. Those who quote, "Thou shalt not kill" should take note that this did not mean "Thou shalt not kill the Philistine." Within the "we-group," or the "in-group," however, there developed a taboo against killing certain people or, at length, anyone whatsoever. This, be it noted, has come out of societal necessity and is not natural at all. A, a member of a savage tribe, is killed by B, a fellow-member. Now A's relatives will try to kill B or, in default of B, any of B's relatives. This makes a feud, as it goes on, and

general internal strife. Groups which permit such discord are
weakened and fall before those that forbid it; and the latter keep
on forbidding it as they extend their power. A steady process of
societal selection destroys the feud-habit and what led to it. Also,
since B's relatives are endangered by his act, they feel a group-
responsibility for him and for each other which leads to restraint.
Gradually the A's cease to be assaulted by the now restrained B's;
then the A's have a right to life. It is enforceable by the group at
large. The right to life is conceded for the sake of expediency, unconsciously and not planfully, as the result of automatic selection.
Behind A stand avengers, ready to make trouble. Those in a group
who have no party to stand up for them, for example, captured
enemies or slaves, have consequently no rights at all; the right to
their lives—and liberty and happiness—lies in the hands of their
masters.

This is the way rights to life, or to anything else, arose; they
are not natural at all, but societal; they do not occur outside of
society. They are not acquired without protracted struggle and
selection, but have to be won and conferred by society. They are
relative, in the form they take, to the stage of civilization. At first
they have nothing to do with religion and certainly not with philosophy. Often they are not at all in the form under which our
age knows them; the prototypes of rights commonly recognized
by us may seem not to exist at all. In other words rights are evolutionary—not absolute, immutable, universal, inalienable, or anything of the sort.

Perhaps the right to life was as early as any other to receive
extension, at least to all grown men, throughout the "in-group."
The taboo that assures it is omitted at peril of group-existence.
Then, as the smaller societies were compounded and re-compounded, the scope of the taboo widened. Not to take human life
at all came at length to be the desirable course. When the presumption that life shall not be taken from anybody has won general concurrence society is conceding to all a right to life. Then
if life is to be taken, it shall be in the interest of a superior and
societal expediency only. Though this widened conception of a
right to life is independent of laws and statutes, it is evidently a
product of society's evolution and of culture; it is historical of

development and not at all natural in the sense of original or instinctive. There were always, even within the society, persons whose right to life was not recognized as such; it was merged in the property-right of their superiors and was long part of that right. The *patria potestas* included rights to others' lives. The bride still is "given." So that it needed the eye of speculation, never very keen to detect awkward exceptions, and great ignorance of the early stages of society's evolution, to elaborate a doctrine of the "natural right" to life. In some way the philosophers succeeded in getting the notion into people's uncritical heads and it has persisted, as a tradition, with great tenacity.

The "sacredness" of life is an idea that follows upon the right to life. All inhibitions that are old enough receive religious sanction. Note the several proscriptions of the Tables of the Law. The ancestral spirits guarantee the expediency-taboos—the rights that come, entirely secularly, out of custom, precedent, and law—guarantee them, as spirit-beings, with all the interest they had in them as living men, but now with infinitely augmented might. These taboos have come, under automatic selection, out of the growth and conflicts of custom and the mores; now that they are sanctioned, to break them is a sin against the supernatural powers. Thus a divine guarantee comes to enfold the idea of life; together with all other things thus enfolded, life becomes "set apart" or "sacred." In the view of the early ages it is a possession of the god which it is not right for man to touch, any more than an Ark of the Covenant, but which the god may take unless it is "ransomed" or "redeemed."

Elaborations in theology have then followed, to any conceivable extent. Many people are as inalterably convinced that God made life sacred as they are that religion made, and makes, marriage; whereas religion only sanctioned what already existed in fact, worked out by selection, in the one case as in the other. This is in no wise to deny the great mystery of birth, life, or death; face to face with such, let any man say "I know not," or "I believe," as he may choose. All that is outside the field of science. We are here interested, not in speculating about how life began or when it is to end, but in knowing how the idea that life is sacred really evolved in human history.

It is a fact, easily established by cases, that the ascription of such a conception to primitive times and peoples is but another instance of projecting our own sentiments into the minds of other peoples whom we do not understand. Savages see lives snuffed out all the time, and as a sort of matter of course. We must remember that they are engaged in a real struggle for existence which civilization has, for us, turned into a mere name. Civilized society is supposed to guarantee existence against hunger, cold, and violence; but no organization ever existed able to safeguard primitive men against these perils and primitive people are familiar with death. Life as life is not sacred at all; no idea exists that birth and death are great mysteries, somehow divine; the capacity for wonder is as yet undeveloped. It is at first astonishing to discover the small valuation that is set upon life, either of others or of one's self. It is not so "precious" that it thus becomes "sacred." Life is easily taken, and

as readily laid down. Suicide is committed under what seem to us highly
frivolous incitements. A native, seeing from a tree-top that his wife, at the
foot of the tree, is smoking up his cigarettes, casts himself down to death in a
pet.[148] A debtor threatens a creditor that if he goes on persecuting him, he
will commit suicide on the creditor's threshold and thereafter haunt the
place.[149] As cases prove, he will carry out the first part of the threat; and
the creditor is sure enough that he will do both things to be ready to ease up
on him. Nor do all highly civilized nations hold life in such estimation as we
do. Readers of Chinese and Japanese history need not be told that the Oriental
ideas on this matter are not ours. They have a different philosophy of life.

To an age materially successful enough to philosophize and be humanitarian
there appears to be some compelling ethical reason, if not a religious one, to
consider all these matters of rights as somehow settled in an absolute form,
irrespective of circumstances. But there is no valid reason for supposing that
the course of societal evolution has changed its mode and direction so that a
right no longer needs an enforcing might behind it. The right to life could
not have been, nor could it now be, without the might of society to support it;
no right in society that is not so supported can persist. To judge of any case
of rights without considering the interests of society, and where society's
power in the matter is going to be put forth, is to ignore the most vital factor
in the field. The very sacredness of life is a societal product; of what use to
play with the term, ignoring that which lends it content?

§173. Society's Interests and Rights. If preceding contentions are accepted, it is not sufficient to approach a case—and let
us still keep that of the right to life before us as a typical example—with a phrase such as "sacredness" as a touch-stone. To
arrive at a sound judgment it is necessary to renounce terms
which are mere symbols or of secondary intention, and to consider why society has developed its prescriptions and prohibitions; in the present case to understand the essence of the societal
provisions as to life-preserving and life-taking and then try to
exercise judgment upon the particular case in hand. If it is preferred to renounce all rational procedure, and go back at once
and fully to revelation, that is as one wills; anyone who wishes to
do that will regard all that is said here as superfluous. But the
tendency has long been to seek rational grounds, if only to justify
revelation. The attempt, for example, however uncritical of its
own cases, to show that society stands a possible chance of losing
a valuable member by allowing a hopelessly defective infant to die,
recognizes the interest of the society in the quality of its members.

---

[148] Hagen, *Papua's,* 254; §§202, 203, below.
[149] §§83, 105, above, and 177, below.

Once it was thought that any approach to the control of the size of families was wrong and even criminal; even continence could, by a logical extension, be a crime against the souls waiting to be born, saved, and glorified. This was a sort of quantitative theory of life. Common sense, basing its findings upon actual knowledge and rejecting dogma, has latterly come to see and perhaps to exaggerate the societal interest that lies in the quality of life rather than in its quantity. When the societal interest projects itself clearly enough upon the scene, all dogmas fall into the shadow and are at length dissipated.

Throughout the ages the interest of society has been an ever more successful adaptation to environment, resulting in a rising standard of living. It has called for members of a superior physical and mental character and for better organization. It has demanded quality. Where the struggle to maintain the society has been severe, the weak have had to be eliminated; men have both practised infanticide and killed the old; they have abandoned the sick. Even when the struggle has been more successful and has aimed at something more than mere existence, a society has yet exposed its weakly infants and refused to burden the fit by making them support the unfit. This policy has been successful in the sense of permitting the race to become what it has become. We must not quarrel too much with the ladder upon which we have climbed nor hold in too deep contempt its base degrees.

On the necessity of competition, with ensuing selection, Petrie[150] writes as follows: "The one means by which all natural progress has been gained is weeding; the only means by which improved races have come forward in the world is by weeding. The hardest weeded race, which has endured most, has always overcome the less weeded race. The fatal curse of Rome was the state-maintenance of a people among whom weeding was thus at an end. The maximum of opportunity to the most able, the full penalty of incompetence when deserved, is the only rule for a state which intends to avoid the far more terrible fate of a catastrophe when it touches a more competent people. The most recent panaceas of political ignorance, equality of wages and the right to maintenance are the surest road to racial extinction. The higher the walls of artificial restrictions—the exclusion of the more industrious races, the limitation of free labour, the penalizing of the capable in order artificially to maintain the incapable—the more certain and the more sweeping will be the migration of a stronger and better race into the misused land. The one great lesson of all this world-agony of migrations is the necessity of weeding; and

[150] In JAI, XXXVI, 220.

the statesman's duty is to see that this is done with the least disturbance, the least pain, and the most whole-hearted effect."

The age-long struggle has succeeded to a degree permitting society in some instances to abrogate its own criterion, ignore quality, and cast upon the fit, who support it, a considerable burden of the unfit; also to develop a number of so-called ethical theories of conduct which if carried out to their logical conclusion could entail only destruction. It is solely success and a surplus in the struggle that allow of such departures from the mode of nature and of the earlier ages.

In these days one society even aspires to carry part of the burden of another, the "white man's burden." This is well enough while the struggle goes well; but it is dangerous, and may bring disaster if the complexion of the conflict changes. What can be done by a comparatively new country with great natural resources cannot be undertaken later on; a man cannot expect at fifty or sixty to bear burdens which lie light upon his back in youth. Even a nation must beware of strapping obligations on too securely and irrevocably, especially if they are sure to increase by the natural course of events in the lapse of time. It may even be a disservice or dangerous to save lives in an alien society where life is cheap because population is almost at the saturation-point—certainly so unless at the same time the local organization is so bettered that it can take care of its own local increase; otherwise there is in preparation either a wholesale sacrifice of life or a geometrically increasing burden for the benevolent life-savers. This conclusion is not arrived at by divination; it is simply mathematics.

It has been for the interest of society, as one sees on looking back over the course of evolution, that men shall, ever and anon, die—whether miserably as the criminal or gloriously as the patriot. A state can never make men of any kind; a state consumes men. The lives of generations are spent to maintain it and carry it on. Death, however much men have been trained to fear it or to be horrified at it, is but an incident in organic or societal evolution. Society can freely send out its best to die for it. To say that society has no right to do this, or to rid itself of dangerous and antisocial elements—by execution or by sterilization, for example —is about equivalent to saying that nature has no right to let the lion-cub, born without a palate, die. The death of the unfit implies the life and increased opportunity of the fit. It was for the benefit of the fit alone that the "Thou shalt not kill" of primitive law was laid down; for those whom society could not spare as a sacrifice to internal animosities. It was they who were automatically assured of the right to life, guaranteed to them by the might of society. If, inflated with ethical theory or high-sounding principles, men try to thwart this age-long selective process, they ought to count well the comparative cost of interfering or letting alone. Somebody who is a societal asset pays for all these reformatory and "uplift" proceedings. Who? And what does the cost mean to him and to society? Shall we refuse to protect him? Even if you can make the offspring of a low-class moron contribute some negligible service to society, is that better than to have denied procreation to his parents and thus to have spared the cost to the normal and fit?

It is far easier to snap up a high-sounding phrase and go ahead by feeling, without thought, than it is to think. Rational action is always hard. Perhaps that is why it is so highly rewarded in its results; it is bound to be, if its outcome is harmony of adjustment. If men are going to secure such an outcome, they cannot act from subjective feelings and pleasant and lofty but inapt theories. They must always have within the horizon of their judgment the vision of society and its interests, which should always remain gravely immanent, like Goethe's great gray face of the Earth-Spirit in the clouds. And its interests are to be conceived, not as the result of hit-or-miss observations of contemporary things, viewed with a prepossessed mind, but in the light of its evolution, studied with cool and clear dispassionateness. If we cannot know in many cases what positive action we should take, we can at least know in the extreme cases what ought not to be. It is always easier to define the issue if it is put in negative form like the primitive taboo. It may not be possible to say, for instance, who shall marry whom, to get wholesome results; but it is safe to require that extreme defectives shall not marry extreme defectives. A beginning can always be made, and made safely, with the extremes about whose identity rational people can have no great doubts. Though this will not satisfy the ardent person with the mission to humanity it ought to appeal to the discerning.

It is a presumptuous and prospectively fatal policy, in order to maintain the inefficient and dependent, to overburden the efficient and self-supporting, in so far reducing their possibilities of bettering themselves. It is imbecile to say that the "state" does this.

What is the state but "all-of-us"? We cannot afford to forget those who are unostentatiously pulling their own weight in the boat, even though, in humble callings, their independence leaves them in an obscurity out of which the less worthy emerge to engage our pity. If we know what a society is and have some idea of its evolution and life, we shall always guard ourselves against forgetting them, being assured that their safety is that of us all. They have rights behind which lies the might of society; and if we infringe those rights, we are in the way of a massive and irresistible force. Wait till the pinch comes, and our ethical constructions will be of about the same utility as a sword of lath would be in stopping the on-rush of a lion. There are notions which, though men can afford to play with them while all goes well and the struggle is easy and successful, must be incontinently abandoned under the stress that carries society into some inevitable crisis-time.

Assertion of the inherent "sacredness" of life is a negation of society's interest and an abdication of judgment based upon a knowledge of the nature and evolution of society. Assertion of the "natural right to life" for all, is but little better; for a doctrine of this order is generally regarded as a sort of revelation and it is not desired to look into its origins. To insist that life must be preserved so long as there is even a thin, theoretic chance of recovery is not a practicable policy. There is always, it is granted, a chance of error in diagnosis; it is pretty hard to find anything in this world of incompleteness of which one can be quite sure. So also there is always a chance that the criminal, unanimously condemned by several juries, is innocent. Some there are who prefer to do nothing positive unless an impossible certainty can be attained. But life cannot be carried on by such highly hazardous and speculative methods. Men always have to do the best they can with the light they have. The system of society cannot be perfect; it can simply become better adapted. Evolution does not produce superlatives, but comparatives; not absolutes, but relatives. It is the overvaluation of human life which we hold in theory that leads us to such cases of long-chance gambling. Error is normal enough. It is too bad that it is; yet the cost to society of an occasional error is nothing compared to the cost to be incurred by trying to adhere only to certainties in a world of uncertainties.

After all, the talk about life's sacredness and the natural right to life is largely theoretical and occasional; where it could be readily translatable into the practical safeguarding of life, were it not for the inconvenience attendant, little is heard of it.

Year in and year out death removes the socially useful—those demonstrated to be so, not by chance, guess, or pious hope, but by test—under the operation of preventable causes. Sentimentalists who are shocked at infrequent executions of guilty men view calmly the steady toll of the innocent taken by the motor-vehicle.[151] If it should come to a clearly defined issue, even the prepossessed might be gravelled by being required to decide where he ought to apply his energies in championing the "sacredness" of life or the "natural right" to it.

§174. Equality.[152] It is doubtful whether anyone ever believed all men to be equal, though many have thought that they ought to be. That is like thinking that gravitation ought not to pull objects down. It has been asserted that they were "originally" equal, by "creation," by "God's intention"; that their "natural rights" were the same; that now sin has come into the world, with all our woes and, among the latter, inequality, together with property and other perversions of primitive innocence and felicity. Arguments about original equality may be "logical" enough but, like many other logical structures, they are irrelevant to the facts of life. The assertion of primitive equality is quite unattested. If death is taken to be the zero mark, there is something to be said for the view that dead men are all equal to nothing, and so equal to each other, but beyond such parity it is difficult to discover any other.

There is no warrant in nature for a belief in equality. Nature shows us heterogeneity, superiorities and inferiorities, surpluses and deficiencies, rule and subordination. There is no room for the equality-idea; it is foreign and fits nowhere. No one who understands the evolution theory is in any doubt about the endless variation which is always creating new inequalities; further, he knows that without this variation there would be no possibility of the adjustive process. Differentiation is the condition of all that is called advance in structure. Men are alike only to a degree per-

[151] Towle, "Motor Menace," in *Atl. Mo.*, CXXXVI, 98 ff.

[152] Sumner, *Coll. Ess.*, II, 87 ff. The *Atlantic Monthly* (CXXXVIII, 432) prints a letter vouching for the fact that Jefferson, when asked what he was thinking of when he said that all men were created equal, answered: "I don't know what I was thinking of. I thought it sounded well."

mitting them to be classed all together under the species *homo;*
taken all together, they can be handled alike only to a corresponding degree. They can, that is, be handled alike only in so far as
they are actually, not theoretically, alike; and any general assumption of likeness—between races, for example—is a very perilous one to go on, as many failures in dealing with the "lower
races" have demonstrated. Hitherto unknown inequalities are
being discovered all the time.[153] Not only what a man is, but what
he does, and wills, and has, must be taken into account. Inequality
is not a fashionable doctrine today, though we affirm it in practice
against Orientals, Jews, and others. So long as men are molded
during life by the interplay of organism and environment, while
they will be brought to a superficial uniformity within limits, yet
within those limits, say of race-type or nationality, there will be
diversity and inequality. Descent always tells.

"It is in the most unqualified manner," writes Galton,[154] "that I object to
pretensions of natural equality. The experiences of the nursery, the school,
the University, and of professional careers, are a chain of proofs to the contrary. . . . Everybody who has trained himself to physical exercises discovers
the extent of his muscular powers to a nicety. When he begins to walk, to
row, to use the dumb bells, or to run, he finds to his great delight that his
thews strengthen, and his endurance of fatigue increases day after day. So
long as he is a novice, he perhaps flatters himself there is hardly an assignable
limit to the education of his muscles; but the daily gain is soon discovered
to diminish, and at last it vanishes altogether. His maximum performance
becomes a rigidly determinate quantity. He learns to an inch, how high or
how far he can jump, when he has attained the highest state of training. He
learns to half a pound, the force he can exert on the dynamometer, by com-
pressing it. He can strike a blow against the machine used to measure impact,
and drive its index to a certain graduation, but no further. So it is in running,
in rowing, in walking, and in every other form of physical exertion. There is
a definite limit to the muscular powers of every man, which he cannot by any
education or exertion overpass. . . . The years go by; he competes in the
examinations of school and college, over and over again with his fellows, and
soon finds his place among them. He knows he can beat such and such of his
competitors; that there are some with whom he runs on equal terms, and others
whose intellectual feats he cannot even approach."

It is so far from being true that all human beings were created
equal that from the very beginning inequality, domination, and
subordination have characterized the relation of the sexes. It is
impossible to measure the sexes in any way so as to judge of their

153 Hartmann, *Phänom.,* 391, 392, 395.   154 Galton, *Hered. Gen.,* 14-15.

equality; they are different enough to be incommensurable.[155] If women are equal to men in certain respects it is because they have been equalized by conventional adjustments which are the product of civilization: by arbitrary concessions to the weaker and sanctions applied according to law and societal standards. The greatest inequality in nature is that of women to men; it is an inevitable one. Nor can the old and young ever be equal to those in the prime of life. It is averred that agriculture, or iron, or private property in land made slavery and inequality. Labor and war made slavery. If each person gets his own living there is none of it. As soon as division of labor appeared, women fell into servitude; and later the subjugated were assigned the drudgery. Inequality is the most inevitable fact of societal life; it is founded at once both in the organism and the environment. Human infants are unequal from the start in the physiological elements of strength for maintaining the struggle for existence, that is, in heredity; and the number that encounter identical conditions of environment must be a vanishing one, both in place and time.

Culture brings out inequality, for when it comes men cannot but exhibit their degree of capacity for participation in it. This involves differences in societal status based upon success or failure in war, acquisition or non-acquisition of property, position taken in the advancing specialization of economic function, and so on through all the cultural activities. Napoleon and a grenadier are approximately equal if each has no weapons or each has a rifle; they are not equal if each is in command of a hundred thousand men. Much of the complaint about inequality rests on the fact that some do not need to work while others do. The justice we pride ourselves on and somehow believe to be capable of securing equality does not pretend to confer that but only *suum cuique*, to each his own. Advocacy of equality often means an insistence that there shall be nothing to *show* inequality. There can never be equality between the governing and the governed, even though the former are elected by popular suffrage. One directs; the other obeys. The governor or mayor may be an officer whom we can personally flout and insult in order to show him that he is no better than we; but at last, at some point, the power of the state which

155 §§57 ff., above.

resides in its officials seizes us and we are forced to subject ourselves or go to prison. This is so under any governmental organization, however democratic, or else there is anarchy and the organization crumbles. So long as government exists, its agents
coerce, and rulers and ruled are unequal as being the coercing
and the coerced respectively—and this despite all abstractions
like "law" and the "state." The law has to be made, interpreted,
and administered by certain men; and in the end there is a constable or soldier who is the superior of the recalcitrant. Wherever
political equality is combined with unequal taxation there is reproduced the old injustice of unequal political power and equal taxation.

There is about the equality-idea a *reductio ad absurdum.* Why
not sell all the seats for a popular play at the same price? A
ticket-seller's answer, as reported, was: "When they build a hall
with all front seats, then we will sell them so." Further, inequality
is as essential to the process of societal evolution as it is to the
organic process. Variation is requisite, in the one case as in the
other, to start the process going; there is then something to select,
with the resulting possibility of adjustment. There is no reaction
in the homogeneous; if all were equal and there were no classes
there would be no competition, entailing selection. It is an error
that society gains more by equality than it does by a class-differ-
entiation allowing of higher organization and greater efficiency—
in the result of which all, not the higher strata alone, share. The
formation of classes stimulates competition.[156] In the United
States the development of classes by wealth is what overcame the
sluggishness of the eighteenth century. That and freedom of individual enterprise explain in good part the broad lines of American
life.

An individual can never have abstract equality as his ideal; if he
professes it, he is simply adopting a fighting doctrine by which to
get up on a level with a superior. If he wants to come down to an
inferior level, all he has to do is to stop struggling and he will
presently be there. When many profess a love of equality it means
that they are all inferior or that they fear lest their equals are

[156] Ammon, *Gesellsftsord.,* 79.

about to rise above them. Nor can equality be the ideal of a group, for a group never has anything such.

The dogma about all men being equal may be rationalized in two ways: first, that each shall have all the chances to make of himself what he can without regard to status by birth, and that each shall be esteemed for just what he is and does; second, that all ought to be and shall be treated as being equal. But either of these interpretations, both of which have a great deal of sense in them, recognizes original inequality. Civilization distributes the opportunities with greater fairness than uncivilization; and yet the equality of men under the highest civilization can never go beyond parity in the satisfaction of primary needs that are simple and universal.

The origin of the doctrine of equality is not far removed from that of the dogma of "natural rights." That doctrine marked a revolt against status and hierarchy, and represented, again, the class-struggle and the effort of the powerless classes to climb up. Equality meant the negation of special privileges such as the mediæval barons, cities, and gilds had held.

The French Declaration of the Rights of Man, of August 4, 1789, states in its first article that "men are born and live free and equal in rights. Social distinctions can be founded only upon common utility"; and later on (art. 6): that all the citizens being equal in the eyes of the law, "are equally admissible to all public dignities, positions, and employments according to their capacity and without other distinctions than those of their virtues and their talents." Even in this sweeping document natural equality is subject to some reservations. Later the law ordered *pain gris* as the *pain d'égalité* for the people while the rulers had white bread.[157]

In establishing the right of equality recourse was again taken to that imaginary "state of nature" which was invoked to prove the naturalness of all the "natural rights."

A socialist writes:[158] "All animals, except man, have an equal opportunity. We want economic equality, that is all. We have been despoiled of it for thousands of years." The comment runs: "There you have it. It is the true cry of atavistic Socialism. It would level the individuals of the human race to the plains they occupied millions of years ago."

The reader realizes by this time the fancifulness of all reconstructions of primitive life as it "must" or "ought," "logically," to

[157] Taine, *Origines*, III, 278.   [158] N. Y. *Times*, Nov. 4, 1906.

have been. If we recall the gist of our evidence concerning the chieftainship, plutocracy, caste, and other social distinctions, we know that they have always existed; that "among the savages, the spontaneous political constitution reproduces all the natural differences of force, courage, sagacity, or experience, giving the power to the bold and the capable."[159] It is true that the chief is not always sharply distinguished from the rest, except in wartime, and that the social distinctions are perhaps in lower relief than they later become; but in the cases where the authors report a lack of such distinctions the rest of the picture does not correspond to the notion of the happy innocence of the race. We present several cases of alleged primitive equality.

"Real distinctions of rank and class are as lacking among our Papuans as the distinction of poor and rich. The jealousy and envy that are deeply rooted in the Papuan character, on the one hand, and the fear of magic on the other allow neither power nor well-being to grow up among them. In this way it comes to pass that . . . the one never has a superfluity while the other suffers great want. They cannot at all express such distinction, for their language lacks a word for it."[160] "One striking feature of life in canoes at sea is that all men become equal. A chief or 'big man' on land is no more important than anyone else when he is at sea. Thus, if a canoe sinks at sea and some one in a canoe which remains afloat says, 'Take in that "big man,"' others will say, 'Let him swim. He is not a "big man" when he is out at sea.' "[161] This instance recalls several stories of shipwreck, with ensuing rearrangements of authority and prestige under novel conditions, that have been exploited in fiction; also the redistribution of powers among immigrants of various social prominence in a new and rough country. Each village of one tribe of India is a small republic. Each man is as good as his neighbor; "indeed, it would be hard to find anywhere else more thoroughly democratic communities. Headmen . . . do exist, but their authority is very small."[162] In one Indian sect, "a belief in the strict fundamental equality of all things, which is the basis of their creed, leads to a life of utter self-abasement and great austerity, with a view to winning the favor of Siva."[163] A number of the tribes of India are reported to be living "in primitive equality," but their culture is always low. The Buddhistic Nirvana is a sort of immaterial equality. The Turcomans say: "We are a people without chiefs. . . . We are all equal and with us each is king." "There is not among the Fuegians either king, chief, aristocracy, castes, social hierarchy, or slaves; it is the régime of equality in all its purity."[164] Islam and Christianity, in theory, regarded the faithful as equal, and in the first century of Islam its army divided the booty equally. The believers might not be enslaved.[165] In the Chinese colonies in Borneo "the republican equality is so great

159 Oliveira Martins, *Raças,* I, lxxiv.   160 Krieger, *Neu-Guinea,* 191.
161 Rivers, *Melan. Soc.,* I, 171.   162 Risley, *Ethnog. Ind.,* I, 212.
163 Balfour, in JAI, XXVI, 346.   164 Letourneau, *Polit.,* 29, 77, 97.
165 Ratzel, *Vkde.,* III, 126; Van den Berg, in *Bijd.,* XLI, 463.

that one sees the association in common of all classes and a chief sits down at
table with the poorest coolie. . . . In daily life the Chinese know no distinction of class or rank."[166]

Ratzel,[167] explaining how the desert educates to freedom and independence,
so that there are none other than slaves and masters, and all are chiefs or
sheiks if they are not slaves, says that the system has at the same time a
democratic or an aristocratic phase according to the point of view. This remark seems to us to explain the talk about "republican" and "democratic"
tribes,[168] the equality in the primitive "horde,"[169] and the like.

A return toward equality is the result of adjustment to cruder natural conditions, for instance on the frontier, by civilized men.[170] "It is undoubtedly
true that while this country was under the royal jurisdiction, there was much
less of aristocratic pride in the intercourse of the inhabitants with each other,
than since we have enjoyed the privileges of a free government, and by our
constitution, have declared that all men are born free and equal."[171]

We think that our examples show social differentiation in a
good many of the peoples cited, as exhibiting equality, by writers
who miss in them the degree of distinction to which they themselves are used. Such distinction is developing along with civilization and is one of the factors promoting it. As culture increases
certain kinds of inequality are on the wane. This leads to the conclusion that "society began with tyrannies, and the equalization of
the conditions is a result of history, not a fact of nature."[172]

"Society, fixing the ideas of the relation between men, formulated the conception of man as a citizen; and for that the word
Equality is the expression which makes objective the moral code
in a society, in opposition in a certain sense to the laws of unconscious nature. That social code, or Equality, it is which causes us
to respect our neighbors; it condemns by doctrine the enslavement
of lower races and the exploitation of the weak and unhappy
classes, elevating us to the formulation of abstract human rights,
in contradistinction to the laws of life-competition which express
the conflicts of individual wills on an inferior grade of definition
or of conscience."[173] If this is true there is a closer approach to
equality under the modern state than there ever was before, and

166 De Groot, *Kongsiwezen*, 140.   167 *Vkde.*, III, 53.
168 Letourneau, *Prop.*, ch. III.
169 Gumplowicz, *Soc.*, 124; Gumplowicz, *Staatsidee*, 126.
170 Keller, *Soc. Evol.*, ch. IX.
171 Dudley, "Memoir," in *Hist. Coll.*, I, 157.
172 Oliveira Martins, *Raças*, I, lxxiv.
173 Oliveira Martins, *Raças*, II, 162; Ratzenhofer, *Soc. Erkennt.*, 123, 126,
249.

also more human rights. But such equality is not "natural." As usual, the imagined primitive superiorities prove upon serious investigation to be only apparent ones and the casting-back to a mythical golden age a mere device or gloss in presentation.

In one of the stories of Sieroshevski[174] about lepers in the country of the Yakuts, a woman says: "When all become sick then it will be better for us, for all will be equal." A man answers her: "I do not by any means wish that all should be as we are. Let them be well. God grant it to them. Will my sores hurt me any less if others have the same pain?"

§175. **Liberty.** For a more exhaustive review of this topic than can be undertaken in this book the reader may consult a series of essays by one of the authors.[175] There are two kinds of liberty: the anarchistic, which is the absence of any restraint on will and action; and civil liberty. The latter is liberty under law and institutions, and is a status created by law, with security, peace, order, and a guarantee against arbitrary action contrary to the conceptions of justice at the place and time. It is evident that the first type of liberty is a mere figment, like natural rights and equality. In a number of matters where he is not ruled at all by his fellows man has only liberty to begin or to let alone; having begun, his freedom to leave off is not complete. This is true of his appetites and habits. The first sort of liberty is only a fighting doctrine, like those of natural rights and equality, belonging to a transitional era. The defeated and discontented cry out for liberty against their limitations; they want to apply the civil machinery to the competition of life in order to realize freedom, equality, justice, and also civil and institutional ideals which are unreal and metaphysical. What they want is to elevate themselves, to do what they want to instead of what they have to. They repudiate the right to leisure of a man who has accumulated capital and stopped work; yet they really want to be what he is. So they idealize savage life and proclaim a natural right to liberty.

There is no object in rehearsing again the futility of such a reconstruction of how it "must have been" in the happy state of

---

174 *Dawn* (*Russ.*), 113.
175 Sumner, *Coll. Ess.*, II, 109 ff.; IV, index, *sub* "Liberty."

nature. By his very entrance into human society the individual pays for his desirable status therein by a sacrifice of liberty.[176] He is not glad to do so, but it is inevitable. The savage is bound on every side, and is subject to many restraints which do not limit the civilized man. He is a slave to custom, tradition, and religion. What looks superficially to be primitive unrestraint turns out to be a tangle of restrictions.

Of the Australians it is said that "there are endless sources of enjoyment when a large meeting takes place; but on the whole the life of a savage is one of trouble. He is either very hungry or has eaten too much. He is often very cold, or suffering from the heat. He is never sure of his life. He may be speared by an enemy lurking in the bush . . .; a sorcerer may have taken some of his hair, or a distant doctor may be arranging measures for securing his kidney-fat—and there are noises at night that terrify him. His wives, too, give him trouble, and his children need guidance."[177] A passion for freedom is found in the Bushman of Africa, though his culturally more advanced neighbors do not have it.[178] They are better off and better disciplined. Says Ratzel[179] of the West Africans: "We have here a weak monarchy enveloped in strong forms; a mighty oligarchy, and at the same time great freedom and independence of the individual. What a capricious mixture! Before a state is built by conquest we see the negro in almost unbridled freedom; nobody else has any right over the field which he has won from nature by his labor. What he does or does not do is no one's affair; no one gives him orders. He cannot be limited in any of his favorite tastes by the prohibition of any magistrate, except when he binds himself in the fetters of the fetish. He can begin to cultivate the ground wherever he likes and act as he pleases, provided always, that he remains within the limits of the customs handed down from his ancestors. But these customs which are nowhere and everywhere, constitute for his understanding a system of complicated entanglements which he cannot disengage, and in the case of the least transgression against these of which the palaver may find him guilty, not only his own person, but his entire family and all his property, fall without redemption under the absolute control of the chosen king, who will seldom have any scruples about selling him at once as a slave, provided a purchaser can be found." The negro father "makes slaves of his children, the husband of the wife, in order himself to be free; and he is free until he meets one more powerful, who then becomes for him just as inexorable a master." He falls powerless under subjection to the priests' caprices, "and becomes a slave because he wanted to be free without possessing the moral courage to submit himself to the limitations necessary to the good of the whole. He knows his neighbor only as his enemy. The dogma of general equality stands farther off from no one than from the savage and the state of nature."[180] The Kabyle village assembly "which can execute a man or deprive him of all his goods, has not the right to detain him for an hour. . . . Among

[176] §§6, 7, 8, 10, above.
[178] Fritsch, *Eingeb. S.-Afr.*, 423.
[180] Bastian, *Afr. Reisen*, 67, 68.

[177] Smyth, *Vict.*, I, xxxi.
[179] *Vkde.*, I, 606.

the mountaineers liberty is the most precious thing in life,"[181]—that is, in this case, liberty of movement. In the case of the Veddahs, "within his hunting-boundaries the individual has full freedom; toward the community he has no duties except one: to let alone the hunting-range of his neighbor and above all also his wife—to refrain from all varieties of violence toward neighboring families. If he permits himself such trespasses, death at the hand of the injured party awaits him, and that from ambush. The nature-Veddah is thus a self-avenger."[182] He is on a very low stage of culture, like the Bushman.

Says Kubary,[183] in connection with the Caroline Islanders: "In reality the 'son of nature' who appears so free from care has far more cares than a diligent laborer amongst us who, when he has satisfied his duties to the state, is his own master and has only to care for his family." The desire for a secure, orderly existence where rights are equal appears in early society; but it is not possible to get it for all because it cannot exist without the responsibility and moral superiority of all. The only way men have found to get it is to set all free so that those who had the requisite moral value could win it and keep it. Except in a few cases, it has never been secured over generations.

It will be seen that even if the savage has fewer restrictions upon his will by reason of being under a poorly organized system of regulation, his destiny as a whole is nothing that any civilized man might yearn for. He pays for his lack of restriction by his defective security. If this is the reality of anarchistic liberty, then, even if such liberty can be attained, no one in his senses wants it. Further, one should remember that those who report upon the freedom of the Bushmen and other backward peoples often neglect to mention the restrictions that root in tradition, especially as backed up by ghost-fear; the savage is restricted in many a detail of his life about which, in civilization, freedom exists as a matter of course. What made men free was the appropriation of energies out of nature and the development of apparatus to save work. Land passed from a means of livelihood to a source of wealth while laborers were moving from servitude to freedom and status was turning into contract.

Liberty under regulation is the only variety possible to men or expedient for them; it is not the unbridled and ferocious pursuit of self-will that makes men strong and great but the reaction, in pursuing their interests, against the limitations that surround them. Strength comes only from a combination of liberty and discipline. Nor may liberty be thought of as a clean-cut, simple, obvious, unvarying relation; all things, whether men, combina-

[181] Hanoteau et Letourneux, *Kabylie,* III, 128.
[182] Sarasin, *Weddas,* 490.   [183] *Karolinen-Arch.,* 2, 23.

tions, societies, or states impinge upon one another, that is, they grow till they strike limits; and there is really no liberty except as an imaginary negation of constraint or as a real definition of the limit of constraint. Hence liberty is not a simple or absolute affair; it is a relation of two or more things which meet at shifting lines.

History is a long series of "reconciliations between the two extremes of omnipotence of the organization and freedom of the individual."[184] No one is civilly free except by institutions; economically free except by capital; socially free except by good breeding—and all these cost. People among whom peace and order prevail are policed. Those who are policed can proceed in security to do whatever the policing power will let them do. They are policed to get freedom from violence and anarchy, and they pay for it; the policing power takes part of their freedom away and may take more at any time. Absolute freedom would mean absence of obligation as a group-member, that is, no duties to society. Hence an increase of duties to the community always militates against liberty. In the sixteenth century in Scandinavia, "each one believed in his heart that all public ordinances for cleanliness and order were so many invasions of the individual's rights and therefore should be broken as soon as he saw the chance."[185] There is no true conception of a free man except the technical one which can be formulated within the notions of the time and in accordance with the contemporary laws and institutions, and in no other way. The strong man could serve his individual interests with his fists, let us say; but the society wants peace and enforces it, and so the individual loses his advantage. Though he loses liberty in the absolute sense he does not lose his civil liberty, and in the end he wins more as a sharer in the society's welfare. The state, by bringing about a concord of interests, is relatively an emancipator of all interests from a coercion that is societally inexpedient, that is, from violence; and even the state is restrained by the society of a wider culture-area, which thus champions the individual[186]— as the concourse of nations restrained Germany in recent years.

Foregoing references to liberty under the state should not lead

[184] Lippert, *Kgchte.*, II, 118.   [185] Lund, *Norges Hist.*, II, 61.
[186] Ratzenhofer, *Soc. Erkennt.*, 236.

to the impression that society needs a formal and developed regulative system in order to occupy the relation to individual freedom which has been sketched. Through its code of mores any undeveloped society discharges in its degree the function of the more highly developed system of regulation. Civil liberty is not confined to modern states; much more than its germ is found in uncivilization. If civilized man gets his liberty under law, uncivilized man gets his under the code of mores out of which law develops. Both of them experience the play of their energy and will against the limits of rights set by the society in which they live—limitations which take no account of the individual, for they have been evolved in societal adjustment to society's life-conditions. If marriages are forbidden, up to a certain age, without parental consent, that is a limitation of individual liberty in the interest of society as a whole. Lynching is an exhibition of liberty but it is punishable as against the interests of society, the latter having taken individual settlement of private wrongs into its own hands and courts. Sometimes laws make men do what they want to do; precariousness of tenure or eviction is no hardship to a tenant who wants to go, or villainage or a law of compulsory settlement to one who wants to stay. But laws do not seem generally to work out thus pleasingly; there is usually a compensatory disadvantage, representing the incompatibility of the society's interest with the individual's, to offset any advantage conferred. A labor orator once said that the wage-receiver was no better off than a slave: the latter had no liberty but had security, while the employee had liberty but no security. The modern laborer's absorbing preoccupation is to get work; by becoming free he has incurred a danger, not present under forms of servitude, of falling out of the industrial organization altogether, and he struggles to get back into it by contract, not by status. Liberty and equality are in many respects opposites; yet they are both called for in the same manifesto. The basic error which affects masses of mankind is the notion that liberty, together with order, wealth, security, rights, and equality, come about by being put into constitutions.

The most important fact to be noticed in connection with the modern industrial organization is the coercion it exercises on all men over the earth. Rent-slavery and wages-slavery are denounced by those who have been taught that liberty is a product of philosophy and conventional resolution and who have supposed that, since slavery has been abolished and liberty is in the constitution, there should be nothing but freedom now. Current periodicals are about equally filled with two complaints. The first is lodged against competition, involving irritated contradiction of its alleged benefits and declarations that it may be disloyal, excessive, fatal, and therefore should be checked by the sanctions of society. Then there are complaints of monopoly: denials that it need ever exist; assertions that it is always harmful, inconsistent with freedom and democracy, unfair as between man and man. There are all degrees of competition and of monopoly; they merge into one another, with no gulf between. If there is objection to both of them, what shall men have? Monopoly is in nature and never can be eliminated. Competition is the only practical freedom there is.

The power that set men free from slavery has prepared a new servitude for them. The free man must earn his living and to do so he must get into the industrial organization. That organization is now world-wide; shocks may be imparted to it in China which will be felt in New England. The risk-element has not been eliminated; it has been increased. One who wants to live on his capital must venture it in enterprises, which means that he must let it go; whether he will get it back or gain interest on it depends on the correctness of his judgment of the point at which and the way in which to put it into the industrial organization. The same is true of the laborer. Every man who grows up and learns a trade or educates himself for a profession seeks a place in the organization; then when he gets in he finds that he must follow the lines it sets for him. If he rebels and falls out he is trodden under foot. At every interruption or variation in the working of the organization the laborer runs the risk of being unemployed. He pays a heavier penalty than anyone else for errors of policy which disturb the regularity and healthfulness of operation of the industrial organization. On account of the element of adjustment or progress the organization will not stand still; there is no chance to learn, once for all, what it is and then settle down to a routine of safe action based on knowledge. Every decade the changes are more numerous and far-reaching in their effects and more rapid in their succession. What room is there for "freedom" when everyone is at the sport of these circumstances? The free man has a tyrant whom the slave never knew, namely, Care; and every step that is made in industrial progress adds new weight to the tyranny of Care.[187]

Liberty is something about which men dream, not realizing its real nature. Individualism contends that men shall have liberty and rights. Barriers are enthusiastically broken down; then it is found that liberty only sets free the forces, and favors the strong while crushing the weak. Next comes disappointment and people cry out against liberty, not against the foolish dreams of liberty. Later still arrive prophets with more and higher dreams and proclaim that it is not liberty that is needed but equality, which will

[187] Goethe, *Faust*, II, act V, 326 ff.

realize the dreams through collective force. In any case the dreams must be saved.

Gumplowicz[188] sees liberty in several aspects which serve to fill out the general conception. For the mass of mankind, he says, it is inevitable that individual freedom will dash itself against natural necessities and suffer for it; the vital question is whether in many relations of life a recognition of natural necessity would not enable us to avoid the superfluous evil which comes from exercising individual freedom in vain. Intelligent adjustment to the inevitable is the only winning policy.[189] The most important object of the efforts of men, next to the preservation of life, is the satisfaction of natural needs. Here the forms which have been created by the freedom of men run directly counter to natural necessity and fill the life, especially of civilized men, with useless torment and struggle. In the organization of the state, for instance, human liberty in self-direction always either over-hastens the natural development of the social relations or unnaturally restrains them and makes them stagnate. Hence that continual oscillation in the inner life of the state which is the natural operation of human freedom. Comte attributed it to the conflict of the theological and the metaphysical principles.

If any member of a society had full liberty, no other member could have it. Each wishes to follow up what he considers his interests as far as they lead him. This brings him into conflict with someone else who is doing the same. At the point of contact of such spheres of freedom there must be a fight or a compromise. The society sees to it that there shall not be a fight, for if it allowed that, presently all would be a chaos of violence. The spheres of interest and of freedom to pursue it flatten out against one another like soap-bubbles in a basin. Each person or group is free within a deformed sphere and no one is going to be allowed to invade it. The most that can be hoped for is the largest measure of self-determination consistent with the balancement of claims favorable to the welfare of the society.

[188] *Soc.*, 207, 208; Oliveira Martins, *Quadro*, ix, x, 121; Oliveira Martins, *Raças*, I, lxxv; Ratzenhofer, *Soc. Erkennt.*, 324, 325, 327, 328, 331.
[189] Keller, *War to Peace*, ch. XVIII.

CHAPTER XIX

ADMINISTRATION OF JUSTICE

§176. Group-Control. Even the least developed societies known to us act upon the principle—of which their members are unconscious because their doings are merely customary and traditional, not reflective—that the whole membership has an interest in the behavior of each associate;[1] and in particular that individual members may not settle their private wrongs without reference to the interests of the whole. This is true in the family, which reveals a distinct solidarity of all its constituents. So too in the larger kin-group it is only the composite that counts; the individual is something only as he belongs to it and the outcast is the legitimate prey of anyone who may encounter him, for he has no avengers. Whether or not there is any real government, the society makes its interest felt over that of the individual; and its interest is not served if he is allowed either to define his own rights, to defend them, or to avenge their infringement. Society has moved steadily forward toward a monopoly of the power both to defend and to avenge; indeed it was already reaching out for that power upon very early stages of its evolution.

The only way in which peace and order can be maintained within a society is by the apportionment and guarantee of rights, every grant of rights in favor of any individual or group involving curtailment of the liberty of the rest. This is accomplished by the imposition of a taboo. The right is conferred, not by positive assurance to the recipient but negatively, by the laying of restrictions upon all others. "Thou shalt not kill" confers the right to life; "thou shalt not steal" the right to property. Whether or not the society in question possesses a regulative system fit to be called a government, it must as a condition of its own existence and well-being prevent internal quarreling and violence. Automatically in the mores there develop an apportionment of rights and a guarantee of them at the hand of public opinion. This is the prototype of

---

[1] On the tendency to think group-wise, see Lévy-Bruhl, *Ment. Prim.*, 465-466, 475.

the administration of justice; "justice" having nothing to do with equality in apportionment but simply with the guarantee of the rights as they appear in the code. Public opinion supports the latter and expresses itself immediately and not by way of constituted functionaries. As the ghosts are always found sanctioning the mores, it is to be expected that primitive regulation shall exhibit a strong religious tinge.[2]

In view of the sense of group-solidarity harbored by primitive peoples, it is natural enough that an action directly harmful to the society as a whole should be especially hateful and should be visited by prompt and severe vengeance. Such public crimes are represented in their extreme by treason. Where a number of men have associated themselves in a joint-enterprise, especially if it is of an aggressive character against others, any individual among them will find chances to profit by turning against his comrades and "selling them out." The immediate interest of the individual is antagonistic to that of his group; but if he follows it the power of the whole society is concentrated against him in a fury of indignation. It is readily enough understood by the most primitive peoples that individual interests must clash with one another; these are mere flurries on the surface of things and are settled by routine methods without the appearance of any special anxiety as to the general welfare. But the several varieties of public wrong which are taken to involve directly the destiny of the whole group are punished swiftly and severely. The case is parallel with that of heresy wherein the mere presence of the infidel invited an indiscriminate visitation of divine wrath. Among these public crimes was included, as an important item, any form of disobedience or disrespect to constituted authorities.

It is asserted that, in Australia, "outside the family, the power which enforces custom in our tribes is for the most part an impersonal one, and that the delegation of authority to chief or council belongs notoriously to a stage of progress which the Australian race has not reached. . . . Except Mr. Smyth and two other writers . . . no one that I can recollect has seriously asserted that government exists in our tribes."[3] In the New Hebrides, "it is not the sense of right and justice, but fear and sentiment, that keep down wrong."[4] In the Torres Strait region, "there is no administration of justice; doubtless

2 §272, below.   3 Curr, *Aust. Race.*, I, 52-53.
4 Gray, in AAAS, 1892, 663.

the old men of the island often meet and talk, and formulate public opinion, but there is no legal machinery for punishment of offenders, or for dispensing justice or settling disputes."[5]

In Melanesia as a whole "there is no tribunal for the administration of justice, or for the punishment of offences against other individuals or against the community as a whole, but the administration of justice has a spontaneous character which is wholly foreign to our own point of view." In one of the islands, which is representative, "certain offences, especially the theft of fruit from trees protected by taboos, are believed to receive punishment at the hands of the ancestral ghosts, and do not enter into the category of crime. So far as one could tell, the only grave offences formerly recognized were incest and murder, meaning by the latter term killing of a person by a member of his own community. For both incest and murder, and especially for the former, the punishment was death. I was unable to discover that the infliction of this punishment took place as the result of any formal decision by chiefs, elders, council, or meeting of the community in general. To my informants it seemed obvious that one who had committed incest would be killed, and that any kind of machinery for the determination of guilt or for reaching a decision concerning punishment was quite unnecessary. The punishment followed automatically the discovery of the crime, and it seemed that the relatives . . . of the offender took the leading part in the infliction of the punishment. . . . We may be enabled the better to understand the spontaneous, or, as it might be called, intuitive mode of inflicting punishment by such knowledge as we possess concerning the deliberations of councils or less formal bodies in such regions as Melanesia. In these councils there are none of the formal means of reaching decisions by voting or other means which are customary among ourselves. At a certain stage of the discussion it seems to be recognized by some kind of common sense . . . that the group has reached agreement. The conclusion which has been reached is intuitively known to all, and the meeting passes on to the next business. A friend who has had the opportunity of observing the social activity of the Russian peasants tells me that the same complete absence of governorship and apparently unregulated reaching of conclusions is characteristic of their assemblies. . . . Among such a people as the Melanesians there is a group-sentiment which makes unnecessary any definite social machinery for the exertion of authority, in just the same manner as it makes possible the harmonious working of communal ownership, and ensures the peaceful character of a communistic system of sexual relations. . . . The members of an individualistic society may be as unable to understand the activity of a tribal council as a member of a communistic society may . . . be unable to understand the concept, to us so simple and obvious, of the sale of land."[6] This view of the spontaneous nature of the administration of justice is confirmed from a somewhat diverse angle by Seligmann:[7] "A reconstruction of the old morality as it can still be obtained from men not much past middle age, shows that it was almost entirely a group morality, and that the idea of individual responsibility and individual effort had scarcely emerged. The natives lived and still live their whole life in a condition of publicity, which, even when with them, it requires an effort to realize, so that in spite of the comparatively loose structure of the hamlet-group, every man, woman and

---

[5] Haddon, in JAI, XIX, 334. [6] Rivers, *Soc. Org.*, 167-170.
[7] *Melanesians*, 565, 566.

child is being constantly judged in regard to matters which appear to be of the smallest importance by a relatively large number of his fellows, whose verdict constitutes the public opinion of the community." This is what is meant by saying that public opinion operates directly, without instrumentalities. The group shows a solidarity which will be more fully illustrated a little later on; for instance, "in inter-community war, the death of any member, man or woman, of the opposing community formerly constituted adequate revenge," and "the inheritance of the whole or almost the whole of any individual's property is automatically provided for from the moment it comes into his possession."

Sir Charles Dundas[8] treats of the organization and laws in East Africa from a point of view so commanding that what he says transcends any local reference. "A clear dividing line between custom and law is difficult to establish in a society of which it may be said that custom is as binding as law. . . . Owing to many circumstances customs may have changed, and therewith the law was subjected to variations. These would, however, be no more frequent than was demanded by necessity, and every alteration was finally based on one guiding principle, namely, that the foundation of law was custom. But at the present day variations of native law are too frequently mere evasions of inconvenient rules. They are made on the spur of the moment for the benefit of one, or at most a few. . . . The decision the elders have to give is principally the point of custom in dispute. Where the fact is in issue they will generally rely on their knowledge of the probable course of events in the case, but unless this is very clear the elders will not take upon themselves to decide a fact. I am afraid that the main object is the evasion of responsibility, which, in fact, is one object of the secret consultation. No one can say who decided the case, and therefore no one can be blamed. Whenever then a doubtful fact has to be determined, a test of veracity has to be decided by an oath or ordeal. . . . We think of injustice and cruelty as inseparable from primitive government, yet the laws . . . do not seem to me to display any characteristic trace of this. In fact, if it is deficient in anything it is in the direction of severity. . . . In native custom there is unquestionably a morality of a certain quality, and could we but preserve this, much deplorable degeneracy might be averted, since when native morality is destroyed European immorality too easily takes its place. . . . The tribes we have discussed have not yet reached the age of kingship and despotic rule; they are guided merely by what always has been, and they are wise in assuming that what always was cannot be entirely evil." This opinion should be aligned with the impatient intolerance of the inexperienced observer of primitive mores.

The author quoted goes on to express the thoughts of a veteran administrator on the modification of native customs. "Many of our own laws may be calculations of some astute mind, but those of our Africans are born of custom. How remote must be the time of that birth, and what multitudes of circumstances and events must have arisen before the infant custom became mature! Customary law is the experiences of generations which successively have cast this and that aside, tried many methods and found them to fail, until at last some course remained open which proved itself the most workable and acceptable, not because it met merely one requirement, but because it fitted into all other circumstances. Therefore it is a deeply-thought-out code,

8 In JAI, XLV, 235, 251, 304-305, 306.

and the experience and intellect of generations have worked to make it one link in a chain of usages and ideas. For the law as approved by custom is but part of the mechanism of society. It is nothing separate as with us, and how far any alteration in this part may prove to be irreparable injury to the whole we cannot say. It is one of the most pernicious errors to tamper with native custom. We are not in touch with it, have never experienced the conditions of life to which it is adapted, and therefore cannot completely enter into its reasons. To interfere with native customs is too often like blundering with an instrument the use of which we have long forgotten. . . . To us it falls . . . to make or modify such changes as are inevitable. This is a delicate task indeed, requiring much sympathy with the past, for we are to frame new laws for the ancient. To that end it seems to me that first and foremost we shall require a knowledge of what we are dealing with; if we set out even only with the idea of destroying, let us by all means know what it is we destroy."

If a Galla wants to avoid a trial he may appeal to the public judgment of his fellow-tribesmen, and if they find for him he adopts a headgear calculated to put his opponent to shame.[9] "Where forcible means are lacking, the influence of the opinion of others, at other times their help, are two great factors upholding order in the Kayan society."[10] Of the East Greenlanders, Holm[11] writes: "Despite the fact that they are not subjected to enacted laws, yet . . . their social life is founded on rules whose compulsion they tacitly recognize as legal, and whose transgression exposes them to society's displeasure. These rules will even be found to set, in certain respects, narrower bounds to the individual's liberty than the laws of civilized society."

As regards group-solidarity the South Africans offer striking illustration. They hold the head of the family accountable for the conduct of all its branches; the village is responsible for all its residents; the clan for each of its villages. A man may not profess ignorance of his neighbor's doings; the law requires him to know all about his neighbors.[12] Perhaps the natives do not pry into each other's affairs wholly out of idle curiosity. The East African "Egungun" is an example of the supernatural sanction of the code. "Egungun really means 'bone,' hence 'skeleton,' and Egungun himself is supposed to be a man risen from the dead. The part is acted by a man disguised in a long robe, usually made of grass, and a mask of wood, which generally represents a hideous human face, with a long pointed nose and thin lips, but sometimes the head of an animal. Egungun appears in the streets by day or night indifferently, leaping, dancing, or walking grotesquely, and uttering loud cries. He is supposed to have returned from the land of the dead in order to ascertain what is going on in the land of the living, and his function is to carry away those persons who are troublesome to their neighbors. He may thus be considered a kind of supernatural inquisitor who appears from time to time to inquire into the general domestic conduct of people, particularly of women, and to punish misdeeds. Although it is very well known that Egungun is only a disguised man, yet it is popularly believed that to touch him, even by accident, causes death. . . . Egungun is thus at the present day a sort of 'bogey,' or make-believe demon, whose chief business is to frighten termagants, busybodies, scandalmongers, and others, but it seems probable that originally he

[9] Paulitschke, *Nordost-Afr.*, II, 156.　　[10] Nieuwenhuis, *Borneo*, I, 78.
[11] *Ethnol. Skizze*, 43.　　[12] Macdonald, in JAI, XIX, 287.

was regarded as the incarnation of the dead, and that the whole custom is connected with manes-worship."[13]

A mark of group-solidarity is the unwillingness of one member to incriminate another. Evidence, to the native, "depends largely on who the witnesses are; for instance, as weighty as a man's evidence might be against his brother, just so worthless it would be in his favour, it being assumed that the witness is biased. To the native a trial is in this respect much like a fight: your brother may be in the wrong, but loyalty forbids you to go against him. So also it were shameful to testify against a clansman; indeed, some natives . . . always seem to reckon up which of the two contending parties is more nearly allied to them by blood, family, clan, community or tribe, and they give evidence accordingly. Loyalty is simply more weighty than truthfulness, and if a kinsman denies a thing, it is not right to go against him: the blame for the untruthfulness falls on the kinsman. After many years' experience of natives I have come to the conclusion that in nine cases out of ten in which the truth is spoken in a court, it is spoken by the accused and not by the witnesses. Therefore the native goes so much by what the contending parties say and less by what their witnesses depose to, unless these witnesses have no more interest in the one than in the other. Yet the fewest natives can conceive the rejection of a suit for lack of evidence, and there is undoubtedly a theory that it is for the accused or defendant to clear himself, it being assumed that he is not accused without any cause at all. So often I have had cases referred to me with these words, 'and now we appeal to you because this case defeats us,' and invariably I have found that the defeat lies in the fact that there is no evidence at all. . . . Under all these conditions it is explicable that the natives resort to superhuman devices for discovering the truth, and it may be said that in the vast majority of cases where any doubt as to fact exists, some such remedy is sought. These devices may take the form of oaths or ordeals or special tests of a supernatural nature devised by medicine men, and finally fatal curses which only affect the guilty one." The author[14] relates personal experiences in point.

Says Wilken,[15] with the peoples of Sumatra chiefly in mind: "The other groups are modelled on the family-group. The tribe, the community are really regarded as nothing else than the extension of the family. Both groups and each of their members then answer for one another. This solidarity-system holds not only in civil but also in penal relations." Most misdemeanors result in fines and debt, and fall under this solidarity-system. The community's responsibility "extends over everything that happens within its territory and of which the perpetrator remains unknown." Justice was originally in the literal sense of the word folk-justice, the court being composed of the whole people, but gradually the custom developed that the oldest and the chief took account of complaints, adjudged guilt or innocence, and applied the penalty. There are still to be encountered in the Archipelago peoples who administer justice as a body, at any rate as a body of males. This author, in discussing the Malay penal code, remarks repeatedly upon the system of solidarity which it reveals, which is "merely a necessary sequel of the strongly marked family life, the stability of the family-tie, among peoples who are still in their childhood. . . . The members of a family not alone dwell together, but have common needs,

13 Ellis, *Yoruba*, 107, 108.   14 Dundas, C., in JAI, LI, 226-227.
15 In VG, II, 391-394, 460-462, 489; and *Vkde.*, 455, 456.

form a whole in the administrative as well as the economic sense, if we may use such Western expressions here. By virtue of such an intimate union the responsibility of the family for the actions of one of its members is no more than natural. This system of solidarity is peculiarly marked in Sumatra; solidarity exists within the family, the larger kin-groups, the villages, and the small combination of villages. "The solidarity-system thus forms one of the most prominent bases for native justice in civil as well as in penal cases. It is self-evident that people must have quite speedily arrived at the necessity of setting certain bounds to their responsibility; hence the usage of expelling one who by creating obligations or by the repeated practice of misdemeanors, brings the family or the clan into embarrassment." The same system applies to the debt-relation. If the creditor cannot lay hand upon the goods of the debtor himself, he seizes those of a member of the latter's group. If, for instance, a debtor is behindhand in repayment the creditor may take a buffalo from any one of the defaultor's village-mates, that is, from any person who is within the range of solidarity with the debtor. A special case is where the creditor goes to one of the debtor's co-responsibles and takes a bar of iron, a copper vessel, or the like. This proceeding has been arranged with the owner, but the latter ostensibly knows nothing about it and raises a great clamor. "The debtor, who is thus put to shame before the whole village, hastens to pay up." The more valuable the property seized the greater the uproar and the speedier the settlement. This procedure by seizure may even take place between larger communities, to be followed by conferences and repayment.

In Peru, "not only is the delinquent regarded as answerable for his deed, but also his parents and brothers and sisters, and in wider extension even his whole kin-group, and that too when the latter was wholly without part in his crime."[16]

The modern world has moved away from an arrangement where each is his brother's keeper and the system, both in its legal and religious manifestations,[17] seems strange. Even now, however, a family feels shame at the misdemeanors of one of its members and sometimes pays his debts. It hardly needs be said that if everyone is responsible for everyone else there is a sharp, if informal, scrutiny of mutual conduct. This is the spontaneous administration of justice of which some of the authors quoted have spoken.

§177*. Retaliation. By its conventions society is always controlling and disciplining instinctive impulses,[18] so that their expression does not injure its interests but contributes to them rather. In all ages the undisciplined individual has been found ready to pursue his personal advantage as he sees it, regardless of

[16] Cunow, *Verf. Inkareichs,* 117.   [17] §274, below.
[18] Keller, *Soc. Evol.,* 28 ff.

the commotion he might cause in the group at large. He has been callous in his aggressions upon others, fierce in resenting encroachment upon himself, quick to take recourse to retaliation and vengeance, and totally devoid of any appreciation of society's interests. He could not be allowed to raise the commotion; yet he could neither see for himself nor be shown the interests of the whole that his unrestrained yielding to impulse would injure. Neither provocation nor retaliation could be wholly done away with. They were original in the field. What society did was to define aggression by the apportionment of rights and then to utilize retaliation in modified form to sanction the rights.

The talion law, says Letourneau,[19] is the foundation of the development of justice; a real reflex action going back to self-defense as its source. It is in force in nearly all primitive societies, retaliation first in kind and then in property. It is profitless to speculate as to whether the custom of "paying-back," so common among boys, is or is not an instinct; what the facts reveal is that the most primitive societies are found both restricting the practice and utilizing the principle, and that the principle is by no means obsolete even at the present day. It is reasonable to contend that without a "law of retaliation" to start with and to modify, the evolution of justice might have been very different from what it has been.

Often enough in this book is there occasion to reflect upon the necessity of starting with something strong and positive, however rough and crude or even wrong and repulsive it may seem to our eyes. Such a rugged block is something that can be shaped, after a while, into a form more comely as well as more expedient, without losing the toughness of fiber necessary to institutional structure. In any case, society laid hand upon the tendency to take an eye for an eye or a tooth for a tooth and harnessed it, somewhat as it yoked the ox or subjected fire to control. It left vengeance and retaliation wholly free outside the peace-group, controlling and directing it inside, in the interest of peace and order. It assumed a monopoly of in-group retaliation and became the sole lawful avenger. The presence of the retaliatory element will be easily detected in a number of forms of punishment accorded to

19 *Morale,* 222 and ff.

crime;[20] the general tendency toward retaliation and the special case of blood-vengeance are indefinitely illustratable.

Among many savage peoples vengefulness is a veritable passion. Says one of the Basuto whose son had been wounded on the head by a staff: "With the same staff and on the same spot where my son was beaten, will I give a blow on the head of the man who did it."[21] Of the Brazilian Indians, for instance, "we may say that the sole strong and deep-rooted belief held by them was the obligation to avenge themselves on strangers who have offended some one of their band. This spirit of vengeance raised to excess was their true faith. . . . The impulse to avenge themselves was so extreme that they judged themselves obliged to murder every animal that should molest them, even though it was merely a filthy insect. . . . And so engrossing was the thought of revenge and expiation that among their sacrifices the most prominent was that of an enemy whose body they would disinter after many years to take vengeance upon the corpse, crushing the skull and assembling as many trophies as possible."[22] Latent vengefulness is always breaking through the barriers of the mores and of law. In the Malay Archipelago it reveals itself in the form of running *amok*. Whenever an Indian islander is placed, with arms in his hands, in a situation where he thinks his life or honor is in danger, the chances are that he will devote himself to be avenged upon those he deems his oppressors, totally regardless of all consequences. "In our intercourse with them we must always be prepared for such a result, and the natives are themselves so fully aware of this feature of character, that the very first step taken with a prisoner, however trivial his offence, is to disarm him."[23]

This tendency toward retaliation, which does not call for much illustration, is made use of under socictal supervision in a number of ways. The Australians stage a sort of retaliation-ordeal. Persons accused of wrong-doing get a month's notice to appear before the assembled tribes and be tried, on pain of being outlawed and killed. The guilty party is painted white and, along with his nearest male relative as second, is armed and placed opposite to the injured person and his friends, who may number twenty warriors. Spears and boomerangs are thrown at him "like a shower." If he succeeds in warding them off, he must then, protecting himself with a shield, allow each of his enemies to strike a single blow at him. Blood must be spilt to satisfy the injured party, and the trial ends when the culprit is hit. Then the wound is dressed and all shake hands.[24] Here the community sustains, as it were, and regulates the primordial method of settlement of injuries. There is also, among the Australians, a review by the old men of the reasons for a fight. "If . . . the victor happens to be the aggrieved party only in his own opinion, and not in that of those to whom he is answerable, and who do not believe the grounds on which he commenced the fight to be sufficient, he has to undergo exactly the same mutilations subsequently at the hands of the vanquished as he himself had inflicted: it devolves upon his 'brother' to bring him back to undergo the punishment, though if a coward he may run away from camp, but he dare then never return. Thus, in all these individual quarrels or fights, whatever

20 §184, below.
21 Spencer, *Prin. Soc.*, II, §533.
22 Varnhagen, *Brazil*, I, 121-122.
23 Crawfurd, *Ind. Arch.*, 70.
24 Dawson, *Aust. Aborig.*, 76.

injury may be perpetrated upon the vanquished, the latter, supposing he has justice on his side—and this is regulated by the general opinion of the elders in camp—has the opportunity always afforded him of retaliating by similar injury with similar weapon—'an eye for an eye, a tooth for a tooth.' " And "the women fight among themselves on the same general principles as the men. . . . As in the case with the stronger sex, there is a subsequent adjustment of the rights and wrongs of the dispute, and, unless sufficient cause be proved, the victorious amazon will be similarly treated."[25]

In New Guinea a man often fears to push his case against a powerful antagonist lest the latter avenge himself through sorcery, which is employed "as a last means of self-help."[26] It is to be noted throughout the cases having to do with justice that intent does not come into account; it is the act, not the purpose that fills the mind of the practical savage. Thus, in Melanesia, "recently a case came under notice in which payment was made by a man who was not actually the cause of death. This man was in his canoe with three others, one of whom was a youth of about 14 years. Seeing a shark in shallow water this man drove his spear into it; the spear broke off leaving five inches or so in the shark, which plunged upward and struck the canoe, knocking the youth into the water. The shark turned quickly and seized the boy, tearing out the whole of one side from shoulder to groin. He died, of course, and the owner of the canoe, the man who had speared the shark, paid the relatives just as if he himself had speared the boy."[27] In South Africa, "a very effective law is the following:—If a debtor does not pay his creditor, the latter will take anything of the same value as the debt, say a cow, from anybody who is living in the same kraal as the debtor. The owner of the cow misses it, and searching, finds his cow at the cattle kraal of a stranger. He goes and asks the reason why his cow has been brought there. The creditor tells him the name of his debtor, and informs the owner of the cow, who is only an inhabitant of the debtor's kraal, that the cow will be kept impounded by him until the debtor has paid his account. The owner of the cow is bound by Bawenda law to leave it in the hands of the stranger until the debt has been paid. Consequently, if he wishes to have his cow back, the only way for him to get it is to force the debtor to pay his creditor. This is called . . . the law of 'tit for tat.' "[28] Again, "a master was responsible for the actions of his slaves. I remember a case . . . when a slave attempted the life of a headman in his master's town. His attempt failed and he escaped to a very distant town. The master was tied up, killed, and eaten."[29]

Retaliation or repayment may be indefinitely under dispute. "Nothing which is owing can ever be remitted, it matters not how long ago a claim arose or whether the original parties in such a case are dead and gone, for debts, claims and property are all inheritable from one generation to another. To hear two men enter upon an endless dispute regarding some paltry article which was owed by one of their grandsires to the other takes one's breath away."[30] Again, "if a murderer refuses to pay up he is killed in the same manner that he killed his victim. If a wife commits a murder and her husband refuses to

[25] Roth, *N. W. Cent. Queensland*, 140, 141.
[26] Krieger, *Neu-Guinea*, 205.
[27] Seligmann, *Melanesians*, 669, note.
[28] Gottschling, in JAI, XXXV, 378.   [29] Weeks, in JAI, XXXIX, 429.
[30] Dundas, C., in JAI, XLIII, 489.

pay up the fine, he is killed, the woman is not punished. If a man escapes after committing murder and gets away altogether, his nearest male relation will be called upon to pay up the fine; if he refuses he is killed. If the murderer has no male relations his clan will be called upon to pay the fine; if they refuse, one of their male members is killed by members of the clan of the deceased."[31] This case illustrates both group-solidarity and also the basic nature of blood-for-blood retaliation; if blood-money is not paid, the situation reverts to original principles.

The retaliation-idea has some curious applications. In the Congo region, at the time of the appointment of a chief, who is a judge, "the heads of all the families living in the district who wished to come under his jurisdiction cut down his plantains and banana trees. This action gave him a *casus belli* against all the towns that acknowledged him as judge. By the cutting down of his plantains he became the offended party, and as such had the right of aggressive action against the offenders. No subsequent quarrel could be taken up until the first was settled. Hence the above chief appointed as judge might enrage a town by his decision, and might call on the other towns to help him enforce his verdict, yet the said town could not attack the chief judge's town because of the old standing palaver of cutting down his plantains and bananas. This ensured the chief judge's immunity from quarrels with people who did not like his decisions, and as there was no fear of such quarrels there was a guarantee of a certain amount of justice and impartiality in the decisions given. He was paid to act as judge by those who needed his services, and this pay refunded his temporary loss from his destroyed plantains and bananas."[32] In Angola, "if a weaker man wants to avenge himself upon an enemy too strong for him, he betakes himself to a prince and declares himself his slave." The new master gives him a box on the ear, tears his cap, or performs some other symbolic action indicative of the desired relation. Then the injured man "can reckon on sufficient help and support to get himself satisfaction."[33]

"Cases of murder are differently regarded by the Chukchee, according to whether they are committed within or without the family group. In the latter case murder is subject to blood-revenge on the part of the family group of the victim. Murder within the family group is usually considered a matter to be dealt with by that group alone. . . . It is usually a 'bad man' who is murdered by members of his own family group. They think it is better to dispose of a troublesome individual in this way than to be forced to undertake a blood-feud by leaving such a person to be killed by a member of another family. . . . Other examples cited, however, show that the victims were sometimes not 'bad men,' but that the murderers were simply acting for their own material interests, or in anger."[34] This method of evading the action of retaliation enforces again the essential solidarity of the group.

On Easter Island "crimes of any sort, but especially the graver ones, are of great rarity, and murder, at the present day, unknown. Petty thieving is common, is considered a venial offense, and the injured party seeks redress by stealing in kind, if possible, but in any event, stealing from the thief. There are no punishments, so called.[35]

[31] Barrett, in JAI, XLI, 34. [32] Weeks, in JAI, XXXIX, 430.
[33] Bastian, *Deut. Exped.*, I, 195.
[34] Czaplicka, *Aborig. Siberia*, 24-25. [35] Cook, in USNM, 1897, I, 719.

Jones[36] mentions two instances illustrative of the indifference of natives to the intentions of a malefactor. "A man attended the funeral of another. He felt so sad that he resorted to the whiskey bottle to drown his sorrow. He succeeded in more thoroughly doing so than he had planned, as it killed him. Whether it had more than the usual amount of poison in it, or he drank too much, we do not know. At any rate, his tribe wanted damages for the death of their member, so they held responsible the clan of the man whose funeral he had attended. The argument was that if their man had not attended the funeral he would not have been so sad; and had he not been so sad, he would not have drunk the whiskey; and had he not drunk the whiskey he would not have died. Consequently the family that gave the funeral were to blame." Again, "a native was working in the great Treadwell mine at Douglas. He quit, and was on his way to the steamer returning home when he stepped into the post-office and found a letter containing a dun for one hundred dollars. Not having the money, he concluded to go back to work, earn the money and pay the bill. In less than a week he fell . . . down a shaft in a hoisting cage and received injuries which paralyzed him for life. At this writing he is living, but absolutely helpless, and cannot live long. The one who wrote him the letter is held responsible for his injuries and will be for his death. The tribe of the writer of the letter will have to pay heavy damages."

The Guiana Indians do not dispense justice to the individual through community-action, or through the chief; it is the business of the person injured or of his relatives to get their own redress. The law of talion prevents increase of population. "As a matter of fact, though the Indian may lead a life of apparent amity, an injury is neither forgotten nor forgiven, but only bottled up, so to speak, to be subsequently sampled at the next drinking party, where his tongue is unbridled, his mind inflamed, and his actions are more or less irresponsible. So well is this known and recognized that at every drunken orgie one of the first concerns of the women is to hide all the paddles, cutlasses, and other weapons with which the men might damage one another."[37]

"Self-help is admitted by the ancient law of Indo-European nations in connection with civil as well as with criminal litigation. In fact it looks almost as if it were the original basis of possession itself. It is at least characteristic that some of the expressions referring to ownership in Indo-European language go back to the notion of conquest, the taking of booty. The Italian *roba,* meaning chattels, goods, is nothing but the Teutonic *Raub,* the produce of robbery, and the Latin *praedium,* estate, is related to *praeda,* booty. No wonder that the symbol of property in Rome came to be a spear, *hasta.*"[38]

It is clear enough from such cases as the above that early society is quite willing to tolerate retaliation provided it is accomplished in authorized ways. It is in the interest of the group that aggression shall not go unresisted, and retaliation is the instrument nearest at hand and is as if provided for the purpose. It is therefore appropriated and controlled, which is the first step

36 *Thlingets,* 196, 197-198.
37 Roth, in BAE, XXXVIII, 557, 558.
38 Vinogradoff, *Hist. Jurispr.,* I, 357; §§108, 109, above.

toward getting the private righting of private wrongs out of the hands of the individual and into those of the society. The case is one where punishment, though not yet imposed by society's functionaries, is permitted, under conditions that safeguard society's interest, by public opinion. Later on, when punishments have come to be imposed by regular functionaries, the penalties reveal their relationship to permitted retaliation.

A curious form of retaliation is suicide. To understand how anyone might take recourse to this method which seems to us, with our ideas and traditions, exactly the way not to do it, one must bear in mind that all peoples do not share our convictions about the sanctity and worth of earthly existence, while they possess a faith in their beliefs about the next life which, however loudly we may profess it, we do not exhibit. Their faith is, at any rate, strong enough to act upon and it does not seem to occur to them that they are taking chances. If a person is not powerful enough to avenge himself in life, he believes that as a ghost he will be able to do so;[39] and thus believing, threatens suicide. Since the individual whom he menaces shares his beliefs quite unshakenly, the threat is often sufficient to secure redress; but if not, there is no hesitancy about carrying it out. This is a sort of *post mortem* retaliation.[40] If an offended person mutilates or kills himself, the offender must imitate him or there is great popular indignation. If a ruler is tyrannical, the population may come and sit down about the palace to die of hunger.[41] This is a form of coercion upon others that assures rights to the weak.

Steinmetz[42] goes into the various motives for suicide. We are interested here only in the one of revenge. Lasch[43] cites a number of cases, remarking in summary that since it is believed that one's ghost can stay about and injure his enemies, it is understandable "when the injured party suicides in or before the house of the one inflicting injury; for his soul will hover about the scene of the deed, torture the ill-doer, and thus take the vengeance which the injured person from lack of power or from fear of blood-vengeance was not in a position to inflict in life."

In the Trobriand Islands, "suicide seems to be very common. It is per-

39 §§201, 206, 207, 208, 214, below.
40 On the custom of dying to redress a grievance see Hopkins, in *Jr. Am. Or. Soc.*, XXI, 146.
41 Letourneau, *Morale*, 298.   42 In AA, VII, 53 ff.
43 In *Globus*, LXXIV, 37 ff.

formed as an act of justice, not upon oneself, but upon some person of near kindred who has caused offence. As such it is one of the most important legal institutions among these natives."[44] In West Africa, "should a person commit suicide, and before so doing attribute the act to the conduct of another person, that other person is required by native law to undergo a like fate. This practice is termed 'killing oneself upon the head of another,' and the person whose conduct is supposed to have driven the suicide to commit the rash act, is visited with a death of an exactly similar nature. Such suicides are rare, and the family of the suicide generally forego their right to the death of the person indicated as the cause of the calamity, receiving money damages instead."[45] In one tribe of India, "should alms be refused, the men, to frighten the people into giving, threaten to run an iron skewer through their own cheeks and sometimes carry out the threat (several men of a gang showed scars to prove this)."[46] One female divinity was breastless, having, as the legend goes, cut off her breasts to bring blood-guilt upon those who would not respect her safeguard.[47]

"The one who rejects a suppliant and compels him to kill himself, goes to hell. The only one who has a right to exercise constraint of this sort is a priest. Clearly then the practice of door-besieging is a restriction for a special cause of a practice once recognized as universal, suicide with especial intent to compel the victim of the practice to yield under pain of future punishment after death."[48] This interpretation is a little out of line with the preceding. "The inviolability of the Brahmin is a fixed principle with the Hindoos, and to deprive him of life, either by direct violence or by causing his death in any mode, is a crime which admits of no expiation. To this principle may be traced the practice called dharna, which may be translated caption or arrest. It is used by the Brahmins to gain a point which cannot be accomplished by any other means, and the process is as follows; the Brahmin who adopts this expedient for the purpose mentioned proceeds to the door or house of the person against whom it is directed, or wherever he may most conveniently arrest him; he then sits down in dharna with poison or a poignard or some other instrument of suicide in his hand, and threatening to use it if his adversary should attempt to molest or pass him, he thus completely arrests him. In this situation the Brahmin fasts, and by the rigour of the etiquette the unfortunate object of his arrest ought to fast also, and thus they both remain till the institutor of the dharna obtains satisfaction. In this, as he seldom makes the attempt without the resolution to persevere, he rarely fails; for if the party thus arrested were to suffer the Brahmin sitting in dharna to perish by hunger, the sin would for ever lie upon his head. This practice has been less frequent of late years, . . . but the interference of the Court and even of the Resident has occasionally proved insufficient to check it."[49] Wilken[50] mentions the dharna as one of the applications of animism; the soul of one who dies at the threshold will not quit the place, but stay about to torment the owner. He believes that the Nias custom of taking up one's abode at the house of a debtor until paid is a relic of a practice once religious but now secular. The

[44] Malinowski, in JAI, XLVI, 360.   [45] Ellis, *Tshi*, 302.
[46] Gunthorpe, in JASB, I, 162.   [47] Campbell, in JASB, IV, 62.
[48] Hopkins, in *Jr. Am. Or. Soc.*, XXI, 146 ff.
[49] Maine, *Early Inst.*, 298-300.   [50] In VG, II, 402-403, notes.

sojourning creditor must be fed with the best pork and rice, even if the debtor and his children go hungry. In any case the debtor is responsible for the death of his creditor, should this occur; he may not be afraid of his haunting ghost, but he is answerable on the basis of the mores.

The custom is most marked among the Chinese. They "think that after death every man's soul can take vengeance upon surviving enemies. Hence a remedy for quelling lengthy disputes, which seldom fails, is for one party to say that he will commit suicide that he may avenge himself afterwards. Frequently the paltriest quarrel, especially between women, becomes an occasion for suicide. A few leaves of a poisonous plant which grows on almost every road-side are sufficient to put an end to life."[51] "Chinese law and morals hold individuals responsible for all suicides of which they may have been even the indirect cause." Strikers often hold out and die of hunger.[52] A proprietor is responsible for indemnity if a man is found dead on his premises. Hence suicide is a method of insurance for a man's children.[53] A published letter from China relates several cases of attempted suicide by an overdose of opium, taken to secure revenge upon a neighbor. "The only amusing thing about these sad affairs is that almost invariably it is the other party to the quarrel who brings the victim in for help, and who never tires walking him or her up and down the corridor, pleading, commanding, and threatening the subject to keep awake and take an antidote or emetic. For woe to him if the victim dies and he has a suicide laid at his door."[54]

With these cases may be aligned the Irish custom of fasting on a man's door-step to coerce him.[55]

§178*. Blood-Vengeance.

Perhaps the most striking case of retaliation and its modification is afforded by the treatment of manslaughter. No society can maintain order and security that permits such an exhibition of violence within its jurisdiction. As in other forms of retaliation, it is quite commendable to take vengeance upon the alien; but if there is to be a peace-group at all, members of the same kin-association or tribe must act toward each other upon a different principle. The cases will show how difficult it was for society to control the situation in the matter of homicide; for a long time it continued to tolerate even the blood-feud, however heavily that practice might be fraught with peril to its existence. Even today some forms of homicide for vengeance are tolerated, being referred to the "unwritten law."

The matter of blood-revenge was intimately associated with the

[51] Rehatsek, in JASB, I, 318.
[52] Letourneau, Prop., 169 (where references are given).
[53] Bordier, Géog. Méd., 493.
[54] Inglis, "From China," in Osage City Free Press for Dec. 22, 1898.
[55] Maine, Early Inst., 39.

religious ideas prevalent among those who practised it. It was necessary to attain such revenge in order that the ghost of the slain might be "laid."[56] This obligation, resting as it did upon all members of the kin-group, helped, by emphasizing its solidarity, to make that group a stronger society. Protection was thus afforded to its members. In later times the duty involved was regarded as due to the blood-tie, whereas originally that tie was only the definition of those upon whom the duty, as fellow-members of the group, devolved. In time the state came to assume the obligation and then the original motive force, which was fear lest the unappeased ghost do damage, was lost to sight. If the ghost could for any reason not be appeased by retaliation upon his murderer, then those on whom the duty of blood-vengeance had descended had to be purified by water or otherwise, that is, delivered from the anger of the incensed ghost. Condemnation consisted often of handing over a culprit to the free vengeance of the injured man or his friends. Then, by means of sanctuary and time-taboos[57] the privilege of vengeance was limited both spatially and temporally. As property increased, the condemned could ransom himself if the injured parties would agree; and, later on, the tribunal might compel the acceptance of such commutation or put the insistent avenger out of the fold. Money-composition was the next step, and ransom from the blood-avenger came to be regarded as payment for the wrong suffered.[58] In all cases the settlement is found to be passing out of the hands of the injured parties into those of society. The various aspects of the matter should be brought into relief in the following representative illustrations, in which should be noted both the insignificance of the individual in the group and also the insistence upon the fact of homicide, irrespective of motive or any other circumstance later deemed to be extenuating.

In Australia, "if two or more men fight, and one of the number be accidentally killed, he who caused his death must also suffer death. But should the offender have an elder brother, then he must die in his place; if he have no elder brother, his father must be his substitute; but in case he has no male relative to suffer for him, he himself must die. He is not allowed to defend himself, nor indeed is he informed of the time when sentence will be executed. On some night appointed, an armed party surround and despatch him. Two

---

56 §§228 ff., below.   57 §§251, 255, 273, below.
58 Lippert, *Kgchte.*, II, 326, 327, 591.

sticks, each about six inches in length—one representing the killed and the other the person executed—are then buried, and upon no occasion is the circumstance afterwards referred to." The solidarity of the whole group is revealed by the fact that "a law prevails, among some tribes at least, which renders it compulsory on the nearest male relative to take the life of some one of the tribe to which the slayer belongs. And even if a man dies a natural death, they believe he has been killed by some unseen hand, in which case they resort to divination, to ascertain the tribe from which the slayer came. The avenger is generally not actuated so much by personal ill-feeling as by the desire to perform a supposed duty, and thereby maintain his good name among his own people. He therefore sometimes kills the first of the tribe he meets, without for a moment considering whether or not his victim was even an accessory. Justice is then supposed to be vindicated. Blood for blood is their universal law; revenge becomes a sacred duty; and if a man withhold his hand from taking life as a satisfaction for his brother's, he is ever after looked upon as a coward."[59] It is well worth noting that a wife is not a blood-relation to her husband;[60] if she is killed he is not bound to avenge her; her own blood-relatives must do that. No institutional relation is as close as the blood-tie. Hagen[61] says that not even the low societal organization of the Papuans can exist in the presence of blood-vengeance. If this is the case, then that organization must have advanced considerably, for blood-revenge is a constructive societal institution at one stage. "From the outside, in the period between the kin-group stage and the first beginnings of state-formation, the union of group-members is exhibited chiefly in blood-revenge."[62] A seeming paradox, readily explicable if the native standpoint be occupied, is where there is no payment for the murder of a kinsman; for here "the persons who should pay the blood-price would likewise be the recipients of it; consequently no payment is possible in these circumstances." A man, however, had to pay for killing his wife; the blood-money went to her kin who divided it among themselves by mutual agreement.[63]

In West Africa, "each family is held by the community responsible for the misdeeds of its members. However unworthy a man may be, his 'people' are to stand by him, defend him, and even claim as right his acts, however unjust. . . . Revenge, especially for bloodshed, is everywhere practised. It is a duty belonging first to the 'ijawe' (blood-relative), next to the 'ikaka' (family), next to the 'etomba' (tribe). . . . The murdered man's own family take the lead,—in case of a wife, her husband and his family, and the wife's family; sometimes the whole 'ikaka'; finally, the 'etomba.' "[64] The order here reveals the order of regulative development, from family to tribe.[65] "The family collectively is responsible for all crimes and injuries to person or property committed by any one of its members, and each member is assessible for a share of the compensation to be paid. On the other hand, each member of the family receives a share of the compensation paid to it for any crime or injury committed against the person or property of any one of its members." The system of family-responsibility was, however, in some cases, subsequent to that of community-responsibility, "under which each member of a village, or other

[59] Smyth, *Vict.*, I, 129; II, 229.   [60] Curr, *Aust. Race*, I, 100.

[61] *Papua's*, 256.   [62] Krieger, *Neu-Guinea*, 199.

[63] Jenness and Ballentyne, *D'Entrecasteaux*, 79-80.

[64] Nassau, *Fetichism*, 4, 19.   [65] §§146-149, above.

community, was assessible for a share of the fine to be paid in compensation of injuries committed by one of the community upon others not belonging to it."[66] It is quite evident that this joint-accountability, whether of family or other group, tends to enforce the control of the individual by the society; and it is to be noted that the injuries in question, where group-responsibility is in vogue, are supposed to be inflicted upon, or suffered from, members of the out-group.

In East Africa, "blood revenge was restricted to the slaying of one person, but it naturally tended to further reprisals, and so to feuds or open warfare, which was not to the interest of the chief, sultan or king, who thereby lost subjects, and consequently intervened. And the degree to which such intervention was effectual was according to the power of these supreme authorities. . . . The right of private revenge was undisputed, but was frequently simply interdicted by the chief wherever he had sufficient authority to enforce his decision. Sanctuary was known in so far as a murderer might seek refuge with the chief, and the latter, not wishing further bloodshed, would decline to surrender the offender, so that the pursuers were obliged to content themselves with payment of blood-money." This blood-money was mostly paid by the family or clan, and to the next of kin as representative of the family; he then distributed it to the various relatives of the deceased. "Homicide is, in fact, a crime which concerns the whole family or even the whole clan on both sides; the clan and family have been weakened by the loss of a member, and this is a loss which is felt beyond the circle of immediate relatives. In this respect murder is treated differently from all other crimes, and has probably retained a significance surviving from the most primitive times in that it reflects so vividly the individual solely as one of the family group or clan. . . . The killing of a human being is always one and the same offence, regardless of the circumstances under which it is committed. Neither in this nor any other offence are provocation, self-defence or unintended acts, accepted as extenuating circumstances. Severe as this general rule may seem, it has its reasons. Undoubtedly any relaxation in this respect would result in increased bloodshed, and its maintenance prevents fine distinctions being drawn between intentional, and unintentional or negligent acts, while it enforces care and restraint upon men's actions. . . . So strict is this broad rule that Kikuyu elders have told me that if a man were seized by a lion, and his friend wishing to save him were to throw a spear, he would be liable for compensation if he inadvertently struck the man instead of the lion. . . . It is by no means necessary that death should ensue immediately or within a given period, it is sufficient that a blow or wound inflicted is ultimately the cause of death, no matter how many years may have elapsed between the two events. To European ideas these rules may appear unreasonable, perhaps pointless, but in view of the lenient methods adopted to prevent homicide it is a wise precaution to give a wide meaning to this offence. . . . The custom of the Akamba provides an exception to the general rule of liability, accidental killing being here compensated by only half the amount of bloodmoney." There are a few junctures when liability is set aside: "If two men kill each other in a fight, compensation is dispensed with, and a man may kill another whom he sees in the act of killing his brother, without paying compensation. So also, if a murder is committed and compensation refused, it may be taken by force, and if anyone is

<hr>

[66] Ellis, *Ewe*, 208, 209.

killed in the fight no bloodmoney is paid. Akikuyu elders have also told me
that a man may refuse to accept bloodmoney, and may instead kill the murderer or his relative. In short, any two deaths may be treated as a set-off one
against the other, provided that the slayer in the second instance was nearly
related to the first victim; in reality, this is, of course, only so because equal
compensation is due from both sides, and therefore payment would only be an
exchange.

"Thus it will be observed that compensation was far from being the accepted
penalty for murder: either the right of revenge prevailed or this was superseded by the power or influence of the authorities, or it was voluntarily waived
in favour of payment. But it is only natural that the waiving of this right was
held not to be respectable, and that it would easily be interpreted as cowardly.
It is, therefore, quite wrong to speak of murder as a matter of compensation
only." Tables are presented, showing compensation for various offences, which
add valuable detail to a first-class treatment.

The author quoted[67] goes on to say that "although the circumstances under
which a man is killed are immaterial, the relationship between him and the
slayer is a point upon which the crime and manner of compensating it greatly
depend. In all three tribes a man may kill his wife without paying any compensation, for the simple reason that no one could claim for the death but
himself. Any balance of dowry due at the time must, however, be paid, and in
Ukamba the father of the woman claims by right one cow, whereas he could
only receive it by gift if the dowry had been paid in full. In this tribe no other
relationship entirely exempts from compensation. If a man kills his own
daughter, her brother is entitled to two cows and a bull, but if he kills his
mother he must pay four cows and a bull. If a son is killed by his father,
half bloodmoney is claimed by the deceased's son, or failing a son, by a full
or half brother; failing any of these the claim is made by a nephew, but an
uncle can make no claim. A man who kills his father must pay seven cows and
a bull (half bloodmoney) to his brothers, or, if he has none, to his uncle's sons.
In all these cases it appears that the claim can be made only by near relatives,
but in absence of these the maternal grandfather may claim one cow in exchange for a bull. The clan is excluded from any share, although it contributes
as in any other case of homicide. If a man kills any distant relative, or a
clansman living in the same locality, he must pay half bloodmoney, but if he
slays a clansman not residing in his district he is liable for full bloodmoney."

The comments of the author are applicable to retaliation in almost any age
and place. "It must appear as curious that relationship and clanship tend to
reduce the amount of compensation due, but this is largely because blood-
money, being intended to replace by goods a life, and the slayer having an
interest or share in that life, the amount is reduced accordingly as his share
is greater or less. Thus a husband has sole share in his wife's person, and
therefore he can compensate no one. From these facts we must, however, the
more clearly perceive that compensation is not to be confounded with punishment, for it is least where relationship is closest, and among people with whom
the family bond is so remarkably close we cannot assume that the slaying of a
father or son is regarded as a minor offence. Indeed it is said that a parricide
is doomed to die himself. An incident related to me as absolutely authentic,

[67] Dundas, C., in JAI, LI, 236, 237, 238, 241; and in JAI, XLV, 263-266,
279 ff.

told of a man who, having speared his father, was cursed by the dying parent, and forbidden ever to drink water or eat food excepting from remote localities. For some time the unhappy man lived on sugar cane juice, but one day, forgetting the curse, he drank water from the river, and being unable to swallow it, died of suffocation. Leprosy is believed to be one of the results of parricide. Compensation, it must be remembered, wipes out the offence, but where nothing is paid the crime remains, and we can imagine the resentment shown to a man who deprives his own family of a member, yet cannot replace him in any way. In Kikuyu if the one who kills his father survives, his family deprives him of his inheritance, and in Ukamba if he refuses to pay, his brothers will kill him. A man who kills his mother is said never to find a woman who will marry him."

"The Jibaro Indian is wholly penetrated by the idea of retaliation; his desire for revenge is an expression of his sense of justice. The principle is eye for eye, tooth for tooth, life for life. If one reprehends a Jibaro because he has killed an enemy, his answer is generally: 'He has killed himself.' But blood revenge among these Indians is not merely owing to moral or ethical, but also to religious reasons. The soul of the murdered Indian requires that his relatives shall avenge his death. The errant spirit, which gets no rest, visits his sons, his brothers, his father, in a dream, and, weeping, conjures them not to let the slayer escape but to wreak vengeance upon him for the life he has taken. If they omit to fulfill this duty the anger of the vengeful spirit may turn against themselves. To avenge the blood of a murdered father, brother, or son, is therefore looked upon as one of the most sacred duties of a Jibaro Indian. . . . A man has perhaps been murdered while his sons were still small, and he has perhaps likewise lacked brothers or other male relatives who had been able to revenge his death. As soon as the sons become full grown they know what their duty toward their murdered father requires of them. However, in such cases it sometimes occurs that the affair is settled in a peaceful way. . . . The Jibaros do not find anything repugnant in . . . estimating the life of a parent with material equivalents, and an agreement like this is especially possible in cases where the crime to be punished has been committed very long ago."

The author[68] quoted renders an account of the blood-revenge system which is extraordinarily replete with suggestion. "Among the Jibaros blood revenge is not strictly individualized in the sense that it always directs itself exclusively against the slayer. The Jibaro certainly first of all wants to take revenge on the person who committed the crime, but if he can not be caught it may instead be directed against some one of his relatives—his brother, his father, even his mother or sister. To understand this we have to consider that the conception of individual personality and consequently of individual responsibility does not exist among the primitive Indians in the same sense as among civilized peoples. The individual forms an inseparable part of a whole, namely, of the family or tribe to which he belongs. Especially the members of the same family are regarded as, so to speak, organically coherent with each other, so that one part stands for all and all for one. . . . Such a view prevailing among the Indians, it is easy to understand that a Jibaro, with regard to the murder of one of his relatives, asks not so much which individual has committed the deed, but rather reasons in the following way: 'A member of that

[68] Karsten, "Jibaro," in BAE, Bull. LXXIX, 10-11, 11-13, 13-14.

family has murdered my relative; consequently, in revenge, some member of that family must die' . . . but he does not take the life of more than one member of the family, even if he has an opportunity of killing more. If he, for instance, killed not only the murderer himself but also some one of his brothers, this would awaken indignation in the whole tribe, and it would be considered righteous that the family thus offended in its turn should take revenge. The blood guilt in such a case has passed to the original avenger. This principle, which requires that there shall be justice in the retaliation so that life is weighed against life, of course, in itself has a tendency to limit blood revenge." There is no blood-revenge within the family, the basic peace-group; "among these Indians it sometimes occurs that a man kills his brother, if the latter, for instance, has seduced his wife or bewitched one of his children. But in this case blood revenge generally fails, inasmuch as the natural avengers—that is, the father and the remaining brothers—abstain from carrying it out. 'It is enough that one member of our family has died,' they say, 'why should we deprive ourselves of one more?' . . . That the blood feuds which take place within the tribe have an entirely different character from the wars of exter-mination waged against foreign tribes also appears from the fact that only in the latter case, but not in the former, the victors make trophies . . . of the heads of their slain enemies. . . . Nor is there any victory feast in this case." The trophy, among these Indians, is ultimately the shrunken head, called *tsantsa*. "The making of a *tsantsa* of an enemy's head, and especially the feast which follows the acquiring of such a trophy, implies the grossest insult, not only to the murdered person himself and his family, but to his whole tribe." This long quotation should justify itself, if in no other way, by the clear portrayal of primitive group-solidarity—a conception so foreign to modern minds and yet so necessary of apprehension if one hopes to enter into the essentials of societal evolution.

Blood-revenge appears in the Old Testament.[69] In case of doubt as to the slayer of a man in the fields, the nearest village has the duty of wiping out the blood-guilt. This is done by sacrifice and water-purification, as among the Greeks. "This custom is based upon the idea that the soul of the slain finds no rest and may do harm to the nearest community. Therefore the blood-guilt must be removed." Blood-revenge is the duty of the whole house. Originally it was directed against the whole family of the slayer. Blood-vengeance is taken even upon the animals. Whatever—not whoever—spills human blood must die. But the talion led to results which, with the alteration of life-condi-tions, were injustices and absurdities, and was gradually given up. There was some attempt to distinguish between murder and other forms of homicide, and on the distinction rested the right of asylum—chiefly at old cult-places. This device seems to have been taken over and developed from aboriginal models. With respect to other injuries the rule was: eye for eye, tooth for tooth.[70]

Among the Arabs, the duty of blood-revenge stands dominant among the other obligations. The holiness of blood transcends all other holy things; for example, it thrusts religion wholly into the background. The kin-group is the realized ideal, the gods pale beside it. . . . Among the Arabs the crime is cowardice and avarice, the virtue is earnest of goods and blood for one's own.

[69] II Sam., III, IV.
[70] Maurer, *Vkde.*, I, 110-111, 155, 164; Num., XXXV, espec. 22-25; Deut., XXIV, 16; II Kings, XIV, 6; Jer., XXXI, 30; Ezra, XVIII, 19 ff.

A bad man is one who asks first concerning the grounds, the merits of the case, when he is summoned to help by his cousins. He must stand by them, whether they are right or wrong; he must carry out the affair he has advised against, bear the burdens that others lay on him."[71] Abstention was required of one who was prosecuting a blood-feud.[72]

Whatever Æschylus[73] may have had his characters say about the impossibility of atoning for blood-guilt, in practice the Greeks from Homer's time employed the wergeld. Public opinion in Homer seems to be coming to approve of a commutation, though the cases of retaliation in kind are much commoner. "Many a man has received an indemnity from the murderer of his own brother, or even of his son, when he [the victim] was dead; and he [the murderer] has remained there, in the country, after paying a great reparation, and his [the avenger's] heart and noble soul have been stayed by the receiving of the penalty."[74] Banishment was employed in ancient Scandinavia to limit blood-revenge.[75] Life and honor, as well as property, were under the protection of the kin-group. Blood-revenge was a holy duty; in the oldest times a son could not inherit while his slain father remained unavenged. The murderer was outlawed and had to take to the forest until there was a settlement by fine or fight, and his father and brother or nearest relatives must flee with him. When the wergeld was in question the avengers must swear to let the matter drop after payment.[76]

The blood-feuds of the Middle West[77] do not seem so strange in the light of such cases as the above. Kohler,[78] after citing several parallels to the Albanian custom, concludes: "The further we penetrate into the history of justice, the more are we astonished by the universal character of the jural ideas."

The evidence reveals the form of retaliation before us as peculiarly correlated with kinship-organization. The incoming of tribal government, after the amalgamation or fusion of the constituent kin-groups, seems to throw the primordial system out of adjustment. Especially to be noted is the fact that the exaction of blood-money is not a punishment; it is a replacement. If the homicide is flagrant enough, compensation will not be accepted. Punishment is often in the hands of the spirits, when the crime is a sin.[79] Jenks[80] believes that the earliest object of recorded law is the suppression of the blood-feud. And while, as has been noted, the tribe and state still make use of the traditional expedient, they tend to control its employment and to modify it. After a time it becomes obsoles-

[71] Wellhausen, *Skizzen,* III, 194.   [72] Smith, *Relig. Sem.,* 482.
[73] In *Choephori* and *Eumenides.*
[74] *Iliad,* IX, 632-636; Keller, *Hom. Soc.,* 283 ff.
[75] Magnusson and Morris, *Grettir the Strong,* 250.
[76] Geijer, *Svensk. Hist.,* I, 300.
[77] Clemens, *Huckleberry Finn,* ch. XVIII.
[78] "Blutrache," in *Pol.-Anth. Rev.,* I, 204; Lane, *Shala,* ch. VII, *et passim.*
[79] §274, below.   [80] *Law and Pol.,* 197.

cent, though it lasts on sporadically and in survivalistic form into late stages of evolution.

§179. Justice. When the individual settlement of private quarrels had been taken from the hands of the aggrieved into those of the community at large, the latter may be said, in the modern phrase, to have assumed the administration of justice.[81] What it did was to insist upon its monopoly of the right to administer the code of mores; it was the provisions of the code that represented "justice." If, then, codes are in evolution, the conception of justice must have been in evolution, that is, subject to change and to the necessity of adjustment to mutable life-conditions. History shows it to have been in precisely that state. A man gets justice when he gets his rights; and since rights are not natural and immutable but are also matters of adjustment, justice could scarcely be absolute and invariable.

Gumplowicz,[82] with his usual tendency to ignore the services of incipient and partially organized government and its regulations, which do not really deserve the name of "state" and "laws," says that if we should take away from our past the development of the state and of the civil law, every trace of a notion of justice would pass away from our minds. The fact of rights as they have grown up in the state alone creates in us the idea of justice. It is nothing to the contrary that we often regard a law as unjust, because our sense of justice, developed under the influence of civil law, may run ahead of the development of that law; for all institutions of law exist only by virtue of written statute or tradition, while civil relations and our sense of justice have gone on farther, and a new legal definition of right must soon be made.

In our parlance any law which represents a maladjustment, whether it is survivalistic or is a new variation that is inexpedient, will seem unjust to many; and a law that is generally expedient and regarded as just by the great body of society, will seem unjust to outlying individuals and groups who are out of harmony with most of their fellows.

The state alone, Gumplowicz goes on, gives the standard of justice; and the limits of the notion of justice, therefore, are the conditions of the existence and maintenance of the state. The society automatically distributes rights in its own interest, and men come to consider that the ensuing arrangement represents justice.

[81] Lugard, *Brit. Trop. Afr.*, chs. XXVII, XXVIII.
[82] *Soc.*, 193, 194, 227.

When men come to reflect and dream over the facts of life, they may imagine an equilibrium in which no one encroaches or is encroached upon. This is a utopia. The oppressed have always risen, struggled, invented dogmas to prove their oppressors wrong and themselves right. Perhaps they win their way up to equality. Then, gaining power, they reach out to get more, aggrandize themselves, encroach, and perhaps come to oppress their former oppressors. One might almost visualize the series: slave, serf, villain, yeoman, employee, capitalist, master, boss, oppressor. No equilibrium can exist while there is motion and competition, that is, life; only in death can it be realized, if anywhere. And while life goes on readjustment must continue and the idea of justice must change. It is a modern notion, in hating what we call injustice or oppression, to think that all men must have hated what we hate. It is a shock to such sentiments to find, for instance, that savage women do not harbor resentment at the injustice which, according to our ideas, they suffer, or that savage men value what we should call a bloody despotism. In the Middle Ages it was assumed to be natural and inevitable that he who had power should use it. The chivalrous protection of women was largely humbug, the limits within which it was practised revealing its essential character.

There can be, therefore, no abstract, absolute, and final justice, any more than anything else that is absolute, except as certain essential arrangements in the code may disengage themselves from inessentials during the process of automatic selection, and appear as adjustments upon whose persistence that of the society depends. Since no society can persist which does not forbid murder within, and since that confers the right to life; then it is always and ever unjust to infringe upon that right and just to respect and defend it. But the mind easily runs wild when it deals with generalizations, begins to brood upon equality, somehow to be attained, and evolves conceptions of perfect and even god-given justice. There is an old conception of "distributive justice" which goes back to the Greeks, and which some recent writers have brought out again. "Distributive justice is justice in which all personal circumstances are duly allowed for so that all are made 'equal' on an absolute standard. Of course equality must necessarily be carried to some such conception at last. It is evident that God alone could give distributive justice; and we find, in this world in which we are, that God has not seen fit to provide for it at all."[83]

Reparatory or compensatory justice is another vagary of the meditating mind intent upon ideals never to be realized. Do we not owe compensation to the negroes in this country because our forefathers did them the injustice of bringing them over here as slaves? This question can be answered by another: Can the living of one group assume to compensate the living of another group for wrong done by the ancestors of the former to the ancestors of the latter—such ancestors having acted in accordance with notions of their time which have lost hold upon the minds of the now-living or are actually offensive to them? Adjustive change in the mores has intervened and a change in the conception of justice has followed.

Still more foolish is it to look for justice in the world at large, outside of the peace-group which maintains its code as a condition of its own persistence. In nature forces act upon material things precisely according to their constitution. A rotten limestone perishes more quickly under the operations of the weather than a hard granite. A hillside without trees is more quickly stripped of soil by the rain than one covered with a forest. No one would speak of justice in this connection. It is just as improper to speak of justice in connection with the fate of a people. Such fate is the result of causes which are partly in the object, partly in the forces of nature and history. The only justice there is is the conformity of the results to the causes.[84]

§180. "Natural" Law. The administration of justice means, to the civilized man, the enforcement of law. Law, as we view it, is a sort of crystallization or precipitation of the mores. Here yet again one is obliged to take account of certain ideas which parallel those about "natural" rights. This field of study is so plagued by such conceptions that no representative of them should be allowed to pass without specific challenge.

Justice Holmes[85] has paid brief, genial, but illuminating respects to "Natu-

---

[83] Sumner, *Coll. Ess.*, II, 89.   [84] Gumplowicz, *Soc.*, 227.
[85] "Natural Law," in *Harvard Law Review*, XXXII, 40 ff.; the following is taken from Keller, "Law in Evolution," in *Yale Law Jr.*, XXVIII, 769 ff.

ral Law." He thinks that in all men there exists an ingenuous and naïve demand for a superlative—"so much so that the poor devil who has no other way of reaching it attains it by getting drunk." In this world of relativities the soul strains after finalities and absolutes. "It seems to me that this demand is at the bottom of the philosopher's effort to prove that truth is absolute and of the jurist's search for criteria of universal validity which he collects under the head of natural law." It is evident enough that the Justice takes but limited stock in natural law as represented by such "collections." The implication of his writings is that law is evolutionary.

The most accessible point on which to join issue as to this contention is the term "natural." This term is under suspicion, and deserves it. About it has collected a clutter of intellectual rubbish, heaped up by the winds of doctrine and rooted at, from time to time, by the vagrant dialectician. We men have stock ways of concealing ignorance and of dissimulating indolence and prepossession. "It is easy," writes Darwin,[86] "to hide our ignorance under such expressions as the 'plan of creation,' 'unity of design,' etc., and to think that we give an explanation when we only restate a fact." Camouflage is nothing new in the intellectual world, as is sufficiently indicated by the avidity with which the term has been seized upon as a metaphor. What is under the painted cheese-cloth this time?

In earlier and simpler ages men knew little and frankly referred the explanation of what they could not account for on the basis of concrete experience, to the world of spirits which, as they conceived of it, surrounded and permeated their existence. In so doing they regularly sought for an agent rather than a cause. The fellow-tribesman died of some disease; and the survivors asked forthwith, not *what* killed him, but *who* had done him to death—by witchcraft. How did the world and man come into being? Unkulunkulu made them. How did man acquire fire? Prometheus stole it from heaven. Where did the laws come from? Minos "gave" them.

This tendency to seek a supernatural agency for all phenomena not explicable with the aid of present or accumulated experience, under the tests of reality current in ordinary life, is represented by copious survivals among more sophisticated peoples. Among these is the habit of personalizing abstractions. Says Darwin,[87] again: "It is difficult to avoid personifying the word Nature";

[86] *Origin of Species*, 497.   [87] *Origin of Species*, 75.

and he goes on to state that by nature he means "only the aggregate action and product of many natural laws, and by laws the sequence of events as ascertained by us." Manifestly this is not what Aquinas meant when he made proclamation that "by the law of Nature all things are common," thence deriving the sentiment that it was avarice which brought in the property-conception of mine and thine. What he had in mind was theological dogma, and his Nature was the Creator.

Scientifically speaking, the ascription of phenomena to the arbitrary action of a personal Power is only a grandiose way of saying: "I do not know." Sooner or later men have to say that, as they face the encircling dark; but the only way they have got as far as they have is by resolutely refusing to say it till they had to—and then by saying it squarely and without self-deceiving circumlocution.

It is the tendency of ignorance and of intellectual torpidity to throw itself forthwith upon the "higher causes," or the absolute, or the universal, or revelation—why search painfully for the special key if you have the pass-key?—and thence secure a major premise, out of which, then, anything and everything can be readily deduced. "You can always get out of a major premise everything you have put into it." This propensity, taken together with the personalization of the higher causes, or the absolute, has been the mode of primitive thought from the outset up to, and including, the present. It is easier. It is the line of least resistance. It is our human way to be engrossed in the definite and immediate things amidst which we live; and then we think with less strain if we think in terms of persons. In fact, the race has always personalized the less tangible and more abstract things, for by such means it has been possible to tie up floating and evasive conceptions so that they can be found again and dealt with. The vast impersonalities that control our destiny—Nature, Chance, God—are rendered into terms that men are more used to handle. The de-personalization of what has been long personalized has demanded a tedious process of mental discipline and development.[88]

We have slowly and laboriously extended the range of the "lower causes" to explain what was formerly referred forthwith to Zeus, or Fortuna, or to some Law-Giver. We have progressively

[88] Keller, *War to Peace*, 14.

eliminated the explanatory subterfuge; we have discarded the easy excuse and have girded ourselves to the arduous performance. But there are many modern men who yet resist the process; it is of such that Darwin[89] speaks when he refers to "one whose disposition leads him to attach more weight to unexplained difficulties than to the explanation of a certain number of facts"—that is, one who, in the face of difficulties, races incontinently back to the refuge of his chosen universal. Such an one refuses to remove an issue from the domain of Natural law into that of natural law.

An attenuated and a paler survival of this same attitude is to be found in the rooted persuasion that, even among the "lower causes," there is some absolute or universal to be detected. Many a man who rejects "Natural" in the sense of supernatural, yet readily uses "natural" to cover the unknown. Why is the right arm generally stronger than the left? It is "naturally" so. But that is no answer. It is an evasion; it is no more than equivalent to the childish retort: "Because it is." And then, when "natural" or "instinctive" is felt to be insufficiently protective, there will be a little hedging and a reference to "second nature." It is a sop, automatically and unconsciously thrown to vanity, to employ an expression that sounds as if it meant and explained something, and that darkly suggests vistas of profound reflection, rather than to admit ignorance baldly and without adornment.

Push the man who says that it is natural to be right-handed, and very likely he will abandon his subterfuge and be candid about his ignorance; or he will rake about in his mental outfit and try to construct some rudimentary theory. Either alternative is hopeful: the one ethically, the other scientifically. Theories can be corrected. This is the way we have got our science: we have corrected astrology into astronomy, alchemy into chemistry, magic into medicine. Push the man who talks about natural law, and he will either admit his ignorance, fly to the "Natural" of which his "natural" is but a thin and bloodless survival, or set to work to dig out some real evidence. As temperament and previous experience determine, he will show a blockhead's indifference, the antique recourse to unverified authority, or the modern procedure of the positivist. If he adopts the last course, he is on the way to the

[89] *Origin of Species,* 497.

truth of the matter, for he will shortly find that "natural law" exists about as little as "natural rights," or any other of those philosophical figments that have not been checked up with realities. He will soon come to see that law, like all other living things, is evolutionary, persisting only as it secures adjustment to a changing environment. Then he will change his tune about absolutes, finalities, and universals.

The origin of species was by creation, or it was by evolution. Species are either permanent and invariable, or they are not. Nobody who is informed has doubt any longer on this issue. Codes of law are either a created, permanent, and invariable product; or they are evolutionary, relative, changing, and adaptive. There is no third possibility. If law is evolutionary, then its course will show, as that of organic nature shows, a series of forms developing out of forms, in a connected series, with survival of the fitter, in adjustment to life-conditions.

No man can execute a *tour de force*, like that of Darwin, and confine resultant intellectual clarification, even if he wills, within the range of phenomena immediately under observation while the theory was being constructed. Ranges of knowledge are sufficiently akin to be subject to ready mutual infection. In the middle of the last century evolution was in the air, and Spencer was discovering it in the societal—or, as he called it, the superorganic—realm while Darwin and Huxley were demonstrating its presence in the organic. No man who has seriously followed Spencer's sociological writings, however much he may dissent from Spencer's specific contentions, has any excuse for not knowing that law, along with all other social forms and institutions, is a matter of growth from unpromising beginnings, through illimitable time—time that stretches not only from the present back to the beginnings, but also from the present forward to the last days of the last human society that shall inhabit this planet.

§181. The Mores and Laws.[90] What is said of the mores in general applies *a fortiori* to law. Mores are the society's traditional ways of acting in the presence of interest. But now one of

[90] Sumner, *Folkways*, §62; in §277 of text and *Case-Book* occur instances of the passage of ecclesiastical into secular law.

the major interests of any society is that there shall be cohesion, order, discipline, and coöperation within. Otherwise it is subject to aggression from without. The extreme case is that of war, when internal regulation reaches its acme of extension and severity. What is a crime in war-times is perhaps not even a misdemeanor in peace. In that sense, war represents a reversion to the crudities of the primal regulative system, with its frequent death-penalties for what are to us trivial offenses, its undeveloped apparatus of courts, advocates, and the rest. Here, in any case, is shown an insistence, under special stress, upon the regulative system that governs conduct in the interest of society's self-preservation.

Excluding war from the general case, it is clear that any society at any time must show discipline and order in the conduct of its members, if it is to persist under an unintermittent competition. For these qualities have survival-value in them. Only under the protection of extreme isolation, which minimizes the competition, may the societally or the organically obsolete last on. The mores take care of the more scattered and intimate questions of conduct. There is an extensive field where law does not enter at all, as, for instance, that of the domestic arcana. The essence of marriage is the personal, not the legal, relation. Man and wife have to live together in adjustments, involving good-breeding, self-sacrifice, and other qualities, which the law cannot touch. All such intimate relationships are matters of the mores. But certain more external cases, and classes of cases, enter more visibly and tangibly into the arena of public accessibility and regulation; and these become public precedents.

There is, at first, no distinction between the personal and the public (if these two classes of cases may be roughly so termed) or between mores and law. It is *themis* in Homer for a child to kiss his father; but yet the king is charged with upholding the *themistes*, and does it as an executive officer.[91] Naturally, though, he does not enforce caresses between parent and child. That the law is at first mere precedent is strikingly illustrated in the judgment-scene wrought on the shield of Achilles: there are a number of elders there; they all hear the case and each then speaks the precedent

91 Keller, *Hom. Soc.*, 252, 289 ff.

as he sees it. That is, he applies the current code whose tradition he as an elder is supposed to know best, to the specific circumstance. The audience applauds or not; and in the midst lie two pieces of gold, to be given to the judge who speaks the precedent "straightest."[92]

Precedents touching salient lines of conduct are presently codified in some fashion: in formulas or verses or, at length, on "tablets." This was long ago; but the very first codifications must have been preceded by an unreckonable period of test in usage. No one knows or can know their origins, except as he can infer it from what he can see of their subsequent course. Because they are so old they look to be inevitable and "natural." And so they are currently referred to some mythical, supernatural source—they were "given" on Tables amidst terrific exhibitions of supernatural potency. Further, if we examine such codifications, we find them pretty much alike; and that strengthens the impression that they are somehow inevitable, and therefore "natural." But human societies are nearly enough alike to be obliged, as a condition of self-preservation, to taboo practices that might be termed antisocial. Such taboos might be thought to be the result of acculturation (contagion, borrowing) if any possible agency of communication could be discovered or even imagined between remote parts of the earth in primitive ages. The better explanation of concurrences is that they are parallelisms—taboos that have sprung up under similar conditions as the only adequate response to them.

The taboo: "Thou shalt not kill (thy fellow-tribesman)" represents the very essence of social necessity, if internal cohesion and order are to be maintained; "Thou shalt not steal (from a tribal brother)" establishes the right to property, thus excluding aggressions, reprisals, and consequent chaos and disorganization. No society can long persist in the competition without such inhibitions. Here are laws, then, which have an eternal survival-value in them, so far as we can predict in the light of the past, over space and through time; they are as good in a modern society, as a *conditio sine qua non,* as they have been in the most rudimentary group. It will be noted that they contemplate merely the fellow-tribesmen—the members of the so-called "we-group," or "in-

92 Homer, *Iliad,* XVIII, 497 ff.

group"—for it is proper and praiseworthy to kill the alien, to rob
him, and to do to him all the other things which the code forbids
within the group. There is here no outcome of a yearning altruism; the code is as un-moral from that point of view as are any of
its analogues in nature—the lion's claw, the viper's tooth, the law
of the pack.

If we confine our attention to the elements common to all codes
of laws, over all earthly space and through such a vista of time
as we can span by recourse to our records, ethnographic and historic, and if we are artless, we may readily conclude that this presence of similar or even identical provisions in them supports the
assumption that they were put there by some Power. That is the
way similarities in organic nature used to be explained; it was
"unity of design" that accounted for all that—a pseudo-explana-
tion restating the question. Or we may say that part of law is
"given," as species were given; and admit that the rest was made
by man or at least not by "Nature," as formerly it was admitted
that varieties of animals and plants could be produced under the
operation of natural or "lower" agencies. Or we may dodge the
whole explanation by drawing a blank check on "natural law."

From the evolutionary standpoint, these similarities and identi-
ties are simply variations that have persisted in the conflict because endowed with lasting survival-value under any life-conditions
of society yet known to us. Tradition has passed them down unim-
paired, because they respond to a perennial necessity for the very
self-preservation of society. In that sense, they are natural and
not Natural law; but now we know what the "natural" means. We
are on the familiar scientific ground so strongly fortified by Lyell
and others, who championed the competency of forces which we
see daily in operation about us to produce any and all results
that come before our eyes. In that position inheres intellectual
liberation; and it is not recorded that the possession of a long and
orderly perspective has ever constituted a handicap when science
has come to practical application.

It is as impossible to draw a sharp line of distinction between
mores and laws as it is to determine at just what point in life a
youth becomes a man. The best that can be done is to distinguish
types which run into one another by almost imperceptible grada-

tions. "If the term 'mores' is to be applied only to formulations of very general ways having widely diffused conscious approval, then there are thousands of 'laws' that are not mores because they are formulations based upon limited precedents and known only to a few. We all say that an enacted dead letter is no longer law. Is not this the distinction between the mores and law? The difference is in the form of sanction, not in the form of enactment or of statement, or even in generality of application or conscious approval. A rule that is administered by societal functionaries consciously chosen for the purpose is law; a rule enforced only by public opinion or by amorphous mob-action is in the mores alone."[93] A distinction on some such lines enables us to hold two types of rule apart, chiefly, in the present case, in order that we may more intelligently perceive the passage, in societal evolution, of the simpler into the more complex.

It is probably useful to try, while making this distinction, to sharpen it somewhat, even at the risk of exaggeration. "When folkways have become institutions or laws they have changed their character and are to be distinguished from the mores. The element of sentiment and faith inheres in the mores. Laws and institutions have a rational and practical character, and are more mechanical and utilitarian. The great difference is that institutions and laws have a positive character, while mores are unformulated and undefined. . . . The laws, being positive prescriptions, supersede the mores so far as they are adopted. It follows that the mores come into operation where laws and tribunals fail. The mores cover the great field of common life where there are no laws or police regulations. They cover an immense and undefined domain, and they break the way in new domains, not yet controlled at all. The mores, therefore, build up new laws and police regulations in time."[94]

The "law-givers" have simply codified principles which had long been current and which already constituted a code of experience. Practical effort led life-maintenance into certain paths; then experiences were sifted and the repeated exercise of that which was more conducive to satisfaction impressed upon the sense of generations the rightness of certain lines of conduct.[95] Then the salient features of the code of experience were set down. But constant adjustments have always remained necessary; "judge-made law" represents the recognition of that necessity.[96] Judge-made law is based upon experience, where legislation is often mere experiment. "In England the cumbersome practice of judge-made law has been constantly and rightly defended as the means of ensuring a progressive adaptation to altered conditions combined with a traditional continuity."[97]

[93] Professor A. L. Corbin, personal communication.
[94] Sumner, *Folkways*, §63.   [95] Lippert, *Kgchte.*, I, 25.
[96] Corbin, "Law and Judges," in *Yale Rev.*, III, 234 ff.
[97] Vinogradoff, *Hist. Jurispr.*, I, 116.

"The true grounds of decision are considerations of policy and of social advantage, and it is vain to suppose that solutions can be attained merely by logic and the general propositions of law which nobody disputes. Propositions as to public policy rarely are unanimously accepted, and still more rarely, if ever, are capable of unanswerable proof. They require a special training to enable any one even to form an intelligent opinion about them. In the early stages of law, at least, they generally are acted on rather as inarticulate instincts than as definite ideas for which a rational defence is ready."[98]

Law-makers, says Gumplowicz,[99] amend and correct, constructing a patchwork out of which the actual facts and relations will develop a law to meet needs. Only in so far as law-makers limit themselves to satisfying the immediate necessities, the actual interests, do they produce statutes which can be used. As soon as they mount the high horse of doctrine and set up ideal principles in order to deduce laws from them, that is to say, soar into the realm of "free" intellectual activity, then mankind gets laws which Savigny said show our lack of vocation for law-making.

We turn now to observe, in the cases, the raw material out of which law, as we are accustomed to understand it, was formed. Among the more backward races there is nothing that deserves the name of law, and even in the case of the half-civilized there is seldom any enacted or codified regulation. The authorities, whether the elders or the chiefs, have as one of their chief functions the safeguarding of the mores; and they control the punishment of those who challenge the code.

A Fiji chief sent to Queen Victoria his favorite war-club, which he had called "the former, and until recently the only known, law of Fiji."[100] Even where the faith of the Prophet has overcome previous native beliefs, the Mohammedan laws have been ingeniously defeated and a return made toward ancient custom.[101] Caravans in Central Asia sometimes break down and the goods in process of transportation have to be left until they can be sent for. "Custom, stronger than law, binds all travellers to respect the property thus temporarily left in the road."[102] Some of the oldest law-books, so called, are merely aphoristic prose or even verse, and bear but slight resemblance to statutes.[103] In Japan, "legally, a man can go where he pleases. But as a matter of fact he can nowhere do as he pleases; for individual liberty is still largely restricted by the survival of communal sentiment and old-fashioned custom."[104] The Malays have not the notion of law in their language, and have no class of judges, but their system of rights rests on custom. The chief, in giving judgment, says, "It is the custom."[105] The effect of the taboo must not be ignored; it is the power behind most conduct; it "often did good service in the absence of positive public law, and was the most formidable weapon

98 Holmes, J., in Vegelahn vs. Guntner, 167 Mass., 92.
99 Soc., 205.   100 Weld, in PSM, XLVIII, 230.
101 Hanoteau et Letourneux, Kabylie, II, 135-136, 237.
102 Huntington, Pulse of Asia, 83.   103 Maine, Early Law, 10.
104 Hearn, Japan, 106.   105 Ratzel, Vkde., II, 452.

which church and state could yield. The rule of the father of the family suf-
ficed for ordinary needs, public laws scarcely existed, and the few relating to
land and its incidents were well understood. There were no judges and no
police. Councils, of greater or less importance or scope, were convened according to the subject to be considered."[106]

If one attempts to gather together the laws of some savage people, he finds
himself cataloguing a set of precedents regarding inheritance, marriage, the
position of woman, pregnancy, children, divorce, adoption, tattooing, and other
folkways.[107] These are adhered to more closely than are our laws. "A war-
party of Sioux surprised a squad of sleeping soldiers, who were all killed at
the first volley from the Indians. Their arms, blankets, and other property
were untouched, because, the attacking party being large, it could not be
decided by whose bullets the soldiers were killed." Stricken game always fell
to the one who killed it, and for this reason arrows were marked. Among the
tribes of North America there were three special methods of terminating quarrels. "When controversy arises in relation to ownership, the property is usually
destroyed by the clan or tribal authorities. Thus, if two men dispute in bartering their horses, a third steps in and kills both animals. It seems probable that
the destruction of property the ownership of which is in dispute is common to
all tribes. A second method of ending controversy is by the arbitration of
personal conflict. For example: if two persons disagree and come to blows
(unless the conflict end in the maiming or killing of one of the parties), it is
considered a final settlement, and they cannot thereafter appeal to their clans
for justice. By conflict a controversy is barred. This law seems to be universal.
The third method of terminating controversy is by the establishment of some
day of festival—sometimes once a month, but usually once a year—beyond
which crimes do not pass. The day of jubilee is a day of forgiveness. The
working of this principle might be illustrated in many ways."[108] The Indians
of Washington "have several unwritten laws regarding the beach. If a seal or
an otter be found by an Indian, the profits must be divided with any companions who chance to be with him. Formerly different parts of the beach
belonged to different factions. This rule is not now adhered to as formerly.
Drift-wood when chopped and piled against a log on the beach, is never disturbed by others in search of fuel; but any lost article is considered as belonging to the finder, even if the owner be known to him. If the article be
given up to the owner, it is expected that he will pay its full value."[109] The
Tlinkit "would sooner sustain great personal loss than face the opprobrium
which would be heaped upon them for the violation of any popular custom.
Public scorn is the most dreadful thing imaginable to them. And nothing invites it like the violation of their customs."[110]

The Homeric case, briefly alluded to above, is a typical one. We have already
seen that law is here in its infancy, inasmuch as the settlement of individual
disputes has not yet been taken out of the hands of the parties immediately
concerned. The rise of a régime of law and order is indicated, however, by
the fact that the talion may give way, in the case of homicide, to less primi-

[106] Williamson, *Cent. Polyn.*, III, 22.
[107] Senfft, in *Globus,* XCI, 139 ff., 149 ff., 171 ff.
[108] Powell, in BAE, III, lvii, lviii, lx.
[109] Willoughby, in *Smithson. Rep.,* 1886, pt. I, 273.
[110] Jones, *Thlingets,* 146.

tive methods. Punishments were, in the main, private matters. The germ of law to come lay in norms derived from the past and clothed with all the sanction of ancestor-reverence and religion; these went under the names of *dikē* (what has been "pointed out") and *themis* (what has been "put" or established). These terms were used commonly as equivalent to "hereditary custom" or "hereditary precedents of procedure," and covered the whole of social existence. Disputes involving social relations of importance were referred to the elders, who best knew the code, and were settled according to precedent. They were decided in the presence of the people, who took sides with one or the other party; the disputants were eager to get a decision from "one who knows"—the term translated "judge." The elders sat in the sacred circle upon polished stones and each in his turn spoke his judgment. The presence of heralds and of the scepter seem to betoken the presence of royal power, delegated to the elders. Chiefly to be noticed is the interpretation of the unwritten law of ancestral custom, treasured in the memories of the old and experienced, and reverenced by the people. There is a distinctly religious tinge to all early law; the *themis* is under the strong sanction of the gods who loved not deeds of violence; if men pronounced "crooked" judgments, Zeus punished them severely. There was no reasoning about general principles; there was merely an application of accepted precedent—and that might be enforced by some tale of how it was done in the old, heroic days—to the case in hand. To judge was to expound the *themistes* and the place of judgment was called *themis*.[111]

The "commandments" are the first brief statements of certain selected taboos, defining rights in accordance with the code, and are largely religious in nature;[112] in law as in religion the antique and holy form is resolutely clung to. But under all such "tables" or codifications lies the "unwritten law," the origin of which is so remote that it is referred to the gods.

Says the king, who had forbidden the burial of the heroine's brother, to Antigone: "And did you truly dare to transgress these edicts?"

Antigone: "Yes, for Zeus it was not who proclaimed them to me, nor did Dikē, who dwells with the gods below, formulate such laws for men. Nor did I think your edicts of such power that one, being a mortal, could overstep the unwritten, infallible canons of the gods."[113]

Vinogradoff[114] develops the characteristics of the primitive "trial" in some fulness; he sees the court as an agency of arbitration. "This aspect of arbitration is also deeply ingrained in the constitution of ancient courts of law, and the forms of procedure. It may be said that an ancient trial was not much more than a formally regulated struggle between the parties in which the judges had to act more as umpires and wardens of order and fair play than as investigators of the truth. . . . If the parties have agreed to submit their dispute to the regularizing action of a court instead of prosecuting their interest by private means, and when they have given solemn promise to appear at the trial, the next step in Greek, Roman and Teutonic law was to provide for the amount of possible compensation and loss in the forthcoming struggle.

[111] Keller, *Hom. Soc.*, 282 ff., 289-290 (where references to the text are cited).

[112] Maurer, *Vkde.*, I, 183; Spencer, *Study Soc.*, 109.

[113] Sophocles, *Antigone*, 449-455.

[114] *Hist. Jurispr.*, I, 348, 350, 354, 361.

It was not only a question of carrying through one's contention and retaining or acquiring the objects in dispute, or making good one's claim to the performance of an obligation, the conquering party meant to get compensation for the danger and risk of the enterprise, and for their efforts in carrying it out. The losing party had to incur a penalty for mischievous and useless resistance to the better right. Both parties usually made an agreement on entering on the trial to make a deposit with the court, in order that the losing side should incur a fine at the end of the litigation. This pledge was symbolized in Greek law by . . . [*prytaneia*], in Rome law by *sacramentum* and in Teutonic law by *vadium* (*gage*). In all these cases we have the very elements which characterize international law at the present time: no direct compulsion, no necessity to bow to a superior or sovereign will, but a voluntary submission to rules established by consent of the parties and guaranteed by their good faith, and by a certain regard for public opinion as far as it represented the views of persons not directly affected in the struggle, and therefore better able to judge it with impartiality. Looking back on ancient law, it may be said that criminal and civil procedure are still at a stage corresponding to a great extent to the modern state of international law and procedure. Procedure begins to develop at a time when the element of public compulsion is absent or insignificant. The transitions from one stage to the other—from a legalized struggle to arbitration and ultimately to full jurisdictional authority are very gradual. Two circumstances contributed powerfully to effect the transition from international law to a law regulated by the commonwealth: the growth of a mediating power to which parties were forced to submit, and the increasing strength of the view that even imperfect compromise is better than open struggle. . . .

"So wide is the range of self-help in early society, that it may sometimes even go to the length of putting pressure on a tribunal, and, as it were compelling it to give judgment. The litigant is bound to ask for the decision of a court to authorize his own action:—and this is evidence of the necessity of some control by constituted authority; but, on the other hand, the individual had to extract from the tribunal the judgment he desired;—and this is evidence of the power of personal self-help. In Frankish law, litigants frequently put pressure on the courts in order to obtain the required verdict. This seems a glaring anomaly to us at the present day, for we are accustomed to speak and think of the supremacy of the courts in litigation. The appeal to a tribunal had to be made by the particular means of a solemn formula, the 'tangano,' and the arbitrators, or *Rachimburghs*, were required to deliver judgment in the manner specified by the claimant. It would seem that in many cases they did so against their will: often the parties appearing before them were persons of great influence, and in primitive society it was no light matter for a judge to provoke powerful individuals by adverse decisions. . . . The actual method of the declaration of the law was not so much the issue of a positive command as a process of ascertaining established views and customs. The ancient lawgiver never considers himself as issuing an order to particular persons or the community in general: his primary function is to *find the law* and give expression to the sense of the community in regard to juridical acts."

It is evident that the term law, meaning enacted statute, is out of place before the development of definite enactments and codes.

"Legal right is defined as a capacity residing in one . . . person . . . of controlling, with the assent and assistance of the State, the actions of others. In popular usage we speak of a man having a right to use his property as he likes and so forth; whereas his right is, accurately speaking, to prevent other people from interfering with his use."[115] If law demands, as here indicated, the presence of the integrated state, then it can exist only in its germ under the family, clan, or tribal system; but its growth from this germ, that is, from custom, should never be lost sight of by one who would understand its nature and evolution. Law is always developing, even in the highest civilization, from the same fecund matrix.

Law, says Carter,[116] "begins as the product of the automatic action of society and becomes in time a cause of the continued growth and perfection of society. Society cannot exist without it, or exist without producing it. *Ubi societas ibi lex.* Law, therefore is self-created and self-existent. It is the form in which human conduct—that is, human life—presents itself under the necessary operation of the causes which govern conduct. It is the fruit of the myriads of concurring judgments of all the members of society pronounced after a study of the consequences of conduct touching what conduct should be followed and what should be avoided. . . . The conclusion is clear that habit and custom . . . furnish the rules which govern human conduct, and that they still exert over enlightened man the same imperious dominion that they did among the primeval hordes which peopled the world before the dawn of civilization, or that they now do among the barbarous tribes which inhabit the wilds of Patagonia or Australia. To the absolute generality of this conclusion an exception is to be made for the influence of legislation; but the extent of this exception diminishes to a point where we may, for all large and general purposes, dismiss it from attention, when we consider that its principal function is to supplement and aid the operation of custom and that it can never supplant it, and . . . that its own efficiency is dependent upon its conformity to habit and custom. . . . Inasmuch as conduct is necessarily controlled by previous thought, and such thought is determined by individual constitution, that is, character, and the environment, nothing can directly control conduct, which cannot control both character and environment. It is not, therefore, possible to *make law* by legislative action. Its utmost power is to offer a reward or threaten a punishment as a consequence of particular conduct, and thus furnish an additional *motive* to influence conduct. When such power is exerted to reinforce custom and prevent violations of it, it may be effectual, and rules or commands thus enacted are properly called laws; but if aimed against established custom they will be ineffectual. Law not only cannot be directly made by human action, but cannot be abrogated or changed by such action."

115 Pollock, *Essays in Jurisp.*, 11.   116 *Law*, 119, 129-130.

The mores, so far as they conferred rights, covered at first only relations between members of the in-group, thus making it a peace-group. Outsiders had no rights at all until inter-group relations came to need regulation in the interest of the societies concerned. Then came the rules of war and the various customs of hospitality and blood-brotherhood, which extended the peace-group to some degree and eventually worked out into an inter-group code. Efforts are being redoubled in these days to get international relations out of the stage of custom and precedent into that of enforceable law, that is, to do for the wider society of nations what was long ago done within the state. Intra-group mores, as has been seen, had to wait for the development of the state before they could become real law; and the inference is not a long one that an inter-group or international code must have the sanctioning power of highly organized world-opinion behind it before it has much claim to the title of law.[117]

§182*. **Crime.** That crime is an in-group affair, since it is right and praiseworthy to kill or rob the out-groupers, needs mention only; the conception of crime is correlative with that of the peace-group. It is a public wrong—an assault upon the rights of the other group-members. Within the peace-group, as must be evident from what has gone before, the distinction between a sin and a crime was not by any means as clear once as it has since become. Hence the two topics of crime and sin,[118] though separated in deference to modern usage, should be studied together. There were really no specifically secular offenses. Any infringement of the mores was hateful to the ancestral ghosts who sanctioned them and if the chief or elders inflicted punishment they did it quite as much in the name of the dead as of the living. Among the Indians the fear of the departed spirits often prevents murder more effectually than the prospect of hanging does among white peoples.[119]

---

[117] Keller, *War to Peace,* chs. VIII, IX, X.

[118] §§268, 274, below; on crimes and punishments, see Wines, *Punishment and Reformation.*

[119] Schoolcraft, *Indian Tribes,* II, 195-196.

Crimes in Fiji are theft, adultery, rape, magic, arson, want of respect toward important persons; they are offenses against a master or in violation of property, theft and adultery being aligned under the latter category.[120] "The enormity of all crimes depends on who commits them, and against whom they are committed."[121] "In Dahomi it is criminal to attempt to commit suicide, because every man is the property of the king. The bodies of suicides are exposed to public execration, and the head is always struck off and sent to Agbomi; at the expense of the family if the suicide were a free man, at that of the master if he were a slave. . . . Any person whose house takes fire, even by accident, is punished with death."[122]

In short, that which ran counter to the mores was a crime. It follows that the conception of crime was a shifting one, with certain unvarying elements in it that corresponded to persistent taboos expedient in any society, such as the taboo on in-group homicide or theft. As in the case of sin, the offense was ritual, not rational; and so there appear in the list of crimes as in that of sins certain items that seem to us in the highest degree grotesque. This has occurred in relatively recent times.

"Juvenal exhausts his vocabulary of invective in denouncing the atrocious criminality of a certain noble, who, in the very year of his consulship did not hesitate—not, it is true, by day, but at least in the sight of the moon and of the stars—with his own hand to drive his own chariot along the public road. Seneca was scarcely less scandalised by the atrocious and, as he thought, unnatural luxury of those who had adopted the custom of cooling different beverages by mixing them with snow. Pliny assures us that the most monstrous of all criminals was the man who first devised the luxurious custom of wearing gold rings. . . . If we were to measure the criminality of different customs by the vehemence of the patristic denunciations, we might almost conclude that the most atrocious offence of their day was the custom of wearing false hair, or dyeing natural hair."[123] Such actions constituted crimes along with such obvious mischief-making as tampering with the water-supply for irrigation.

No extensive catalogue of crimes is called for in this place, for the notions of what is criminal will come out in a subsequent connection, in dealing with punishment. There is one aspect of crime, however, as of sin, which needs reiteration. The exclusive interest in primitive times lay in the action itself, whereas among civilized peoples interest has shifted to the condition of mind whence the action arises.[124] The objectively-minded savage did not exercise

---

[120] Letourneau, *Soc.*, 432, 465; §383, below.
[121] Hopkins, *Relig. India*, 263.   [122] Ellis, *Ewe*, 224.
[123] Lecky, *Europ. Morals*, I, 260-261.
[124] Starcke, *Samvittighedslivet*, 2, 4.

himself at all over motive; he was evidently of the opinion, could he have expressed it, that there is no relation between purposes and consequences. Homicide was murder, whether it was accidental or not. Hardly any better case is to be found than the one related by Homer.[125] The father of Patroclus, the story goes, had to take him from his native country because in a childish fit of anger over a game he had struck and killed a young companion, "not intending." Of course all the relations of the dead boy would have taken up the trail against the offending child as against an adult and wilful murderer. Even more striking is the ascription of crime to animals, the beast sometimes being tried, condemned, and executed. Such a culprit was significantly termed a "deodand."[126] An Associated Press despatch of January 10, 1926, solemnly records a jury verdict against a collie dog, followed by the imposition of a death sentence by a county judge and execution by electrocution.[127] Xerxes, in flogging the Hellespont, was carrying the idea into the inanimate realm itself. Even for striking a corpse blood-money may be claimed. The reason for refusing to take motives into account was briefly expressed by some elders in East Africa: "If we pardon one man who kills by accident there will be nothing but accidents."[128]

The division of law into criminal and civil throws light upon the conception of what crime is thought to be. "Since the law of 'might is right' was suppressed in Europe, an offence became mainly a breach of a law, and it is primarily this, and not the injury resulting to anyone, which constitutes the offence. We have, however, means of claiming damages for injuries done to us without the commission of an offence coming into question, and our law is thus divided into criminal and civil law. It is natural, on the other hand, in a community in which there is no supreme authority, to stamp this or that act as an offence. It is not the disobedience to any law which constitutes the offence, but the injury done to a person. In consequence the whole attitude of the law is transformed from its public to a private character. By agreement the public authority steps in to arbitrate between private persons, and no offence concerns the public, unless its frequency threatens the public welfare; and while we cannot make good our defaults toward the State, we can compensate the individual. The distinction between that which can be amended, and that which cannot, therefore does not exist in native law, and hence there

125 *Iliad*, XXIII, 85-88.
126 §256, below; Oliveira Martins, *Quadro*, 168; White, *Sci. and Theol.*, II, 113.
127 N. Y. *Times*, Jan. 11, 1926.
128 Dundas, C., in JAI, LI, 239, 240.

is no division into criminal and civil law. Any such distinction is therefore quite out of place and unmeaning when applied to native law. . . . Punishment, especially with natives, is apt to be forgotten; it is of a certain duration only, but compensation is lasting. As long as a man lives, and after his death, his children will see his cattle increasing in the village of another. However cruel English law was in times gone by, it was incapable of deterring from crime those whose ignorance forced them to it, and this applies in a greater degree to primitive men whose feelings and emotions are largely beyond their control. The native has no natural inclination to crime. In his proper mode of living the criminal class is practically non-existent, but on the other hand he is not easily to be deterred from doing that which his inclinations for the moment suggest. . . . The decrease of a man's wealth by frequent demands for compensation would affect the interests of clan and family alike, and we may be sure that both would do their utmost to restrain their members from excessive crime. The greatest deterrent must, however, have been the fear of private revenge, just as it was among ourselves before organized government substituted public revenge for it. . . . There being no State to protect the individual, he was safest who had fewest enemies, and he who had many went in constant fear of his life. Attempts are now made to restore the useful elements of the old order of things, but while we have allowed the law of compensation, we have abolished the fear of private revenge, without which compensation is indeed an insufficient means of restricting crime."[129]

The point is made that it is impossible to set up any fixed scale of crimes and punishments as existent in a primitive community; differences seem to appear in various districts; upon closer inspection, however, "what at first seem differences are really their regard for all the circumstances of the case, persons and conditions, such as:—(a) The existing supply and demand in cattle and marriageable women. (b) The local estimate as to the gravity of any particular offence, dependent on the conditions of the district." The whole situation is based upon "(a) The possession of women and cattle. (b) The purchase of wives by means of cattle. (c) Inheritance of women and children and cattle. (d) Compensation for injury and homicide, by means of women and cattle."[130] This being the case, the conception of what constitutes crime and degree of crime is very difficult to infer from a list of penalties.

The conception that there is no crime except within the in-group is brought out sharply by the Congo tribe's use of the adjective meaning "good, right, just, reasonable, fine, proper, admirable, beautiful." "In all our translations," says the missionary, "we had to take the best words, the nearest equivalents, and group round them the moral ideas we wished them to convey." There was some trouble concerning this conception of the good and admirable; for if a man "stole from a stranger and lied wholesale to him he would be admired by his neighbours as a clever, sharp-witted fellow, but if he robbed his neighbour, or slept with his neighbour's wife without first paying him, he would be condemned by public opinion and regarded as one who had . . . bad habits."[131]

Remarkable pictures of primitive simplicity and absence of crime are reported by some writers. In one place on the Malay Peninsula, "every portion of the primitive social fabric reared by these tribes bears the clear impress

129 Dundas, C., in JAI, XLV, 261-262.
130 O'Sullivan, in JAI, XL, 174-175.   131 Weeks, in JAI, XXXIX, 445.

of the child-like simplicity and trustfulness that lies at the root of their character; and in no department is this more evident than in that which pertains to law and public order. The evidence discovers an unappreciable amount of crime, few laws, and still fewer hard-and-fast penalties fixed for the non-observance of the latter."[132]

A sort of traditional stage between the crime against an individual and that against the state is formed where much is made of correctness of conduct in relation to the chief. In the Society Islands "the official system of administration of justice was put into motion in connection with offences against the chiefs rather than as between the people themselves. . . . There was no regular code of laws, and, except in cases of offences against the king or chiefs, rulers were seldom appealed to; . . . criminal punishment was unknown, except in the selection of obnoxious characters for occasional sacrifice; . . . the people obtained satisfaction with their own hands, whether justly or unjustly, for every injury received. Sometimes disputes were referred to a bystander, and the party he declared to be in the wrong submitted and made his opponent a peace-offering of a plantain stalk. There were no regular police; the chief of each district was accountable to the king for the conduct of the people within that chief's jurisdiction, and the final appeal was to the chief ruler, whose decision was generally regarded as binding." But the chief ruler was in a position to resent and punish any injuries that he thought he had received; "the king, if he felt himself strong enough, would banish instantly any one who resisted his authority, and send some one else to take possession of the culprit's lands, and occupy his station as chief of the district. Death or banishment was the punishment usually inflicted by the chiefs, and often the objects of their displeasure were marked out as victims for sacrifice. . . . Rebellion, or shaking the government, withholding supplies, or even speaking contemptuously of the king or his administration, were by general consent considered criminal; and so heinous was such an offence that the culprit was not only liable to banishment, or the forfeiture of his life, but a human sacrifice had to be offered to atone for the guilt, and appease the displeasure of the gods against the people of the land in which it had been committed." This last provision is a reflection of the sacred nature of the chief and also of the feeling of group-responsibility.[133]

Grinnell[134] presents a picture of Cheyenne conditions which illustrates a number of aspects of crime and punishment. "Crime as understood by civilized people scarcely existed in the Cheyenne camp. Such a thing as theft was unknown." If one man used the horses of another too much, the owner simply clubbed him. In disputes there was a council-decision to pay something, which was generally accepted at once; "public opinion was the law of the camp, and few were bold enough and reckless enough to fly in the face of it." All was conformity. There was no legal death-penalty; if one murdered a tribal comrade, he had to flee for a time, as he was likely to be killed by the deceased's relatives. He lost standing in the tribe and must camp apart for a long time; no one would smoke with him, as he was impure; no woman would live with him. He must have his own cup and other utensils, as if infected; indeed, he was supposed to suffer from inward decay and to be destined ultimately to

[132] Skeat and Blagden, *Malay Penin.*, I, 495.
[133] Williamson, *Cent. Polyn.*, III, 16-17, 20-21.
[134] *Cheyenne*, I, 349-358.

die and blow away. He had a bad smell, so that he could never get near the bison. There are cases of very eminent men in a tribe who lost all credit and influence by homicide; and it was the same if they killed an adopted member of the tribe. Small matters were settled privately by the parties to them or by relatives; the council did not concern itself with private quarrels unless they had a distinct bearing on general welfare; there was no tribal machinery for punishing crimes against individuals. So-called "soldiers" interfered to prevent or punish acts of the individual against public welfare—those which seemed to threaten the tribe as a whole. The killing of fellow-tribesmen was most unusual; the author cites two cases, one in 1836-1837, one in 1879; "only five or six cases in more than forty years." The Araucanians had the same general ideas; carrying off a married woman, as well as stealing and murder, were always "considered only as crimes towards the community, and were punished as such, but without it occurring to the Indian that it was wrong in a religious sense. It was not the act itself that was condemned, but the fact of its being committed in one's own or in a friendly clan. On the contrary such an act committed in a strange tribe was considered as perfectly allowable, and generally upheld by arms, if necessary, by the clan to which the offender belonged."[135]

"Public reaction against homicide asserts itself in the necessity for purifying the soil from that pollution. Primarily—in so far as the individual injury is concerned—homicide is a private wrong: but in the consequences which it entails, it affects the whole body of society."[136]

It is evident enough that a civilized man cannot carry over into his estimate of primitive conditions the ideas of crime with which he is familiar; and yet it is readily enough seen that the primitive conceptions are nothing but the lower terms of the civilized. The primitive community was fumbling about in the effort to smooth the pathway of life and using what it had in the way of instrumentalities. In the main it was relying upon a simple and direct expression of public opinion. Nowadays that expression is so hampered by the very means provided for its emergence that its incidence is belated, confused, difficult to interpret. The thing itself is lost in a maze of method, except that it is wont to break through its appointed channels at a pinch and to appear in its stark simplicity and even brutality, with momentum the more disastrous by reason of its suppression. It is not seldom enlightening to view the savage working according to first principles.

§183*. Detection of Crime: the Ordeal. If the general lines of the administration of justice have been adequately brought out

[135] Latcham, in JAI, XXXIX, 349.
[136] Vinogradoff, Hist. Jurispr., I, 361.

in what precedes, it will be evident to the reader that not much in the way of formalities is to be looked for among primitive peoples. He will not expect to encounter courts and court-proceedings; he will not expect to find judges on a bench or advocates prepared to argue cases. The expression of public opinion in the raw, together with a strong reliance upon supernatural sanctions, takes the place of elaborate systems. There are, however, certain tentatives in the direction of providing instrumentalities for adjudication; there is the chief, who has certain judicial functions and there is the council of elders. What these functionaries generally accomplish is the alignment of any given case with precedent and tradition; the elders are the custodians of the mores and they are also those who will, ere long, attain the spirit-status with all its powers of sanction over the prevailing code. The chief has some resemblance to the judge; he can perhaps take closer account of rising situations, especially as they seem likely to affect the tribal interests as a whole—which, from his position, he is better able to visualize—or as they promise to affect his own position and prerogatives. He is specialized enough in function to be less engrossed in everyday detail and more conversant with wider aspects. It might also be said that the elders are specialists in tribal interests as the younger and more active men cannot be; they have leisure to reflect, discuss, and compare. In any case, however, differentiation has not gone far, and the structure has never risen much above the direct expression of public opinion. The following rather miscellaneous aspects of judicial procedure, if it may be dignified by that name, will illustrate this contention from a number of angles. Always interesting, and important as well, are the sometimes quaint-appearing expedients which have been developed for reducing the friction of clashing interests and keeping the peace.

Most of the following is taken from the often-quoted articles of Sir Charles Dundas.[137] "In Theraka they have a curious custom of speaking through a proxy. A, a plaintiff, will address his remarks and refutations to B, who has nothing to do with the case, and C will address D; but both A and C address B and D by the names of A and C respectively. The Theraka are remarkable for their hot temper, and it is more than likely that if the parties addressed each other they would be unable to restrain themselves, and therefore this roundabout method is used."

[137] In JAI, XLV, 250, 259, 260, 261, 292-293; and in JAI, LI, 219, 224-226.

An appeal to force underlies all the formalities, such as they are. "Since there is no higher authority in the tribe than that of the elders, it follows that their decision is in theory final; there is no further appeal, and a suggestion for the formation of an appeal *kiama* met with decided disfavour in Kikuyu. Nevertheless, the judgments of the elders are wrangled over, submitted to other elders, retried and reversed, until one is inclined to doubt if there is such a thing as a final decision. It is also inconceivable to a native that a claim should ever be allowed to drop, or fail for lack of proof, wherefore he will never content himself with a philosophic resignation to inevitable loss. . . . Supposing, then, that one party refused to pay what the council had awarded, the elders would tell the other to take it by force while they were present to prevent fighting. . . . If we now consider the methods adopted by the elders and the means available to them, we shall see that we must regard the council in a light quite different from that of a court as generally understood by us. They have no measures whereby they could command the submission of any-one: they met on the invitation of both parties, and they consulted as to the case, but they did not decide obscure facts; they left these to divine judgment. When they actually settled a case they did not enforce that settlement, though they might support the successful party in his endeavour to demand satisfac-tion. If the elders can be induced freely to express themselves on the subject, they will always say that their chief duty was to prevent strife between credi-tors and debtors, and to prevent both from resorting to supernatural powers and open hostilities; nor was it their duty to condemn and punish this one and that. It was for them to say how the matter could be settled in accord-ance with recognised custom, and they were in fact witnesses to such a settle-ment. The judicial council of elders may therefore be described rather as a court of arbitration than a court of decision. . . . The mediatorial character of the council of elders is in evidence to-day, and must be continually borne in mind when dealing with them. It often appears that the elders are negligently indifferent to what results from their deliberations, and that they wantonly debase their authority by allowing it to be defied. At one time it was feared that they would abuse their powers of imprisonment, but it soon appeared that they reluctantly exercised this power, and in fact elders have expressed doubts as to whether they would not be liable for blood-money should a man convicted by them die in gaol. This betrays merely the old desire to evade responsibility, and unfamiliarity with the idea of decisive and authoritative action."

The size of the community inevitably determines much of the theory of procedure. "The native council, when it assembles, must contain many mem-bers who know the facts of the case before them. Often they are known to all of them, and in fact a council in which there are no such persons is regarded as incompetent to deal with the case. This marks a great difference from our own courts, which are supposed to be unacquainted with matters which come before them. The result is, of course, that the magistrate asks questions which make obvious his ignorance of the matter, and the native does not see the advantage of enlightening him where such would damage his cause. Hence much perjury is occasioned, more by our peculiar methods than by the natural untruthfulness of the native, to whom nothing could be more astonishing than that a case should be settled by one who himself knows nothing about it. When, therefore, an elder acting as an assessor in a high court case, blandly told the judge that he could give no opinion as to the 'guilt' of the accused, 'because I was not there,' he was merely speaking as a member of the council, and expressing what to him was the only reasonable opinion."

The case of debt-recovery is characteristic. "Debts may be recovered at any time and are inherited. They may be claimed by or from descendants as well as principals, but the claim can only be made good against the one who has inherited the debtor's property. . . . Debts are, however, frequently settled by giving the creditor a daughter, and in such case the girl cannot be redeemed by subsequent payment of the debt. A girl thus paid cannot be forced to marry the one she has been given to, and if she refuses him he must content himself with appropriating the dowry paid for her. Bloodmoney is often settled in this way. . . . When the payment of a debt is disputed, the elders will require the defendant to state which elders were witnesses to the payment, and if he cannot name them it is not admitted that the debt has been paid. Hence debts are not paid except in the presence of elders, or before the council. This is often erroneously taken to mean that no native will pay a debt unless sued. That is not so, but, on the other hand, it is not the duty of the debtor to pay without demand—the creditor must go and demand what he claims."

The author cites some minor differences in procedure in the eighteen tribes which he covers. "The main difference is to be found in this, that the tribes which have evolved actual chiefship are judged by their chiefs; those who have no chiefs recognize the jurisdiction of a council of elders. The former are in the minority, and invariably the chief as judge is assisted or guided by a council, so that individual jurisdiction is hardly known. The effectiveness of the judgment given will depend upon the power and influence of the judicial authority, but as a general rule it is no more than an authoritative establishment of a claim the enforcement of which is left to the claimant: the judicial authority neither brings offenders to justice nor enforces its decree. Almost invariably the claimant has the right to redress his own wrong; in fact this is very frequently the ordinary method or that attempted in the first instance, and by consequence the case is submitted to trial rather by mutual agreement than in obedience to any law. . . . The judicial authority hardly takes upon itself to give a decision on facts in dispute, this being left to some such test as ordeal. Therefore the judicial authority in the main restricts itself to decision concerning undisputed facts voluntarily submitted for decision by the parties interested, and this decision will in almost all cases and in all tribes be in regard to a payment in the nature of compensation. Now at the present day in Europe a crime is considered primarily as an offence against a definite law: it is the breach of a law rather than the injury to a person which is in issue; but in Africa it is the personal injury which counts: the injured party takes action independent of the public authority; his redress lies mainly in his own hands, and thus the whole procedure and essence of the law bears a purely private character by comparison with ours. Under our system we cannot, excepting in rare cases, make private amends for our misdeeds, but we can for wrongs which come under the classification of civil suits, such as debts. In Africa all wrongs can be amended by payment of compensation much as though all cases were compoundable with us; but this is principally a matter for the person wronged to decide. In Africa the injured party has, as it were, the power to convert a criminal case into a civil suit. For instance, if we regard blood-revenge as an admissible penalty on the guilty party, the aggrieved party has the right to inflict this penalty or to convert it into a civil suit for compensation, as he pleases. These are some of the salient points of variance between European and Bantu law, and they are significant if we would form a true estimate of native ideas on the subject."

Compensation looks to a modern eye like an ineffectual means for the restriction of crime, "but there are aspects of this question which should not be overlooked. Actual crime in olden times would be limited almost to injury of one sort or another which was inflicted in the heat of anger by men whose minds were little capable of controlling their actions, and to them the fear of punishment would hardly be a deterrent. It must, however, never be forgotten that compensation was really an alternative, which the offender could not count on. The most effectual deterrent was the fear of private revenge, which was generally lawful and often a duty. He who offended against many had so many more to fear, and was never safe. And whether redress took the form of revenge or compensation, the burden might fall on the offender's relatives, whose interest it therefore was to dissuade him from wrongdoing. It thus comes about that at the present day when we admit the application of the old rule of compensation we do not fully retain the essential element of primitive law, for we have eliminated the fear of revenge."

The conclusion is as follows: "The divergent characteristics of African and European jurisprudence are patent: on the one hand a voluntary means of redress through arbitration and induced by expediency, on the other . . . law manipulated by judges of decision. Once this distinction is clear to us we are capable of appreciating a certain perplexity the native must feel in regard to our handling of his affairs, and we shall understand how essential it is that as far as is practicable their disposal should be entrusted to his own tribunals. It may be objected that the native prefers the tribunal of the white man, but it must be borne in mind that it is mostly only the successful party who expresses an opinion, and under all circumstances the more intimately the court is acquainted with and guided by the native view of a case, the more surely its decision will give satisfaction. The weakest side of the native tribunal is of course its venality, not that the majority or even a large percentage of litigants fail to find justice; but none is so well aware as the native that complete integrity in his own tribunal is not assured, and it is here that he shows preference for the European courts. On the other hand, it must be confessed that as often as not the underlying idea of the litigant who has recourse to European courts is to derive advantage from the ignorance of the white judge. Another reason for such preference is the more absolute decision thereby ensured, but that a final and irrevocable solution is not appreciated appears from the fact that when, as invariably happens, the losing party again brings forward his case at a later date, often representing the judicial award as an arbitrary seizure by the other party, the latter as often as not omits to refute it, merely repeating the statement of his original case, so that finality is by no means ensured in our courts. Similarly, all the venality of the native court may and often does imperceptibly appear in our courts, in which case the result is, if anything, far less satisfactory than it would have been before a native tribunal."

The author gives the following description of normal procedure: "In the first instance the *Mkonde* will endeavour to obtain redress unaided by his relatives and friends. If he fails to come to an agreement he will have recourse to a solicitor, who may be of any clan, and is selected for his eloquence and ability. Having received an advance or promise of payment, the solicitor approaches the defendant, whom he plies with arguments and threats. If he proves obdurate and unwilling, the claimant will appeal to the senior members of his family, an elder brother, uncle, or the head of his clan according to the importance of the matter. These endeavour to arbitrate. If such efforts are fruitless, a new solicitor is engaged who goes to the defendant's family and clan, to whom he represents the true aspects of the case. The defendants on their side put up a pleader, and the two solicitors now wrangle over the case for days together, supported by their respective parties. The plaintiff's solicitor resorts to all manner of objective and historical arguments, which he combines with persuasion and threats, and if these fail he will speak of the standing of his client, his numerous and wealthy kinship, intimating the consequent disadvantages of opposing him. If all this is of no avail, open hostility is threatened and finally carried into practice. By force or cunning, slaves and members of the opposing family are kidnapped to extort payment. This final phase may be reached for any cause from the murder of a brother to the loss of a knife." Judicial decision plays little part here; to be noted is the final appeal to force as an *ultima ratio*. "The facts of a case of recent date are not often in dispute before a native tribunal, for the judges themselves are as often as not aware of them and there remains only the rule of custom to be decided; but the majority of disputes brought up are of very ancient origin. As often as not two men will agree to leave a dispute as to a certain claim or property because they are friendly, but later in life the friendship may cool and then come claims and counterclaims. Moreover, a claim never lapses, and consequently what A did not demand from B, the descendants of A may very well demand from the descendants of B. Thus B may accidentally have killed A's brother, but A made no claim because he was B's friend; but his sons or grandsons will probably not omit to claim from B's descendants. Here, then, the whole matter is in dispute, because none of them is really aware of the facts in issue."

The administration of justice is evidently more or less of a forensic exercise; it is also a great source of entertainment. The palaver is the center of tribal life. Torday and Joyce[138] present "a typical case, such as occurs every day in this country. . . . A, of the village X, steals a goat belonging to B, of the village Y. Under pledge of the greatest secrecy, he boasts to some friend of his feat, and the result is that before the end of the day B knows who the thief is. B then sends a messenger to A asking for *Kama-Kumi*, that is, . . . a little salt, a fowl, or in fact, anything of little value. If A refuses, and this is rarely the case, war is made on his village; if, as usual, he consents, it means that he admits the crime and is willing to accept responsibility for the act. B's next act is to send an arrow to A's chief, marked with a number of incisions indicating the number of days in which the *Milonga* palaver will be held. When the day arrives, not only the whole population of the villages of A and B, but of all the neighbourhood, flock to B's village, all armed with bows and arrows, . . . to take part in the trial. There is no judge, but the decision is left to the crowd. Men of noted eloquence speak in behalf of each party, and the discussion begins. A admits that he has stolen the goat, but did not B's grandfather seduce his, A's, grandfather's wife? B allows this, but

138 In JAI, XXXV, 414-415.

asserts that his father had a fowl stolen by A's grandfather. A does not deny the offence, but recalls the fact that a pig was stolen from his uncle by a slave of B's grandfather's brother-in-law. And so the case proceeds, the assembly declaring after each charge and counter-charge that the matter is compensated. Eventually he who can bring the greater number of charges against his adversary is declared the winner, and claims compensation. This gives rise to further discussion; if one demands twenty goats the other offers one, and the argument often lasts several days, but they generally arrive at some agreement at the end of it; on the rare occasions when they cannot come to terms war results. . . . As a general rule every crime except parricide and diabolical possession can be compensated by a fine." These "trials" evidently maintain and refresh the memories of all parties as to the genealogies and history—not to say the police-blotters—of their social groups.

In Buru, "the evidence of two persons known to possess good name and reputation, is sufficient for the acquittal of an accused person; if there are none, or none of adequate quality, and if the affair cannot be brought to clarity in any other way, they resort to the ordeal." All sorts of shaky evidence are accredited; they have marks by which they recognize guilt, such as a change of color on the part of the accused or his avoidance of people. They lay great stress on such evidence in comparison with oaths and witnesses. The oath-taking is a case of group-solidarity; oaths are self-cursings with symbolic acts which fall upon the group in which the oath-taker resides as well as upon himself. His fellows are *consacramentales* or *conjuratores*, as in ancient Germany. The changes which have occurred under contact with Islam and the Europeans are few, for the *adat* (mores) persists; only when it and the strange code are similar, does the latter seem to win. Islam has really penetrated the mores but slightly. The author[139] quoted goes on to remark that it is confession alone that gives complete proof. It is wholly inexplicable in the eyes of the natives that we should demand still other proofs over and above confession. Next to confession comes the evidence of witnesses, who, as a rule, are not put under oath. In general, more stress is laid upon the number of the witnesses than upon the value of individual testimony. "It is said by the Balinese that it is impossible to win a suit without witnesses, and that a man who knows how to produce the most witnesses in a case can be sure of winning."

"When the Araucanos began to adopt a more sedentary life, it became necessary to establish more firmly their *admapu* (customs of the land), or code of laws. Their quarrels were formerly settled by an appeal to arms; now however the *ulmen* called together the elders of the clan and they deliberated on the evidence given, and imposed punishment for the crime committed. It was not considered necessary to hear the offender."[140]

With this we may leave the question of procedure, in so far as the incipient formalities of trial and court-practice go. In several of the passages cited it has been intimated that behind an appeal

[139] Wilken, in VG, I, 38; II, 491 ff., 489-490.
[140] Latcham, in JAI, XXXIX, 355.

to human ways and judgment there lay a possibility of appeal to the supernatural. It seems that the primitive peoples made groping attempts to avoid both violence and recourse to the spirits, but that both these ultimates lay just below the surface. The reason for evading hostilities is readily comprehensible; that for halting immediate reference of a question to the ghosts and gods is less clear. It seems that as long as a suit brought out merely questions of fact known to many if not all, human minds felt themselves competent to pass judgment without troubling the supernatural powers; but when it came to the unknown and mysterious —whether, in the absence of evidence or in its conflict, an accused party was or was not guilty—men felt themselves at the end of the tether and cast responsibility upon omniscience.

The deodand, or condemned animal, is, by its very name, a witness to the connection of criminal procedure with religion. This relation comes out with especial clearness in the methods of detecting the criminal; for in the main, among the backward races, they are magical and it is part of the duties of the medicine-man, if not of the god, to act as detective.[141] Magic is one of the most effective means ever devised for settling a case "out of court"; a thief, hearing people talking about a recourse to magical means, "and being convinced of the effects of the magic will hasten to return the stolen property to its owner."[142] In particular is the ordeal, or judgment of God, utilized in fixing responsibility for crime. To men who regarded the ills of life as proof of the wrath of the ghosts or gods, the ordeal was a rational procedure. They could wait and see what the higher powers were going to do in view of the fact of crime, being assured that the criminal, though he were unknown, would not escape. In the case of a suspected man they could watch to see whether he suffered ill. Or they could hasten the result by setting up an experiment, by deliberately referring the case to the gods. This was in reality the administration of justice through the cult.[143] The ordeal was utilized also as a test before confiding important functions and as such it might be of an intellectual type.[144] The following cases, mainly of the or-

---

141 §§277, 305, 313, below.   142 Hobley, in JAI, XLI, 436.

143 Lippert, Kgchte., II, 491, 588.   144 Letourneau, Polit., 194.

deal,[145] will present judicial procedure in its simplest and crudest aspects.

In Australia, persons accused of wrong-doing are summoned to appear and to withstand a flight of weapons, having only a little shield for defense. Blood must be spilled to satisfy the injured party and the trial ends when the accused is hit. He seldom receives more wounds than his crime calls for. "If the accused refuses to be tried, he is outlawed, and may be killed, and his brother or nearest male relative is held responsible, and must submit to be attacked with boomerangs."[146] In the Solomon Islands an accused person goes to a man who possesses a magic stone and engages him to undergo an ordeal. "The people assemble and the accused denies the charge, and he submits to the ordeal through his compurgator. The latter heats the stone and throws it from hand to hand; if his hands are not burnt the accused is pronounced innocent, and pays a porpoise-tooth fee. There is much preparation with a very young cocoa-nut, the flower of sugar-cane and chanted charms to make the proceeding *saka,* hot, with supernatural power. It is probable that sometimes the accusers make their preparations also with a bribe." There is also an alligator-ordeal, employed in a region where the reptiles abound. "A man accused of serious crime is taken there; the wizard who manages the ordeal calls the alligators with his charms, and the accused who is confident in his innocence and in the wizard's power dares to swim across. No one will hold him guilty if he escapes. In this ordeal also it is sometimes not the accused, but the man who knows the charm who submits himself to the test. In Lepers' Island a man to prove his innocence will submit to be shot at with arrows; if he be hit he is of course guilty; if he be innocent, Tagaro will protect him, just as he protects in fighting any young man whom he preserves that he may be prosperous and great. The favour of Tagaro in either case is sought for with the appropriate charm."[147]

In southern Africa a drink is offered to those suspected of witchcraft. "Those who vomit it are considered innocent, while those whom it purges are pronounced guilty and are burned to death. . . . The practice of ordeal is common among all the negro nations north of the Zambesi." The accused eagerly desire it, relying implicitly upon the vindication of the innocent.[148] It is reported that, in addition to the decoction, which acts as an emetic or purge, the ordeal of boiling water is put into practice in South Africa. A man dips his arm into the water; "if, when the chief takes hold of his arm when withdrawn from the pot, the skin comes off, then he is guilty, but if not, then innocent." The author[149] saw a case where the accused suffered not the slightest injury; he cannot account for it unless there was some drug applied to the arm. He is not ready to accept "the opinion of a certain missionary, who, when I told him of this, informed me that he had also seen it done, and put it down to supernatural agency." It is strange how persons of uncritical mind, when

[145] Goitein, *Prim. Ordeal and Mod. Law;* "Ordeal," in Index, Pinkerton's *Voy.,* XVII; Mauss, "Relig. et Origines du droit pénal," in *Rev. Hist. Relig.,* 1897, nos. 1 and 2.

[146] Howitt, *S. E. Aust.,* 336; Ratzel, *Vkde.,* II, 80.

[147] Codrington, *Melanesians,* 212, 213; Oliveira Martins, *Quadro,* 155.

[148] Livingstone, *Mission. Travels,* 666.   [149] Garbutt, in JAI, XXXIX, 556.

they have lived for a time among native tribes, become superstitious. Thus Nassau[150] seems to have lost his judgment on one occasion.

In West Africa almost every death rouses suspicion of witchcraft. "Then woe to the unpopular man, the weak women and slaves! On some one of them will fall the accusation that means ordeal by poison, or fire, followed, if these point to guilt, as they usually do, by a terrible death." "In the neighborhood of Benin, there is a Ju-Ju ordeal pond or river, said to be infested with dangerous and poisonous snakes and alligators, through which a man accused of any crime passing unscathed proves his innocence." A so-called feather-ordeal is performed as follows: "The Ju-Ju man takes a feather from the under part of a fowl's wing, choosing a stronger or weaker one according as he intends the ordeal shall demonstrate, then, drawing the tongue of the accused as far out of his mouth as he can, forces the quill of the feather through from the upper side and draws it out by grasping the point of the feather from the under side of the tongue; if the feather is unbroken the accused is proved guilty; if the feather breaks in the attempt to pass it through the tongue, it proves the person's innocence. It may be seen from this how very easy it was to prove innocence or guilt."[151] Among the Yoruba, the ordeal-draught "is prepared by a priest, who thus has it in his power to make it harmless or effective. It is a powerful poison, and if not at once rejected by the stomach, as often happens, causes death, in which case the *orisha* is considered to have declared his guilt by slaying him. A guilty man does not dare to 'drink *orisha*,' but the innocent will submit to the ordeal without fear, and, indeed, frequently demand it in order to prove their innocence, whence it follows that it is the guiltless who ordinarily perish."[152] Again the smith's hammer is dipped into water which the accused must drink; "they firmly believe that if anyone has done a wrong and yet denies it, the hammer will strike him down with sickness, and death will follow.[153]

In the East Indies the water-test is universal; men plunge into the water simultaneously, and the one who comes up first to get breath or first faints loses the case. Professional divers are sometimes employed. The diving-ordeal "can be traced from India to Borneo through the Burmese, Siamese and Malays." A brief description will reveal the essentially religious element involved: "In the case of disputed ownership of a fruit tree, which after 20 years begins to bear fruit, several begin to claim ownership, as doubtless the owner has been dead for some years and no one has paid any attention to the tree. The two principal disputants agree to settle the matter by diving, and call together hundreds of people to witness the trial. The two men take their positions in about 4 feet of water, each holds forth to the effect that he is the rightful owner, and prays that the water may trouble and enter the mouth and nostrils of his opponent; he calls on the birds and animals to witness his testimony. Two sets of cross-sticks have been driven into the mud at the bottom of the river leaving room enough for a man to get his head through; on a given signal the disputants, one at a time, dive into the water and each holds on as long as he can, placing his head under the cross sticks. A friend holds the legs of each, and in this way is enabled to tell whether his principal is

---

150 *Fetichism*, 136-137; §246, below.
151 Kingsley, *Travels W. Afr.*, 463; and *W. Afr. Studies*, 457, 490, 491.
152 Ellis, *Yoruba*, 191.   153 Spiess, in *Globus*, LXXV, 63.

going to faint; should he faint immediately the second must pull him out at once. The man who can keep under water longest is the winner. Sometimes the two men faint simultaneously, and the man who first recovers consciousness is the winner. Severe measures are taken to make them regain consciousness; a fire is lighted under a platform, and as soon as one of the men faints he is put on this platform and almost roasted alive, so anxious are his friends to restore him and so have him win the prize. During the ordeal there is the wildest excitement." There are also tests by boiling water and molten metal. If a woman accuses a man of being her seducer, she (or a fellow-tribesman of hers) and the accused are set opposite one another with knives, with which they try to stab each other. The first one wounded is false. This is a sort of duel. And there are running-tests. Drawing a red-hot iron over the tongue is also found, as well as fire-ordeals similar to those of mediæval Europe. Among the Land Dyaks there is a method by which "many disputed matters are settled very quietly. It is called *Pangat,* and is thus performed: two small wax tapers are made, of equal length and size; they are lighted together, one being held by the plaintiff, and the other by the defendant, in the case thus brought to trial; he whose taper is first extinguished is adjudged to be in the wrong, and, as far as I have seen, he always implicitly accepts the decision." The stroking of hot resin and the extraction of a gold weight from boiling water one and one-half inches deep are ordeals reserved for cases of greater importance.[154]

The ordeal has persisted far down into history. The laws of Hammurabi included it; the ancient Hebrews and the later Semites practised it. The Icelandic sagas exhibit it in full sway, and it lasted on into the Middle Ages. A curious story, preserved by the Saxon annalist Widukind, "shows that, even in the 10th century and under Otto the Great, Law was regarded as a truth to be discovered, not as a command to be imposed. The question was, whether the children of a deceased person ought to share in the inheritance of their grandfather, along with their uncles. It was proposed that the matter be examined by a general assembly convoked for the purpose. But the king was unwilling that a question concerning the difference of laws should be settled by an appeal to numbers. So he ordered a battle by champions; and, victory declaring itself for the party which represented the claims of the grand-children, the law was solemnly declared in that sense. The original proposal would have been an appeal to custom; but the plan adopted reveals the thought that even custom is not conclusive proof, that Law is a thing which exists independently of human agency, and is discoverable only in the last resort by an appeal to supernatural authority." Ordeals were abolished by the Lateran Council in 1215,[155] but they persisted in popular practice long thereafter.

There is always sense in such universal practices. A veteran missionary[156] writes as follows: "To drink this ordeal and be either

[154] Wilken, *Vkde.,* 474 ff.; Ratzel, *Vkde.,* II, 454; Roth, *Sarawak,* I, 187, 235 (quoted), 236, 237; II, clxxxviii; Perelaer, *Dajaks,* 147; Hose, in JAI, XXIII, 163.

[155] Winckler, *Hammurabi,* 10; Maurer, *Vkde.,* I, 160, 161, 162; Smith, *Relig. Sem.,* 178, 181; Ersch and Gruber, *Encycl., sub* "Ordalien"; Laing, *Sagas,* IV, 44, 261; *Laxdaela Saga,* 46; Leo, *Island,* 418; D'Alviella, *Concep. God,* 181, 182; Jenks, *Law and Pol.,* 9-10 (quoted), 127.

[156] Weeks, in JAI, XL, 364-365.

right or wrong according to its action settles the affair once for all, ends all possible deadly feuds and bloodshed, and saves many a man from what is worse than death, viz., an ever-present anxious fear of what his enemy or enemies may do to him. If a man accuses another of giving him a disease or of causing the death of his wife by witchcraft, how can the accused disprove such a charge? Not by talking, no matter how much he may swear that he is innocent. If he calls the chiefs and headmen together he knows the verdict will be given in favour of the one who pays the most; if he runs away he will soon be captured by some other town and probably sold to furnish a cannibal feast; if he runs to a friendly town he will lose caste, he will be treated with contempt as a coward, and his life be rendered miserable. So he boldly steps forth and takes the *nka* and the affair is settled. . . . No stigma attaches to a man who is found guilty, for 'one can have witchcraft without knowing it.' Moreover, no one lightly brings a charge of witchcraft against another, for, if the ordeal test goes against the accuser, the damages are so very heavy as to deter frivolous accusations." There are no ill feelings after the affair is over. Plainly the ordeal is as reasonable a device, granted the religious beliefs of the people, as any of the enlightened adjustments of civilization which go with corrected major premises.

"Some of these practices must appear to us as entirely ridiculous and merely calculated to defeat the ends of justice, so that we are unable to countenance them or permit their application. But we should not condemn them all too hastily, especially as long as the natives retain a genuine belief in their efficacy. Let it also be considered that originally they were not intended as indisputable deciding factors in trials, for the ultimate outcome of every suit lay with the parties themselves. And in point of fact, natives frequently speak of such devices as 'witnesses,' according as they are considered fallible or not. One reason for suspicion as to the reliability of these tests lies in the fact that either the medicine man who administers them may be biased or the one party may risk the supposed evil consequences rather than give way, or for some supernatural reason their potency may fail, or, finally, the victim may be cured of the ill effects by the aggrieved party. Hence, although the decision may be guided by some such test, its execution need not necessarily follow, and mostly does not ensue through the judges. It is therefore only when we convert the native tribunal into a European court that the application of these means is apt to defeat the ends of justice. Nevertheless, they have their uses, partly because the one who is in the wrong may fear their supernatural power and therefore give way, knowing himself to be at fault; partly because many are in the nature of solemn or sacred affirmations which the native will not flippantly pronounce. Not every witness in a European court is a sincere believer in the divine nature of his oath on the Bible, and yet the oath does call to mind very potently the sacred obligation he undertakes in the court. So with the native, even if he has become sceptical, the ceremonial and traditional performance of his oath, test or ordeal is not without veneration in his eyes, and we shall not be well advised if we discard such ceremonies entirely."[157]

The reader of literature or history is well aware of the practice of ordeal by duel for it is one of the picturesque motives seized upon by the recounter, for example, by Walter Scott. Issues of all sorts were "proved," in the times of chivalry, by recourse to single combat; and it required a Cervantes to reveal by parody the emptiness of the whole system. The duel goes far back beyond the Middle Ages in society's evolution. It has appeared as a mitigation of war, in the case where two champions fight instead of two tribes.

A few scattering cases may serve to illustrate some of the aspects of the duel as an ordeal. It is thought that the Tungus must have had formerly a higher culture; "one need only take the duel which without doubt, in the case of so very sanguine a people, speaks for a certain grade of mitigation of custom in comparison to the blood-vengeance which is present among the rudest nature-peoples, but does not appear among the Tungus."[158] It is known how in Europe, among the ancient Germans and even up into the Middle Ages, the duel appeared as an ordeal of God; of this the duel of our day is to be regarded as a moribund reminiscence. Among the people of the Indian Archipelago too this is the case."[159] In the Homeric age there is at least one good example of the ordeal-trial. "Greeks and Trojans, under solemn oaths and truce, agreed to leave the settlement of their disputes to the duel of the injured Menelaus and the seducer Alexander. This duel was to end the war. As the gods had been solemnly called upon to sanctify the oaths of truce, so they were present to conclude the ordeal. So much trust was placed in the outcome of the trial, that Greeks and Trojans, in defiance of their own knowledge as

157 Dundas, C., in JAI, LI, 231-232.   158 Hiekisch, *Tungusen,* 68-69.
159 Wilken, *Vkde.,* 476, 477.

to who was the guilty party, could pray, 'Whoever brought on these woes, let him die.' The outcome of the combat itself was a just one; Menelaus had Paris at his mercy. But Aphrodite snatched him away; thus the trial had not the literal decision necessary, though it was claimed upon the advantage of the Greek champion, and even Paris acknowledged that the gods had decided against him."[160] After using the ordeal of red hot iron and scalding water, the Franks adopted the judicial duel, which was imposed first on the disputing parties, then on the witnesses, and sometimes on the judges themselves. From the reign of Otho the Great (967) the duel, which had been at first restricted to the most serious cases, was had recourse to in almost all suits. No one was exempt from it, either for himself or his champion. If the legend of the dog of Montargis is to be believed, the judicial duel seems to have been resorted to even against an animal.[161] The anathemas of the Church were almost impotent to discourage duels; but "in our own century they are rapidly disappearing before the simple censure of an industrial society."[162]

"The old Russians knew single combat on the battle-field, but the duel as a means of repairing injured honor had remained to them something incomprehensible. If anyone wanted to take sharper vengeance upon an insulter than the . . . laws allowed, he simply put him out of the way by treachery or assassination. The noblest, it is true, knew of a sort of duel as private justice; not, however, a duel with sabres or pistols, but with whips. . . . 'Often great lords, on horseback, beat each other with whips and flayed each other in cruel fashion.' " The most tragic of the duels in the defense of family-honor, contests later introduced into Russia from abroad, was that in which the poet Pushkin lost his life.[163]

The duel is not solely an expedient for revealing the will of heaven and appealing to divine authority; it was also "a substitute for private war and irregular self-redress";[164] it is here treated under the former aspect because in its quality of ordeal it is, perhaps, of deepest significance. Its later history furnishes a remarkable example of a custom persisting in spite of attempts, not always sincere, to suppress it. The right of private redress was one which the peace-group could not tolerate if it were to take to itself the control over rights and remedies; but it compromised for a time, assuming power over some and allowing others to remain in private hands. It was not until the duel had completely disappeared that the state could be said to have fully assumed the right of punishment. Blood-revenge was a very ancient practice and the duel had been an ordeal with sacred character for the solemn decision and settlement of disputes; then too the duel satisfied honor, or vanity, in cases where the personal element bulked so

[160] Keller, *Hom. Soc.*, 165.
[161] Lacroix, *Middle Ages*, 353.
[162] Lecky, *Europ. Morals*, II, 254.
[163] Stern, *Russland*, 263, 264, 265.
[164] Vinogradoff, *Hist. Jurispr.*, I, 349.

large that the individual would allow nobody else to decide for him what he could tolerate and what not. It ought not to be denied that cases arise in which the sense of humiliation under wrong suffered is so great that it is unendurable consistently with life. It is not good for a man to accept and submit to such a wrong. Our mores do not provide for redress; the civil law fails most conspicuously in the worst cases. It cannot be gainsaid that the abolition of the duel has given license to a large class of base persons to perpetrate insults and injuries with impunity. These facts by no means outweigh the great evils and abuses of duelling but they account somewhat for the tenacity of the custom. Like lynching, it represents an unwillingness to surrender private retaliation to the state, which may, indeed, not be ready to guarantee satisfaction. It is thus a passing, transitional form. It is not a rational remedy but only a conventional one. As such it has come to satisfy vanity only.

§184*. Punishments. From a review of the punishments accorded to crimes by the less developed societies there emerges a real perspective of primitive administration of justice.[165] As the following cases are scanned, the persistence of the idea of retaliation should be noted, together with the fact that it is not the intention but the actual deed of which account is taken. It will be noted that the elders as the repositories of custom and the chiefs as the representatives of their societies are the administrators of justice if any such are singled out; and also that the penalty is primarily an atonement and an expiation, as for a sin, whose sense is to be found in current religious ideas. Compensation, it will be recalled, is a replacement rather than a punishment.[166] To us commutation in property or money seems unjust in the case of murder, especially if the wergeld is fixed according to a tariff based on the rank and wealth of the person killed. On the earlier stages of society's evolution and down into almost modern times it was not so regarded; for men were then familiar with the idea of ransoming a person captured by enemies or robbers, whose life was forfeit or at mercy, for sums varying according to his wealth and rank. Cases of execution where no ransom was forthcoming were no

[165] §160, above.   [166] §178, above.

novelty to them. It is not so unheard-of that a life should be regarded as having a money-value; until recently slaves were worth a price, and life-insurance assumes the principle. Other aspects of the penal code of backward peoples will appear in the cases;[167] except that cannibalism as a punishment for crime and the penalties for adultery have been saved out for treatment in other connections.[168] In citing punishments we have not sought to arrange them according to the crimes in question. In regard to theft, it should be noted that it is punished more severely in primitive society, in part at least because on that stage the relative value of men and goods is weighted on the side of the latter.[169] Theft and murder outside the group are, of course, essentially commendable.

It is to be noted that "offences against religion do not come within the law, for those who offend the spirits bring their own punishment upon themselves."[170]

The Abyssinian tendency toward exact retaliation in punishment is illustrated by the story of the boy who fell out of a tree upon a companion and killed him. The judges decided that the mother had the right to send another boy up the tree, to fall upon the slayer's neck.[171] A similar punishment is recorded in the pre-Conquest Saxon law, though Professor Llewellyn[172] finds "this passage to look like the attempt of a theoretician to reduce a case to absurdity."

In the case of crimes other than murder, the Australian atonement is "by the criminal appearing and submitting himself to the ordeal of having spears thrown at him by all such persons as conceive themselves to have been aggrieved, or by permitting spears to be thrust through certain parts of his body—such as through the thigh, or the calf of the leg, or under the arm. The part which is to be pierced by a spear is fixed for all common crimes, and a native who has incurred this penalty sometimes quietly holds out his leg for the injured party to thrust his spear through. . . . If the criminal is wounded in a degree judged sufficient for the crime he has committed, his guilt is wiped away; or, if none of the spears thrown at him—for there is a regulated number which each may throw—take effect, he is equally pardoned."[173] The Australians hale a persistent offender against tribal law or one who has used magic too freely to a trial. Those who have lost a relative through his witchcraft are given the task of executing retribution. From that time the offender is an outlaw and, unless he can get into sanctuary, is killed. There are certain places

[167] Also in Steinmetz, *Strafe;* Wines, *Punishments; Pinkerton's Voy.,* XVII, index, *sub* "Punishments."

[168] §§292, 383, below.   [169] De Greef, *Soc.,* II, 267.
[170] Dundas, C., in JAI, XLIII, 518.   [171] Tylor, *Anth.,* 417.
[172] Personal Communication. The reference given is *Leges Henrici* (Holdsworth), XC, 7.
[173] Smyth, *Vict.,* I, 80-81; Eyre, *Cent. Aust.,* II, 389.

where he is safe.[174] Ostracism is generally equivalent to death, for a man has then no fellows to stand by and avenge him; sometimes, however, where conditions are less primitive, it is the punishment for lesser crimes. Rivers[175] tells of a man who took a second wife, though he had neither of the qualifications necessary, namely, chieftainship or the possession of ten heads taken in battle. He was then ostracized or boycotted by the rest of the island, and came to the white man's camp; "but after about ten days he became tired of his isolation, gave up his second wife and returned to his village, to carry for the rest of his life . . . a social stigma for having tried unsuccessfully to regard himself as superior to the traditions of the community. . . . The man had committed an offence against the community, and the community had, intuitively it would seem, decided to have no more social dealings with the offender till the offence was purged." In New Caledonia the thief and adulterer were treated alike, that is, murdered. In a neighbouring district the parties guilty of adultery were tried, dressed up, fed before the multitude, and then publicly strangled. A man of the friends of the woman took one end of the cord, and a man of the friends of the man took the other."[176]

Under Kikamba law, in East Africa, offences are dealt with by fine, compensation, or the death-sentence. The first applies only to theft and amounts to seven times the value of the article stolen. Compensation, we now know, is an attempt at replacement following murder. There is a religious ceremony attendant; if it is not performed neither family will drop the feud; "their hands are fierce," as the natives say. Hanging is of no avail in such cases: "it is probably only adding evil to evil." The compensation is both an atonement and a sacrifice. "There is left, so to speak, a death-dealing spirit, and it is quite a logical supposition that when nothing is done to curb this power it will continue as before, death-bringing to those with whom it began thus, and death-dealing by those who first caused death. Any other view could only spring from ideas of justice, but the Mkamba reckons on no justice from supernatural powers." The death-penalty follows upon habitual robbery or theft of honey-barrels, incorrigible witchcraft, repeated murders, or where a man is recognized as a public danger. The sentence is carried out with the consent of the offender's relatives by the community; he is hunted down by his fellows in a body. "Here, we see, again, that the great aim is to remove the blame from the individual. . . . It was done by common consent, and no one could be blamed; if there was any responsibility it rested with the brother or father of the offender, who alone had the right to sentence him, because to them the blood money would be due. . . . It is my impression that this is regarded as a crime committed of necessity by the people as a whole, and sanctioned by the only one who could take vengeance or claim compensation, namely the nearest relative. . . . Among the Sumbwa a family may secure itself against blood revenge by disowning a member who has committed repeated murder or witchcraft."[177] A writer on Dinka laws,[178] after giving pages of detail, finds that "there is no leader who can give a death sentence, nor order any tribal fine for any offence to be paid to him."

[174] Horne and Aiston, *Cent. Aust.*, 145, 147.
[175] *Soc. Org.*, 168.   [176] Turner, *Samoa*, 343.
[177] Dundas, C., in JAI, XLIII, 512-515; and in JAI, LI, 233-234.
[178] O'Sullivan, in JAI, XL, 190.

Wilken[179] has written one of his thorough studies upon the subject of the penal laws of the Malay race. "Among peoples in their childhood, in a raw, uncivilized, as yet little organized society, punishment is vengeance, and indeed private vengeance. . . . Not everywhere and at all times may the ill-doer be visited by this right of revenge; only within a not too extended period after the misdeed, and in particular at discovery in the act, is it regarded as allowable. After this interval the right ceases and the acceptation of the gift of reconciliation, the fine, is a duty." This is the case in the Indian Archipelago. If the thief or adulterer is caught in the act he may be killed; if not, there is a time-limit, say twenty-four hours; or if one kills the thief he must report to the king, with proofs of the crime. There are many cases illustrative of the principle that if the individual is to inflict punishment he must do it at once. If the murderer gets to the judge's house, he is in sanctuary. This setting of a term during which punishment remains in private hands is like the provision connected with elopement, whereby vindictiveness must be renounced unless the parties are apprehended within a certain time. After further development of the system has taken place, that term is reduced to zero and then compensation must be received, no heed being paid to the feelings of the injured. The penal code of the Malays is characterized by the fine or compensation, whereby every misdeed, in all its shadings, has its property-equivalent. The compensation or fine has, however, a purely private stamp, and is a making good of loss rather than a penalty. Crimes are regarded as committed against individuals, not the community, "so that the pursuit of the culprit is regarded as in itself no state-affair. Therefore there exists no distinction between a civil and a penal action." This is particularly the case with the wergeld. "A natural result of this principle is that the distinction which the European penal code makes between murder, homicide, and involuntary killing is not known by the peoples of the Indian Archipelago. Against every killing stands the wergeld," barring a few exceptions. The amount of this compensation varies with circumstances, but it is noteworthy that if it cannot be paid the guilty person is executed or enslaved.

It is significant to find adultery and theft aligned as respects penalty.[180] Just as for theft, so for adultery, it is universal to apply vengeance to those caught in the act, while in other cases they are simply fined. The thief may have simply to give back the stolen goods or to make good their value; if this cannot be done, the thief may serve the owner as a slave or pawn.

There are crimes that may be called public, such as those against rulers; to such the compensation does not apply. It is to be recalled that compensation is based on the right of vengeance, and that the taking of it was a matter of the pleasure of the injured party. It stands to reason that when the injured were the more powerful they were less likely to be complaisant; among many tribes, "while crimes against equals or inferiors in rank are generally made up for by compensation, those against the higher-placed, especially against chiefs and ruling persons, are mostly punished by death." Where there is a settled rule, crimes against the ruler or his relatives are not settled by compensation; it is a case of *lèse majesté;* even errors in etiquette may be capitally punished.

[179] In VG, II, especially 449, 450, 454, 456-458, 464 ff., 470 ff., 479 ff., 486 ff.
[180] §383, below.

Wilken cites numbers of cases of the first importance, lists the various varieties of penalty, and concludes that East Indian punishments reduce to the following categories: (1) property-punishment: fines and compensations, especially in the case of crimes against individuals; (2) the death-penalty and other corporeal punishments: in connection with political crimes and trespasses against good morals, and also subsidiarily in connection with crimes against individuals; (3) liberty-penalties: slavery and debt-bondage, chiefly a subsidiary punishment in case of crimes against individuals." There is not much imprisonment, though the stocks are used very cruelly; but there are a number of what are called punishments by insult, where, for instance, a thief has to carry stolen property on his neck in a parade about the village. It is stated that his relatives become so ashamed that they buy the culprit off. The private nature of most Malay crimes is shown by the type of punishment and by the identity of the parties determining or inflicting them.

In the Malay Islands a nettle is found which compares to ours as a tiger to a cat. Thieves are punished by flogging them with freshly cut branches. Says a traveler: "I saw such unlucky persons writhing on the earth like worms attacked by ants. Their condition was beyond any description, and they were on the verge of losing their senses."[181] In one district of Borneo, the sultan's two sons executed the sentence of flogging thieves; the crime was against their father; it was his money that was stolen.[182] In Sumatra the thief deserves death, according to native law, even if not caught in the act; the Moslem law provides for progressive amputations of hands and feet in case of repeated offenses.[183] Certain tribes in the Philippines forfeit property in the case of murder inside the group; if an outsider kills a tribal member they unite to kill the slayer or his relatives.[184] In Núkuóro, "a slight misdemeanor calls down individual expressions of censure from the neighbors, while a more important one brings to pass a common interposition by the community. The evil-doer is . . . bound to a tree and chastised with a rope according to the degree of his transgression. The punishment is sharpened by hunger and exposure in the sun. . . . According to the crime and behavior of the culprit is the protraction of his punishment for several days, and in some cases he dies in consequence of the sufferings he has endured. In case of backsliding the same punishment is repeated three times in ever severer degree and then banishment out to sea . . . is proclaimed by the chief. This banishment occurs in a manner whereby the evil-doer is set bound, without food or paddle, in a canoe, launched on the high sea, and there left to his fate." Transgressions and punishments are very rare; in thirty years no banishment has taken place and the flogging has been applied only three times.[185]

Throughout most of Polynesia a thief is turned over defenseless to those he has wronged. He may be thrown to the sharks, or forced to bathe where they congregate.[186] "Chiefs of considerable rank had sometimes been detected in the act of stealing, or had been known to employ their domestics to thieve, receiving the articles stolen, and afterwards sheltering the plunderers. This, however, had generally been practised on the property of foreigners. Among

[181] Ratzel, *Vkde.*, II, 367.　　　　[182] Bock, *Borneo,* 8.

[183] Snouck-Hurgronje, *Atjèhers,* I, 108.

[184] Worcester, *Philippine Isl.,* 413.

[185] Kubary, *Núkuóro,* 21-22.　　　　[186] Letourneau, *Morale,* 160-161.

themselves, the thief, if detected, experienced no mercy, and was often murdered on the spot; and even, if detected afterwards, was sometimes dreadfully wounded or killed. The London missionaries say that the Tahitians held thieving among themselves to be a bad thing, and did not scruple to kill a thief if they found him; but they did not suppose that their deities were angry with them for stealing, and indeed prayed to them for success. . . . Theft of food was sometimes punished by death, and this was generally the penalty adopted in cases of theft by persons outside the tribe. The more usual punishment of members of the tribe was destruction of everything edible on the land of the family of the thief." The author[187] speaks of a man "who lined the banks of his fine *taro* patch with the bodies of thieves slain by his own hand"; and adds that none of these murders was avenged. "This last statement suggests that the justice of the punishment was recognized by the friends of the thief."

In the Hervey Islands, he goes on, the supernatural was invoked in the punishment of thieves; the "sorcerers had a method of destroying a thief by burning his spirit on a red-hot iron. If a person had been robbed and could not discover the thief, he would give a present to a sorcerer sufficient to pay for one or more ovens, according to the value of the article stolen. The sorcerer would then repair to his house; and in the darkness of the night would make a fire in a pit dug in a shed used for the purpose of the operation, and place upon it stones which became red hot. As the flames arose and the stones waxed hot he danced round the oven, uttering the most dreadful imprecations against the unknown thief; he even gave each of the gods a round of curses in order to excite their anger against the thief and cause them to bring his spirit to the oven. As the pile consumed, the sorcerer saw the spirit of the thief actually writhing upon the burning stones, and, perhaps to make certainty more certain, he thrust it through and through with his spear until it was presumably dead. This operation would sometimes, if the property stolen was valuable, or the anger of its possessors was very great, be repeated two or three times. It is stated that the terror inspired by these performances was so great that attempts would often be made to kill the sorcerer, and so break the spell, before he had completed his purpose, and sometimes the actual thief died of sheer fright."

Among the Eskimo the punishment for murder, which, despite their peaceableness, sometimes occurs, is left to the relatives of the deceased; but in very atrocious cases the men of the village may kill the murderer. Women are the most common cause of bloodshed.[188] Among the Hudson Bay Eskimo a form of boycott like the ancient practice of withdrawing fire and water is in vogue. "When a person becomes so bad in character that the community will no longer tolerate his presence, he is forbidden to enter the huts, partake of food, or hold any intercourse with the rest. . . . Should he be guilty of a murder, several men watch their opportunity to surprise him and put him to death, usually by stoning. The executors make no concealment of their action, and are supported by public opinion in the community."[189] The Eskimo cannot comprehend "white man's justice"; "the Eskimo, especially when he or one of his fellows has admitted killing a white man, finds it extremely difficult to under-

[187] Williamson, *Cent. Polyn.*, III, 21, 22-24.
[188] Nansen, *Esk. Life,* 163.
[189] Turner, in BAE, XI, 186; Lippert, *Kgchte.*, I, 268.

stand why the red-coated mounted policeman, representative of the white man's law, should not shoot him on sight, but instead should bring him out to civilization where a big white chief, dressed like a woman, sits on a bench and hears another white chief say, on the Eskimo's behalf, that though he killed the white man in question he should not be punished. Several natives having been brought out to civilization for trial, given good treatment and then returned to their own people fatter than when they left, the Eskimo mind has been unable to understand this situation when all of the murderer's friends had given them up for dead, in some cases the men having confessed to the murders of whites."[190] It is naturally impossible for men to understand a system which represents an adjustment so far ahead of them on the road of institutional evolution.

In British Guiana, property was holy and there was little theft. If it occurred, the men's council took notice of it and the opposing parties submitted to its sentence.[191] To prevent theft, one tribe works its grain, stalks and all, into figures of animals. Then part cannot be removed without detection of the fact of theft—something especially difficult among people who cannot count very well. It is the same expedient which appears when civilized owners put up butter or the like in certain forms corresponding to definite weights or sprinkle piles of coal with white coloring.[192] In Peru punishments were generally public humiliations; for example, the culprit had to carry a heavy burden through the village under the scorn of his fellows. Public chastisement was rare. "When any general calamity occurred, the members of the community were rigorously examined, until the sinner was discovered and compelled to make reparation."[193]

The ancient Hebrews allowed no atonement for murder: "ye shall take no ransom for the life of a manslayer, which is guilty of death; but he shall surely be put to death."[194] It is not necessary to recount the long line of penalties exacted by more highly developed nations; but a pair of examples may be cited to illustrate the persistence of outlawry and of sheer physical cruelty.

"Outlawry is the last weapon of ancient law and one that it must often use. As has been well said it is the sentence of death pronounced by a community which has no police constables or professional hangmen. To pursue the outlaw, to knock him on the head as though he were a wild beast, this is the right and duty of every law-abiding man. 'Let him bear the wolf's head,' this phrase is in use even in the thirteenth century. But as the power of the state increases, as the number of its weapons increases, outlawry loses some of its gravity; instead of being a substantive punishment, it becomes mere 'criminal process,' a means of compelling accused persons to stand their trial."[195] In the reign of Queen Anne, "a remnant of the barbarous use of torture still remained (indeed it was not abolished until the year 1772) in the 'peine forte et dure' . . . or pressing to death. When a Felon, punishable with Death, takes a

Despatch in N. Y. *Times,* Oct. 8, 1922. Compare the circumstances attending the murder of Dr. Marvin, as revealed in the confession of his Eskimo slayer, published and commented upon in late September, 1926.

[191] Schomburgk, *Brit.-Guiana,* II, 321.

[192] Schmidt, in *Globus,* LXXXVI, 124.

[193] Cunow, *Verf. Inkareichs,* 114; Payne, *New World,* I, 443.

[194] Num., XXXV, 31.

[195] Pollock and Maitland, *Eng. Law,* I, 459.

Resolution not to make any Answer to his Judges, after the Second Calling
upon, he is carry'd back to his Dungeon, and is put to a Sort of Rack called
Peine forte et dure. If he speaks, his indictment goes on in the usual Forms;
if he continues dumb they leave him to die under that Punishment. He is
stretched out naked upon his Back, and his Arms and Legs drawn out by
cords, and fasten'd to the four Corners of the Dungeon: A Board or Plate
of Iron is laid upon his Stomach, and this is heap'd up with Stones to a certain Weight. The next day they give him, at three different times, three little
Morsels of Barley Bread, and nothing to Drink: the next Day, three little
Glasses of Water, and nothing to Eat: And if he continues in his Obstinacy,
they leave him in that Condition 'till he dies. This is practis'd only upon
Felons, or Persons guilty of Petty Treason. Criminals of High Treason, in the
like Case, would be condemn'd to the usual Punishment; their Silence would
Condemn them."[196]
Penalties for adultery have been treated in another connection.[197] It is to
be noted, as several preceding examples have also intimated, that this crime
was assimilated to theft.

That the religious element enters into procedure, not only in the
detection of crime but also in the matter of punishment, is a fact
now familiar. Sometimes it exercises a mitigating influence, as in
the provision of sanctuary.[198] It is especially significant that the
society reserves to itself the punishment of the crimes most menacing to the integrity of the peace-group, leaving minor misdemeanors to be dealt with by the family or other local bodies; and
it is enlightening to observe how, with the failure of criminal law,
punishment falls back into the hands of groups or even individuals, as in lynching,[199] who assert that they are acting under a
higher or unwritten law. In their character, primitive penalties
are retaliatory and intimidating, not reformatory; the principle
of an eye for an eye is unmistakable in them. They also partake
of the nature of the ordeal. Comparatively speaking, they are not
severe, especially if one realizes that the estimate set on human
life is not his own, and if he compares them with the tortures inflicted upon aliens. The ritual nature of penalization is revealed
in the provision that one may secure a substitute; and that he can
procure one in the case of the death-penalty is again evidence of
the light value set on life. It is evident throughout the cases that
while the responsibility and solidarity of the group persist, they
are giving way in some instances to the conception of individual

[196] Ashton, *Queen Anne*, 410-412.   [197] §383, below.
[198] §§251, 272, 273, below.   [199] Cutler, *Lynch Law*.

accountability; and that some small notice is taken of extenuating circumstances or, at any rate, of motives. But these latter phenomena are variations that yet require a long stretch of evolution before they secure a dominant place in the mores.

CHAPTER XX

ANTECEDENTS OF THE STATE

§185. Transition to the State. The regulative system as developed in preceding chapters has shown nothing that deserves the dignity of the term "state." Our plan does not contemplate more than an introduction to the study of that developed political form. Covering as it does a stretch of societal evolution, and not the whole,[1] this book begins with the simplest institutional forms that are well attested in ethnography and history and stops short of the modern period, except in so far as the conclusions here drawn throw forward toward the present or as certain modern societal phenomena, survivalistic or other, cast a special light upon the general course of institutional evolution. In particular, we stop where the science of economics begins its more special analysis of the developed self-maintenance organization and where the study of comparative religion undertakes its estimates of the several distinctive systems of Buddhism, Islam, and the rest. So here; for we do not wish to enter upon the domain of political science. That discipline virtually begins with the state, while it is with the conditions precedent to the development of the state that we conclude. Our chief interest lies in background-building and in the indication of lines of development which are projected forward into the modern period.

As there are no chasms or even sharply marked lines of demarkation between periods of evolution, but zones of transition merely, it is as impossible to say at what point the state first appears as it is to determine when mores become laws, or at what hour the child becomes a youth or the youth a man. Formerly he was a youth; now he is a man. Between then and now a development has taken place which makes it necessary to employ a new designation; at any time between then and now he may seem the one or the other according to his behavior on some occasion or according to the viewpoint of the observer. Similarly with the developing regulative institution: it is uncertain just where it takes on the

[1] §§454, 455, below.

state-form. This book invades, to some degree, the transition-period between less developed forms of regulation and the state.

It is possible to contend that the first real state was the Roman. In it alone was realized the concentration by civil organization of a great group over a great territory, so that the total power for work or war could be directed with prompt reaction to selected ends. Its cohesion was so intense that it only gradually dissolved. Its organization was a model for the structure of modern states many of which have been formed as petty imitations of it. "In no one of the primitive societies was there a more rapid formation of the civil city in which the molecule was the man and the principle of cohesion was local contiguity in place of domestic proximity and consanguinity."[2] Compared with some such idea of the state, "neither the Aztecs nor the Nahuas formed a state, a nation, or even a political society."[3] After two centuries of rule in Asia, the Persians had done nothing to make the complex populations which they had controlled into a state; they were varnished with Babylonian half-culture but had no security of life and property. The fact that an "authority" was present to plan all the irrigation-enterprises and carry them through is evidence of government but it does not justify the assertion that "on this spot the State first appeared in history."[4] Yet one encounters commonly enough the use of the term state in connection with regulative organizations antecedent to and far less perfect than the Roman.

There is evidently a zone of transition from such tribal government as has been reviewed to even the less perfect state. With the outlines of the former now before us, we can perhaps gain a clearer idea of the transition by noting certain of the characteristics of the state-form toward which the developing regulative system was working.

The outstanding feature of state-development is the decline of the blood-bond in favor of the territorial bond; it has been seen that, although the family and clan tended to disappear in the tribe, the consanguineal tie has long persisted, at least in name. The term "nation," from the Latin verb "to be born," is evidence of this, and the terms of family-relationship are used loosely to cover political connections; many a scion of stock but recently transplanted into this country refers to his American "forefathers." Men do not readily alter their terminology, though they may shift connotations without taking any account of it. The distinction between state and nation should be clear in the mind before attempting to discuss either; it comes out clearly in the

2 Oliveira Martins, *Quadro,* 109.   3 Nadaillac, *Preh. Amer.,* 310.
4 Beloch, *Gr. Gchte.,* II, 597; Ihering, *Aryan,* 160-161; Rogers, *Babylonia,* I, 300-301, 308-309.

case of the Jews who have long formed a nation but never a real state. For centuries they have had no regulative system of their own, though they once had a tribal government. The Zionist movement of recent years aims at the establishment of a Hebrew territorial state.

A nation is a group of people who cherish the same code, so far as the salient and essential mores are concerned: speak the same language, adhere to the same type of institutions, have a fund of common convictions, principles, and aims.[5] There is no denying that if they are at the same time under a single government they are likely to be the more homogeneous; yet parts of the same nation may be distributed among a number of states. A state, on the other hand, is a regulative organization existing within a certain territory and its body politic may include a number of nationalities. It is at the end of a series of forms of societal organization beginning with the family, and is different enough from what goes before to get a special name. There is nothing metaphysical about it. A nation by its very homogeneity is more like a kin-group; and if the state could be the regulative organization of a single nation it would be considerably more stable and satisfactory. This is recognized by the modern principle of self-determination of peoples.

It is not necessary to follow up this distinction between state and nation in the present connection, since we shall attend only to the development of the regulative system toward the state-form; but the nation-concept may be somewhat sharpened.

There is, we are told, "practically no Dahomi nation. The original stock disappeared through the great loss of life incurred in the incessant wars, and the waste of reproduction represented by the enforced celibacy of some three thousand Amazons and two thousand palace women has been replaced long since by slaves, mongrels, and Yorubas. It is really a political organization, and if the monarchy were overthrown, Dahomi would cease to exist."[6]

The Civil War taught the American people what a nation is. "A nation is not a certain extent of territory on the earth's surface; nor is it the mere aggregate of the persons who may live within a certain territory. A nation is a community of various ages, occupations, talents, and circumstances, but all united in a common interest. . . . It is enduring in its existence, spanning over individual lives and generations. It accumulates the contributions of various individuals and of various generations and it brings them all to the

5 Sumner, *Coll. Ess.*, III, 354 ff.   6 Ellis, *Ewe*, 198.

service and benefit of each. It is, therefore, in the strictest sense, a commonwealth, in which each participates in the prosperity of the whole and all suffer through the misfortune of one. It brings down from generation to generation the accumulation of art, science, and literature and its store of these treasures should be a steadily increasing one. It brings down the public buildings, the machinery of government, the stores of defensive means, the galleries of painting, the museums of art and science, the libraries, as a continually increasing endowment of posterity. Moreover it cherishes traditions which, if they become petrified, form a prison-house which must be broken, but which, if they are fresh, living, and flexible, are the framework of society. For instance, the rights of conscience, the equality of all men before the law, the separation of church and state, religious toleration, freedom of speech and of the press, popular education, are vital traditions of the American people. They are not brought in question; they form the stock of firm and universal convictions on which our national life is based; they are ingrained into the character of our people and you can assume, in any controversy, that an American will admit their truth. But they form the sum of traditions which we obtain as our birthright. They are never explicitly taught to us, but we assimilate them in our earliest childhood from all our surroundings, at the fireside, at school, from the press, on the highways and streets. We never hear them disputed and it is only when we observe how difficult it is for some foreign nations to learn them that we perceive that they are not implanted by nature in the human mind. They are a part and the most valuable part of our national inheritance, and the obligation of love, labor, and protection which we owe to the nation rests upon these benefits which we receive from it."[7]

In a striking review, GilFillan[8] develops the nationalizing effect of a common language. A good part of Europe is bilingual, inasmuch as the people are obliged to acquire in school a common cultured language in addition to the vernacular. The former is different from the latter in grammar, pronunciation, idiom, and vocabulary; the vernacular may be Slovene and the reading language German. Eight languages, with numerous dialects, are spoken in France; only one is much written or used by the upper classes or in wide intercourse or in cities. It is this "printed and aristocratic medium, that binds the French territory into a particularly homogeneous and patriotic nation." There are seven languages in the British Isles, six in Italy, nine in old Germany; but it is the single culture-tongue that is the determinant and cement of any such great nation. Eastern Europe has no such binder. There uncouthly speaking peoples are building little nations about local languages. Esthonian or Slovak is satisfactory for local concerns; and people of limited cultural horizon demand an Esthonia or Slovakia. With the loss of prestige by the upper classes, since about 1880, disintegration has set in. Five new states were recognized by the Peace treaties; eleven others have appeared since 1917, "of which eight survive to hinder the reconstruction of the continent by their petty, obstructive independence. . . . Nationalism on the small, vernacular basis, the natural product of democracy wherever the culture tongues had not won an impregnable hold, as in the great western states, is one of the . . . most baneful disintegrating forces with which the twentieth century has to deal." This statement of the case was made to offset the accusation that about two million

[7] Sumner, *Coll. Ess.*, III, 353-354.
[8] In *Sewanee Rev. Qtly.*, XXXI, 252 ff.

Magyar-speaking people had been incorporated in states other than Hungary, owing to the rapacity of their neighbors. It is a challenge to the modern principle of self-determination, but bears as strongly upon the function of common language in nation-building as does that principle.

As an instance of confusion between state and nation, Brinton's[9] "The Nation as an Element in Anthropology" may be cited. The author means the state but is mixed between the two concepts. Some functions which he finds in the nation are distinctly those of coördinating force and belong to the state. Others are organic relations of a complex body integrated as to blood, language, religion, and other matters.

There seems to be an inevitable tendency to refer likeness or homogeneity to the primordial notion of kinship. It appeared in the term "family," as used prior to Darwin's time, and therefore, quite metaphorically, to include similar organic beings. It seems to be as difficult for mankind to get away from the ideas of the race's childhood, as illustrated in this tendency to use the terms of kinship, as for the individual to divest himself of lurking notions deriving from his own early days.

§186. Characteristics of the State. While a nation has no necessary relation to a defined territory, a state cannot exist apart from such a relation. Further, almost all states have had their origin in the conquest of one nation by another, resulting in a combination of rulers and ruled, the former devoting themselves to the organization and administration of power, the latter working and sustaining under coercion. The difference between the state and the nation, in the case of old and strongly marked nations, bears witness often to the struggle through which state-organization has been won, for the process has been one of violence and conquest. A state is a group occupying a defined territory, in so far as it is organized so as to make its force available to execute its will, within and without, as formulated by its constituted authorities. More specifically, the word state refers to the organization of regulation alone; states are viewed as organizations of defense and offense in relation to interests. Their functions include executive and administrative coercion and also transfers of political power by elections or otherwise as the institutions may provide.

It is evident that the state is an adjustment of a higher complexity and potency than any form of the regulative system

9 *Smithson. Rep.,* 1893.

hitherto considered. It is correlative with enacted law or legislation, whereas the forms of government thus far described go with
customary law or traditional precedent. The term state is properly reserved for a somewhat highly developed regulative organization; a conqueror-group, being compounded and composite, rises
perforce to a higher complexity and combines all the powers to
wider ends. It is an organization with authority and discipline
essential to large-scale achievements, as compared with the family,
for example, which is an organization on the same lines but simpler
and less potent. Morgan[10] sees an immense change from the gentile
or tribal system to the nation or state, and thinks the Greeks and
Romans took this step for us. The state in its development assumed many of the functions held previously by the patriarch and
became an abstraction, in institutions, of those functions. The
gens had to deal with the patriarchal head of each household, not
with individuals; nor could the state, when it was developing—in
the Middle Ages, for example—deal readily with individuals; only
after struggle did it do so, by taxes, conscription, and otherwise,
and ended by emancipating the individual and then taking him
under its own dominion. It constantly extended its sway to new
domains: trade, transportation, education, recreation. Modern
schemers, ignorant of history, think they may extemporize judgments on the expediency of all this.

States have aimed at internal uniformity by repressing tendencies to variation on the part of individuals or minor groups which
have developed enterprise or efforts at reform. They also resist
all the stresses and strains to which they are subjected by the culture-area to which they belong; a state-system of absolutism has
resisted constitutionalism, one of slavery has resisted free labor.
Like all other institutions, therefore, states which are, on the one
side, indispensable agents and bearers of societal interests, appear
on the other side as destroyers and opponents of those interests.
Hence, while the civilized culture-area of the present time shows a
complete and instantaneous transmission to all its members of all
the gains of any of those members, in literature, science, and art,
yet the industrial coöperation which would melt the whole into one
society, with incalculable benefits to all societal interests, is trav-

10 In *Contrib. N. A. Ethnol.,* IV, 23.

ersed by state-originated tariffs, military regulations, restrictions
on immigration, laws of domicile and settlement, which are in the
interest of state-jealousy and isolation.

The state obviously belongs to a relatively sophisticated stage
of society's evolution and, like the evolved economic organization,
forms the subject-matter of a special science; political science devotes itself in good part to the analysis and assessment of state-
forms as of immensely complicated modern adjustments. That,
however, the state finds its antecedents in the simpler regulative
systems of undeveloped peoples must now be evident. It develops
out of the compounding of tribes, generally by conquest, sometimes by confederation, into a larger peace-group; and it thus
represents, in either case, the outcome of war. There appears to
be a triangular relation between agriculture, slavery, and the
development of the territorial state; it is the idea of one writer[11]
that agriculturists live scattered and unorganized and do not
make states and that conquering nomads have overcome agriculturists and coerced them into state-organization. This author
seems to be thinking of the Manchus in China and the several invading tribes that came down into Assyria, Egypt, and Greece
and ruled the agricultural populations already there. But whoever
the conquerors were and whatever their type of self-maintenance,
the basic occupation in the earliest states was tillage. The conquered were reduced to the slave-status and set to cultivate the
fields. Systematic enslavement, as has been explained,[12] does not
appear until the development of agriculture. Hence the triangular
relation. With the slaves emerges also the primal division into
classes, a phenomenon characteristic of the state. Agriculture
further demands a sedentary life, and that sort of life is regarded
as the "direct antecedent of the state and the central point of the
German as well as of the Keltic, Indian, Greek, or Roman
civitas."[13]

Ihering[14] conceives of the possibility of a "migratory state," as exhibited
by the Aryan nomads. "All settled nations which they encountered during
their march were overcome by them; they alone held their own throughout;

[11] Ratzel, *Vkde.*, I, 18.   [12] §§100, 103, above.
[13] Ihering, *Vorgchte.;* Zimmer, *Altind. Leben;* Kowalewsky, *Ökon. Entwick.*,
I, 54.
[14] *Aryan*, 160.

history affords no more impressive example than this of the independence of the idea of State from the territorial element, and at the same time its supremacy over it." If this is the best example there is of a non-territorial state, we think we need not withdraw our contention. The nomadic government is characteristically tribal. Says Schrader:[15] "It was obviously a common occurrence for a number of village-communities, weary of the work of agriculture, or led by desire of better soil, to cut their crops, like the Helvetii of Caesar, pull down their lightly-built huts, pack child and chattel on the wagon, with its team of oxen, and seek their fortune in a distant land." The conception of "fatherland" had no compelling influence upon men until it acquired a territorial basis for the political unit in place of the tie of kinship.

§187. Origin of the State. It is as easy to guess at the origin of the state as at that of marriage or of religion. Along with them, it has been ascribed to the supernatural or, what is the same, to legendary figures like the "law-givers." If, renouncing otiose speculation, one gets down to the actual study of the series of forms that lead up to the state, he observes a set of expanding peace-groups characterized by systematized authority and resulting in the supersession of strife: family, clan, gens, tribe. In all of them power and authority are essential and the concentration of both is as necessary as it is spontaneous and unplanned. Weak in the clan and under the mother-family, it grows stronger with the patriarchate and is capable, along with it, of extension by conquest and enslavement. It tends therefore to transcend the bounds of the kin-group and to take on the characteristic of territoriality. Power that has been concentrated in the hands of the despot is wont to be delegated and distributed, though its earlier disposition always returns when the more complicated system weakens: "whenever a total change is made in government, it breaks down altogether and a resort to the despotism of one man is the result."[16] All forms of the state aim at power, authority, and discipline; it is an organization to collect the working and fighting force of the society so that it can be managed and directed. While all forms of government have this function, the state is that type which secures such ends under more evolved and complex conditions. The state is nothing else than an adjustment farther along in the series which begins in the family and works on through the clan and tribe.

[15] *Aryans*, 403.
[16] Petrie, in *Smithson. Rep.*, 1895, 595.

It has been asserted that the state evolved out of the patriarch-ate. No one would deny that in respect to the organization of power the patriarchate is nearer to the state than is the system whose center is the woman; for the patriarchate has a capacity for conquest and consolidation that the latter has not.[17]

The power of the father in the family breaks up, says Lippert,[18] and the state and the individual struggle for its fragments. The stress that urged toward the territorial state was that which resulted in a single simple peace-bond for groups compounded by war or otherwise; and so men gradually broke away from the blood-bond which was the only one they could know upon the earlier stages.

This, however, is far from saying that the state came out of the patriarchate. As the state results from conquest, and since the patriarchal organization was the form necessary to that end, it may be contended that the development of the patriarchate was a necessary antecedent to the development of the state. The latter, however, was a long way down the line of development from the former and seems to have come much more immediately from the compounding of tribes. The patriarchal principle existed in the tribes, either actively or in survivals; whatever forms and survivals remained when the state was formed were naturally taken over by it;[19] but they had, as a system, done their work and had been transmuted into political forms long before the state arose.[20]

To our way of thinking, the theory of Gumplowicz[21] accounts most satisfactorily for the rise of the state. It is, briefly, that the state is the result of conquest followed by stratification into classes and, at length, by amalgamation of the originally diverse elements. We shall not follow this author into his analysis of the state but shall reproduce such of his views as bear upon state-formation.

Gumplowicz[22] sees in the state an arena for a continuous mutual influence of manifold and heterogeneous social groups or ethnic elements, which is the condition of a rapid and manifold development. There is an unremitting strain

[17] §§421, 422, below.
[18] *Kgchte.*, II, 118; also II, 59, 163, 532, 560, 563, 569, 601.
[19] Rossbach, *Röm. Ehe*, 45 ff.   [20] Ch. XVI, above.
[21] *Soc.*, 40, 73, 78, 100, 114 ff., 119 ff., 126 ff., 133, 138, 147 ff., 155 ff., 187, 220-221, 245; *Staatsidee*, 20, 25, 96, 99, 102, 104, 116, 121, 128, 134; *Rassenkampf*, 298, 318 ff., 344; *Soc. u. Pol.*, 55, 74, 75, 80, 93.
[22] *Staatsidee*, 1 ff., and *Soc.*, 115 ff.

after power with all the means at disposal, by groups and parties; the latter seek justification by theories and watchwords, but it is power that decides. In this struggle some subjugate others, getting their services; if this had not been so, no states would ever have arisen. The further we go back into history the heavier are the services laid under requisition. Hatred for the alien led to war and subjugation; as culture advanced, needs grew along with satisfactions and groups extended their efforts at self-maintenance into robbery and eventual conquest of other groups. "The effort of every social community to render subject to itself and useful to itself every other social community which comes within the sphere of its existence, which effort has its ultimate origin in the struggle of the first community for self-maintenance, is the law which explains the composition of a state." Every state is a complex of institutions which have for their object the rule of some over others; and, furthermore, of a minority over a majority. This is the sole, correct and universal definition which fits all forms of the state. No state was ever founded in order to establish general prosperity or realize justice, as the political scientists have said; there are plenty of states which never have pursued any such aim. Every organization for ruling, under favorable conditions and in the course of time, necessarily takes upon itself exertions toward those ends but the definition should apply to all states at all stages of development.

We must not overlook another characteristic of the state, namely, the ethnological heterogeneity of the ruling and ruled, which can be perceived in every organization for rule. "Nowhere and never have states arisen otherwise than by the subjugation of outside tribes by means of one or more allied and united tribes." This lies in the nature of the case; over the whole globe there are no states without original ethnical heterogeneity of the ruling and ruled, and it is only the social development of the state which brings about an amalgamation of the nation. Spencer[23] holds the same view. He says no tribe becomes a nation by simple growth, and also no great society is formed by the direct union of the smallest societies, by which he means that a great nation is a union of heterogeneous elements which themselves were already complex, so that a great nation is a combination of a higher power. The state can never think of increasing its external power and dominion until it has succeeded in bringing its own heterogeneous components to unity. If a weak state is in the midst of or at the border of several powerful states and has not strengthened itself by alliances, then an agreement of the mighty neighbors to divide it up is inevitable. Such events are incidents in nature, produced by the operation of blind forces. Some people call them crimes. They might as well call an earthquake a crime because thousands perish in it. The only difference is that in the case of the political event we seem to see the people who did it; in the case of the earthquake we do not.

It is to be noted that the state-forms in a higher civilization have greater stability because the rulers have more means of maintaining their supremacy. In primitive states, after a short exploitation, the conquerors have used up the people and the land and have to move on to subjugate others.

The two simple classes, rulers and ruled, speedily evolve into a variety of social strata whose powers reside in property, religion, and discipline, as well as in general custom. All these classes take part in the regulative system according to their power and acquire rights and privileges. The power of the

[23] *Prin. Soc.*, I, §263.

constituent groups varies according to the number of interests upon which they can concentrate in common; but that number varies inversely as the numerical magnitude of the group. Thus a small group or minority may be strongly united upon a considerable number of interests while a large group can hold only a relatively few in common.[24] Out of the struggle of its constituent groups the society unerringly follows its own broad interests. The social struggle is intensely immoral, that is, it wounds our moral feelings. For societies have no such feelings but roll on like avalanches in the direction of their interests and overwhelm opposition with destruction. "The blind law of nature predominates over the actions of wild hordes, of social groups, and of states." The state has been developed out of facts and by facts; by natural and necessary efforts to satisfy experienced necessities. It has become the protector of rights and of tradition, and also of prosperity and civilization. This has produced a moral theory of the state—a myth—according to which the state arose from a social compact, the members of the society having created it, that it might protect rights and administer justice. The German mystical state has revived the French ideas of the eighteenth century.

The state establishes and confirms inside itself the inequalities under which a united social life is possible. There are then no inequalities or injustices that are "established," but they arise all the more from the free play of natural forces. The thing that happens in a state is never what the monarch or statesman intends but that which is immanent in the circumstances, that is, the product of the relations of power between the contending parties. "All social development uses the state as the highest factor for the attainment of its aims, and there is no object too ideal to be reached through the state; what through it is not reachable is entirely unattainable, is a utopia. . . . Sovereignty is the distinguishing characteristic of the state, and sets it apart, sky-high, from all other human associations." When one of two social groups subjugates the other, social development begins. The action of the two groups on each other sets loose a number of latent social powers which push social evolution on in all directions and produce an ever advancing development of civilization.

The state, being a structure of such nature, originated in the earlier subjugations of tribe by tribe which allowed of the formation of a territorial in place of a consanguineal bond. Classes resulted. These were strata differentiated by their language, religion, and general mores. Then amalgamation set in, first, perhaps, through the adoption of common language. Gradually the rest of the mores, under the process of competition and selection, took on a common type and the original differentiation was succeeded by integration. Attention now turned to further conquests, for the state, even in embryo, is by nature predatory. New conquests were followed by new differentiations and repeated amalgamation.

Gumplowicz makes fun of the vague and mystical definitions of the state, and contrasts the theological, biological, rationalistic, and juristic theories with the scientific. The state is not a divinely instituted thing nor is it the product of rational judgment, as Rousseau would give us to understand. It is not a product of an act of law; still less is it "a Will, which is borne by physical persons but is set loose from them and condensed into a single whole." This mystic German conception is paralleled by the Teutonic "organic theory of the state": "The state is a hyperorganic community in which we see an animal life

[24] Keller, *Soc. Evol.*, 78-80.

of a higher order. As such it possesses all organs which provide for the functions of the animal-organism and fulfil those functions of the state-organism which are analogous to those of the animal." Equally with the mediæval notion of a *civitas Dei* which, like "Jerusalem the Golden," is not a view of the world as it is, is the socialistic notion of the state bereft of objectiveness and scientific quality. The state cannot be part of the economic organization, however strongly it rests upon that organization; it is regulative of social life in general.

What this author calls "the sociological idea of the state" is attained by advance in knowledge and does not concern itself much with policies or reforms. "Inasmuch as it expects from the development of the state according to natural law the correction of many ills and evils, it renounces any solution of the problem how to make the state better." That is, it is not the advocate of either the state or the individual but studies the relations which in fact exist between them. "It does not conceive of the state as means and the individual as purpose, or *vice versa,* as the true relation, but takes its beginning from the social groups which precede the state and lie outside of it; it regards the state as a means for the purposes of those groups, and regards the individual as dependent upon his group and as material used, with or without his conscious consent, by it for its ends. . . . It regards as the constitutive elements of the state, not the individuals but those social groups whose mutual relations form the constitution of the state. . . .

"The sociological conception of the state presents the state, it is true, as a reduction of inequality to order but also as the only reduction to order which is possible amongst human beings. Accordingly it demands resignation and submission to the inevitable. . . . In the sociological conception the origin of the state is an historical event produced by the superior power of a group of human beings having a warlike organization. In connection with this mode of origin, the essential character of the state appears as a division of labor, brought about and maintained by force, between different social components which are coördinated into a whole." The development of this whole goes on by means of a strife of its components over the delimitation of their respective spheres of power, the position of which delimitation at any time is determined by rights and law. Individuals participate in this strife only as members of a group. The individual counts for nothing in it. The group is all. The entire organization is buttressed by moral forces also, which arise from the joint life of these social components, such as mores, morals, religion, language, and culture.

This view of the state is one which, as has been suggested before, is doubtless somewhat tinged by the experience of living in what was the Austro-Hungarian Empire; but the conception of the state as an automatic development in adjustment to life-conditions stands forth clear of all distortions due to local influences. The socialistic idea of the state, finally, finds this sociological conception pessimistic. "It accepts the contention that the existing state is based upon inequalities but is indignant at the alleged proof that it cannot be otherwise; and it scorns sociology because it undermines the idea of the free and equal state of the future and presents the capitalistic state as a necessary result of social development under natural law."

Though Gumplowicz is not strong along the lines of ethno-

graphical evidence and is likely to argue back from a keen perception of modern political structure to what must have been on the
earlier stages, in this case it is difficult to suggest any conclusive
evidence against the views thus arrived at. That the state is, in its
origin, intimately connected with war and conquest, with the resultant formation of a compounded group incapable of being
handled upon the old tribal basis and therefore calling for a regulative organization of higher potency, is not to be questioned.

Ratzenhofer,[25] an Austrian soldier, offers a number of suggestions as to the
origin and nature of the state. He notes that the more the members of society
individualize the greater is the need of the preservation of order and of property and of the composition of strifes. The great impulse to political development comes with the conquest of a sedentary by a nomadic people, where the
victors politically annihilate the vanquished but where the latter live on as a
stratum of the society. Such a condition of social inequality calls for a stronger
regulative organization, which we find developed in China, India, Egypt, and
Mesopotamia. "The state exhibits itself in this perspective as a social fusion-
product of divergent efforts of primitive communities." The original differentiation between component elements is kept up by new differentiations
corresponding to newly arising conditions and new associations about newly
perceived interests. Such groupings petrify into castes. But any such social
forms, even the strictest despotism, is no more than the expression of the life-
conditions of the group and must change in response to their change. The state
comes out of the conflict of hostile interests and is an organization of coercion,
not at all one of free assent; "subjection to an authority is the fundamental
principle of the state; in the social process it is only the identity of this
authority that changes. At first it is the authority of bodily strength and
courage, then it becomes the authority of political sagacity, and at length the
authority of civilization, which subjects peoples to the power of the state."

According to Jenks,[26] "the Clan is a community of groups, the State is a
community of individuals. All that is known of the Clan organization leads us
to believe that it stopped short at the Household. With the individual members of the Household, it dealt only through their natural head, the House-
Father. They were in his *mund;* his voice spoke for them at the Clan assemblies, he led them to fight in the Clan battles. The Germans of whom Tacitus
writes conducted their warfare by *familiae et propinquitates.* But the King
in the time of the *Leges Barbarorum* dealt directly with the individual. The
man who failed to attend the host at the king's summons paid a heavy fine to
the king. . . . The state is a community of casual units, bound together by
the tie of military allegiance, acting directly upon its individual members,
valuing only personal ability, and willing to take personal ability wherever it
can find it. . . . The State, at least in some cases, apprehends and prosecutes
the offender, investigates the facts, declares the law, pronounces the award,

[25] *Sociol. Erkennt.*, 143, 144, 156 ff., 160 ff., 165 ff., 176, 188, 230, 233 ff., 242,
243, 246, 248, 249, 288.
[26] *Law and Pol.*, 77-79, 100, 237 ff., 308-309.

and carries it into effect. The first truth which the student has to grasp is, that these different processes have different histories, that they were acquired by the State in different ways and at different times. . . . In its struggle with the Clan, the State has created Property, as it is now understood, especially Property in land. For what is meant by Property? Is it not that interest in tangible things which can be bought and sold, taken in execution for debt, left to descend to one's heirs, or disposed of by Will? These are the very essentials of our notion of property; it is seen how they are one by one established in the course of the struggle between State and Clan. . . . We see that the leading characteristics of the Clan are a caste organization (status), a respect for the autonomy of its constituent groups, and exclusiveness. The principles of the State are precisely the opposite—encouragement of individual ability by the offer of splendid rewards, an insistence on absolute and direct obedience by every one of its members to its acknowledged head, and a willingness to purchase ability wherever it can get it. Institutions founded on such opposite principles can never exist peaceably together."

"From tribes at war are born nations, with their classes and castes, on the barbarous stage. . . . From strife comes victory; thus rise nations, greater aggregations, more vast, in which one tribe imposes its eminent dominion over its neighbors." A structure results which is more general than any resting upon consanguinity, an area vaster than that of any family, and new destinies for men.[27]

Ethical and other philosophers have undertaken to explain the state by postulating invented antecedents to it. They have even declared it to be an "ethical person."[28] The analogy between it and an organism has been pushed to the extent of confusing analogy with identity. Jurists have attributed to it, in its origin, ends which it now serves or is believed to cherish; in reality, these have come in during its evolution. There is even a "pathos" of the state, parallel to that in vogue respecting marriage.[29] A scientific study of the facts behind state-development, free from all bias or affectation of non-bias, shows that there was no policy, no principle, and no wisdom in its origination. It was due to helpless incapacity, feebly reaching out now in one direction and now in another. Bewildered as they confronted intricate and contradictory phenomena, people were forced to do something. Automatically, through trial and failure, adjustment was secured; and that adjustment came after a long time to be known as the state. Statecraft has always lain in the domain of expediency; it has had to shift and adapt as it went along, and the wisdom of it has resided in its adaptability rather than in any fixed policies or principles.

[27] Oliveira Martins, Raças, II, 50, 58, 63.
[28] Sumner, Coll. Ess., I, 221; II, 309.   [29] §338, below.

It is assumed that the state can interfere at isolated points and on narrow lines, to regulate and direct the action of society so that it shall run on selected paths and in the direction of ends other than those toward which it would have trended under the free play of self-interest and competition. Where men used to turn to religion in the face of the ills of life, they are now coming to turn to the state. To direct society successfully, however, it is necessary to regulate comprehensively, constantly, and thoroughly, or self-interest and competition will elude regulation. The fact is that society is self-regulated; the only directing of it that men can do lies in knowing its laws and adapting measures to them. Political leadership is in the recognition of the societal necessity of the moment. One might think a state lucky to have no state-necessity; in default of that questionable possession it is to be feared that politicians would have to create one in order to have an issue to fight over. The state, with its institutions, is purely historical and evolutionary, like all the rest of the institutions and the mores out of which they come. It faces practical problems such as this: How can you get peace, quiet, and security for industry, pay the necessary taxes to support the civil authority that guarantees these, and yet prevent the taxes from crippling the industry and restrain the civil authority from becoming parasitical?

The state is a product of force and exists by force. Hence it is not ethical. It begins in the interest of some to exploit others or to organize a common effort out of which to take the benefits. By growth and the resistance of the subject-classes, rights grow up and are defined, and the state becomes ethical, in a certain sense. Life under it turns into a free and rational coöperation toward common ends. As an organization, the state must remain in the hands of a few and must execute decisions by force; and it may at any time relapse into an engine of exploitation in pursuit of interests felt by classes or parties.

The state is an adjustment like any other. That its weight falls on the producing mass of its people is no "injustice." No one arbitrarily made it so. It is inevitable. The rulers may, by choosing the tasks of the state and its enterprises, increase or lessen the people's burdens; their highest function is to alleviate such inevi-

table costs and it is the privilege of those who pay the costs to see
that this is done. The state nowadays is always a party in power
and a party always has interests or represents them; it is only a
group or congeries of groups having ends to serve, not an over-
ruling, just providence or an upright arbitrator. It is not an
"ethical person" but a successful party in the struggle for power
which means to use its strength for its own interests against or in
indifference to other interests. Once such other interests could not
make themselves felt short of a revolution; now the modern system
provides for "bloodless revolutions," where ballots count instead
of bullets. Thus is an expedient in adjustment presented by which
neglected or injured interests may assert themselves. Public opinion has been enfranchised and readjustments rendered speedier
and easier. Much is to be gained in understanding an evolutionary
product by realizing first its broad inevitability and then the conditions in accordance and only in accordance with which neglected
or injured interests can be served.

§188. Confederation. Though the prevailing form of group-
compounding is by conquest, yet there are a number of instances
where confederation on relatively peaceful lines has taken place.
It is to be noted that such alliances, creative of a larger peace-
group than the tribal, were generally contracted in the face of
danger; that the bonds between the confederates were often those
which Kipling detected as existing between the scattered members
of the British Empire, namely, "ties of common funk." The most
striking confederation of which we know is, perhaps, the Iroquois
League of the Six Nations, and to that we shall give most of our
space, beginning, however, with several minor cases.

In the region of Sierra Leone are five peoples who form a confederation,
although each has its own government. When any two of the five get into war,
a great warrior-council of twenty-five—five from each tribe—intervenes, inter-
dicts the war, investigates its origin, decides which party is to blame, and
ordains as a penalty that it shall be plundered for four nights by a band
recruited from the neutrals.[30] Among the Yakuts, clans sometimes made alliances called "reconciled," "peaceful." This was done by groups more or less
closely related by blood, in the need of defense against outsiders or for some
economic cause, and the alliances were cemented by sacrifices and festivals.

[30] Frobenius, *Masken*, 138 ff.

"All the traditions point to the great solidarity of alliances between the chiefs of clans; also to their independent attitude with regard to each other. Superior to them all was the council of the confederation."[31] In the East Indies, the city-communities join wider bonds among themselves, chiefly for war. Formerly there were large confederations. As usual among barbarous peoples, such unions were closely connected with religion. One of the forms of union was through *connubium*. Tribesmen do not, in some cases, live tribewise but mingle in the villages; the tribal division is lost in the territorial. Wars have often led to efforts to unite in peace-bonds.[32] Something similar is found in the Mortlock Islands but here the constituents of an alliance or confederation will not fight tribally related persons in another alliance.[33] Siouan "institutional development went forward through incorporation of peoples and differentiation of institutions. The same process was followed as tribal society passed into national society; and it is the same process which is today exalting national society into world society, and transforming simple civilization into enlightenment. Thus the evolution of social organization is from the simple and definite toward the complex and variable, or from the involuntary to the voluntary; or from the environment-shaped to the environment-shaping; or from the biotic to the demotic." In Mexico "the conditions favor patriarchal or feudal organization and oppose extensive confederation or national union; and throughout northern Mexico, conformably to these conditions, the smaller settlements gathered about a single spring or well are usually patriarchal even to-day, while the larger villages have strong feudal characteristics, and have been welded slowly and incompletely into republican confederation only through persistent and intelligent effort by one of the world's greatest leaders during the last quarter century."[34] The ancient Toltecs formed a confederation of tribes, over which the chiefs could reign only for a cycle of fifty-two years. At the end of the cycle power and insignia of office were handed over by them to their successors.[35]

The League of the Iroquois has been described by a number of writers, some of whom instance other less perfect examples of Indian confederation. "The last and ultimate stage of organization was the confederacy of nations. It was usually, if not invariably, composed of nations speaking dialects of the same stock-language. The Iroquois, Otawa, Powhattan, and Creek Confederacies, the Dakota League of the Seven Council Fires, the Aztec Confederacy between the Aztecs, Tezcucans, and Tlacopans, and the Tlascalan Confederacy are familiar examples."[36] "One of the most valuable results of modern ethnological research is the proof, now indisputable, that practically all of these confederacies were similar in general character. . . . The Aztec political and industrial systems had developed further, but along much the same lines, as in the more northern tribes."[37] If the Iroquois confederacy was not so highly developed as the Aztec

[31] Czaplicka, *Aborig. Siberia*, 57-58.
[32] Wilken, *Vkde.*, 345-348; and in VG, I, 296-297, 303, 304, 305, note.
[33] Finsch, *Ethnol. Erfahr.*, III, 303, 311.
[34] McGee, in BAE, XV, 201; McGee, in AA, X, 215.
[35] Nadaillac, *Preh. Amer.*, 278.
[36] Morgan, in *Smithson. Contr. Knowl.*, XVII, 141, 203.
[37] Farrand, *Basis*, 213.

organization, it was considerably beyond the rudimentary type, and may stand as a representative instance.[38]

The name of the League, "Kanonsionni," means "league of united households," and the occasion of its founding was somewhat as follows. From the time Europeans first knew them until about 1650, the Iroquois had been waging a savage and unrelenting warfare with their near kinsmen, the Hurons; but they succeeded at length in destroying most of their enemies and forcing nearly all the rest into exile. They then turned upon the so-called Neutrals and the Eries and by 1655 had defeated and expelled most of them. By 1676 the Susquehannocks of southern Pennsylvania and Maryland had submitted, and the Iroquois sway reached into Virginia. Thus far the tale is one of war and destruction though, it will be noted, there was no actual conquest and enslavement. But the alternatives were not confined to death or exile; for the Neutrals and the Eries were offered the choice between extermination and admission to the League and a portion of the Eries voluntarily surrendered after their defeat and were incorporated with the Senecas who were members of the League, while others were carried off and incorporated. Accessions came also from the Neutrals and even the Hurons.

The Iroquois employed this incorporation or adoption more than other Indians. It was often a sort of selective process; captives had to run the gantlet after which, if successful, they received new names which were proclaimed at the next festival of the family into which they were adopted. Those who survived this ordeal were likely to be strong, picked men. Further, a whole tribe might be incorporated in the League upon terms approaching equality, as were the Tuscaroras whose inclusion made of the original "Five Nations" (Cayuga, Mohawk, Oneida, Onondaga, and Seneca) "The Six Nations." Others were taken under protection and given territory. The Iroquois name for themselves as a political body signifies "We are of the extended lodge"; for their association, like their "long-house,"[39] could be built to, or extended, to almost any degree. This principle of adoption knit the interests of the vanquished with those of the victors and the League threatened, at its acme of power, to dominate the whole country east of the Mississippi. It was powerful enough to have contributed in no small degree to shatter French plans for an empire in North America.

As for the origin of the League, it seems to have risen as a revolt against war and tyranny, and is inseparably connected with the name of Hiawatha, an Onondaga sub-chief who, despite the mythological accretions that came to surround him, was a historical character belonging to the middle of the fifteenth century. Disregarding the details of the league-founding, which include a flight of Hiawatha from the vicinity of a tyrannical Onondaga head-chief to the country of the Mohawks—a flight which was to the Five Nations "what the flight of Mohammed from Mecca to Medina is to the votaries of Islam"— we find presently a coalition of tribes all of which feared the prowess and

[38] Morgan, *League of Iroquois;* Morgan, in *Smithson. Contrib. Knowl.,* XVII, 141, 150 ff., 172, 203; Hale, *Iroquois Book of Rites;* Hale, in JAI, XXVI, 221 ff.; Hewitt, in AA, VII, 61; Hewitt, "Confederation," in HAI, I, 337; Henning, in *Globus,* LXXVI, 225; Dellenbaugh, *North Amer.,* ch. XV. The following account is based chiefly upon Hale.

[39] §§414, 417, below.

cruelty of the Onondaga leader. At length, the Onondagas and their ruler were
enticed into the association by grants of preferential position, and their and
his powers diverted to the enlistment of further accessions. The avowed design
of the League's proposer was to abolish war altogether. "He wished the federation to extend until all the tribes of men should be included, and peace should
reign everywhere. Such is the positive testimony of the Iroquois; and their
statement is supported by historical evidence." Family-nomenclature persisted
between the members of the association; thus the Oneida was the son and the
Onondaga the brother of the Mohawk. "No other Indian community, so far as
known, has ever pursued the policy of incorporation to anything like the same
extent, or carried it out with anything like the same humanity." "Inquiry
shows that in every instance when, after the League of Peace was established
by Hiawatha, the Iroquois entered upon a war, it was begun in self-defence,
and that as soon as their enemy's resistance ceased, slaughter ceased with it."

The League was a sort of religion with its members, and the alternative
offered to opponents, however they became such, of incorporation or destruction reminds one, again, of the conquering Moslems. Wars against the Hurons
and Algonquin tribes succeeded, as we have seen, the establishment of the
confederacy; and "the Mohegans inflicted some serious blows upon the eastern
nations of the confederacy. It took a long and sanguinary struggle to reduce
the Delawares to subjection." Attacks were made by the nomadic Sioux and
Algonquins upon the settled Iroquois hunters, fishers, and tillers. Doubtless
there were cases of aggression from without constant enough to lend to all
these wars the character of defensive operations.

The mechanism of government developed by the League has been often
described. Morgan[40] summarizes its general features as follows, with illustrations:

"I. The confederacy was a union of Five Tribes, composed of common gentes,
under one government on the basis of equality; each Tribe remaining independent in all matters pertaining to local self-government.

"II. It created a General Council of Sachems, who were limited in number,
equal in rank and authority, and invested with supreme powers over all matters
pertaining to the Confederacy.

"III. Fifty Sachemships were created and named in perpetuity in certain
gentes of the several Tribes; with power in these gentes to fill vacancies, as
often as they occurred, by election from among their respective members, and
with the further power to depose from office for cause; but the right to invest
these Sachems with office was reserved to the General Council.

"IV. The Sacnems of the Confederacy were also Sachems in their respective
Tribes, and with the Chiefs of these Tribes formed the Council of each, which
was supreme over all matters pertaining to the Tribe exclusively.

"V. Unanimity in the Council of the Confederacy was made essential to
every public act.

"VI. In the General Council the Sachems voted by Tribes, which gave to
each Tribe a negative upon the others.

"VII. The Council of each Tribe had power to convene the General Council;
but the latter had no power to convene itself.

[40] *Anc. Soc.*, 128-129.

"VIII. The General Council was open to the orators of the people for the discussion of public questions; but the Council alone decided.

"IX. The Confederacy had no chief Executive Magistrate, or official head.

"X. Experiencing the necessity for a General Military Commander they created the office in a dual form, that one might neutralize the other. The two principal War-chiefs created were made equal in powers."

"The systematic transmission of official rank was, in fact, the vital principle of government. It was in this system that their federal union differed from the frequent and transitory confederacies common among the Indian tribes. In general, among nearly all the tribes, the rank of a chief was personal. It was gained by the character and achievements of the individual, and died with him. Hence their government and policy, as far as they can .be said to have had any, were uncertain and fluctuating. . . . The principle that 'the chief dies but the office survives',—the regular transmission of rank, title and authority, by a method partly hereditary and partly elective,—was the principle on which the life and strength of the Iroquois constitution depended."[41]

The League, according to Morgan's view, "was rendered possible by a limited agricultural cultivation through which their means of subsistence had been permanently enlarged," whereas the Dakotas, though they came to the verge of confederation, were arrested and rendered unsettled by the possession of the horse and of the productive bison-hunting which the horse made possible. This would seem to accord with the wider generality developed above, that a developed regulative system goes with agriculture and sedentation. To this we shall return. But it is to be noted that the incorporations made by the Iroquois were those of "captives belonging to tribes of the same stock, speaking similar dialects, and having usages closely resembling those of their captors." Thus amalgamation of diverse ethnic elements was not a necessity demanding the power of a real state. "The warriors who were willing to unite their fortunes with the confederates were at once welcomed. Some were adopted into the families of those who had lost children or brothers. Others had lands allotted to them, on which they were allowed to live by themselves, under their own chiefs and their native laws, until in two or three generations, by friendly intercourse, frequent intermarriages, and community of interests, they became gradually absorbed into the society about them."[42]

What the League might have become, if the tribes composing it had been left to work out their own destiny, can only be inferred; but it looks as if it were on its way toward genuine statehood. The irruption of the white man brought about a contact of two unequally developed cultures in consequence of which that of the native Americans was destroyed or completely modified. In any case, the native regulative system was not able to amalgamate with the European. It was an excellent adjustment to Indian life-conditions and was proving itself, and it was in concord with the rest of the native mores; but when the European had altered these life-conditions, by his presence and by what he did, the case was changed. One Indian writer[43] puts his finger upon the system of private property in land as the salient solvent element in the contact of cultures. "One might inquire just why the Iroquois League became disrupted, and why it has not endured unbroken. Ah, this is another story.

[41] Hale, *Iroq. Rites,* 67, 68.   [42] Hale, *Iroq. Rites,* 95.
[43] Ga-wa-so-na-neh, in letter to N. Y. *Times,* Jan. 21, 1923.

The pale invader came with the doctrine that land is personal property and may be sold. One great nation after another from across the great salt sea came crying for dominion over land. We became confused, and, from a peace-loving agricultural people, we became demoralized hunters—even hunters of our own fellowmen. We became selfish of our own tribal interests, because of the superior situation of our brethren we grew to hate them; we sought revenge, and finally, after having varnished our souls with the white man's religions, we became intolerant."

The writer just quoted had been citing the League of the Iroquois as a prototype of the League of Nations. It fully deserves the honor; taking into account the circumstances under which it rose, it is perhaps a greater accomplishment than any modern form can be. It is a notable case of the extension of the peace-group beyond local boundaries into the international realm.

§189. Essentials in State-Formation. Morgan[44] sees in the American confederacy, resting as it does upon the gentile system, an exhibition of the capabilities of the gens (clan) "as the unit of a social system," and then institutes a comparison with the case of the Greeks and Romans which issues virtually in an explanation of why the ancients were headed directly for the state-form of regulation as the Iroquois were not. The former were once much on a par in matter of government with the latter. Of the ancients Morgan says, in his alignment: "The same scheme of government composed of gentes, phratries and tribes in a gentile society will be found among them as they stood at the threshold of civilization, with the superadded experience of two entire ethnical periods.[45] Descent among them was in the male line, property was inherited by the children of the owner instead of the agnatic kindred, and the family was now assuming the monogamian form. The growth of property, now becoming a commanding element, and the increase of numbers gathered in walled cities were slowly demonstrating the necessity for the second great plan of government—

[44] *Anc. Soc.*, 150; for the change, among the ancient Hebrews, from a kin-tie to a territorial bond, see Schrader, *Keilinschriften*, 154-155, 164, 205, 206, 210-211.

[45] These periods are, according to Morgan (*Anc. Soc.*, 8-13), the Middle and the Upper Status of Barbarism, wherein were developed domestication of animals, somewhat advanced tillage, the smelting of iron, and several minor and related adjustments.

the political. The old gentile system was becoming incapable of meeting the requirements of society as it approached civilization. Glimpses of a state, founded upon territory and property, were breaking upon the Grecian and Roman minds before which gentes and tribes were to disappear. To enter upon the second plan of government, it was necessary to supersede the gentes by townships and city wards—the gentile by a territorial system. The going down of the gentes and the uprising of organized townships mark the dividing line, pretty nearly, between the barbarian and the civilized worlds—between ancient and modern society."

A comparison of the system of the ancients with that of the Iroquois reveals with considerable clarity the essential conditions for state-formation. By something more than implication Morgan finds the Six Nations lacking male descent, inheritance by a man's own children, monogamy, high development of property, density of population, and a gentile system likely within discernible time to pass into a territorial one. This amounts to saying that the mores were not consistent with the development of the state-form of regulation. Morgan's list might be extended, or its implications developed, by citing the absence, among the Iroquois mores, of conquest, enslavement, classes, agriculture, and private property in land. The conclusion emerges that unless all these conditions are represented the formation of a real state is out of the question. A survey of the bearing of these conditions amounts then to a review of the essentials to state-evolution, some of which have already been encountered singly in what has gone before.

Certain of these conditions link up with others: private property in land and slavery go regularly with agriculture,[46] and developed tillage admits of a greater density of population than any other type of self-maintenance.[47] Slavery goes also with conquest as distinguished from the wide alternatives of slaughter or adoption that attended Indian warfare; and slavery is the germ of the class-system.[48] Male descent is a common accompaniment of the pastoral stage of culture, which no Indians ever of themselves developed[49] and is generally found under advanced tillage; for man it carries with it the system of inheritance by his own offspring,

[46] §§118, 103, above.
[47] §§31, 32, above.
[48] §§106, 164, 165, 167, above.
[49] §§27, 28, 30, above.

replacing that of sisters' children. It likewise renders possible the expansion of a group through conquest, which is not a phenomenon of a matrilineal society.[50] And conquest is territorial as no preceding system of irregular raids and robberies, accompanied by massacre or adoption, could have been. Neither density of population, developed agriculture, conquest, enslavement on the large scale, or private property in land belong to the earlier stages of societal development. Evidently all these forms of the mores hang together and are in a large way consistent with one another.

The above correlations may be more readily seized as a whole if gathered into tabular form. Out of them emerge, chiefly by comparison with the deficiencies of the Iroquois organization, the essential prerequisites to the state. These may be arranged in a sort of genetic table and then exhibited by a parallel-column comparison of the Iroquois and the classical system.

Father-Family (§419)

Developed agriculture with domesticated animals (§§67, 97)   Conquest (§138)

Density of Population (§§26, 31, 32)   Private Property in Land (§§123, 124)   Slavery (§103)   Slavery (§141)   Territoriality

Classes (ch. XVIII)

Iroquois	*Greeks and Romans*
Mother-Family (nephew-inheritance).	Father-Family (son-inheritance).
Hoe-culture (no domestic animals).	Agriculture (domestic animals).
Relatively sparse population.	Relatively dense population.
Communal Property in Land.	Private Property in Land.
Massacre or Adoption.	Slavery.
No Conquest.	Conquest.
No Territoriality (kinship only).	Territoriality.
No Classes.	Classes.

It is a matter of history that the Greeks and Romans developed a political organization which has been generally accepted as constituting a state. Hence the items in the right-hand column, as contrasted with those in the other, represent the necessary antecedents of the state. Their indispensability has appeared in various parts of this chapter.

The Six Nations pursued agriculture of a relatively crude grade and their population was not dense; they practised extermination or adoption rather than enslavement, and therefore lacked classes

[50] §§419, 421, 422, below.

composed of heterogeneous ethnic elements, for the vanquished who
were adopted had mores, including language, almost identical with
those of the adopting people; they did not understand private
tenure of land; they clung to the matrilineal system, with its weaknesses as respects inheritance and conquest. They were on the way,
perhaps, to form a state but were far back along the road as compared with the Greeks and Romans. Their system could not stand
up against the competition it met from the cultural heirs of those
ancients; it was doomed as soon as it came into rivalry with the
more developed organization, just as were the bow and arrow and
the spear when they came to be measured against the fire-arm. In
particular, no form of regulative organization that has come to
bear the title of state has proceeded upon the cardinal principle
of adoption into full rights as the only alternative to death or
exile, in place of social differentiation issuing in classes. The Iroquois failed of the advance in societal organization which was
rendered possible by the social type of differentiation and integration as compared with and as complementary to the biological
type of sex-specialization and coöperation.[51] And there was no
such cross-fertilization of culture as results from the amalgamation of heterogeneous ethnic elements and their codes.

Further, it must be recalled that a number of correlations accompany several of the items listed in the above comparison. They
need not be developed again in this place. Withdrawal from a
communal system, for example, entails liberation of individual initiative; and where such liberation takes place, there is a veritably
new societal system. More detailed analysis would undoubtedly
yield a medley of finer criteria of discrimination between the two
types of society here thrown into broad contrast.

It is enlightening to realize the variation of the whole course
of things that cannot but result from the presence of adoption or
enslavement respectively in the disposition of the vanquished.
What the Indians had and had not, as well as what the Greeks and
Romans had not or had, is clearly a matter of stages of adjustment to life-conditions. If the Indians, with their confederacies,
had been destined to pursue a long course of development undis-

[51] §§70, 71, 73, above.

turbed by the heirs of the Greeks and Romans, they could hardly have failed to work along through the stages that lay between them and the political adjustments called for by a general advance in numbers and culture. In any case, there can be drawn from the comparison of confederacy and state some very positive inferences about the preconditions of state-formation.

§190. Feudalism. Historians of Western Europe tell us that feudalism was a substitute for the state and that, with the break-up of the Empire of Charlemagne, the lord-and-vassal relation took the place of the weakened bond between subject and king.[52] It was once assumed that this European arrangement was unique; but students of society's evolution now know that few if any institutional developments are wholly that. It is enlightening, again, to realize that a feudalism grew up in Japan independently of but coincidently with that in Europe, out of a set of causes similar in nature and principle to those which gave rise to the latter.[53] Collectors of ethnographical parallels find among a number of primitive peoples examples of what they call feudalism.[54] They have encountered in primitive life societal phenomena and relations which have reminded them strongly of the details of the European feudal system; in parts of Africa, for instance, there occurs a "rough sketch" of this system. In seeking to classify what they find the ethnographers have seen nothing better to do than to align it with its like. This is quite legitimate and indeed inevitable; it is not by any means, however, an assertion of complete parallelism.

There are in southwest Africa, "despite its anarchical condition, really no free people at all apart from the very prominent ones. Each person is in some way bound by a vassal and serf relation to an over-lord, and all legal protection consists essentially in this patriarchal relationship. No one may desert his master without having to fear lest he become outlawed thereby."[55] Letourneau,[56] noting that in mediæval Europe isolation was equivalent to death, and how small proprietors were obliged to surrender their estates to powerful men or to the Church, becoming then tenants bound under certain services and

[52] Maine, *Early Institutions*, 152 ff.
[53] Asakawa, *Land Tenure in Japan*, 1.
[54] Letourneau, *Soc.*, 178, 392, 394, 398, 433, 443; Ratzel, *Vkde.*, I, 308, 405, 431, 432, 470, 563.
[55] Büttner, *Walfischbai*, 59-60.
[56] *Prop.*, 307, 301-302; *Soc.*, 443; *Polit.*, 92, 99.

dues, finds that "this is exactly what happens to this day in Abyssinia, where existence is only possible on the condition of being docketed in the feudal pigeonholes." And he finds similar conditions in Madagascar, among the Tartars, in Malaysia, China, and ancient Japan—in all which cases the protection of the great is sought amidst conditions of insecurity; and grades of servility result which cannot but recall the European system. In parts of Africa everyone is under the protection of someone. If by death a negro is suddenly left without protection, he runs great risk of being sold into slavery. Everyone must have an elder to "speak his palavers" for him. There is a sort of ceremony of commendation when the protector-client relation is formed; the free man who dares not stay free places his hands upon the head of the elder whose guardianship is sought.[57]

In the Upper Congo region, "there were no absolutely independent men and women, apart from chiefs or headmen. All the rest were attached to headmen as relatives, slaves, pawns, or by a voluntary surrender of themselves to a chief. If the family of a free man died off, or became very weak—too weak to defend itself against the aggressiveness of the other families in the town, such a free man would go and attach himself (and any relatives he might have left) to the headman of any one of the stronger families he might select. He then became a member of that family. Their quarrels were his, and his quarrels were theirs. His position was that of a free man owing fealty to the head of his adopted family. He was never treated as a slave. If he had tried to stand alone some quarrel would have been picked with him, and eventually he would have become a slave."[58] "Politically the Jaluo are in a semi-feudal state; the tribe is divided up into larger or smaller chieftaincies or clans, which correspond to the old baronies, but there is no one overlord to make the resemblance complete. Nominally the chiefs have absolute power, but in reality their influence is not great. Each chief subdivides his territory, placing each portion under a sub-chief. These sub-chiefs or headmen are supposed to attend frequently at the chief's village in order to hear and carry out his orders. If a crisis arises, an informal council of the heads of the village is called and the *patres familiarum* can express their views, though the decision rests with the chief. There is no kind of voting. This council will also assemble if the rule of the chief becomes intolerable. They may threaten to secede, but their resistance is always passive; the usual result, however, is that one or more of the headmen set up as chiefs on their own account, and quietly disregard the orders of their quondam superior."[59] "In a region of so broken a character as the Tuareg country no very special political régime can develop: the sole organization that is suited to the mentality of the Tuareg, as to the inhospitable environment in which he lives, is the feudal system. And it might be affirmed that they have pushed it to its extreme consequences. . . . The status of war was, moreover, the only one that suited the bellicose minds, the modest needs, and the difficult economic situation of the Tuareg. Ancient authors attest that the Sahara was always a nest of brigands, and its progressive impoverishment, by reason of the diminution of humidity, could not but stimulate the combative tastes of the Berbers, forced to pillage to live."[60]

[57] Du Chaillu, *Journey*, 426-427.   [58] Weeks, in JAI, XXXIX, 428.
[59] Northcote, in JAI, XXXVII, 59-60.
[60] Zeltner, in JAI, XLIV, 354.

The Jews of Morocco enjoyed immunity from robbery and pillage, though no "practical government" existed, through a special custom called "sacrifice," which is not unlike guestfriendship as a measure for admitting outsiders into a peace-group. "This means that the ancestors of Jewish families have, by means of a 'sacrifice' fallen under the actual protection of certain Berber families who guarantee them from ill-treatment or robbery in return for a certain annual payment. Any injury to the Jew is looked upon as a personal matter, and the protecting Berber takes up the quarrel as if it were his own. The system is excellent, and the Jews reside in greater security in these wild regions than is the case where lawless Arabs rob and ill-treat them in other parts of Morocco."[61] In Tibet, "certain tracts of land are assigned to officers of high rank for their support, in lieu of salaries, and others are given as endowments to lamaseries. On many, if not all, of these the beneficiaries have not only all the revenues derivable therefrom, but exercise also judicial rights over the people inhabiting these estates, who are their serfs, subject to all such *corvées* as they may see fit to order, such as working the land, going on caravans, on which they have also to supply pack animals or saddle ponies, supplying food to officers when passing through their place of residence, etc."[62]

Hutton[63] speaks of the "manor" as the unit of Sema society: the organized community, with its chief at its head, but not necessarily co-terminous with the population or land of the village. He finds the origin of this arrangement in colonization by sons of chiefs, who were followed by run-aways and broken men. The new chief reserves all the land he wants for himself and the people are dependent upon him. They are his "churls" in the older sense; they do him homage and call him "father," they themselves being denominated "orphans." They help the chief in the fields and in war, and so get land. The chief's relations to them are more or less private and personal. As "lord of the manor" he decides what land is to be cultivated in successive years. Full details of the arrangement are given. In the Indian hills, "the position of a Chin chief with regard to the people is very similar to that of a feudal Baron. The chief is lord of the soil and his freemen hold it as his tenants and pay him tithes, while they in common with the slaves are bound to carry arms against all his enemies. If a fugitive or an outcast takes refuge in a village, he pledges himself as the vassal or slave of his protector." In other regions the chiefs "were in a similar position to the Barons of old who ruled their tenants and were subordinate, both they and their dependents, to the King. The Sokte chiefs ruled their tenants, received their tithes, and fought their own private quarrels, and at the same time paid tax to the Tashons and obeyed their summons to collect their forces to fight in the Tashon interests."[64] "We find that among all the tribes of Indo-Germanic blood which have conquered and ruled Indian provinces, the tendency is to establish a feudal system extremely similar to that which prevailed in Europe. In Rajpootana the system is still in full force."[65]

As has been intimated the feudalism of China and Japan was quite similar to that of Europe.[66] In Japan, "formerly the family furnishing servants to a

[61] Harris, in JAI, XXVII, 71.   [62] Rockhill, in USNM, 1893, 680.
[63] *Sema Nagas,* 144-150.
[64] Carey and Tuck, *Chin Hills,* I, 201.
[65] Probyn, *Land Tenure,* 216; Fenton, in *Antiquary,* IV, 90.
[66] Letourneau, *Soc.,* 479-481; *Prop.,* 160, 169; *Polit.,* 156, 157, 167-168.

household of higher rank, stood to the latter in the relation of vassal to liege-lord; and between the two there existed a real bond of loyalty and kindliness. The occupation of servant was then hereditary; children were trained for the duty from an early age. After the man-servant or maid-servant had arrived at a certain age, permission to marry was accorded; and the relation of service then ceased, but not the bond of loyalty. The children of the married servants would be sent, when old enough, to work in the house of the master, and would leave it only when the time also came for them to marry."[67] In Malaysia, "before the Dutch came the princes, being owners of the territory of their states, divided it into fiefs which they granted to vassals, called regents, in return for dues and military service. These regents farmed out their villages to tillers of the soil."[68] Feudal practices have been observed in the Philippines and Polynesia.[69]

On the American northwest coast the advent of the whites and the abolition of slavery have stopped a tendency toward feudalism and have introduced industrialism.[70] The prince of the Chichimecs, after defeating the Toltecs, in order to establish his power, divided the country into provinces which he gave in fief to his principal officers on condition of subordination to him.[71] Maspero[72] finds feudal arrangements in Syria after the Egyptian conquest, and among the Hittites; and the Assyrian system was not dissimilar, since conquered kings were reduced to feudatories, bound as vassals to do services and send troops.[73]

Maitland[74] regards feudalism as a natural stage in evolution. "If we use the word in its widest sense, then (the barbarian conquests being given us as an unalterable fact) feudalism means civilisation, the separation of employments, the division of labor, the possibility of national defence, of art, science, literature and learned leisure"—the cathedral, the scriptorium, the library as well as the baronial castle. It is not a retrogression or a disease, he thinks, but a normal, healthy growth.

It is clear enough to one who aligns the feudal system of Europe with parallels to it in other lands that they are all adjustments to similar conditions. Whether they appear antecedently to the state or under conditions where the state has dissolved, throwing peoples back upon expedients that may have been practised and discarded long before, they are always adaptations calculated

[67] Hearn, *Japan,* 87-88; Asakawa, *Japan,* index *sub* "feudalism."

[68] Letourneau, *Prop.,* 111; Day, *Dutch in Java,* ch. I; Moszkowski, in *Globus,* XCVI, 261.

[69] Blumentritt, *Philippinen,* 21; Letourneau, *Soc.,* 394; Letourneau, *Polit.,* 74-75; Finsch, *Ethnol. Erfahr.,* III, 230, 275.

[70] Niblack, in USNM, 1888, 339.

[71] Nadaillac, *Preh. Amer.,* 283; Letourneau, *Polit.,* 133-135.

[72] *Hist. Anc.,* II, 271, 356; Meyer, *Aegypten,* II, 167 *et passim;* Letourneau, *Polit.,* 148 ff.

[73] Tiele, *Bab.-Assyr. Gchte.,* 493; Von Kremer, *Kgchte.,* II, 160.

[74] *Domesday,* 223; Vinogradoff, *Villainage,* 127 ff.

to maintain peace and order of some sort and to afford security. Whether they are in vogue because nothing more expedient has yet been evolved or for the reason that a state has broken up and the more effective system has been lost for a while, is no matter; they are adjustments, just the same, to a similar set of life-conditions. This does not mean that a system comparable with European feudalism, in all details and in complexity, ever existed in a less developed civilization; it means only that European society, after the fall of the central power, automatically evolved expedients suggested by the circumstances which earlier societies, before there had been any development of a central power, had adopted at the suggestion of similar circumstances. In both cases there was a lack of organization: in the one because it had been lost; in the other because it had not yet come to be. One society was doing the best it could to develop a substitute-adjustment; the other was groping toward what the more evolved society had lost.

Though manifold ways of meeting exigencies have been tried out, in general there are not many expedient methods of dealing with a given situation. Parallelisms teach us that when societies are faced with similar conditions they tend to develop similar adjustments. It is no more incredible, therefore, that primitive societies should have evolved details of their regulative systems that recall details of the European feudal system than that their marital or religious mores should reveal similarities with those of more advanced peoples. If one has almost any modern system in mind while studying savage life, he will find plenty of reminiscences of it in that life. If he falls into error on this account it will be because he sees more in the savage institution than is there and concludes that the crude primitive adjustment, because it shows likenesses to the modern type, is the same; it can be so only in the broadest way, as belonging to the same genus or species, with many general and some specific likenesses. If feudalism is taken to mean the European system in all its detail, no primitive society ever exhibited feudalism; if, on the other hand, it is seen as a type of societal regulation, then many primitive societies have shown adjustments classifiable under that type—some more and some less. Dealing in types, as we do, we have no hesitation in speaking of such adjustments as being of a feudal character and might well have called attention to the feudal nature of a number of details in the tribal regulative system as hitherto described. Some writers seem to enjoy themselves in demonstrating such parallelisms. If we have not done so, it was because we are less interested in developing parallels to more modern institutions than in the evolution of institutions for themselves.

§191. Aristocracy and Democracy. All governments are democratic, in the broad etymological sense, for in the long run the masses, carrying the mores, have their way; but when one is given to understand that primitive systems are republican or democratic in the sense which moderns attach to those terms, his skepticism should be roused. After what has been said about chiefs, classes, equality, plutocracy, and feudalism, the reader should be fortified against such assertions. It is quite possible to catch sight of primitive practices that remind one of some detail of democracy, as of feudalism; but sentimental generalization from such details is, scientifically speaking, entirely out of order.

The Kaffirs have a cattle-aristocracy which is as well marked as any money-aristocracy.[75] The palaver of the west coast of Africa may be a splendid specimen of the tyranny of democracy, but no one would seriously contend that the local governmental form is democratic. In the Desert of Sahara men are trained to liberty and independence; all are sheiks or slaves.[76] Among the Berbers "where instruction is nil, where education is the same for all, and where wealth is often only a degree of destitution a little less complete than that of the poor, men's pride has found a means of creating classes by stigmatizing certain professions."[77] In China the masses may be undistinguished and may possess village autonomy, but the mandarins rule them through their own self-chosen heads.[78] Among the central and northern Arabs, poorness of dress never lowered a man; but they reveal an old and intense aristocratic feeling wherever any superiority can be claimed. Tribal feeling is for caste and nobility.[79]

It pleases the Americans, says Ratzel,[80] to represent the monarchies of Mexico and Peru as exotics in a field democratic by nature, but facts contradict such a notion. We are told that research among the records of the Mexicans show that the government was very democratic, appointments being given by election. Among the Central Americans no office of the tribe was hereditary. Offices were obtained by election, with the exception of one high title, meaning "grandfather," and "which was given as a reward for acts of bravery before the enemy, for long and important services either in the council or in the

75 Letourneau, Soc., 436.   76 Ratzel, Vkde., I, 591; III, 53.
77 Hanoteau et Letourneux, Kabylie, II, 23.
78 De Groot, Kongsiwezen, 101-102.   79 Ratzel, Vkde., III, 130, 153.
80 Vkde., II, 635.

embassies."[81] Viewed from a selected angle, Indian life has a certain democratic aspect: "A simple democracy exists among these people, and they have a variety of tribal offices to fill. In this way the men of the tribe are graded, and they pass from grade to grade by a selection practically made by the people. And this leads to a constant discussion of the virtues and abilities of all the male members of the clan, from boyhood to old age. He is most successful in obtaining clan and tribal promotion who is most useful to the clan and the tribe. . . . In this manner all of the ambitious are stimulated, and this incentive to industry is very great."[82] So-called primitive democracy, however, was a gentile brotherhood, with no state-monarch or privileged class to enforce labor for his or its luxury. "The principle of democracy, which was born of the gentes," manifested itself in the right to elect sachems and chiefs, in the safeguards that were erected to prevent usurpation, and in the checks on election held by the remaining gentes.[83] Euripides[84] makes Helen say that among barbarians all are slaves but one—which often fairly covers the case. "Under the tribal system the structure of society was rather that of aristocratic gradations of rank than of equality in the modern democratic sense."[85]

Among peoples with a democratic tradition which they accept unreflectingly there is often prevalent a notion that the raw human being is the standard human being. If that is the case, then evolution and democracy are at war. Though the theories of democracy may flatter human nature, the business of life demands inequalities; if the race is to live by deliberation and rationality rather than instinct, it needs head-power, and that quality is rare.[86] Referring to the Athenian democratic plan of electing annually ten *strategoi*, or generals, Philip of Macedon is reported to have said: "Lucky Athenians, who find ten annually whom they can elect generals. In long years I have found one—Parmenius."[87] "Of a surety the safety of communities is reposed in the councils of the best."[88] There is no democracy upon a ship, because some there can navigate it and some cannot; the same is equally true, though less obvious, in a factory or any other enterprise run by men. An aristocratic impulse, if it may be called that—not to be one of the crowd, but to win prestige and be distinguished[89]—is always stressing men of power. It resembles a primary impulse.

If democracy attempts to ignore forces in political organization such as knowledge, talent, wealth, they nevertheless have their

81 Nadaillac, *Preh. Amer.*, 309, 315.   82 Powell, in BAE, VII, 35.
83 Morgan, *Anc. Soc.*, 73; Morgan, in *Contrib. N. A. Ethnol.*, IV, 44.
84 *Helen*, 276.   85 Seebohm, *Tribal System*, 105.
86 Sumner, *Soc. Classes*, ch. V.
87 Burckhardt, *Griech. Gchte.*, I, 222, note.
88 Cicero, *De Rep.*, I, 34.   89 §449, below.

effect, only it is indirect and concealed and perhaps corrupting. And if there gathers about democracy a "pathos"[90] which insulates it from critical examination, and if there develops a species of fetishism with respect to the "people," or the "masses," or the "poor," or the weak and ignorant, then the notions of men are departing ever more widely from correspondence with the facts and the society's chance of expedient adjustment to its life-conditions is lessened. Poverty and simplicity may have dignity when there is no chance of winning wealth and advancing in rank, that is, where status rules; if the chances are opened, lowliness and penury are signs of supineness or incompetence.

It has been said that, since the masses of men never act on rational grounds but by instinct, habit, and tradition, therefore democracy is sure to be irrational; that even where it appears as a revulsion against aristocracy, it is likely to run down into a glorification of the commonplace as against all superiority; that when the masses get the power to choose their rulers, they choose very badly and often on irrelevant grounds, whereas they ought to choose men who will not always do what they want but will reason with them; that democracy is a mass of superstitions, dogmas, myths, formulas, half-truths, and phantasms, with a little truth capable of verification, and that it can change its "doctrines" at a moment's notice because it is capricious and vain and flies to that which tickles its self-love and ambition most. There is no denying the elements of truth in such strictures. For the moment it is of interest to notice that none of them apply to any primitive system. This reflection causes one to conclude from yet another point of view that what is called democracy among less developed peoples is specifically nothing of the sort, though there may be broad generic similarities and some likenesses in details between the primitive organizations and later-developing members of the evolutionary series. In the earlier days there was in the people no power capable of being deliberately and systematically applied. They had the power then, as always, only there was no recognized way in which it could be exercised. Public opinion had not been freed and given definite and regular means of self-expression.

90 §338, below.

§192. **Public Opinion.** As we conclude the topic of societal self-regulation, we return to the basic force which underlies all of its forms—public opinion—and shall first look into the method of its formation.[91]

The code of any peace-group must contain of necessity taboos on violence and also upon conduct likely to lead to violence; otherwise the existence of the group would always be in jeopardy. "Thou shalt not kill" and "thou shalt not steal" are such taboos. Any member who transgresses these formulations of adjustment to life-conditions is removed from the group or some attempt is made to force him into harmony. The code of any peace-group whatsoever must contain these taboos as a condition of being a peace-group; this has been tested over and over throughout human history, has become traditional, and is never questioned. Other items in the code of a modern nation, such as freedom of conscience, are of much later development, having been acquired within the recent historic period. No variations are permitted that may tend to weaken these fundamentals; in fact, every variation is tested on the criterion of its consistency with the fundamentals. Thus is many a proposed law declared unconstitutional, that is, inconsistent with the national principles or the genius of national institutions.

Where, however, the fundamentals of the code are not obviously in question, a flexible and adaptable societal system will show free and versatile variation. Such variability has a high selective value, for its presence means a heightened chance of securing, through multiplied expedients, a speedy and adequate adjustment. But that result cannot come about unless unhampered freedom of expression is accorded to the producers of any new expedient for living, whereby they may seek to offer it for imitation and concurrence, spontaneous or induced, in competition with other variations. Such competition aims at power, political or other; but that power can be gained only by winning over public opinion. Now, public opinion is commonly supposed to be responsive to reason, and people who accept that supposition are led to lay much stress upon reasoned and purposeful individual initiative as a moving force in societal evolution. If such a position is sound, then society

[91] The rest of this chapter is adapted from Keller, *War to Peace*, ch. VIII.

practises a rational selection among its mores, and therefore a rational adjustment to its life-conditions. It is necessary to consider this matter somewhat before going on.

In conceiving of public opinion men are inclined to think of it as the opinion of their own circle of life, and if one's circle is composed chiefly of educated people, as is generally the case with any theoretical writer, he is apt to assume that public opinion includes a large element of the intellectual or of the rationally discriminative. But genuine public opinion cannot be anything else than the consensus of the whole society; and the vast bulk of any society is composed of so-called "common people," not at all or not very well educated, of horizons much limited, and without the time, surplus energy, or even capacity to grapple intellectually with broad and general issues. This is no indictment of those who form the solid strength of any society; in fact there are not a few of those who are regarded as intellectuals because of eminence in certain restricted fields who are both artless and childlike when they set out to pass judgment on the societal order. The scope of any human intellect is circumscribed. Few men can deal intelligently with the broadest issues of societal adjustment. There is no immediate test or verification to go by and it is generally only after the issue is long past that the "verdict of history," the only sure one, can be rendered.

Public opinion, in brief, is a matter of feeling rather than of intellect; and the feeling is developed in connection with a more or less localized interest. If such interests are being realized, public opinion is favorable to or acquiescent in the societal order; if not, there is "unrest" and a threat of conflict to secure change. Men adjust consciously only to what they can see, or visualize, or think they see. This may be thoroughly irrational, as with the primitive people who have a whole set of adjustments to a world of ghosts and demons—a construction that can withstand none of our accepted tests of reality.

And yet it is possible to contend that public opinion is prevailingly "right"—even that the *vox populi* is the *vox dei*. Public opinion supported primitive religions. We cannot at all agree with the feeling back of it. But the religions were of the highest societal effectiveness, constituting as they did, among other things, a powerful disciplinary factor just when and where discipline was most needed. They had a high survival-value and public sentiment was "right" in supporting them. Society automatically used the public opinion, intellectually mistaken as it was, with the result of securing adaptation to conditions that really existed, and to them as they existed. Men in those elder ages never saw the societal expediency of their religion; it was all the time being put to uses quite other than those which had won it the favor of the public. No matter whence or how they arose or how they were viewed by the individual mind, the religious institutions represented a real adjustment to life-conditions and therefore persisted, surviving all sorts of selective tests along their course.

This is not to say that enlightenment has not enabled a modern society to proceed more intelligently and consciously toward its destiny; but any one who faces the facts will have to conclude that intelligent and conscious action is still, among the masses of mankind, confined for the most part to local issues and even to personal exigencies. The wider view is the rare view; it is, for example, the view of the statesman as contrasted with that of the "practical" politician. Most of us are but little concerned in action that contemplates a distant or universal result; few people can take a deep intelligent interest in a social program, like that of eugenics, which aims at an improvement of the whole human race some centuries hence. The human tendency is to shrink such a program down to a proximate, immediate aim; to make it bear on the present situation and upon the local interest of the adherent. Certainly the adjustment of a nation's code, let alone that of a race, to life-conditions is one of those matters that transcend the mental outfit and powers of most, if not of all men. How, then, can public opinion be trusted to settle such an issue? The answer is, because the process is typically automatic and impersonal, of a larger potency than any intellect-directed process can be, and must of necessity work out into adjustment.

Consider the adjustment secured by natural selection, which is so apt that it was at first unhesitatingly ascribed to infinite intelligence, and so rational in its outcome that the best brains of mankind have been employed for centuries in simply following out the process and seeing how it was done. Science has limped along after natural fact; after the act it has offered, at length, its rational explanation; but would it trust itself, even now, to vie with the process which it has followed and learned?

What science has learned is how things are and how they go, in the natural order. These processes cannot be altered, but they can be fallen in with, or adjusted to, with the result of human well-being. There is here no negation of the value of human knowledge and of action in its light. And the case is similar in the societal realm. The process, here too, is "right" as the natural process is "right" because it is of the same impersonal, elemental nature. The test is, in one case as in the other, the magnificently simple and conclusive one of persistence or non-persistence. Our business is to learn how things are and how they go, in the societal order; these processes, like the natural ones, cannot be altered, but we can fall in with them or adjust to them, with the result of societal well-being.

§193. The Liberation of Public Opinion. Recurring now to public opinion, which comes near to being the elemental force in societal evolution, it is found to be based upon sentiment and interest rather than upon intellectual analysis of complicated conditions. Upon interest—but here is precisely the touchstone of society's adjustments: do they subserve interests or do they not? Each local group, while incompetent to survey the interests of the whole society, is clear enough upon its own immediate status, for it has to live from day to day in that status and it knows without much cerebration whether life is comfortable or not. It is the only agency that can pass upon that question; for it is well-nigh impossible for a member of one group to see the life in another as a member of the latter sees it. If each group is to judge of its own interests, the responsibility lies precisely where the real experience is. The resulting inferences as to what ought to be done may be wrong; in fact, through the suggestion of interested parties a group or class may be persuaded that it has cause for discontent when none would be felt if it were let alone; but it is just the virtue of the automatic process that under it such unrealities at once encounter, along with the realities, an unplanned test by conflict. If there is anything in proposed variations of the code, it will come out, at length; if there are only phantasms, they will be dissipated under the test. If all the interests, locally felt and locally defended, have their chance within the arena marked out by the limits set in the national code, the composite product of the consequent selection, neither foreseen nor planned by anyone, will represent a more expedient adjustment for the whole society. And if the arena is too narrow or the restriction too cramping, that too will take care of itself; the pressure of discontented groups is bound to increase under repression until the conflict issues in a revolutionary modification of the broader outlines of the society's code or even in the violent disruption of the peace-group itself. Adjustment to life-conditions is a necessity of life, for organism or society. It is bound to come.

The peace-group is an expedient for living whose efficacy is unquestioned by anyone except perhaps certain crazy anarchists. But its adaptability, through freedom accorded to public opinion, has been a matter of growth. At an early period in the world's history it was not in the mores to allow of the free expression of general opinion. "Sit down thyself and cause the rest of the people to sit down," suggests Odysseus, blandly, to the excited noble, "for not yet dost thou clearly know what is the mind of the son of Atreus"; but with the common man he uses harsher measures, and thunders: "Sit still and harken to the words of others who are your betters! On no account shall all the Achæans be king here. Not good is the rule of many; one is to be leader, one king."[92] Yet even in Homer's time, and in war, the assembly of the people could make itself felt by peaceable means, even though the threat of violence lay not far away.

The course of civilization has been marked by a progressive enlargement of the range of expression accorded to the popular will. This has assured the stability of peace-groups to a higher and higher degree, for it has amounted to enlarged opportunity for the realization of interests without resort to violence. It is the justification for a freedom of speech almost bordering upon license, that popular discontent may thus blow itself off into thin air and do no such damage as it might if confined. Limitation of freedom of expression is popular only when the group-code and

[92] Homer, *Iliad*, II, 188 ff.

the sentiment of patriotism supporting it are endangered and out-raged.

Formerly, then, there was little apparatus for the expression of public opinion. The society was conceived to be in the hands of its rulers. Theoretically the Homeric king was the only person who had a right to speak, even in the assembly, and if anyone else wanted the floor, he had the privilege conferred upon him by being handed the royal scepter. The assembly of all tribal members, in earlier European times, often had no other mode of expression than applause or silence in the face of an announcement of intent. But this state of inarticulateness was succeeded by the evolution of various devices which limited the power of the ruler by allowing registration of the popular will. When the king ceased to be a religious fetish and lost "divine right," there fell away, for the emancipated peoples, a formidable barrier to the free expression of public opinion.

The modern form of adjustment in this matter of enfranchising public opinion is democracy, where, as the etymology of the term indicates, recognition is accorded to no ruler at all except the *demos* or people. But no society can get along without an execu-tive of its will. There has always been an executive of the society's code; the only difference between types of executive worth men-tioning in this connection has lain in the degree of responsibility imposed. The executive is but a man, and he belongs to some class in the society. If not responsible, he may try to impose a capri-cious personal will or the special code of his class. As a matter of fact, there was always a limit to this sort of thing, even if it had to be established by assassination. Deposition of some sort has been common enough under unlimited monarchies. Under the con-stitutional monarchy, the constitution or charter of rights laid down the essentials of the national code and the executive was held responsible for its defense and upholding, as well as limited to action within it. If he or his class abused their position of power to tamper with the code of rights, there was always the expedient of revolution. But, in the recession from violence or from situa-tions fraught with the threat of violence, all of which menaced the very peace-group itself, the device of "peaceful revolution," or election, arose as a better adjustment. Nowadays the executive—

president or premier—is subject to periodic examination at the bar of public opinion; the issue is as to whether he has executed its mandates or not. Meanwhile the king, where there is one, is a survival except as he symbolizes continuity and in some other relatively unimportant respects.

The election, though it is associated with persons, is essentially a selection in the details of the national code—details surrounding the unquestioned essentials to which allusion has several times been made. Some elections are frankly the decision of an issue, as, for example, woman-suffrage; and the party platforms sometimes make a plain presentation of an issue, as where protection and free trade have stood over against one another. A party espouses a certain type of societal policy and draws its adherents from certain well-recognized groups in the population that have, or think they have, interests in common. A revolt against the traditional code may bring about a new alignment of parties. However, when certain men have been elected, while it is understood that their special policies are to prosper with them, they are yet bound to uphold the national code and to look after the essential interests of all their constituents, of whatever political faith. The representatives are those to whom is delegated the selective power of public opinion, so far as their constituencies go, but the delegating body can hold them responsible, for it has regularly recurring opportunities to continue or discontinue its representatives. The move toward the referendum and recall indicates discontent with the traditional system of representation and impatience over having to wait awhile for a chance to rebuke and change representatives. It is an important new variation at the end of a long line of development, stretching from an era of restriction of the popular voice toward ever greater freedom.

Election is the typical modern method by which societal selection is accomplished within the peace-group, and an altered adjustment is attained. It is not asserted, however, that a single such expression of public opinion must be "right." The candid examination of an American election[93] makes one dubious as to the efficacy of public opinion to secure expedient societal adjustments by this method. It can be swayed to a considerable extent by in-

[93] Keller, *Soc. Evol.*, 105-114.

terested and unscrupulous parties—let one refer to Lecky[94] on the function of the demagogue in a democracy, or consider "Legislation by Clamor."[95] But we have as yet no surer device for appraising public sentiment within a peace-group. It is needful for anyone who wishes to see what there is in any evolutionary process to realize that much has been done in the lapse of time which we cannot perceive going on under our eyes. We have gained many an expedient adjustment of society at the hand of public opinion when, to contemporaries, it appeared that the popular will, in the contradictoriness of its expressions, practically cancelled out. A societal process must be allowed its time and be viewed over a long perspective; it should not be judged by a series of isolated and perhaps erratic swings. Only it cannot be accredited with purposeful rationality in the attainment of adjustments and least of all can it be referred to the individual. It shows a general trend and some very actual results, when viewed over a long enough course and in perspective. Evolution does not produce perfection. It does not even bring forth a superlative, but only comparatives. Before despairing, one should always compare the evolutionary product with what went before. Defective, for example, as the election is, in specific instances, one would be a bold man to advocate going back to the theory and practice out of which this and other freer expressions of public opinion once developed.

[94] *Democracy and Liberty,* I, 22-23.   [95] Sumner, *Coll. Ess.,* III, 186-187.

END OF VOL. I